CULTURAL
Anthropology

Third Canadian Edition

CULTURAL
Anthropology

A Perspective on the Human Condition

Emily A. Schultz
Robert H. Lavenda
Roberta Robin Dods

OXFORD
UNIVERSITY PRESS

OXFORD
UNIVERSITY PRESS

Oxford University Press is a department of the University of Oxford.
It furthers the University's objective of excellence in research, scholarship,
and education by publishing worldwide. Oxford is a registered trade mark of
Oxford University Press in the UK and in certain other countries.

Published in Canada by
Oxford University Press Canada
8 Sampson Mews, Suite 204,
Don Mills, Ontario M3C 0H5 Canada

www.oupcanada.com

First Canadian Edition published in 2009
Second Canadian Edition published in 2012

Cultural Anthropology 6/e was originally published in English in 2004 by Oxford University Press, Inc.,
198 Madison Avenue, New York, N.Y. 10016-4314, USA, with the ISBN number 9780195170115.
This adapted edition is published by arrangement. Oxford University Press Canada is solely responsible for this
adaptation from the original work. Copyright © 2005 by Emily A Schultz and Robert H. Lavenda

Library and Archives Canada Cataloguing in Publication

Schultz, Emily A. (Emily Ann), 1949-, author Cultural anthropology: a perspective on the
human condition / Emily A. Schultz, Robert H. Lavenda, Roberta Robin Dods. — Third Canadian edition.

Includes bibliographical references and index.
ISBN 978-0-19-900972-5 (pbk.)

1. Ethnology—Textbooks. 2. Ethnology—Canada—Textbooks.
I. Lavenda, Robert H., author II. Dods, Roberta Robin, author III. Title.

GN316.S38 2015   306   C2015-900042-4

Cover image: Blend Images – Jade/Getty Images

Oxford University Press is committed to our environment.
Wherever possible, our books are printed on paper which comes from
responsible sources.

Printed and bound in the United States of America
1 2 3 4 — 18 17 16 15

Brief Contents

PART I | The Tools of Cultural Anthropology 1

1 | The Anthropological Perspective on the Human Condition 2

2 | Fieldwork: A Meeting of Cultural Traditions 26

3 | Anthropology in History and the Explanation of Cultural Diversity   50

PART II | The Resources of Culture   75

4 | Language   76

5 | Culture, the Individual, and Identity 96

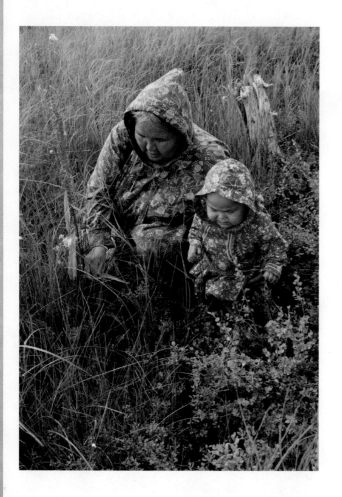

6 | Social Relationships: Marriage, Family, Kinship, and Friendship 130

10 | World View 239

PART III | Organization of Life: Local to Global 265

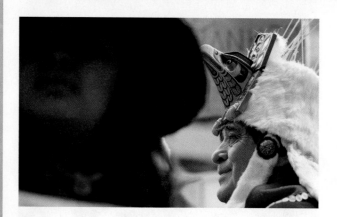

11 | Social Organization and Power 266

12 | Inequality in the Contemporary World   292

13 | A Global World   318

MAPS

Map 1.1
Dakhleh   9

Map 2.1
Utkuhikhalingmiut   39

Map 6.6
Ju/'hoansi   142

Map 11.4
Bolivian Tin Miners   282

FOREWORD

Emily A. Schultz and Robert H. Lavenda

We are pleased to see the third Canadian edition of our *Cultural Anthropology: A Perspective on the Human Condition*. In our view, Roberta Dods has done a very fine job in adapting our book for Canadian students. While we wrote a book that has had success internationally, we recognize the advantages of tuning a book for a particular academic environment; the Canadian educational system is sufficiently different from that of the United States to justify differences in textbooks at the university level. But it is also the case that Canada has long had its own anthropological history and set of problematics, not reducible to the Anglo-American narrative that has dominated English-language anthropology.

Our original book aimed not only to show beginning anthropology students something of the varieties of human culture around the world, but also to draw their attention to the intensifying flows of people and culture from many parts of the world on unpredictable journeys, producing sometimes surprising encounters. When we began, we did not realize the journeys our book would take outside the United States, and even outside the English-speaking world, as translations allowed it to encounter audiences we never anticipated being able to address. The Canadian edition of our book has undergone a somewhat different kind of customization process, since it is still in English, but has, thanks to Roberta Dods, been more fully customized for Canadian readers, thus enriching our original efforts with a wealth of new ethnographic examples by a wide range of Canadian anthropologists. It is a pleasure to learn from our own book!

While we have taken an explicitly global perspective in the book, we recognize that what anthropology does best when it looks at the global is to concentrate on the local in order to grasp the effects of the global. So making our anthropology text more Canadian paradoxically makes it more global as well.

Dr Dods is correct in commenting that we take students seriously. We believe that when students are challenged, they rise to the challenge. Anthropology is a vibrant, challenging discipline, perhaps the earliest discipline to take the diversity of human culture seriously. We have tried to capture that in the text we wrote in a clear, straightforward, and uncluttered manner, and we are delighted that Dr Dods has also taken these same challenges seriously and has presented all of us with a successful hybrid text for a hybrid discipline!

PREFACE TO THE CANADIAN EDITION

Roberta Robin Dods

This third Canadian edition of *Cultural Anthropology: A Perspective on the Human Condition* continues to situate students in a world view informed by a concern for social justice within a discussion of the discipline of anthropology, specifically cultural anthropology. This aim has come into sharper focus in recent times as globalization has brought us into closer relationships with peoples around the world. Some of these relationships have challenged our better selves to reach out in times of change and upheaval while we consider the complications of living in a world of deep diversity. Anthropology offers a unique opportunity to situate each of us in this better place of understanding and analysis of the humanity of ourselves and others.

In this new edition, some chapters have been reorganized to add new material but, as with the earlier Canadian editions, the conceptual integrity has been maintained. We continue with the 14-chapter structure designed to fit the semester system of most Canadian universities. Each chapter begins with an outline and a set of learning objectives and concludes with a list of key terms, a chapter summary, critical thinking questions, and lists of suggested readings and related websites. These framing materials challenge students to integrate learned concepts while providing them with a window to a wider world of inquiry. In preparing the third edition, I was asked to add a critical comment at the end of each chapter, and thus there are fourteen new commentaries on topics that tie in with the concepts discussed in the specific chapters. These mini-essays reflect my commitment to the discipline, to positioning anthropological study within a larger community of inquiry, and to exploring themes that will inform—and in many cases challenge—the reader.

In Chapter 1, we begin with a discussion of anthropology and its four traditional subfields—biological anthropology, archaeology, linguistic anthropology, and cultural anthropology—as well as what could effectively be considered its fifth subfield: applied anthropology. The theme of applied anthropology in its various forms echoes throughout this text. We continue with an introduction to cultural anthropology—its scope and its goals. Further, we explain the concept of *culture* and examine the critique of its use within a wider historical perspective, and we emerge with an understanding of the efficacy of a holistic approach to anthropological study. We also introduce the methodology of fieldwork and its resulting reportage—ethnography—and conclude with a discussion of ethnocentrism.

We examine ethnographic fieldwork in detail in Chapter 2, offering insight into forms of data collection, ways to prepare for "the field," professional ethics, and culture shock. We also compare three principal modes of ethnographic research—positivist, reflexive, and multi-sited. Our explanation of the "dialectic of fieldwork" considers the roles people play when acting as an anthropologist's guide in the field, the effects of fieldwork on all involved, and the value and open-ended nature of anthropological knowledge.

Our focus in Chapter 3 is on colonialism, capitalism, and modernity. Viewing historical developments through a critical lens, we examine the rise of political economies and place anthropology as a "player" in the colonial encounter. We then critique the development and use of various classification systems including the "culture areas" classifications that evolved in North America. In conclusion, we reflect on post-colonial realities as a counterpoint and a challenge.

In Chapter 4, our objective is to understand the theoretical and practical aspects of language and its use. Here, we discuss the relationship between language and culture and the importance of symbolic representation. We introduce some of Charles Hockett's design features of language, and we overview the components of language (phonology, morphology, syntax, semantics, pragmatics, and ethnopragmatics). We also consider linguistic inequality and areas of negotiated meaning exemplified by pidgin languages. The chapter concludes with a brief statement on the dialectic between experience and language and the creation of ambiguity in symbolic systems.

Beginning from the observation that every individual views the world from a unique position, we investigate the nature of identity and the individual in Chapter 5. First, we explore how individual psychology is situated in the context of a symbolic, cultural world and how cultural schemas and prototypes shape the ways we perceive our experiences. Then, we outline interpretations of intelligence, cognitive (learning) styles, reasoning, and logic. Next, we examine emotion as the product of the dialectic between bodily arousal and cognitive interpretation mediated by, and embedded within, a cultural matrix. In addition, we discuss ranges of sexual and gender identities and how those identities are culturally informed. Norms and normative constructs are also considered. Finally, we reflect on the self and how this "entity" interprets the world and, specifically, how the *self* survives in the face of violence and trauma.

In Chapter 6, we analyze the complexities of human social relationships, focussing on different interpretations of marriage, family, kinship, and friendship. Throughout the chapter, we investigate what determines relatedness and group membership, with an awareness of the role of sex and gender in systems of social organization. We discuss marriage as a social process in the context of economic exchange and family alliance. As we explore the dimensions of family life, we outline various family structures and note how families change over time and in response to new global circumstances. We also compare kin-based versus non–kin-based societies and conclude with an appreciation for the nuances of the dimensions of group life.

Making a living is our central focus in Chapter 7. We begin with a consideration of subsistence strategies before moving on to discuss the relationship between production, distribution, and consumption. Additionally, we note the differences between internal (needs) and external (resources) explanations of consumption patterns. We also explore the cultural and symbolic nature of consumption and then elucidate distribution and exchange at local and global levels by examining various forms of exchange—from reciprocity to redistribution to market exchange.

In Chapter 8, we discuss play, art, myth, and ritual. We begin with play, which is an open system that allows us to communicate about communicating (metacommunication) and provides an introduction to meaningful reflexivity. From play, we move on to discuss first sport as embedded in the prevailing social order and then art as play that produces significant transformation-representation. We also explore the relationships between myths, as charters for social action and providers of stories of truth, and rituals, culturally defined schemas that bring text and performance together and that can function as powerful forms of metacommunication.

Chapter 9 focusses on an applied discipline that has been gaining attention in recent years: medical anthropology. While a chapter is not enough to cover all the diverse topics of study that medical anthropologists investigate, we discuss many themes at the heart of the discipline and offer examples of how researchers have applied these themes to real-world situations. We emphasize holism, particularly in our discussion of the impact of physical, social, and cultural environments on the well-being of individuals. We also consider various culturally informed approaches to health care and ways of labelling and defining illness and disease. In addition, we revisit some ethical considerations as we explore the challenges involved in studying human health. Above all, we emphasize the importance of being open to traditional knowledge and non-Western ways of healing.

In Chapter 10, we consider the seemingly simple—yet actually very complex—subject of world view. We explore the role of metaphor, metonymy, and symbolic thought and comment on the anthropological analysis of religion and secularism within the context of world view. As we come to understand world views as instruments of power, we also come to understand how key metaphors and world views are maintained and modified in a world of change.

We turn to social organization and patterns of human interdependence in Chapter 11, noting that no single cause can explain the complexities of human social relations. We consider the human power to act, various forms of social power, and explanations of why human beings submit to institutionalized power. As we investigate how humans invest the world with meaning, we also discuss how people bargain for reality as they negotiate the meaning of history and tradition.

In Chapter 12, we delve into social inequality and explore the multi-dimensional nature of inequality in terms of class, caste, race, ethnicity, and nationality. We begin by considering the implications of class-stratified societies and class mobility. Next, we present examples of caste, focussing in particular on how divisions of caste impact peoples' ways of living in India. We then survey the discredited concept of *race* and its manifestation in today's world, keeping in mind the ethical implications that often arise when race is perceived as a social division. Finally, we reflect upon definitions of *ethnicity* before concluding with an examination of what constitutes a *nation*, what a *national identity* is, and how national identity may manifest in *nationalism*.

We explore the emergence of the *global world* in Chapter 13. In the context of the history of the development of political economies, we consider globalization and the pressures on nation-states as new cultural processes emerged and continue to emerge. A key issue is the challenge of human rights in a "globalized" world, and we discuss cultural imperialism, cultural hybridization, and cosmopolitanism as responses to this challenge.

In the concluding chapter, we emphasize the idea that anthropology encompasses so much more than what students will learn in a classroom. Anthropology is about the lives and worlds of the people who gift us with their world views. It is a portal to effective global citizenship in a world of uncertainty. Finally, it offers perspective and a way to develop awareness (reflexivity) in order to confront issues and challenge views on freedom and constraint.

A Final Note

Each new edition of *Cultural Anthropology* has moved forward in some small and/or large way to illuminate the trends of the discipline. Nonetheless, what has been constant is the book's core value: a respect for students. Like Schultz and Lavenda, I, too, take students seriously. I believe that students have the capacity to read and think as involved adults. It has been my experience using this book over the years that students are happy to be seen as capable of the reflexivity the book espouses. They may sometimes complain about or struggle with the content and the concepts, but I have found they are charmed into learning as they come to appreciate that the text grounds them in an intellectual, emotional, and practical perspective that finds resonance in their—quite substantial—understanding of the world. What we offer are the tools for analysis. Inevitably, students appreciate how this book, and anthropology as a subject, situates them in a world of change and challenges them to employ the anthropological perspective as an increasingly important tool for effective global citizenship.

ACKNOWLEDGEMENTS

Once again I want to thank the people I met and worked with in the field who gifted me with their friendship and insights into their lives while teaching me to see their worlds and ways of being human. They have been my true teachers, and their kind involvement has been a sacred gift. As this book has always inferred, such generosity helps us face the world with humility, while the study of anthropology situates us in a place of analysis that fosters the development of humble concern and deep hope. None of this could be possible without the kindness of others.

I would like to thank Schultz and Lavenda for providing the foundation upon which the Canadian editions of *Cultural Anthropology* have been built and for their ongoing insightful comments on the progress made in the current edition.

The work could not have proceeded without the exceedingly positive relationship that I developed with my first editors at Oxford University Press. Here, I note three people specifically: Peter Chambers, developmental editor, Higher Education Division; Amanda Maurice, assistant editor, Higher Education Division; and Janice Evans, senior editor, Higher Education Division. Peter worked with me on the first two Canadian editions. Without his input and the contribution of Amanda on the first Canadian edition, I could not have worked through the difficult process of making this book "Canadian" while keeping the tone of the original authors. The second edition became what it was because of Janice Evans, and she continued to provide great assistance in working through the final processes for this third edition. To her and our new additions to the editorial team for this book, Tanuja Weerasooriya and Dani Pacey, fell the monumental task of smoothing out the tone of three voices, setting a better order for the material while reconciling the struggle of the reorganization of chapters, and the adding of new and, at times, controversial materials. Thanks to all.

All the people thanked in previous editions have their place in this edition as well. I would like to join the publisher in thanking the following reviewers, as well as those who wish to remain anonymous, whose thoughtful comments and suggestions helped shape these, now three, Canadian editions.

Hugo De Burgos, University of British Columbia Okanagan

Steven Ferzacca, University of Lethbridge

Diana French, University of British Columbia Okanagan

Dawn Grimes-MacLellan, St Mary's University

Nicole Hayes, University of Waterloo

Chris Holdsworth, University of Calgary

David Howes, Concordia University

Magdalena Kazubowski-Houston, Wilfrid Laurier University

Carlota McAllister, York University

Laurie Milne, Medicine Hat College

Charles R. Menzies, University of British Columbia

Timothy Panas, University of Saskatchewan

David Ryniker, University of British Columbia

Alan Smart, University of Calgary

Pamela Stern, Simon Fraser University

Douglass Drozdow-St. Christian, Western University

Susan Walter, St Mary's University

Terry Webb, Western University

Roberta Robin Dods

FROM THE PUBLISHER

What does it mean to be human? How do we define ourselves and others? Which of our qualities remain fixed across time and space, and which are subject to change? These questions are at the very heart of anthropology. Of course, some of what makes us human is biological—our physiology is distinctively human, we possess a complex brain that is capable of high-level thinking, and so on. Yet much of our humanity comes from how we choose to interact with our fellow human beings and the world around us—the relationships we nurture, the traditions we learn and pass on, the ways in which we adapt to and transform our surroundings. In many ways, it is our capacity for *culture*, in all its forms, that makes us human.

Building on the solid foundation of past editions, this third Canadian edition of *Cultural Anthropology: A Perspective on the Human Condition* invites students to embark on a journey of cross-cultural comparison. Some of what they will encounter may be surprisingly familiar; some of it will be startlingly new. Everything will be thoroughly human.

Key Features

EXPANDED COVERAGE OF GENDER, SEXUALITY, RELIGION, AND OTHER ESSENTIAL TOPICS.
New discussions of topics such as queer theory, gendered violence, women in the working world, and religion in contemporary society offer students further insight into important areas of study within anthropology.

FIGURE 5.11 A hijra onlooker watches another hijra apply makeup.

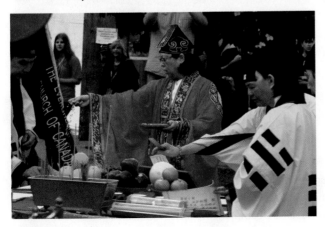

FIGURE 10.7 Priests are experts in carrying out religious rituals.

---

3 | ANTHROPOLOGY IN HISTORY AND THE EXPLANATION OF CULTURAL DIVERSITY   69

IN THEIR OWN WORDS   "Bisexuality" and the Politics of Normal in African Ethnography

Marc Epprecht is head of the Department of Global Development Studies at Queen's University. In the following discussion, he examines the lasting impact of the common stereotype, created and spread by Europeans in colonialist times, that Africans did not practice same-sex sexuality.

Anthropologists have played a central role in documenting the diversity of human sexuality as it is understood and expressed in different cultures around the world.... However,... anthropologists at times "conscripted" select evidence and even fabricated "facts" about the people they studied in order to advance ideals and preferences around sexuality in their own societies. By conjuring idealized or exoticized Others, they helped to create an understanding of "normal" and "modern" by way of contrast. This has resulted in a body of purportedly empirical or scientific data that in retrospect we can see as deeply flawed, morally normative, and sometimes actually complicit in the construction and maintenance of racist colonialist structures....

[Consider] the commonplace assumption or assertion as an unqualified fact that Africans south of the Sahara either did not practice same-sex sexuality in their traditional societies, or that they only did so rarely that it was inconsequential.... [More recently,] a growing body of research, activism, and art has comprehensively demonstrated the falseness of the "fact" of Africans' exclusive heterosexuality.... A growing, pan-African network of lesbian, gay, bisexual, transgender, and intersex (LGBTI) associations also attests to diverse, indigenous, same-sex, and bisexual cultures and practices in Africa. A range of images written or produced by Africans in fiction, theatre, and film further destabilizes the stereotype of the "pure" African heterosexual.

These sources on the whole do not propose a timeless, archetypal African gay or lesbian in opposition to that older stereotype. Rather, the women and men who have same-sex sexual relations most often also continue to marry, to have children, and to engage in heterosexual relationships. Whether this should properly be termed "bisexual" is a matter of debate. However, whether men who sometimes have sex with men but do not identify as homo- or bisexual (MSM), and whether women who sometimes have sex with women but do not identify as lesbian or bisexual (WSW) exist in Africa in greater numbers than commonly assumed or asserted cannot in good scholarship be disputed. That it *does* continue to be disputed is a cause for far greater concern than academic quibbling over numbers. Indeed, scholars, activists, and community leaders who deny the existence of MSM and WSW in Africa, who rationalize it as imported or recent, or who simply disregard the evidence, may be fuelling unhelpful or even dangerous homophobic and xenophobic

rhetoric. Such rhetoric stigmatizes already vulnerable groups and self-evidently impedes HIV/AIDS awareness and prevention campaigns....

Clearly, many factors contribute to the tenacity of the no same-sex sexuality in Africa argument. The ethnography, however, is unquestionably foundational in that it provides a scientific-sounding canon that gives authority to contemporary claims about what is normal and traditional, and what is deviant, non-existent, or modern. But how trustworthy is that canon? [There are] key discrepancies in the documentary record dating as far back as the eighteenth century... [that] offer insight into the complex relationship between colonial rulers and subjects, and can help us to understand why some Africans today still remain attracted to and defensive of colonial notions of normal. Awareness of this history could also move us toward more pointed research about sexuality in the present that could, in turn, improve our ability to design more effective interventions against HIV/AIDS. A queer analysis of African ethnography could also sharpen the postcolonial critique of anthropology more generally by alerting us to hitherto unsuspected essentialist, "Westocentric" terms and concepts....

[This] new anthropology... represents the kind of bold challenges to mainstream scholarship predicted by Kath Weston in her reflections on queer ethnographic research (1998). These would include:

First, establishing beyond reasonable objection that most African societies had normative ways of dealing with sexual difference that were discreetly hidden within the dominant heteropatriarchal norms. Sweeping claims about non-existence... [of] same-sex sexuality are thus empirically unfounded. Expressions of same-sex sexuality, moreover, changed over time in response to many factors, almost certainly including interventions by Western anthropologists.

Second, the research raises compelling questions on a number of contemporary issues. Are men who sometimes have sex with men but do not admit it and do not consider themselves homosexual or bisexual a more significant vector for HIV than has previously been considered? Do women who have sex with women yet consider themselves straight or normal engage in practices that would more accurately be termed bisexual or lesbian-like? It seems likely.

The new anthropology also causes us to reflect on whether the attitudes and political agendas that obscured MSM and WSW from the view of earlier anthropologists and other researchers had a bigger role in shaping heteronormative gender roles and identities in the majority population than has thus far been investigated.

Source: Epprecht, Marc. "'Bisexuality' and the Politics of Normal in African Ethnography," *Anthropologica* 48, 2: 187–201.

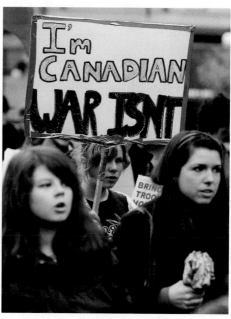

FIGURE 5.1 Today, many Canadians are passionate about their anti-war stance.

CANADIAN FOCUS. An array of Canadian examples, points of view, and issues offer insight into the many ways in which Canadians have contributed to the field. Students will also enjoy learning about the breadth and depth of anthropological research being carried out in this country today.

FIGURE 8.5 Cecil Paul, a Haisla elder, stands next to the G'psgolox totem pole, which now stands in the Kitlope Valley near Kitimaat, British Columbia. The totem pole was returned from Sweden's Museum of Ethnography in 2006. Why might some people object to displaying "art by appropriation" in museums?

BROAD THEORETICAL COVERAGE. The authors bring together traditional anthropological perspectives and cutting-edge theories that reflect the most recent trends in the discipline. The result is a comprehensive, holistic approach that sheds new light on standard topics.

A CHAPTER ON MEDICAL ANTHROPOLOGY. Chapter 9 gives students solid grounding in the fundamental principles of one of the fastest-growing subdisciplines of cultural anthropology. Numerous examples from the field demonstrate how medical anthropologists can contribute to the resolution of some of our most pressing global health concerns.

FIGURE 9.9 The Lucky Iron Fish is part of a relatively simple health initiative to supplement iron-deficient diets in Cambodia. What have the creators of this initiative done to tailor it to the culture whose people they are trying to help?

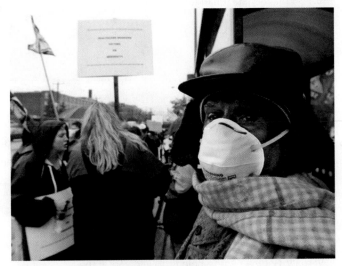

FIGURE 9.14 A Toronto resident dons a medical mask to protect himself from the SARS virus in 2003.

NEW "A CRITICAL LOOK" BOXES. End-of-chapter commentaries written by Roberta Robin Dods challenge students to think critically about a range of engaging and relevant cultural topics.

A CRITICAL LOOK

"ETHNOPROFILE" BOXES. Brief overviews of relevant geographic, linguistic, demographic, and organizational information offer students contextual information on various societies discussed in the text.

ETHNOPROFILE

"IN THEIR OWN WORDS" BOXES. Short commentaries from experts in the field provide students with alternative perspectives on key issues and also furnish insight into what it means to be an anthropologist.

IN THEIR OWN WORDS

VIBRANT FOUR-COLOUR DESIGN. A wide array of photos, illustrations, maps, tables, and graphs helps bring anthropology alive!

ENGAGING LEARNING TOOLS. Learning objectives, marginal definitions of key terms, critical thinking questions, annotated suggestions for further reading, lists of related websites, and a new end-of-book glossary encourage students to actively engage with what they are reading and explore resources beyond the text to enhance their learning experience.

EXTENSIVE ANCILLARY PACKAGE. The third Canadian edition of *Cultural Anthropology* is supported by an array of supplementary resources for the student and the instructor, all designed to enhance and complete the learning experience. The companion websites for *Cultural Anthropology* are found at:

 www.oupcanada.com/Schultz3Ce

FOR THE STUDENT

Student Study Guide. An updated and expanded package of review material—including a list of relevant films, self-testing quizzes of multiple choice and true-or-false questions, essay topics and discussion questions, kinship diagrams, new video links, and weblinks to resources such as online ethnographies—is designed to reinforce student understanding of each chapter and provide direction for further research.

FOR THE INSTRUCTOR

The following instructors' resources are available online to qualifying adopters. Please contact your OUP Canada sales representative for more information.

- **Instructor's Manual.** This comprehensive package features chapter summaries, suggestions for discussion and debate, suggested lecture topics and teaching resources, and a sample syllabus and grading rubric.
- **PowerPoint Slides.** These dynamic lecture slides summarize key points from each chapter and incorporate figures and tables from the text.
- **Image Bank.** This expansive resource contains a wealth of full-colour figures, photographs, and tables that will make classroom lectures more engaging and relevant for students.
- **Test Generator.** This comprehensive bank of test questions provides hundreds of multiple choice, true-or-false, short answer, and mini essay questions along with suggested answers and page references guiding students to related in-text discussions.

COMPANION WEBSITE	Emily A. Schultz, Robert H. Lavenda and Roberta R. Dods *Cultural Anthropology: A Perspective on the Human Condition*, Third Canadian Edition ISBN 13: 9780199009725

Inspection copy request

Ordering information

Contact & Comments

About the Book

Cultural Anthropology: A Perspective on the Human Condition, Third Canadian Edition, A Perspective on the Human Condition introduces students to the history, methods, and theoretical approaches of the discipline. Drawing on experiences from their own fieldwork and the work of other top researchers, the authors explore how cultural creativity, human agency, and the material conditions of everyday life interact to shape cultural practices. Discussions of ongoing controversies - including tribalism vs globalization, the vulnerability of transborder citizens, attempts to use cultural relativism as an excuse for human rights violations, and increasing inequality between 'have' and 'have not' regions - show how cultural anthropologists can apply their knowledge and skills to tackle the world's most pressing social problems.

Sample Material

Get Adobe PDF reader [US | UK]

Instructor Resources

You need a password to access these resources. Please contact your local Sales and Editorial Representative for more information.

Student Resources

I | The Tools of Cultural Anthropology

IN PART I, WE INTRODUCE ANTHROPOLOGY—SPEC-IFICALLY CULTURAL ANTHROPOLOGY—AS A WAY OF EXPLORING AND GAINING KNOWLEDGE ABOUT OUR WORLD AND OURSELVES. We also consider the possibilities made available by fieldwork, cultural anthropologists' principal method of data collection. Finally, we discuss the historical context for how anthropologists have attempted to make sense of human cultural diversity.

1

The Anthropological Perspective on the Human Condition

CHAPTER OUTLINE

Explanations of the Human Condition

The Anthropological Perspective: The Cross-disciplinary Discipline

Anthropology and the Concept of Culture

The Challenge of Cultural Differences

Culture, History, and Human Agency

The Promise of the Anthropological Perspective

LEARNING OBJECTIVES

By the end of Chapter 1, you will be able to

- define anthropology's aims and scope of study,
- explain culture as a concept within anthropology,
- distinguish cultural anthropology as a subfield of anthropology,

- articulate connections and relationships between the four major subfields of anthropology in North America,
- explain the world views of dualism and holism, and show ways that the

conflict between them has shaped anthropology, and
- explain the relationship between cultural relativism and ethnocentrism, and give examples of both.

A Samburu shepherdess watches over her herd of goats as they graze in rural Kenya, where her people have raised goats, cows, and sheep for many generations. Her particular cultural experience is only one of a vast array of such experiences that shape human behaviours and beliefs in different ways across the globe.

Explanations of the Human Condition

Dualistic, Idealistic, and Materialistic Explanations of Our World

What is the world like? And what is the human condition within the world? Indeed, does it make sense to speak of a *single* "condition" shared by all human beings? Members of all societies pose questions such as these. And all societies develop their own answers. If asked what they believe about human nature, for example, many North Americans would answer that human nature has two parts: *mind* and *matter*, *soul* and *body*, or *spirit* and *flesh*. The belief that human nature, or reality as a whole, is made up of two radically different yet equal forces is called **dualism**. The pair of forces is often referred to as a **binary opposition**.

For thousands of years, from the time of the Greek philosopher Plato (428–347 BCE) onward, people of the Western tradition have debated the importance of each half of human nature. They have understood each person as made up of a material (physical) body inhabited by an ethereal mind or spirit. According to Plato, the drama of human existence consists of the internal struggle between the body (drawn naturally to base, corruptible matter) and the mind or soul (drawn naturally to pure, unchanging forms). Christian theology later incorporated the view that each human being consists of a soul that seeks God and a physical body that is tempted by the material world. This view of earthly life as a struggle between spirit (good) and flesh (evil) is sometimes called *conflict dualism*.

Subsequently, Platonic and Christian theories of human nature came to emphasize that although human beings are equipped with physical bodies, their true nature is spiritual, not material; the body is a material obstacle that prevents the full development of the mind or spirit. This view is known as **idealism**. Conversely, others have argued that the activities of our physical bodies in the material world make us who we are. From this perspective, human existence becomes the struggle to exercise our physicality as fully as we can; to put spiritual values above bodily needs would "go against human nature." This view is known as **materialism**. In their most extreme forms, idealism and materialism propose competing forms of **determinism**: idealists claim that human nature is *determined by* the causal force of mind or spirit; materialists argue that human nature is *determined by* the causal force of physical matter.

Many idealists and materialists have sought to strip away our seemingly minor or unnecessary attributes in order to reveal an unchanging core or **essence** of human nature. Indeed, across the history of Western philosophy, various philosophers have assumed that our species has an essence but have disagreed about just what that essence is. Yet other thinkers have argued that human beings come into the world with *no fixed essence*. For them, we are shaped by various forces we encounter throughout our lives. But what those forces might be, how many there are, and which of them is the most powerful remains part of the debate.

Some nineteenth-century thinkers argued that the most powerful material forces that shape human nature were to be found in the surrounding *natural environment*. Rich soil, a temperate climate, drought, and the absence of animals that can be domesticated are examples of the environmental factors understood to shape past and present societies and, ultimately, their inhabitants' sense of self and society. German philosopher Karl Marx (1818–1883) and his followers, by contrast, argued that forces shaping human beings' self-understanding were rooted in social relations shaped by the mode of economic production that sustained a society (Figure 1.1). Because different groups, or *classes*, played different roles in that production process, members of each group would develop a different sense of what life was all about. An extreme idealist reaction against such materialist thinking, influential in cultural anthropology, has argued that human beings have no fixed essence when they come into the world, but they become different kinds of human beings as a result of the particular *ideas*, *meanings*, *beliefs*, and values that they absorb as members of particular societies (see Benedict 1934).

As liberating as the proposition of being born without a fixed essence may sound, such accounts are not always optimistic. A number of scholars have adapted this basic assumption

dualism
The philosophical view that reality consists of two equal and irreducible forces.

binary opposition
A pair of opposites used as an organizing principle (e.g., body–soul; yin–yang; male–female).

idealism
The philosophical view that pure, incorruptible ideas—or the mind that produces such ideas—constitute the essence of human nature.

materialism
The philosophical view that the activities of our physical bodies in the material world constitute the essence of human nature.

determinism
The philosophical view that one simple force (or a few simple forces) causes (or determines) complex events.

essence
An unchanging core of features that is unique to things of the same kind and makes them what they are.

FIGURE 1.1 Factory workers in Woodstock, Ontario, during World War I. Karl Marx believed that modes of production shape social relations and, in turn, individuals' perceptions of themselves and their place in society. Can you identify some of the modes of production that impact your own life?

holism

A perspective on the human condition that assumes that mind and body, individual and society, and individual and environment interpenetrate and even define one another.

culture

Sets of learned behaviours and ideas that humans acquire as members of a society.

to portray humans as passive, pliable creatures who are *wholly* moulded by environmental, sociohistorical, cultural, or other forces beyond their control. According to these scholars, the open possibilities with which we begin are

inevitably closed down tight as human possibilities are overwhelmed by environmental determinism, sociohistorical determinism, or cultural determinism.

Holistic Explanations

Yet there is another approach to the human condition that is less distorting than dualism and less simplistic than idealism or materialism: **holism** (see Figure 1.2). Holism assumes that no sharp boundaries separate mind from body, body from environment, individual from society, my ideas from your ideas, or our traditions from the traditions of others. Rather, it proposes that mind and body, body and environment, and so on, interpenetrate and even define one another. Holism holds great appeal for those who seek a theory of human nature that is rich enough to do justice to its complex subject matter—namely humans themselves.

Holism sees the whole as greater than the sum of its parts. Human beings are what they are because the mutual shaping of genes and **culture** and experience has produced something new, something that cannot be reduced to the materials used to construct it. Similarly, a society is not just the sum of the behaviours of its individual members but a unique entity, and

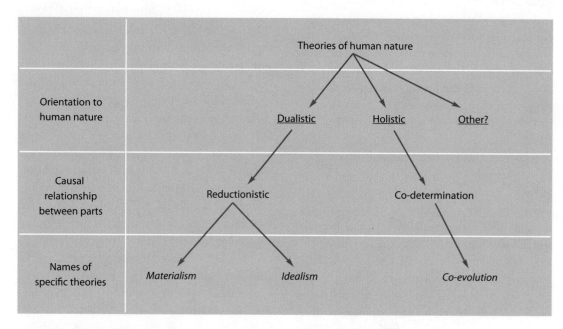

FIGURE 1.2 Perspectives on the human condition. While the dualistic approach reduces the human condition to the sum of its parts, the holistic approach considers the human condition to be co-determined through a complex interplay among many internal and external influences. Can you think of any other way(s) of looking at the human condition?

human beings living in groups are so deeply affected by shared cultural experiences that they become different from what they would have been had they matured in isolation. Cultural anthropologist Clifford Geertz notes that human beings raised in isolation would be neither failed apes nor "natural" people stripped of their veneer of culture; they would be "mental basket cases" (1973: 40). Social living and cultural sharing are necessary for individual human beings to develop what we recognize as a *human* nature—in all its wonderful diversity.

Holism as a perspective allows us to consider human nature as the result of a **co-evolution**: Human beings are creatures whose bodies, brains, actions, and thoughts are equally involved in learning, co-determining, and co-evolving. Thus, we can view human nature as embedded in a wider world and profoundly shaped by culture. We can also infer that human beings are open to becoming something more than what has gone into making them what they are at a given point in time. Ultimately, holism offers a refreshingly positive belief in human potential.

The Anthropological Perspective: The Cross-disciplinary Discipline

From the optimistic promise of holism we can engage with the subject matter of **anthropology**, a scholarly discipline that aims to describe, in the broadest possible sense, what it means to be human. Anthropologists want to learn about different human ways of life. Essentially, the anthropological experience is a gift from teachers who live or lived in different social, economic, or geographical circumstances. Anthropologists are often treated to the sweet discovery of familiarity and the joy of making the unfamiliar familiar. They often face, as well, the experience of the familiar becoming unfamiliar; as frightening as this discovery can be, it is also a source of great insight and immense pleasure.

Anthropologists are not alone in focussing their attention on human beings and their creations. Human biology, literature, art, history, linguistics, sociology, political science, economics—all these disciplines and many more—concentrate on one aspect of human life or another. The **anthropological perspective**, unique in the social sciences, draws on the findings of these other disciplines and attempts to fit them together with its own findings in order to understand how different forces collectively shape human life. Anthropologists are convinced that explanations of human activities will inevitably be superficial unless they are holistic—that is, unless they acknowledge that human life is greater than the sum of its parts. Thus, the anthropological perspective recognizes that so long as they are alive, individuals and societies always remain open to influences and opportunities that may take them beyond what they are at the present moment or what they have been in the past.

To generalize about humanity requires evidence from the widest possible range of human societies. Thus, in addition to being holistic, anthropology is **comparative**. As anthropologists, we understand that it is not enough, for example, to observe only our own social group, discover that we do not eat insects, and conclude that all human beings do not eat insects. When we compare human diets in different societies, we discover that insect-eating is quite common and that our North American aversion to this practice is specific to our own society (Figure 1.3). In making such comparisons, anthropologists recognize that all social groups deserve equal treatment and respect, and they reject terms such as *exotic*, *primitive*, and *savage* to describe practices that differ from those of their own group.

co-evolution
The relationship between biological processes and symbolic cultural processes in which each makes up an important part of the environment to which the other must adapt.

anthropology
The integrated study of human nature, human society, and human history.

anthropological perspective
An approach to the human condition that is holistic, comparative, and evolutionary.

comparative
A characteristic of the anthropological perspective that requires anthropologists to consider similarities and differences in a wide a range of human societies before generalizing about human nature, human society, or human history.

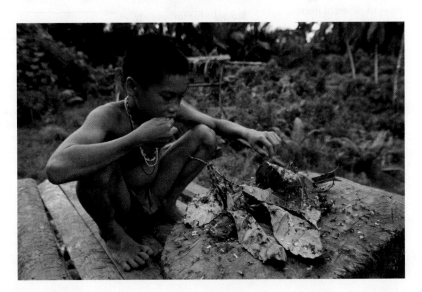

FIGURE 1.3 A Mentawai boy in Sumatra, Indonesia, eats ants from their nest. Insects are commonly eaten as a source of protein in many regions of the world. Can you think of any Western dietary staples that might be considered unusual elsewhere?

biological evolution
Change (through mutation) in genetic makeup (the DNA/RNA) of a population that is passed on through the generations.

cultural evolution
Evolution of the beliefs and behaviours we incorporate into human development through the experiences of teaching and learning.

evolutionary
A characteristic of the anthropological perspective that requires anthropologists to place their observations about human nature, human society, or human history in a flexible framework that takes into consideration change over time.

biological (or physical) anthropology
The specialty of anthropology that looks at humans as biological organisms and tries to discover what characteristics make us different from and/or similar to other living things.

Thus anthropological study involves (1) gathering data from many cultures, both past and present, (2) comparing those data to derive informed and testable hypotheses about what it means to be human, and (3) investigating what, if anything, can be said about the human condition that might be valid across space and over time.

This interest in change over time leads anthropologists to explore how individual humans, their societies, and their cultures have evolved. Consequently, some anthropologists study the **biological evolution** of the human species, paying attention not only to human origins but also to the patterns of biological variation in living human populations; others study **cultural evolution**, tracing how elements of culture have changed over time. In general, one of anthropology's most important contributions to the study of human evolution has been to demonstrate the critical differences that separate biological evolution, which is situated in environmental *circumstances*, from cultural evolution. This distinction remains important as a way of demonstrating the inadequacy of arguments that assert that everything people do or think can be explained biologically—for example, in terms of "race" or "sex." Because anthropologists are interested in documenting and explaining change, the anthropological perspective is

evolutionary at its core. And today, as we move into an era in which even our biological being can be altered through technology, anthropologists' interest in human evolution has taken on additional cross-disciplinary implications.

The diverse ways we come to understand the meaning of being human through the anthropological perspective can be seen in Figure 1.4. This diagram shows the connections among the four traditional specialties, or subdisciplines, of anthropology and their combined linkage to applied anthropology. As this figure illustrates, at the most inclusive level anthropology is the holistic study of human nature, human society, and human history. The following subsections will explain each of the four major specialties—biological anthropology, archaeology, linguistic anthropology, and cultural anthropology—as well as applied anthropology.

Biological Anthropology

Biological (or **physical**) **anthropology** focusses on human beings as living organisms and what makes us different from or similar to other living things. This specialty of anthropology has its roots in the nineteenth-century interest in human physical variation, which was

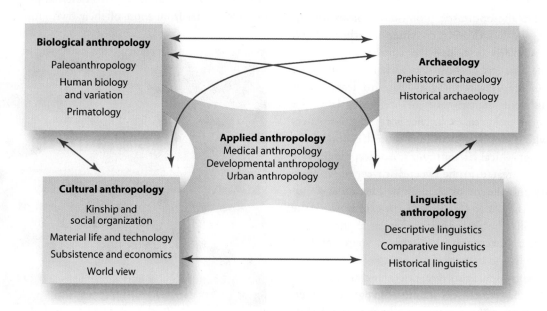

FIGURE 1.4 In North America, anthropology is traditionally divided into four specialties: biological anthropology, archaeology, linguistic anthropology, and cultural anthropology. Applied anthropology draws on information provided by the other four specialties.

a by-product of centuries of exploration and encounters between people from geographically distant societies. At the time, variation in the physical appearance of peoples around the world was a matter of interest, and early physical anthropologists invented elaborate techniques to measure observable features of human populations, including skin colour, hair, and body type. This "scientific" evidence facilitated the classification of all peoples into supposedly unambiguous categories based on distinct sets of biological attributes. Such categories were called *races*, and many nineteenth- and early twentieth-century physical anthropologists were convinced that their studies would reveal clear-cut criteria for racial classification.

The peoples whom these early physical anthropologists were trying to assign to racial categories were, in most cases, non-European peoples, peoples coming under increasing political and economic domination by colonizing European (and European-ancestry) capitalist societies. These peoples differed from "white" Europeans in ways other than physical appearance—they had their own languages and customs, and they possessed technologies that were, in most cases, no match for the might of the industrialized West. As a result, racial categorization not only noted individuals' physical characteristics but also made judgments on people's mental and moral attributes, and races were ranked in terms of these attributes. Not surprisingly, "white" Europeans and their "white" descendants in power outside Europe were seen as superior, while other races were considered to represent varying grades of inferiority. In this way, the first physical anthropologists helped develop theories that would justify the social practice of racism (see Chapter 12). Indeed, racism influenced official social policies in many Western nations well into the twentieth century. In Canada, one of the most destructive of such policies was the government's implementation of mandatory residential schools for Aboriginal children. Oneida scholar Roland Chrisjohn and his colleagues observe that these schools destroyed the circles of life and life-affirming metaphors of unity and wholeness, substituting instead Euro-Canadian "circle games" of the "empty non-existence of zero" (1997: 115).

Yet even as racist policies continued to affect the lives of individuals, many physical anthropologists in the early twentieth century began realizing the fallacy of racial categorization. New theories, many based on principles of holism, led these anthropologists to question past assumptions. In addition, new scientific advancements, such as the discovery of blood types, led them to add data on individuals' internal features to their calculations. The more they learned about the inner biological attributes of human beings, the more they realized that races with distinct and unique sets of such attributes simply did not exist. Thus they concluded that the concept of "race" was not a reflection of fact but instead a cultural label invented to sort people into groups.

Support for non-racial understandings of human populations has a long history among anthropologists in North America. Pioneering anthropologist Franz Boas, for example, who in the early 1900s founded the first department of anthropology in North America (at Columbia University), had long been uncomfortable with racial classifications. Boas and his students devoted much energy to debunking racist stereotypes, using both their knowledge of biology and their understanding of culture. As the discipline of anthropology developed in the United States and then Canada, students continued to be trained in both human biology and human culture, to provide them with the tools to fight racial and ethnic stereotyping. Rejecting the racial thinking of the nineteenth century, many modern anthropologists who study human biology prefer to call themselves *biological anthropologists* and focus on patterns of variation within the human species as a whole.

Today, some biological anthropologists, such as Biruté Galdikas (Simon Fraser University), work in the subfield of **primatology**; others, such as Pamela Willoughby (University of Alberta), work in the field of **paleoanthropology**. Other specialties focus on human adaptability in different ecological settings, on human growth and development, or on the connections between a population's evolutionary history and its susceptibility to disease. Forensic anthropologists, as noted below in the applied anthropology discussion, use their knowledge of human skeletal anatomy to aid law enforcement and human rights investigators (see Figure 1.5). Molecular anthropologists trace chemical similarities and differences in

primatology
The study of non-human primates, the closest living relatives of human beings.

paleoanthropology
The study of the fossilized remains of human beings' earliest ancestors.

FIGURE 1.5 Forensic anthropologists work with human remains to aid police investigations. How do you think the study of human biology could add to discussions of culture?

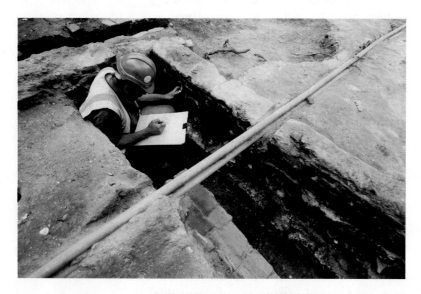

FIGURE 1.6 Excavation work and analysis of material remains are central to archaeologists' study of the human past. What sorts of insights can material remains offer about the ways cultures change over time?

archaeology
The specialty of anthropology interested in what we can learn from material remains left behind by earlier human societies.

cells, tissues, and organs; what they have learned about the immune system, for example, has enabled them to contribute actively to HIV/AIDS research. In all these ways, biological anthropologists can illuminate what makes human beings similar to (and different from) one another, other primates, and other living organisms.

Archaeology

Archaeology is the study of the human past through the analysis of material remains (Figure 1.6). Archaeologists must also be knowledgeable about the history of the sites they investigate—they must be familiar with past technologies and environmental as well as economic indicators (e.g., plant and animal remains)—so they can recognize valuable details and situate their findings within the greater scientific landscape. Archaeologists frequently work in teams with other scientists who specialize in specific areas of research. Their findings complement those of paleoanthropologists and indeed sometimes become common interest. For example, archaeological information about the use of stone tools in a particular region may correlate with fossil evidence of prehistoric human occupations.

One such example of an archaeological research project involving experts from various fields is the Dakhleh Oasis Project in Egypt (see EthnoProfile 1.1). Project director Anthony J. Mills, who initiated the project in 1978, describes it as

> a long-term regional study of the interaction between environmental changes and human activity in the closed area of the Dakhleh Oasis . . . since the first incursion of humans in the Middle Pleistocene, perhaps 400,000 years ago, down to the twenty-first century oasis farmers, and all the human activity and all the changing environmental conditions for which there is evidence within the time period. (Mills 2013)

Participants in the study include environmentalists, physical anthropologists, linguists, historians, and archaeologists specializing in various areas of study. The project has attracted researchers from around the globe, and several Canadians—including anthropologist Maxine Kleindienst—have signed on to contribute to the massive undertaking.

Scientific dating techniques allow archaeologists to make hypotheses about the age, territorial ranges, and patterns of sociocultural change in ancient societies, thus tracing the spread of cultural inventions over time and space. American archaeologist Jeremy Sabloff tells us that archaeology is an "action" science in the modern world, as it "can play helpful roles in broad, critical issues facing the world today . . . inform[ing] us in general about lessons to be learned from the successes and failures of past cultures and

EthnoProfile 1.1 | Dakhleh

Region Northeastern Africa

Nation Egypt

Language Nearly all of the 14 colonies that constitute the Dakhleh Oasis—including Mut, Al-Qasr, and Qalamoun—have their own dialect of Arabic

Population 75,000 (2002)

Environment Desert oasis

Livelihood Farming (dates, oranges, mangoes, wheat)

Political organization Region in a modern nation-state

For more information Chandler, Graham. 2006. "Before the Mummies: The Desert Origins of the Pharaohs," *Saudi Aramco World* 57, 5: 2–11; Mills, Anthony J. 2013. "Dakhleh Oasis Project," *Monash University Arts*, available at http://artsonline.monash.edu.au/archaeology/excavations-in-dakhleh-oasis-egypt.

provid[ing] policy-makers with useful contexts for future decision-making" (2008: 17). In such a context, archaeology becomes applied anthropology, which we discuss later in this chapter!

Linguistic Anthropology

Perhaps the most striking cultural feature of our species is language (see Chapter 4). Anthropologists have long recognized the connections between language and human culture, and many early anthropologists were the first researchers to transcribe non-Western languages and to produce grammars and dictionaries of those languages. When investigating living cultures, linguistic anthropologists often connect with one or a few members of the culture who can act as guides to the language and customs of specific social groups (Figure 1.7). The loss of languages is also a concern, as each language is a unique way of understanding ourselves and our place in the universe. Contemporary linguistic anthropologists and their counterparts in sociology (called *sociolinguists*) study the way language differences frequently correlate with differences in gender, race, class, or ethnic identity.

Linguistic anthropology has become so highly specialized that modern linguistic anthropologists are deeply trained in both linguistics and cultural anthropology, and many cultural anthropologists receive linguistics training as part of their professional preparation. Linguistic anthropologists are applied anthropologists in some instances, working to maintain endangered languages and attempting to help us understand the nature of language and its links to our cultural identity.

Cultural Anthropology

Now we come to the central topic of this book: **cultural anthropology**. Sometimes called *sociocultural anthropology*, *social anthropology*, or *ethnology*, cultural anthropology focusses on sets of learned behaviours and ideas that human beings acquire as members of a society. Recognizing that people ordinarily take their

linguistic anthropology
The specialty of anthropology concerned with the study of human languages.

cultural anthropology
The specialty of anthropology that studies how variation in beliefs and behaviours is shaped by culture and learned by different members of human groups.

FIGURE 1.7 Canadian linguistic anthropologist William Thurston with his friend Avel, a Lusi speaker, travelling in Papua New Guinea. During their travels, Avel acted as guide and introduced Thurston to the community where he collected material on the Mouk language. How can understanding a group's language help anthropologists understand that group's culture?

culturally shaped beliefs and behaviours for granted, anthropologist Michael Herzfeld has suggested that cultural anthropology might be usefully defined for us as "the study of common sense," although "sense" as a concept is not *common* to all cultures, and what one group considers to be "common sense" may not seem *sensible* to anyone outside that group (2001: 1).

Because people everywhere use culture to adapt to and transform everything in their wider world, the field of cultural anthropology is vast. Cultural anthropologists tend to specialize in one domain of human cultural activity or another. Many cultural anthropologists study language, music, dance, art, poetry, philosophy, religion, or ritual. Some study the ways particular groups of human beings organize themselves to carry out collective tasks, whether economic, political, or spiritual. This focus is in some ways similar to the discipline of sociology, and from it has come the identification of anthropology as one of the social sciences. In fact, sociology and anthropology developed during the same period of the late nineteenth and early twentieth centuries and thus share some similar interests in social organization. However, interest in *comparing* different forms of human social life sets anthropology apart from sociology.

FIGURE 1.8 A Bedouin woman in Jordan makes bread on the top of an oil drum, which she has reshaped and placed on top of rocks; in the past, she would have used more traditional materials. What might this use of materials tell us about the environment in which this woman lives?

Transcending the racism that permeated early anthropological studies, modern cultural anthropologists are concerned with studying *all* human societies, including their own, and they do research in urban and rural settings around the world. They reject, as do other anthropologists, labels such as *civilized* and *primitive* for the same reason they reject the term *race*. These concepts carry offensive connotations and do not help us make sense of the everyday realities of human life.

In recent years, many cultural anthropologists have studied contemporary issues of gender and sexuality, transnational labour migration, urbanization, globalization, and the lasting impact of colonialism. Others have investigated the patterns of material life found in different human groups. Among the most striking are worldwide variations in clothing, housing, tools, and techniques for getting and preparing food and making material goods (Figure 1.8). Like archaeologists, cultural anthropologists interested in material life describe the natural setting for which technologies have been developed, and they analyze the way technologies and environments shape each other.

In addition to investigating how certain technologies have developed in specific areas, cultural anthropologists also look at the effects of foreign technologies on local populations. Historically, colonialism brought many Western technologies (e.g., railroads, mechanical clocks, firearms) to non-Western peoples, often with enormous impact. Contemporary cultural anthropologists study these sorts of influences from a postcolonial perspective, examining the cultural legacies of these sorts of technologies. With the age of globalization upon us, another area of interest is the spread and influence of electronic media and communications technologies. Studies have shown, for example, the creative and unanticipated ways peoples use popular media and online communication tools (e.g., email, instant messaging) to make sense of their own local cultural context and situate it in a wider world.

As cultural anthropologists have become increasingly aware of the many influences that stretch across space to affect local communities, they have also become sensitive to those that stretch across time. As a result, many contemporary cultural anthropologists make serious efforts to place their cultural analyses in detailed historical contexts. These anthropologists often work closely with archaeologists and historians who have related interests.

Cultural anthropologists, no matter what their area of specialization, ordinarily collect their data during an extended period of fieldwork (the topic of Chapter 2). Its central feature is the anthropologists' involvement in the everyday routine of those among whom they live. Fieldwork is a period when the anthropologist receives one of the most meaningful gifts that any human can receive—entry into the lives of others. This gift is part of an act of *reciprocity*, an exchange of mutual benefit. The researcher can enhance the reciprocal relationship by participating in social activities and negotiating the meaning of what they observe with the people they work with. Fieldwork also requires that the anthropologist engage in what is termed *reflexivity*—thinking about why and how one thinks about specific things.

People who share information about their lives have traditionally been called **informants**; however, some anthropologists object to the use of this term because it suggests a role that is limited to supplying information for the benefit of the researcher. Therefore, some contemporary anthropologists choose to describe the people they encounter in the field as *partners, participants, consultants,* or simply *the people I work with* because these terms emphasize a relationship of equality based on mutual respect. Others prefer the term *teachers*, making it explicit that fieldwork is an active dialogue between the researcher (the student) and the people who are the experts on their own lives (the teachers). Of course, these experts, like all teachers, also learn and develop new perspectives as they interact with their students.

The recordings cultural anthropologists make in the field to document the lives of the people they work with are of prime importance. Most researchers make written notes, but many use videos or photographs as well (Figure 1.9). Indeed, the use of "shadow catching" technologies—devices that capture a visual representation of life—in the discipline dates back to the earliest period of photography in the nineteenth century. Such photographs have been an invaluable record. In many cases, however, visual records

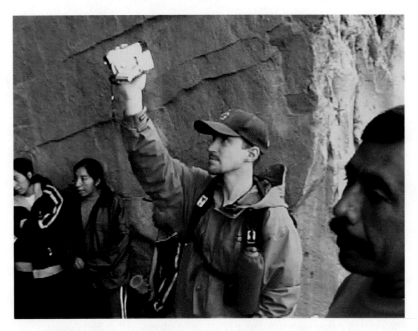

FIGURE 1.9 Anthropologist Ryan Cook videotapes the spectators and ritual performers at the Popocatepetl volcano in Mexico. How do you think using technology like this could impact the research process?

say more about the photographer or videographer than about his or her subject. This notion is well illustrated by some of Franz Boas's pictures taken for the US National Museum (e.g., Figure 1.10). Another historical example is photographer Edward Curtis's movie *In the Land of the War Canoes* (1914), which depicts a fictionalized account of the lives of the Kwakiutl (Kwakwaka'wakw) peoples (Northern Vancouver Island).

Two related terms for anthropological studies are *ethnography* and *ethnology*. An **ethnography** is a recorded description of a particular group of people's way of life; **ethnology** is the comparative study of two or more such groups. Thus, cultural anthropologists who write ethnographies are sometimes called *ethnographers*, and cultural anthropologists who compare ethnographic information on many different cultural practices are sometimes called *ethnologists*.

Applied Anthropology

Applied anthropology could be termed *action anthropology*. In applied anthropology, anthropological information is put to practical use to propose solutions to important social and cultural problems. You may be familiar with the practical applications of forensic anthropology—perhaps

informants
People in a particular culture who work with anthropologists and provide them with insights about local ways of life.

ethnography
An anthropologist's recorded description of a particular culture.

ethnology
The comparative study of two or more cultures.

applied anthropology
The use of information gathered from the other anthropological specialties to solve practical problems within and between cultures.

FIGURE 1.10   Franz Boas demonstrates a position in the Kwakiutl (Kwakwaka'wakw) Hamatsa dance ritual, as he observed it at Fort Rupert, British Columbia, in 1894.

you've even encountered media coverage of forensic anthropologists such as Mark Skinner (Simon Fraser University) who have worked on highly publicized crime cases or genocide investigations. Although generally exposed to less public attention, other areas of application can also make important contributions to social life. For example, when working with a traditionally structured non-Western community, applied anthropologists could

- use the culture's ideas about illness and health to introduce useful public health practices in a way that makes sense to, and will be accepted by, members of that culture (more on this in Chapter 9);
- draw on the knowledge of traditional social organization to ease the problems for refugees trying to settle in a new land; and
- integrate traditional and Western methods of cultivation to help farmers increase their crop yields.

biocultural organisms
Organisms whose defining features are co-determined by biological and cultural factors.

Because of the power of applied anthropology to solve problems and help those in need, many such anthropologists become advocates or activists for a cause. They use their professional skills to draw public attention to the plight of the people they study, to seek social justice, to fight discrimination, or to support human and cultural rights. In Canada, applied anthropologists have frequently acted to support First Nations land claims and resolve public policy issues (Hedican 2008).

While many anthropologists would argue that applied work can be done *within* any of the four traditional specialties, an increasing number of anthropologists have come to view applied anthropology as a separate field of professional specialization (see Figure 1.4). Thus more universities in Canada and the United States have begun to develop courses and programs specifically in applied anthropology.

Anthropology and the Concept of Culture

Unquestionably, the emergence of culture has had a profound impact on the evolution of human nature and human society. Thus, it is not surprising that the idea of culture as a marker of our humanness has been central to anthropological thought since the early days of the discipline. Pioneering anthropologist Edward B. Tylor defined culture as "that complex whole which includes knowledge, belief, art, morals, law, customs, and any other capabilities and habits acquired . . . as a member of society" (1958 [1871]: 1). Most later definitions have built on this theme.

From the anthropological perspective, culture is central to explanations of why we are what we are and why we do what we do. Anthropologists have shown that members of a social group behave in a particular way *not* because the behaviour is an inevitable result of human biology but because it is *learned*—individuals observe and then copy certain actions performed by others. At the same time, no one would deny that biology plays a role in determining what we *can* learn. Thus, most anthropologists view human beings as **biocultural organisms**. Our biological makeup, formed by our genes and cellular chemistry, contributes to our capacity to create and use culture. Conversely, our survival as biological organisms depends upon learned ways of thinking and acting that help us find food, shelter, and mates, and that teach us how to rear our children.

Of course, other living species learn, but our way of interacting with the wider world is distinct for two reasons:

1. our large, complex brains are capable of extremely intricate open symbolic thought and
2. our hands are capable of manipulating matter in both powerful and delicate ways.

Our being capable of open symbolic thought means that we are able to make sense of our world through **symbols**. We use symbols in many ways. For example, many of us use alphabetic symbols to represent the sounds of spoken languages. The sounds themselves are symbols, and they stand for meanings a speaker tries to express. The fact that we can translate from one language to another suggests that the same or similar meanings can be expressed by different symbols in different languages. However, we do not use symbols only to form language. Everything we do in society has a symbolic dimension, from how we conduct ourselves at the dinner table to how we bury the dead.

Culture's beginnings are deep in time. They can perhaps be glimpsed, in our modern world, among Japanese macaques who have invented a custom of washing sweet potatoes and among wild chimpanzees who have developed techniques to gain access to food or water (Figure 1.11). Our primate ancestors surely shared similar aptitudes when they started walking bipedally over 5 million years ago. Two and a half million years later, their descendants were making stone tools, and through human palaeontology and archaeology we can follow our cultural path to the silicon chip and beyond. Thus, as paleoanthropologist Richard Potts puts it, "an evolutionary bridge exists between the human and animal realms of behaviour" (1996: 197). Potts urges us to think of the modern human capacity for culture not as a uniform monolith but rather as a structure whose various pieces were added at different times in our evolutionary past (Figure 1.12). The foundation of culture, he proposes, contains five elements:

1. *transmission*, the ability to copy behaviour by observation and/or instruction;
2. *memory*, the ability to remember new behaviours (which allowed traditions to develop);
3. *reiteration*, the ability to reproduce or imitate behaviour or information that has been learned;
4. *innovation*, the ability to invent and modify behaviours; and
5. *selection*, the ability to select which innovations to keep and which to discard.

To the five basic elements, Potts adds three elements that evolved later and made *human* culture possible:

6. *symbolic coding*, or *symbolic representation*, the ability to use symbols to represent elements of reality;

symbol
Something that stands for something else.

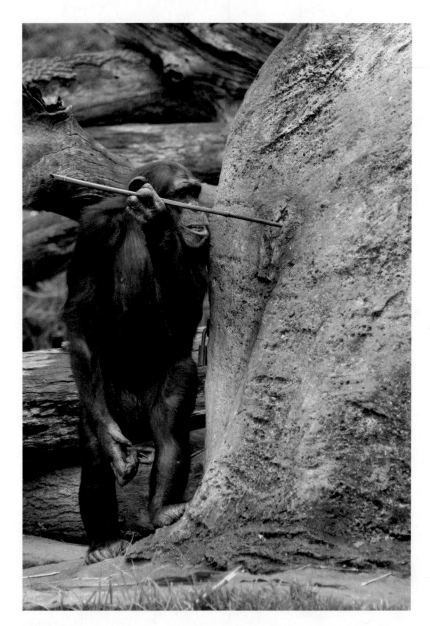

FIGURE 1.11 A chimpanzee uses a piece of bamboo to get termites out of a hole in a large rock.

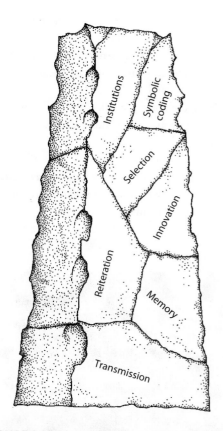

FIGURE 1.12 The modern human capacity for culture did not appear all at once. Rather, the various pieces that make it up were added at different times in our evolutionary past.

habitus
Everyday, routine social activity rooted in habitual behaviour.

cultural pattern
A behaviour or idea that members of a specific society repeatedly pass on to one another, across generations, and that is thus recognizable to all members of that society.

7. *complex symbolic representation*, the ability to communicate freely about the past, the future, and the invisible or imaginary; and
8. *institutional development*, the ability to create complex and variable forms of social organizations unique to our species.

Symbolic coding is something we share with other species, in particular the great apes. *Complex symbolic representation* distinguishes human language, for example, from the simpler vocal communication systems of apes. While apes have a limited ability to remember complex symbolic structures and to hold information on remote things, human beings can think about, invent, and discuss a great number of complex ideas in great detail. Indeed, humans evolved to be far more capable than any other species of learning and manipulating symbolic representations. Moreover, as biological anthropologist Terrence Deacon suggests, the huge adaptive value of complex symbolic representation for our ancestors appears to have led to genetic changes that improved our brain's symbolic capacities. Put another way, culture and the human brain *co-evolved*, each shaping the development of the other (Deacon 1997). Yet it is the final element given by Potts—*institutional development*—that made it possible for human culture to develop in such elaborate ways. As a result of our ability to create complex social organizations, culture has become "the predominant manner in which human groups vary from one another . . . it *swamps* the biological differences among populations" (Marks 1995: 200). We are truly biocultural organisms.

Throughout our history, culture has helped humanity survive and prosper in often difficult situations. As cultural traditions are passed on to new generations, we can modify them to meet our changing needs. Many of the practical survival skills we learn, such as what is good to eat and where it is safe to sleep, are never explicitly taught; nonetheless, they are dependent on contact with other members of our social group. Such learning is sometimes called **habitus** since it is rooted in habitual behaviour. In addition, because cultural traditions encompass the varied situational knowledges and skills of many different individuals, they allow the group to adapt and accomplish beyond any individual's limitations.

Looking at human cultures across time and space, we can also note that they appear *patterned*; that is, related cultural beliefs and practices repeatedly show up within a cultural group. An example of a common **cultural pattern** is a particular group's language. (Also see the discussion of *schemas* in Chapter 5.) Some cultural patterns are rooted in specific historical events: that English and French are widely spoken in Canada is connected to the colonial conquest and domination of Canada by speakers of English and French. Cultural patterns also vary across space: for example, the English of Newfoundland and Labrador differs from the English of southwestern Quebec, and from the various dialects used in different First Nations communities. It differs in rhythm and in vocabulary. Many factors contribute to such variation. In the case of First Nations communities in Canada, researchers have found that "the heritage languages, language socialization, and cultures of Aboriginal peoples living in Canada influence the ways in which Aboriginal children and families use English" (Bernhardt, Ball, and Deby 2007).

Because of this patterned cultural variation, anthropologists frequently distinguish different "cultural traditions" from one another. Although distinguishing such traditions can be useful as a kind of shorthand, we must remember that the boundaries between cultural traditions can be very fuzzy, ultimately resting on someone's judgment about how different one set of customs is from another. Indeed, customs in one area of a culture may contradict customs in another area, as when religion tells us to share with others and economics tells us to look out for ourselves. In addition, people have always borrowed cultural elements, so there may be much overlap between apparently distinct traditions.

As we think about what defines a cultural tradition, we must also remember not to assume conformity over time. Cultures constantly change, and many people refuse to be limited by cultural practices of the past. Yet there is also the question of *traditional culture*—what aspects of the past do specific peoples want to protect, maintain, or retrieve? (Note Regna Darnell's discussion in the "In Their Own Words" box, below.) Worldwide this is a fundamental dilemma for peoples who have been subjugated or forced to abandon elements of their traditional cultures (e.g., under colonization). In the Canadian context, this question is of particular concern to First Nations peoples. Ron Ignace, a member of a First Nations band in British Columbia, expressed such concerns in an interview with anthropologist Noel Dyck:

They [some anthropologists and museums] don't seem to understand that we still exist as a people, that we adapt and change and we have that right to adapt and change, while still maintaining some of our principles that were tried and true over the years. Particularly principles that are necessary for survival as a people. (Ignace et al. 1993: 168–9)

IN THEIR OWN WORDS | Invisible Genealogies

Canadian anthropologist Regna Darnell speaks to the concepts of "tradition" and "traditional" culture.

"Traditional" culture is a moving target, always changing and adapting to new circumstances. It is located in the contemporary practices of the communities whose interests and concerns direct the work of anthropologists. The label "traditional" is used with considerable rhetorical force in contemporary Native American communities and in their interactions with non-Native institutions and individuals. "Tradition" does not imply returning to some idealized pure culture that existed before Columbus spearheaded the invasion of the "new" world. Native Americans recognize that their societies, like those of white people, whether in Europe or America, have changed in 500 years; all peoples have a history in which living traditions are continuously invented and reinvented.

This discourse is, of course, very different from the non-Americanist one about "invented traditions" that somehow lack authenticity because they are continually constructed by contemporary communities, often without attention to the scientific authority of the anthropologist to define their culture. In my view, anthropologists, in the field and in their writing alike, must respect both the cultural heritage and the contemporary practice of the peoples with whom they work. "Tradition," in such a discourse, refers to that which is continuous with the past, in line with the practices and values of a moral community. Native people themselves can and should define what is traditional within their own communities. They do so in terms of innovations that serve to maintain the identity of the community and its members in relation to their collective histories and personal agencies. "Tradition," in Native American terms, holds much of the meaning that "culture" embodies for anthropologists. If it is invented, we must celebrate its creativity and adaptability under conditions of change. That anthropologists sometimes produce alternative interpretations for other purposes is, of course, another matter.

Source: Darnell, Regna. 2001. *Invisible Genealogies: A History of Americanist Anthropology* (Lincoln: University of Nebraska Press), 16–17.

As Ignace's comments suggest, the question of how anthropologists can best represent the cultures they study to an outside population is a matter that requires great consideration, sensitivity, and consultation.

Anthropology and Culture/Cultures: Critique and Response

For many years, the concept of "culture" anchored the anthropological perspective and illuminated the human condition in powerful ways. Yet, over time, the term *culture* came to mean somewhat different things to different people, and culture has become the most contested concept of contemporary anthropology.

Essentially, the critique centres on the specific definition of *culture* (singular) and of *cultures* (plural). The former refers to the distinguishing human characteristic of being able to create and imitate patterned, symbolically mediated ideas and activities that promote the survival of the species, while the latter indicates a particular, learned way of life belonging to a specific group of human beings. Of the two definitions, the second has elicited the most objections. Those who "write against culture" (Abu-Lughod 1991) defend the validity of *culture* as a concept, but they object to the use of the term *cultures* because it highlights the differences, rather than shared humanness, between groups of people. To some, this focus on differences suggests a lingering racism in the field of anthropology.

The controversy is heated because many anthropologists have viewed the use of *cultures* (plural) as not only analytically helpful but politically progressive. Their view reflects a struggle that developed in nineteenth-century Europe: supporters of the purportedly progressive civilization of the Enlightenment, spread in large part by Napoleonic conquest (c. 1803–1815), were challenged by inhabitants of European nations who resisted both Napoleon and the Enlightenment in what has been called the Romantic Counter-Enlightenment. Romantic intellectuals rejected what they considered to be the imposition of "artificial" Enlightenment *civilization* on the "natural" spiritual traditions of their own distinct national or regional *cultures* (Kuper 1999; Crehan 2002). This political dynamic, which pits a steamroller civilization against vulnerable local cultures, carried over into the usage that later developed in anthropology, particularly in North America.

The decades surrounding the turn of the twentieth century marked a period of expanding European colonial empires, as well as westward expansion and consolidation of control in North America. At that time, the social sciences were becoming established in universities, and different fields were assigned different tasks. Anthropology was allocated what Trouillot (1991) has called "the savage slot"—that is, the so-called "primitive" world that was the target of colonization. Anthropologists thus became the official academic experts on societies whose members suffered appalling racist denigration as "primitives" and whose ways of life were being undermined by contact with Western colonial "civilization." And rightly, many anthropologists were determined to denounce such practices and to demonstrate that the "primitive" stereotype was false.

Some found inspiration in the work of English anthropologist Edward B. Tylor who, as we noted earlier, presented a lasting definition of the term *culture*. His definition had the virtue of blurring the difference between "culture" and "civilization," and it encouraged the view that even "primitives" possessed "capabilities and habits" that merited respect. Thus, in response to stereotypes of "primitives" as irrational, disorganized, insensitive, or promiscuous, anthropologists such as Franz Boas and Bronislaw Malinowski were able to show that, on the contrary, so-called "primitives" possessed "cultures" that were reasonable, orderly, artistically developed, and morally disciplined. The plural use of *culture* allowed them to argue that, in their own ways, "primitives" were as fully human as "civilized" people.

By the end of the twentieth century, however, the plural use of *culture* began to appear pernicious rather than progressive. To some, the boundary that was once thought to protect vulnerability came to look more like a prison wall, condemning those within it to live according to "their" culture just as their ancestors had done, like exhibits in a living museum, whether they wanted to or not (recall the quote above from Ron Ignace and his colleagues). Contemporary critics argue that the plural concept of culture not only highlights the differences between groups of people but also assumes that group members uncritically accept those differences, want to preserve them, and naturally view cultural change as the loss of authenticity. Consequently, if group members disagree with one another publicly, import ideas or practices from other societies, or challenge traditional ways (e.g., by protesting against social inequality), they may be condemned by insiders and outsiders alike as flirting with cultural treason. It is this absolute, inflexible concept of culture that is the problem: it seems to endorse an oppressive kind of cultural determinism.

Anthropologists Michel-Rolph Trouillot (1991) and Adam Kuper (1999) have suggested that anthropologists who continue to use any form of the concepts of *culture* (singular) or *cultures* (plural) as a part of their professional analytic vocabulary risk lending credibility to the way the concepts have been used to oppress rather than to liberate. They present serious considerations. We must, as anthropologists, be constantly vigilant that oppression is not the outcome of our work. Allowing or facilitating any outcomes of oppression from our research is a betrayal of the great gift, essentially the gift of "self," entrusted to us by our teachers in the communities where we have lived and learned to be anthropologists.

In another take on the issue, anthropologist Sherry Ortner notes that the essence of the critique was that in the atmosphere of post-colonialism, "many ethnic groups, and many contemporary post-colonial intellectuals, react very strongly against being studied as specimens of cultural differences and otherness" (1999: 8). Thus the critique of racism was not infrequent. However, Ortner also points out that it is not an issue of "banishing" the concept of cultures but rather of thinking on the process of "reconfiguring this enormously productive concept [*cultures*] for a changing world, . . . a changing landscape of theoretical possibilities" (8). What she calls for are three "imperatives":

1. "[E]xoticize and objectify the culture of the ethnographer, placing it in the same analytic framework" (8). This imperative would allow anthropologists to highlight differences between cultures without implying that their own culture is better or more "normal" than others.
2. "Emphasize the issue of meaning-*making*," an active process (8–9). This imperative would ensure anthropologists represent cultures as dynamic rather than static, and that they recognize individuals as active participants in making sense of their own lives.
3. "[S]ituate cultural analysis within . . . larger analyses of social and political events and processes" (9). This imperative would force anthropologists to work toward a greater purpose, rather than simply engaging in cultural analysis as an "end in itself." It would also force them to recognize the reality that no community exists in isolation.

Attempts by anthropologists to deal with these complications will be a focus in future chapters, especially in our discussions of anthropological approaches to ethnicity and nationalism (Chapter 12), globalization (Chapter 13), and democracy and multiculturalism (Chapter 14).

The Challenge of Cultural Differences

The same objects, actions, or events frequently mean different things to people within different cultures. In fact, what counts as an object or event in one culture may not be recognized as such in another. Even within a single cultural tradition, the meaning of an object or an action may differ depending on the context. Quoting philosopher Gilbert Ryle, anthropologist Clifford Geertz notes that "there is a world of difference between a wink and a blink, as anyone who has ever mistaken one for the other has undoubtedly learned" (1973: 6).

Thus, human experience is inherently ambiguous. To resolve the ambiguity, experience must be interpreted. Human beings turn to their own cultural traditions in search of an interpretation that makes sense and is coherent. They do this daily as they go about life among others with whom they share traditions. But this interpretive activity does not cease at the boundary of their specific place in their culture, and serious misunderstandings may arise when two individuals are unaware that their cultural traditions or cultural ground rules differ. Noting the potential for misunderstanding in such encounters, anthropologists are careful to distinguish between two approaches: *ethnocentrism* and *cultural relativism*.

Ethnocentrism

ethnocentrism
The opinion that one's own way of life is the most natural, correct, or fully human way of life.

Ethnocentrism is the term anthropologists use to describe the opinion that one's own way of life is natural or correct, indeed the only way of being fully human. Ethnocentrism is one solution to the inevitable tension between individuals from different cultural backgrounds. Yet this "solution" is problematic because it reduces other ways of life to distorted versions of one's own.

The greatest problems with ethnocentrism arise when the members of one society go beyond merely interpreting another way of life in ethnocentric terms and decide to do something about the differences they observe. For example, if individuals from one group conclude that the other way of life is wrong, they might try to convert the members of the other group to their own way of doing things. If the others are unwilling to change their ways, the failed attempt at conversion may transform into an active dualism: *we* versus *they*, *civilization* versus *savagery*, *good* versus *evil*. The ultimate result may be war and *genocide*—the deliberate attempt to exterminate an entire group based on race, religion, national origin, or other cultural features. Throughout history, such assumed differences have also been used as an excuse for economic and political gains by one group over another. Anthropologist and genocide specialist Alexander Laban Hinton goes so far as to call genocide "the Janus face"—the darker flip side—of the Western **metanarratives** of "civilization" and "progress" that drove the rise of the modern nation-state (2002: 1). Even in more recent times, ethnocentric justifications for war and genocide have persisted, playing a large part in such conflicts as the Rwandan and Bosnian genocides in the 1990s and the continuing tragedy in Darfur.

cultural relativism
"Understanding another culture in its own terms sympathetically enough so that the culture appears to be a coherent and meaningful design for living."

metanarrative
A grand-scale story or theme that members of a given culture recognize and that often drives ideas and actions within that culture.

Is it possible to avoid ethnocentric bias? A holistic approach to relationships between us and others, both across and within cultural traditions, holds promise. So too does our lifelong ability to learn—if we honour this potential in ourselves and others. People with a cultural background very different from your own may help you see possibilities for belief and action that are drastically at odds with everything your tradition considers possible. By becoming aware of these unsuspected possibilities, you become a different person. In effect you may be gifted with an "Aha!" moment—a moment of sudden clarity and discovery. In addition, when you share elements of your own culture with people from another cultural background, those individuals are likely to be affected in a similar way.

Learning about other cultures opens us up to new possibilities. Once such learning occurs, we can no longer claim that any single culture has a monopoly on truth. Rather, we must recognize that the truth embodied in any cultural tradition is bound to be partial, approximate, and open to further insight and growth.

Cultural Relativism

Anthropologists must come to terms with the consequences of learning about cultural differences as they do their fieldwork. One result has been the formulation of the concept of **cultural relativism**. Boas taught that cultural relativism was the considered response to racism and prejudice. One of his students, Ruth Benedict, commented that all cultures are "equally valid patterns of life, which mankind has created for itself from the raw materials of existence" (1934: 279). Definitions of cultural relativism have varied over time as different anthropologists have tried to draw conclusions based on their own experiences with other ways of life. One definition that attempts a holistic approach states that cultural relativism involves "understanding another culture in its own terms sympathetically enough so that the culture appears to be a coherent and meaningful design for living" (Greenwood and Stini 1977: 182).

Taking a relativistic approach can help us understand what at first might seem incomprehensible from an outsider's perspective. For example, cultural relativism can help us understand how genocide could develop in a society. Consider the example of the Holocaust in Europe. The Holocaust was intimately related to certain cultural patterns and historical processes that were, and perhaps are yet, deeply rooted in

German and European society (Figure 1.13). Answering questions on the causes of the Holocaust involves investigating the historical roots of anti-Semitism and nationalism in Germany.

Some people might be inclined to take a deterministic approach to explaining such an event, arguing that the killers cannot be blamed for their own actions because they had no choice but to do what their culture dictated. These same people might also argue that all members of the culture committing the genocide are responsible because it was their collectively constructed culture that led to the genocide. Yet to accept the argument that "their" culture made them do it is to accept a pessimistic version of cultural determinism that can offer only a simplified account of any complex phenomena. This sort of cultural determinism makes three major faulty assumptions about human nature and human society:

1. cultures have neat boundaries between them and are sealed off from one another;
2. every culture offers people only one way to interpret experience (cultures are uniform and permit no variety, harbour no contradictions, and allow no dissent); and
3. people living in these closed cultural worlds are passively shaped by culture, helpless to resist indoctrination into a single world view, and incapable of inventing alternatives to that view.

Yet lived human experience undermines all three of these assumptions. To begin with, cultures are not sealed off from one another. Their boundaries are fuzzy, indeed porous, and people with different cultural backgrounds regularly exchange ideas and practices. Internally, they are not uniform. Even without the alternatives introduced from the outside, every culture offers a variety of ways to interpret experience, although not all may be officially sanctioned. In addition, cultures are constantly being redefined by their members. Finally, human beings are not passive lumps shaped unresistingly to fit a single cultural mould. After all, there is no such thing as a single cultural mould in a society acquainted with variety, and in a society where options exist, choices must be made.

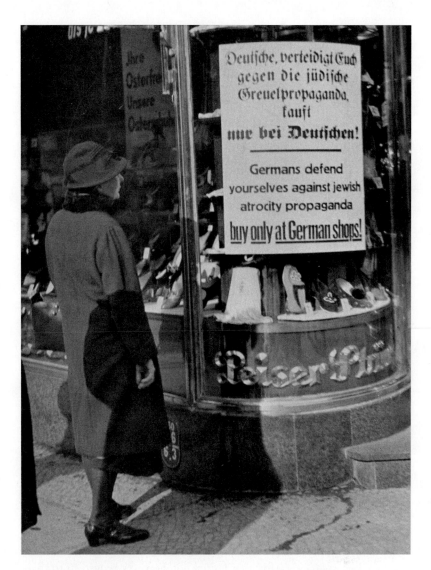

FIGURE 1.13 A sign posted in Berlin, Germany, in 1933 assaults passersby: "Germans defend yourselves against jewish [sic] atrocity propaganda, buy only at German shops!" Such public displays of combined anti-Semitism and nationalism are evidence of the cultural preoccupations that led to the Holocaust. How can taking a relativistic approach to other cultures help us make sense of this sort of hateful display?

In contrast to the deterministic approach, a relativistic understanding of the Holocaust—and mass genocides in general—accomplishes several things. It makes the events more comprehensible, even coherent. It reveals, to our horror, how the persecution and murder of human beings can appear perfectly acceptable when placed in a particular context of meaning, thus challenging our own views on violence. The one thing that this relativistic understanding does not do, however, is allow us to excuse mass killers for what they have done on the grounds that it was all due to their culture.

Understanding something is not the same as approving or excusing it. When we grow to understand a cultural practice that we at first found repellent, we may arrive at a number of different conclusions. We may change our minds and decide that the practice is desirable, at least in some contexts. We may conclude that the practice in question is more suitable for the people who employ it than any of our own practices would be. We might even recommend that the practice be adopted in our own society. But the opposite may also be the case.

We may understand perfectly the cultural rationales—for example, those behind such practices as slavery, infanticide, headhunting, or genocide—and still refuse our approval. We may not be persuaded by the reasons offered to justify the practice, or we may be aware of alternative practices that could achieve the desired outcome using less drastic methods. Indeed, it is likely that any cultural practice with far-reaching consequences for human life will have critics as well as supporters within the society where it is practised. This is certainly the case in North American societies where such sensitive topics as abortion, capital punishment, gun laws, and same-sex marriage have been and continue to be discussed in many contexts.

Cultural relativism makes moral reasoning more complex and, not infrequently, less comfortable. It does not, however, require us to abandon every value our own society has taught us. Our culture, like every other culture, offers more than one way of evaluating experience. Exposure to the interpretations of an unfamiliar culture forces us to reconsider the possibilities our culture recognizes in light of new alternatives. It invites us to search for areas of intersection as well as areas of disagreement. What cultural relativism does discourage is the easy solution of refusing to consider alternatives from the outset. Also, it does not free us from sometimes facing difficult choices between alternatives whose rightness or wrongness is less than clear-cut. In this sense, "cultural relativism is a 'tough-minded' philosophy" (Herskovits 1973: 37). As cultural anthropologist Renato Rosaldo (2008) comments,

> Relativism . . . argues for engagement, for dialogue between cultures. This is not the kind of easy cosmopolitanism that implies enormous privilege—the capacity, for example, to spend three days in the Bali Hilton. It's a deeper form of knowing that entails some recognition that I am one among others. I'm not the centre of the universe.

Thus, at its core, cultural relativism is an argument against ethnocentrism.

Culture, History, and Human Agency

The human condition is rooted in time and shaped by history. As part of the human condition, culture is also historical, worked out and reconstructed in every generation. As paleoanthropologists have shown, the human species is itself a product of millions of years of evolution. Hence, human history is an essential aspect of the human story.

Anthropologists sometimes disagree about how to approach human history. Nineteenth-century thinkers such as Herbert Spencer argued that an examination of the evolution of social structures over time was central to the study of the human condition. Other anthropologists were not interested in change over time. In the 1930s, British anthropologist A.R. Radcliffe-Brown justified this lack of interest by pointing out that in societies without written records, knowledge about past life is non-existent; according to him, any attempt to reconstruct such past life would be an unfounded attempt at "conjectural history."

Approaches such as this, which ignore the significance of *oral* (as opposed to *written*) histories, lost support by the end of the twentieth century. As French philosopher Jean-François Lyotard observes, it is "impossible to judge the . . . validity of narrative knowledge on the basis of scientific knowledge [since] the relevant criteria are different" (1987: 80). In other words, we cannot conclude that knowledge shared orally, through storytelling, is any less meaningful than more rigidly recorded history. Different ways of transmitting knowledge from person to person, generation to generation, simply reflect the diversity of the human condition. No matter what the method of transmission, all societies choose what aspects of their history they want to remember, and the collective memory of a people is transmitted "in their historical, social, and political context" (Rodriguez and Fortier 2009: 7).

Other early anthropologists had no interest in history for a different reason. Western capitalist culture, with its eye on the future and its faith in progress—a theme from the Enlightenment—has had little use for the past. It is therefore no wonder that some anthropologists built clockwork models of social structures that could be trusted to run reliably without "losing time." In these models, human beings and societies are both likened to machines. If a living organism is used as the model of society, and if organisms are nothing but machines, then a machine model of society, with individuals as robot-like moving parts, is not at all far-fetched (Figure 1.14).

A holistic approach—one that focusses on inclusive assessment of counter points of view—to human history, however, rejects these clockwork models. Our biocultural heritage has produced a living species that uses culture to overcome biological and individual limitations. The result has been the emergence of beings capable of studying themselves and their own biocultural evolution.

But just how free from limitations are humans? Opinion in Western societies often polarizes around one of two extremes: either we have *free will* and may do just as we please, or our behaviour is *completely determined* by biology or society. Many social scientists, however, are convinced that a more realistic description of human freedom was offered by Karl Marx, who wrote, "Men make their own history, but they do not make it just as they please; they do not make it under circumstances chosen by themselves but under circumstances directly encountered, given, and transmitted by the past" (1963 [1852]: 15). As humans we regularly struggle, often against great odds, to exercise some control over our lives (Figure 1.15). We are *agents*, but agents

FIGURE 1.14 In the 1927 film *Metropolis*, a lower class of labourers works within a machine-like power plant, which strictly limits what they can do, to supply the ruling classes. Does this sort of technological metaphor accurately represent the way your own life works?

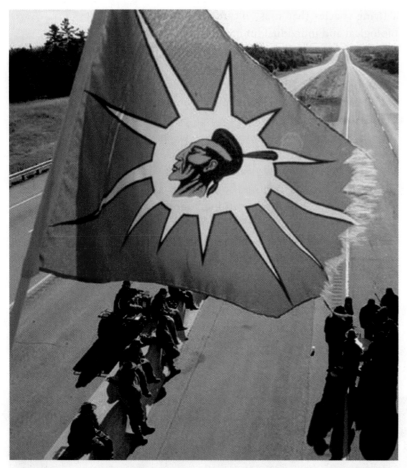

FIGURE 1.15 In 2007, Mohawk protesters successfully shut down Highway 401, one of Canada's busiest highways, as part of their protest of a housing development near Deseronto, Ontario. Besides protest, what other ways do humans demonstrate agency in their lives?

Some anthropologists even liken our existence to a minefield that we must painstakingly try to cross without blowing ourselves up. In such cultural contexts, with their ragged edges and fuzzy boundaries, we human beings must make interpretations, formulate goals, and set out in pursuit of them. A holistic, dialectical approach to the human condition recognizes the existence and importance of **human agency**—the stuff of our dreams and the realm of our potential for growth.

The Promise of the Anthropological Perspective

The anthropological perspective on the human condition is not easy to maintain. It forces us to question the common-sense assumptions with which we are most comfortable. It increases the difficulty we encounter when faced with moral and political decisions. It does not allow us an easy retreat to ethnocentrism when the going gets rough. Once we are exposed to the kinds of experiences that the anthropological undertaking makes possible, we are changed—for better or worse. We cannot easily pretend that these new experiences never happened to us. Once we have had a genuine glimpse of "the other" as human beings equal to ourselves, there is no going back, except in bad faith.

So, anthropology is guaranteed to complicate your life. Nevertheless, the anthropological perspective can give you a broader understanding of human nature and the wider world—of society, culture, and history—and thus help you construct more realistic and authentic ways of coping with those complications.

human agency
Human beings' ability to exercise at least some control over their lives.

who cannot escape from the cultural and historical contexts within which we act. We must frequently select a course of action when the "correct" choice is unclear and the outcome uncertain.

A CRITICAL LOOK | The Canadian Mosaic

Where the United States has termed its national character a melting pot, Canadians have chosen the image of a cultural mosaic—a rich, colourful collage made up of pieces from many different cultures. But where did this notion of Canada as a multicultural nation come from? And just how inclusive of different cultures *is* our national identity?

The idea of the cultural mosaic was first developed by Scottish-Canadian writer John Murray Gibbon (1875–1952), in his book *Canadian Mosaic* (1938). Gibbon was, in many ways,

a model of a certain type of "British" colonial-era immigrant. He was born in British colonial Ceylon (now post-colonial Sri Lanka); his father was a British colonial bureaucrat. As a child, he was sent "home" to be educated in Scotland, and he later attended university in England and then in Germany. In 1913, the year before World War I broke out in Europe, Gibbon came to Canada to work for the Canadian Pacific Railway (CPR).

The CPR was—and remains—an iconic Canadian company. Between 1881 and 1885, it built a national railway linking eastern Canada to the west coast. The CPR was a model of late nineteenth-century capitalism. Driven by profit, it imported 15,000 Chinese labourers willing to work for little pay and under dangerous conditions. In the five years it took to complete the project, at least 600 of those workers died. The CPR accepted these deaths as the cost of progress, as did they accept the disruptions the railway brought to Aboriginal peoples' ways of life. And in the end, most Canadians did, too. After all, the railway helped to unify Canada as a nation, and it allowed European immigrant families to move west.

In the decades following the completion of the railway, Canadian officials actively encouraged the settlement and development of western Canada. They offered free land to Europeans looking for a new start (but not to the Chinese who had built the railway), and their campaign was very successful. As Canadian academic Antonia Smith (2007) notes, however, members of the British-Canadian elite soon felt threatened by the influx of so many new people from southern and eastern Europe. One response to this perceived threat was to implicitly accept Canadian-British culture as the country's dominant culture, while characterizing non-British cultures as "other." By extension, people from "other" cultures were "outsiders," while British-Canadians remained "insiders."

It was against this historical backdrop that Gibbon, the quintessential colonial company man, began to consider the emerging character of Canada in the post–World War I period. Undoubtedly, Gibbon's status as a British-Canadian immigrant in a country ruled (for the most part) by British-Canadians coloured his view of what he termed a "mosaic." To Gibbon and his like-minded contemporaries, encouraging diversity meant organizing and supporting festivals of "folk" (usually meaning "non-British") culture and crafts. These events consolidated specific images of "Canadian-ness," creating "multiple discourses of race, citizenship, cultural belonging, and national identity" at a time of "demographic flux" (Smith 2007: 37). Subsequently, Gibbon's work contributed to definitions of *multiculturalism* and, indeed, culturally "inclusive" legislation. Thus emerged a Canadian identity based in pluralism. However, in some senses a binary remained—between "English" Canadians and the "folks."

Questions about the place of different cultural traditions in relation to our national identity remain relevant today. A major concern, which Canadian anthropologist Regna Darnell (2000) discusses, is why our national identity doesn't reflect a greater influence from First Nations peoples. If, as we so often hear, Canada's national identity is founded on multiculturalism, why are Aboriginal peoples still viewed as "others"? These peoples were, after all, here long before the British or the French began colonizing the land. And we could, as a nation, learn a great deal from them—from "the application of First Nations strategies of consensus, environmental stewardship, community rights and obligations, respect for the wisdom of age, and the autonomy of individuals" (Darnell 2000: 166). Suggesting the need for a more holistic, inclusive approach, Darnell notes that anthropologists are uniquely situated to participate in "reconstituting the Canadian national identity" (173). Ultimately, anthropological work may lead to a national identity that truly reflects the cultural diversity of the Canadian people.

—Roberta Robin Dods

KEY TERMS

anthropological
  perspective 5
anthropology 5
applied anthropology 11
archaeology 8
binary opposition 3
biocultural organisms 12
biological evolution 6

biological (or physical)
  anthropology 6
co-evolution 5
comparative 5
cultural anthropology 9
cultural evolution 6
cultural pattern 14
cultural relativism 18
culture 4

determinism 3
dualism 3
essence 3
ethnocentrism 18
ethnography 11
ethnology 11
evolutionary 6
habitus 14
holism 4

human agency 22
idealism 3
informants 11
linguistic anthropology 9
materialism 3
metanarrative 18
paleoanthropology 7
primatology 7
symbol 13

CHAPTER SUMMARY

1. Various models have been devised to explain humans and their cultures: dualism, idealism, cultural determinism, for example. Since anthropology aims to describe, in the broadest sense, what it means to be human, anthropologists have developed a perspective on the human condition that is holistic, comparative, and evolutionary.

2. North American anthropology is usually considered to have four major specialties or subdisciplines: biological anthropology, archaeology, linguistic anthropology, and cultural anthropology. Some anthropologists consider a fifth to be applied anthropology. Each of the four traditional subdisciplines can inform the others, and each can contribute to problem-solving within and between cultures.

3. Many anthropologists have criticized the use of the term *cultures* to refer to particular, learned ways of life belonging to specific groups of human beings. Critics argue that the plural concept of *cultures* seems to endorse an oppressive kind of cultural determinism. Yet many groups have incorporated the term *cultures*, with its plural meaning, into their own self-definitions. Many anthropologists defend this use of the term as valuable and progressive.

4. Ethnocentrism is a form of reductionism. Anthropologists believe it can be countered by a commitment to cultural relativism, an attempt to understand the cultural underpinnings of behaviour. Cultural relativism makes moral decisions more difficult because it requires us to take into account many things before we make up our minds. Cultural relativism does not require us to abandon every value our society has taught us; however, it does not permit the easy solution of refusing to consider alternatives from the outset.

5. Through fieldwork, cultural anthropologists gain insight into another culture, both by participating with their informants in social activities and by observing those activities as outsiders. Ethnographies are published accounts of what an anthropologist learned during fieldwork. Ethnology involves comparing ethnographic information from two or more different cultures. Because human experience is often ambiguous, adaptation requires cultural interpretation, which is a constant, necessary process, whether it is an attempt to understand people or symbols within one's own culture or those of another culture.

CRITICAL THINKING QUESTIONS

1. Using the concepts of *idealism* and *materialism*, how would you develop definitions of what it means to be human? How deterministic are your definitions?

2. What is the difference between *culture* (singular) and *cultures* (plural)? Why has this distinction become contentious in anthropology, and how could this problem be resolved?

3. What are the advantages of taking a holistic approach in anthropology? How does the concept of holism relate to the concept of cultural relativism? Can holism succeed in anthropology without cultural relativism?

4. How do the four original subdisciplines of anthropology—biological anthropology, archaeology, linguistic anthropology, and cultural anthropology—contribute to an understanding of humans? How does applied anthropology add to this anthropological perspective, and what would you consider to be its ethical position in anthropology?

SUGGESTED READINGS

In Recent (and Relatively Recent) Publications

Benhabib, Seyla. 2002. *The Claims of Culture: Equality and Diversity in the Global Era* (Princeton, NJ: Princeton University Press). This book examines what we mean by "political membership" and what constitutes a "political community": How do we bring people we term "aliens"—strangers, immigrants, asylum seekers—into our political processes? What boundaries must be negotiated?

Borofsky, Robert, Fredrik Barth, Richard A. Shweder, Lars Rodseth, and Nomi Maya Stolzenberg. 2001. "When: A Conversation about Culture," *American Anthropologist*, New Series, 103, 2: 432–46. A discussion of what culture is and is not, as well as how and when anthropologists should use the culture concept.

Feder, Kenneth L. 2014. *Frauds, Myths, and Mysteries: Science and Pseudoscience in Archaeology*, 8th edn (New York: McGraw-Hill). An entertaining and informative exploration of fascinating frauds and genuine archaeological mysteries seen through an application of the scientific method.

Marks, Jonathan. 2002. *What It Means to Be 98% Chimpanzee: Apes, People, and Their Genes* (Berkeley: University of California Press). A lively and provocative text by a molecular anthropologist who explains what can and cannot be concluded from the fact that the genomes of chimpanzees and humans are nearly identical.

Ortner, Sherry. B. 2006. *Anthropology and Social Theory: Culture, Power, and the Acting Subject* (Durham, NC: Duke University Press). So you want to be an anthropologist? This is a must-read, either now or when you are in an advanced theory course!

Relethford, John. 2013. *The Human Species: An Introduction to Biological Anthropology*, 9th edn (New York: McGraw-Hill). An excellent, clear introduction to biological anthropology.

Sahlins, Marshall. 1999. "Two or Three Things That I Know about Culture," *Journal of the Royal Anthropological Institute* 5, 3: 399–421. A thoughtful consideration of the lasting importance of culture as an anthropological concept.

Skinner, Mark, and Kristina Bowie. 2009. "Forensic Anthropology: Canadian Content and Contributions," in *Handbook of Forensic Anthropology and Archaeology*, ed. S. Blau and D.H. Ubelaker (Walnut Creek, CA: Left Coast Press), 87–103. A survey of forensic anthropology in Canada, Chapter 8 in an in-depth handbook for forensic anthropologists.

Smedley, Audrey. 1998. "'Race' and the Construction of Human Identity," *American Anthropologist*, New Series, 100, 3: 690–702. An examination of how "race" came to be associated with human identity, and the problems with this association.

Taylor, Christopher C. 2002. "The Cultural Face of Terror in the Rwandan Genocide of 1994," in *Annihilating Difference: The Anthropology of Genocide*, ed. Alexander Laban Hinton (Berkeley: University of California Press), 138–78. Exploring a topic central to Canadian discussions of participation in peacekeeping, this chapter from a book on genocide challenges us on the nature of culture.

Watson, Patty Jo. 1995. "Archaeology, Anthropology, and the Culture Concept," *American Anthropologist*, New Series, 97, 4: 683–94. This article relates how an anthropologist/archaeologist evolved in her thinking about the nature of the subject of her discipline and her specialty within that discipline.

RELATED WEBSITES

Archaeology at Parks Canada www.pc.gc.ca/eng/progs/arch/index.aspx

Canadian Anthropology Society www.cas-sca.ca

Residential Schools www.cbc.ca/news/canada/a-history-of-residential-schools-in-canada-1.702280

American Anthropological Association www.aaanet.org

Informant (Debated Terminology) www.anthrobase.com/Dic/eng/def/informant.htm

Society for Applied Anthropology www.sfaa.net

Historical Perspective (1940s–1960s)

Boas, Franz. 1940. *Race, Language and Culture* (New York: Macmillan). A collection of Boas's most influential essays on anthropology.

Kroeber, Alfred L. 1948. "White's View of Culture," *American Anthropologist*, New Series, 50, 3 (Part 1): 405–15. American cultural anthropologist Alfred L. Kroeber, who studied under Boas, examines and clarifies a view of culture put forth by Leslie A. White (see below).

Montagu, Ashley. 1962. "The Concept of Race," *American Anthropologist*, New Series, 64, 5 (Part 1): 919–28. An examination of "the concepts of race as they are used with reference to man," written by a highly accomplished British-American anthropologist.

Stocking, George W., Jr. 1966. "Franz Boas and the Culture Concept in Historical Perspective," *American Anthropologist*, New Series, 68, 4: 867–82. German-American scholar George W. Stocking, Jr, takes a close look at Boas's view of culture, just over twenty years after Boas's death.

White, Leslie A. 1959. "The Concept of Culture," *American Anthropologist*, New Series, 61, 2: 227–51. Another classic analysis of the culture concept, this time from American anthropologist Leslie A. White, writing a decade after Kroeber (see above) published his comments on White's earlier view of culture.

Online Videos

Cross-cultural Comparisons of Mass Murder in the US and Canada (Lecture) www.youtube.com/watch?v=XWv8sYCNUsc

Cultural Differences (National Geographic Video) video.nationalgeographic.com/video/movies/cultural-differences-ggtu

Uncontacted Tribes: First Ever Aerial Footage of Uncontacted Amazon Tribe www.uncontactedtribes.org/brazilfootage

2

Fieldwork: A Meeting of Cultural Traditions

CHAPTER OUTLINE

LEARNING OBJECTIVES

By the end of Chapter 2, you will be able to

- understand the value of ethnographic fieldwork,
- describe how fieldwork is used in cultural anthropology,
- outline key stages in the process of preparing to do fieldwork,

- understand the importance of professional ethics,
- compare and contrast three modes of ethnographic research: positivist, reflexive, and multi-sited,

- consider the effects of fieldwork on all involved, and
- appreciate the value and open-ended nature of anthropological knowledge.

A researcher engages with an Ainu chief in Hokkaido, Japan. Fieldwork offers anthropologists the opportunity to gain insight into new cultural worlds and to reflect on their own culture in a new way.

Ethnographic fieldwork can seem unusual. Someone shows up in a community, plans to be there for a year or more, claims to be interested in the community's way of life, and then spends all of his or her time interacting with people, making observations, and taking notes (Figure 2.1)! Yet by bringing people from different cultural backgrounds together, this process creates new spaces for deep learning. Here, a great gift is given: people give of themselves and their resources, sharing their families and friendships, homes and food, as well as insights into their lives and culture. Receiving the gift is a humbling experience. The process of *reciprocal* action and influence in this space changes all in essential ways. Thus, **fieldwork** broadens understandings of cultural worlds and transforms the self-understandings of anthropologists and the people with whom they work.

When you think about fieldwork, it is important to remember that anthropologists get to go home, while the people they study and learn from *are* at home. Thus, transformations that occur during fieldwork may have a strong impact on these people's lives. There is, then, the deep responsibility of behaving ethically in seeking and accepting the gift of insight into other people's lives.

Methods of Collecting Information

When conducting fieldwork, anthropologists use various methods to gather data. They consult published literature and archives. They conduct **structured interviews**, which can draw out a great amount of information on topics of particular interest to the anthropologist. As American anthropologist Charles L. Briggs comments, structured interviewing

> can inform such anthropological issues as ethnographers' constructions of space and time, fieldwork as "immersement" and doubling [i.e., as wholly engaging and deeply informative], science/antiscience debates, questions of scale, and explorations of similarities of methods between anthropology and other forms of "expert" knowledge. (2007: 551)

In addition to interviewing, sometimes questionnaires and psychological tests are used in the field. However, such methods are never used alone. The information they uncover may not have an appropriate context and therefore may be highly misleading. Thus anthropologists use **participant-observation** (Figure 2.2).

Participant-observation involves direct, face-to-face interaction between the researcher and his or her local research partners, as they go about their daily lives. The method was pioneered by cultural anthropologists and remains characteristic of anthropological work. It allows anthropologists to understand interactions in a wider context of social networks and cultural beliefs and values. As we will discover, participant-observation is the most productive method available to anthropologists who seek a holistic understanding of culture and the human condition.

Modes of Ethnographic Fieldwork: A Short History

When anthropology began to take on its own identity as an intellectual discipline during the nineteenth century, it aspired to be scientific. As a result, early anthropologists adopted **positivism**, the traditional philosophy of the physical sciences. Indeed, this perspective heavily influenced the pioneering ethnographers who established

fieldwork
An extended period of close involvement with the people in whose way of life anthropologists are interested, during which anthropologists ordinarily collect most of their data.

structured interviews
A method for gathering information whereby an anthropologist (or another researcher) asks a set of predetermined questions and records participants' responses.

participant-observation
The method anthropologists use to gather information by living and working with the people whose culture they are studying while participating in their lives as much as possible.

positivism
The view that there is a single reality "out there" that can be detected through the senses and that there is a single, appropriate scientific method for investigating that reality.

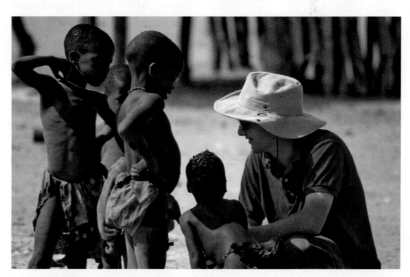

FIGURE 2.1 Ethnographic fieldwork involves entering into a community and forming reciprocal relationships with the people of that community. What kinds of effects do you think fieldwork can have on the people whose lives are being observed? How might anthropologists be affected by the process?

FIGURE 2.2 Participant-observation has long been a hallmark of research in cultural anthropology, whether in the 1920s with pioneering cultural anthropologist Margaret Mead on the island of Samoa (left) or in the 1980s with Canadian anthropologist Naomi McPherson in Papua New Guinea (above). What could be some of the benefits and challenges of participant-observation over other information-gathering techniques (e.g., interviewing, handing out questionnaires)?

the fieldwork tradition—for example, Bronislaw Malinowski (who, it is often said, invented long-term participant-observation–based fieldwork); Franz Boas (who based much of his fieldwork on the Kwakiutl [Kwakwaka'wakw] in British Columbia); Margaret Mead (Boas's best-known student, who conducted extensive fieldwork in the South Pacific); and Frank G. Speck (who worked with the Algonquians of eastern Canada).

Since the early twentieth century, anthropologists' approaches to fieldwork have changed. While anthropologists still aim to be scientific in their study of human nature, human society, and human history, they now understand "science" very differently. They recognize, for example, that there is not just one but a *variety* of scientific methods, each able to produce reliable knowledge about the world (e.g., Knorr Cetina 2000). Similarly, they recognize that there are not one but *many* understandings of reality. The approach that developed out of this new way of thinking came to be known as the **reflexive** approach. In the following discussion, we will examine in greater detail both the positivist approach and the reflexive approach, both of which have played major roles in the history of anthropology. (Note

reflexivity
Critically thinking about the way one thinks; reflecting on one's own experience.

that we will examine a third, more recently developed mode of ethnographic fieldwork, multi-sited fieldwork, later in the chapter.)

The Positivist Approach

The positivist approach has its roots in the writings of French philosopher Auguste Comte (1798–1857) and his "positive philosophy." In the late nineteenth and early twentieth centuries, it was refined by a group of influential thinkers known as *positivists*. Today, *positivism* has become a label for a particular way of looking at and studying the world scientifically.

First, positivists are committed to explaining how the material world works in terms of material causes and processes that we can detect using our senses. Second, to achieve this goal, positivists are also committed to a separation of facts from values as part of their scientific approach. They justify this separation on the grounds that facts relate to the nature of physical, material reality—what *is*—whereas, in their view, values are based on speculation about what *ought to be*. To positivists, scientific research is concerned only with the former. As a result, they think that all valid scientific inquiry, no matter the focus, should be understood as different aspects of a single, disinterested quest for knowledge, a quest that cannot be compromised simply because it offends some people's moral or political sensibilities. In other words, the truth remains the truth whether people like it or not, whether it conforms to their idea of what is good and proper or not. Thus a third feature of positivists: they are convinced that a single scientific method can be used to investigate any domain of reality, from planetary motion to chemical reactions to human life. The most ambitious positivists are convinced that all scientific knowledge will ultimately be unified in a "theory of everything."

The traditional goal of the positivist program has been to produce **objective knowledge**. Positivists believe that their approach is the route to such knowledge because it seeks to describe the way the material world actually is, unobscured by any human-applied values, beliefs, or assumptions.

Applying Positivist Methods to Anthropology

For the positivist, the standard research scenario involves a scientist in a laboratory. This approach creates obstacles for those who study human life by means of participant-observation. Early cultural anthropologists were aware of these obstacles, and they tried to devise ways to get around them. Their first step was to approximate lab conditions by testing hypotheses in different cultural settings. These settings were carefully selected to display the same range of variation, naturally, that a laboratory scientist could create artificially. As a result, the field could be seen as a living laboratory. Each research setting would correspond to a separate experimental situation, a method called *controlled comparison*. Margaret Mead used this method in the 1930s when she studied four different societies in an attempt to discover the range and causes of gender roles.

Anthropologists such as Mead were encouraged by the enormous successes that the physical scientists had attained through positivist approaches. From the mid-nineteenth to the mid-twentieth century, positivistically inclined anthropologists studied cultures their contemporaries had neither heard of nor cared to know. Rejecting the unstructured, impressionistic work of an earlier period, they attempted to produce accounts that were systematic and accurate. Overall, they were

more or less successful, although they were sometimes accused of insensitivity.

Yet there remained a problem. In order to remain true to positivism, anthropologists had to record objective facts from the perspective of an invisible observer; yet in order to get closer to the truth, they had to admit that they were personally involved in the situation. In fact, they regularly developed close ties to the people among whom they worked, often defending their full humanity to outsiders and, at times, even intervening on their behalf with the government. Yet none of these efforts showed up in their ethnographies. To resolve these apparent conflicts, they needed to find a new approach.

Questioning the Positivist Approach

The 1960s and 1970s marked a turning point in anthropological concepts of fieldwork. Many assumptions about the way the world worked were called into question, as was the nature of scientific inquiry. New Zealand anthropologist Derek Freeman's critique (1983; 1998) of Margaret Mead's early fieldwork in Samoa illustrates the tone of the debate (see Côté [2000] for a summary of the Mead–Freeman controversy; also see Shankman [2009] for a discussion of the problems with Freeman's critique). Anthropologists began to write ethnographies highlighting the ways their own involvement with others in the field had contributed to the growth of cross-cultural knowledge. They were able to show how different observers, working from different assumptions, often produce different ethnographies about the same society. At the same time, they noted that differently situated fieldworkers also came to many similar conclusions, and these conclusions allowed them to link their work in productive ways.

Consider the case of American anthropologist Annette Weiner, who conducted fieldwork in the Trobriand Islands nearly sixty years after Bronislaw Malinowski. Malinowski and Weiner were anthropologists of different nationalities and different genders working in different villages with different informants during different periods. Weiner made an important contribution to our understanding of Trobriand life by describing and explaining activities involving Trobriand women's "wealth" (Figure 2.3)—activities that were central to the continued healthy functioning of Trobriand life,

objective knowledge
Knowledge about reality that is absolute and true for all people, in all times and places.

FIGURE 2.3 Trobriand women's wealth, consisting of dried, processed banana leaves, being collected at a funeral.

subjective meaning
Meaning that seems true to a particular person, based on his or her personal values, beliefs, opinions, and assumptions.

intersubjective meaning
Meaning rooted in the symbolic systems of a culture and shared by participants in that culture.

but about which Malinowski had written nothing. Weiner might have published her findings by declaring that Malinowski had got it wrong. But this route did not appeal to her, primarily because, as she alluded, he got so very much right. Malinowski's own preoccupations led him to write about aspects of Trobriand life different from those that interested Weiner. As a result, he left behind a portrait of Trobriand society that Weiner later felt obliged to supplement. Nevertheless, much of Malinowski's work remained valid and insightful to Weiner. In tribute to him, she quoted long passages from his ethnographies (see Weiner 1976; 1988; see also the EthnoProfile on the Trobriand Islanders in Chapter 7).

Beginning in the 1960s, anthropologists also began to reconsider the ethics and politics of positivist science in general and of participant-observation in particular. They began to pay close attention to the nature of the relationships they developed with their informants, and they re-examined the laboratory model of fieldwork, noting the differences between anthropology and other more traditionally scientific disciplines. In the physical sciences, for example, it is fairly easy to justify a hierarchy elevating scientists over their subject matter. Indeed, it seems difficult to imagine the ethical or political obligations that a geologist might have to a rock. Matters are otherwise when human beings are the subject of inquiry. To approach human beings as objects, lacking

the same inquisitive intelligence as the scientists who study them, is to mischaracterize the subject matter of anthropology. Anthropologists *do* have ethical obligations to other human beings; political factors *can* complicate the relationships ethnographers develop during fieldwork. Further, there *is* a mutual inquisitiveness that needs to be acknowledged in the fieldwork experience. It is *human interaction* that is central to cross-cultural understanding. Thus, by extension, anthropologists came to understand that they are *human beings* in relationships, not impersonal recording machines. In doing so, they become aware that observation "has a subjective component by virtue of the observer's . . . decision to recognize certain distinctions" (Allen and Hoekstra 1991: 49). In effect, anthropological observation cannot be entirely value free.

Questioning positivist science is not taken lightly. Those who do raise objections are often accused of abandoning scientific discipline entirely, allowing material facts to be obscured by the researcher's individual, *subjective* values and preferences. But does the rejection of positivism turn anthropological fieldwork into just one person's subjective impressions of other people? Most anthropologists would answer a firm *no*, because fieldwork is a *dialogue*; ethnographers engage in real conversations with their local research partners. Such dialogues are often characterized by mutual patience and painstaking collaborative attempts to sort things out and to piece things together in mutually coherent pictures of reality. When successful, the outcome is a new understanding of the world that both anthropologist and informant can share. This means that field data are not **subjective** but **intersubjective**: they are the product of long dialogues between researcher and informant. Through dialogue and negotiation, intersubjective meanings are achieved.

The Reflexive Approach

The intersubjective meanings on which informants rely are public, not private. Informants take them for granted, but they may not be obvious to an outsider. In order to make these meanings explicit, anthropologist and informants together must occasionally step back from the ordinary flow of daily life and examine them critically. They must think about the way members of the culture normally think about their lives. This thinking about thinking is known as *reflexivity*; thus, fieldwork in cultural anthropology is a reflexive experience.

Reflexive fieldwork retains a respect for detailed, accurate information-gathering, but it also takes into consideration a broader range of contextual information than does positivist fieldwork. It pays explicit attention to the ethical and political context of research, the background of researchers, the full partnership of informants (who are really our teachers), and the collaborative relationships that produce anthropological knowledge. Consideration of these factors is essential to producing scientifically valid knowledge about human beings. Ethnographic knowledge shaped by reflexivity becomes what science and technology scholar Donna Haraway (1991) has called **situated knowledge**. Here, "situating" involves making explicit exactly who you are as an ethnographer—that is, your gender, nationality, political preference, class/ethnic/educational backgrounds, and so forth. Once you have identified your own social location, you will be better able to understand your unique perspective—your *situated subjectivity*—that informs your research choices. You will also be better able to present who you are to the people with whom you will be working. Both these distinctions inform you as an ethnographer and shape the relationships you have in the field.

Being *aware* of who you are will help you identify the limits of what you can discover. For example, in some societies, being a female ethnographer may bar you from studying certain social activities that are central to the local culture. In such a case, your ethnographic account is bound to be partial and could be seen as weak under the test of "scientific objectivity." Nevertheless, a detailed, reflexive account of what you were able to learn may be far more reliable than a strictly "objective" account. After all, such an account would explicitly acknowledge the fact that you did not talk to everybody or see everything, and it would openly admit that your observations are not universal but *situated*. This approach avoids suggesting sweeping generalizations about an entire social group on the basis of partial knowledge. As such, it allows anthropologists to develop a fuller, truer account of people's lives.

The commitment to reflexivity means anthropologists are obligated to reveal to everyone involved the ways in which they gather data. Some anthropologists have argued that they must also share their conclusions with their informants and include their informants' reflections on those conclusions in their published ethnographies. For example, after conducting fieldwork in a poor neighbourhood in the US, cultural anthropologist Bettylou Valentine (1978) persuaded several of her informants to comment on her manuscript before publication. She visited them for lengthy discussions and found that, in general, they agreed with her conclusions. In the published volume, *Hustling and Other Hard Work: Life Styles in the Ghetto*, Valentine includes both her own conclusions and her informants' voices in the final chapter. Valentine's ethnography presents a vivid example of the open-endedness of the dialogue between anthropologist and informant: no single interpretation of human experience is final. This kind of mutual reflexivity is at the heart of anthropological knowledge, and it invites future anthropologists and others to continue the dialogue from their own uniquely situated position.

As a final note, you should know that while the reflexive approach is accepted by most contemporary anthropologists, it is not without its critics. Most criticism centres on the reliability of anthropologists' self-reports as to **positionality**, since our descriptions of ourselves are not always reliable. Indeed, most people, when describing themselves, tend to overlook their own faults and embellish their better qualities (Salzman 2002). Yet even though the critics note flaws in the reflexive approach, most would agree that it is far more useful than the positivist alternative. Indeed, we would argue that the best ethnographies have always been reflexive, whether or not the ethnographers realized it at the time.

The Fieldwork Experience: A Brief Overview

Today, as in the past, ethnographic fieldwork continues to be the quintessential anthropological experience for many cultural anthropologists. Many students first experience fieldwork when they are in their undergraduate or early graduate studies, when they work on research projects or in field schools run by established anthropologists. An extended period of fieldwork is the final phase

situated knowledge
Knowledge that is set within or specific to a precise context or situation.

positionality
A person's uniquely situated social position, which reflects his or her gender, nationality, political views, previous experiences, and so on.

of formal anthropological training, and many anthropologists incorporate additional periods of field research into their subsequent careers. Beginning anthropologists usually decide during graduate school where they want to do their research and on what topic they wish to focus.

Many students who have never participated in fieldwork have an idealized image of the experience: at first, the disoriented fieldworker faces suspicious potential informants, but uncertainty soon moves to understanding and trust as the anthropologist's good intentions are made known and accepted. Soon, the fieldworker becomes so well loved and trusted and accepted as an equal that she or he is allowed access to the culture's secrets. Yet this is naive thinking. Fieldwork is entangled with the realities of diverse, complex relationships (Pack 2006). Thus gaining acceptance in the field takes time and effort, and there is no guarantee that the fieldworker will be accepted by everyone. In addition, as anthropologist Pierre Bettez Gravel (1976) notes, fieldwork can be rather dull: "The substantive part of fieldwork has no glamour. It is made up of . . . the same little administrative tasks [e.g., cleaning, filing, making notes] we try to get away from . . . the tedium of daily life with suddenly no one to share it with" (121).

Many novice researchers do not anticipate the amount of preplanning required. Something as seemingly simple as finding a place to live may be challenging. Sometimes, a researcher will simply move into a pre-existing residence in the research locale; but other times, particularly when the researcher will be working among remote peoples in a rainforest, desert, or tundra area, he or she may need to bring along materials to establish adequate living quarters.

A field project's success depends to a larger extent on two things. First, the researcher must gain the appropriate authorization to work in a particular place—for example, permission from academic and government offices in the host country. Second, she or he must gain acceptance from the people who will be participants in the study. In the past, such acceptance was not always sought, and the people who were to be studied did not always know an anthropologist was on the way. Arriving in Pond Inlet, on Baffin Island, in 1963, anthropologist John Matthiasson noted, "No one in the settlement knew of my impending arrival although I was equipped with an Explorer's and Scientist's licence properly signed by the appropriate officials in Ottawa—a bureaucratic prerequisite for research in the Northwest Territories" (1992: 13). Today this would never do! Researchers need to seek funds to support their studies, and funding agencies have strict codes of ethics for research involving human participants.

Obtaining grants from private or government agencies involves, among other things, persuading them that (1) the work will focus on a topic of current interest within anthropology and (2) the work is connected to their funding priorities. As a result, "field sites . . . end up being defined by the cross-hatched intersection of visa and clearance procedures, the interests of funding agencies, and intellectual debates within the discipline and its subfields" (Gupta and Ferguson 1997: 11). Since funds are finite, not all topics of current interest can be funded; to get around this limitation, some anthropologists pay for their research themselves by finding a job in the area where they want to do fieldwork or by supplementing small grants out of their own pockets.

Anthropologists are accountable not only to the agencies or people who fund their projects but also to the communities and individuals who allow them entry into their lives (see, e.g., Carrithers 2005). To help researchers protect the rights and dignity of their informants, professional associations—such as the Canadian Anthropology Society/Société canadienne d'anthropologie (CASCA) and the American Anthropological Association (AAA)—provide networks through which researchers can connect with one another to discuss best practices. Some associations also offer guidelines for conducting ethical research. The AAA's *Code of Ethics* states that "Anthropological researchers have *primary ethical obligations* to the people, species, and materials they study and to the people with whom they work" and must "ensure that they do not harm the safety, dignity, or privacy of the people with whom they work, conduct research, or perform other professional activities" (2009: III, A.1, A.2; italics added). In Canada, the *Tri-Council Policy Statement* (*TCPS*), first published in 1998, sets ethical guidelines for researchers and informs the research ethics boards (REBs) of all federally funded institutions. It explicitly states that "researchers are expected, as a condition of funding, to adhere to the *TCPS*" (CIHR, NSERC, SSHRC 2010).

As you might expect, policies evolve from the problems, constraints, and considerations that arise from fieldwork, but no policy can suit every researcher or address every problem one might encounter. Mike Evans (2004), reflecting on his research into the Island Cache in British Columbia, has noted the problem of giving voice and representation to informants while also meeting the *TCPS* requirement of maintaining their confidentiality. Evans, like most anthropologists, feels strongly that informants have the right to protect their identities. Indeed, the need for protection is paramount when informants belong to marginal or powerless groups that might suffer retaliation from more powerful agencies. However, Evans emphasizes that in certain situations, such as community-centred research when informants wish to express their identities and ideas, anthropologists need to record people's stories without depriving individuals of their right to be acknowledged.

Of course, before researchers can look for funding or contemplate any ethical issues, they must choose a focus and a setting for the fieldwork. Classic anthropological fieldwork emphasized working "abroad" in societies that were culturally and geographically distant from that of the ethnographer. Such an orientation bears clear traces of European colonialist attitudes, but it can also draw attention to ways of life among peoples whom elite groups in powerful Western nations have traditionally dismissed or marginalized. Additionally, such approaches allow anthropologists to develop cross-cultural understandings and forge links between different types of knowledges (see Gupta and Ferguson 1997).

More recent discussions of anthropological fieldwork have noted the significance of working "at home," particularly when the ethnographer focusses on local forms of social inequality and marginalization. This orientation has the added benefit of providing insight from an insider's perspective; increasingly, anthropologists working in their own societies interpret and write about their experiences both as observers and as members of those societies (see, e.g., Kumar 1992, Turgeon and Pastinelli 2002, Undie 2007). Such an orientation also notably incorporates traditions of anthropological research that have developed in countries such as Mexico, Brazil,

India, and Russia, where fieldwork at home has long been the norm. In the twenty-first century, developments such as these are helping create "decolonized anthropology in a deterritorialized world" (Gupta and Ferguson 1997: 35).

Interactions in the Field: Interpretation and Translation

Fieldwork is a risky business, as anthropologist Vesna V. Godina warns us (see the "In Their Own Words" box, below). Fieldworkers face the shock of the unfamiliar and their own vulnerability. Indeed, they must embrace this shock and cultivate this vulnerability if they are to achieve any kind of meaningful understanding of their informants' culture. They resist ethnocentric impulses by recalling "that if what we observe appears to be odd or irrational, it is probably because we do not understand it and not because it is a product of a 'savage' culture in which such nonsense is to be expected" (Greenwood and Stini 1977: 185).

Anthropologist Michael Agar (1996) uses the expression "rich points" for unexpected moments when problems in cross-cultural understanding emerge. These moments occur when words or actions signal gaps between the anthropologist's assumptions about how the world works and those of the local people, These moments are "rich" because they offer opportunities for a great number of valuable insights. Agar observes that rich points are the raw material of ethnography. As he says, "it is this distance between two worlds of experience that is exactly the problem that ethnographic research is designed to locate and resolve" (1996: 31). That the anthropologist doesn't understand what is going on is the anthropologist's problem, not the local people's; therefore, it is up to the anthropologist to identify rich points, to interpret these moments, and to investigate the accuracy of his or her interpretations.

Interpreting Actions and Ideas

How does one go about interpreting the actions and ideas of other human beings? As anthropologists, we need to find a form of interpretation based on reflexivity rather than objectivity.

IN THEIR OWN WORDS   Anthropological Fieldwork at the Beginning of the Twenty-First Century: Crisis and Location of Knowledge

Slovene anthropologist Vesna V. Godina discusses anthropological fieldwork in the modern age. She begins by noting that this fieldwork is no longer a uniform practice. Rather, it typically takes one of three forms:

1. fieldwork in a non–Western European society in which the observer is an anthropologist from Western Europe (or North America);
2. fieldwork in a non–Western European society in which the observer is a native anthropologist; and
3. fieldwork in a Western European (or North American) society in which the observer is a Western European (or North American) anthropologist.

She then continues by focussing on complications anthropologists commonly encounter when engaging in fieldwork.

First of all, there are difficult, and sometimes dangerous, living conditions (Salzman 1994: 31). Then there is the so-called "alienating nature of the field situation" (Obeyesekere 1990: 235), connected to the fact that an anthropologist in the field is a "marginal outsider—incompetent, awkward, rude—and largely irrelevant" (Salzman 1994: 31; see also Eriksen 1995: 14; Obeyesekere 1990: 228). Additionally, all kinds of personal problems occur which are closely related to this marginal position: "problems of sex, aggression, loneliness, and despair" (Obeyesekere 1990: 235).

For the essence of fieldwork involves work with informants; this fact complicates the anthropologist's situation even more. This complication is connected to the fact that "contrary to the traditional anthropological views of fieldwork, our informants are not simply giving us 'facts'; they are involved with us in a crucial intersubjective relationship and are engaged in continuing dialogue with us" (Obeyesekere 1990: 226). This involvement is related to sympathies and antipathies, and to positive and negative transference; there are some informants whom anthropologists love, and there are some whom they hate. . . . This ambivalence is characteristic . . . [and] persist[s] long after the fieldwork is finished.

There are, however, other difficulties related to informants. Every informant knows, first of all, that he or she is being observed. In such situations he or she isn't going to behave "as usual" but is going to exhibit behaviour which he or she thinks is expected. Moreover, even the most truthful informant is (unconsciously) going to tailor information given to the anthropologist. In this connection, [anthropologist Gananath] Obeyesekere speaks about "interpreter effect" (Obeyesekere 1981: 11), the influence of the interpreter in the progress of fieldwork. An anthropologist is dependent on his or her informant/interpreter, a dependence commonly linked to knowledge of the local language. "The more the anthropologist is ignorant of the language, the more dependent he is on this person" (Obeyesekere 1990: 236).

To the above complications which occur in fieldwork situations we can add others, which do not occur regularly, but which are, when they do occur, of extreme importance. First of all, there is the possibility that the anthropologist may practise different roles in the field. So many possibilities are opened that the anthropologist does not have enough time to realize all of them. Among these are some which can ruin a field situation; such as, for example, the role of the expert who enables an anthropologist to see those "aspects of society which the locals are ashamed of showing to high-ranking strangers" (Eriksen 1995: 15). In contrast, problems connected to interpersonal situations between an anthropologist and an informant/interpreter can also spoil the field situation, for example, "if the informant/interpreter is more intelligent than the anthropologist, or if he is a better politician" (Obeyesekere 1990: 231).

If anthropologists in these romantic, but somehow "unnatural" circumstances finish their fieldwork—"if young fieldworkers do not give up in despair, go mad, ruin their health, or die," they do, "after a fashion, become anthropologists" (Mead 1995: 142). But neither is this the end of the story: on returning home, the anthropologist first has to survive another identity crisis, another type of "field shock," when "the return produces critical self-reflections on his own culture" (Obeyesekere 1990: 235). The anthropologist will then have to live for the rest of his or her life "somewhere in between": thus, "the anthropologist lives and works in two worlds" (Nader 1994: 151).

Source: Godina, Vesna V. 2003. "Anthropological Fieldwork at the Beginning of the Twenty-First Century. Crisis and Location of Knowledge," *Anthropos* 98, 2: 473–87.

In *Reflections on Fieldwork in Morocco* (1977), Paul Rabinow addresses this problem:

> Following [French philosopher Paul] Ricoeur, I define the problem of [interpretation] . . . as "the comprehension of the self by the detour of the comprehension of the other." It is vital to stress that this is not psychology of any sort. . . . The self being discussed is perfectly public. . . . [It is] the culturally mediated and historically situated self which finds itself in a continuously changing world of meaning. (1977: 5–6)

In the field, then, interpretation becomes a task of coming to comprehend the *cultural self* by way of comprehending the *cultural other*. In other words, the anthropologist's understanding of the cultural other is intersubjectively constructed, using elements drawn from the cultural systems of anthropologist and informant alike. As we come to grasp the meaning of the other's cultural self, we simultaneously learn something of the meaning of our own cultural identity. While the gulf between self and other may seem unbridgeable at first, and absolute understanding between one who is "apart from" and one who is "a part of" the culture under study may never be possible, anthropologist and informant can work together to negotiate meanings and arrive at shared, albeit at times partial, understandings.

In the field, anthropologist and informant may find they talk past one another, as each describes activities from a different perspective using a different language. However, all cultures and languages are open enough to entertain a variety of viewpoints and a variety of ways to talk about them. Continued discussion eventually reveals areas of intersection for understanding and describing the same behaviour. Any intersection, however small, can form the foundation on which to build a new intersubjective symbolic language. This process is what Rabinow refers to as "the **dialectic of fieldwork**" (1977: 39). Both fieldworker and informant may begin with few shared experiences, but if they are willing to work together, they can begin to understand each other. Indeed, it is this effort to arrive at a deeper cross-cultural understanding that sets anthropological work apart, as more than merely documenting a culture from an outsider's perspective (Figure 2.4).

FIGURE 2.4 A crowd of tourists watches as Burmese monks stand in line for lunch at the Mahagandhayon monastery in Amarapura, Myanmar (Burma). What are some of the ways in which anthropologists' interactions with their informants differ from tourists' interactions with local people in a foreign land?

Let's take a look at how this process might unfold in a typical fieldwork situation. Traditional fieldwork often begins with collecting data on kinship relations (i.e., significant family and social ties) in the host society. The anthropologist comes to the field with certain ideas about kinship in mind. These ideas derive mainly from the anthropologist's own experience, and from his or her knowledge of other anthropologists' theories about kinship. As the fieldworker begins to ask informants questions about kinship, he or she may discover that they have no word in their language that accurately conveys the range of meaning carried by the term *kinship*. This does not mean that the anthropologist must give up. Rather, he or she must enter into the dialectic process of interpretation and translation. The process works something like this:

- The anthropologist poses a question about kinship using the term in the informants' language that seems to come closest in meaning to *kinship*.
- The informants do their best to interpret the anthropologist's question in a way that makes sense to them. That is, each informant

dialectic of fieldwork
The process of building a bridge of understanding between anthropologist and informant so that each can begin to understand the other.

has to be reflexive, thinking about how people in his or her society think about a certain domain of experience.

- Having formulated an answer, the informants respond to the anthropologist's question in terms they think the anthropologist will understand.
- The anthropologist interprets this response, deciding whether it carries the kind of information he or she is looking for or whether it carries information that he or she can use to rephrase the initial question to get closer to an understanding.

As you can see, both anthropologist and informant are active agents in this process. Each party tries to figure out what the other is trying to say. If there is goodwill on the part of both, each party also tries to provide responses that make sense to the other. In many ways, anthropological fieldwork is *translation*. Translation is complicated and delicate, full of false starts and misunderstandings. As time passes and the partners in this effort learn from their mistakes and successes, their ability to communicate increases. The anthropologist learns what types of questions to ask and how to ask them; the informant learns how to provide answers that the anthropologist can understand. Gradually, these interactions build a new world of knowledge that is meaningful to both anthropologist and informant.

While informants are equally involved in this dialogue and may end up learning much about the anthropologist, we must remember that the dialogue is initiated by the anthropologist. Anthropologists come to the field with their own sets of issues and concerns, which are determined not by the field situation but by academics within the discipline of anthropology and others who are supporting the research project. This continues to be true even when anthropologists find that their project is changing direction in response to developments at the field site. Furthermore, when anthropologists are finished with a particular research project, they are free to break off the dialogue with informants and resume discussions with fellow scholars. In many cases, the only link between these two sets of dialogues is the anthropologist who conducted the research in the field.

Academics have traditionally relied on fieldworkers to interpret and speak for informants, often assuming that informants would not speak for themselves. In recent years, however, some scholars have begun to question this assumption, noting that many members of marginalized societies are perfectly willing and capable of discussing their cultures with the wider world. Although language and other barriers may prevent informants from speaking directly to an audience of professional scholars, such difficulties are becoming easier to overcome in our increasingly globalized, wired world. In light of such changes, some anthropologists have suggested replacing the traditional dialectic of fieldwork with a new, more inclusive model for generating anthropological knowledge. To do so, they argue, we must move beyond the Western-centric roots of the discipline and create a more global community of colleagues—both academic and non-academic—who can work together to generate and spread anthropological knowledge. Cultural anthropologist Arjun Appadurai, for example, has called for a global effort to encourage academics, researchers, and informants to become equal partners in an ongoing "conversation about research"—a conversation in which "scholars from other societies and traditions of inquiry" could discuss *their own* ideas of "what counts as new knowledge" and how to measure the researcher's accountability to those among whom they work (2002: 281).

An essential step toward creating a more inclusive approach to generating knowledge is identifying and moving beyond cultural biases that can distort a researcher's interpretation. Such biases can have a particularly enduring influence on anthropologists who study Indigenous cultures within their own country. Roberto da Matta, a Brazilian anthropologist who has studied Indigenous cultures in Brazil, has addressed problems associated with characterizing Indigenous peoples as "others" (see the "In Their Own Words" box, below). The issues that da Matta suggests resonate with Canadian researchers who have examined our country's Indigenous cultures. As inheritors of the colonial concept of *terra nullius*, the "empty land," early Canadian anthropologists engaged with Indigenous peoples as the "mythical other" or the "noble savage." Even while approaching Indigenous cultures as "new," these anthropologists essentially saw them as representative of an earlier stage of human evolution. While echoes of such interpretations persist today, most contemporary anthropologists actively try to avoid suggesting that Indigenous cultures are any less "evolved" than non-Indigenous cultures (see, e.g., Liebersohn 1994; Darnell 2009).

In light of such concerns, researchers have re-evaluated the responsibilities they have toward their informants. One question comes up often: Is it enough to build cross-cultural understandings and discuss field observations in academic contexts, or should anthropologists go so far as to act as advocates for the people they study? Anthropologists Kirsten Hastrup and Peter Elsas (1990), who have explored issues of advocacy in relation to their fieldwork with the Arhuacos of the Sierra Nevada of northern Colombia, note that this question is not easy to answer:

There is a continuum of anthropological interest from [1] the countering of Western, colonial ethnocentrism by providing systematic knowledge about other cultures to [2] the active pleading of the cause of a particular ethnic group vis-à-vis a government (Van Esterik 1985). In principle this continuum leaves no anthropologist untouched by the problem of advocacy. . . . When anthropologists use their knowledge for a particular cause, they can be charged with furthering "the colonial processes still at work by stealing crucial decisions and political initiatives from Indigenous peoples" (Henriksen 1985: 124–5). . . . There is . . . an inherent dilemma in anthropological advocacy. Anthropology is concerned with context rather than interest, while advocacy means making a choice among interests within the context. (Hastrup and Elsas 1990: 302–7)

Our sense of ethics, as well as our concern for preserving human decency, leads us to understand that some things require us to choose among interests within contexts. Indeed, we must sometimes choose to stand with others to achieve justice.

IN THEIR OWN WORDS | Some Biased Remarks on Interpretism

Roberto da Matta explores what it means for him to be a Brazilian anthropologist studying Indigenous cultures in Brazil.

In order to grasp deep motivations in ethnographic styles, one has to deal with how Natives are represented as "others"—as different, as distinct—in divergent national contexts. In Brazil, the "other" is incarnated by a small Native population, scattered in the empty Amazon and Central Brazil, a population generically called by the name "Índio" (Indian). But the "Indian" is not alone, for with the category "Negro" they form the basis of a singular and intriguing view of the immediate human diversity for Brazilians. The "Negro" (who is fundamentally the ex-slave) is an intrinsic element of Brazilian social structure, haunting with his massive presence the "whiteness" of a bourgeois lifestyle. The "Indian" is an outsider, giving rise to the romantic fantasies of the noble savage who has to be either isolated and protected from the evils of civilization or eliminated from the national landscape for incapacity to take part in modern progress.

In this context, to be with "Indians" is, for a Brazilian anthropologist, more than having the opportunity of living with another humanity. It is also to have the privilege of getting in touch with a mythical other. And by doing so, have the honour of being the one to overcome all manner of discomforts in order to describe a new way of life in the midst of Brazilian civilization. Thus, for Brazilian anthropologists, "to be there" is also an opportunity of being a witness to the way of life of a different society. This is particularly true when that way of life runs the risk of succumbing to a contact situation that is brutally unequal in political terms.

Source: da Matta, Roberto. 1994. "Some Biased Remarks on Interpretism: A View from Brazil," in *Assessing Cultural Anthropology*, ed. Robert Borofsky (New York: McGraw-Hill), 119–32.

Examples from the Field

Fieldwork is, by definition, an active process that takes place out in the real world, in the middle of the action. Therefore, let's turn to two examples of researchers' experiences in the field to help illustrate some of the interests and concerns at the heart of the dialectic of fieldwork.

Nita Kumar is an anthropologist from Delhi, India. She works in different regions within her home country. Kumar chose to do fieldwork in the Banaras (or Varanasi) region of India, a region very different from the one where she grew up:

> Banaras was such a mystery to me when I arrived there in 1981, ironically *because* I was an Indian and expected to have a privileged insight into it. In fact, from Banaras I was *thrice* removed: through my education and upbringing, than which there is no greater moulder of attitudes; by language and linguistic culture; and by region and regional culture. (1992: 15)

Although her social connections smoothed the way for her in official circles, she had no special advantage when trying to make contact with the artisans whose way of life interested her (Figure 2.5).

FIGURE 2.5 Prayer and worship on the Ganges River, Banaras, India. Indian anthropologist Nita Kumar found Banaras to be a mystery because of her background and her unfamiliarity with local cultures. In what ways might you feel similarly out of place studying in a region of Canada other than the one in which you live?

Finding informants and establishing a good relationship with them is a necessary first step in fieldwork, but there are no foolproof procedures that guarantee success. In her fieldwork memoir, *Friends, Brothers, and Informants* (1992), Kumar shares her four failed attempts—and her final successful effort—to contact weavers. In her first attempt, the weavers she approached turned out to have well-established ties to rickshaw pullers and taxi drivers who regularly brought tourists to visit their shop and buy souvenirs. Not wishing to become just another business contact, she left. Her second attempt was with the owner of a weaving business whose suspicions of her motives caused her to turn elsewhere. Her third attempt was made through a sari salesman who took her to a market where silk weavers sold their wares. Unfortunately for her, he would periodically announce to all assembled who she was and invite weavers to come up and speak with her, a procedure she found deeply embarrassing. Her fourth attempt followed her accidental discovery of several members of a family who were weavers. When she was invited to see one brother's loom, however, she grew "uncomfortable with all the obvious evidence of bachelor existence and their readiness to welcome [her] into it" (99). On her fifth attempt, a silk-yarn merchant introduced her to weavers living in a government-subsidized housing project next to his house. In the home of a weaver named Shaukatullah, surrounded by members of Shaukatullah's family, she finally found a setting in which she felt welcome and able to do her work. A few weeks after meeting Shaukatullah and his family, she "was given the status of a daughter of Shaukatullah" (105). That status was not only important to Kumar's research, but it also made her feel comfortable in the local setting. Ultimately, she developed a unique perspective as both outsider and insider.

Jean Briggs is an anthropologist who was also adopted by a family of informants. Briggs worked among the Utkuhikhalingmiut (Utku, for short) in northern Canada (Figure 2.6; EthnoProfile 2.1). When she first arrived in their community, the Utku thought she was strange, entirely unlike them. Once she had been adopted by her new "father," Inuttiaq, and "mother," Allaq, however, the community began to see her as able to be educated in their ways of life:

> From the moment that the adoption was settled, I was "Inuttiaq's daughter" in the camp. Inuttiaq and his relatives, with much amusement, drilled me in the use of kin terms appropriate to my position, just as they drilled his three-year-old daughter, who was learning to speak. (1980: 46)

The context of their interactions changed as a result of the adoption, and Briggs's family had new expectations both of Briggs and of themselves:

> Allaq, and especially Inuttiaq . . . more and more attempted to assimilate me into a proper adult parent–daughter relationship. I was expected to help with the household work . . . and I was expected to obey unquestioningly when Inuttiaq told me to do something. . . . Inevitably, conflicts, covert but pervasive, developed. (47)

Briggs became increasingly uneasy in her situation. She began to realize that part of the problem had to do with differences between her ideas of how parents ought to relate to their daughters and Utku beliefs on this matter. She also experienced contradictions between her role as daughter and her role as anthropologist. Unlike Kumar, Briggs found that assuming the role of daughter was uncomfortable. While it initially provided her with an opportunity to "fit into" the community she was studying, it also posed challenges to the very continuation of her fieldwork.

One incident in particular marked a turning point in Briggs' relationship with her adoptive family. It arose in part out of differing ideas about acceptable behaviour, and in part out of a misunderstanding. A few summers before Briggs's arrival, sportsmen from Canada and the United States began to fly into the inlet where the Utku lived. Once there, they borrowed canoes belonging to the Utku. Although there had at one time been several usable canoes in the community, only two remained when Briggs arrived. That summer some sportsmen borrowed one canoe

FIGURE 2.6 Summer in the traditional lands of the Utku Inuit in Nunavut.

ETHNOPROFILE 2.1 | Utkuhikhalingmiut (Utku Inuit)

Region North America

Nation Canada (Nunavut); the area between Franklin Lake and Chantrey Inlet (Tariunnuaq) on the east side of Adelaide Peninsula

Language Utkuhiksalingmiutitut, a dialect of Inuktitut

Population 35 (1970)

Environment Tundra

Livelihood Seasonal fishing, hunting, and gathering

Political organization Communal, with hunting territories

For more information Briggs, Jean. 1970. *Never in Anger: Portrait of an Eskimo Family* (Cambridge, MA: Harvard University Press); 2000. "Emotions Have Many Faces: Inuit Lessons," *Anthropologica* 42, 2.

but ran it onto a rock. They then asked if they could borrow the remaining canoe, which happened to belong to Inuttiaq.

Briggs was annoyed that their carelessness had led to the ruin of one of the last two good canoes. Because the Utku used the canoes for getting food, the loss had serious economic consequences for her informants. When the outsiders asked to use the last good canoe, Briggs "exploded." She lectured the sportsmen about their carelessness and insensitivity, and she explained how important canoes were to the Utku. Then, remembering Inuttiaq's often-repeated warning never to lend his canoe, she told the sportsmen that the owner of the remaining canoe did not want to lend it. When Inuttiaq insisted that the canoe be lent, she was shocked.

But this was only the beginning. Briggs discovered that following her outburst, her informants seemed to turn against *her* rather than the sportsmen:

> I had spoken unbidden and in anger. . . .
> Punishment was a subtle form of ostracism.
> . . . I was isolated. It was as though I were
> not there. . . . But . . . I was still treated with
> [great care and concern]. (56–7)

Prior to her outburst, Briggs had understood from her informants that anger was dangerous and must never be shown. She was also aware of the various ways her informants diverted or diffused angry feelings. Nevertheless, it wasn't until she had seriously violated the Utku value of avoiding angry displays that she understood its importance.

This breach might well have ended Briggs's fieldwork if a Westernized Utku friend, Ikayuqtuq, had not come to her rescue. She wrote to Ikayuqtuq to explain her version of the story, which was that she had been trying "to protect the Utku from the impositions of the *kaplunas* [white men]" (58). In her letter, she asked her friend for help explaining her position to the Utku. Ikayuqtuq agreed to help. Once Ikayuqtuq's letter arrived, everything changed. Briggs's friend had found a way to translate her intentions into terms that Allaq and Inuttiaq could understand. As Briggs recalls, "the effect was magical." Inuttiaq began to tell the others what a dangerous task Briggs had taken on to defend the Utkus against the white men. Briggs was no longer frozen out of Utku society. And she knew that relationships had been restored (and perhaps deepened) when Inuttiaq called her *daughter* once again.

The struggle that ensued when Briggs tried to be a good Utku daughter stems in part from what happens when ethnographers struggle to keep the full expression of their own cultural selves in check, in an effort to avoid offending their informants. The situation is complicated by the fieldworker's imperfect awareness of the sort of behaviour that is likely to offend informants. As a result, fieldworkers have frequently felt that their motto ought to be "The informant is always right" (see Rabinow 1977). Many fieldworkers therefore forbid themselves to express anger, disgust, or disagreement. But such self-imposed restrictions are likely to cause problems. After all, what sort of person is always smiling, never angry, without opinions? Anthropologists who refuse to challenge or be challenged by their informants dehumanize both themselves and their informants. Thus, anthropologists must be careful to find a balance between being themselves and avoiding offence.

These examples illustrate how a researcher's reflexive awareness can affect the ways in which the dialectic of fieldwork produces anthropological knowledge. They also show how reflexivity can enhance the ethnographies anthropologists write. Unlike in earlier ethnographies committed to the positivist approach, in reflexive ethnographies the presence, personalities, and voices of ethnographers and informants alike become vivid elements. Finally, these accounts highlight the complications and misunderstandings that are a regular part of the dialectic of fieldwork.

While the above examples reveal a clear move away from the positivistic approaches of the past, they also resemble earlier studies in their basic form: a researcher arrives at a specific site of interest, gets to know the ways of the local people, and writes an account of her or his time in that location. Much valuable work of this kind continues to be done in anthropology. But changes in the world as a whole in recent decades have led many anthropologists to undertake fieldwork projects that include more than a single site.

Multi-Sited Fieldwork

Some of the factors pushing toward multi-sited fieldwork came from within anthropology and related social sciences as they responded to wider social and political changes. One spark for such changes came in 1974, when American sociologist Immanuel Wallerstein published a highly influential study called *The Modern World System*. In this text, Wallerstein argues that the rise and expansion of the European capitalist economy between 1450 and 1750 had incorporated vast regions of the globe into a world system held together by *the market*. This work had important implications for anthropologists, for Wallerstein argued that many parts of the world where anthropologists worked had been remade to occupy specialized niches within the capitalist world system (*the market economy*). Thus, anthropological attempts to account for the current beliefs and practices of small-scale societies in these parts of the world could not ignore the historical impact upon them of world-system influences such as European colonialism.

Another spark came from the publication of Austrian-born anthropologist Eric Wolf's book *Europe and the People without History* (1982). This ironically titled text opens our eyes to the histories of non-European people—people inaccurately described in colonialist times as being "without history." In this groundbreaking work, Wolf draws attention to how non-European groups changed and adapted over time, and how they were very much involved in the history of European expansion. Tracing some of the same world-system interconnections discussed by Wallerstein, Wolf regularly abandons the abstract view of the overall system in order to focus on the historical ethnographic details of specific societies affected by that system. Thus, in Wolf's discussion, Indigenous peoples of North America appear as actors creatively coping with the challenge of the fur trade and European settlement, developing some of their now characteristic forms of social organization.

The influence of Wallerstein and Wolf on ethnographers was profound. American anthropologist George Marcus notes that single-site fieldwork continued, but from the perspective of the world system (1995: 96). Anthropologists began to supplement their own data-gathering with archival research that allowed them to historically situate their "field." Moreover, they began to rethink existing social arrangements and cultural understandings as the products of *active response* to outside pressures rather than as timeless practices. Such work reanimated their awareness of the *lack* of isolation of the societies they studied, both in the past and in the present, and it reinforced an awareness of their informants' *agency*. The result was that neat boundaries between particular societies and the larger world system began to dissolve as ethnographers contextualized their own field data in relation to places and processes that stretched far beyond their original field site. By the early 1990s—after such developments as the break-up of the Soviet Union, the somewhat piecemeal move of capitalism into China, and an extraordinary surge of migrants around the world—all traditional boundaries seemed on the verge of crumbling.

This is more the case today, as global processes—including global social movements, international trade, and climate change—increasingly link disparate groups of people. For example, think of the many ties between various fundamentalist activists—frequently described as "terrorists"—who are dedicated to promoting their individual causes by redefining political, ethnic, linguistic, economic, and religious boundaries. Think also of capitalists who promote continued economic growth at all costs, bringing the world together so they can gain access to dwindling resources and create markets for their products. (Note Benjamin R. Barber's discussion in the "In Their Own Words" box, below.)

How do you proceed with fieldwork, then, when the study of any cultural group demands the mapping of various disconnected, fragmentary processes in a disorganized, globalized world? For increasing numbers of anthropologists, the answer is **multi-sited ethnography**, which focusses on widespread cultural processes and leads the researcher from site to site as new considerations present themselves. As Marcus describes it, "Multi-sited research is designed around chains, paths, threads, conjunctions, or juxtapositions of locations" as ethnographers trace "a complex cultural phenomenon" that

multi-sited ethnography
Ethnographic research on cultural processes that are not contained by social, ethnic, religious, or national boundaries, in which the ethnographer follows the process from site to site.

IN THEIR OWN WORDS | Jihad vs McWorld

Writing in 1992, American political scientist Benjamin R. Barber describes the conflict between tribalism and globalism. In that year, a number of observers were concerned with these issues, although many anthropologists were dubious about claims of "retribalization." How much has changed since Barber made his rather simplistic argument?

Just beyond the horizon of current events lie two possible political futures—both bleak, neither democratic. The first is a retribalization of large swaths of humankind by war and bloodshed: a threatened Lebanonization of national states in which culture is pitted against culture, people against people, tribe against tribe—a Jihad in the name of a hundred narrowly conceived faiths against every kind of interdependence, every kind of artificial social co-operation and civic mutuality. The second is being borne in on us by the onrush of economic and ecological forces that demand integration and uniformity and that mesmerize the world with fast music, fast computers, and fast food—with MTV, Macintosh, and McDonald's pressing nations into one commercially homogenous global network: one McWorld tied together by technology, ecology, communications, and commerce. The planet is falling precipitantly apart AND coming reluctantly together at the very same moment.

These two tendencies are sometimes visible in the same countries at the same instant: thus Yugoslavia, clamouring just

recently to join the New Europe, is exploding into fragments; India is trying to live up to its reputation as the world's largest integral democracy while powerful new fundamentalist parties like the Hindu nationalist Bharatiya Janata Party, along with nationalist assassins, are imperilling its hard-won unity. States are breaking up or joining up: the Soviet Union has disappeared almost overnight, its parts forming new unions with one another or with like-minded nationalities in neighbouring states. The old interwar national state based on territory and political sovereignty looks to be a mere transitional development.

The tendencies of what I am here calling the forces of Jihad and the forces of McWorld operate with equal strength in opposite directions, the one driven by parochial hatreds, the other by universalizing markets, the one recreating ancient sub-national and ethnic borders from within, the other making national borders porous from without. They have one thing in common: neither offers much hope to citizens looking for practical ways to govern themselves democratically. If the global future is to pit Jihad's centrifugal whirlwind against McWorld's centripetal black hole, the outcome is unlikely to be democratic.

Source: Barber, Benjamin R. 1992. "Jihad vs McWorld," *Atlantic Monthly* 269, 3: 53–65, available at www.theatlantic.com/magazine/archive/1992/03/jihad-vs-mcworld/303882.

has many connections across the globe (1995: 105–6). Like all good researchers working on complex issues, multi-sited ethnographers follow *people, things, metaphors, plots,* and *lives* (107).

Marcus (1995) admits that multi-sited fieldwork may present certain limitations. Compared to single-sited fieldwork, it appears to dilute the intensity of involvement and the depth of understanding fieldworkers develop with their informants in each situated study. Further, some activist anthropologists who use their ethnography to draw public attention to the plight of the people whose lives they study see multi-sited research as weakening their political commitments to their primary informants. Yet Marcus does not see these drawbacks as fatal. After all, he notes, multi-sited fieldwork is usually *based* in

one primary site; its major innovation involves doing fieldwork in additional sites and bringing information from all these sites together in a single study.

Concerns about the way multi-sited ethnography may dilute the researcher's ability to defend a single group raise more complex issues. Multi-sited ethnography highlights the multi-centred, complex conflicts of the contemporary world in which clear-cut "good guys" and "bad guys" are increasingly hard to identify. In addition, by narrowly focussing on the needs of one group, a researcher may draw attention away from another group in equal—or even greater—need. For example, to defend the views of working-class women in a single site is to downplay or ignore the views of unemployed women. Or, such a focus may gloss over differences *among* those women based on class, "race," ethnicity, or religion. Further, it ignores entirely the points of view of all men. On a global scale, the spread of industrial capitalism across the globe means that the growth of an urban immigrant workforce in one place is probably connected to a lack ofemployment somewhere else. Multi-sited ethnography offers the possibility of juxtaposing more than one place, more than one time, and more than one point of view, thereby bringing to light connections among them that would otherwise remain unknown.

The nature of our world is changing, becoming increasingly complex, and anthropologists must continue their studies despite what anthropologist Michael Fischer has called our "break in the ability to write about . . . traditional topics as if they were a stable source of values and social integration" (1999: 471). Of the modern world, Fischer notes:

> No longer is it possible to speak of modernity in the singular. . . . [The term] *alternative modernities* acknowledges the multiple, different configurations that modernities have taken and the recognition that modernization and globalization are not homogenizing processes. . . . It challenges old area-studies frameworks, as well as old-style social theory, and requires re-studies of canonic anthropological societies, to provide a sense of the transformations of the past century, as well as new ways of doing fieldwork, engaging colleagues and interlocutors in new relationships. (470–2)

So contemporary ethnographic research must rework traditional notions of comparative work for a world that is both increasingly aware of difference and increasingly shaped by widespread social forces. Fischer suggests the complexity of these social forces when he calls attention to three key overlapping arenas that should be of concern to contemporary anthropologists: (1) the centrality of science and technology; (2) decolonization, post-colonialism, and the re-construction of societies after social trauma; and (3) the role of the relatively new electronic and visual media (458). Each of these arenas has many sides, and each has a complex relationship

with contemporary cultures. Multi-sited fieldwork encourages anthropologists to identify and explore these relationships.

The Effects of Fieldwork

The Effects of Fieldwork on Informants

Fieldwork changes both anthropologists and informants. What kinds of effects can fieldwork experience have on informants? Anthropologists have not always been able to report on this, as the effects may take many years to manifest. Yet in some cases, it becomes clear in the course of fieldwork that the anthropologist's presence and questions have made the informants aware of their own cultural selves in new ways that are surprising, and perhaps even uncomfortable.

Upon reflecting on his work in Morocco, Paul Rabinow (whose ideas we have discussed earlier in this chapter) recalled some cases in which his informants' new reflexivity led to unanticipated consequences (Figure 2.7). One key informant, Malik, agreed to help Rabinow compile a list of landholdings and other possessions of the villagers of Sidi Lahcen Lyussi (see Map 2.2). As a first step in tracing economic statuses within the community, Rabinow suggested that Malik list his own possessions. Initially, Malik appeared to be neither rich nor poor, and he considered himself "not well-off."

FIGURE 2.7 Paul Rabinow's reflections on his fieldwork in a Moroccan village much like this one led him to reconceptualize the nature of anthropological fieldwork. At what point should anthropologists start thinking about the potential impacts of their work in the field?

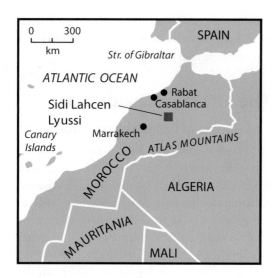

MAP 2.2 Sidi Lahcen Lyussi

culture shock
The feeling of physical and mental dislocation/discomfort a person experiences when in a new or strange cultural setting.

As we began to make a detailed list of his possessions, he became touchy and defensive. . . . It was clear that he was not as impoverished as he had portrayed himself. . . . This was confusing and troubling for him. . . . Malik began to see that there was a disparity between his self-image and my classification system. The emergence of this "hard" data before his eyes and through his own efforts was highly disconcerting for him. (1977: 117–18)

Malik's easy understanding of himself and his world had been disrupted, and he could not ignore the disruption. He would either have to change his self-image or find some way to integrate this new information about himself into his old self-image. In the end, Malik managed to reaffirm his conclusion that he was not well-off by arguing that wealth lay not in material possessions alone. Although he might be rich in material goods, his son's health was bad, his own father was dead, he was responsible for his mother and unmarried brothers, and he had to be constantly vigilant in order to prevent his uncle from stealing his land (117–19).

The Effects of Fieldwork on the Researcher

What are the consequences of the fieldwork experience for the fieldworker? While the experience is often exciting and enlightening, is not uncommon for field researchers to feel overwhelmed by the unfamiliarity of the situation. They need to adjust to local water, food, and climate, and many encounter plants, animals, insects, and diseases with which they have had no previous experience. In addition, the cultural differences a researcher faces—the very reason the researcher has entered the field in the first place—can be a source of added stress. As a result, many field researchers experience **culture shock**. In fact, many anthropologists feel very anxious and isolated in the field, at least in the early stages of a project, as they find they have nothing familiar to turn to, no common sense on which to rely, and no relationships that can be taken for granted.

The researcher's sense of isolation may lead her or him to search for close contacts in the research setting. Interpersonal relationships can often help researchers adapt to local culture, but they can also make a researcher more vulnerable to feelings of hurt or betrayal. They might also re-emphasize the distance between researcher and informant. Rabinow provides an example of such a situation when he recalls the relationship he formed with his first Moroccan informant, a man called Ibrahim, whom he had hired to teach him Arabic. Rabinow and Ibrahim seemed to get along well together and, because of the language lessons, they saw each other a great deal, leading Rabinow to think of Ibrahim as a friend. When Rabinow planned a trip to another city, Ibrahim offered to go along as a guide and stay with relatives. This only confirmed Ibrahim's friendliness in Rabinow's eyes. But things changed once they arrived at their destination. Ibrahim told Rabinow that the relatives with whom he was to stay did not exist, that he had no money, and that he expected Rabinow to pay for his hotel room. When Rabinow was unable to do so, however, Ibrahim paid for it himself. Rabinow was shocked and hurt by this experience, and his relationship with Ibrahim was forever altered. Rabinow remarks:

Basically I had been conceiving of him as a friend because of the seeming personal relationship we had established. But Ibrahim, a lot less confusedly, had basically conceptualized me as a resource. He was not unjustly situating me with the other Europeans with whom he had dealings. (1977: 29)

Rabinow's experience illustrates what he calls the *shock of otherness.*

To some degree, researchers can prepare for the mental stress of entering an unfamiliar setting by anticipating as many potential circumstances as possible. Nancy Howell, a demographer involved with anthropological research in areas such as Botswana (Figure 2.8), has explored risk factors involved in fieldwork and has observed:

> Anthropologists need to be mentally prepared to cope with . . . risks (diseases, criminal and political threats, vehicle accidents, etc. . . . .) to their health and safety and to the health and safety of . . . others who accompany them on field trips. We don't need to write the kind of guidebook that systematically warns about sunburn, jet lag, and the inoculations needed in various countries. . . . What is needed for anthropology is the sensitizing to the hazards that are likely to be encountered, systematic sharing of experiences with hazards in the field, the best available advice on prevention and responses when they are encountered, and some mental rehearsals of what to do under those circumstances. (1988: 786–7)

Yet in most cases, the immensity of what they will encounter is difficult for researchers to fully anticipate. Initially, just getting through the day—finding a place to stay and food to eat—may seem an enormous accomplishment. With time, however, researchers adapt, become more confident in their position, and feel more comfortable in their new surroundings.

The Humanizing Effects of Fieldwork

Anthropological knowledge is the product of the mutual attempts of anthropologists and informants to understand each other. Often, it

FIGURE 2.8 Elephants on a road in Botswana. Many anthropologists encounter unfamiliar plants, animals, and insects in the field. How do you think you would react if you found yourself living in a place entirely different from anywhere you have ever been before?

can provide answers to questions about human nature, human society, and human history. Thus fieldwork offers extraordinary opportunities. As researchers, we are in privileged positions. Such positions do not come easily or automatically. They must be cultivated with great effort. We have made an important first step if we can come to recognize, as Rabinow did, that "there is no primitive. There are other [people] living other lives" (1977: 151). All human beings live in their own modernity—their own place—in this world we share (Figure 2.9).

Multi-sited ethnography can complicate the picture by simultaneously offering rich portraits of "other people living other lives" and by demonstrating that members of these groups share important cultural commitments. In the best ethnographic writing we can grasp the humanity—the generosity, greed, compassion, suffering, pleasure, confusion, and ambivalence—of the people who have granted the anthropologist the privilege of living with them for an extended period of time. It may also become more natural for us to talk about cultural differences by saying "not 'they', not 'we', not 'you', but 'some of us' are thus-and-so" (Smith 1982: 70).

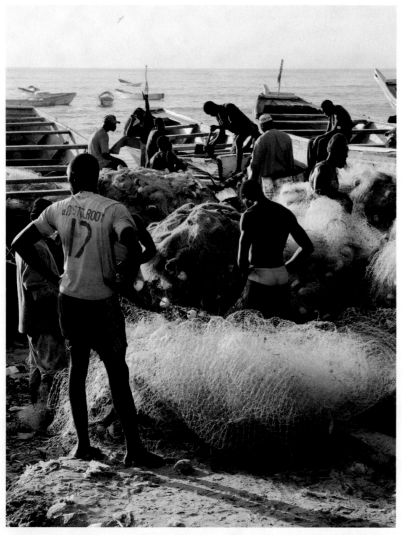

FIGURE 2.9 Unlike most Western commercial fishers, these men in Tanji, Gambia, use small boats and nets to catch fish for local markets. All people experience their own modernity.

item of common knowledge (1997: 101–2). Ethnographers' field notebooks will be full of facts collected from different informants, as well as facts based on their own cultural experiences and professional training. But what happens when facts from these various sources contradict one another?

Facts turn out to be complex phenomena. On the one hand, they assert that a particular state of affairs about the world is true. On the other hand, they do not speak for themselves. They speak only when they are interpreted and placed in a context of meaning that makes them intelligible. What constitutes a cultural fact is ambiguous. Anthropologists and informants can disagree; anthropologists can disagree among themselves; informants can disagree among themselves. The facts of anthropology exist neither in the culture of the anthropologist nor in the culture of the informant. "Anthropological facts are cross-cultural because they are made across cultural boundaries" (Rabinow 1977: 152). In short, anthropological facts are not just out there waiting for someone to come along and pick them up. They are made and remade

- in the field,
- when fieldworkers re-examine field notes and reflect on the field experience,
- when fieldworkers write about their experiences or discuss them with other anthropologists, and
- when fieldwork is redone to mark the changes that have occurred.

For anthropologist Daniel Bradburd, fieldwork begins with "being there." But simply being there is not enough. As he puts it,

> my experiences among the Komachi [in Iran] shaped my understanding of them, and that part of field experience consists of a constant process of being brought up short, of having expectations confounded, of being forced to think very hard about what is happening, right now, with me and them, let alone the thinking and rethinking about those experiences

The Production of Anthropological Knowledge

If anthropological knowledge is the intersubjective creation of fieldworker and informant together, so too are the **facts** that anthropologists collect. The dialectic of fieldwork, however, often involves extended discussions about just what counts as "the facts." We can follow anthropologist David Hess and define *fact* as a widely accepted observation, a taken-for-granted

fact
A widely accepted observation that becomes intelligible only when it is interpreted and placed in a context of meaning.

MAP 2.3 Komachi

when they have—sometimes mercifully—passed. (1998: 161–2; see Map 2.3)

After all, fieldwork is field*work*—there are notes to be taken, interviews to be carried out, observations and interpretations to be made. There is also the transformation of the experience of being there into the beginnings of an understanding. According to anthropologist Harry Wolcott, it is what ethnographers *do* with data that makes fieldwork experience different from just experience and turns it into ethnography. Indeed, ethnographers are concerned with

> making considered generalizations about how members of a group tend to speak and act, warranted generalizations appropriate for collectivities of people rather than the usual shoot-from-the-hip stereotyping adequate for allowing us to achieve our individual purposes. (Wolcott 1999: 262)

Multi-sited fieldwork elaborates upon and further complicates this experience because it involves work in more than one place. As the researcher moves from site to site, new facts come into view, facts that would otherwise never be known. Such discoveries add a further layer to the thinking and rethinking that all fieldwork sets in motion.

Anthropological Knowledge as Open-Ended

Because we can never escape from our humanity to some point of view that would allow us to see human existence and human experience from the outside, the knowledge we uncover can never be objective. Nor should objective knowledge be our goal. As we have seen throughout this chapter, we must be *reflexive* rather than *objective* when seeking anthropological knowledge. Cultivating reflexivity allows us to produce less distorted views of human nature and the human condition. And reflexivity is a never-ending process—the more we experience, the more we have to reflect on.

In the field of anthropology, there will always be more to discover. After all, human beings are constantly learning and evolving, and human societies are constantly changing. Ultimately, then, the ethnographic record of anthropological knowledge is perhaps best understood as a vast, ongoing commentary on human possibility. As with all commentaries, it depends on an original text—in this case, the "text" of human experience. This experience is and always will be ambiguous, speaking with many voices, capable of supporting more than one interpretation. Growth of anthropological knowledge is essentially no different from the growth of human self-understanding in general—of where we have come from, and where we may be going. In both cases, there is no one true version.

This could be considered a sobering possibility, making it appear as though we can never succeed in understanding another culture. It also suggests that informants are equally condemned to never fully know their own way of life. Yet although we may never know everything, it does not follow that our efforts can teach us nothing. As Canadian philosopher Wilfred Cantwell Smith observes,

> Two of the fundamental qualities of humanity are the capacity to understand one another and the capacity to be understood. Not fully certainly. Yet not negligibly, certainly. . . . There is no person on earth that I can fully understand. There is and has been no person on earth that I cannot understand at all. (1982: 68–9)

A CRITICAL LOOK | A Sense of Fieldwork in Our Daily Lives

In early 2013, Anthony Bourdain, the American chef and host of the popular travel-dining show *Parts Unknown*, headed off to Quebec. There, in a wooden ice shack in the middle of a frozen lake, he enjoyed an exquisite meal filled with local delicacies and wine. At one point during the meal, Bourdain boldly declared: "Is there a billionaire or a despot anywhere on Earth who at this precise moment is eating better than us? . . . No." The epic meal ended with another sort of delicacy—imported Cuban cigars—followed by "a dessert as rare as it gets": the Gateau Marjolaine, a traditional French cake with layers of almond, hazelnut meringue, and chocolate buttercream.

While Bourdain chose to travel to a remote location to enjoy his meal, most of us need not go to such lengths to venture into the unfamiliar territory of new cuisine. Many "exotic" and "ethnic" foods are readily available in most urban centres and moderately sized towns across the country. Simply search the Internet or download a take-out app to begin exploring the possibilities open to you where you live.

Seeking out and trying new foods is a sort of fieldwork. It can lead us to think reflexively on the history, cultural significance, and production of "ethnic" foods, as well as what these foods mean in a global world. Often, the meals we find at "ethnic" restaurants are not truly "authentic." That is, they are adapted to our local tastes. Eating these sorts of dishes feels sort of like staying in a Holiday Inn while travelling to a remote and mysterious location—there is an element of unfamiliarity, but it is cushioned within the familiar comforts of home. Yet when we have the opportunity to taste something truly unfamiliar, we can rise to the challenge and consider the deeper significance of the experience.

Canadian ethnologists Laurier Turgeon and Madeleine Pastinelli (2002) have looked closely at this sort of fieldwork. Taking a multi-sited approach, they have examined the intercultural experience of ethnic dining in Quebec City. They see ethnic restaurants as "microspaces of intercultural encounter and exchange, places where people can see, touch, and consume the cuisine of the 'other'" (2002: 247). At the same time, they observe, most ethnic restaurants make "the foreign" more familiar, transforming traditional foods of distant cultures into something more recognizable to local diners. In some senses, the authors argue, this transformation is a form of cultural appropriation, a way for powerful Western societies to selectively change and consume aspects of less powerful cultures.

This appropriation of foreign foods also impacts what we think of as local foods. Regional cuisines, like cultures, inevitably change over time, in response to both external influences and internal developments. Thus Bourdain's experience in rural Quebec likely did not reflect what the locals were eating. The French Canadian cuisine of the past is not the cuisine of modern Quebec. Rather than feasting on traditional tourtières (meat pies), oreilles de crisse (fried pork strips), and pâté chinois (a layered dish of meat, potatoes, and vegetables), Quebecers are more likely to eat foods with an "international" flavour. And this sort of culinary shift is nothing new—what we think of as "traditional" French Canadian cuisine is itself a blend of French, Aboriginal, and other traditions that developed long ago to meet the needs of a past society.

—Roberta Robin Dods

KEY TERMS

CHAPTER SUMMARY

1. Anthropological fieldwork traditionally involves extended periods of close contact with members of another society. This method of gathering information is known as *participant-observation*. This type of interaction in the field has the potential to change both researchers and informants in unpredictable ways.

2. In modern anthropology, researchers understand that they must recognize that informants are human beings and relate

to them as such. Successful fieldwork involves anthropologists who are reflexive—who think about the way they think about other cultures. Informants must also reflect on the way they and others in their society think and try to convey their insights to the anthropologist.

3. Multi-sited ethnography encourages anthropologists to acknowledge that societies are not isolated. It focuses on cultural processes that are not contained by social, ethnic, religious, or national boundaries, and the ethnographer follows the process from site to site.

4. The ethnographic record of anthropological knowledge is perhaps best understood as a vast, unfinished commentary on human possibility. We may never learn all there is to know, but we can always learn more.

CRITICAL THINKING QUESTIONS

1. Why do many anthropologists consider participant-observation to be the central method for ethnographic data-collection? What alternative methods could they use? What are some potential weaknesses of each method?

2. First, take a moment to reflect on how you see the world. Why do you think the way you do about certain people and things? How do you reach conclusions when you are trying to answer questions or solve problems? Next, answer the following: How do these personal reflections inform your understanding of the reflexivity discussed in this chapter and its use to the anthropologist?

3. Three modes of ethnographic fieldwork have been developed over the last hundred years or so: positivist, reflexive, and multi-sited. What are the benefits and drawbacks of each approach? Would you expect different results from each?

4. Anthropological professional organizations and government-fund granting agencies have codes of conduct. Why are carefully designed moral and ethical obligations a critical part of ethnographic fieldwork?

SUGGESTED READINGS

Bradburd, Daniel. 1998. *Being There: The Necessity of Fieldwork* (Washington, DC: Smithsonian Institution Press). An engaging personal study of how the many seemingly small details of experience during field research add up to anthropological understanding.

Godina, Vesna V. 2003. "Anthropological Fieldwork at the Beginning of the Twenty-First Century: Crisis and Location of Knowledge," *Anthropos*, 98: 473–87. A "where are we now?" discussion that contextualizes fieldwork experience.

Kumar, Nita. 1992. *Friends, Brothers, and Informants: Fieldwork Memoirs of Banaras* (Berkeley: University of California Press). A moving and thought-provoking reflection on the experience of fieldwork in the author's own country but in a culture quite different from her own.

Lévi-Strauss, Claude. 1974. *Tristes Tropiques* (New York: Pocket Books). A multi-faceted work about voyaging, fieldwork, self-knowledge, philosophy, and much more. Originally published in French in 1955, this work is considered by some to be the greatest book ever written by an anthropologist.

Liebersohn, Harry. 1994. "Discovering Indigenous Nobility: Tocqueville, Chamisso, and Romantic Travel Writing," *American Historical Review* 99, 3: 746–66. A discussion of the development of the construct of the "noble savage."

Nurse, Andrew. 2008. "'Their Ancient Customs Are Gone': Anthropology as Cultural Process," in *Around and about Marius Barbeau: Modelling Twentieth-Century Culture*, ed. L. Jessup, A. Nurse, and G.E. Smith (Seattle: University of Washington Press). An examination of the cultural significance of Canadian anthropologist Marius Barbeau's representation of First Nations in his ethnographic research.

Rabinow, Paul. 2007 [1977]. *Reflections on Fieldwork in Morocco, 30th Anniversary Edition* (Berkeley: University of California Press). An important, accessible, powerfully written reflection on the nature of fieldwork. The thirtieth anniversary edition contains a new preface in which the author reflects on his classic work from a contemporary perspective.

RELATED WEBSITES

American Anthropological Association www.aaanet.org

Interagency Advisory Panel on Research Ethics www.pre.ethics.gc.ca

Canadian Anthropology Society www.cas-sca.ca

3

Anthropology in History and the Explanation of Cultural Diversity

CHAPTER OUTLINE

The Roots of Canadian Anthropology

Capitalism, Colonialism, and "Modernity"

Anthropology and the Colonial Encounter

Toward Classifying Forms of Human Society

Studying Human Societies Today

LEARNING OBJECTIVES

By the end of Chapter 3, you will be able to

- situate North American anthropology in an historical perspective,
- describe in brief how colonialism and capitalism have transformed societies around the world,

- understand the influence of colonialism on early anthropological work,
- identify various typologies and classification systems that have been applied to human societies, and

- explain why many contemporary anthropologists reject attempts to apply categories to human societies.

A young child reflects on the remains of Machu Picchu in Peru. Originally built around 1450 by the Inca, the elaborate structures of Machu Picchu were abandoned around the mid-sixteenth century, following the Spanish conquest of the region. Today, the remains give us a rare glimpse into a past culture.

Third-Century BCE Chinese scientific thought focused on the Five Elements: wood, metal, fire, water, and earth. These elements fit into a circular relational structure where each "conquered" the preceding element (Ronan and Needham 1978: 151)—much like our rocks, paper, scissors circle. The Five Elements gradually took on greater significance and "came to be associated with every conceivable category of things in the universe that it was possible to classify in fives" (153), such as the seasons, the points of the compass, tastes, smells, numbers, kinds of musical notes, and heavenly bodies. The typology eventually was associated with periods of dynastic history, styles of government, and social order in general; therefore, many saw the Five Elements typology as logical and useful for retrodiction (historical explanation) and for prediction (future planning). In effect it was what anthropologists call a *key metaphor*—a symbolic representation that is widely understood within a culture and central to that culture's world view (see Chapter 10). As with any apt metaphor or good scientific theory,

> these correlations met with criticism, sometimes severe, because they led to many absurdities.... Yet in spite of such criticisms, it seems that in the beginning these correlations were helpful to scientific thought in China.... [I]t was only when they became over-elaborate and fanciful, too far removed from the observation of Nature, that they were positively harmful. (156–7)

In the end, these criticisms resulted in a shift away from the traditional five-point classification system.

Like the Chinese sages, anthropologists in the nineteenth century first sorted human cultures into different categories based on what they believed to be their similarities and differences. Over time, the purposes and the categories have been modified in ways that reflect changes in the wider world, changing research interests among anthropologists, and critical analyses of past approaches. In this chapter we situate the discipline of anthropology within contexts that have shaped its development. Thus we can gain a clearer understanding of the kinds of situated knowledge anthropologists have developed.

The Roots of Canadian Anthropology

Before we delve into the history of anthropological study in general, you should understand a bit about the way anthropology became established in Canada. Canadian institutions were somewhat late to the game, although cultural research had been conducted in Canada since the nineteenth century. The work of Sir Daniel Wilson (1816–1892; Figure 3.1)—who studied Native peoples in Canada from the view that they were "important not in and for themselves but rather because they exemplified living, primitive cultures that had once existed in prehistoric Europe" (Berger, 1990)—is illustrative of this early period. In 1936, Thomas McIlwraith (1899–1964; Figure 3.2) founded the first Canadian department of anthropology, at the University of Toronto. Like earlier ethnographers, McIlwraith was interested in the Native peoples of Canada, but his work provides greater context for these peoples' experiences. The later research of A.G. Bailey (1905–1997) on French–Indian contact (1969 [1937]) shows the mettle of what Canadian anthropology was to become. Bailey was influenced by his association with McIlwraith, his time at the University of Toronto (where he completed his

FIGURE 3.1 Sir Daniel Wilson (1816–1892) is considered by many to be the first professional scholar in Canadian archaeology and ethnography.

capitalism
An economic system dominated by a supply and demand market designed to create capital and profit.

colonialism
The cultural domination of a people by larger, wealthier powers.

imperialism
A system in which one country controls other, less powerful territories through colonization, often augmented by military force.

FIGURE 3.2 Thomas McIlwraith (1899–1964), like A.G. Bailey, was interested in ethnology and how Native peoples in Canada were affected by change. This approach assumed that Aboriginal peoples would survive the devastation of the past and remain part of the evolving Canadian reality.

PhD in ethnohistory and Native culture), and his professional roles at both the University of New Brunswick and the New Brunswick Museum. Bailey became highly respected in Canada and abroad for his ethnographical work, and his research "prefigure[d] . . . the development of American Indian ethnohistory" in North America (Trigger 1975).

Over time, three major anthropological schools of thought came to influence the development of Canadian anthropology: American, British, and French. Thus our proximity to the United States and our historical ties to England and France helped to shape anthropological study in Canada. The result, a happy happenstance of time and place, was an integrative, flexible approach that has remained productive for Canadian researchers even as advances have continued in the discipline. But first there came a colonial prologue.

Capitalism, Colonialism, and "Modernity"

In *Europe and the People without History* (1982), Eric Wolf reflects on the ways in which **capitalism** and **colonialism** emerged as global forces. In his analysis, he finds the seeds of anthropology in **imperialist** Europeans' first meetings with other cultures as they "reached out to seize the resources and populations of the other continents" (1982: 18). He also finds in these encounters the beginnings of the problematic, "tacit anthropological supposition that [Indigenous] people . . . are people without history," a notion that disregards the changes and developments these people have experienced over time (18). If, as Wolf contends, anthropologists are the children of an imperialist/capitalist parent, what is our legacy?

As we discussed in Chapter 1, in the division of labour between the new social sciences at the end of the nineteenth century, anthropology was assigned "the savage slot" as its "field" of inquiry. In North America, this meant that anthropology's primary task was to examine the Indigenous inhabitants of the Americas. They occupied what was characterized by Europeans as a wilderness—unimproved, unused, empty, "uncivilized" land. This wilderness became in anthropologist Gaile McGregor's analysis the "view from the fort" (1985: 5)—the observance, without contemplative engagement, of the world beyond the safety of the Euro-Canadian enclave. This wilderness then became the "field" of emerging Canadian anthropology.

The strong desire for westward European expansion dates to the reign of Queen Elizabeth I of England (r. 1558–1603). At this time, America came to be thought of as a potential source of fresh resources and a distant place to effectively discard unwanted populations. In 1606, Elizabeth's successor, King James I, granted the Virginia Company, essentially a group of gentlemen entrepreneurs, permission to establish a settlement in the New World. This settlement, known as "Jamestown," would become the first permanent British settlement in what is now the United States of America. In this and later settlements, the principle of *terra regis*—the belief that all newly discovered territories were the King's land by divine right—was assumed.

In 1670, King Charles II signed a royal charter establishing the Hudson's Bay Company (HBC). The HBC soon gained control of the area surrounding Hudson Bay, known as "Rupert's Land" (Figure 3.3). The objectives of the HBC were the exploitation of resources and exploration for the Northwest Passage (Rich 1961: 56). Of course, there were two vital differences between the Virginia and the Rupert's Land enterprises:

1. The Hudson's Bay Company was *all* about commerce. Although their charter gave equal weight to trade and colonization, the HBC was almost solely interested in trade (55). In contrast, the Virginia Company's Jamestown, in an effort to graft upon the wild the tame, included colonization along with commerce.

2. The Hudson's Bay Company project required the participation, albeit manipulated, of Indigenous peoples. The Jamestown enterprise, on the other hand, dealt with Indigenous peoples as troublesome and mostly expendable threats to the safety of colony property and colonist life.

In these and other instances of colonization, early settlers "knew virtually nothing of the Native languages of the Americas, even as they freely translated them" with seeming accuracy that was a mere fiction of power (Cheyfitz 1991: xv). Language, as we will see in Chapter 4, was a key element of the process of colonization. As American studies scholar Eric Cheyfitz observes:

> What the English and Europeans could not achieve in actuality they achieved textually . . . [through] early narratives: the translation of the Indians into proper English. . . . [T]hese narratives became models of actuality, models for legal decisions in which the Indians were literally forced to speak proper English, to speak, that is, whether they could speak English or not, in the letter of a law that recognized only the terms of property. (10)

We can find the same themes of unwarranted entitlement and misunderstanding played out in all colonial contexts—in South America, Africa,

FIGURE 3.3 Commercial operations had an enduring presence in the lives of many Indigenous peoples in Canada. Here, a group of Inuit from the Belcher Islands of Hudson Bay stands in front of an HBC store in 1946. Aside from giving rise to a number of department stores across the country, what are some of the lasting effects of the HBC's domination of trade relations in the seventeenth and eighteenth centuries?

Australia, New Zealand, the South Pacific, and Asia. We can also find them today, in continuing land-claims disputes across North America. The ramifications of European colonial aspirations and ideas of progress have been felt across time and space, even into what we consider our modern era.

The Key Metaphor of Capitalism

Fundamental to these enterprises was and remains what has become a central component of capitalism—shareholder-owned company enterprises operating under government approval. On capitalism, Wolf comments that "The guiding fiction . . . [and] one of the key tenets . . . is that land, labour, and wealth are commodities, that is, goods produced not for use but for sale" (1969: 277). The world is a market, and everything within the world has, or should have, its price.

For early colonialists, capitalism very much became a key metaphor. Today, the metaphor of capitalism persists, but it is no longer aligned with just a few cultural traditions; it permeates everyone's life. It is global.

The genius of capitalism has been the comprehensive way in which its supporters have been able to convert anything that exists into a commodity with a price tag: land becomes real estate; material objects become inventory. Price tags are attached to ideas (e.g., patented inventions). Even human beings have been treated as merchandise (e.g., as enslaved labourers or sex-trade workers). Ultimately, capitalism reduces all workers, even those who are not slaves, to objects; their value is in their labour power, which is worth whatever price the laws of supply and demand determine. The market system also restricts buyers' abilities to make decisions for themselves, forcing them to follow the fundamental rules of capitalism: buy low, sell high, and do not be diverted from the bottom line by any personal or social considerations.

To be sure, complex commercial activity was not invented by Western capitalists. Stratified societies have always devised sophisticated socioeconomic systems. In the early days of capitalism, therefore, elite members of such societies around the globe were prepared to take advantage of new economic opportunities offered by Western entrepreneurs. Thus these elites traded with Westerners, often helping to establish capitalist practices in their own societies and benefitting as a result. However, the consequences of capitalism were frequently negative for non-elite members of these societies, who lost many traditional socioeconomic supports.

Capitalism was even more devastating in **small-scale societies**. Members of these societies saw their land turned into a commodity for sale on the capitalist market. They experienced the devaluation of their traditional social identities based on kinship, descent, alliance, and residence. And they witnessed the erosion of traditional ways of life that protected them from destitution. In short, they experienced colonialism.

European conquests created colonial empires in two historical phases. In the first phase, led by Spain, Portugal, and Holland, colonies were required to pay tribute to the ruling empire through trading companies. In the second phase,

small-scale society
A community of several dozen to several hundred people usually held together by family (kinship) ties and often engaged in traditional subsistence activities.

driven by England and France, colonies were treated like "plantations" and governed to meet the demands of industrial capitalism (Gledhill 1994: 74). To function within the capitalist world order, colonized peoples had to begin seeing the world as a storehouse of potential commodities. Much of recent world history can be usefully viewed as a narrative of non-Western responses to this new world view and the practical actions it encouraged and justified. Some people responded with enthusiasm, some were resentful but compliant, while others were violent in rejection.

Responses to European Colonialism: The Fur Trade in North America

Like many Indigenous peoples, the First Nations populations of Canada have been through social, cultural, and environmental disruptions as a result of colonialism. It has been a journey of both immense tragedy and tremendous courage, and along the way they have made many compromises as they were forced to adapt to changed circumstances. Initially, one of the most invasive disturbances to Native peoples' lives came from the fur trade.

The international fur trade's expansion into North America's new and untapped territory sent European profits skyrocketing (see Wolf 1982: 158ff.). The "winners" in all of this were the British. They defeated both the Dutch and the French for control of resources, mostly beaver. Beaver were not only a keystone species—a species on which the balance of an entire ecosystem depended—but also a feature of the key metaphor of many Algonquian peoples (Dods 2003; 2007a; Overholt and Callicott 1982: 74–5). At contact, beaver seemed to be an inexhaustible resource; the estimate of the beaver population was 60 million to 400 million (Naiman et al. 1986: 1254). However, by the nineteenth century, the beaver populations in areas such as northern Ontario were reduced to the point of regional extinction.

The capitalist response to declining resources was to open new territory—the fur traders moved on. Yet this response was not viable for Native peoples who were and are deeply connected to the land. In many places Native peoples were forced to change food strategies.

Canadian anthropologists Edward Rogers and Mary Black (1976: 13–14) recount an example of such a forced shift that occurred in northern Ontario between 1880 and 1920. In what has been referred to as the "fish and hare" period, the Anishinaabe (Ojibwe) were forced by starvation to turn to fishing and trapping after the depletion of their primary food source—the caribou.

Resource depletion and the dietary changes that followed also caused many social issues to develop. For example, anthropologist Charles A. Bishop (1973) has identified the post-contact collapse of the food chain as the major factor contributing to a condition that has been labelled "the Wendigo complex"—a state in which a person is said to crave human flesh. This condition, first documented in the early nineteenth century (Bishop 1970: 8), has been interpreted by modern psychologists as a psychosis (see Chapter 9). However, Bishop (1973) considers the condition to be the direct result of protein starvation, and his interpretation is somewhat supported by work done with Arctic peoples in Lapland, Siberia, and North America. In a similar case, Norwegian physician and nutrition researcher Arne Høygaard (1941) examined reports of "hysterical fits" and "periodical madness" among Arctic peoples; he found the cause to be a lack of certain minerals and vitamins that are essential to the nervous system.

Foreign diseases also had a negative impact on Native peoples, altering population patterns and interrupting social cohesion. The high mortality rate "devastated and decimated some groups, modifying social organizational features and ecological relationships" (Bishop 1981: 45). Further, Canadian anthropologist Bruce Trigger notes that "failure to cope with epidemic diseases led to a spiritual crisis" (1981: 36). In general, settlements located close to active trade routes were most susceptible to infection. This problem continued into the twentieth century. During the Spanish flu pandemic (1918–19), Manitoba's Norway House Cree Nation lost 18 per cent of their adult population (ages 20 to 64) in the span of six weeks; the average loss among other Indigenous populations in that year was closer to 3 per cent (Herring 1994: 96). "Its key position in the fur trade network and frequent contact with locations to the west, northwest, northeast, and south left it particularly vulnerable to imported micro-organisms" (97).

The Slave and Commodities Trades

While the fur trade unfolded in the north, the slave trade and the trade in commodities such as sugar and cotton accompanied the rise of capitalist industry in the south (Figure 3.4). Humans and crops were exchanged in world markets as commodities. The slave trade dominated commerce between Europeans and coastal Africans by the eighteenth century. This trade had a devastating effect on the societies of the African hinterland, whose members were captured and sold to meet European market demand. But the slave trade did not alter social relations in Africa alone. In the Americas, it profoundly reshaped the lives of both local Indigenous peoples and European colonists. The growth of plantation economies in areas that had been used for hunting, gathering, and small-scale farming altered local ecologies as well as local societies. And the wealth produced in these economies transformed both the local gentry and the European nations who claimed ownership of the land. As a result, Africa, the

FIGURE 3.4 A slave family works in a cotton field near Savannah, Georgia. The slave trade had a devastating effect on many Indigenous peoples around the world. What are the short- and long-term social impacts of treating human beings as commodities?

Americas, and Europe became inextricably intertwined. In many ways, this may have been the beginning of globalization.

Colonialism and "Modernity"

What is "modernity"? Its prototype was the European-style industrial city, which existed both in Europe and in colonial settlements founded by Europeans. Colonial cities were markedly different from the great Indigenous cities of pre-colonial times (e.g., the Aztec capital Tenochtitlan, over which the Spanish later built Mexico City). In colonial cities, colonial administrators, merchants, and local elites united to defend their joint interests against those they perceived as "outliers"—both the geographically removed "others" of the resource-rich hinterland and the socially removed "others" within the colonial cities. Elaborate systems for extracting raw materials and recruiting labour, sometimes by force, were devised. These and other capitalist-colonialist processes disrupted or destroyed existing Indigenous communities. At times, they also created new centres of population struggling to become communities, as was the case with the mining towns of Southern Africa. Thus, little by little, in an effort to organize the systems of exploitation, society was restructured.

To some, the term *modern* reflects the modernization—both of technologies and of ideas—that came about in the Enlightenment, which began in the late seventeenth century. The spirit of the Enlightenment was humanist, and its primary goal was to come to an understanding of the "moral, genetic, and historical unity of mankind" (Mafeje 1976: 310). However, this intellectual environment also provided the rationale behind the European notion of the "civilizing mission." This notion led to the "rationalization of more mundane things such as economic plunder, political imposition, and other inhuman practices" (311). Thus we can see at work the dual forces of modernity—development and destruction.

In the colonial context, "modernity" has often been understood as nothing more than adopting the practices and world view of Western capitalism. As a result, the so-called backward rural peoples often turned out to be either those who escaped capitalism's embrace or those who actively opposed it. For many of them, the colonial city and the life it represented symbolized everything that

was wrong with the colonial order. Not surprisingly, this perception persists today among peoples who feel invaded by Western capitalism.

The Colonial Political Economy

Because the colonial order focussed on the extraction of material wealth, it came to link communities around the globe in a diverse market system. Yet this new economic order did not spring up painlessly by itself; it was imposed and maintained by force. For this reason, many anthropologists describe the colonial order as a **political economy** that created three kinds connections:

1. between conquered communities within a conquered territory,
2. between different conquered territories, and
3. between conquered territories and the country of the colonizers.

Eric Wolf describes a particularly striking example of how some of these connections came together in the sixteenth century: silver mined in Spanish-American colonies was shipped to the Spanish-controlled Philippines, where it was used to buy textiles from the Chinese (1982: 153). If we take Wolf's example one step further and suggest that the profits from the sale of the Chinese textiles in the European market were in turn used to fund colonialist projects in North America, we can see how the political economy might come full circle.

One way that colonial enterprises connected communities *within* a conquered territory was by drawing labour from neighbouring regions. For example, in Africa, mine owners recruited Africans from some distance; money earned in one area was thus sent away to support families in another area. These linkages did not come about spontaneously; rather, they were established and reinforced through political manipulation. In the early days of colonialism in Africa, Africans were still largely able to guarantee their own subsistence through traditional means, so they were unwilling to work for wages in the mines except on a short-term basis. Therefore, profitability in mining required that African self-sufficiency be eliminated so that Africans would have no choice but to work for whatever wages mine owners

political economy
A social structure that is organized around material (economic) interests, in which these interests are protected and enhanced through the use of power (politics).

offered. The colonial government achieved this goal through two policies:

1. It imposed taxes on conquered African populations, insisting that the taxes could be paid only in cash.
2. It deliberately prevented the growth of a cash economy in African areas. Thus, the only way Africans could obtain the cash to pay their taxes was by working for wages in the mines.

As destructive as these policies were, they did not arise out of a desire to be cruel: colonial administrators were generally convinced that the work of empire would benefit those they dominated—if not now, then in the future.

However, as the misguided efforts of past Canadian governments have taught us, policies that restrict the freedom of dominated people benefit no one. Consider the example of residential schools for Native children (Figure 3.5). Such schools, first introduced in the first half of the nineteenth century, are seen by First Nations peoples as factories of cultural genocide designed by the Canadian government to eliminate the "Indian Problem" once and for all (Chrisjohn

et al. 1997: 42). Like the colonial governments that implemented pro-mining policies in Africa, the authorities who set up the residential school system believed that they were doing good work. Consider the widespread ideal espoused by Canadian politician Alexander Morris in 1877: "let us have a wise and paternal Government . . . doing its utmost to help and elevate the Indian population, who have been cast upon our care, . . . [and doing] its duty by the red man." Notice how Morris's sentiments echo the colonialist hubris of the **"white man's burden"**! Some First Nations peoples have argued that the actual agenda was much more selfish:

> the "problem" was (and is) that there were (and are) Aboriginal owners (and their legal descendants) inhabiting the land to which the Europeans wished to lay claim.... [The] genocide of Aboriginal peoples grew out of ... [a] need to extinguish Aboriginal title to the land without violating the letter and spirit of established British policy. (Chrisjohn et al. 1997: 51–2)

Others have likewise argued that the government's intent was cultural genocide; not the

white man's burden Europeans' sense that it was their duty to colonize, rule, and "civilize" all peoples they viewed as "savage."

FIGURE 3.5 Native parents camp by a residential school to visit their children in Birtle, Manitoba, in 1904. How do the impacts of the residential school system continue to be felt in contemporary Canada?

physical eradication of Native peoples, but their death "spiritually, mentally, economically, and socially" (Waubageshig 1970: vi).

Women and Colonization

Ethnographic data show that colonial conquest did not affect all groups equally. Notably, Indigenous women's experience with colonialism was different from that of Indigenous men. In addition, colonialism did not treat all groups of women in all conquered territories in the same way. Trobriand women of New Guinea (see EthnoProfile 7.1), for example, were able to maintain status roles under colonial rule. Baule women of Ivory Coast in Western Africa (see EthnoProfile 3.1) were less fortunate.

Before France colonized Baule society in 1893, production among the Baule centred on two products: yams and cloth (Etienne 1980). These products were indispensable for subsistence as well as for exchange in various traditional social contexts, such as marriages. Both sexes worked together in the production of each, with men taking greater responsibility for yams and women taking greater responsibility for cloth. The traditional division of labour found men preparing farm plots for planting and women tending the crops. The women raised the cotton and spun it into thread, and the men did the actual weaving. The result was a highly egalitarian balance of power.

In 1923, the French built a textile factory that sold factory-spun thread for cash. Baule men with cash could therefore buy their own thread, and they, not their wives, would control any cloth woven from it. French colonial administrators also encouraged Baule farmers to plant new varieties of cotton as a cash crop. Baule women had traditionally practised crop rotation with the yams and cotton. Now the fields were devoted to growing only the new cotton. This industrial crop required new farming techniques, which the French taught only to Baule men. Consequently, women's roles in cotton production were reduced considerably. Now women had to work in their husbands' cash-crop fields and the traditional yam plots. The agricultural work for women increased, and they had less time to spin traditional thread.

The colonial government required men to pay taxes in cash for themselves and for their wives, a move that seemed to justify the right of Baule men to control the production of crops that could be sold for cash. Under colonial rule, growing cash crops became increasingly important. As a result, Baule women found that their traditional rights to use their husbands' land for their own production gradually eroded, and they became increasingly dependent on their husbands.

By the 1970s, many Baule women had become wage labourers in the textile factory in order to earn cash to buy their own cloth, which they could then control. They were aware of the loss of status and power they had suffered over the years, and their discontent had undermined traditional Baule marriage. As anthropologist Mona Etienne reported in 1980,

ETHNOPROFILE 3.1 | Baule

Region Western Africa

Nation Ivory Coast; originally from the area where the Koussou Dam was built (1971), the project resulted in the relocation of many Baule to the forests in the southwestern area of the country

Language Fante-Akan

Population 3,615,000 (2011 estimate)

Environment Savannah

Livelihood Farming (yams in particular); coffee, cocoa, and cloth production

Political organization In the pre-colonial period, no state and no clear stratification; today, part of a modern nation-state

For more information Vogel, Susan M. 1997. *Baule: African Art, Western Eyes* (New Haven: Yale University Press).

The wife–husband production relationship has become a constant source of conflict. Because the production relationship has always been the foundation of marriage, and because cloth and cash now tend to be the measure of a husband's affection and respect, the whole personal relationship is also conflict-laden. Inevitably, many women prefer to remain unmarried and all seek to acquire their own cash. (1980: 231)

In this way, the traditional Baule mode of production was transformed by contact with the capitalist market. The previously egalitarian relations of production linking women and men (wives and husbands) were destroyed.

Anthropology and the Colonial Encounter

This section's title has been borrowed from the title of a book edited by anthropologist Talal Asad (Figure 3.6). Published in 1973, Asad's book was the first high-profile work by anthropologists to consider the connections between anthropology and colonialism. It constituted an important exercise in disciplinary self-scrutiny. Three decades after its publication, Asad (2002)

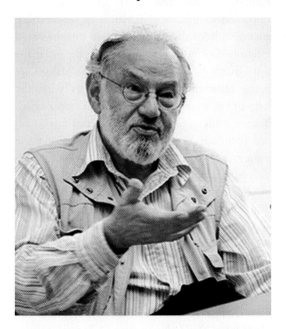

FIGURE 3.6 Anthropologist Talal Asad, who edited *Anthropology and the Colonial Encounter* (1973), has investigated the relationship between anthropology and colonialism.

revisited the questions raised in the earlier publication. In particular, he addressed the charge, made frequently from within and without the discipline, that anthropology was nothing more than a form of "applied colonialism." He concluded that the charge was false for two reasons:

1. anthropological findings were too specialized to be used by colonial administrators, especially compared to the enormous amount of information supplied to them by merchants, missionaries, and other government functionaries; and
2. colonial governments were interested only in research that would help them rule with as little difficulty as possible; they did not share anthropologists' wider interest in conquered peoples' histories and cultures.

European anthropologists sometimes played ambiguous roles in the colonial setting. Colonial administrators often valued them for the expert knowledge they could provide, but those same administrators also viewed them with suspicion because their expert knowledge might easily work against administrative goals. Meanwhile, anthropologists felt they needed to avoid upsetting colonial officials so that they would be allowed to access colonial settings and further their own goal of reducing the impact of colonial rule on subject peoples. Ultimately, then, anthropological work has always felt the impact of colonialism, but this does not mean that anthropologists worked to support colonialist interests.

One way of coping with colonial power was to address it indirectly, as part of a wider topic of study. For example, in the early to mid-twentieth century, a number of North American anthropologists promoted an impartial and scientific program of research that would, they hoped, discover the laws governing how cultures change. They considered situations encountered under colonialism, but they also considered situations where contact and change occurred in the absence of political conquest. The latter cases involved autonomous groups whose members could be freer about what they selected and rejected. The anthropologists did not see themselves as supporting any particular political position, but they were sympathetic to the plight of colonial subjects. Many openly defended the right of Indigenous peoples to control their own destinies.

decolonization
The withdrawal of a colonial power from a territory that had been under its control.

neocolonialism
The persistence of profound social and economic ties linking former colonial territories to their former colonial rulers despite political sovereignty.

social forms
Culturally conforming collective ways of interacting with our surroundings and the people we encounter; these forms of interaction, often taken for granted, are encoded forms of behaviour that are enforced by the group.

In the years following World War II, colonized peoples increasingly rejected the role they had been forced to play as students of European civilization. The colonial order was no longer a given, and its ultimate benevolence was sharply questioned. This critical attitude persisted after the **decolonization** of most European colonies. It became clear that formal political independence could not easily undo the profound social and economic entanglements linking the former colonial territories to the countries that had colonized them. The persistence of ties in the face of political sovereignty came to be called **neocolonialism**.

The study of neocolonialism led to a new awareness of just how strongly the fate of the colonized and the fate of the colonizers are connected. For example, the "underdevelopment" that now characterizes many African and South American nations has developed in large part from conditions established under colonialist rule. The effects of colonialism also continue to impact once-subjugated Native peoples living in more "developed" countries such as Canada, Australia, and the United States. In Canada, we cannot deny the realities of the remains of colonialism. We have only to read the newspaper or watch the evening news to know that the aspirations of the First Nations peoples of Canada have yet to be

addressed in an adequate way (Figure 3.7). Today, through the efforts of organizations such as the Assembly of First Nations (**AFN**), Native peoples have a greater voice than they did in the past, but there is much work ongoing and remaining.

Toward Classifying Forms of Human Society

We can now consider several conclusions that have informed current anthropological approaches.

First, all peoples live in their own modernity. Therefore, the peoples studied by anthropologists are not now—nor were they ever—leading timeless, unchanging ways of life unaffected by the presence of others.

Second, *cultural patterns* have been affected everywhere by the arrival of Europeans and/or the transformations set in motion by the spread of European colonialism and capitalism. For example, many peoples whose native language is not English have incorporated English words into their vocabularies. In turn, English speakers have incorporated words from other languages into their own vocabularies.

Third, many groups have shaped new identities and devised new **social forms** to deal with the effects of contact and conquest. These new social forms sometimes draw on very ancient traditions, reworked to meet the demands of new experiences. Additionally, ways of life that were invented long ago continue to prove their worth, and many ways that were lost as a result of colonialism are being reintroduced today—at times with the help of information gathered by anthropologists. Yet some ancient modes of living continue to fall before the advance of Western technology and the rigours of market capitalism (see, e.g., Lee 2013).

Fourth, colonial empires have been replaced by the empires of transnational corporations. The reach of these corporations is vast, and their actions affect peoples in all regions of the world. As anthropologists, we must work to understand how these corporations influence everyday life and social relations; we must also devise new forms of recourse to challenge the agents of such change. As American anthropologist Laura Nader (1972) has observed, modern anthropologists must "study up" the column of power—that is, they must investigate who has power, where power comes from, and how the powerful make

FIGURE 3.7 A group of 25 First Nations people arrive at Parliament Hill on 24 February 2014, after having walked over 1,500 kilometres from Attawapiskat, Ontario. The group journeyed with concerns about broken treaties, land and water protection, and human rights issues. What recent news stories have you seen that highlight the lasting impact of colonialism on Native peoples in Canada today?

IN THEIR OWN WORDS | The Anthropological Voice

American anthropologist Annette Weiner (1933–97) traces the history of anthropological challenges to colonialism and Western capitalism, pointing out why the perspective of anthropologists has so often been ignored.

Colonialism brought foreign governments, missionaries, explorers, and exploiters face to face with cultures whose values and beliefs were vastly different. As the harbingers of Western progress, their actions were couched in the rhetoric of doing something to and for "the Natives"—giving them souls, clothes, law—whatever was necessary to lift them out of their "primitive" ways. Anthropologists were also part of the colonial scene, but what they came to "do" made them different from those who were carrying out the expectations of missions, overseas trade, and government protectorates. Anthropologists arrived in the field determined to understand the cultural realities of an unfamiliar world. The knowledge of these worlds was to serve as a warning to those in positions of colonial power by charging that villagers' lives were not to be tampered with arbitrarily and that changing the lives of powerless people was insensitive and inhumane, unless one understood and took seriously the cultural meanings inherent in, for example, traditional land ownership, the technologies and rituals surrounding food cultivation, myths, magic, and gender relations.

All too often, however, the anthropologist's voice went unnoticed by those in power, for it remained a voice committed to illuminating the cultural biases under which colonialists operated. Only recently have we witnessed the final demise of colonial governments and the rise of independent countries. Economically, however, independence has not brought these countries the freedom to pursue their own course of development. In many parts of the world, Western multinational corporations, often playing a role not too dissimilar from colonial

enterprises, now determine the course of that freedom, changing people's lives in a way that all too often is harmful or destructive. At the same time, we know that the world's natural resources and human productive capabilities can no longer remain isolates. Developed and developing countries are now more dependent on one another than ever before in human history. Yet this interdependency, which should give protection to Indigenous peoples, is often worked out for political ends that ignore the moral issues. Racism and the practice of discrimination are difficult to destroy, as evidenced by the United States today, where we still are not completely emancipated from assumptions that relegate blacks, women, Asians, Hispanics, and other minorities to second-class status. If we cannot bridge these cultural differences intellectually within our own borders, then how can we begin to deal politically with Third World countries—those who were called *primitives* less than a century ago—in a fair, sensitive, and meaningful way?

This is the legacy of anthropology that we must never forget. Because the work of anthropology takes us to the neighbourhoods, villages, and campsites—the local level—we can ourselves experience the results of how the world's economic and political systems affect those who have no voice. Yet once again our voices too are seldom heard by those who make such decisions. Anthropologists are often prevented from participating in the forums of economic and government planning. Unlike economists, political scientists, or engineers, we must stand on the periphery of such decision-making, primarily because our understanding of cultural patterns and beliefs forces on others an awareness that ultimately makes such decisions more formidable.

Source: Weiner, Annette. 1990. "The Anthropological Voice," guest editorial in *Cultural Anthropology: A Perspective on the Human Condition*, 2nd edn, by Emily Schultz and Robert Lavenda (St Paul: West), 392–3.

---

decisions. When combined with more traditional approaches of "studying down," or examining the lives of the marginalized and powerless, this approach can give anthropologists a very detailed, accurate understanding of a society.

Evolutionary Typologies: The Nineteenth Century

Early anthropologists, like all children of the Age of Enlightenment, liked to devise **typologies**. They believed that such classification systems would facilitate their study of similarities and differences among different cultures. Of course, every system of classification reflects the qualities believed to be most significant by its creator. Therefore, different assessments can lead to different classifications. In the nineteenth-century, most Europeans described the differences they noticed between themselves and the various peoples they conquered in terms of *deficiencies*: lack of formal schools, lack of sophisticated technology, lack of organized religion, and so forth.

typology
A classification system based on systematic organization into types on the basis of shared qualities.

These terms reflected the cross-cultural experience that Western capitalists were having with non-Western peoples. For example, a colonial official eager to establish a trading post and to maximize profits in the fur trade would be most aware of the facets of a people's life that kept him from reaching his goals. How do you "pay" for beaver pelts when the "sellers" are not interested in money? Europeans faced with such practical problems were bound to see life outside Europe in terms of a series of deficiencies compared with what they could count on in their home countries.

More contemplative nineteenth-century observers pondered why such deficiencies existed in the first place. As they sat in their libraries studying the reports of travellers and reading books about history, they learned that many of the aspects of daily life they took for granted had not always existed, even in Europe. So they came to believe that they might, by going back beyond the Middle Ages, discover that their more distant ancestors had lived much the same way as many peoples of the Americas or Africa. Indeed, they found evidence to support their theories in the written accounts of Julius Caesar (100 BCE–15 BCE), who had painted a picture of Indigenous life in early Europe that resembled what Europeans were discovering in the Americas and Africa, and in archaeological discoveries of ancient artifacts on European soil.

Thus, the experience of social change, together with historical and archaeological evidence of past social change, led these thinkers to a new idea: perhaps the ways of life of the non-Western peoples they were reading about were not only similar to but repeats of the ways of life of Europeans long ago. That is, perhaps the West had already moved through *stages* of history in which ways of life had been the same as those of contemporary non-Western societies. According to these scholars, if non-Western societies were left to themselves and given enough time, they would make the same discoveries and social changes that European society had made in the past.

This way of thinking about social and cultural change has been called **unilineal cultural evolutionism** (Figure 3.8). It quickly gained in popularity as an explanation for the widespread cultural diversity that Europeans had been finding since the beginning of the Age of

FIGURE 3.8 E.B. Tylor (1832–1917), one of the founders of anthropology in Great Britain, was convinced that societies moved through a series of unilineal stages. What advantages might there be to unilineal systems? What disadvantages?

Exploration in the fifteenth century. The theory accounted for this diversity by arguing that different kinds of societies represented different stages of societal evolution through which every human society either had passed or would pass if it survived. Proponents of the theory viewed their own late nineteenth-century European capitalist industrial society as the most advanced stage of cultural evolution. Living societies that had not already reached this level were seen as primitive relics of the stages the West had already left behind.

To understand how the stages involved in unilineal cultural evolutionism were conceptualized in the nineteenth century, we will consider two popular schemes:

1. the "three-age system" developed by Danish scholar C.J. Thomsen (1788–1865) and
2. the "ethnical stages" of the American anthropologist and social theorist Lewis Henry Morgan (1818–1881).

unilineal cultural evolutionism

A nineteenth-century theory that proposed a series of stages through which all societies must go (or had gone) in order to reach civilization.

Thomsen's "Three-Age System"

In 1836, around the time Charles Darwin was developing his theory of biological evolution, C.J. Thomsen published his ideas on cultural evolution in *A Guide to Northern Antiquities*. The most notable feature of this text was Thomsen's outline of his three-age system, which he had developed based on his systematic study of artifacts in the National Museum of Denmark. While conducting his study, Thomsen noticed that the raw materials from which people had made tools changed over time. The oldest tools were made of stone, while later tools were made of bronze, and still later tools were made of iron. This observation led Thomsen to propose that Europeans had passed through three technological stages or "ages":

1. the Stone Age,
2. the Bronze Age, and
3. the Iron Age.

Later the Stone Age was subdivided into the *Paleo*lithic (*Old* Stone Age—itself divided into Lower, Middle, and Upper divisions), *Meso*lithic (*Middle* Stone Age), and *Neo*lithic (*New* Stone Age).

Morgan's "Ethnical Stages"

Even more influential than Thomsen's typology was that proposed by Lewis Henry Morgan in *Ancient Society: Researches in the Lines of Human Progress from Savagery through Barbarism to Civilization* (1877). Morgan proposed three "ethnical stages":

1. "Savagery,"
2. "Barbarism," and
3. "Civilization."

The first two were also subdivided into Lower, Middle, and Upper categories and were defined by technological features, in particular food-acquisition technologies. One striking feature, however, effectively kept "Civilization" for Europeans alone—the use of the phonetic alphabet. *Ancient Society* was based in equal parts on Morgan's mid-nineteenth-century field observations of the Iroquois of the Finger Lakes District of New York, the emerging concepts of evolution (biological and cultural), and the ideas of progress from the Age of Enlightenment. In effect it was an attempt at "anthropological" synthesis of the evolutionary stages of human society.

Morgan's typology was immensely influential in its time, and its popularity spread as other writers and thinkers expanded on his ideas. Notably, Friedrich Engels was greatly influenced by Morgan's work. Well into the twentieth century, Morgan's classification, because of its link through Engels to Marxism, was *popular* in some sectors of the academic world. For example, Morgan was the main authority cited in Chinese archaeological reports well into the 1970s. In the Americas, Morgan's typology gained renewed attention in the 1940s and 1950s with the unilineal evolutionary perspective of anthropologist Leslie White, whose approach differed markedly from that of his teacher, Franz Boas.

Sometimes the stages of Morgan's typology were used to justify racism. Under this typology, some people were considered to have "stagnated" or even "slid back" from a later to an earlier stage. Others were considered to be "eminently gifted" (de Gobineau 1967 [1915]: 27). Racial inferiority, French writer and theorist Arthur de Gobineau pronounced, "is shown, not only by defeat, but also by the lack of the attributes that may be seen in the conquerors" (31). He asks: If all men are brothers and the brain of the "Huron Indian" is the same as that of an Englishman or a Frenchman, "Why then, in the course of the ages, has [the Huron] not invented printing or steam power?" (37). Of course, de Gobineau neglected to note that printing was actually the invention of a group classified by Europeans as Upper Barbarians—namely, the Chinese! Such omissions are indicative of the ways in which Europeans assumed credit for all social and technological "advancements." Europeans saw themselves, their technologies, and their social constructs as unique, unmatched in other civilizations.

Reactions against Unilineal Evolutionism

As you might expect, contemporary anthropologists find labels such as *savage*, *barbaric*, and *civilized* to be not only inadequate but also misleading. They avoid using such labels in their research, and many also object to the use of such labels in other, less scientific contexts. In 2007, for example, the British-based Association of Social Anthropologists and the activist group

Survival International initiated a campaign to "challenge racist descriptions . . . of tribal peoples in the media," citing the use of such terms as *Stone Age* and *primitive* as offensive (Kesterton 2007; Survival International 2014). Regardless of such efforts, these classification schemes continue to resonate among Westerners, as they seem to some to offer coherent frameworks for classifying all societies.

What has replaced unilineal cultural evolutionism in modern anthropological thought is the realization that all cultures develop along their own paths. These paths are shaped in large part by the resources available to a given population. Many scholars have noted, for example, that Europeans' seeming superiority is tied to their particular geographic location. A major advantage for early Europeans was their access to temperate environments. Such environments allowed for the domestication of animals and the development of highly effective farming practices to spread with relative ease; as a result of these and other time-saving developments, Europeans had more free time to explore new ideas, develop new technologies, and benefit from new economies. Thus, the colonial advantage did not come from the innate superiority of Europeans but from their control of technological development, which would not have been possible without their luck of an amenable physical geography.

For more objections to unilineal evolutionism of the nineteenth century, see the later discussion on Boas and his students (pp. 67–8).

Social Structural Typologies: The British Emphasis

Although unilineal cultural evolutionism may have justified the global ambitions of Europe and made colonial rule appear inevitable and just (at least, to the Europeans of the time), it was inadequate for meeting the practical needs of colonials once they were in power. By the end of the nineteenth century, most of Africa and much of Asia had been divided up among European powers. At the same time, the United States and Canada assumed a similarly powerful and dominating role in their relationships with the Indigenous peoples of North America.

In order to effectively oversee their subject peoples, administrators required accurate information about those peoples. For example, one goal of a colonial administrator in Africa was to keep peace among various groups. To achieve this goal, the administrator needed to know how those diverse peoples resolved disputes. This knowledge could then help the administrator develop a policy for dispute resolution that would be accepted by local peoples. Reaching other goals—for example, introducing elements of European law and political economy—without totally disrupting life in the colonies also required a deeper understanding of local practices.

Recognizing that this deeper understanding would require Europeans to observe and interact with local peoples, colonial governments began supporting anthropologists' research in the field. Thus, the changing relationships between the West and the rest of the world fostered the development of a new anthropological research model—one that grew out of a desire to gather detailed information on many different societies. Yet willingness to work with colonial governments did not mean that anthropologists supported colonialism. To the contrary, their sympathies often lay with the colonized peoples with whom they worked. For example, British anthropologist Edward Evans-Pritchard, who worked in central Africa for the British government in the 1920s and 1930s, saw himself as an educator of colonial administrators. He tried to convey to them the humanity and rationality of Africans. His goal was to combat the racism and oppression that seemed an inevitable consequence of colonial rule. Not surprisingly, such criticisms of colonialism often caused colonial officials to be wary of anthropologists and distrustful of their motives.

Based on early observations, colonial officials quickly learned that administering their rule would be easier if they could rely on traditional leaders to act as intermediaries to keep the peace among their people (Figure 3.9). Thus the British policy of *indirect rule* was developed. To help officials discover the best way to adapt indirect rule to each group, anthropologists were charged with the task of uncovering information on the traditional political structures of different groups. As a result, British anthropologists developed a new way of classifying forms of human society. Their focus was on the **social structure**, especially the political structure, of

social structure
The enduring aspects of the social forms in a society, including its political and kinship systems.

FIGURE 3.9 Colonial officers often relied on traditional rulers to keep the peace among their subjects. This 1895 photograph shows the British governor of the Gold Coast (seated on the right) together with a contingent of Native police. What are the advantages—both for the foreign officers and for the locals—of this sort of arrangement? What might be the disadvantages?

groups under colonial rule. That British anthropologists came to call themselves *social anthropologists* reflects these developments. This focus on social structure influenced many anthropologists in the early twentieth century. For example, in 1940, in a classic work on African political systems, anthropologists Meyer Fortes and Edward Evans-Pritchard distinguished between *state* and *stateless* societies. This distinction had some similarity to Morgan's ethnical stages, and it described stateless societies in negative terms (i.e., what they lacked in comparison to state societies), but it notably did not refer to "progress" in relation to either system.

Thus a productive emphasis on social structures emerged, and questions of evolution and social change were replaced by concerns about the enduring traditional structures of the societies in which anthropologists worked. Anthropologists came to believe that having a detailed knowledge of social structures would allow them to identify the social type of any particular society. They compared the similarities and differences of these types, and out of this comparison emerged a new classification of social forms.

The Classification of Political Structures

An example of a typical social structural classification is shown in Figure 3.10. In this system, outlined by American anthropologist Ted Lewellen in 1983, the major distinction is between *centralized* and *uncentralized* (*egalitarian*) political systems. Lewellen's system is similar to that established by Fortes and Evans-Pritchard in 1940; however, note that uncentralized societies are now distinguished in positive terms, not in terms of what they lack. A major difference between the two political systems is that centralized systems have distinct, permanent public decision-making institutions (e.g., a chief, a king or a queen, a formal government), while in uncentralized systems groups and even individuals enjoy relative autonomy and equal status.

Within Lewellen's classification, uncentralized political systems can be divided into two types:

1. **Band**: a small social group whose members neither farm nor herd but depend on wild food sources. Lewellen refers to three subtypes of a band, including the *family band*.

band
A form of social organization that consists of a small group of foragers (usually fewer than fifty people), in which labour is divided according to age and sex, and social relations are highly egalitarian.

FIGURE 3.10 A typical classification of forms of human society.

Source: Adapted from Lewellen 1983: 16.

tribe
A form of social organization generally larger than a band, in which members usually farm or herd for a living; social relations are relatively egalitarian, although there may be a chief who speaks for the group.

chiefdom
A form of social organization in which the leader (a chief) and the leader's close relatives are set apart from the rest of society and allowed privileged access to wealth, power, and prestige.

state
A stratified society, controlled by a formal government, that possesses a territory that is defended from outside enemies with an army and from internal disorder with police.

structural-functional theory
A position that explores how particular social forms function from day-to-day in order to reproduce the traditional structure of the society.

2. **Tribe**: a group that lies somewhere between a band and a centralized political system. A tribe is generally larger than a band and has domesticated plants and animals, but its political organization remains largely egalitarian. Lewellen identifies five subtypes of a tribe but comments that there are likely others (1983: 26).

Centralized political systems have a central, institutionalized focus of authority such as a chief or a king. Some members of centralized societies have greater wealth, power, or prestige than other members. Thus hierarchy is evident. Centralized systems are divided into two types:

1. **Chiefdom**: usually only the chief and the chief's family are set above the rest of society, which remains fairly egalitarian.
2. **State**: different groups suffer permanent inequality of access to wealth, power, and prestige; this signals the presence of social stratification.

The major advantage of Lewellen's typology is that it does not attempt to make any hypotheses about evolutionary relationships. Tracing change over time is not its purpose. Instead, the focus is on structural similarities and differences observed at one point in time. Yet we can see in

this approach the lasting influence of colonialism on anthropology, as classifications of this kind were originally made to help colonial authorities rule local peoples. By asking, "How do African political systems work today?" these officials were trying to answer the more practical question, "What do we need to know about these systems to make them work for us?"

Structural-Functional Theory

The theories of British social anthropologists dealt with how particular social forms function from day-to-day in order to reproduce their traditional structures. Such **structural-functional theory** was perhaps most highly developed by British social anthropologist A.R. Radcliffe-Brown in the 1930s and 1940s. Around this time, many social anthropologists were beginning to question why things did or did not change. For example:

- Why do some social structures last for centuries (e.g., the Roman Catholic Church) and others disappear quickly (e.g., the Shakers of nineteenth-century United States)?
- Why did some societies abandon foraging for agriculture thousands of years ago, while others are still hunting and gathering today?

A balanced approach in anthropology involves equal consideration of reasons for change and reasons for a lack of change. This approach recognizes that an emphasis on *social stability* tends to downplay or ignore questions of *change*, while an emphasis on *social change* tends to downplay or ignore questions of *stability*.

In the first half of the twentieth century, the structural-functional focus in British social anthropology produced a variety of non-evolutionary classifications of human social forms. As diverse data on social structure grew, however, such typologies seemed to overflow with more and more subtypes. It is not surprising that most contemporary anthropologists question the point of developing such typologies at all.

Attempting to Do without Typologies: Culture Area Studies in North America

In the late nineteenth and early twentieth centuries, most American anthropologists were becoming increasingly dissatisfied with unilineal evolutionism. The most significant figure in the attempt to move away from this approach was Franz Boas. Boas and his students worked primarily among American Indigenous peoples, including West Coast First Nations. They collected data about these societies, especially data relating to the histories of individual groups and their languages. They found that these societies did not pass through uniform, shared stages as they changed over time. For example, they found that two societies with similar forms of social organization might have arrived at their current positions through different historical routes: one through a process of simplification (i.e., becoming less complex), the other through a process of elaboration (i.e., becoming more complex). To account for such situations, Boas developed the approach of **historical particularism**.

Boas emphasized that many seemingly new cultural forms were actually borrowed from neighbouring societies (Figure 3.11). He and his followers were quick to note that if cultural borrowing, rather than independent invention, played an important role in culture change, then any unilineal evolutionary scheme was doomed. In addition, their focus on cultural borrowing emphasized the porous boundaries around individual societies that made such borrowing possible.

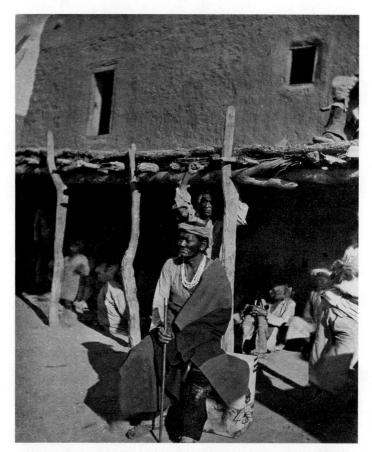

FIGURE 3.11 Franz Boas observed that the culture of the Zuni people of New Mexico seemed to be deeply influenced by Spanish culture, which the Zuni would have encountered under colonialism.

As a result of such observations, the view of society that became dominant in North America was quite different from the one that dominated in Great Britain. Boas and his followers rejected the unilineal cultural evolutionists' view of societies as isolated representatives of universal stages, closed to outside influences, responsible for progressing or failing to progress. Critical of the structural-functional view of societies as bounded, *timeless* social types, they saw social groups as fundamentally open to the outside world. Change was considered more a result of idiosyncratic borrowing from neighbours than a result of inevitable, law-governed *progress*. Therefore, the Boasians focussed their attention on patterns of cultural borrowing, a form of research called *cultural area studies*. They began by developing lists of **culture traits**, such as particular rituals or styles of housing. They then determined how widely those cultural traits had spread into neighbouring societies. A **culture area** was defined by the limits of borrowing, or the *diffusion*, of a particular trait or set of traits (see Map 3.2).

historical particularism
The study of cultures in their own historical contexts.

culture traits
Particular features or parts of a cultural tradition such as a dance, ritual, or style of pottery.

culture area
A geographical region in which cultural traditions share similar culture traits.

Thus North American anthropologists, most famously Alfred Kroeber (1939), were able to discuss social groups without evoking "timeless" classification schemes. Yet new difficulties arose, as they found it impossible to discuss in unambiguous terms societies perpetually open to cultural borrowing. These new orderings were either broader than an individual society (culture areas) or narrower than an individual society (culture traits). Rather than finding a typology-free methodology, then, these anthropologists had simply arrived at a new system of classification, albeit one in which societal boundaries were ignored.

Post-colonial Realities

Around the middle of the twentieth century, the world changed again. World War II was closely followed by the break-up of European colonial empires in Africa and Asia. Former colonies were now independent states, and their citizens rejected the traditional Western view of them as "primitives." Around the world, there developed deepening awareness of the need to promote human rights and principles of equality. Changing realities thus created for Westerners new views of the "other" that made the pretensions of unilineal evolutionism completely unacceptable.

In many new states, leaders began to frame a national consciousness, pulling together supposedly disparate peoples within their borders. Their successes highlighted the weaknesses of colonial-era anthropologists' interpretations of these societies as structurally separate from one another. Decolonization forced anthropologists to pay direct attention to colonialism as a form of political domination—one that eliminated the autonomy of Indigenous social groups and forcibly restructured them into subordinate positions within a larger entity.

At the same time, anthropologists with roots in the non-Western world began to add their voices to those of Western anthropologists (Figure 3.12). They have been highly critical of unilineal evolutionist and structural-functionalist approaches, noting that these approaches helped to spread cultural stereotypes (see the "In Their Own Words" box, below). They have also been critical of the fact that "ranking" typologies have not disappeared altogether in contemporary cultural and social anthropology.

MAP 3.2   The Native American culture areas for North America, north of Mexico.

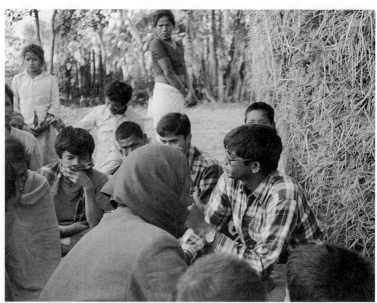

FIGURE 3.12   Sri Lankan anthropologist Arjun Guneratne converses with some of his informants in Nepal. In what ways can researchers from the non-Western world help us gain broader perspectives on the human condition?

IN THEIR OWN WORDS | "Bisexuality" and the Politics of Normal in African Ethnography

Marc Epprecht is head of the Department of Global Development Studies at Queen's University. In the following discussion, he examines the lasting impact of the common stereotype, created and spread by Europeans in colonialist times, that Africans did not practice same-sex sexuality.

Anthropologists have played a central role in documenting the diversity of human sexuality as it is understood and expressed in different cultures around the world. . . . However, . . . anthropologists at times "conscripted" select evidence and even fabricated "facts" about the people they studied in order to advance ideals and preferences around sexuality in their own societies. By conjuring idealized or exoticized Others, they helped to create an understanding of "normal" and "modern" by way of contrast. This has resulted in a body of purportedly empirical or scientific data that in retrospect we can see as deeply flawed, morally normative, and sometimes actually complicit in the construction and maintenance of racist colonialist structures. . . .

[Consider] the commonplace assumption or assertion as an unqualified fact that Africans south of the Sahara either did not practice same-sex sexuality in their traditional societies, or that they only did so so rarely that it was inconsequential. . . . [More recently,] a growing body of research, activism, and art has comprehensively demonstrated the falseness of the "fact" of Africans' exclusive heterosexuality. . . . A growing, pan-African network of lesbian, gay, bisexual, transgender, and intersex (LGBTI) associations also attests to diverse, indigenous, same-sex, and bisexual cultures and practices in Africa. A range of images written or produced by Africans in fiction, theatre, and film further destabilizes the stereotype of the "pure" African heterosexual.

These sources on the whole do not propose a timeless, archetypal African gay or lesbian in opposition to that older stereotype. Rather, the women and men who have same-sex sexual relations most often also continue to marry, to have children, and to engage in heterosexual relationships. Whether this should properly be termed "bisexual" is a matter of debate. However, whether men who sometimes have sex with men but do not identify as homo- or bisexual (MSM), and whether women who sometimes have sex with women but do not identify as lesbian or bisexual (WSW) exist in Africa in greater numbers than commonly assumed or asserted cannot in good scholarship be disputed. That it *does* continue to be disputed is a cause for far greater concern than academic quibbling over numbers. Indeed, scholars, activists, and community leaders who deny the existence of MSM and WSW in Africa, who rationalize it as imported or recent, or who simply disregard the evidence, may be fuelling unhelpful or even dangerous homophobic and xenophobic rhetoric. Such rhetoric stigmatizes already vulnerable groups and self-evidently impedes HIV/AIDS awareness and prevention campaigns. . . .

Clearly, many factors contribute to the tenacity of the no same-sex sexuality in Africa argument. The ethnography, however, is unquestionably foundational in that it provides a scientific-sounding canon that gives authority to contemporary claims about what is normal and traditional, and what is deviant, non-existent, or modern. But how trustworthy is that canon? [There are] key discrepancies in the documentary record dating as far back as the eighteenth century . . . [that] offer insight into the complex relationship between colonial rulers and subjects, and can help us to understand why some Africans today still remain attracted to and defensive of colonial notions of normal. Awareness of this history could also move us toward more pointed research about sexuality in the present that could, in turn, improve our ability to design more effective interventions against HIV/AIDS. A queer analysis of African ethnography could also sharpen the postcolonial critique of anthropology more generally by alerting us to hitherto unsuspected essentialist, "Westocentric" terms and concepts. . . .

[This] new anthropology . . . represents the kind of bold challenges to mainstream scholarship predicted by Kath Weston in her reflections on queer ethnographic research (1998). These would include:

First, establishing beyond reasonable objection that most African societies had normative ways of dealing with sexual difference that were discreetly hidden within the dominant hetero-patriarchal norms. Sweeping claims about non-existence . . . [of] same-sex sexuality are thus empirically unfounded. Expressions of same-sex sexuality, moreover, changed over time in response to many factors, almost certainly including interventions by Western anthropologists.

Second, the research raises compelling questions on a number of contemporary issues. Are men who sometimes have sex with men but do not admit it and do not consider themselves homosexual or bisexual a more significant vector for HIV than has previously been considered? Do women who have sex with women yet consider themselves straight or normal engage in practices that would more accurately be termed bisexual or lesbian-like? It seems likely.

The new anthropology also causes us to reflect on whether the attitudes and political agendas that obscured MSM and WSW from the view of earlier anthropologists and other researchers had a bigger role in shaping heteronormative gender roles and identities in the majority population than has thus far been investigated.

Source: Epprecht, Marc. "'Bisexuality' and the Politics of Normal in African Ethnography," *Anthropologica* 48, 2: 187–201.

Studying Human Societies Today

Some contemporary anthropologists, especially those interested in political and economic issues, continue to find typologies useful. Others reject typologies altogether, arguing that such categorizations are too limited to be of any use. Still, most would agree that the points of comparison on which any given anthropologist chooses to focus are closely related to the type of questions that she or he asks and the theoretical approaches she or he applies.

For example, let us turn again to Lewellen's classification of social types. Lewellen argues that his system is designed to reflect structural, organizational similarities and differences among various societies. To defend such criteria, he employs an analogy in which houses represent societies:

> Two houses built of different materials but to the same floor plan will obviously be much more alike than two houses of the same materials but very different designs (say, a townhouse and a ranch house). . . . In short, a house is defined in terms of its organization, not its components, and that organization will be influenced by its physical environment and the level of technology of the people who designed it. (1983: 17)

Lewellen assumes that structural similarities and differences are both *significant* and *obvious*, seemingly affiliating him with the British social anthropology tradition. He also assumes that the materials out of which the houses are made can safely be ignored. To Lewellen, these assumptions seem justified under his theoretical approach.

Yet not everyone would agree on what is significant and obvious in every case, and not everyone would choose to employ the same categories of classification. For example, the similarities and differences that seemed obvious to many political anthropologists in the British tradition would not seem so sharp to an anthropologist interested in classifying the ways different societies make a living. Indeed, anthropologists interested in how societies make a living employ concepts such as *subsistence strategy* or *mode of production* to order their typologies, focussing on the strategies and technologies people use to produce, distribute, and consume or use food, clothing, housing, tools, and other material goods. Defining different domains of relevance always results in different typologies.

One such domain that became of great interest to Western countries during the mid-twentieth century was *political ideology*. In particular, people were concerned with the divide between *capitalist* and *communist* societies. During the Cold War (1948–91), a new set of categories came into existence that classified states into the First World (capitalist democratic countries that supported the United States), the Second World (communist countries that supported the Soviet Union), and the Third World (countries that remained neutral). After the Cold War ended, a nation's political ideology became of less general significance than its economic development, and these categories shifted to reflect these shifting interests: the label *First World* came to signify the "developed" world, *Second World* came to signify "developing" countries (in particular those that had supported or continue to support communism), and *Third World* came to signify "underdeveloped" countries. In addition, a fourth category—*Fourth World*—was added to signify the "neocolonial" world (e.g., pockets of Indigenous peoples living within First World countries).

As these categories came to redefine how we view modern nations, anthropologists were forced to adjust to this altered context. Yet many of them eventually became highly critical of the way "development" and "underdevelopment" were understood and addressed by scholars and government officials alike. These distinctions have become even more problematic in recent decades, as we face complex divisions in a globalized world economy, and as we confront increasing tensions between capitalist and fundamentalist-religious ideologies.

Sometimes it is easy to emphasize the shortcomings of past approaches to classifying human societies, but we must also acknowledge the lasting contributions they have made. Despite its excesses, unilineal cultural evolutionism highlights the fact that cultures change over time and that our species has experienced broad cultural developments. Structural-functionalist typologies may seem overly rigid and static, but the structural-functionalist ethnographies show just how intricate the social institutions and practices of so-called "simple" societies can be. The cultural distinctions of Boasian culture area studies may be at times too narrow or too broad to apply to individual societies, but they successfully de-emphasize societal boundaries and demonstrate that there are no distinct lines that separate one culture from the next. A focus on "developed" and "underdeveloped" societies may have raised more problems than it solved, but it was in the very attempt to explain why problems of inequality existed that new anthropological understandings were achieved.

Today, virtually all of the familiar anthropological classifications are dropping away as anthropologists explore the continuing cultural creativity of all human beings in all societies, particularly as these societies face rapidly changing conditions. Thus, as we will discover in subsequent chapters, contemporary anthropologists have had to develop new and innovative approaches as they continue to study the meaning of being human.

A CRITICAL LOOK | Classifications and Colonial Reality

In the distorted, self-deluded gazes of eighteenth-century colonialists, the Americas were empty lands—blank spaces that lacked definition and purpose. Moreover, the peoples of the Americas were seen as ineffective overseers of their world, lacking the Europeans' drive to possess and conquer the land. But this view missed—or perhaps willfully ignored—the fact that Indigenous peoples had their own ways of managing themselves and the resources of the land. Why were Europeans so blind? In short, it was in their best interests to be blind. After all, recognizing the value of Indigenous peoples and their approaches to the land would have threatened European's intent to exploit the "new world" for economic gain.

By labelling the land as "empty," the Europeans effectively classified it as less valuable than their own lands back home, which were "full" of factories, businesses, houses, streets, and farms. Similarly, by labelling Indigenous peoples as "ineffective," "passive," and "without purpose," the Europeans were classifying them as inferiors who lacked the qualities they prided in themselves. Such classification schemes reveal a fundamental flaw with systems that try to categorize human beings in terms of *better* and *worse*: the people defining the categories are inevitably the ones who come out on top.

Of course, there were subtle differences in the ways the colonizers of the United States and those of Canada labelled and interpreted the lands and the peoples beyond their settlements. To the former, the borderlands were a *frontier* to new possibilities—the place where Euro-Americans could prove their worth by making the land useful to them. With enough effort, they believed, they could achieve their manifest destiny of civilizing all corners of the new world. To the latter, these lands were a dangerous *wilderness*—a vast and frightening wild land that needed to be survived before it could be tamed and tamed before it could be understood. In both views, Indigenous peoples were at best labelled simply as "others"; at worst, they were labelled as troublesome "savages" to be either "civilized" or destroyed.

The act of labelling Indigenous peoples as "others" is not as harmless as it may at first seem. For one thing, "other" is a rather empty label. It dismisses what is being labelled (in this case, human beings) as not worthy of serious thought or consideration. Further, in the colonial context, it separates the colonizer from the colonized, and it implicitly establishes the colonizer as the standard against which all others should be measured. By giving colonizers the higher status, it also implicitly gives them permission to treat the colonized as lesser beings. As history has shown, again and again, this sort of approach will lead only to tragedy.

Our challenge as anthropologists—and as human beings—is to learn from the mistakes of our ancestors. We must be wary of classifying people as "different" from ourselves and instead focus on the similarities. We must resist ethnocentric impulses. Above all, we must remain open to other people's ways of living and perspectives on life. Only by remaining open can we arrive at a deeper understanding of cultural differences.

—Roberta Robin Dods

KEY TERMS

band 65	decolonization 60	social forms 60	typology 61
capitalism 52	historical particularism 67	social structure 64	unilineal cultural
chiefdom 66	imperialism 52	state 66	evolutionism 62
colonialism 52	neocolonialism 60	structural-functional	white man's burden 57
culture area 67	political economy 56	theory 66	
culture traits 67	small-scale societies 54	tribe 66	

CHAPTER SUMMARY

1. Modern Western history has been characterized by the rise of capitalism. To function under capitalism, colonized peoples had to learn to view everything—including land, objects, ideas, and human beings—as a potential commodity. As colonialists imposed this new world order and increased their control over colonized regions, Indigenous peoples lost much of their autonomy.

2. The context of colonialism has been an ever-present reality for anthropologists. Today, formerly colonized peoples remain tied to their former rulers in many ways. These ties have, in some cases, persisted for over a hundred years and are called *neocolonialism*.

3. Anthropologists have considered various ways of classifying societies. The earliest important anthropological typologies were based on ideas that different kinds of societies represented different stages along a single path of cultural evolution. Following Boas, North American anthropologists rejected such ideas on the grounds that societies could easily borrow from one another, thus skipping supposedly universal evolutionary stages. Consequently, the aim of much research shifted to making lists of culture traits and mapping the culture areas through which they had spread as a result of cultural borrowing.

4. Although some anthropologists still find some typologies useful for investigating particular kinds of issues, classifying forms of human society is not an ultimate goal for most anthropologists today. The fuzziness of category boundaries reminds us that classification systems are human constructions, not pure reflections of objective reality.

CRITICAL THINKING QUESTIONS

1. What were the three major schools of anthropological thought that influenced the development of anthropology in Canada? Why do you suppose these schools were so influential in Canada?

2. What were the crucial differences between the British colonial enterprise in Virginia and that in Rupert's Land? How might these early encounters have affected later relationships between Native peoples and Europeans?

3. What are some of the criticisms anthropologists faced for the roles they played under colonial rule?

4. What are some advantages to being able to classify societies into different types? What are some difficulties anthropologists have faced when trying to develop new systems of classification?

SUGGESTED READINGS

Barnard, Alan. 2000. *History and Theory in Anthropology* (**Cambridge: Cambridge University Press**). A concise overview of the history of anthropological ideas, tying together developments on both sides of the Atlantic.

Driver, Harold E. 1961. *Indians of North America* (**Chicago: University of Chicago Press**). A comprehensive overview of Indigenous traditional life in North America.

Kroeber, Alfred. 1939. *Cultural and Natural Areas of Native North America* (**Berkeley: University of California Press**). This popular work explores the relationship between environment and culture. It has influenced work in cultural diffusion, cultural sharing, and analysis of cultural responses to environmental settings.

Lewellen, Ted C. 2003. *Political Anthropology*, **3rd edn** (**Westport, CT: Praeger Publishers**). Contains much useful information about the different kinds of societies that scholars have identified.

Quimby, G.I. 1954. "Cultural and Natural Areas before Kroeber," *American Antiquity* **XIX, 4: 317–31.** An overview of the development of the culture area concept.

Weatherford, Jack. 1988. *Indian Givers: How the Indians of the Americas Transformed the World* **(New York: Fawcett Columbine).** An engaging account of the consequences of contact between the Old World and the New World. Also worth reading are Weatherford's *Native Roots: How the Indians Enriched America* (1991) and *Savages and Civilization: Who Will Survive* (1994), which explore similar themes.

Wolf, Eric. 1982. *Europe and the People without History* **(Berkeley: University of California Press).** A classic text about European expansion and the impact this expansion had on European societies and the rest of the world. This work also discusses the effect of European contact on Indigenous societies.

———. **1999.** *Envisioning Power: Ideologies of Dominance and Crisis* **(Berkeley: University of California Press).** An analysis of the historical relationship of ideas, power, and culture in which Wolf argues that power is central to shaping the circumstances and form of cultural production.

RELATED WEBSITES

A Brief History of Anthropology at the University of Toronto http://anthropology.utoronto.ca/home/about/history

Assembly of First Nations (AFN) www.afn.ca

Association of Social Anthropologists of the UK and Commonwealth www.theasa.org

Survival, the Global Movement for Tribal Peoples' Rights www.survival-international.org

Truth and Reconciliation Commission of Canada www.trc.ca /websites/trcinstitution/index.php?p=4

II

The Resources of Culture

THE CHAPTERS IN PART II FOCUS ON A RANGE OF HUMAN CAPACITIES THAT LIE AT THE CENTRE OF HUMAN CULTURAL CREATIVITY, FLEXIBILITY, AND DIVERSITY. We all live in a material world. We make our way through this world by assigning meaning to the things—objects, places, ideas, ourselves, other people, and so on—that we encounter. As a result, our contact with the material world is always mediated by a web of meanings of our own creation. Cultural meaning is perhaps most directly encountered in language, but it is also revealed in habitual patterns of thought and action as well as in social relationships, and it is at its most elaborate in those creations that Westerners traditionally call *art*, *myth*, *ritual*, and *world view*. Through created meaning, we fashion our individual and group identities. Because we depend on culture for survival, a proper awareness of the depth, breadth, and complexity of human cultural resources is, from the anthropological perspective, indispensable for an adequate understanding of the human condition in all its guises.

4

Language

CHAPTER OUTLINE

LEARNING OBJECTIVES

By the end of Chapter 4, you will be able to

- explain why cultural anthropologists are interested in language,
- outline the design features and components of language,
- describe why language must be examined in context,

- understand the concept of linguistic relativity,
- recognize the role inequality plays in shaping language use,

- appreciate the flexibility of language, and
- consider how language can change over time.

An Afar woman in Ethiopia looks intently at the camera, seemingly speaking volumes with her gaze. While words allow us to communicate highly complex ideas and information, facial expressions and other non-verbal means of communication have the power to convey deeply significant messages across linguistic barriers.

Language provides us with basic tools for diverse forms of creativity. It allows us to name and consider the various aspects of our world, and it allows us to communicate with one another. Yet language also creates barriers to communication. One major barrier is linguistic diversity (Figure 4.1). After all, there are some 3,000 different languages currently spoken in the world today. This chapter will help you understand why so many languages exist, and it will reveal to you the power of human language in forming individual and group identity.

Language and Culture

Human language is a biocultural phenomenon. Our brain and the anatomy of our mouth and throat make spoken language possible for us. At the same time, every human language is clearly a cultural product. It is shared by a group of speakers, encoded in symbols, patterned, and transmitted through teaching and learning.

Anthropological Interest in Language

Language is of primary interest to anthropologists for at least three reasons:

1. Fieldwork proceeds through oral communication. Often, anthropologists must learn a new language to do fieldwork among people whose language is different from their own.
2. Language involves grammatical and conceptual complexities that anthropologists can analyze to gain insight into a culture. Indeed, some schools of anthropological theory have based their theories of culture explicitly on ideas taken from **linguistics**.
3. All people use language to structure their understanding of the world and of themselves, and to engage with one another. Language is the best tool anthropologists have to access informants' perceptions and interpretations.

By learning another language, we learn something about the culture of the people who use that language, often while gaining unsuspected insights into the nature of our own language and culture.

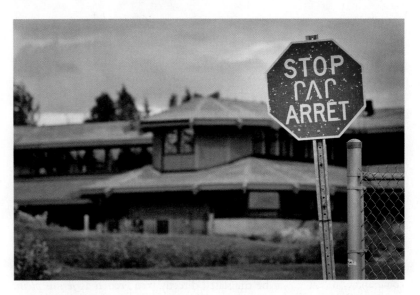

FIGURE 4.1 Language allows people to communicate with one another, but it can also create barriers to communication. What are some of the ways in which language can create barriers? How can commonly understood symbols help to transmit information across linguistic barriers?

As with the concept of *culture* (see Chapter 1), discussions of the concept of *language* have regularly involved a distinction between the singular (*language*) and the plural (*languages*). *Language* (singular) was viewed as an abstract property belonging to the human species as a whole, while *languages* (plural) was used to indicate the actual symbolic systems groups of people use to communicate. This distinction initially enabled anthropologists to recognize that all human groups possess fully developed *languages* rather than "primitive," "broken," or otherwise defective forms of vocal communication. Indeed, just as there is no such thing as a "primitive" human culture, there is no such thing as a "primitive" human language. Today, linguistic anthropologists realize that problems also arise when we think of specific *languages* as being entirely separate from one another. Indeed, the difficulties associated with marking the boundaries between one language and another, or with distinguishing between dialects and languages, become particularly obvious in studies of pidgins and creoles, as we will see.

It remains useful, however, to distinguish *language* from *speech* and from *communication*. We usually think of spoken language (speech) when we use the term *language*, but language can be transmitted by various non-spoken media, such as written words, Morse code, or gestures (as is the case in sign languages). *Human communication* can be defined as the transfer of information

language
The system of symbols we use to encode our experiences of the world and of one another.

linguistics
The scientific study of language.

native speaker

A person who has spoken a particular language since early childhood.

vocabulary

The words used in a particular language or by members of a particular speech community.

grammar

A set of rules that describes the patterns of linguistic usage observed by members of a particular speech community.

design features of language

The characteristics of language that, when taken together, differentiate it from other known animal communication systems.

from one person to another, either verbally or non-verbally (e.g., through facial expressions, body language, and mannerisms).

Native speakers of a language share not just **vocabulary** and **grammar** but also a number of assumptions about how to speak. These assumptions may not be shared by speakers of a different language. Students learning a new language discover early on that word-for-word translation from one language to another does not always work. Sometimes there are no equivalent words in the second language; even when there are, a word-for-word translation may not carry over the original meaning. For example, an English speaker who has eaten enough might say "I'm full." This may be translated directly into French as *Je suis plein*. To French speakers, this sentence has the nonsensical meaning "I am a pregnant [male] animal." Alternatively, if uttered by a man who has just consumed a lot of alcohol, it means "I'm drunk."

Learning to speak a second language is often frustrating and even unsettling, and the experience can result in a sense of culture shock that is as disorienting as being physically immersed in another culture! Often, it is less a matter of learning new labels for old objects than it is of learning how to use the components of the new language to convey the intended meaning in any given situation. Therefore, in order to increase fluency in a language, the student must

move beyond abstract understandings and situate that particular language in its cultural context.

Talking about Experience

Language, like the rest of culture, is a product of our attempt to come to terms with experience. Each language, having the ability to change and adapt, is adequate for its speakers' needs, given their particular way of life. Naturally, people tend to develop larger vocabularies to discuss those aspects of life that are important to them. For this reason, it may be easier to talk about the Polynesian concept of *mana* in Polynesian languages (e.g., Hawaiian) than in English. In addition, different languages have developed to be more or less complex in different ways. For example, some languages require their speakers to master a larger (or narrower) range of sounds than other languages do; some have more complex (or less complex) sentence structures than others have, and the range of meanings associated with a particular expression in one language may be hard to map onto a single expression in another language (Figure 4.2). Yet despite their many differences, all languages appear to be equal in their open potential to communicate experiences.

Traditionally, languages are associated with actual groups of people called *speech communities*. Nevertheless, all members of a speech community do not possess identical knowledge about the language they share, nor do they all speak the same way. Consequently, there is a tension between diversity and commonality. Individuals and subgroups within a speech community make use of linguistic resources in different ways as they attempt to create unique, personal voices. These efforts are countered by the pressure to negotiate a common code for communication within the larger social group. In this way, language is produced and reproduced through the activity of its speakers. Any particular language that we may identify at a given moment is a snapshot of a continuing process.

Design Features of Human Language

In 1966, anthropological linguist Charles Hockett listed 16 different **design features** that in his estimation set human language apart from other forms of animal communication. Six of these design

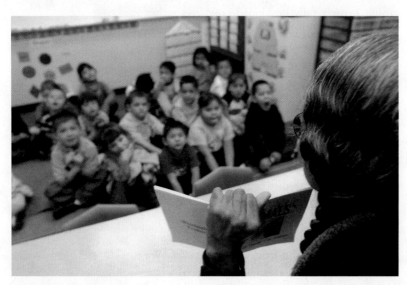

FIGURE 4.2 Languages such as Salish (spoken by Native peoples along Canada's west coast), which in this photo is being taught to a group of second-grade children, contain sounds that are particularly difficult for non-native speakers to pronounce.

features seem especially useful for our discussion: openness, displacement, prevarication, arbitrariness, duality of patterning, and semanticity.

Openness, probably the most important feature, is the ability to talk about the same experiences from different perspectives, using different words and various grammatical constructions. This feature allows people to conceptualize, label, and discuss the same experience in different ways. Thus no single human interpretation of an experience is necessarily more correct in every respect than all others. To understand how truly significant the feature of openness is to communication, compare our spoken language to the vocal communication systems (or *call systems*) of monkeys and apes. Whereas our language allows us to endlessly combine and recombine elements of our experiences in new and various ways, the possibilities of meaning are much more limited when it comes to call systems. Primates have several calls, all of which are appropriate to specific situations: when the animal is in the presence of food; when it is in danger or pain; when it wants to show friendly interest; when it wants to mark its location; and so on. Each call is appropriate in only one situation, and primates cannot combine one call with another to express more complex messages. For these reasons, the call systems of primates are said to be *closed* when compared to *open* human languages.

Anthropologist Terrence Deacon (1997) points out that modern human beings still possess a set of six calls: laughing, sobbing, screaming, crying, groaning, and sighing. These calls, together with gestures and the changes in speech rhythm, volume, and tonality, all appear to have co-evolved alongside our use of language, which is probably why they integrate with one another so smoothly when we speak. Deacon emphasizes, however, that closed primate call systems—which contain between 15 and 40 calls, depending on species—do *not* map onto any of the elements of human language and are even controlled by different parts of the brain.

Closed call systems also lack *displacement*, our ability to talk about absent or non-existent objects and past or future events as easily as we discuss our immediate situations. As Canadian anthropological linguist William Thurston noted in a recent conversation,

displacement allows us to communicate about things that are not here and now; it also allows us to talk with great precision about things that do not exist, like unicorns. The important thing here is that it permits the extension of linguistic creativity to such phenomena as narrative, religion, rhetoric, politics, poetry, history, and science itself.

Although non-human primates have good memories, and some species such as chimpanzees seem to be able to plan social action in advance (as when hunting for meat), their call systems do not appear to be involved in these activities.

Perhaps the most striking consequence of linguistic openness is the design feature *prevarication*. Hockett's remarks about this design feature deserve particular attention: "Linguistic messages can be false, and they can be meaningless in the logician's sense" (1966). Not only can people use language to lie, but they can also use it to form statements that are grammatically correct but semantically nonsensical. Consider linguist Noam Chomsky's example: "Colourless green ideas sleep furiously" (1957: 15). This is a grammatical sentence on one level—the right kinds of words are used in the right places—but on another level it doesn't make sense. The ability of language users to prevaricate—to speak falsely or to make statements that violate convention (e.g., by speaking nonsense, or by writing poetry, or by developing testable scientific hypotheses)—is a major consequence of open symbolic systems.

Also notably absent from closed call systems is *arbitrariness*, the lack of an inherent connection between a symbol (e.g., a word) and its function or meaning. As Shakespeare's Juliet says: "What's in a name? That which we call a rose by any other name would smell as sweet."

Arbitrariness is evident in *duality of patterning*. Language, Hockett claimed, is patterned on two different levels: *sound* and *meaning*. On the first level, each language has a set of sounds called **phonemes**. In combination, phonemes compose **morphemes**, the shortest *meaningful* units of speech. On the second level, morphemes combine in grammatical ways to form meaningful clusters and ultimately sentences. The essentials remain the same: phonemes are patterned

phonemes
Basic units of distinct sound that are characteristic of a language and that come together to form words (e.g., /b/ and /ɔɪ/ in *boy*).

morphemes
The shortest meaning-bearing units in any language (e.g., /bɔɪ/ refers to a young male).

to create morphemes, or units of meaning, and these units of meaning are patterned to create sentences and thus discourse.

Arbitrariness shows up again in the design feature of *semanticity*—the association of linguistic signals with aspects of the social, cultural, and physical world of a speech community. People use language to refer to and make sense of objects and processes in the world. Nevertheless, linguistic descriptions of reality are always selective as they highlight some features and downplay others. For example, a trained primatologist would distinguish apes (such as chimpanzees) from monkeys (such as baboons). In contrast, a person with no special knowledge of primates might use the words *monkey* and *ape* interchangeably to refer to chimpanzees or baboons. Each speaker links the same words to the world in different ways.

Language and Context

linguistic competence
Mastery of adult grammar.

communicative competence
Mastery of adult rules for socially and culturally appropriate speech.

Anthropologists are powerfully aware of the influence of context on what people choose to say. Linguists have noted that social and cultural context has a strong impact on how children develop **linguistic** as well as **communicative competence** (Figure 4.3).

From an early age they appear to communicate very fluently, producing utterances which are not just remarkably well-formed according to the linguist's standards but also appropriate to the social context in which the speakers find themselves. Children are thus learning far more about language than rules of grammar. [They are] acquiring communicative competence. (Elliot 1981: 13)

The term *communicative competence* was coined by American anthropological linguist Dell Hymes (1972). Hymes objected to Noam Chomsky's (1965) suggestion that competent language use consists only of being able to use correct grammar. He observed that competent adult speakers do more than follow grammatical rules when they speak: they also choose words and topics of conversation appropriate to (1) their social position, (2) the social position of the person they are addressing, and (3) the social context of interaction.

For example, consider the issue of using personal pronouns appropriately when addressing another person. For native English speakers, the matter is clear, as we address all people as "you." But any English speaker who has ever tried to learn French has worried about when to address an individual using the second-person plural (*vous*) and when to use the second-person singular (*tu*). To be safe, most students use *vous* for all individuals because it is more formal and they want to avoid appearing too familiar with native speakers whom they do not know well. But if you are dating a French person, at which point in the relationship does the change from *vous* to *tu* occur, and who decides? Moreover, sometimes—for example, among university students—the normal term of address is *tu* (even among strangers); it is used to indicate social solidarity. Rules for the appropriate use of *tu* and *vous* seem to have nothing to do with grammar, yet the choice between one form and the other indicates whether the speaker is someone who does or does not know how to speak French.

Linguistic Relativity

During the first half of the twentieth century, two American anthropological linguists—Edward Sapir and Benjamin Whorf—noted that the grammars of different languages often described the same situation in different ways. Sapir and

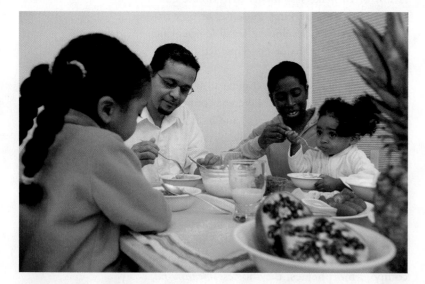

FIGURE 4.3 The contexts in which a child learns to communicate impact the ways in which she or he masters the rules of grammar and the rules for using language in different settings. How might the process of learning socially and culturally appropriate table behaviours, for example, also impact what a child learns about language?

Whorf concluded that language has the power to shape the way people see the world. This claim has been called the **linguistic relativity principle**, or the Sapir–Whorf hypothesis. This hypothesis has been highly controversial because it is difficult to test, and the results of testing have been ambiguous.

The so-called "strong" version of the Sapir–Whorf hypothesis is also known as *linguistic determinism*. It is a rather inflexible view of language that holds that the patterns of our thoughts and our culture are *determined by* the patterns of the language we speak. If a grammar classifies nouns and/or pronouns in gender categories, for example, linguistic determinism concludes that speakers of that language are *forced* to think of males and females as radically different kinds of beings. In contrast, a language that makes no grammatical distinctions on the basis of gender presumably trains its speakers to think of males and females as exactly the same. If linguistic determinism is correct, then a change in grammar should change thought patterns: if English speakers replaced *he* and *she* with a new, gender-neutral pronoun such as *te*, then, linguistic determinists predict, English speakers would begin to treat men and women as equals.

There are a number of problems with linguistic determinism. First, there are languages such as Fulfulde (spoken in West Africa) in which only one third-person pronoun, *o*, is used for males and females; however, Fulfulde speakers tend to follow male-dominant social patterns. Second, if language determined thought in such an absolute way, it would be impossible to translate from one language to another or even to learn another language with a different grammatical structure. Yet human beings *do* learn foreign languages and translate from one language to another. Third, even if it were possible to draw firm boundaries around speech communities (which it isn't), every language provides its native speakers with alternative ways of describing the world. Finally, in most of the world's societies, people grow up speaking more than one language, yet they do not also grow up struggling to reconcile two different views of reality (Figure 4.4). Indeed, bilingual children ordinarily benefit from knowing two languages; they do not confuse them, they can switch readily between them, and they even appear to demonstrate greater creativity and cognitive flexibility than do monolingual children (e.g., Adesope et al. 2010; Elliot 1981; Leikin 2012).

In the face of these objections, many researchers offer a "weak" version of the Sapir–Whorf hypothesis that rejects linguistic determinism but continues to claim that language shapes thought and culture. In this view, grammatical gender might not determine a male-dominant social order, but it might make it easier for people to accept such a social order because the grammatical distinction between *he* and *she* might make separate and unequal gender roles seem "natural."

Neither Sapir nor Whorf favoured linguistic determinism. Sapir argued that language's

linguistic relativity principle

The assertion that language has the power to shape the way people see the world.

FIGURE 4.4 Bilingual children can switch from one language to the other with relative ease. What benefits can there be for children who grow up learning more than one language?

importance lies in the way it directs our attention to some aspects of experience rather than others. He was impressed by the fact that "it is generally difficult to make a complete divorce between objective reality and our linguistic symbols of reference to it" (1966 [1933]: 9, 15). Whorf's discussions of linguistic relativity are more complex and ambiguous, and his views have been more sharply criticized by later scholars. However, interest in the "Whorfian" question has revived in recent years, and scholars have recognized that there are several different ways to ask about the relationship of language to thought. For instance, linguist Dan Slobin has proposed a "thinking for speaking" hypothesis, suggesting that the influence of linguistic forms on thought may be greatest when people prepare to speak to others on a specific topic in a specific setting. "One fits one's thoughts into available linguistic forms. . . . 'Thinking for speaking' involves picking those characteristics that (a) fit some conceptualization of the event, and (b) are readily encodable in the language" (Slobin 1987: 435). For example, an English speaker who is trying to say "I like fast food" in Spanish will have to use a passive encoding—*me gusta la comida rápida*—("fast food pleases me"). This encoding is not easy for many English speakers to learn, precisely because it is not the standard English way to encode the thought.

Dedre Gentner and Susan Goldin-Meadow (2003) point out that some researchers still take a traditional Whorfian approach, viewing language as a lens through which people view the world. Others think of language as a tool kit, a set of resources that speakers make use of to build more elaborate conceptual structures. Still others think of language as a category-maker that influences the way people classify experiences and objects in the world. Gentner and Goldin-Meadow note that research producing the most consistent evidence of the influence of language on thought comes from those who view language as a tool kit—that is, as a set of resources that speakers make use of for conceptual or communicative purposes (10). Nevertheless, they emphasize that defining the research question in such variable ways means that "we are unlikely to get a yes-or-no answer to the whole of Whorf's thesis. But if we have delineated a set of more specific questions for which the answer is *no* to some and *yes* to others, we will have achieved our goal" (12).

phonology

The study of the sounds (phones and phonemes) of a language.

Components of Language

Linguistic study involves a search for patterns in the way speakers use language. Linguists aim to describe these patterns by reducing them to a set of rules called a *grammar*. Over time, linguists came to recognize a number of components that form part of the grammar of any language. The most widely acknowledged components of language are phonology, morphology, syntax, semantics, and pragmatics.

Phonology: Sounds

The study of the sounds of language is called **phonology**. The sounds of language are special because they are produced by a set of organs—the speech organs (Figure 4.5)—that belong only to the human species. The actual sounds that come out of our mouths are called *phones*, and speakers of a particular language recognize phones that are very similar to one another as functionally the same. These functional groups of phones are known as *phonemes*, the characteristic speech sounds in the language.

Part of the phonologist's job is to map out how speech sounds are produced and interpreted. Another part is to examine individual languages to discover the particular sound combinations they contain and the patterns into which those sound combinations are organized. Phonologists have found that no language makes use of all the many sounds the human speech organs can produce, and no two languages use exactly the same

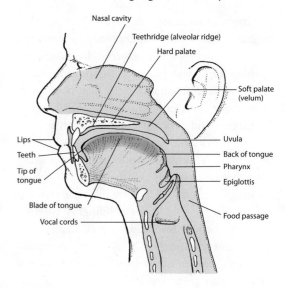

FIGURE 4.5 The speech organs.

set of sounds. Canadian English uses only 38 sounds (more or less, depending on the dialect).

Speakers of the same language often differ in the way they pattern their phonemes, producing "accents," which constitute one kind of variety within a language. This variety is not random; the speech sounds characteristic of any particular accent follow a pattern. Speakers with different accents are usually able to understand one another, but their distinctive articulation is a clue to their ethnic, regional, or social class origins.

Morphology: Word Structure

Morphology is the study of the smallest units of meaning in a language. These units are known as *morphemes*. In English, some words consist of a single morpheme (e.g., *book, top, up*), while others consist of two or more morphemes (e.g., *book/ing, top/coat/s, up/root/ed*). Many other languages are made up of words that are formed in this way. But not all languages are. Consider Shawnee, a language spoken by some Indigenous peoples in North America. A sample utterance in Shawnee is *nikookitepeena*, which translates into English as "I dipped his head in the water" (Whorf 1956: 172). Although the Shawnee utterance is composed of parts, the parts do not possess the characteristics we attribute to words in, say, English or French (Table 4.1). As this example illustrates, describing the smallest units of meaning as *morphemes* rather than *words* allows us to compare the morphology of different languages.

Morphemic patterning in languages such as Shawnee may seem hopelessly complicated to native English speakers, yet the patterning of morphemes in English is also complex. Why is it, after all, that some morphemes can stand alone as words while others (e.g., *-s, -ing, -ed*) cannot?

Syntax: Sentence Structure

A third component of language is **syntax**, or sentence structure. While sentence structure helps us fit meanings together, it also leaves space for possible confusion. In languages such as English,

for example, rules governing word order cannot explain what is puzzling about the following sentence: "Smoking grass means trouble." For many native English speakers, this sentence exhibits what linguists call *structural ambiguity*. In our example, we must ask ourselves what kind of *trouble* is involved: the consequences of smoking an illegal substance or the danger of a prairie fire? In the first reading, *smoking* is a noun that conveys an action (the act of smoking); in the second, it is an adjective that describes the grass (grass that is smoking).

As this example illustrates, structural ambiguity can result when it is not clear how a word is functioning within a sentence—as a noun, a verb, an adjective, an adverb, and so on. But an examination of a word's grammatical function within a sentence cannot account for the ambiguity in a sentence such as the following: "The father of the girl and the boy fell into the lake." How many people fell into the lake? Just the father, or the father and the boy? Each interpretation depends on how the reader groups the words of the sentence together. Linguists have discovered numerous other features of sentence structure that are difficult to explain, leading to a growth of interest in the study of syntactic patterns in different languages.

Semantics: Meaning

Semantics, the study of meaning, can be a particularly tricky area of study, as *meaning* is a highly ambiguous term. What do we mean when we say that a word or a sentence means something? We may be asking about what each individual word in the sentence means, or what the sentence as a whole means, or what I mean when I utter the sentence, which may differ from what someone else would mean if he or she uttered the same sentence.

Semanticists examine how words link to each other within a language. They explore relations such as *synonymy*, or "same meaning" (*old* and *aged*); *homophony*, or "same sound, different meaning" (*would* and *wood*); and *antonymy*, or "opposite meaning" (*tall* and *short*). They look closely at words' **denotative meanings**, and they also consider **connotative meanings**. The

---

morphology
The study of the smallest units of meaning (morphemes) in a language.

syntax
The study of sentence structure.

semantics
The study of meaning.

denotative meaning
The formal meaning(s) of a word, as given in a dictionary.

connotative meaning
Additional meanings of a word that derive from the typical contexts in which they are used and rely on personal and cultural associations.

TABLE 4.1 Morphemes of Shawnee Utterance and Their Glosses

ni	kooki	tepe	en	a
I	immersed in water	point of action at head	by hand action	cause to him

denotative or dictionary meaning of the word *pig*, for example, might be "an omnivorous, domesticated animal with short legs, a broad flat nose, sparse hair, and a curly tail." This formal definition conveys a meaning that all English speakers would associate with the word *pig*. In contrast, the connotative meanings associated with the word *pig* might be "dirty," "fat," "offensive," and "greedy." Not all English speakers associate these qualities with the word *pig*, but many do.

pragmatics
The study of language in the context of its use.

To complicate matters further, words often have informal or slang definitions that may or may not be listed in a dictionary, and of which not all English speakers may be aware. For example, an informal meaning of the word *pig* is "police officer." From a denotative point of view, to call police officers *pigs* is to create ambiguity, because a police officer is not a farm animal. This sort of ambiguous reference is an example of *metaphor*—a form of thought and language that asserts a meaningful link between two expressions from different semantic domains (see Chapter 10). In this case, the metaphor links the unrelated semantic domains of *law enforcement* and *livestock* (Figure 4.6). To understand what this metaphor means, we must understand that some people see police officers (particularly when the police are considered to be corrupt) as greedy and offensive—characteristics also attributed to pigs. But to English speakers who do not understand this connection, the phrase "police are pigs" would make little sense. Our ability to use the same words in different ways (and different words in the same way) is a hallmark of the openness of language.

FIGURE 4.6 The phrase "police are pigs" is a metaphor. What metaphors do you use in everyday speech? What do you mean when you use them?

Thus, to understand what words or sentences mean, we must always be aware of the context in which they are used.

Pragmatics: Language in Contexts of Use

Pragmatics can be defined as the study of language in the context of its use. Each context offers limitations and opportunities concerning what we may say and how we may say it. Everyday language use is thus often characterized by a struggle between speakers and listeners over definitions of words within a given context.

An understanding of context is particularly important for determining the referential meaning of language. We must consider two kinds of context here: linguistic and non-linguistic. *Linguistic context* consists of the other words, expressions, and sentences that surround the expression whose meaning we are trying to determine. We cannot, for example, determine the meaning of *it* in the sentence "I really enjoyed it" by considering the sentence on its own. However, if we know that the previous sentence was "My aunt gave me this book for my birthday," we have a linguistic context that allows us to deduce that *it* refers to "this book." *Non-linguistic context* consists of objects and activities that are present in the situation of speech at the same time we are speaking. Consider the sentence "What is that on the door?" To give referential meaning to the word *that*, we need to inspect the actual door and whatever is on it. Furthermore, even if we know what a door is in a formal sense, we need the non-linguistic context to clarify what counts as a door in this instance (e.g., it could be a rough opening in the wall).

By forcing analysts to go beyond syntax and semantics, pragmatics directs our attention to **discourse**. Linguistic discourse includes a spoken one-word greeting, a series of sentences uttered by a single individual, a conversation among two or more speakers, or an extended narrative. Many linguistic anthropologists accept the arguments of linguistic theorists Mikhail Bakhtin and Valentin Voloshinov (see, e.g., Voloshinov 1986 [1929]) that the series of replies in conversation is the primary form of discourse. In this view, the speech of any single individual, whether a simple "yes" or a book-length dissertation, is only one reply in an ongoing dialogue.

In recent years, linguistic anthropologists have challenged us to consider **metalanguage** as an additional context that helps to shape discourse (see, e.g., Mertz and Yovel 2010). Examples of metalanguage include direct references to words (e.g., "words are symbols," "the word *cat* has three letters") as well as comments on our communication (e.g., "I told you," "I can't understand what he's saying," "does that explanation make sense to you?"). Both types of comments direct attention to the language we are using. The former type does so in an obvious way, signalling that language is the direct topic of discussion. The latter type, which tends to pop up in everyday discussions on various topics, more subtly or even directly, reveals our constant—if unconscious—awareness of words as symbols and of language as open to interpretation.

Ethnopragmatics

Linguistic anthropologists analyze the way discourse is produced when people talk to one another. But they go far beyond formal pragmatics, paying attention not only to the immediate contexts but also to broader cultural contexts, which are shaped by unequal social relationships and rooted in history (Brenneis and Macauley 1996; Hill and Irvine 1992). Anthropologist Alessandro Duranti calls this **ethnopragmatics**: "a study of language use that relies on ethnography to illuminate the ways in which speech is both constituted by and constitutive of social interaction" (1994: 11). Such a study focusses on how language is used in *practice*—in commonplace situations in which the rules of grammar, cultural values, and physical action are all conjoined (Hanks 1996). This perspective locates the source of meaning in everyday, routine social activity, or *habitus*, rather than in grammar alone. As a result, phonemes, morphemes, syntax, and semantics are viewed as linguistic resources people can make use of, rather than factors that impose strict rules on how we use language.

If mutual understanding is shaped by shared routine activity and not solely by grammar, then communication is possible even if the people interacting with one another speak mutually unintelligible languages. All they need is a shared sense of "what is going on here" and the ability to negotiate who will do what. Such mutually co-engaged people shape *communicative practices* that involve spoken language but also include values and shared habitual knowledge that may never be put into words.

Most people regularly engage in a wide range of practical activities with different subgroups within a population, each with distinctive communication practices and linguistic habits. For example, you may eat dinner with your family, attend class with other students, live in an apartment with roommates, attend religious services with fellow worshippers, and work at a part-time job with other employees. Because you simultaneously know which linguistic habits to use in each of these social situations, your overall linguistic knowledge is characterized by what linguist Mikhail Bakhtin (1981 [1975]) calls **heteroglossia**.

For Bakhtin, heteroglossia is the normal condition of linguistic knowledge in any society with internal divisions. Heteroglossia describes a co-existing multiplicity of linguistic norms and forms, many of which are anchored in more than one social subgroup. Because we all participate in more than one of these subgroups, our language use is complex, even when we know only one language! Our capacity for using different varieties of a language is another example of what Hockett called *linguistic openness*: it means that our thoughts and speech are not imprisoned in a single set of grammatical forms and definitions. Here we can see that heteroglossia stands as evidence against absolute linguistic determinism. To the extent, however, that your habitual ways of speaking are deeply rooted in everyday routine activity, they may guide the way you typically think, perceive, and act. And to that extent, linguistic relativity may be seen to operate on the level of discourse (Hanks 1996: 176, 246; Schultz 1990).

As you can see, then, the context in which we communicate heavily influences the words we choose. To understand the degree to which this is the case, consider how speakers tailor their words for a particular audience. Advertising agencies, for example, are notorious for slanting their messages to appeal to the people they want to buy their clients' products or services. In his work in a small Samoan village, Alessandro Duranti (1994) learned just how important a sense of audience is to the professional orators

metalanguage
Language used to talk about language.

ethnopragmatics
The study of language use in a specific culture, grounded in an ethnographic approach, with close attention to the relationships among language, communication, and social interaction.

heteroglossia
The co-existence of multiple varieties of a specific language.

who argue cases before the titled people, called *matai*, in the village council, or *fono* (Figure 4.7) (see EthnoProfile 4.1). Orators use a form of language midway in formality between everyday speech and ceremonial speech. Because the *fono* renders judgments that assign praise and blame, the main struggle between orators for different sides is "often centred on the ability to frame the

reason for the meeting as involving or not involving certain key social actors" (Duranti 1994: 3). Of all the grammatical resources used by orators, the form called the *ergative agent* most attracted Duranti's attention.

An ergative agent can be understood as a "wilful initiator of an event" (Duranti 1994: 125). In Samoan, ergative agents are marked by the preposition *e*, to distinguish them grammatically. Other forms of agency are marked by different prepositions: for example, *i* or *ia* frames the human agent as the source of the transaction rather than as its wilful initiator. Framing agency in grammatical terms is common in the *fono*, as disputants argue over who should be held accountable for some act. Possible agents include God, particular individuals, or groups. In all cases, final judgments are the outcome of talk—talk that is influenced by both the immediate context and the broader cultural context.

Non-verbal Communication

So far, we have focussed mainly on how people communicate through spoken language. But human beings can also communicate quite effectively through non-verbal means. In some instances, non-verbal communication is necessary because of hearing loss or damage to vocal chords. In other cases, we may want to communicate silently for some strategic purpose. For example, Aboriginal hunting parties in Australia communicate through "hand talk" to avoid startling their prey. Simple hand gestures, movements, and facial expressions can also help people who

FIGURE 4.7 Although nominal power rests with Samoan chiefs, when village elders meet in the *fono*, titled orators such as this man from the island of Tutuila tend to direct its proceedings. These orators carefully tailor their words for their audience.

EthnoProfile 4.1 | Samoans

Region Oceania

Nation Independent State of Samoa

Language Samoan, a language of the Malayo-Polynesian family, part of the Austronesian languages

Population 182,080 (2014 estimate; approximately 92.6 per cent of the total population of Samoa), most living on the main island of Upolu

Environment Tropical

Livelihood Farming (tropical and subtropical crops), fishing, wage labour

Political organization Ranked, with linguistic markers for high- and low-status people; now part of a modern nation-state

For more information Duranti, Alessandro. 1994. *From Grammar to Politics: Linguistic Anthropology in a Western Samoan Village* (Berkeley: University of California Press); Mead, Margaret. 1928. *Coming of Age in Samoa* (New York: Morrow).

speak different languages overcome linguistic barriers.

For people who are unable to hear and/or speak, sign languages offer a way of conveying complex messages. Similar to the way in which spoken languages use words as symbols, sign languages use hand gestures, facial expressions, and bodily movement to represent objects and ideas. Globally, there are many different types of sign language. In North America, the most commonly used type is American Sign Language (ASL). Studies show that deaf children learn sign language in much the same way that hearing children learn spoken language, simply by being exposed to the language. One difference, however, is that infants may be able to use sign language much earlier than they can produce speech, because hand-eye coordination develops sooner than the ability to speak. For this reason, some parents have begun to teach their hearing babies to use a simplified version of ASL known as "baby sign language" to communicate their needs and wants at a very early age.

We also communicate non-verbally in more subtle ways. Think of how much we "say" through gestures, movements, facial expressions, and gaze. We communicate whether we are happy or sad, friendly or unfriendly, interested or bored through our facial expressions. By touching or avoiding touch we communicate affection or dislike. By holding out our hand in a certain way we either welcome others or warn them to stay away. We even communicate our gender, age, class, and ethnicity through our physical appearance—our body shape, clothing, hairstyle, and so on. We also construct much of our public identity through body language and gestures, habits we learn based on the cultural norms we see around us. Indeed, body language and gestures are often culturally specific—a fact that we must be aware of when interacting with people from different cultures.

Non-verbal messages can interact with or relate to verbal messages in a variety of ways (see, e.g., Ekman 1965; Knapp et al. 2013). For example, non-verbal behaviours can

1. *complement* what is being said (e.g., raising eyebrows while asking a question),
2. *accent* what is being said (e.g., pounding a table while making an important point),
3. *contradict* what is being said (e.g., nodding while saying "no"),
4. *repeat* what has been said (e.g., nodding after saying "yes"),
5. *substitute* for something that might have been said (e.g., pointing at someone and gesturing to the door instead of asking that person to leave), and
6. *regulate* a discussion (e.g., looking at another person in anticipation to encourage her or him to speak).

In many cases, non-verbal behaviours help people understand verbal messages. Difficulties arise, however, when a non-verbal message conflicts with a verbal message, resulting in a *mixed message*. Mixed messages can lead to breakdowns in communication as well as feelings of distrust, as the confused listener begins to doubt the truthfulness of the speaker's verbal message.

American anthropologist Edward T. Hall (1959) has also found that we communicate non-verbally through our uses of *time* and *space*. In Euro–North American societies, we tend to treat time as a commodity that can be "bought, sold, saved, spent, wasted, lost, made up, and measured," and we use it to structure our daily lives (137). We similarly treat space as a commodity, and we measure and divide it to suit our needs. These approaches to time and space communicate three fundamental aspects of the Western outlook: (1) everything has an economic value, (2) everything can and should be broken down into component parts in order to be better understood, and (3) humans have the right to use everything in the natural world for their own purposes. Recall from Chapter 3 that it was this sort of thinking that drove colonialism, particularly the view that territories were "empty" until they had been mapped and named (see, e.g., Dods 2002). As you might expect, other cultures treat time and space differently, and their approaches reflect different world views. For many North American Native peoples, for example, time is much more flexible, and there is a sense that things will happen when they happen. Similarly, many Native peoples understand space in spiritual rather than material terms, seeing themselves as guardians rather than owners of the land.

Hall (1959) further notes that our use of *personal space* communicates a great deal about our feelings toward other people. When we stand close to a friend or family member, we may communicate good will and affection; when we stand close to a casual acquaintance or a stranger, on the other hand, we may communicate hostility. But *close* is a relative term. What we consider to be *close* in North America may seem to be an uncomfortably great distance to someone from a culture in which standing very close is the norm. As Hall observes,

> In Latin America, the interaction distance is much less than it is in [North America]. Indeed, [Latin American] people cannot talk comfortably with one another unless they are very close to the distance that evokes either sexual or hostile feelings in the North American. The result is that when they move close, we withdraw and back away. As a consequence, they think we are distant and cold, withdrawn and unfriendly. We, on the other hand, are constantly accusing them of breathing down our necks, crowding us, and spraying our faces. (163–4)

Of course, as anthropologists, we must overcome these sorts of ethnocentric impulses, and we must avoid judging other peoples' behaviours based on our own cultural norms.

Pidgin Languages: Negotiated Meaning

When members of communities with radically different language traditions are forced to communicate, they must work together to negotiate new meanings. These sorts of situations may arise when one community is conquered by another (e.g., through war or colonization), or when groups that speak different languages want to initiate trade relationships. While there is no way to predict the outcome of such contact on either speech community, it is likely that new forms of communication—including a new form of language, **pidgin**—may develop.

A pidgin language is different from the languages that gave birth to it. Its shape reflects the context in which it arises (e.g., colonial conquest, commercial exchanges). Vocabulary is usually taken from the language of the dominant group, making it easy for that group to learn the new language. Syntax and phonology may be similar to the subordinate language (or languages), however, making it easier for subordinated speakers to learn the new language. Morphemes that mark the gender or number of nouns or the tenses of verbs tend to disappear (Holm 1988). Accordingly, pidgins are traditionally defined as reduced languages that develop in a single generation. When speakers of a pidgin language pass that language on to a new generation, linguists usually refer to the language of the new generation as a **creole**. The creolization of pidgins involves increased complexity in phonology, morphology, syntax, semantics, and pragmatics, such that the pidgin comes to resemble a conventional language.

Linguist Derek Bickerton (1981) has suggested that the way in which pidgins form could shed light on the universal biological bases of language. He notes that Hawaiian Pidgin English differs in many ways from Hawaiian Creole, which descended from it. Because, in his view, none of these differences can be connected to the languages available to those who invented Hawaiian Creole, Bickerton concludes that they were produced by the innate linguistic "bio-program" of the creole creators. He further claims that these same "bio-program" forms can be found in other creoles.

Other students of pidgins and creoles have tried to test Bickerton's hypothesis. While their work has not confirmed his views, it has revealed that the distinction between pidgins and creoles is more complex than previously thought. For example, linguists have found that creolization can take place at any time after a pidgin forms, creoles can exist without having been preceded by pidgins, pidgins can remain pidgins for long periods and undergo linguistic change without acquiring native speakers, and pidgin and creole varieties of the same language can co-exist in the same society (Jourdan 1991: 192ff.). In fact, it looks as if heteroglossia is as widespread among speakers of pidgins and creoles as it is among speakers of other languages.

Awareness of heteroglossia in pidgin/creole speech communities has led to the redefinition of a pidgin as a *shared secondary language* in a speech community in which speakers also use

pidgin
A fairly simple language with no native speakers that develops in a single generation between members of communities that possess distinct native languages.

creole
A complex language with native speakers that has developed over one or more past generations from two or more distinct languages.

some other main language, and a creole as a *main language* in a speech community, whether or not it has native speakers. According to this view, creolization is likely when pidgin speakers find themselves in new social contexts requiring a new language for *all* the practical activities of everyday life. Without such a context, it is unlikely that creoles will emerge (Jourdan 1991: 196).

Contemporary linguistic anthropologists view pidgin creation as an active form of communicative practice, and they have explored the role of pidgin creators as agents in the process. It appears that as people negotiate meaning across language barriers, they have intuitions about which parts of their speech carry the most meaning and which parts can be safely dropped. Neither party to the negotiation, moreover, may be trying to learn the other's language; rather, "speakers in the course of negotiating communication use whatever linguistic and socio-linguistic resources they have at their disposal until the shared meaning is established and conventionalized" (Jourdan 1991: 200). Such analysis can be extended to other spheres of creative co-communication, such as popular music. The musical styles and lyrics used in the modern music genres of hip hop (Petchauer 2011) and grime (Barron 2013), for example, bring together elements from different cultures and different music genres to create new ways of communicating through music.

Linguistic Inequality and Oppression

Pidgins and creoles are far more complex—and the result of far more active human input—than previously thought, which is why they are so attractive to linguists and linguistic anthropologists as objects of study. Where they co-exist, however, alongside the language of a dominant group (e.g., Hawaiian Pidgin English and English in Hawaii), they are ordinarily viewed by members of society as defective and inferior languages. Such views frequently stem from the situation that led to the formation of most of pidgins: systems of race, gender, and class discrimination that are usually tied to colonial domination.

In such settings, the language of the powerful is often considered to be superior to all others. Colonizers and their descendants generally look down on "other" languages (frequently Indigenous) as lesser forms of communication, and they characterize pidgins and creoles as broken, imperfect versions of their own language. The situation only worsens for dominated populations when formal education is carried out in the "correct" language. Consider the lasting impact of the residential school system in Canada, where administrators firmly and sometimes violently discouraged Native children from using their original languages. In addition, speakers of a pidgin, a creole, or an Indigenous language who do not master the language of the powerful may find themselves effectively barred from participating in the civic life of mainstream society.

To take one language variety as the standard against which all others are measured is linguistic ethnocentrism. It involves making value judgments about other people's speech in a context of dominance and subordination. Thus, it contributes to linguistic inequality.

We can find a powerful example of the effects of linguistic inequality in the history and controversies surrounding African American English (AAE) in the United States. In the 1960s, some psychologists claimed that African American children living in urban areas of the northern United States suffered from linguistic deprivation. They argued that these children started school with a limited vocabulary and no grammar. As a result, they continued, these children could not perform as well as Euro-American children in the classroom. In short, the psychologists claimed that these children's language was unequal to the challenges of communication. Some sociolinguists, including William Labov and his colleagues, found such claims incredible and undertook research of their own. They proved that the form of English spoken in the inner city was not a defective "lesser" language (Labov 1972). Further, they showed how a change in research context permitted inner-city African American children to display a level of linguistic sophistication that the psychologists had never dreamed these children possessed.

When African American children were in the classroom (a Euro-American dominated context) being interrogated by Euro-American adults about topics of no interest to them, they said little. This did not necessarily mean, Labov argued, that they had no language. Rather, their minimal responses were better understood as defensive attempts to keep threatening Euro-American questioners from learning anything about them. For the African American children, the classroom was part of a broader racist culture. The psychologists, due to their ethnocentrism, had been oblivious to the effect this context might have on their research. Reasoning that reliable samples of African American speech had to be collected in contexts where the racist threat was lessened, Labov and his colleagues conducted fieldwork in the children's homes and on the streets of the inner city. They recorded enormous amounts of speech in AAE produced by the same children who had had nothing to say in the classroom. Labov's analysis demonstrated that AAE was a variety of English that had certain rules not found in Standard English. These rules do not make it "defective"; they simply make it distinct.

Linguistic differences exist between most social subgroups in a society that is characterized by heteroglossia. These differences mark a speaker's membership in a particular speech community. Since Labov's time, AAE has gone through stages of invention, borrowing, and evolution—stages common to all "living" languages (Childs and Mallinson 2004). Indeed, many elements from AAE have entered into more mainstream usage, both in North America and in other English-speaking regions of the world.

The situation is quite different for Native peoples in Canada. Today, many Native communities are struggling to retain original languages that have been pushed to extinction or near extinction by the consequences of colonialism (Figure 4.8). In many communities, English continues to be thought of as the language of domination. In contrast, original languages are thought of as tools that can preserve the collective memories of the culture: "Memory needs a place, a context. Its place, if it finds one that lives beyond a single generation, is to be found in the stories that we tell" (Kenny 1999: 421). Further, learning original languages becomes one route to healing the injured individuals and groups who have suffered loss through the colonial process. Thus, many First Nations communities are engaged in programs to retain and/or recall and teach their languages (see the "In Their Own Words" box, below).

language ideology
A system of beliefs about how language features relate to social features and what they reveal about the people who use them.

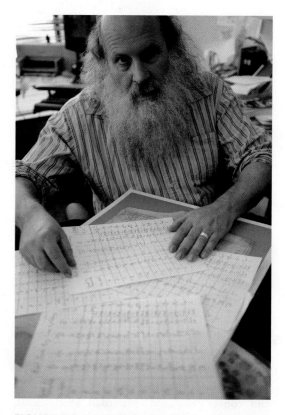

FIGURE 4.8 Scholar John Steckley, a native English speaker, is the world's last-known Huron-language speaker. The extinction or near extinction of languages is one of the many consequences of colonialism. How can anthropologists work with communities to help people retain their languages?

The various perceptions of languages and of their speakers we have discussed in this section lead us to consider the study of **language ideology**: the intersection "between social forms and forms of talk" (Woolard 1998: 3). The study of language ideology reveals speakers' basic understandings of their world, and it highlights how our speech is always embedded in a social world of power differences. It also uncovers struggles between social groups with different interests, as these struggles are often revealed in what people say and how they say it. The way people monitor their speech to bring it into line with a particular language ideology illustrates that language ideologies are "active and effective . . . they transform the material reality they comment on" (11). In settings with a history of colonization, where groups with different power statuses and different languages co-exist in tension, the study of language ideologies has long been significant (16). Linguistic anthropologists are particularly well suited to study

---

IN THEIR OWN WORDS | **Community Consensus and Social Identity in Alphabet Development: The Relationship between Kala and Jabêm**

Canadian linguistic anthropologist Christine Schreyer writes about her efforts to help local peoples strengthen an Indigenous language in the Huon Gulf area of Papua New Guinea.

[T]he majority of indigenous languages from around the world were oral languages, and the development of literacy practices were but one of the impacts of communities' interactions with colonial powers. . . . In many places, literacy [i.e., the ability to read and write] did not occur first in the indigenous language, but rather in the dominant colonial language. In these instances, the indigenous language was simultaneously replaced with the dominant language via assimilatory processes such as residential schools in Canada (Aboriginal Languages Task Force 2005). However, in other cases, such as in New Zealand, the indigenous language was the first language of literacy (King 2000). . . . Jabêm, an indigenous language originally located on the northern coast of the Huon Gulf in Papua New Guinea, became a lingua franca when German missionaries began using it as a language of liturgy and, later, education. However, Kala, an indigenous language from Papua New Guinea related to Jabêm, did not have a writing system until recently.

Throughout Papua New Guinea, there have been many different critiques of the mother-tongue approach to early-years education, including the ideas that indigenous languages are useless; that they are backwards; that they stop people from learning English; that they stop people from learning anything; and that making people learn them is oppressive, hegemonic, and limiting in the wider world (San Roque 2010). Kala speakers do not seem to hold these viewpoints, however, and two of the communities, Alēso and Kui, had active Kala language education programs running in 2010. A third community, Kamiali, was in the process of building a Kala language school while the Kala language teacher was out of the community for language training. In 2006, two other communities, Apoze and Lambu, also had Kala language schools, and both communities hoped to start these again in the near future. Therefore, the goal of our (Dr John Wagner and myself) research in 2010 was to aid in the development and strengthening of the Kala language schools, and developing a standard orthography for all of the communities was a critical part of that goal.

Before we began the process of deciding on the orthography, I outlined key points about the process. I reminded the Kala Language Committee members that they were the ones who were in charge of the decisions for the orthography, and that although I would provide suggestions, the final decision was up to them. I also went over some key concepts in linguistics, such as the difference between letters and phonemes and what minimal pairs are. I also stressed the practice of linguistics to encourage a "one sound—one symbol" ideology for new orthographies (Hinton 2000) and illustrated how the English writing system is very inconsistent in how it represents sounds, particularly vowels. I commented on how the new Kala orthography would be an orthography that would be shared by all dialects of Kala so that resources could be shared among the different villages and how this would allow Kala speakers to learn more about the dialects other than their own.

The rest of the world has not yet heard much about the Kala language . . . but Kala is finally stepping out of the shadow of its better-documented siblings (Jabêm and Bukawa). This is happening both in indigenous speakers' own communities (in terms of writing and speaking) and also within the world of academia.

Source: Schreyer, Christine. In Press. "Community Consensus and Social Identity in Alphabet Development," *Written Language and Literacy*.

---

language ideologies because (1) their linguistic training allows them to describe linguistic features (e.g., phonemes, morphemes, syntax) in detail and (2) their training in cultural analysis allows them to explain how those linguistic features come to be used symbolically by a particular social group.

Language and Gender

Language habits differ not only among ethnic groups but also between culturally identified genders. Indeed, one of the early objections to work on African American English was that it focussed only on the ways African American men use language. Since the 1970s, the language habits of African American women and girls have figured in numerous studies (see, e.g., Morgan 1995: 336ff.; Washington and Craig 1998; Lanehart 2009).

Sociolinguist Deborah Tannen has written several popular books based on her studies of speech patterns of men and women. Tannen focusses on typical male and female styles of discourse, arguing that men and women use language for different reasons: men tend to use language as a competitive weapon in public settings, whereas women tend to use language as a way of building closeness in private settings (e.g., Tannen 1990). Tannen has found examples of how miscommunications can occur when men and women assume that members of the other gender understand language use in the same way they do. For example, when a husband and a wife get home from work at the end of the day, the wife may be eager to talk while the husband is just as eager to remain silent. She may interpret his silence as a sign of distance or coldness and be hurt, while he may interpret her eagerness to talk as pressure to perform and be irritated.

Some researchers have suggested that differences in the ways men and women use the right and left sides of their brains may be the cause of differences in communication styles. However, after analyzing a number of studies on the topic, psychiatrist Iris Sommer and colleagues (2004) found little evidence for this interpretation. Thus it seems that the reasons for the observed differences may be based more in learned behaviours—that is, in cultural factors—than in biology.

Researchers have also looked at the ways women and men communicate online. Because the Internet allows for a certain degree of anonymity, meaning that people can communicate online without clearly stating their gender, some researchers have suspected that gender differences in language use would be eliminated or at least greatly reduced in online forums. Similarly, some have suggested that male-dominated power dynamics would break down online. Yet neither appears to be the case (see, e.g., Herring and Stoerger 2014; Sussman and Tyson 2000). Indeed, men and women often choose different words and use different language patterns when communicating online. In addition, men tend to write longer entries, while women tend to post more frequently (Sussman and Tyson 2000). Such findings suggest that gendered differences in language use are rooted very deeply in our communication habits.

The Flexibility of Language

As you have seen throughout this chapter, language is a very flexible and versatile tool. It allows us to describe and make sense of our world in various ways. To at least some degree, it even shapes our understanding of reality. After all, it is language that connects our thoughts to the world beyond our mind. Therefore, it is difficult—if not impossible—for us to think of something as "real" if we cannot describe it with words.

Language is also a living system, capable of shifting and evolving as our experiences and observations change. Every time biologists discover a new species, for example, they must create a new word to describe it—a taxonomic term. Similarly, every time researchers develop a new technology, they must name it—sometimes by creating a new word, such as *telephone*. Often, words are combined or repurposed to take on new meanings. Today, when we hear words such as *tablet*, *smartphone*, or *laptop*, we immediately think of the objects these words name. However, these same words would have meant something very different to people living fifty years ago. In the case of *smartphone*, the term would likely have seemed nonsensical—how can a *phone* be *smart*? Other terms are added to describe new concepts. A relatively recent example is the word *wackadoodle*, meaning "an eccentric or fanatical person," which was added to the *Oxford English Dictionary* in 2014.

Language's capability for shifting and evolving highlights its essential quality of ambiguity. We saw examples of this quality when we considered *structural ambiguity* and *metaphor*. Of course, such ambiguities are not experienced only by people in Western societies. Anthropologist Edward Evans-Pritchard (1963) describes the use of metaphor among the Azande of central Africa (see EthnoProfile 10.1). The Azande people are well aware of the ambiguity inherent in language, and they exploit it by using metaphor (what they call *sanza*) to disguise speech that might be received badly if uttered directly. For example,

> A man says, in the presence of his wife, to his friend, "Friend, those swallows, how they flit about in there." He is speaking about the flightiness of his wife and in case she should understand the allusion, he covers himself by looking up at the swallows as he makes his seemingly innocent remark (1963: 211).

Evans-Pritchard later observes that *sanza* adds greatly to the difficulties of anthropological inquiry. Despite learning to speak the local language, anthropologists may be unaware of the nuances embedded in that language. Even if they suspect that a word or phrase has more than one meaning, it is difficult for them to be sure. Indeed, even locals can sometimes be unaware or unsure of what a speaker means (228).

However much we learn about language, we will never be able to exhaust its meanings or circumscribe its rules once and for all. Human language is an open system, and as long as human history continues, new forms will be created and old forms will continue to be put to new uses.

Language and Change

Change can be both a negative and a positive process with language—we gain some and we lose some. Yet the losses of entire languages are hard to take, even if we never were a speaker of those languages. Linguist Anthony Woodbury (2012), writing on behalf of the Linguistic Society of America, estimates that about 5,000 to 6,000 languages are spoken in the world today. But he predicts that several thousands of these languages will be lost over the next century. As he notes,

> the pressure on languages can be economic, social, cultural, religious, political, military, or any combination of these. The peoples directly affected are minorities almost by definition, yet they are the bearers of most of the linguistic diversity that has developed over the course of human history.

So much of who we were, who we are, and how we pronounce our place in the cosmos and in our cultures is the creation of language. Voice marks our identity in relation to place and time. For those languages on the brink of silence, anthropologists and native speakers struggle with maintenance and revitalization in a world where the languages of the powerful dominate. Linguist Christine Sims notes that "revitalization at its heart involves re-establishing traditional functions of language use in the context of everyday

speaker interactions" (2005: 104). However, as linguistic anthropologist Michael Walsh warns us, "it remains unclear why some attempts at language revitalization succeed, whereas others fail. What is clear is that the process is profoundly political" (2005: 293; 313).

Survival and modernity may go hand in hand. A language may not survive completely, but it may survive in a form that contains the essentials of identity. An example of this sort of survival can be seen in the history of the English language. As anyone who has ever tried to read a text written in Old or Middle English knows, the English language has changed considerably over time. Indeed, these earlier forms of the language are almost entirely unintelligible to modern English speakers. Over time, obsolete words such as *brabble* (meaning "to quarrel noisily") were dropped, while new words were added to meet changing needs. Many of the greatest changes occurred around the time of the Norman invasion in the eleventh century. Following their conquest by Norman French–speaking invaders, the people of England gradually adapted their indigenous language to reflect their changed social and cultural circumstances. In particular, they incorporated aspects of Norman French into the language. Essentially, they adjusted their language to ensure it would survive in the new modernity of the day.

Similar processes have occurred—and continue to occur—throughout the world. The many regional variations of English that exist around the word are evidence of such changes. Linguist Jamie Shinhee Lee (2006) has identified an ongoing example of language mixing in South Korea. Drawing on observations from Korean television commercials, Lee argues that "mixing English with Korean is a linguistic mechanism for the construction of modernity in contemporary South Korea" (59; 90–1). Just as mixing English with Norman French was a sign of modernity for eleventh-century inhabitants of England, mixing Korean with English appears to be a sign of modernity for contemporary South Koreans. These examples one again highlight the openness and flexibility of language and the endless adaptability of human culture.

A CRITICAL LOOK | The Language of Hurt

Sticks and stones may break my bones, but words will never harm me. You've likely heard this popular children's rhyme, but have you ever stopped to question it? *Can* words cause harm? While they may not be able to break your bones, they can certainly be powerful. As one linguistic anthropologist has stated: "One of the things that drew me to linguistic anthropology and keeps me fascinated is that my chosen field often explores the interface between language and power, where power is understood as the ability to influence the behaviour and attitudes of others without applying actual physical force" (Judy 2010). As this comment suggests, words carry with them great force; at times, they carry enough force to change a world.

Too often, however, we use words to change the world for the worse. Consider harsh insults. Vicious labels. False accusations. Racial slurs. Cruel words that send messages of hatred and intolerance. Such words can cause intense, often lasting emotional harm. Indeed, researchers at the University of California, Los Angeles (UCLA) have shown that emotionally charged "taboo" words—words that convey forbidden meaning—tend to stick in people's minds longer than more neutral words (MacKay et al. 2004). Yet as linguist and philosopher Adam M. Croom points out, such terms may also have the power to reaffirm: "slurs are frequently picked up and appropriated by the very in-group members that the slur was originally intended to target, . . . for instance, as a means for like speakers to strengthen in-group solidarity" (2013: 177).

An example of the sort of positive appropriation Croom describes is the LGBTQ community's reclamation of the word *queer*. In the 1950s, and for several decades thereafter, the word *queer* was commonly used as an insult against people who broke—or were thought to be breaking—the sexual and/or gender conventions of the time (Wagner 2012). In the early 1990s, however, beginning with the reclamation efforts of the American activist organization Queer Nation, the term began to take on more positive connotations. Today, the negative power of the word *queer* has dissipated, and its use as an insult "seems archaic to most" (Wagner 2012).

Feminist Mary Daly (1978; 1984; 2001) was an early advocate of re-examining and reclaiming derogatory terms in order to reclaim aspects of ourselves. She used the example of *spinster*. Originally used to refer to a woman who spins thread—an essential task necessary for the production of cloth—the term *spinster* has become a derogatory term for an unmarried woman of a certain age. Thus, a word that once referred to a highly valued position of creation has been twisted to convey a sexist, ageist view of older single women. By reclaiming the term *spinster* and defining it in a more positive light, women once shamed by the term can reclaim a more positive identity as esteemed creators.

Unfortunately, the meaning of the term *spinster* has not changed much since Daly first wrote about the issue, and people continue to use words with far worse meanings to insult others. In part, undoubtedly, the problem is ignorance. Some people use hateful words because they don't fully understand the words' meanings, or because they don't understand that language can cause harm. But the greater problem is fear and intolerance of people who are seen as "different." Indeed, this is the same fear that drives the ethnocentric impulses to wage war against "others" based on race, religion, nationality, or other cultural features. It would seem, then, that society at large could benefit from taking a more holistic approach—an anthropological approach—to learning about other peoples' ways of life.

—Roberta Robin Dods

KEY TERMS

CHAPTER SUMMARY

1. Language is a uniquely human faculty that that people use to encode their experiences, to structure their understanding of the world and of themselves, and to engage with one another. It is a fundamental part of culture. In addition to communicating verbally, we also communicate non-verbally, through formal sign languages as well through our body language, facial expressions, and behaviours.

2. In anthropological investigations of language, the most significant design features of language are openness, displacement, prevarication, arbitrariness, duality of patterning, and semanticity. Also important is Edward Sapir and Benjamin Whorf's hypothesis, known as the *linguistic relativity principle*, that language has the power to shape the way people see the world.

3. Formal linguistic analysis is usually divided into five specialties: phonology, the study of the sounds of a language; morphology, the study of the smallest units of meaning in a language; syntax, the study of sentence structure; semantics, the study of meaning; and pragmatics, the study of language in the context of its use. Ethnopragmatics pays attention both to the immediate context of speech and to the broader cultural contexts that are rooted in history and shaped by everyday social interactions. Different social groups generate different communicative practices, contributing to heteroglossia.

4. Pidgin languages display the radical negotiation of new meaning. These languages are actively constructed, and they often develop into complex languages known as *creoles*. Against the backdrop of colonialism, members of more powerful groups tend to look down on the languages of less powerful groups, resulting in linguistic inequality and oppression.

CRITICAL THINKING QUESTIONS

1. What is language? What is communication? What is conversation? How do these concepts relate to and differ from one another?

2. What are the design features of language? How do these features separate human language from communication systems used by other animals?

3. Why do speakers of a particular language have different "accents"? What factors—historical and current—might contribute to the variety of accents across Canada today?

4. How many friends do you interact with in person? How many do you interact with online? Does the way you use language in face-to-face conversations differ from how you use it online? Do your feelings of connection with other people change depending on the medium of communication?

5. In what ways does language change over time? How has language evolved in your lifetime?

SUGGESTED READINGS

Akmajian, A., et al. 2010. *Linguistics: An Introduction to Language and Communication*, 6th edn (Cambridge, MA: MIT Press). A fine introduction to the study of language as a formal system.

Lakoff, George, and Mark Johnson. 2003 [1980]. *Metaphors We Live By*, rev. edn (Chicago: University of Chicago Press). An important, clear, and very accessible book that presents a radical and persuasive view of metaphor. The revised edition contains a new afterword that places the text in a more contemporary context.

Salzmann, Zdenek, James Stanlaw, and Nobuko Adachi. 2014. *Language, Culture, and Society: An Introduction to Linguistic Anthropology*, 6th edn (Boulder, CO: Westview Press). An up-to-date and thorough text on linguistic anthropology.

Turkle, Sherry. 21 April 2012. "The Flight from Conversation," *New York Times*, available at www.nytimes.com. An insightful opinion piece on how modern communications technologies have impacted the ways in which we connect and converse with other people.

RELATED WEBSITES

Franglais www.yrad.com/franglais

Newfoundland Word Game www.nfld.com/nfld/other/words/word.html

New Words in English www.learn-english-today.com/new-words/new-words-in-english.html

Semiotics for Beginners www.aber.ac.uk/media/Documents/S4B/sem07.html

Tok Pisin–English Dictionary www.tok-pisin.com

5

Culture, the Individual, and Identity

CHAPTER OUTLINE

Perception

Cognition

Emotion

Motivation

Personality/Self/Subjectivity

Sex, Sexuality, and Gender Roles: The
Creation of Subject Positions

Structural Violence and Social
Trauma

Individual Psychology and Context

LEARNING OBJECTIVES

By the end of Chapter 5, you will be able to

- understand how perception organizes information and frames the "self,"
- appreciate cognition as a complex mental process that helps us make sense of our world,

- consider that emotion and motivation are influenced by cultural contexts,
- recognize the roles that socialization and enculturation play in shaping cognitive development,

- understand how sex and gender roles influence our sense of identity, and
- identify how violence and trauma affect the individual.

Muxe partygoers enjoy the festivities at a cultural celebration in Mexico. Commonly thought of as members of a "third gender," muxe individuals a
widely respected within Zapotec cultures of southern Mexico. Gender identity is one of many factors—including ethnicity, occupation, class, and
socioeconomic status—that shape the subject positions through which we view and engage with the world around us.

We do not all learn the same things, even if we live in the same society. Our learning is socially and culturally shaped by differences in status and experience. Anthropologists are interested in the patterns and variations in patterns of how individuals engage in cultural learning—how individuals learn from one another within a culture. Historically, anthropology addressed this phenomenon by seeking answers for a series of persistent questions: "What characteristics of our species are found in all times and places? What features are limited to specific groups of humans? How can we best take account of individual uniqueness?" (Bock 1994: ix).

Anthropologists who want to understand how individuals perceive and make sense of their world have incorporated psychological theories into their studies. Some of the first of the twentieth-century anthropologists to take an interest in psychological matters, such as Margaret Mead and Ruth Benedict, were influenced by the psychology of Sigmund Freud. These anthropologists attempted to test Freudian ideas about personality development, which were based on social relations in late nineteenth-century Viennese society, in non-Western settings. These early studies initiated a pattern of analysis that remained central to much psychological anthropology: that of critically examining Western researchers' claims about human nature. This critical role is especially important in situations where researchers make extreme claims about all members of the human species. When faced with such claims, anthropologists must ask, "Is this claim universal in all human groups, or is it relevant only to certain people in certain times and places?

In Western societies, claims about universal human psychology compete with assertions of individual uniqueness. This competition is clear in ongoing "nature versus nurture" debates, in which one side claims that biology (nature) is responsible for some aspect of human behaviour, while the other side claims that culture (nurture) is responsible. Such extreme claims and counterclaims never seem to be resolved, perhaps because they are too crude to illuminate much lasting interest. Further, relying on such broad "either/or" approaches can cause us to miss the variation and complexity we actually see in our fieldwork experiences.

As we discussed in Chapter 1, most anthropologists view human beings as biocultural organisms. Thus, psychological anthropologists have typically concentrated on areas where it is possible to identify relationships between biological (internal) and cultural (external) influences. One of the more promising approaches has come from recent work in developmental biology: developmental systems theory (DST), which focusses on genetic as well as environmental contributions to an organism's development (Oyama et al. 2001). This approach recognizes that socially constructed environments—along with their social, economic, and political resources—get passed on to subsequent generations as faithfully as genes. This social transmission influences how individuals develop. Thus DST explains how biological *and* cultural processes are intertwined, and how they can shape the directions of our lives in decisive ways.

In this chapter, we will consider the basic areas of human experience: perception, cognition, emotion, and motivation. As we will discover, what results from experience is a personal position, called a *subject position*, from which one views the world. "Once having taken up a particular position as one's own, a person inevitably sees the world from the vantage point of that position and in terms of [its] particular images, metaphors, storylines, and concepts" (Davies and Harré 1990: 46). In turn, these images, metaphors, storylines, and concepts become a conceptual repertoire for future use. As with language, this repertoire is an *open* system. How we think or feel at any given time is shaped by the cultural factors we have encountered. In addition, our ways of thinking and feeling develop in the context of culturally shaped activities that draw our attention to some parts of the world while leading us to ignore others. What we think or feel about something depends greatly on what we have learned to pay attention to in the past and the associated values (Figure 5.1). As a result, different groups in a society—with different histories and experiences—are likely to develop different subject positions.

As we discuss human psychological processes, you may find it useful to keep in mind the design features of language (see pp. 78–80). Besides openness (mentioned above), the features of displacement and prevarication can inform your understanding of these processes. Consider that when we learn from culturally shaped experience,

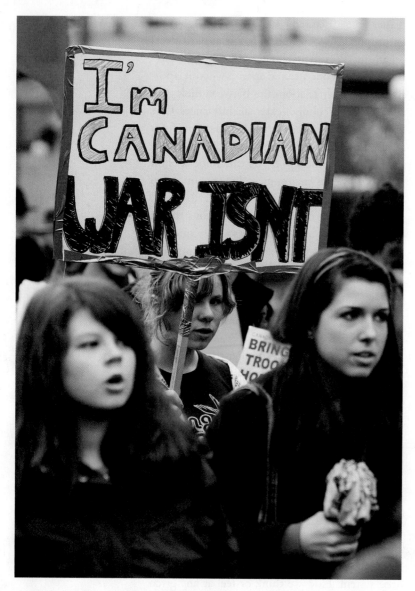

FIGURE 5.1 Today, many Canadians are passionate about their anti-war stance.

perception

The "processes by which people organize and experience information that is primarily of sensory origin."

cultural synaesthesia

A culturally shared response to a sense other than the one being stimulated (e.g., hearing a sound and seeing it as a colour).

schemas

Patterned, repetitive experiences that are shared and easily understood by members of a particular culture.

a butcher knife means when it is (1) lying on a cutting board or (2) being wielded by an intruder.

Perception

Perception can be defined as the "processes by which people organize and experience information that is primarily of sensory origin" (Cole and Scribner 1974: 61). Traditionally, people have tried to deal with perceptions in two principal ways: through intellect (rationality, logic) and through emotion (passion, intuition). Although some people tend to overvalue one approach at the expense of the other, experience shows that both our rational thoughts and our emotions help us to make sense of our perceptions.

Anthropologists are also aware of how culture affects **perception**. Indeed, it influences not only *what* we perceive, but also how we *respond* (intellectually and emotionally) to those perceptions. Australian anthropologist Diana Young's (2005) study of **cultural synaesthesia** with Aboriginal people of the Western Desert of Australia (see EthnoProfile 5.1) provides us with an excellent example of the link between perception and culture. Young found that the odour of wet earth after a rainfall elicits a sense of "greenness" in these people. Smell and colour become one as they perceive in the odour of wet soil the new green growth that is to come (61). Russian psychological anthropologist Anton Sidoroff-Dorso (2014) has also examined cultural synaesthesia. He finds in this phenomenon evidence that (1) we perceive what our culture tells us to perceive, and (2) we frame our sensing through cultural constructs. Further, he sees synaesthesia as reflecting "both biology and culture," since the "brain is shaped by exposure and experience," and "human experience comes from . . . shared practices, beliefs, [and] ecology [i.e., physical surroundings]."

Within a given culture, certain chunks of perceptual experience appear to hang together as wholes, exhibiting the same properties in the same configuration whenever they recur. These patterned collections of perceptions are called **schemas**. As human children grow up, they gradually become aware of the schemas that their culture (or subculture) recognizes. Such schemas are often embedded in practical activities and labelled linguistically, and they may serve as a focus for discourse. People living in North America, for example, cannot avoid a

we can use pre-existing categories to help us interpret new experiences. This is a version of *displacement*. Moreover, all our senses can play tricks on us, and we can mistakenly perceive something that "does not exist." Thus, *prevarication* is a built-in feature of human psychological processes.

Human psychological processes are heavily influenced by symbols, and the meaning of what we see, touch, smell, taste, or hear depends on context. As with language, two contexts are normally invoked: the *immediate* context of the perception itself and the broader *displaced* context stored in memory and shaped by culture. The "same" object or symbol can mean different things in different contexts. Consider what seeing

EthnoProfile 5.1 | Pitjantjatjara (Anangu)

Region Central Australia, which includes the Western Desert area

Nation Australia; area around Alice Springs extending to the west

Language Pitjantjatjara

Population 4,000 (2014 estimate)

Environment Arid desert of interior Australia—the outback

Livelihood Farming, hunting, gathering; originally nomadic but now more settled in small communities

Political organization Since 1981, under the management of a central political authority

For more information Young, Diana. 2005. "The Smell of Greenness: Cultural Synaesthesia in the Western Desert (Australia)," *Etnofoor* 18, 1: 61–77.

schema called *Christmas*, a chunk of experience that recurs yearly. The Christmas schema can include features such as snowy weather, colourful decorations, and Christmas cards as well as activities such as baking cookies, singing carols, going to church, putting up a Christmas tree, and exchanging gifts. In the experience of a child, all these elements may appear to be equally relevant parts of a seamless whole. At the same time, not everyone will interpret a schema in the same way. For example, in North America, devout Christians may struggle to accept the secularization of what was originally a religious holiday, while non-Christians might question why they must be subjected to the Christmas schema every year (Figure 5.2).

People take for granted most of the schemas that their culture recognizes, using them as simplified interpretive frameworks for judging new experiences as typical or not (D'Andrade 1992: 48). Schemas thus become **prototypes**. Prototypes can help us navigate routine cultural practices. However, when we organize sensory information on the basis of prototypes, the categories we use have fuzzy (open) boundaries because our experiences do not always neatly fit our prototypes. Does a library that contains fewer books than DVDs, videotapes, and electronic databases fit with our prototypical idea of a library? In a case such as this, suggests linguist R.A. Hudson (1980), a person must simply recognize the openness of language and apply linguistic labels creatively. Similarly, when confronted with novel perceptions—that is, experiences for which no ready-made cultural

interpretation is available—human beings must extrapolate creatively to make sense of what is going on around them.

Inevitably, observers situated in different social and/or cultural positions will draw on different background knowledge and different prototypes. As a result, they may interpret the same sensory information in different ways. Classic research on variations in perception has related people's interpretations of their experiences to their understandings of *context*. For example, American psychologists Michael Cole and Sylvia Scribner (1974) recount a study in which researchers tested non-literate South African miners using two-dimensional line drawings of three-dimensional objects (Figure 5.3). The test results indicated that the miners consistently interpreted

prototypes
Examples of a typical instance, element, relation, or experience within a culture.

FIGURE 5.2 In North America, the Christmas schema involves public events, such as the annual rush to complete holiday shopping. What might people who do not observe Christmas think when they encounter others engaging in Christmas-related activities in public spaces?

FIGURE 5.3 Line drawings used to elicit verbal responses in the depth-perception test in Africa.

the drawings in two dimensions. For example, when asked at which animal the man was pointing his spear on Card 1, subjects would usually respond "the elephant." The elephant is, in fact, directly in line with and closest to the spear point in the drawing. However, the researchers thought that the subjects should interpret the elephant as standing on top of the distant hill. Did the subjects' responses mean that they could not perceive in three dimensions?

To address this question, researchers devised the following test. First, they presented different African subjects with the same drawings and asked them to describe what they saw. Again the subjects responded with two-dimensional verbal reports. Next, the researchers presented the same subjects with the line drawings in Figure 5.4. This time, they asked the subjects to construct models based on the drawings. The subjects had no difficulty producing three-dimensional models.

In these tests, the "correct" solution depended on the subject's mastery of a Western convention for interpreting two-dimensional images. For the drawings in Figure 5.3, the Western convention includes

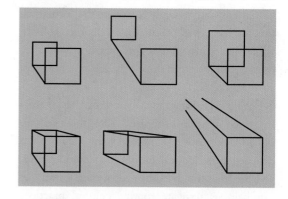

FIGURE 5.4 Line drawings used for the construction of models in the depth-perception test in Africa.

assumptions about perspective that relate the size of objects to their distance from the observer. Without such a convention in mind, it is not obvious that the size of an object has any connection with distance. Thus, far from providing insights about Africans' perceptual abilities, the tests highlight the assumptions behind Western perceptual conventions. As Cole and Scribner (1974) point out, the images make sense to us only once we accept certain rules for interpreting them. And we need to remember that *perspective* in Western drawing is a relatively recent "invention" dating to the fifteenth-century Italian Renaissance—through our capacity for openness, our conventions changed.

Illusion

If you examine Figure 5.5, you will see that marks on a piece of paper can be ambiguous. The signals we receive from the outside world—be they shapes, smells, tastes, sounds, or words—tend to be open to more than one interpretation. The contrast between literal and metaphorical language is not unlike the contrast between reality and illusion as it relates to perception. In both cases, knowledge of context permits us to distinguish between the literal and the metaphorical, the real and the illusory.

Richard Gregory (1983), a cognitive psychologist, argued that visual illusions are produced when the wrong cognitive processes are selected and applied to a particular set of visual signals. Perceptions are symbolic representations of reality, not direct samples of reality. Perceivers must often work very hard to make sense of the visual signals they receive. When they are wrong, they are subject to illusion.

Consider the visual illusion Gregory called *distortion*, in which what you see appears larger or smaller, longer or shorter, and so on, than it really is. Look at the Ponzo illusion in Figure 5.6. Typically, the upper parallel line appears to be longer than the lower one when in fact they are equal. The illusion occurs because we interpret the two-dimensional drawing as if it were in three dimensions. The shapes

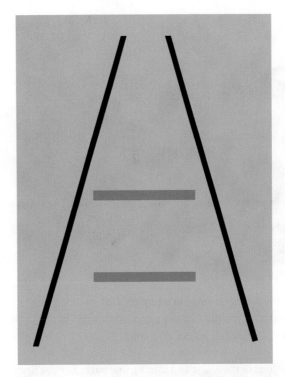

FIGURE 5.6 An example of distortion: the Ponzo illusion.

trick us because they are very similar to what we perceive when we stand on a railroad track and look toward its vanishing point on the horizon. The Africans discussed by Cole and Scribner (1974) did not attempt to interpret the Ponzo-like lines on Card 2 of Figure 5.3 as representations of three-dimensional reality. On the contrary, they seemed to work very hard to keep the relationships between objects on the card in two dimensions, even if this meant that the sizes of the objects themselves appeared distorted. When we compare the Western interpretation of the Ponzo illusion with the African interpretation of the pictures in Figure 5.3, we discover something important: the ways in which people interpret ambiguous drawings depend on pre-existing experiences and cultural conventions.

Anthropologist Colin Turnbull worked among the Mbuti of the northeastern Democratic Republic of the Congo for many years around the middle of the twentieth century (see Figure 5.7; see also EthnoProfile 5.2). He discovered that these people, who lived all their lives in a dense forest, had no experience of distance greater than a few feet and were therefore not accustomed to taking distance into consideration when estimating the size of an object. Turnbull took one of his informants, Kenge, on a trip that brought them

FIGURE 5.5 Ambiguous marks.

FIGURE 5.7 A Mbuti pygmy mother paints her daughter's face with a black juice from the gardenia fruit. Can you think of any customs your parents or other older members of your family passed down to you?

visuality
The ways that individuals from different societies learn to interpret what they see and to construct mental pictures using the visual practices that their own cultural system favours.

out of the forest and into a game park. For the first time in his life, Kenge faced vast, rolling grasslands. Kenge's response to this experience was dramatic: "When Kenge topped the rise, he stopped dead. Every smallest sign of mirth suddenly left his face. He opened his mouth but could say nothing. He moved his head and eyes slowly and unbelievingly" (Turnbull 1961: 251). When Kenge finally saw the far-off animals grazing on the plain, he asked Turnbull what insects they were. When told that they were buffalo, Kenge laughed and accused Turnbull of lying. Then he strained to see better and inquired what kind of buffalo could be so small. Later, when Turnbull pointed out a fishing boat on the lake, Kenge scoffed at him and insisted it was a piece of floating wood (252).

Visuality: Learning to Look

Anthropologist Susan Vogel has studied the sculpture of the Baule people of Ivory Coast (see EthnoProfile 3.1) since the early 1970s, and her research has taught her that looking and seeing are culturally learned modes of sensory perception (1997: 108–11). She terms this interpretive process **visuality**. Vogel notes that, for the Baule, objects are powerful and affect the people who see them. Spiritually significant objects, which include much of what Westerners would call *sculpture*, are thus potentially dangerous. "Even an inadvertent glimpse of a forbidden object can make a person sick, can expose them to huge fines or sacrifices, or can even be fatal" (110).

For the Baule, looking is the most important of all perceptual activities: seeing something may be more significant and more dangerous than touching, eating, or drinking something. There is an explicit etiquette governing how one ought to look at things, and staring is highly inappropriate. It is disrespectful for younger people to look directly at their elders. In many cases, the rules for looking actually limit the "visibility" of sculpture. For example, while Western worshippers might feel free to gaze intently at the adorned altar of a medieval Christian cathedral, the Baule would consider analogous behaviour to be highly improper:

If someone stopped and looked for a whole minute at the altar erected in plain view in [a certain] courtyard, they would be called before the chief to explain. The fact that the altar stands in a public place, where a hundred people pass daily, does not mean it can be stared at. In fact the

EthnoProfile 5.2 | Mbuti (Bambuti)

Region Central Africa

Nation Ituri Forest (>70,000 km²) in the northeastern Democratic Republic of the Congo

Language Mbuti are actually three distinct cultures differentiated by the dialects they speak: Efe, Kango, and Asoa

Population 30,000–50,000 (2010 estimate)

Environment Dense tropical rainforest with a two-month dry season

Livelihood Hunting and gathering

Political organization Traditionally, communal bands of 7 to 30 families (average 17 families with 15 to 60 members); today, part of a modern nation-state

For more information Turnbull, Colin. 1961. *The Forest People* (New York: Simon and Schuster); 1983. *The Mbuti Pygmies: Change and Adaptation* (New York: CBS College Publishing).

only motives for looking hard at such an object would be malevolent: a desire to kill someone in the courtyard, or to nullify the altar's powers. (111)

The language Baule speakers use to talk about visuality is also highly revealing. Speakers shape vocabulary to reflect their cultural preoccupations. Thus the Baule language contains four words for looking and seeing. These terms distinguish among objects that anyone can look at, objects that must never be deliberately looked at, and degrees in between:

1. The most common verb translated as "to look" is *nian*, which can also mean "to watch." It connotes intentional watching and is used for watching mask dances intended for entertainment and for watching television.
2. The noun *nyin* means "a stare" or "a good hard look." The phrase *nyin kpa*, "a real stare," is used to describe looking at a useful decorated object with no sacred meaning.
3. The noun *kanngle* means "evil looks from the corner of the eye."
4. *Nian klekle* means "to look secretly," to "cast a rapid glance." (91)

The most awesome objects and events—the men's sacred masks, divination dances, and funerals—are not spoken of with any of these words. "One never says one has seen or looked at these potent things; one merely says *N'wo se bo*, 'I went to the funeral,' or *N'su ko awebo*, 'I went to the divination dance'" (92).

For the Baule, life is lived knowing that sculptures—powerful objects—are present but cannot be examined, cannot be looked at closely. However, even incompletely seen, these objects make an extraordinary impression and impact the Baule's particular world view.

Cognition

The study of illusion demonstrates that there can be a gulf between what we see and what we know, what we perceive and what we conceive. In everyday life, these differences seem to be manageable: there is coherence between perceptions and conceptions. Moreover, there is no sharp boundary between what we perceive and what we conceive.

Not only can new perceptions lead us to modify our conceptions (i.e., we learn), but new conceptions can also lead us to perceive aspects of the world around us that we didn't pay attention to before. We are active meaning-makers, internally negotiating our experiences. As a result, **cognition** is perhaps best understood as "a nexus of relations between the mind at work and the world in which it works" (Lave 1988: 1).

Anthropologists began to study cognition in the 1960s, when there was a growing interest in the ways different people classified cultural knowledge. These anthropologists used folk **taxonomies** and generic terms to lump things into categories. Over the past decades, anthropologists have expanded their investigations to incorporate the links between language and culture, focussing on the many ways of "labelling" the social and cultural worlds of their informants. Today, cognitive anthropologists look closely at the mental processes people use to label and make sense of their experiences.

Cognitive Capacities and Intelligence

What makes it possible for us to receive signals from the outside world (or from within our own bodies) and then interpret those signals in a way that makes appropriate action possible? One traditional answer has been that every person either possesses at birth or develops over time certain basic *cognitive capacities*. At one time, these capacities were thought of as substances or properties, and the goal of psychological testing was to measure how much of each cognitive capacity an individual had. Consequently, intelligence has traditionally been "measured" using "*intelligence tests*," and the results of these tests led to the assignment of a number called the "*intelligence quotient*," or IQ. Thus, in the past, some researchers equated differences in *performance on intelligence tests* with differences in *intelligence*. Today, psychologists and others take a more nuanced approach.

Studies show that intelligence tests are not very useful for studying peoples whose cultural backgrounds differ from those of the researchers. Psychologists Michael Cole and Sylvia Scribner repeatedly encountered situations in which the same psychological test produced results that differed between Western and non-Western subjects (see, e.g., Cole 1994). Although they found that the scores of their non-Western subjects were generally lower, Cole and Scribner did not

cognition
(1) The mental process by which human beings gain knowledge, and (2) the "nexus of relations between the mind at work and the world in which it works."

taxonomies
Hierarchical systems that sort groups of things that share at least one quality (e.g., dogs) into subgroups that share a greater number of qualities (e.g., poodles, collies, boxers).

elementary cognitive processes
Mental tasks common to all humans without cognitive impairment.

functional cognitive systems
Culturally linked sets of cognitive processes that guide perception, conception, reason, and emotion.

global style
A field-dependent way of viewing the world that first sees it as a bundle of relationships and only later sees the smaller pieces involved in these relationships.

articulated style
A field-independent way of viewing the world that breaks it up into small pieces, which can then be organized into larger chunks.

conclude that these subjects were less intelligent. Indeed, they noted that outside the laboratory setting, in the routine contexts of everyday life, these individuals' intelligence was obvious.

So why do bright people perform poorly on psychological tests? In the work of the Russian psychologist Lev Vygotsky, Cole and Scribner (1974) found an approach that points toward an answer. Vygotsky distinguishes between **elementary cognitive processes** and **functional cognitive systems**. Elementary cognitive processes include the ability to make abstractions, to categorize, to reason inferentially, and so forth. All humans without cognitive impairment are equipped with these abilities. Different cultures, however, organize these elementary processes into different functional cognitive systems. These systems govern how people respond to different tasks, which means that individuals from different cultures may have different routine responses for tackling the same task. As a result, it seems unlikely that any psychological test could adequately assess individuals from different cultural backgrounds.

More recently, Canadian psychological researchers Cristopher Mushquash and Dana Bova (2007) have taken a closer look at the problems with using intelligence tests in cross-cultural settings. As they note, "culture influences many aspects of an individual's life; thus measurement of various psychological constructs is also likely to be influenced by cultural characteristics" (54). More specifically, they point out that issues arise because every facet of this sort of testing is impacted by culture:

- the content of the test,
- the materials used to administer the test,
- the wording of the test,
- the way the directions and conditions are organized,
- the way the test is scored,
- the behaviour of the test administrator, and
- the behaviour of the participants (56).

Mushquash and Bova conclude that we need to be very "cautious when interpreting standardized test scores of intelligence from culturally diverse clients" (62).

Cognitive Style

Cultures provide people with a range of **cognitive styles** that are appropriate for different cognitive

tasks in different contexts. Psychological anthropologists have attempted to compare cognitive styles cross-culturally. Some have argued that the styles of individuals and of groups can be located on a continuum between a **global style** and an **articulated style**. People who use a global style tend to view the world holistically; they first see a bundle of relationships and only later see the bits and pieces that are related. They are said to be *field dependent* because they consider everything in relation to its context. In contrast, people who use an articulated style tend to break up the world into smaller and smaller pieces, which they can then organize into larger chunks. They also tend to see a sharp boundary between their own bodies and the outside world. People using an articulated style are said to be *field independent* because they are able to consider whatever they happen to be paying attention to apart from its context (Cole and Scribner 1974: 82).

Originally, most people in Western societies were thought to be field independent, whereas most people in most non-Western cultures were thought to be field dependent. However, more detailed research shows that these generalizations are misleading. For instance, the preferred cognitive style of an individual often varies from task to task and from context to context. People who use articulated styles for some tasks also use global styles for other tasks. In fact, they may bring a range of different styles to bear on a single task—that is, they may look at a task or a problem in more than one way.

Research by social anthropologist Jean Lave and her colleagues (1988) demonstrated that North Americans are not field independent in all contexts, even when the task involves mathematics, which would seem to be the most field independent of all cognitive activities. The researchers wanted to test the widespread assumption that cognitive style does not vary across contexts. In particular, they wanted to find out whether ordinary people use the same mathematical skills in the supermarket that they use in the classroom. As part of the research, subjects were given a pencil-and-paper math test to determine how well they could solve mathematical problems in a school-like context. Then, the same subjects were observed while using mathematics to make buying decisions at a grocery store. Finally, the subjects were presented with paired grocery items and asked to calculate the best buy.

cognitive style
Recurring patterns of cognitive activity that characterize an individual's perceptual and intellectual activities.

Surprisingly, the subjects averaged only 59 per cent correct in the school-like context but achieved averages of 98 per cent correct in the supermarket experiment and 93 per cent correct in the best-buy experiment. The high scores were achieved with very little reliance on mathematics taught in school—shoppers were better able to make wise economic decisions using informal calculation strategies. The three most common informal strategies were:

- *inspection* (recognizing that an item was lower in price and/or larger in volume),
- *best-buy calculations* (comparing quantities and prices, and then choosing the better value), and
- *a difference strategy* (deciding whether a marginal difference in quantity was worth the marginal difference in price) (Lave 1988: 107ff.).

To conclude from these results that there was something primitive or illogical about the informal strategies—and, by extension, about the people who used them—would contradict the evidence showing that the shoppers' informal strategies were exceptionally accurate (see Lave 1988: 79ff., 107ff.). In addition, shoppers did occasionally use formal mathematics as an alternative to the other informal strategies, but they did so only when the numbers for quantity and price were easy to transform into unit–price ratios. This did not happen very often, however, because units and prices in supermarkets are often given in prime numbers (i.e., numbers that can be divided only by 1 and themselves), making rapid mental calculation tedious and complicated. Rather than waste time dividing $5.27 by 13 ounces to obtain the price per ounce, the shoppers preferred to rely on other calculation strategies (Figure 5.8).

These observations point to a major difference between "school" math and "grocery store" math. In school, the only purpose of solving a mathematical problem is to obtain a single correct answer. However, shoppers do not visit supermarkets to practise formal mathematics; they go to buy food. Consequently, the choices they make are influenced not merely by unit–price ratios but by their family's food preferences, the amount of storage space at home, the amount of time they can spend shopping, and so on. The supermarket "'problems' are dilemmas to be resolved, rarely

problems to be solved" (Lave 1988: 20). Formal mathematical calculations may help resolve some dilemmas, but in other cases they may be irrelevant or too troublesome to bother with. Shoppers are free to use means other than formal mathematics to resolve a dilemma (58).

One feature all of Lave's subjects shared was the knowledge that school-like tests required a specific problem-solving style—an articulated style. In non-Western societies, individuals who have been educated in the Western system also tend to reserve articulated cognitive styles for the classroom, preferring a variety of more global strategies to resolve the dilemmas of everyday life. So it seems that human beings can choose to employ a range of cognitive styles, depending on the situation. Further, they are able to adopt new cognitive styles as they have new experiences. Studies have shown, for example, that individuals can acquire cognitive styles through social interaction (see, e.g., Levinson 1998). When studying cognitive styles, then, anthropologists must be careful to give their informants the freedom to express a wide variety of global and articulated styles.

Reason and the Reasoning Process—Thinking

In the early days of Europeans' "discovery" of other societies—and for many years thereafter—a common topic of debate was the extent to which

FIGURE 5.8 Shoppers often rely on informal mathematical strategies to calculate the best buy because numbers for quantity and price are not often easy to transform into unit–price ratios. What sorts of strategies do you use to find the best values when you shop?

non-literate non-Western peoples might be said to possess reason. In the context of Western colonialism, this debate was rarely disinterested, for Europeans often justified their position of dominance on the grounds that those dominated were irrational. Faced with this problematic history, how might anthropologists study rational thinking?

Most cognitive psychologists have adopted psychologist Jerome Bruner's (1957) famous definition of **thinking** as "going beyond the information given." This distinction suggests that thinking is different from remembering (which involves referring to information already given) and also from learning (which involves acquiring new information being given). Going beyond the information given thus implies a complex interrelationship between *information* and the *cognitive processes* of a person who is attempting to cope with that information. This definition also reminds us of the nature of cognition as the "nexus of relations between the mind at work and the world in which it works" (Lave 1998: 1; quoted above). Thinking is open and active, and it has no predetermined outcome.

Culture and Logic

One set of cognitive tests has to do with verbal reasoning ability. These tests present subjects with three statements in the form of a **syllogism**—for example:

1. All men are mortal.
2. Socrates is a man.
3. Therefore, Socrates is mortal.

In a syllogism, the first two statements are the *premises*, and the third statement is the *conclusion*. For a syllogism to be sound, the conclusion must follow from the premises. In Western culture, **syllogistic reasoning** is considered to be a perfect example of rational thought. In the past, some researchers suggested that the rational capacities of non-Western peoples could be tested using logical problems in syllogistic form. The assumption was that these peoples' rationality would be confirmed if they could correctly deduce when the conclusion followed logically from the premises and when it did not.

Cole and Scribner (1974) presented logical problems involving syllogistic reasoning to their Kpelle subjects in Liberia (see Map 5.3).

thinking
The active cognitive process of "going beyond the information given."

syllogism
A series of three statements in which the final statement (the conclusion) must follow logically from the first two statements (the premises).

syllogistic reasoning
A form of reasoning based on the syllogism.

MAP 5.3   Kpelle

Typically, the logical problem was embedded in a folktale-like story. The researcher read the story to the subjects and then asked them a series of follow-up questions designed to reveal whether the subjects could draw a "correct" conclusion from the premises given.

Here is one story Cole and Scribner prepared:

> Spider went to a feast. He was told to answer this question before he could eat any of the food. The question is: Spider and Black Deer always eat together. Spider is eating. Is Black Deer eating? (1974: 162)

Given the two premises, the conclusion should be that *Black Deer is eating*. Now consider a typical Kpelle response to hearing this story:

> Subject: Were they in the bush?
> Experimenter: Yes.
> Subject: Were they eating together?
> Experimenter: Spider and Black Deer always eat together. Spider is eating. Is Black Deer eating?
> Subject: But I was not there. How can I answer such a question?
> Experimenter: Can't you answer it? Even if you were not there, you can answer it. (Repeats the question.)
> Subject: Oh, oh, Black Deer is eating.
> Experimenter: What is your reason for saying that Black Deer was eating?
> Subject: The reason is that Black Deer always walks about all day eating green

leaves in the bush. Then he rests for a while and gets up again to eat. (162)

The subject's answer to the question and subsequent justification for that answer seem to have nothing whatsoever to do with the logical problem the subject is being asked to solve.

The researchers devised this story the same way schoolteachers devise mathematical word problems. That is, the contextual material is nothing more than a kind of window dressing. Schoolchildren quickly learn to disregard the window dressing and seek out the mathematical problem it hides. In the research setting, Cole and Scribner expected the Kpelle subjects to act in a similar way and disregard the contextual material about the feast and the identity of the characters involved. However, Kpelle subjects did not understand that they were supposed to disregard this material.

Cole and Scribner interpreted their subject's response to this problem as being due not to irrationality but to a "failure to accept the logical task" (1974: 162). In a follow-up study, Cole and Scribner discovered that Kpelle children who were studying at a Western-style high school responded "correctly" to the logical problems 90 per cent of the time. This finding suggests a strong correlation between Western-style schooling and a willingness to accept context-free analytic tasks in testing situations (164).

But this is not all. David Lancy, one of Cole and Scribner's colleagues, discovered that Western-style syllogisms are very similar to certain forms of Kpelle riddles. Unlike syllogisms, however, those riddles have no single "logically correct" answer. "Rather, as the riddle is posed to a group, the right answer is the one among many offered that seems most illuminating, resourceful, and convincing as determined by consensus and circumstance. This emphasis on edification [i.e., enlightenment or education] as a criterion for 'rightness' is found in Kpelle jurisprudence as well" (Lancy, cited in Fernandez 1980: 47–8). In other words, the "right" answer cannot be extracted from the form of the riddle by logical operations. Rather, the "right" answer is the one that seems most enlightening and informative to the particular audience in the particular setting where the riddle is posed. This approach to identifying the correct answer also reinforces the concept of consensus, or general agreement, thus making problem-solving a group activity.

There is no question that all humans come equipped with the same elementary cognitive processes—for example, the ability to make abstractions, the ability to create conceptual categories, and the ability to reason inferentially. The difficulty is to understand how these elementary cognitive processes are put to work within culturally shared schemas to produce different **reasoning styles**.

Emotion

Psychological anthropologists who try to define **emotion** in cross-cultural terms run into a familiar problem: they discover that not all languages possess a term that might be translated as *emotion*. To get out of this tangle, they have tried to develop a theory of cognitive functioning that accounts for the experiences that some cultures recognize as emotional.

In Western culture, emotion is often associated with the body, and it is generally separated from rational thought, which is typically associated with the mind. Therefore, it is clear that any attempt to explain emotion must deal with the nature of the bodily arousal we associate with it. But there is more to emotion, as we commonly understand it, than mere bodily arousal. Recall the butcher knife scenario referred to near the beginning of this chapter. What do we feel when we see a butcher knife sitting beside mushrooms on a cutting board in our kitchen? What do we feel when we see that same knife in the hands of an intruder bent on attacking us? The knife alone does not trigger our feeling. The *context* in which we encounter the knife becomes the important point. Moreover, it is our *interpretation* of the context—a cognitive activity—that influences our emotional experience.

Emotion engages both bodily arousal and cognitive interpretation. Bodily arousal can trigger an emotional experience by attracting our attention and prompting us to seek the source of arousal (see Mandler 1975: 97). Conversely, a particular interpretation of our experience can trigger bodily arousal. Further, our arousal may increase or decrease depending on how we interpret what is happening around us. Thus we can see that emotions are not caused by *either* bodily

reasoning style
Culture- and context-dependent ways in which we appraise, come to understand, and think about a cognitive task.

emotion
The product of entanglements connecting bodily arousal and cognitive interpretation.

arousals *or* cognitive interpretations; rather, they are the product of entanglements connecting the two. Approaching emotion from this perspective accomplishes three things:

1. it integrates mind and body in a holistic fashion;
2. it acknowledges ambiguity as a central feature of emotional experience (recall that ambiguity is also central to linguistic, perceptual, and conceptual experience); and
3. it suggests how different cultural interpretations might shape what we feel (because cultural interpretations shape our thoughts).

Why should we experience emotion at all? The role of emotion in human life may be rooted in our evolutionary history. Bodily arousal alerts us to something new and unexpected in our environment, something that does not easily fit into any conventional or current schema. Once our attention is caught in this way, we can focus on the interrupting phenomenon and decide how we should react. From this perspective, a person would be foolish to ignore "gut feelings" when trying to sort out a confusing experience. Indeed, "gut feelings" are usually what alert us to confusion in the first place. Our emotions help us engage with the world to develop a full understanding of a situation. Simply knowing what to expect on an intellectual level is not enough—situations must be experienced and felt to be truly understood. Generations of new spouses, new parents, and anthropological fieldworkers can testify to the overwhelming truth of this statement (Figure 5.9).

In sum, we experience bodily arousal when our familiar world is somehow interrupted. Such arousal may either fade away or develop into an emotional experience, depending on the meaning we assign to it. Possible meanings arise out of cultural interpretations of recurring experiential schemas. We should not be surprised to find some overlap in the categories of feeling recognized by different cultures. After all, certain experiential schemas that interrupt the familiar world—birth and death, for example—are human universals. At the same time, the wider cultural context will, in each case, modify the perspective from which such experiences are understood and, thus, the categories of feeling associated with them.

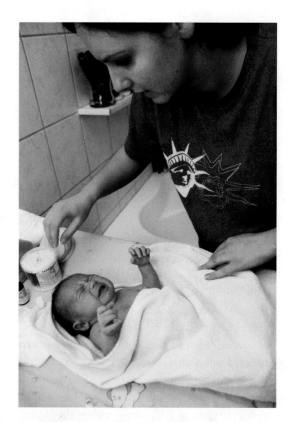

FIGURE 5.9 New parents must learn through whole-body experience how to care for their newborns.

Emotion in an Eastern African Culture

David Parkin (1984) studied the cultural construction of emotion among the Giriama of coastal Kenya (see Map 5.4). Their theory of human nature does not recognize a mind–body dualism of the Western sort. They are unwilling to set up sharp, mutually exclusive oppositions of any kind when discussing human nature. Therefore, such behaviour as spirit possession, madness, hysteria, witchcraft, persistent violence, drunkenness, and thieving are explained

as the result of what we might call imbalances in human nature.... [T]he Giriama do not believe that a person can be intrinsically or irredeemably evil: at some stage, usually remarkably quickly, he will be brought back into the fold, even if he subsequently leaves it again. A large number of terms, roughly translatable as greed, lust, envy, jealousy, malice, resentment, anger, are used to refer to these imbalances of character and the accompanying behaviour. (Parkin 1984: 14)

MAP 5.4 Giriama

As with Westerners, the Giriama associate different feelings with different parts of the body. In the West, people conventionally connect the brain with reason and the heart with emotion. For the Giriama, however, the heart, liver, kidneys, and eyes are the seat of reason *and* emotion. They may distinguish thinking from feeling in discussing the actual behaviour of real people, but they nevertheless presume a common origin for both (17). What about particular emotions? Although the categories of feeling recognized by the Giriama overlap in some respects with the experiences labelled by English terms for emotions, Parkin suggests that there are important differences that stem from the nature of recognized Giriama schemas and from the prototypical thoughts and feelings that are appropriate to those schemas. Consider the term *utsungu*:

> *Utsungu* means poison, bitterness, resentment, and anger, on the one hand, but also grief on the other. It is the feeling experienced at a funeral of a loved or respected relative or friend. A man or woman is grieved at the loss but also bitter that it has happened at all, and angry with the witch who caused the death. Since the witch will be made to pay, the sentiment carried with it both the consequences of the loss of a dear one and the intention to avenge his or her death. (118)

In Western societies, people also feel "grief" at the death of a loved one. But the prototypical Western experience of grief does not contain the additional meaning involving anger at witchcraft or the desire for vengeance. In some cases, however, a person who has lost a loved one may associate grief with a desire for vengeance—for example, if the loved one was murdered. Thus, although we may not believe in witchcraft, we can begin to understand the Giriama people's association of grief with vengeance.

Motivation

Perception and cognition are psychological processes that acquaint us with the inner and outer "worlds" of our experiences and assist us in making sense of those worlds. But human life also involves activity, agency: we set goals and pursue the means to achieve them. Our efforts to set and achieve goals are driven by **motivation**. Where does this motivation come from? Some people assume it comes from something we are born with, called "instinct." But many anthropologists have found that speaking of "instinct" is unhelpful and misleading, especially since different societies appear to establish different culturally defined goals to motivate their members.

In the 1930s and 1940s, pioneering anthropologist Ruth Benedict argued that each culture has its own set of motives. These motives reflect culturally specific models of ideal behaviour, and thus they drive people to pursue some kinds of behaviours rather than others in an attempt to achieve the ideal. Identifying peoples' cultural motivations is an important part of the anthropological task, as it can help us to understand where the people with whom we work are "coming from" (see, e.g., Rosenblatt 2004). As Catherine Lutz (1988) has observed, gaining an understanding of peoples' cultural motivations requires anthropologists to

1. pay close attention to the social and cultural contexts in which individuals learn to interact with other members of their society,
2. learn to understand the local discourse about vice and virtue, and
3. come to terms with local practices and values when attempting to exercise their own agency.

motivation
The inner impulse to set (or accept) and accomplish goals.

socialization

The process by which human beings learn to become members of a group, both by interacting appropriately with others and by coping with the behavioural rules established by the group.

enculturation

The process by which human beings living with one another must learn to come to terms with the ways of thinking and feeling that are considered appropriate in their respective cultures.

self

The result of the process of socialization and enculturation for an individual.

zone of proximal development (ZPD)

The difference between what an individual can achieve on her or his own and what she or he can achieve under the guidance of more experienced individuals.

In short, anthropologists can uncover the mainsprings of motivation by studying **socialization** and **enculturation**.

Socialization and Enculturation

Children use their own bodies and brains to explore their world, but other people actively steer their activity and attention in particular directions. Consequently, their exploration of the world is not merely trial and error: the path is cleared by others who shape their experiences—and their interpretations of their experiences—for them.

Two terms in the social sciences refer to this process of culturally and socially shaped cognitive development: *socialization* and *enculturation*. Becoming human involves both these processes, for children learn how to act, think, feel, and speak at the same time as they participate in the joint activities carried out by social groups to which they belong (Figure 5.10). These two processes are closely related; thus, cultural anthropologists recognize that the study of one is intimately connected to the study of the other.

Anthropologists seek a theory of cognitive development that is holistic; therefore, many have been attracted to the ideas of American philosopher George Herbert Mead and, more recently, to the work of Russian psychologist Lev Vygotsky. For Mead and Vygotsky alike, human life is social from the outset. As Vygotsky wrote,

"The social dimension of consciousness is primary in time and in fact. The individual dimension of consciousness is derivative and secondary" (1978: 30). Like Vygotsky, Mead (1934) believed that human nature is completed and enhanced by socialization and enculturation. Indeed, the successful humanization of human beings lies in people's mastery of symbols, which begins when children start to learn language from others within their culture. As children come to control the symbolic systems of their cultures, they gain the ability to distinguish objects and relationships in the world, and they come to see themselves as objects as well as subjects.

While Mead focussed primarily on face-to-face interaction, Vygotsky was more interested in the wider social, cultural, and historical context in which face-to-face interaction is embedded. This awareness of context makes Vygotsky's work particularly appealing to anthropologists because it provides a way of accounting for the similarities and differences observed when we compare how people from different cultures think and feel. When children learn about the world in a cultural context, they are not working on their own to create an entirely new system of understanding; on the contrary, they are learning how to think and feel like other members of the community.

Vygotsky argued that this learning process creates in the child a new plane of consciousness resting on the dialogue-based, question-and-answer format of social interaction. From this, he inferred that our internal thought processes would also take the format of a dialogue. Mead suggested something similar when he spoke of every person as being able to carry on internal conversations between the *I* (the unsocialized self) and the *me* (the socially conditioned self). Only on this basis can an individual's sense of identity develop as the **self** comes to distinguish itself from the conversational other.

Vygotsky also developed the related concept of the **zone of proximal development (ZPD)**, which is the distance between a child's "actual development level as determined by independent problem solving" and the level of "potential development as determined through problem solving under adult guidance or in collaboration with more capable peers" (Vygotsky 1978: 86). Psychologists everywhere have long been aware that children can often achieve more when they are coached than

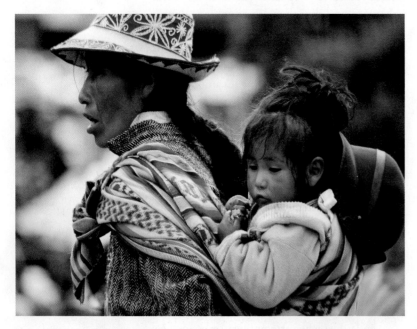

FIGURE 5.10 An Indigenous Andean woman carries her daughter on her shoulder as she walks through a local market.

when they work alone. Vygotsky and his followers see this difference in achievement as demonstrating how growth is rooted in social interaction, especially in educational settings (Moll 1990). The concept of the zone of proximal development enables anthropologists and comparative psychologists to link cognitive development to society, culture, and history because practices of coaching or formal instruction are shaped by social, cultural, and historical factors. To the extent that these factors can vary, we can expect cognitive development to vary as well.

Is Cognitive Development the Same for Everyone?

Most theories portray cognitive development as a progression through a series of stages. Many of these theories also assume that the stages are the same for all human beings or at least all human beings in a particular society. However, anthropological observations suggest that this is not always the case. A Vygotskian perspective helps us explain not only cross-cultural differences in development but also differences in the cognitive development of different subgroups in a single society.

Consider the following illustrative example. In Cuba, a team of researchers followed a sample of 4,299 children from their birth in 1973 through the late 1980s, periodically collecting information on each child's cognitive, social, economic, physical, and academic development (Gutierrez Muñiz, Hurtado, and Beatón 1997). The researchers identified a series of correlations between levels of education, wage employment, living standards, and health of mothers on the one hand and levels of development and achievement of the children on the other. Put in Vygotskian terms, the data show that the zone of proximal development is greater for children of mothers with higher levels of education and participation in the paid workforce than it is for children of mothers with lower educational levels who do not work outside the home. These findings contradicted popular beliefs that the children of educated working mothers would suffer as a result of their mothers' activities (Beatón, personal communication).

Psychologist Carol Gilligan's (1982) comparative study on the moral development of women and men in North American society offers another example. Gilligan argued that middle-class boys and girls begin their moral development in different sociocultural contexts. Boys are encouraged from an early age to break away from their mothers and families and make it on their own. In this context, they learn that independence is good, that dependency is weakness, and that their first duty is to themselves and what they stand for. In contrast, girls mature in a sociocultural context in which their bond with their mothers and families is never sharply broken. They learn that connection to others is good, that the destruction of relationships is damaging, and that their first responsibility in any difficult situation is to ensure that nobody gets hurt.

The Vygotskian concept of the zone of proximal development provides a useful tool for describing how the differential moral development of boys and girls is accomplished. In Vygotskian terms, the moral development of boys and girls proceeds in different directions because boys and girls are coached differently by more mature members of society. That is, when faced with the same dilemmas but unsure of how to act, boys are encouraged to make one set of choices, girls another. In this way, each gender category builds up a different set of schemas as to what constitutes the "good." Gilligan (1982) argued that men are able to present their moral perspective as universally correct because men as a group hold power over women as a group in North American society. She predicted, however, that as women continue to gain social power and status, their "different voice" will acquire ever more legitimacy, and the culturally embedded paths of moral development may themselves eventually be altered.

Personality/Self/Subjectivity

Early psychological anthropologists often spoke of individual **personality** rather than the *self* when discussing an individual's sense of identity and personal place in the world. Many Western psychologists and psychological anthropologists also assumed that the mature self or personality was a bounded, independent, self-contained entity with a clear and non-contradictory sense of identity that persisted through time. According to this interpretation of the self, an individual would naturally strive to be self-sufficient and work to further her or his own individual interests, whether or not those interests benefitted others. Anthropologists working in non-Western societies, however, have found that the development of

personality
The relative integration of an individual's perceptions, motives, cognitions, and behaviour within a sociocultural matrix.

subject position
An individual's unique position in the world, which is shaped by social variables such as class, gender, and socioeconomic status.

such an independent entity was not always the goal of socialization and enculturation. In many cases, the objective was to shape selves that were motivated to look out for others and to work for the well-being of the family, the lineage, or the community. As African psychologist Augustine Nwoye (2006) points out, "the Western notion of the self is largely incompatible with the African view. The Western model is based on the notion of the self as a demarcated entity set off against the world, whereas the African views the self as an entity in close interaction with the multi-faceted aspects of the world" (119).

In recent decades, psychological anthropologists such as Philip K. Bock (1994) have looked very closely at the relationship between culture and the individual in different cultural contexts. What they have found is that an individual's personality is not merely a reflection of a culturally ideal type; it is also shaped by "quasi-universal" factors such as "the individual's position in the social structure, including his or her social class, gender, occupational role, and even birth order" (1994: xiv). Thus it seems that different dimensions of one's personality or self can be activated or de-activated in different contexts and over time as contexts change. What then does this mean for our understanding of "the self" or "personality" as a constant, unchanging entity?

Aware that conceptions of the self as unchanging do not fully encompass our continually shifting sense of identity and place in the world, contemporary psychological anthropologists are more likely to speak of individual **subjectivity** than of individual personality or the self. *Individual subjectivity* has been described as "the felt interior experience of the person that includes his or her positions in a field of relational power" (Das and Kleinman 2000: 1). Thinking of individuals as *subjects* who occupy various positions within society has two major advantages. First, it highlights individual **agency**, as each of us is the initiating subject of our actions. Second, it acknowledges that our power to act is limited by our circumstances. After all, individual agency is not absolute; it is circumscribed by various limitations that result from the distribution of social, economic, and political power in the societies in which we live. These limitations may be greater or lesser, depending on social variables such as class, gender, occupation, or birth order. That is, we are

subject to the workings of institutionalized power in the various **subject positions** we occupy.

Our subject positions are formed in and through our cultural context; consequently, they reflect certain social, economic, and political circumstances, both past and present. People in all societies occupy a variety of different subject positions: a particular individual may, in different contexts, be differently positioned in terms of gender, ethnicity, occupation, class, or some combination of these positions. At the same time, however, all of us can potentially play the insights gained from each subject position against the others and thus gain a measure of reflexive awareness and understanding of our own situations. (See the "In Their Own Words" box for a discussion of the neoliberal view of agency and the self, which has challenged anthropological interpretations of aspects of globalization in recent decades.)

The Presentation of Self

Whenever we interact with others, we present a version of our "self." The clothes we wear, the way we style our hair, the makeup we apply, even the ways we move and speak—these all create an image of self. In certain contexts, a specific presentation is expected. Think of the Catholic pope, who must wear a specific type of costume and assume a specific public demeanour to set himself apart from those he leads (cardinals, archbishops, bishops, priests, the Catholic masses). In Pueblo culture, ceremonial dancers present themselves as kachinas (spirits of the natural world) by wearing specific masks and clothes and performing specific activities not appropriate outside the ceremonial space and time. An example more familiar to North Americans may be the "red carpet" phenomenon, in which celebrities are expected to don expensive clothes and elaborate hair and makeup in a highly formalized presentation of self.

Even in less formal contexts, we all face certain expectations about how we present ourselves. In class, we are expected to present ourselves as intelligent and eager to learn; at work, we are expected to present ourselves as responsible and hard working. On a more general level, we are expected to present a self that reflects the **norms** and the values of our culture. In North America, for example, youth and independence are seen as ideals. Thus, many North Americans strive to present themselves as young, strong, and self-sufficient. Of course, other cultures have

subjectivity
An individual's awareness of his or her own agency and position as a subject.

agency
An individual's ability to make choices and to effect change through her or his actions.

norms
Rules (usually unwritten) for behaviour assumed to be typical within a specific social or cultural group.

different ideals, and those ideals shape expectations of self-presentation differently. In addition, as Western cultural norms have expanded in recent decades to be more inclusive, our presentation of self has become more open as well (Van Wolputte 2004: 264). It has also become easier to achieve our ideal, whatever it may be, "through tattoos, piercings, branding, liposuction, or cosmetic surgery"—a purchased commodification of the "dominant ideology" (264).

IN THEIR OWN WORDS | Neoliberal Concept of Agency

American ethnologist Ilana Gershon explores the neoliberal concept of agency, as it relates to anthropological interests.

The shift from economic liberalism to neoliberalism affects the concept of agency in two important ways. I have already alluded to the first shift—that subjects, markets, economic rationality, and competition are all recognized as socially constructed under neoliberalism. The second shift is a move from the liberal vision of people owning themselves as though they were property to a neoliberal vision of people owning themselves as though they were a business. From a liberal perspective, people own their bodies and their capacities to labour, capacities they can sell in the market. In contrast, by seeing people as businesses, a neoliberal perspective presumes that people own their skills and traits, that they are "a collection of assets that must be continually invested in, nurtured, managed, and developed" (Martin 2000: 582; see also Leve 2011). . . .

A neoliberal perspective presumes that every social analyst on the ground should ideally use market rationality to interpret their social relationships and social strategies. This concept of agency requires a reflexive stance in which people are subjects for themselves—a collection of processes to be managed. There is always already a presumed distance to oneself as an actor. One is never "in the moment"; rather, one is always faced with one's self as a project that must be consciously steered through various possible alliances and obstacles. This is a self that is produced through an engagement with a market, that is, neoliberal markets require participants to be reflexive managers of their abilities and alliances. . . .

Managing the self involves taking oneself to be a collection of skills or traits that can enter into alliances with other such collections. In her elegant genealogy of how communication has come to be a set of work-related skills in the twentieth century, Bonnie Urciuoli addresses how recent college graduates easily describe themselves as "a bundle of skills" as they attempt to find employment (Urciuoli 2008). As Urciuoli illustrates, when one becomes a bundle of ill-defined but highly flexible skills, one becomes a fragmented self of usable traits. . . .

[T]he reflexive aspect of the neoliberal self exists before relationships and contexts and actively decides how he or she will connect to other people, institutions, and contexts. In this sense, the neoliberal self is autonomous. While this self exists before relationships, it is still socially constructed, albeit by itself as reflexive manager. It is only reflexivity that is presumed to be before social or self-construction in this perspective. . . .

If neoliberal selves exist before relationships, what are relationships under neoliberalism? They are alliances that should be based on market rationality. Under liberalism, an employer rented the worker's body and labour capacity for a set amount of time in exchange for a wage. Under neoliberalism, the employer and the worker enter into a business partnership, albeit an unequal partnership. The worker provides a skill set that can be enhanced according to the employer's requirements—part of what is being offered is the worker's reflexive ability to be an improvable subject. . . .

To sum up, a neoliberal perspective assumes that the actors who create and are created by the most ideal social order are those who reflexively and flexibly manage themselves as one owns and manages a business, tending to one's own qualities and traits as owned and even improvable assets. Many aspects of selves and the social world become redefined as a result, even culture has become a trait that can serve as a basis for or enhance people's alliances with others. Another transformation has been to how one has agency—any one or group that is agentive should be agentive as a corporative entity. At the same time, these actors have alliances with others, alliances that ideally should be distributing risk and responsibility so that no corporate entity bears another's risks. These actors cannot be relied on to police themselves and their own alliances effectively, and as a result, laws become the central medium for regulating practices. Laws are uniquely appropriate for neoliberal policing because they contain the potential to overlook the intricacies of social organization—laws can accommodate misrecognitions of scale. In short, a neoliberal perspective of agency depends on transforming liberalism's possessive individualism (Macpherson 1962) into corporate individualism, viewing all agents as commensurate corporate entities so that social organization or differences in scale can be ignored.

Source: Gershon, Ilana. 2011. "Neoliberal Agency," *Current Anthropology* 52, 4: 537–55.

sex

The conventional biological distinction between male and female based on *morphological sex* (observable sex characteristics), *gonadal sex* (ovaries in females; testes in males), and chromosomal sex (XX or XY chromosomes).

gender roles

Sets of behaviours that are commonly perceived as masculine or feminine within a specific culture.

gender

The culturally constructed beliefs and behaviours considered appropriate for each sex.

sexuality

An individual's sense of his or her own sexual desires, orientation, and preferences.

heteronormativity

An ideology that promotes heterosexuality as the social ideal, supported by the cultural definition of "appropriate" behaviour based on culturally defined categories of "male" and "female," "masculine" and "feminine."

In presenting the self, individuals sometimes draw on what cultural anthropologist Mark Edberg (2004) calls a "cultural persona"—"a type of personified cultural model that appears to serve as a distinct nexus between representation and practice" (258). The example Edberg focusses on is the tough-guy persona of the US–Mexican narcotrafficker. As Edberg describes them, "cultural personas are recycled and may surface in a particular setting as a 'type,' . . . which represents a cluster of values and meanings that are expressed through a particular pattern of action that is many steps removed from the persona in its original or 'pure' form" (273). To the insider who is familiar with the cultural meanings on which a particular persona is built, that persona makes sense. However, taken out of context, or from a cultural outsider's perspective, a cultural persona can easily be misunderstood.

In recent years, anthropologists have increasingly turned their attention to the presentation of self in technology-mediated social environments. Electronic media—first radio, then TV, and now the Internet—broaden the reach of the presented self. In our world of Facebook, Twitter, Snapchat, email, selfies, texting, blogging, and online video sharing, it is relatively easy to present whatever self we like to a great number of people. Politicians and other personalities in the public eye are highly aware of the power of selective self-presentation on social networking sites. Stephen Harper, for example, has a Facebook page and a Twitter account that he (or his staff) regularly updates with messages that present him as a strong leader. As social anthropologist Steffen Dalsgaard (2008) argues, the presentation of self via social networking services may even be "a new form of presentation of self . . . that focuses on the social relations of the person rather than the person as an individual" (8).

Sex, Sexuality, and Gender Roles: The Creation of Subject Positions

In many ways, our "selves" or "subject positions" are shaped by our **sex** and our adoption of **gender roles** or roles (see, e.g., Peletz 2006). In most Western societies, concepts of sex and **gender** have traditionally been closely linked.

As philosopher of science Sarah S. Richardson (2012) observes,

> there is a broad popular, scientific, and medical conception of the X chromosome as the mediator of the differences between males and females. . . . The still very contemporary view is that the double X makes females unpredictable, mysterious, chimeric, and conservative, while the single X allows men to learn, evolve, and have bigger brains but also makes them the more risk taking. . . . [This] shows how conceptions of X chromosome structure and function often reflect and support traditional gender stereotypes. (927)

To truly understand the roles sex and gender—not to mention **sexuality**—play in our lives, we must move beyond such simplified conflations of these concepts. We need to differentiate the three fundamental terms of *sex*, *gender*, and *sexuality*. Conventionally, *sex* refers to anatomy (biology), *gender* refers to sociocultural beliefs and practices, and *sexuality* refers to the way sexual desire is experienced, including an individual's preferences in sexual partners. But as we will see, matters are less straightforward than these conventional understandings allow.

Sex, sexuality, and gender identities define subject positions, sorting each of us into categories—and often hierarchies—defined by our cultures. This type of sorting is not an inconsequential matter. Consider how narrow and limiting the traditional categories of "male" and "female" or "heterosexual" and "non-heterosexual" are. In contrast, consider the openness of the identity categories suggested by the acronym LGBTQ (lesbian, gay, bisexual, transgender, queer or questioning), which is now commonly used to draw attention to a range of possible identities (see, e.g., Kulick 2000: 243). Undoubtedly, this inclusive conception of human sexuality is much better equipped to describe our diversity of attractions.

Despite such progressive developments, however, the notion that sexuality and gender must be defined by clear, unmovable lines persists. This is the notion that lies behind the still widely held ideology of **heteronormativity**, which separates sexuality and gender into fixed, hierarchically defined categories based on strict definitions of "male" and "female" and of "masculine" and "feminine." Many people today live in heteronormative cultures where cultural realities and constructs separate the worlds of men and women from each other. In such societies, we can find evidence of heteronormalizing boundaries in the differential use of public and private space, in approved forms of dress, and even in the mutual exclusivity of the definitions of *maleness* and *femaleness* or *masculinity* and *femininity*.

Supporters of the heteronormative view often employ **naturalizing discourses** to reinforce their position (see, e.g., Sullivan-Blum 2006). You have likely heard people argue, often from an ostensibly religious standpoint, that same-sex sexual relationships are "unnatural." These sorts of claims presume that what is *natural* can be meaningfully distinguished from what has been *culturally constructed*. Anthropologist Pamela L. Geller (2009) observes that this sort of confusion arises even in scientific research settings. Looking specifically at examples from biological anthropology, she notes that many biological anthropologists, through their reliance on Western biomedical ideas about the human body, "unwittingly naturalize cultural values that are in fact modern constructs" (504). For example, the biomedical approach tends to see the male body as "standard" and the female body as notable primarily for its reproductive capabilities, a view that disempowers women. Further, it regards sex as "dichotomous, immutable, and interchangeable with gender" (505), clearly blurring the lines between what is "natural" and what is socially constructed.

From a modern anthropological perspective, it is clear that we must question how definitive any categorizations of sexuality or gender can be. As with any attempt to classify human experiences, the categories are ultimately too limiting. For this reason, anthropologists tend to take a broader approach, viewing sexuality and gender in a context that includes local, national, and global views on sexuality and gender roles (see Boellstorff 2007). This is a refreshing development if we consider that "colonial-era anthropologists tended to suppress, minimize, or exoticize evidence of [non-heterosexual] practices in conformity with colonial ideologies, practices, and prevailing debates around gender and sexuality in Europe and America" (Epprecht 2006:187).

We must also question common ideas about biological sex. Biological determiners of sex are not always obvious, and physical sex differences do not always help us to predict the roles that an individual will play in any particular society. For example, sometimes genetic or hormonal factors produce variations in sex characteristics (both internal and external) that blur the line between what we typically think of as "male" or "female." Individuals with these sorts of variations are often referred to as *intersexed*. Steroid 5-alpha-reductase deficiency (5ARD), a rare hormonal condition, is an example where genetic males are born with ambiguous genitalia and at puberty display male morphological changes. Cultural anthropologist Gilbert Herdt (1994) investigated 5ARD in the Dominican Republic and New Guinea. In both places, the sexually anomalous individuals were assigned to a locally recognized third sex. This third sex was called *guevedoche* ("testicles at twelve") in the Dominican Republic and *kwolu-aatmwol* ("changing into a male thing") among the Sambia of New Guinea.

The existence of *supernumerary*—that is, more than two—sexes and/or genders (Peletz 2006)—in cultures where the presence of ambiguous genitalia at birth seems to play no obvious role has been documented. In the Byzantine civilization of late antiquity, phenotypic differences were deliberately created in the case of eunuchs, whose testicles were removed or destroyed, often before puberty (Ringrose 1994). With the *hijras* of Gujarat, India, adult males deliberately cut off both penis and testicles in order to dedicate themselves to the mother goddess Bahuchara Mata (Nanda 1994; Figure 5.11). In both cases, members of the wider society understand these third gender roles to be distinct from feminine and masculine gender roles.

Perhaps the most famous anthropological example of supernumerary sexes and genders without morphological sex anomalies is that of individuals called by the contested term *berdache*. Cultural scholar Will Roscoe points out that the role can be marked by cross-dressing (1994: 332). Individuals in such a role are accepted and respected members of their communities, and their economic and religious pursuits are

naturalizing discourses
The deliberate representation of particular identities (e.g., caste, class, race, ethnicity, and nationality) as if they were a result of biology or nature rather than history or culture, making them appear eternal and unchanging.

FIGURE 5.11 A hijra onlooker watches another hijra apply makeup. In hijra communities, third gender roles—distinct from traditional masculine and feminine gender roles—are considered appropriate for third-sexed individuals. How can other cultures' ideas about sex and gender help us see our own culture's ideas about sex and gender in a new way?

frequently more culturally significant than their sexual practices:

> the key features of male and female *berdache* roles were, in order of importance, *productive specialization* (crafts and domestic work for male berdaches, and warfare, hunting, and leadership roles for female *berdaches*), *supernatural sanction* (in the form of an authorization and/or bestowal of powers from extra-societal sources), and *gender variation* (in relation to normative cultural expectations for male and female genders). (332)

Early French explorers in the Americas used *berdache* to mean "male prostitute." Thus many contemporary anthropologists refuse to use the term, as do those members of contemporary Indigenous societies who want to reclaim this alternative gender role for their cultures. No single alternative term has yet reached universal acceptance, although *two spirit* has been gaining support. Perhaps no single term is adequate; after all, two-spirited males have been described in almost 150 Indigenous North American societies, and two-spirited females in perhaps half that number. For a deeper understanding, see the work of Canadian anthropologist Jean-Guy Goulet (1996), who discusses personhood and gender, arguing that "anthropologists have conceptualized gender variance among Native North Americans without paying attention to the ways in which Indigenous practices construct members of a community "as" woman or "as" man (or member of other gender category)" (683).

In Canada, sex and gender have been topics of public discussion only in the past few decades. Even today, little of this public discourse focusses on intersexuality (biological manifestation of male and/or female physical characteristics in one individual) or transgender people (those whose internal gender identity differs from that suggested by their physiology). Indeed, many Canadians still hold to the traditional views that the existence of only two sexes, each with its own gender role, is both natural and obvious. Yet American historian Thomas Laqueur (1990) has shown that the "two-sex model" took root only after the Renaissance. Prior to that, the bodies of all human beings were evaluated in terms of a "one-sex model" based on the Platonic notion that there was one ideal human form, which all actual human beings embodied to greater or lesser degrees. Moreover, as Roscoe points out, "the presence of multiple genders does not require belief in the existence of three or more physical sexes but, minimally, a view of physical differences as unfixed, or insufficient on their own to establish gender, or simply less important than individual and social factors" (1994: 342). These observations sustain anthropologists Jane Collier and Sylvia Yanagisako's key assertion that "there are no 'facts,' biological or material, that have social consequences and cultural meanings in and of themselves" (1987: 39).

Sexual Practices and Identity

The range of sexual practices in the world is vast. It is vast even across our own continent, as suggested some years ago by the *Kinsey Reports* (1948 on males and 1953 on females) and more recently in various large-scale studies on sexuality. Contemporary anthropologists recognize that sexual activity is an essential part of social behaviour and that a desire for sex is a strong motivation in most individuals. As such, they have made observations on how sexual practices, as situated within the sexual norms of a culture, influence an individual's identity and social position.

Currently, one of the most productive fields of inquiry is the postmodern body of research called *queer theory*. Queer theory challenges and rejects "defined categories of male/female, man/woman, heterosexual/homosexual" (Hatzfeldt 2011). It avoids placing fixed boundaries around ideas of sexuality. If we return to the *Kinsey Reports* (Kinsey et al. 1948; 1953), we could note that these reports supported the conclusion that human sexuality exhibits a wide range of behaviours. And although the Kinsey Scale (Figure 5.12) assigned categories to sexual orientation, these categories were not seen to be impermeable. The scale actually "showed people did not fit into neat and exclusive heterosexual or homosexual categories" (Kinsey Institute, 2014). Subsequently, other organizational systems, such as the Klein Sexual Orientation Grid (Figure 5.13; Klein 1978) were devised.

Queer politics moves to facilitate change in our general ideas about sex, gender, sexuality, and social tendencies (Sullivan 2003: 81). The terminology for sexual orientation and sexual identity used today—for example, androphilia (sexual attraction to men/males), gynephilia (sexual attraction to women/females), pansexuality and polysexuality (sexual attraction to men/males and women/females), third gender, two spirit—somewhat reflects the serious consideration of our sexual and gendered selves. But these terms are subject to change as we move to deeper and more nuanced interpretations of identity (or identities). As anthropologist Ana Mariella Bacigalupo comments "selfhood is gendered dynamically by individual desire and competing cultural and religious norms" (2004: 440). We are challenged by conventional notions—the "rules" of "the norm"—to seek the experiential realities of our own identities. (See the "In Their Own Words" box for an extended discussion that relates to this topic.)

Cross-cultural Approaches to Sexuality

Some cultures take a relatively open approach to sexuality, and the sexual desires of women and men are equally recognized. For example, consider the Ju/'hoansi, who begin sexual activity at an early age (Lee 1992b). As a result of this early sexual openness, the social and sexual constraints of marriage represent quite a shock at first, especially for young women. Some Ju/'hoansi are strictly faithful to one another, but a significant minority take lovers. The Ju/'hoansi have no double standard; both men and women are free to take lovers. However, discretion is necessary when taking a lover because both husbands and wives can become very jealous and start fights. Sexual satisfaction is important to the Ju/'hoansi; female orgasm is known, and women expect both husbands and lovers to satisfy them sexually.

Yet not all societies are as accepting of female expressions of sexuality. For the Mundurucu of the Brazilian Amazon, female orgasm is more

FIGURE 5.12 The Kinsey Scale, developed by pioneering sex researcher Alfred Kinsey and his colleagues in the late 1940s, attempts to describe a person's sexual orientation based on her or his behaviours.

Variable	Past	Present	Ideal
Sexual Attraction			
Sexual Behaviour			
Sexual Fantasies			
Emotional Preference			
Social Preference			
Self-Identification			
Heterosexual/Homosexual Lifestyle			

Please rate the first five variables in the above table according to the following scale:

1	2	3	4	5	6	7
Other sex only	Other sex mostly	Other sex somewhat more	both sexes equally	Same sex somewhat more	Same sex mostly	Same sex only

Please rate the final two variables in the above table according to the following scale:

1	2	3	4	5	6	7
Heterosexual only	Heterosexual mostly	Heterosexual somewhat more	Heterosexual/ homosexual equally	Homosexual somewhat more	Homosexual mostly	Homosexual only

FIGURE 5.13 The Klein Sexual Orientation Grid, developed by psychiatrist Fritz Klein in the late 1970s, attempts to "measure" a person's sexual orientation based on her or his thoughts and behaviours.

accidental than expected (Murphy and Murphy 1974). Many societies insist a woman must be a virgin until she is married. In some Arab societies, a couple must produce bloodstained sheets the morning after the consummation of their marriage to demonstrate that the bride was a virgin.

Many cultures place taboos on certain types of sexual activity, and individuals are expected to respect these taboos. For example, American anthropologist Karl Heider (1979) observed a strict postpartum sex taboo among the Dani, a people of highland New Guinea (see Map 5.5). For five years after the birth of a child, Dani parents do not have sexual intercourse with each other. Such taboos are found in all cultures, but they generally last for only a few weeks or months. (In North America, we say that the mother needs time to heal; other societies have other justifications.) Yet to most Westerners, the Dani's five-year wait would seem to be exceptional. What could explain this difference in opinion? Heider points out that Westerners assume that the sex drive is perhaps the most powerful biological drive of all; the Dani do not share this assumption. The Dani are not

MAP 5.5 Dani

celibate, yet they do not seem very interested in sex (78–81). It seems that the Dani represent an extreme in the cultural construction of sexuality.

Of course, not all sexual practices map onto the Western heterosexual model. Indeed, the fact that people in almost every society have developed complex ideological and ritual structures to encourage heterosexual practices, ostensibly to promote procreation, suggests that human sexual expression would

IN THEIR OWN WORDS | Digisex: Cellphones, Barbadian Queens, and Circuits of Desire in the Gay Caribbean

David A.B. Murray is a Canadian anthropologist whose field-work explores such themes as culture, colonialism, identity, and sexuality. Here, Murray examines the experiences and identities of several Barbadian "queens" (self-identified "effem-inate" gay men from Barbados) who have formed intimate romantic-sexual relationships with men from Jamaica.

[G]enerally, we might observe that the struggles and tensions in [Barbadian] queens' romantic-sexual liaisons mirror certain qualities of heterosexual relationships in the Afro-Caribbean. . . . Not only do they seem to face similar challenges around issues of honesty and suspicion of a partner having outside sexual liai-sons, which are exacerbated by the presence of the cellphone, they also manifest more generally tensions generated between the value of respectability, the importance of material and eco-nomic support, and the ideal of romantic love. . . . While the queens' desired ideal in romantic-sexual relationships mirrored a highly gendered "women's" perspective on relationships (i.e., the search for "true love," emphasizing a search for a faithful, honest male mate with whom they could establish a long-term, secure, and emotionally intimate relationship), their reputation for eco-nomically supporting their male mates disrupted the popular male perception of a woman's objectives in a heterosexual rela-tionship (material and financial gain from their male mates) due to their economic power over their male partners. This economic independence . . . in these queens' narratives . . . appears to pro-duce an ambiguous outcome, as the queens began to complain of having to support their Jamaican boyfriends, most of whom were unemployed or not able to work in Barbados. . . .

Contrary to much of the analysis of working-class Afro-Caribbean relationships which dismisses "romantic" love as sub-ordinate to material needs and economic survival, I would argue that individualized "Western romance" discourses are significant in the queens' beliefs (at least in the initial stages) about rela-tionships, but these ideals are supplemented, supplanted, and challenged by the pragmatics of economic and material circum-stances in which the queen begins to occupy a role she perceives as "masculine," which in turn troubles the relationship. Trouble also comes in the form of suspicion and gossip about male partners cheating and lying, traits which are often explained as "natural" components of masculinity (Chevannes 2001). In sum, love and sex were constituted by the queens in ways that both re-inscribed and complicated tropes of heterosexual gendered relations in the Afro-Caribbean.

We see [in this account] an undermining of the theory of dis-tinct national masculinities that the queens presented to me at the outset of their contact with the Jamaicans when they noted that the latter appeared to be more honest, faithful, and roman-tic than their Bajan counterparts, and yet three months later, were described as just as "wuthless" ["worthless"] and trouble-some. Thus the experiences of this group of marginalized sexual subjects, mediated through new communications technologies, relative mobility, and (the queens') relative economic stability, produced knowledges about sex, gender, and society that simul-taneously enhanced and transformed existing circuits of desire, sexuality, and identity in the Afro-Caribbean: one transformation occurred in the sense that both of these groups—the Jamaican men and the Bajan queens—had not known or met many of their sexual counterparts in person prior to these relationships, and through their experiences with each other, learned some-thing new about themselves and each other's society. . . . [T]his experience enhanced or re-inscribed practices and knowledge about gender, sexuality, and society already circulating through-out the Anglo-Caribbean. . . .

A transformation could also be found in the ways in which intimacy and romance were created, maintained, and broken through technology: cellphones, and in particular [mobile tele-communications operator] Digicel's aggressively competitive marketing strategies across the Anglo-Caribbean, lowered the cost of long distance communication and provided these cou-ples with previously unaffordable and unavailable means (i.e., texting) of maintaining regular, intimate contact. However, the cellphone was also viewed as a technology which could be used to undermine relationships in ways that were not previously possible through its portability and technological capacities (for example, address lists and storage of previously dialled numbers that could be used to discover a partner's lies and deceitful behaviour). At the same time, this inter-island intimacy (and its attendant tensions) was not entirely new. Movement of Caribbean people across the region, whether in search of work, romance, or play, is a long-established practice, and so too, accordingly, is knowledge of other island societies and social practices. The cellphone thus facilitated and enhanced certain possibilities between these groups, who did not enjoy ease of communication and did not readily achieve sociality and a sentiment of community because of their marginality in their respective societies, but it would be problematic to claim that a singular technology "created" new social communities, practices, or identities.

Source: Murray, David A.B. 2010. "Digisex: Cellphones, Barbadian Queens, and Circuits of Desire in the Gay Caribbean," *Anthropologica* 52, 1: 103–12.

resist such confinement if it were not under strict and sometimes life-threatening control. As we mentioned in our previous discussion, anthropological information about supernumerary sexes and genders undermines the "two-sex model" that is dominant in Euro-American cultures. Anthropologists Evelyn Blackwood and Saskia Wieringa (1999) have similarly undermined Western heterosexual assumptions in their exploration of how culture shapes female desires. These researchers concluded that focussing on the ways that female bodies are assigned cultural meanings in different historical and ethnographic settings, and on how those meanings affect the way females constitute their relations with other females, reveals a wide range of "varied and rich cultural identities and same-sex practices between those with female bodies" (1999: ix). Significantly, they note that this sort of research does not assume that having a male body or a female body necessarily determines any individual's traits, feelings, or experiences (x). As a result, it provides a vital comparative context that can illuminate our understanding of sexual practices that Euro-Americans call *homosexuality* and *bisexuality*.

Consider the Nicaraguan concept of *cochónes* within the greater social construct of *machismo* (aggressive masculinity). As anthropologist Roger Lancaster learned while he was doing fieldwork in Nicaragua in the 1980s, working-class Nicaraguans admire *machistas*—"real men" who are active, violent, and dominant. They see the penis as a weapon that can dominate a sexual partner—male or female—who is thereby rendered passive, abused, and subordinate. A "passive" male who allows a "manly man" to have sexual intercourse with him is called a *cochón*. Thus the identity and social position of a *cochón* differs greatly from that of a man who is perceived as sexually dominant. While the "passive" *cochón* is stigmatized, the male who takes the "active" role in sexual intercourse with other males and with females is seen as "normal." These distinctions pervade social interactions, as public challenges for dominance are a constant of male–male interaction in Nicaragua, even when sexual intercourse is not involved. *Cochón* may be used as an epithet not only for a man who yields publicly to another man but also for cats that don't catch mice or indeed anything that somehow fails to perform its proper function. As Lancaster notes, *cochónes* are made, not born:

> Those who consistently lose out in the competition for male status . . . discover

pleasure in the passive sexual role or its social status: these men are made into *cochónes*. And those who master the rules of conventional masculinity . . . are made into *machistas* (1992: 249).

As with the gender roles we recognize in Western cultures, the position of the *cochón* is a social construct.

The examples we have discussed in this section reveal that the physical activity we call *sexual intercourse* is not just doing what comes naturally. Like many things in human life, sex does not speak for itself nor does it have only one meaning. Sexual practices can be used to give concrete form to more abstract notions we have about the place of men and women in the world. They may serve as a metaphor for expressing differential power within a society. That is, sexual practices can be used as an excuse to enact, in unmistakable physical terms, the reality of differential power. As anthropologists, we must remember that sexual practices never occur in a vacuum. They are entrenched in other social practices such as food production, political organization, legal protection, and kinship, all of which act to shape who we are, how we see ourselves, and how we are perceived by others.

Structural Violence and Social Trauma

Earlier in this chapter, we noted that individual subjectivity and identity are heavily influenced by the processes of socialization and enculturation. But social and cultural expectations are sometimes overturned by experiences that intrude on predictable daily routines, and these experiences, too, will shape individuals' subjectivities. Among the most powerfully intrusive experiences are those occasioned by violence and trauma. When these causal agents arise from widespread social and/or political factors, they are commonly referred to as **structural violence** and **social trauma**. As you read through the following examples, consider your responses to such violence and trauma, and keep in mind writer and political activist Susan Sontag's observation on the role of compassion in our "society of spectacle": "Compassion is an unstable emotion. It needs to be translated into action, or it withers" (2003: 101).

structural violence
Violence that results from the way that political and economic forces structure risk for various forms of suffering within a population.

social trauma
Individual and group experience of negative physical, mental, and emotional effects resulting from powerfully disturbing occurrences caused by forces and agents external to the person or group.

Paul Farmer is an anthropologist and medical doctor who has worked in Haiti since 1983 (see Map 5.6; Figure 5.14). In his position, he has witnessed extreme forms of human suffering that are part and parcel of everyday life for those at the bottom of Haitian society. Much of this suffering is in the form of infectious and parasitic disease, but it can also include other forms of extreme suffering such as hunger, torture, and rape (Farmer 2002 [1996]: 424). In Haiti, the operations of structural violence create spaces in which the poorest and least powerful members of society are subjected to highly intensified risks of all kinds, increasing the likelihood that sooner or later they will experience one or more varieties of social suffering. The structural aspect of this violence is important to emphasize since the attention of most Western outside observers, even those who want to alleviate suffering, is often trained on individuals and their personal experiences, with the resulting temptation to blame the victims for their own distress.

Farmer relates the story of a Haitian woman, Acéphie Joseph, who died of AIDS in 1991, when she was 25. Acéphie's parents had been prosperous peasant farmers selling produce in village markets until 1956, when the fertile valley in which they lived was flooded after officials built a dam to generate electricity. They lost everything and became "water refugees" forced to try to grow crops on an infertile plot in the village where they were resettled. Acéphie and her twin brother were born in the village and attended primary school there. Farmer writes that Acéphie's "beauty and her vulnerability may have sealed her fate as early as 1984" (426). She began to help her mother carry produce to the market along a road that went past the local military barracks, where soldiers liked to flirt with the passing women, and one soldier in particular approached her. "Such flirtation is seldom unwelcome, at least to all appearances. In rural Haiti, entrenched poverty made the soldiers—the region's only salaried men—ever so much more attractive" (427). Although Acéphie knew that the soldier had a wife and children, she nevertheless did not rebuff him; indeed, he visited her family, who approved of their liaison. "I could tell that the old people were uncomfortable, but they didn't say no . . . I never dreamed he would give me a bad illness . . . it was a way out, that's how I saw it," Acéphie explained. Only a few weeks after the beginning of their sexual relationship, the soldier died, and Acéphie sought training as a cook in order to qualify for work as a servant in the city, for she had no other viable alternative. Eventually she found work as a maid and began a relationship with a young man, who drove a bus, whom she planned to marry. After three years as a maid, Acéphie became pregnant; she went home to her village to give birth, but she had a very difficult delivery. When she finally sought medical help for a series of infections, she was diagnosed with AIDS. Following her death, her father hanged himself.

Acéphie was an individual, and so it is natural to ask how representative her experiences might be. Farmer's work with many poor women with AIDS allowed him to recognize that all of their cases,

MAP 5.6 Haiti

FIGURE 5.14 Dr Paul Farmer treats a patient at Clinique Bon Sauveur in Haiti. Why is it important for anthropologists and others to investigate the structural aspects of violence and suffering in less affluent areas of the world?

including Acéphie's, showed "a deadly monotony." The women he interviewed "were straightforward about the non-voluntary aspect of their sexual activity." They had been driven to it by poverty (431). Farmer concludes that Acéphie and others like her suffered because they did not have the power to avoid their circumstances. Farmer identifies specifically the relations of power that contributed to the likelihood that Acéphie's suffering and death would take the forms it took. For example, "gender helps explain why Acéphie died of AIDS" (433). Race or ethnicity helps explain why illness is more likely to be suffered by the descendants of enslaved Africans, and social class helps explain why they were more likely to be poor. Acéphie was "at risk" of such a fate long before she met the soldier who altered her destiny. She was, from the outset, a victim of structural violence (431).

Anthropologists are also interested in identifying the causes and effects of large-scale, collective violence. After all, incidents of warfare, genocide, ethnic cleansing, mass rape, and other such forms of mass violence were distinctive features of the twentieth century, leading to widespread death, the disruption of social institutions, the destruction of economic and political arrangements, and the displacement of surviving populations into unfamiliar and often hostile new settings. Anthropologist Robert M. Hayden (2000), who investigates occurrences of mass rape in times of ethnic or nationalist conflicts, argues that mass rape is likely when the state itself is in a transitional or unsettled condition, with both its territory and its governance uncertain. However, when the state is not itself threatened, there is some evidence that rape is avoided, even when murder is accepted. In approaching such topics, some have chosen to speak in terms of social trauma—"events in life generated by forces and agents external to the person and largely external to his or her control and . . . generated in the setting of armed conflict and war" (Apfel and Simon 2000: 103). Psychoanalysts Roberta Apfel and Bennett Simon distinguish social traumas such as "separation and loss, imprisonment and exile, threats of annihilation, even death and mutilation" from the less devastating "ordinary traumas" or "necessary losses" that all people are likely to face, "such as the birth of a sibling, natural death of a parent or sibling, divorce, illnesses, and accidents, whether man-made or natural" (103).

Anthropologists investigating the causes and consequences of such large-scale trauma regularly work together with other specialists, including psychoanalysts such as Apfel and Simon, because such phenomena are so complex. The causes of large-scale collective violence involve psychic, social, political, economic, and cultural factors, and this sort of violence aims to destroy not just individual psychological functioning but also the physical body and the social order. Individual and cultural factors together bring about the trauma and are equally implicated in the ways in which survivors come to deal with trauma's aftermath (Suárez-Orozco and Robben 2000: 1).

This means, of course, that attempts to reduce explanations of large-scale collective forms of violence to either "nature" or "culture" are bound to be inadequate. Like many anthropologists, Marcelo Suárez-Orozco and Antonius Robben seek analysis in the intermediate zone "somewhere between those two analytical dead ends" (2000: 2). For example, attributing large-scale, collective forms of violence to some innate *individual* capacity for violence ignores the many differences between small-scale, face-to-face violent interchanges and the massing of armies and technology to wreak havoc on an "enemy" that is often not known personally. To grasp the complexities involved requires "multi-level approaches" that combine "solid understandings of the inner psychic processes as well as the social and cultural contexts of large-scale violence and trauma" (4).

Western scholarly and medical understanding of large-scale trauma developed over the course of the twentieth century. Phenomena called *shell shock* or *battle fatigue* were first identified in some soldiers during World War I (Figure 5.15). Although initially these soldiers were vilified as cowards who were morally corrupt, some researchers eventually proposed that the suffering these soldiers experienced could not be attributed to individual psychological or moral deficiency but needed to be seen as a consequence of the trauma inflicted by battlefield experience itself. The commitment in World War II to "total war" made the destruction of civilian populations and support structures as important as, or more important than, the destruction of soldiers on the battlefield. Indeed, the number of civilian casualties rose from 5 per cent in World War I to 50 per cent in World War II

(Suárez-Orozco and Robben 2000: 15). After World War II, attention was for the first time directed to the massive trauma to which civilians had been subjected, with particular attention focussed on the experiences of those who had survived Nazi concentration camps. Suárez-Orozco and Robben note that the pioneering work by psychoanalyst Bruno Bettelheim, for example, highlighted the "complex social dynamics between perpetrators and victims of violence" (17). This dynamic was revealed to be even more complex in later wars—for example, in the Vietnam War, during which the number of civilian casualties was over 80 per cent (15) and after which more than one-third of individual veterans suffered from what was officially designated as "post-traumatic stress disorder" (PTSD) in 1980 (20).

Suárez-Orozco and Robben note that societies as well as individuals need to heal. In both cases, successful healing requires the re-establishment of "basic trust": individuals need to find ways to trust other individuals, and all survivors need to be able to find ways to develop trust in the institutions of their society. Some dimensions of healing can be successfully promoted by the efforts of psychiatrists and medical specialists who focus on individuals; for example, interpreting the suffering of veterans in medical terms acknowledges that their suffering was not a consequence of their own personal defects but a consequence of the trauma they had experienced in war. At the same time, a continuing focus on individuals diverts attention away from the sociocultural dimensions of such trauma. "Combat trauma shatters the meaningfulness of the self and the world, and makes its sufferers put their bodies and minds on constant alert for any possible attack. They become distrustful of others, their own memories, and visual perceptions" (Suárez-Orozco and Robben 2000: 20). The taken-for-grantedness of everyday social life is destroyed, allowing "the uncanny"—"the dread and horror of social violence"—to become a recurring and unassimilable feature of their lives:

Those who experience such traumas are faced with an unbelievable and unreal reality that is incompatible with anything they knew previously. As a result, they can no longer fully believe what they see with their own eyes; they have difficulty in distinguishing between the unreal

FIGURE 5.15 World War I Canadian soldiers are brought to the field dressing station at Vimy Ridge, April 1917. Soldiers who have fought in wars often experience psychological disturbances as a result of their experiences on the battlefield. How can a better understanding of how trauma works help anthropologists?

reality they have survived and the fears that spring from their own imagination. . . . When one experiences the uncanny . . . what has been hidden becomes visible, what is familiar becomes strange and frightening. (Gampel 2000: 49–50)

We all experience a mild form of "the uncanny" when we find ourselves in situations of ambiguity—for example, when learning a new language or living in an unfamiliar society. But "the uncanny" experienced by war refugees, concentration camp survivors, or victims of state repression is more intense. "The feeling of uncanniness overwhelms us when we are thrust into a fragmented, violent social context, one without any continuity and which transmits extremely paradoxical messages" (55).

Individuals' responses to experiences of social trauma vary. For example, many survivors of Nazi death camps did not explicitly show signs of their severe trauma, but they revealed the lasting effects of their experiences through their general anxiety and over-protectiveness toward their children. Psychoanalysts can be effective in helping individuals who suffer from traumatic experiences in such ways, but many believe it is naïve and overly optimistic to imagine that a total "cure" is possible. Other survivors exhibit (and pass on to their children) a remarkable resiliency, "the capacity to survive violence and loss, and moreover, to have flexibility of response over the course of a life time," including "a sense of agency and a sense of capacity to choose—among courses of action and among conflicting moral values" (Apfel and Simon 2000: 103).

In still other cases, traumatized persons and groups turn to "hatred and violence as ways of coping with traumatic wounds" (Apfel and Simon 2000: 102). Vamik Volkan has described one way in which this can happen, in terms of what he calls a group's *"chosen trauma"* (quoted in Apfel and Simon 2000: 102). A chosen trauma arises, Volkan argues, from experiences of collective violence and loss that survivors are unable to mourn. This can lead to a collective focus on the group's past experiences of victimization, and the entire identity of the group's members may come to centre on the chosen trauma. Moreover, the chosen trauma can be passed on to subsequent generations along with the expectation that it is up to them to right past wrongs, using violence if necessary. "While the group does not consciously choose to feel victimized, it does choose to psychologize losses and to transform them into powerful cultural narratives which become an integral part of the social identity" (23). Volkan studied Christian Serbs, who for hundreds of years elaborated and passed their chosen

trauma: the loss of their empire to the Ottoman Turks in the early 1500s. Although this chosen trauma was not always in the forefront of Serbian actions during those centuries, it remained a powerful cultural resource that Serbian president Slobodan Milosevic and his cronies successfully exploited for their own political purposes in the 1990s, as the former Yugoslavia broke apart (23; Figure 5.16).

The power of chosen traumas derives in large part from the fact that they remain unmourned, thus cutting off possible forms of social and cultural healing that can rebuild trust in social institutions. Suárez-Orozco and Robben note, for example, that "institutional acknowledgement—in the form of 'truth' commissions and reparations (monetary and symbolic)—and justice—in the form of trials of perpetrators—can begin partially to restore the symbolic order that is another casualty of the work of violence" (2000: 5). These kinds of institutional acknowledgements, most often initiatives taken on the level of the nation-state, may coincide with more local actions (e.g., healing rituals) designed to aid recovery and rebuild social trust (22, 24).

The residential school trauma of First Nations peoples in Canada is an example of a large-scale social trauma that went unmourned for many years (see the "In Their Own Words" box, below). Today, the Canadian federal government is moving to compensation and various forms of reconciliation. Yet has this "institutional acknowledgement" gone far enough? Perhaps healing can emerge only once all Canadians become engaged—at some level—in the process and once the conditions that have resulted from the original trauma no longer limit the agency of the survivors.

All of these examples reveal how very much the personal is political. All violence and trauma affects the person and is therefore personal, but at the same time it is also an issue for societies. Everything from gendered violence (e.g., rape, honour killings) to child slavery to forced relocation due to persecution, war, or violence (refugees) starts with the individual but comes to be recognized through the group. Sociologist Srila Roy (2008) would call violence that happens on the personal level

FIGURE 5.16 The ruins of a house burnt down during the war in the former Yugoslavia stand next to a house newly built for returning Serbian families. Can physical reminders of a group's past experiences continue to impact that group after the original trauma? How?

IN THEIR OWN WORDS | A Place for Memory

Anthropologist Michael G. Kenny, from Simon Fraser University, discusses residential schools to which First Nations children were sent.

Boarding schools were seen as a practical necessity if Indian children were to be acculturated to the new European order. Government and church authorities thought it best for children to be taken away from their families and cultural milieu so that they could be "civilized," meaning that they would be taught to work and to be good Christians. While the Nazi concentration camp guards regarded Jewish inmates as *Urzgeziefer* (vermin), Native children often remember being regarded as dumb, dirty, lousy Indians. Seen in a certain light, the schools were a Dickensian horror: squalid, oppressive, and violent.

The Canadian Federal Government has responsibility for Native affairs. Given the vast size of the country, underfunding, and the absence of constitutional barriers limiting sectarian involvement in public education, the Canadian state in effect farmed Indian education out to the churches and most particularly to the Roman Catholic Church (the United Church of Canada and the Anglican Church were also involved, among others). The schools were often highly regimented, a discipline of much work and, at least at first, little play, insufficient food, and a high mortality rate—particularly from tuberculosis—brought about by the harsh and overcrowded conditions. Children were taken from their families, sometimes with consent, sometimes coercively. While in school, boys were separated from girls, sibling from sibling. The speaking of Indigenous languages was prohibited and little place made for Native culture.

This widely shared school experience has in recent times led to a sense of collective victimization and, inversely, to renewed self-assertion among Canadian Native peoples: "The residential school issue has united Native people across Canada like no other issue in recent history." But the way in which the residential school story has come to be told is a sign of our times. Sexual abuse allegations about what went on in the schools have multiplied, accompanied by numerous confessions and convictions, extending even to a Roman Catholic bishop: "What people make of their places is closely connected to what they make of themselves as members of society." What Native peoples now make of the residential schools has been accompanied by a sea-change in political consciousness.

It is now possible to speak of a Residential School Syndrome, of Native people as its survivors, and of what Euro-Canadians tried to do to them as "cultural genocide." Political and therapeutic discourses have become thoroughly intertwined around the central metaphor of "healing." It is said that, as the white world tried to deny Native history, so recovery of the hidden history of the residential schools affirms the persistence and constitutional status of the First Nations as a necessary step toward the restoration of integral personal and cultural identity. One such account actually attempts to drop the "healing" metaphor since, in the view of its authors, it tends to psychologize what is at root a political issue. What happened in the schools was not the product of an honest mistake on the part of misguided churches and a paternalistic government; instead, it was attempted genocide, as defined by the UN Genocide Convention—an Indian Holocaust.

Source: Kenny, Michael G. 1999. "A Place for Memory: The Interface between Individual and Collective History," *Comparative Studies in Society and History* 41, 3: 420–37.

"ordinary" or "everyday" violence, as opposed to the "extraordinary" violence of political terror that happens on a much broader and more public scale. Everyday violence is often widely accepted within a specific community due to cultural allowances—allowances that tend to normalize the brutalization of certain individuals on the basis of who holds the power to do so. Cultural allowances support such things honour killings, the selling of children into prostitution, and other such violences directed against the powerless. Unfortunately, there is often little recourse to this sort of violence, as the people who are in a position to help the victims (the police, lawmakers, elders, etc.) support the cultural values and/or the more powerful individuals responsible for perpetuating the violence (see, e.g., Zuckerhut 2011).

Individual Psychology and Context

Cross-cultural studies of human psychological functioning all stress the vital importance of *context*—not just the immediate context but also the displaced context of culture and history that may be invisible in local settings but present in people's habits of thought and feeling. Sometimes researchers can identify contextual factors with little effort. When administering a psychological test on visual illusions to the Fang in Gabon, for example, anthropologist James Fernandez (1980) discovered that many questioned his explanation of the "real" reason behind such a bizarre activity as psychological testing. He deduced that years of colonial domination and exploitation at the hands of outsiders made these people suspicious of his research motives.

Contextual factors shape human experiences in subtle ways as well, contributing to nuanced, holistic ethnographic understandings of other ways of making meaning. An excellent description of this kind of holistic experience is given by anthropologist Michael Gilsenan (1982), who worked for a time among urban Muslims in Cairo, Egypt (see Map 5.7). Gilsenan spent many hours with his informants, observing their prayers in the local mosque. Along the inside wall of the mosque were verses from the Quran shaped out of bright green neon tubing. Green is the colour of the prophet Muhammad, so finding that colour used prominently in mosque decoration is not surprising. However, Gilsenan's experiences in Western culture did not include schemas in which neon lights and serious worship went together, and for several months the neon interfered with his attempts to assume a properly reverential attitude. Then one day, Gilsenan reports, "I turned unthinkingly away from the swaying bodies and the rhythms of the remembrance of God and saw, not neon, but simply greenness. . . .

MAP 5.7 Cairo

No gaps existed between colour, shape, light, and form. From that unreflecting and unsuspecting moment I ceased to see neon at all" (1982: 266).

Nothing had happened to Gilsenan's eyes or his other senses, which continued to receive the same signals they had always received, but the meaning of the signals had been altered. Gilsenan's experience in the mosque situated neon light within a new schema, and his growing familiarity with that schema made the neon seem more and more natural. Eventually, Gilsenan was noticing only the colour green. He was still able to report, of course, that the green light was produced by green neon tubing; however, that fact seemed irrelevant given the new schema he used to interpret his experience.

These sorts of transformations of perception and understanding remain mysterious, but they seem to occur whenever we have an insight of any kind. Insights, like good metaphors, reshape the world for us, throwing new aspects into sharp focus and casting other aspects into the background. Our ability to achieve insights, like our ability to create good metaphors, remains a central and highly mysterious aspect of human psychological processes.

A CRITICAL LOOK | Malinowski and *The Sexual Life of Savages*

In 1929, Bronislaw Malinowski's *The Sexual Life of Savages in North-Western Melanesia* was published. For its day, it was a rather startling book, even within the field of anthropology. Academics and general readers alike considered the book's detailed discussion of sexuality to be quite racy. However, a close read of this ethnography gives us keen insights about the ways in which sex is embedded in the culture of the Trobriand Islanders. Throughout the work, Malinowski's commitment to holism shines forth.

In the preface to the book, anthropologist Havelock Ellis notes that sex as an anthropological subject has "always been veiled in mystery" (Malinowski 1929: vii). Ethnographic research on this topic, he continues, could proceed only because sex taboos had lost some of their "stringency" at the start of the twentieth century (x). Further, this sort of work required, in Ellis's view, "a rare combination of qualifications," including

1. access to scientific equipment,
2. familiarity with various new theories on the subject matter,
3. "long and intimate knowledge" of the people at the centre of the study,
4. "facility in the language," and
5. openness toward behaviours and expressions that might seem strange to most Westerners (ix).

Ellis saw that Malinowski had not only these qualities, in a "rare degree," but also patience in observation and sympathetic insight. Here, then, we have an excellent list of the requirements for the field anthropologist—background knowledge of the discipline and the peoples involved, ability to learn foreign languages, openness and lack of ethnocentrism, patience, and sympathy.

In many ways, Malinowski was ahead of his time. After all, he was writing about sex more than twenty years before Alfred Kinsey released his groundbreaking works *Sexual Behaviour in the Human Male* (1948) and *Sexual Behaviour in the Human Female* (1953). Malinowski also emphasized Trobriand women's social power and equality in family life

long before most Westerners wanted to become aware of issues of women's equality. Further, he approached two topics that remain somewhat taboo for us still—sexuality in childhood, and sexuality in the later years of life.

Perhaps Malinowski's most progressive—and at the time most controversial—contribution came from his observations on the sexuality of children and adolescents. To begin with, he notes that Trobriand parents allow their children freedom to engage with one another sexually. Indeed, childhood play is often replaced by amorous adventures that are serious but do not necessarily lead to permanent marriage arrangements. Children are emancipated from direct parental control at an early age, at which time they move away from their families to form their own communities. In these communities, they have plenty of opportunities "to receive instruction in erotic matters from their companions" (55). Further, children often "hear of and witness much of the sexual life of their elders" (54), making sex far less secretive and taboo than it is considered to be in Western cultures. At the same time, "there is no interference by older persons in the sexual life of children," as it is "considered both improper and silly for an older man or woman to have sexual dealings with a child" (59).

Malinowski's attention to the sexuality of older members of societies was also quite progressive for its time. He describes the Trobrianders as considering sex to be a natural part of later life. Sadly, anthropologists' and other Westerners' attention to older individuals' experiences of sex and sexuality remains largely inadequate. This is surprising if we consider how commonly sexual matters are discussed in today's media. Little of this discussion represents the sex life of the aging and the elderly. When the topic is approached, it is often from a medical perspective, as is the case with advertisements for erectile dysfunction drugs, personal lubricants, and sex-hormone replacement therapy. Thus, once again we find that we can learn much from an open anthropological perspective, and from the world views of people from cultures different from our own.

—Roberta Robin Dods

KEY TERMS

CHAPTER SUMMARY

1. Psychological anthropology can be grouped into four basic areas of human experience: perception, cognition, emotion, and motivation. Research overwhelmingly sustains the view that human psychological processes are open to a wide variety of influences.

2. Human psychological perception always takes place in a cultural context. Alternative understandings of a situation are possible because of the ambiguity of many perceptual signals. Both looking and seeing are culturally learned modes of sensory perception.

3. Some anthropologists argue that people in different cultures have different cognitive styles that ranging from global (field dependent) to articulated (field independent). Research suggests that the same individual may use a global style for some tasks and an articulated style for others.

4. Our emotions, like our thoughts, are culturally constructed. Different cultures conceptualize emotions differently. For this reason, it is often difficult to translate the language of emotion from one culture to another.

5. The mainsprings of motivation develop through socialization and enculturation. Humans must learn to pattern and adapt behaviour and ways of thinking and feeling to the standards considered appropriate in their respective cultures. Cognitive development results from a dialogue with others and the coaching they receive from others.

6. Different cultures conceptualize sex roles and gender roles differently. These roles greatly influence how individuals see themselves, how they define their place with a social group, and how they are perceived by others. Individuals' sexual practices vary greatly—both within a single culture and between different cultures.

7. Patterns of socialization and enculturation are sometimes overturned by experiences that intrude on predictable daily routines. Among the most powerful experiences are those occasioned by structural violence and social trauma, the investigation of which has become a significant topic for some contemporary psychological anthropologists.

CRITICAL THINKING QUESTIONS

1. Human psychology, like language, is an open system. How can the design features of language, in particular *displacement* and *prevarication,* help us to better understand human psychology?

2. Why is it sometimes difficult for individuals from different cultures to discuss specific emotions? Which aspects of emotion seem universal to the human experience? Which are defined by the culture in which a person lives?

3. How would you distinguish among sex, gender, and sexuality? How is gender culturally defined? What role do legislative decisions play in defining the boundaries of what the general population perceives as "normal" sexual behaviour?

4. In what ways have your cultural experiences shaped your sense of identity? Does you share a similar world view to that of your peers from similar backgrounds? Does your world view differ in any major ways?

SUGGESTED READINGS

Berlin, Brent, and David G. Casagrande. 2000. "Cognitive Prototypes in Tzeltal Maya Medicinal Plant Selection," available at http://gravlee.org/ang5091/proposals/casagrande_nsf.pdf. This article, an example of applied anthropology, discusses bridging the gap between traditional medicinal plant knowledge and Western biomedical knowledge, an important example of coming to understand taxonomies.

Bock, Philip K. 1999. *Rethinking Psychological Anthropology: Continuity and Change in the Study of Human Action*, 2nd edn (Prospect Heights, IL: Waveland Press). A thorough introduction to psychological anthropology, tracing developments from the early twentieth century to current directions in the field.

Cole, Michael, and Sylvia Scribner. 1974. *Culture and Thought: A Psychological Introduction* (New York: Wiley). A clear, readable survey of the literature and case studies on the cultural shaping of cognition.

D'Andrade, Roy G. 1995. *The Development of Cognitive Anthropology* (Cambridge: Cambridge University Press). An interesting and comprehensive review of the early application of theories of cognition. Chapter 5, which is on folk taxonomies, gives insight into shared salient cognitive features; of particular use here are the early studies of ethnobotany and ethnozoology.

Dods, Roberta Robin. 2004. "Knowing Ways/Ways of Knowing: Reconciling Science and Tradition," *World Archaeology* 36, 4: 547–57. This paper distinguishes two ways of knowing, traditional and scientific, suggesting their compatibility and utility for the development of a wider perspective in both anthropology and archaeology.

Harland, Robert, and Gerard Hutchinson. 2004. "Phenomenology, Science, and the Anthropology of the Self: A New Model for the Aetiology of Psychosis," *British Journal of Psychiatry* 185: 361–2, available at http://bjp.rcpsych.org/cgi/content/full/185/5/361. An examination of the links between psychoses such as schizophrenia and socioenvironmental factors.

Jansen, Willy. 1987. *Women without Men: Gender and Marginality in an Algerian Town.* (The Netherlands: E.J. Brill). An excellent examination of the lives of North African women, with deep comment on gender roles and social restrictions.

Lyons, Andrew P., and Harriet D. Lyons. 2006. "The New Anthropology of Sexuality," *Anthropologica*, 48, 2: 153–7. A good review of the history of anthropological studies of sexuality and a discussion of current work.

Schwartz, Theodore, Geoffrey M. White, and Catherine A. Lutz, eds. 1992. *New Directions in Psychological Anthropology* (Cambridge: Cambridge University Press). A survey of psychological anthropology, with articles by experts in the fields of cognition, human development, bio-psychological studies, and psychiatric and psychoanalytic anthropology.

RELATED WEBSITES

Anthropological Theories (Cognitive Anthropology) http://anthropology.ua.edu/cultures/cultures.php

Culture and Personality School www.encyclopedia.com/doc/1O88-CultureandPersonalitySchl.html

Definition of Terms: Sex, Gender, Gender Identity, Sexual Orientation www.apa.org/pi/lgbt/resources/sexuality-definitions.pdf

Optical Illusions http://allpsych.com/opticalillusions/index.html

6

Social Relationships: Marriage, Family, Kinship, and Friendship

CHAPTER OUTLINE

Marriage

Family Structure

Families and Change

Kinship and Systems of Relatedness: Ways of Organizing Human Interdependence

Beyond Kinship

Theories of Relatedness: Kin-based and Non–kin-based Societies

LEARNING OBJECTIVES

By the end of Chapter 6, you will be able to

- understand "marriage" as a social process,
- identify variations in family structure,
- consider how families change over time and in response to new circumstances,
- appreciate kinship patterns of descent,
- see kinship terminology as statements of rights and obligations,
- situate marriage and kinship in an economic world, and
- understand the value of friendship and voluntary alliances.

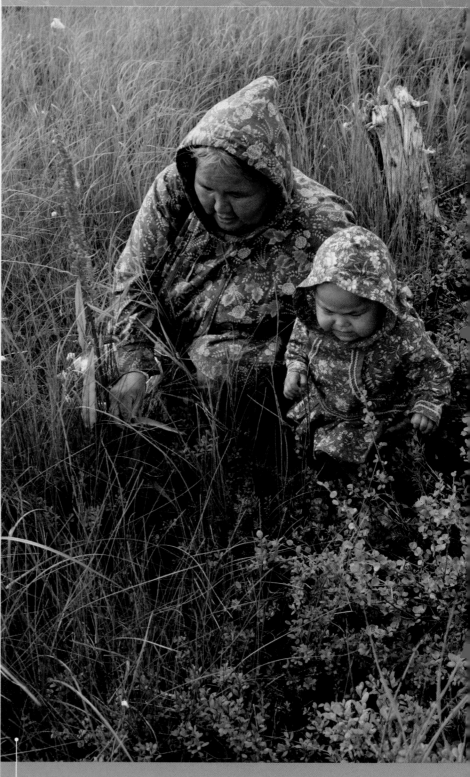

An elder Yupik woman and her granddaughter pick blueberries in south-western Alaska. Young children develop close ties to members of their kinship group, first to members of their immediate families and then to more distant relatives and acquaintances.

Human beings are highly social creatures. As such, we constantly endeavour to establish and maintain relationships with other people, thus warding off feelings of loneliness. Our need for companionship is well explored in Kurt Vonnegut Jr's science fiction novel *Slapstick, or Lonesome No More!* (1976). In the novel, Dr Wilbur Daffodil-11 Swain presents a plan to end loneliness with a new system of interrelatedness, one in which every person has a large number of relatives on whom they can depend. Swain proposes that everyone will be given a new middle name composed of a noun and a number (e.g., Daffodil-11). Everyone with the same noun will be cousins and everyone with the same noun and number will be siblings. A side effect is the development of clubs based on shared characteristics. While the setting is a fictional reimagining of America, the author's comments on loneliness resonate beyond the American context, illustrating that **relatedness** is a central concern for most of us. We all want to belong. Indeed, we define ourselves and our world based on the relationships we form and the positions we hold within specific groups.

We start life physically and emotionally tied to our mothers; as we grow, we become individuals. To survive on our own, we must bind ourselves to others through alliances of **marriage**, **family**, **kinship**, and **friendship**. We become enmeshed in a changing web of friends and relatives—some of whom we are related to through family lines, others of whom we are connected to through mutual affection. It is a web of rights and obligations. In this chapter, we focus on relatedness and how relatedness is selectively understood and culturally formed in our deeply layered social practices.

Marriage

Different cultures have different criteria for defining marriage. Some cultures recognize only heterosexual alliances, while others include same-sex partnerships. Some allow individuals only one spouse at a time, while others permit individuals to have multiple spouses at the same time. Some treat marriage as a prerequisite for sexual activity (especially for females), while others do not. Some insist on a ceremony and/ or a legal document to formalize a marriage, while others accept long-term cohabitation as a marker of such unions. Indeed, the definition of marriage has evolved in Canada over the past few decades, particularly after the Civil Marriage Act (2005) opened civil marriage to same-sex couples across the country. Today, more and more Western couples are choosing less rigidly defined forms of marriage (see tables 6.1 and 6.2).

Marriage always creates new *relationships*—between the individuals marrying one another, among their relatives, and among members of the wider society. Frequently, the community recognizes the new union by participating in the rites of marriage, thus accepting the newly married couple into the community. On the familial level, marriages affect *affinal* relationships

relatedness
The socially recognized ties that connect people in a variety of ways.

marriage
An institution that prototypically (1) involves a man and a woman, (2) transforms the status of the participants, (3) carries implications about sexual access, (4) gives offspring a position in society, and (5) establishes connections between the kin of a husband and the kin of a wife.

family
At minimum, a woman or a man and her or his dependent children.

kinship
Social relationships that are prototypically derived from the universal human experiences of mating, birth, and nurturance.

friendship
The relatively unofficial bonds that people construct with one another that tend to be personal, affective, and a matter of choice.

TABLE 6.1 Marital Status of Individuals 15 Years of Age and Older, Canada, 2011

	Not Living Common Law	Living Common Law
Single (never legally married)	7,816,050	2,255,290
Married (and not separated)	12,941,965	0
Separated (but still legally married)	698,245	128,200
Divorced	1,686,035	679,735
Widowed	1,584,530	79,305
Total	24,726,815	3,142,530

Note: *Common law* refers to two people living together as a couple but not legally married to each other.

Source: Adapted from Statistics Canada. 2013. "2011 Census of Canada." Data retrieved from http://www12.statcan.gc.ca/census-recensement/2011/dp-pd/tbt-tt/Rp-eng.cfm?LANG=E&APATH=3&DETAIL=0&DIM=0&FL=A&FREE=0&GC=0&GID=0&GK=0&GRP=1&PID=102095&PRID=0&PTYPE=101955&S=0&SHOWALL=0&SUB=0&Temporal=2011&THEME=89&VID=0&VNAMEE=&VNAMEF.

TABLE 6.2 Opposite-Sex and Same-Sex Couples, with and without Children, Canada, 2011

	Opposite-Sex Couples	Female Couples	Male Couples
Without Children	3,694,400	24,305	33,855
With Children	4,102,880	5,075	1,340
Total	7,797,280	29,380	35,195

Source: Adapted from Statistics Canada. 2013. "2011 Census of Canada." Data retrieved from www12.statcan.gc.ca/census-recensement/2011/dp-pd/tbt-tt/Rp-eng.cfm?LANG=E&APATH=3&DETAIL=0&DIM=0&FL=A&FREE=0&GC=0&GID=0&GK=0&GRP=1&PID=102659&PRID=0&PTYPE=101955&S=0&SHOWALL=0&SUB=0&Temporal=2011&THEME=89&VID=0&VNAMEE=&VNAMEF.

(relationships created via marriage, therefore based on *affinity*) as well as *consanguineal* relationships ("blood" relationships based on descent, regardless of whether the child is related by birth, adoption, sperm/ovum donation, or surrogacy). If the couple has children, these children will go on to form relationships of their own. Thus, many anthropologists choose to think of marriage as a social process.

Marriage as a Social Process

Seeing marriage as a social process allows us to describe all forms of marriage, including those that do not fit traditional Western definitions (Lamphere 2005; Figure 6.1). Marriage sets in place alliances that define essential social roles. It also establishes and reinforces rights

bridewealth
The transfer of certain symbolically important goods from the family of the groom to the family of the bride, representing compensation to the wife's lineage for the loss of her labour and for child-bearing capacities.

and obligations at the core of social life. Thus it evolves as societal norms change with changing times. For example, before Bill 16 was passed in 1964, a woman who entered marriage in Quebec lost her status as an independent adult unless she had a previously arranged legal contract, similar to what we would call a "prenup" (i.e., a pre-nuptial agreement) today. Under Quebec's Civil Code, a married woman without such a contract could not inherit property, open a bank account, or sign her children into hospital for treatment; these "rights" were reserved for her husband. Today, due in large part to social changes supporting women's equality, women in Quebec share these rights with their husbands.

A couple's post-marital living arrangements may reflect the role each partner is expected to adopt in familial and social relationships (see Table 6.3). In many societies, the couple is expected to live with a specific set of family members. Such arrangements, traditionally called "residence rules" by anthropologists, suggest how that culture understands family bonds.

Some cultures use creative marriage forms to develop specific social relationships. Anthropologist Edward Evans-Pritchard (1951) described two such forms present among the Nuer of East Africa in the early twentieth century. In the first form, a woman could marry another woman and become the "father" of the wife's children. To understand this sort of arrangement, we must distinguish between *pater* (social father role) and *genitor* (biological father or sperm provider role). To establish the marriage, the female husband (the *pater*) gave the bride's lineage cattle as **bridewealth** payments. Then, a male kinsman, friend, or neighbour (the *genitor*) impregnated the wife and contributed labour by performing tasks considered to be men's work. The female

FIGURE 6.1 Muslim brides wait for their turn during a mass wedding ceremony (an event in which many couples are married at the same time) in Hyderabad, India. The Indian government organized this mass wedding for financially poor Muslims. In what ways does this approach to marriage differ from traditional Western approaches?

TABLE 6.3 Patterns of Residence after Marriage

Pattern Name	Residence	Comments	Example
Neolocal (major pattern)	In a place of the couple's own choosing	Found in societies that are more or less individualistic in their social organization	Most Western nations, including Canada and the United States
Patrilocal (major pattern)	With (or near) the husband's father's family	Most common in herding and farming societies; observed by more societies in the contemporary world than any other residence pattern	China (villages and traditional communities); Turkey (villages and traditional communities)
Matrilocal (major pattern)	With (or near) the family in which the wife was raised	Most common in horticultural groups; the core of the social group consists of a woman, her sisters, and their daughters, together with their husbands	Iroquois (NE North America); Hopi (SW North America); Tlingit (NW Coast North America)
Avunculocal (major pattern)	With (or near) the husband's mother's brother	Found in matrilineal societies in which a boy inherits from his mother's brother	Chamorros (Mariana Islands); Taíno (Turks and Caicos Islands)
Ambilocal (minor pattern)	First with the family of one spouse and later with the family of the other	Eventually the couple chooses which family they want to affiliate with permanently	SE Porno and E Porno (California); Mbuti (NE Democratic Republic of the Congo)
Duolocal (minor pattern)	Each partner lives with members of his or her own lineage even after marriage	Seen where lineage membership is the most important societal aspect	Nayar (NE India); Minangkabau (Indonesia)

husband played the social role of a man. She could marry several women if her wealth permitted, and she could demand damage payment if any wife engaged in sexual activity (adultery) without her consent. She was the *pater* of her wives' children, who were of her patrilineage and called her "father." She administered her compound and her herds as any male head of household would, she was treated by her wives and children with the same deference shown to a male husband and father, and she fulfilled all her duties to her relatives through her role as a man.

The second form, *ghost marriage*, was more common. Since a basic obligation of Nuer kinship was for a man to be remembered through and by his sons, a man who died without male heirs became an unhappy, angry spirit. To appease this ghost, the man's kinsman—a brother or a brother's son—would marry a woman "to his name." Bridewealth cattle were paid in the ghost's name. From the marriage ceremony onward, the kinsman acted as husband and the children were commonly referred to as his—but legally they were the children of the ghost husband. The kinsman was *genitor*, but the ghost husband was *pater*, and the ghost husband's name would be remembered in the history of the lineage. Marrying a woman "to his kinsman's name" before the man himself married presented difficulties in subsequently contracting a marriage in his own right. Because he was already married, his relatives would want to allocate cattle for bridewealth to unmarried brothers. Even if he eventually accumulated enough cattle to afford to marry for himself, he would feel that those cattle should provide the bridewealth for the sons he had raised for his dead kinsman. He then died without any sons of his own, thus becoming an angry spirit in his own turn. Someone else (in fact, one of the sons he had raised for the ghost) had to marry a woman to *his* name and so the pattern continued.

This practice is similar to the more widely documented practice of levirate (discussed in the Bible in Deuteronomy 25: 1–5), in which a widow marries her deceased husband's brother. When it is a widower who marries a sister (or sometimes a specific cousin) of his deceased wife, the practice is known as *sororate*. There are advantages to such systems when considerable resources are invested in the marriage. Sororate also has the advantage of the stepmother being a kinswoman of any existing children from the first marriage, meaning that she is very likely to feel protective of those children.

Marriages are sometimes contracted within a particular social group, a practice called **endogamy**. Alternatively, when marriage partners must be found outside a particular group, it is called **exogamy**. In all societies, some close kin are off limits as spouses or sexual partners, specifically members of the nuclear family. This pattern is known as the *incest taboo*. Pressure to marry specific partners can be formally defined, covertly manoeuvred, or at least sensed in almost all societies. Collective identities of ethnicity, religion, language, class, and caste may be bounded by law or custom (see, e.g., Connolly 2009). In some cases, marrying outside the prescribed group can lead to social exclusion or even formal disenfranchisement (removal of rights). This was certainly true for Canadian First Nations women under the Indian Act (1876), which denied these women certain rights, including residency rights, if they married non-Native men. When the Act was amended, the great Mohawk activist Mary Two-Axe Earley (Figure 6.2) observed: "After all these years, I'll be legally entitled to live on the reserve, to own property, die and be buried with my own people" (*The Gazette*, 5 July 1985).

Monogamy and Polygamy

The number of spouses a person may have varies cross-culturally. **Monogamy** signifies one spouse at a time. This is the form of marriage that predominates in Canada. Before the twentieth century, divorce was rare, and people in European-style societies generally married only once unless they were widowed. Today, as some observers have noted, North Americans practise *serial monogamy*—that is, they marry several different people throughout their lives, but they are married to only one person at a time.

Polygamy allows a person to have more than one spouse. Polygamy has two subcategories: *polygyny* (multiple wives) and *polyandry* (multiple husbands). Polygynous societies vary in the number of wives permitted. Traditionally, a Muslim man may have four wives, but only on the condition that he can support them equally. Some Islamic theorists today argue that equal support must be emotional, not just financial. Convinced that no man can feel exactly the same toward each of his wives, these theorists have concluded that monogamy must be the rule. Other polygynous societies have no limit on the number of wives. Nevertheless, not every man can be polygynous—there are simply not enough women. Polygyny is also expensive, for a husband must support all his wives as well as their children (Figure 6.3).

Polyandry is much rarer than polygyny. Polyandrous societies tend to separate a woman's sexuality from her reproductive capacity, and

polygamy
A marriage pattern in which a person may be married to more than one person at a time.

endogamy
Marriage within a defined social group.

exogamy
Marriage outside a defined social group.

monogamy
A marriage pattern in which a person may be married to only one person at a time.

FIGURE 6.2 Mohawk activist Mary Two-Axe Earley, from Kahnawake, Quebec, was a catalyst for the establishment of Bill C-31, which led to the reinstatement of treaty status for First Nations women married to non-Native men.

FIGURE 6.3 The wives and children of a polygynous family. How might polygynous family structures affect the structure of a society?

some researchers have suggested that polyandry is uncommon because, unlike polygyny or even monogamy, it is not concerned with controlling women's sexuality (see, e.g., Levine and Sangree 1980). Anthropologists generally recognize three forms of polyandry: fraternal, associated, and secondary marriage.

Most anthropologists consider fraternal polyandry—particularly that found in Nepal and Tibet—to be the prototype for other forms of polyandry. Here the oldest brother serves as the groom, but all brothers, even those yet unborn, are married to the same woman in a publicly recognized wedding. The wife and her husbands live together patrilocally (see Table 6.3). All brothers have equal sexual access to the wife, and all act as fathers (*pater*) to the children without distinguishing the identity of the *genitor*. A notable exception is found with the Nyinba of Nepal (see Map 6.1), where each child is recognized as having one particular *genitor* (Levine 1980; 1988). Sexual jealousy is rare, and the brothers have a strong sense of solidarity with one another (Levine 1988). If the wife proves sterile, the brothers may marry another woman. Solidarity

of brothers is a central kinship ideal in societies that practise fraternal polyandry, and it helps to keep the household and the landholdings unified. Fraternal polyandry, by its essential structure, diminishes fragmentation of land holdings while limiting population growth (Mishra et al. 2003). Land and resources are limited, so the concentration of resources increases a household's political position and economic viability.

Associated polyandry is open to men who are not brothers (Levine and Sangree 1980). There is evidence it was an acceptable marriage variant with some peoples of the Pacific and North and South America. But it is best described with the Sinhalese of past generations, where polyandry began monogamously and a second husband was brought into the union later. The first husband was the principal husband in terms of authority, while each man looked after his own economic resources. Both husbands were considered fathers to any children the wife bore. Once the primary polyandrous relationship was established, the three spouses could decide to take another woman into the marriage—often the sister of the wife—creating a marriage pattern called *polygynandry*. Depending on relative wealth and the availability of economic opportunity, a traditional Sinhalese household may be monogamous, polyandrous, or polygynandrous.

With *secondary marriage*—as practised, for example, in northern Nigeria and northern Cameroon—a woman marries one or more *secondary* husbands while staying married to her first husband (Levine and Sangree 1980: 400). She lives with only one husband at a time, but she retains the right to return to a previous husband and to have legitimate children by him at a later date. There is no divorce; marriage is for life. However, men are as polygynous as women are polyandrous. A man marries a series of women and lives with one or more of them at his homestead, while the women independently pursue their own marital careers. Technically, secondary marriage is a combination of polyandry and polygyny, resulting from the overlap of men seeking several wives and women seeking several husbands. Thus, it can build extensive networks of marriage-based ties throughout a region (Levine and Sangree 1980).

Flexibility and Negotiation in Marriage

At this point, it may seem as though the rules that govern marriage are often rigid, compelling people to adhere to social norms and, at times, do things they do not want to do. Marriage rules, however, are always subject to some negotiation.

Sometimes, the contrast between the formal rules of marriage and the actual performance of marriage rituals is very revealing. For example, the Iteso (Map 6.2) take the marriage ritual very seriously, using it as the basis for the physical and social reproduction of Iteso patrilineages. Anthropologist

dowry
The transfer of wealth from parents to their child (usually a daughter) at the time of the child's marriage.

Ivan Karp (1978) analyzed the meaning of the Iteso marriage ritual from two perspectives: that of the men and that of the women. He found that the men's perspective presents the "official" view, which emphasizes how marriage brings the bride's sexuality and reproductive capacity under the control of her husband's lineage. By contrast, the women's "unofficial" view in a sense celebrates the fact that although men control women's bodies for reproduction, these bodies belong to outsider women. These same outsiders direct the two ritual events crucial to lineage reproduction—marriage and birth—and men of the lineage are not allowed to attend either ritual. Thus, women control the continued existence of patrilineages whose male members are supposed to control them! Iteso women see the irony in this: they are at once controlled and controlling. In the marriage ritual itself, they comment on this paradox through laughter. In doing so, the official ideology of male control is subverted, at least momentarily.

Marriage and Economic Exchange

Many societies transfer specific categories of symbolically important goods at marriage. These are called *bridewealth* and **dowry**. Bridewealth, briefly noted earlier with Nuer practices, is most common in patrilineal, patrilocal societies, although it is found in other types of societies as well, such as matrilineal societies with avunculocal residence rules (see Table 6.3). The goods exchanged may include shell ornaments, ivory tusks, brass gongs, bird feathers, cotton cloth, and animals. Bridewealth in animals is prevalent in eastern and southern Africa, where cattle have

MAP 6.1 Nyinba

MAP 6.2 Iteso

the most profound symbolic and economic value. In these societies, a man's father, and often his entire patrilineage, gives a specified number of cattle (often in instalments) to the patrilineage of the bride. Anthropologists view bridewealth as a way of compensating the bride's relatives for the loss of her labour and child-bearing capacities. Bridewealth formalizes the new **affinal** link. The bride's relatives, in turn, often use the bridewealth to find a bride for the woman's brother in yet another kinship group. In many societies in eastern and southern Africa, a woman gains power and influence over her brother when her marriage brings the cattle that will allow him to marry and continue their lineage; "Cattle beget children," according to the southern Bantu (Kuper 1982: 3)! This is why anthropologist Jack Goody describes bridewealth as "a societal fund, a circulating pool of resources, the movement of which corresponds to the movement of rights over spouses, usually women" (Goody and Tambiah 1973: 17).

Dowry is a transfer of family wealth, usually from parents to their daughter, at the time of marriage. It is found primarily in the agricultural societies of Europe and Asia but has been brought to some parts of Africa with the arrival of Islamic sharia law. In societies where both women and men are seen as potential heirs, dowry is sometimes regarded as the buyout of the inheritance. Dowries are often considered the wife's contribution to the establishment of a new household, to which the husband may bring other forms of wealth. In stratified societies, the size of a woman's dowry often ensures that when she marries she will continue to enjoy her accustomed lifestyle. The goods included in dowries vary in different societies and may or may not include land (Goody and Tambiah 1973).

Anthropologist and psychologist Leigh Minturn (1993) has examined dowry practices among the Khalapur Rajputs of northern India (see Map 6.3). Here all land is held by a group of brothers with their wives and children living as a joint family. Daughter's dowries consist of transportable items (chattels) such as money, jewellery, clothing, and household decorations. Rajput marriages are village exogamous and *hypergamous*: that is, women normally marry into lineages of higher status than the ones into which they were born, living as low-ranking outsiders in the households and villages of their husbands. How well they marry and how well they are treated by their in-laws depend on the size of their dowries. In the 1950s, when Minturn first visited Khalapur, new Rajput wives were under the strict control of their mothers-in-law, who assigned tasks, limited their contact with their husbands, and controlled their dowries. Every time a wife visited her parents, moreover, she was expected to return with more gifts for her husband's family.

Dowry practices can cause considerable financial strain on the family providing the dowry. As many Rajputs believe, "It is best to have two sons and one daughter, because then you will receive two dowries, but give only one" (Minturn 1993: 130). Yet sons do not always receive dowries. Poor people whose sons cannot attract women with dowries often engage in a practice called *buying*

affinal
Related through marriage.

MAP 6.3 Khalapur Rajputs

FIGURE 6.4 Dowry can take many forms, such as these wedding gifts at a celebration in Tamil Nadu, India.

a wife, in which the husband's family gives money to the bride's family to purchase her dowry goods.

In 1961, the government of India passed a law prohibiting dowries, but it has proven impossible to enforce. Dowry violence and death occur with alarming frequency in India.

> Dowry violence takes a characteristic form. Following marriage and the requisite giving of dowry, the family of the groom makes additional demands for the payment of more cash or the provision of more goods. These demands are expressed in unremitting harassment of the bride, who is living in the household of her husband's parents, culminating in the murder of the woman by members of her husband's family or by her suicide. The woman is typically burned to death with kerosene ... hence the use of the term *bride-burning* in public discourse. ... Police records do not match hospital records for third-degree burn cases among younger married women; far more violence occurs than the crime reports indicate. (van Willigen and Channa 1991: 369)

Also relatively frequent is the murder of widows to keep them from withdrawing their husband's portion of the land from traditional joint holdings. Some families also participate in the widespread practice of "selective female abortion" to avoid having to pay dowries in the future (van Willigen and Channa 1991: 370).

Family Structure

What is a family? At minimum, most anthropologists would point to the **non-conjugal family**: a parent (usually a woman) and dependent children. In this sort of arrangement, a second parent (usually the father) may be occasionally present or completely absent. Cross-culturally, non-conjugal families are usually rather infrequent, but in some large-scale industrial societies, including Canada, they have become increasingly common.

Many families are **conjugal families**. In most societies, the conjugal family members all live together. But in some matrilineal societies, the husband lives with his matrilineage (i.e., members of his mother's kinship line) while his wife and children live with theirs; the husband usually visits his wife and children on a regular basis.

The Nuclear Family

The structure and dynamics of neolocal monogamous families, or **nuclear families**, are familiar to North Americans. Somewhat surprisingly, this type of arrangement remains the prototype for many North Americans, even though only about 25 per cent of North Americans currently live in such families. In a nuclear family, each family member has a series of evolving relationships with every other member, and these relationships frequently involve feelings of jealousy, competition, controversy, and affection. Sibling rivalry, for example, is a form of competition characteristic of nuclear families; it is shaped by the relationships between siblings and between siblings and their parents.

The Polygynous Family

Another fairly common family arrangement is the polygynous family. In polygynous families, co-wives, individually and collectively, interact with each other and with the husband (Figure 6.5). Important distinctions are made between children with the same mother and children with a different mother. Children also have different kinds of relationships with their own mothers than they do with their fathers' other wives. In some polygynous cultures, a close connection with a particular brother or sister is emphasized by saying that he or she is "same father, same mother."

Where there is a significant inheritance, these relationships serve as the channels for jealousy and conflict. The children compete with one another for their father's favour, and each mother tries to protect the interests of her own children, sometimes at the expense of her co-wives' children. Among the Mende of Sierra Leone (see Map 6.4), co-wives come to compete with each other. Anthropologist Caroline Bledsoe (1993) explains that this competition is often focussed on how many children each wife has and how likely it is that each child will obtain things of value, especially education. Here husbands try to avoid overt signs of favouritism, but wives are ranked by order of marriage and by the status of their natal (birth) families. Such rankings lay the groundwork for rivalries.

---

nuclear family
A family made up of two generations: parents and their unmarried children.

non-conjugal family
A woman (or, less commonly, a man) and her (or his) children, with or without a second parent.

conjugal family
A family based on marriage; at minimum, a spousal pair and their children.

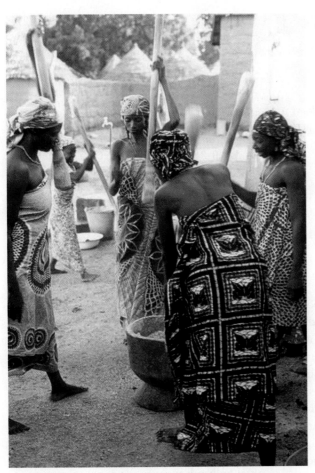

FIGURE 6.5 Co-wives in polygynous households frequently co-operate in daily tasks such as food preparation. What might be some of the advantages and disadvantages to this sort of family arrangement?

To a Mende mother, a child's education is of immense importance. She depends on the income that child may earn to support her. Education often requires a significant cash outlay, and a man may be able to send only one child to school, or he may be able to send one child to a prestigious private school only if he sends another to a trade apprenticeship. These economic realities can lead to bitter feuds—and even divorce—as co-wives blame the husband for disparities in the accomplishments of their children. To avoid these problems, children are frequently sent to live with relatives who will send them to school. Also important are the rights to inherit property and positions of leadership from the father.

Extended, Joint, and Blended Families

Some societies have expanded definitions of the central family unit. Two traditional examples are the **extended family** and the **joint family**. In an extended family, the role each member plays in the family dynamic is tied to his or her position as a parent and grandparent, an adult child and parent, or a child and grandchild. In a joint family, the dynamic is less constant. For example, consider the possible situation of a joint family composed of a father and his married sons, as well as the sons' wives and children. Upon the death of the father, the eldest son inherits the position as household head. His younger brothers may not accept his authority as readily as they did their father's, and they may decide to establish separate households. Each brother usually hopes then to start his own joint family; eventually, his sons will bring their wives into the household, and a new joint family will emerge. Something similar happens among the polyandrous Nyinba discussed earlier. A group of brothers may take a second wife. At first, all brothers have equal sexual access to both wives, but in time they tend to form groups around each wife, eventually choosing to split the household in two.

In recent decades in North America, anthropologists have observed the emergence of a new family type: the **blended family**. The internal dynamics of such a family—which can come to include one or both parents' children from previous unions, as well as children the couple have together—may resemble the dynamics of polygynous families, with complex relations among the children and between each child and each parent.

extended family
A family pattern made up of three generations living together: parents, married children, and grandchildren.

joint family
A family pattern made up of brothers and their wives (or sisters and their husbands) along with their children and sometimes their parents living together.

blended family
A family created when previously divorced or widowed people marry, bringing with them children from their previous marriages.

MAP 6.4 Mende

EthnoProfile 6.1   Ashanti

Region Western Africa

Nation Ghana

Language Various dialects of Twi (Akan), a member of the Niger-Congo language group

Population 3.7 million (2011 estimate)

Environment Slightly inland, partly mountainous

Livelihood Farming, fishing, market trading (women)

Political organization Traditionally, a kingdom; today, part of a modern nation-state

For more information Fortes, Meyer. 1950. "Kinship and Marriage among the Ashanti," in *African Systems of Kinship and Marriage*, eds A.R. Radcliffe-Brown and Daryll Forde (Oxford: Oxford University Press); Clark, Gracia. 1995. *Onions Are My Husband* (Chicago: University of Chicago Press).

Brother–Sister Relationships

In North America, the relationship of the spousal pair ordinarily takes precedence over the brother–sister relationship. Yet in some societies, the most important adult relationships a man or a woman can have are those with his or her opposite-sex siblings. Anthropologist Meyer Fortes (1950) gave us the classic illustration from the Ashanti (EthnoProfile 6.1; Figure 6.6), where the central legal relationship is the tie between brother and sister. Legal power is vested in males, and brothers have power over the children of their sisters since all belong to a common matrilineage. A sister has claims on her brother because she is his closest female relative and represents the only source of the continuity of

his lineage. "Men find it difficult to decide which is more important to them, to have children or for their sisters to have children. But after discussion most men conclude that sad as it may be to die childless, a good citizen's first anxiety is for his lineage to survive" (1950: 274–5). More than this, the Ashanti brother and sister are close confidants on matters ranging from property and financial management to matrimonial difficulties (275). This closeness is reinforced by the Ashanti residence pattern: people live in their matrilineages' neighbourhoods, and, often, husbands and wives do not live together.

According to anthropologist Gracia Clark (1994), the status of women within Ashanti matrilineages has eroded since the 1940s. Clark, who did fieldwork in Kumasi, Ghana, in the 1980s, observed that the women she knew could still turn to their matrilineages for support against the risks of divorce, illness, or bankruptcy. At the same time, support beyond subsistence level is not automatic and must be negotiated between a woman and her kin. Clark concludes that Ashanti girls and women "unfortunately seem to be increasingly marginalized within their lineages, in leadership, residence, and inheritance" (335).

In patrilineal societies, the strength of the brother–sister relationship depends on how the kinship group is organized. Where sisters do not move too far from home upon marriage, and where they are not incorporated into their husbands' lineages, a group of brothers and sisters may control the lineage and its economic, political, social, and religious aspects. The senior members of the lineage—males and females alike—exercise control over the junior members, although the brothers generally have more control than do the sisters.

FIGURE 6.6 The men and women living in the Ashanti's matrilineal society are close confidants, often siding with their opposite-sex siblings over their spouses. What might be some of the advantages and disadvantages to this sort of family arrangement?

Families of Choice

Not everyone defines a family as individuals connected through marriage or genetics (or adoption). For example, anthropologist Kath Weston (1991) looked at family forms among gay and lesbian individuals in the San Francisco Bay Area during the 1980s. A lesbian herself, Weston knew that a turning point in the lives of most gay and lesbian individuals was the decision to announce their sexual orientation to their parents and siblings. Sadly, this announcement sometimes resulted in parents turning their child away, thus rejecting the bonds of blood. Living through—or even contemplating—such an experience has been enough to force many gay and lesbian individuals to think seriously about the sources of family ties.

By the 1980s, some North American gay and lesbian individuals had reached two conclusions:

1. blood ties *cannot* guarantee solidarity, and
2. new kin ties *can* be created over time as friends and lovers demonstrate their genuine commitment to one another by creating **families of choice**.

"Like their heterosexual counterparts, most gay men and lesbians insisted that family members are people who are 'there for you,' people you can count on emotionally and materially" (Weston 1991: 113). Some gay kinship ideologies now argue that "whatever endures is real" as a way of claiming legitimacy for chosen families. Such a definition of family is compatible with understandings of kinship based on nurturance.

Families and Change

Families change over time. New households branch off from old. The same family can take on different forms and provide different opportunities for the interaction of family members at different points in time. Existing households commonly change through death, divorce, remarriage, the departure of children, and the break-up of extended families.

Individuals' sense of family belonging changes over time as well. Edward Evans-Pritchard noted that for Nuer women, affinal ties gradually became kinship ties: *ruagh* (in-law relationships) became *mar* (kinship) (1951: 96). The birth of a child gave the wife kinship with her husband's relatives, and it gave the husband kinship with his wife's relatives. In many patrilineal societies, a woman begins to identify with and become more interested in the affairs of her husband's lineage, partly because she comes to be more intimate with the details of the lineage over the years. More significantly, however, what had been her *husband's* lineage becomes her *children's* lineage. The children create a link to the lineage that is independent of her husband.

Divorce and Remarriage

There are very few societies today in which divorce is not recognized. Depending on the society, nagging, quarrelling, cruelty, stinginess, or adultery may be cited as causes for divorce. In almost all societies, childlessness is grounds for divorce as well.

In some societies, the process is long, drawn-out, and difficult, especially when bridewealth must be returned. A man who divorces a wife in such societies, or whose wife leaves him, expects some of the bridewealth back. But for the wife's family to give the bridewealth back, a whole chain of marriages may have to be broken up. Brothers of the divorced wife may have to divorce to get back enough bridewealth from their in-laws. Sometimes a new husband will repay the bridewealth to the former husband's line, thus letting the bride's relatives off the hook.

In other societies, divorce is easier. For example, the Fulbe of Guider, Cameroon, prefer that a man marry his father's brother's daughter. In many cases, such marriages are contracted simply to oblige the families involved; after a few months, the couple splits up. In general, there is enough dissatisfaction with marriage in Guider to make household transformation through divorce quite common.

Among Muslims in Guider, divorce is controlled by men; women are not legally allowed to initiate divorces. If a husband wants a divorce, he need only follow the simple procedure laid down in the Quran and sanctioned by long

family of choice
A family created over time by new kin ties as friends and lovers demonstrate their genuine commitment to one another.

practice: he appears before two witnesses and pronounces the formula "I divorce you" three times. He is then divorced, and his wife must leave his household. She may take an infant with her, but any children at the toddler stage or older stay with the father. If she takes an infant, she must return the child to the father's household by the time the child is six to eight years old. Yet the wife is not entirely powerless. Although a woman cannot ask for a divorce directly, she can facilitate an escape from an unsatisfactory marriage by neglecting her household duties or by going to live in the compound of her father or brother.

For the Ju/'hoansi of the Kalahari Desert (see EthnoProfile 6.2), most divorces are initiated by women. The most common reasons for divorce among the Ju/'hoansi are a woman's displeasure with her husband and her desire to no longer be married (Lee 1992b; Shostak 1981). After what is often a considerable debate, the couple simply separates. There is no bridewealth to return, no legal contract to be renegotiated. Mutual consent is all that is necessary. The children go with the mother. Ju/'hoansi divorces are generally cordial: ex-spouses may continue to joke with each other and even live next to each other with their new spouses (Lee 1992b).

Traditional northwestern Inuit view all kin relationships, including marital ones, as permanent (Burch 1970). A husband and wife who stop having sexual relations and stop living with each other are considered to be separated and ready for another marriage. If each member of a separated couple remarries, then the two husbands of the wife become co-husbands, the two wives of the husband become co-wives, and the children of the first and second marriages become co-siblings. In such cases, a "divorce" results in more, not fewer, connections.

International Migration and the Family

Families also change their structure in response to external social pressures. In our globalized world, migration to find work in another country has become increasingly common. Anthropologist Eugenia Georges (1990) examined the effects of this sort of migration on people who migrated to the United States from Los Pinos, Dominican Republic (see Map 6.7). Families were divided, with some members moving to New York. Sometimes spouses separated, with the husband migrating and the wife staying home. Consequently, many households in Los Pinos were headed by women. In most cases, the husband worked to help his wife and children migrate. But relocating an entire family across an international border takes a significant amount of time and money. Children who were close to working age migrated, frequently with their mother, and younger children were sent for as they approached working age. After several years in the United States, the couple who started the migration cycle would often take their savings and return to the Dominican Republic while their children stayed in the United States and continued to send money home. Even when the husband was geographically separated from

EthnoProfile 6.2 | Ju/'hoansi (!Kung)

Region Southern Africa

Nation Botswana and Namibia

Language Ju/'hoan, part of the Ju language family

Population 50,000 (1996 estimate)

Environment Desert

Livelihood Hunting and gathering

Political organization Traditionally, egalitarian bands; today, part of modern nation-states

For more information Lee, Richard B. 2013. *The Dobe Ju/'hoansi*, 4th edn (New York: Holt, Rinehart, & Winston); Hitchcock, Robert K. 2003. "Land, Livestock, and Leadership among the Ju/'hoansi San of North Western Botswana," *Anthropologica* 45, 1: 89–94.

MAP 6.7 Los Pinos

his family, he maintained an active role as the breadwinner and the main decision-maker in the household through visits, letters, and occasional telephone calls. Georges found that the divorce rate was slightly lower than average in migrant families, likely because dense and frequent exchange of information between Los Pinos and New York maintained strong ties of spousal affection.

In recent years, the Internet has become increasingly important in the lives of families that are separated by migration, education, work, and so on. Anthropologist Daniel Miller and sociologist Don Slater (2000) studied Internet use in Trinidad, finding that email and instant messaging have strengthened considerably both nuclear and extended families, allowing closer relations between distant relatives. They remark on the experiences of a widow they knew who, depressed after her husband's death, was convinced by relatives to learn to use email to contact a beloved grandchild who had gone abroad. This experience was so valuable to her that she began to contact other relatives, and younger members of her family "swear it has given [her a] 'new lease of life'" (2000: 61). Anthropologist Katy Gardner (2008) also observes, in her work on Bangladeshi people settled in British communities, that online communication can help migrants overcome "the political insecurity and social exclusion" they commonly experience in their new countries (277). Overall, the Internet offers a variety of tools that can help people feel connected to one another over great distances.

Kinship and Systems of Relatedness: Ways of Organizing Human Interdependence

So far, we have discussed systems of relatedness in terms of *marriage* and *family*. But there are other forms of relatedness as well—for example, those based on *nurturance* or *invited kinship*. As you might expect, these sorts of relationships are sometimes difficult to define precisely.

Early anthropologists focussed mainly on relations of biology, believing that Western understandings of "real" relatives—mothers, fathers, sisters, brothers, sons, daughters, and so on—were universally valid. They saw their job as comparative and formal, and they searched for organizational patterns along genealogical (descent) lines. They tried to specify the formal "rules" that would be characteristic of, for example, all patrilineal societies. Although this work did bring some important patterns to light, ethnographic evidence indicated that the principles of relatedness that any group of people used to organize themselves were sometimes at odds with genealogical principles. Indeed, in some cases, relatedness based on *birth* was only one of several ways in which people created strong and enduring ties with one another.

Today, anthropologists tend to take a broader approach when they examine relatedness in a particular culture. They continue to focus on relationships that stem from universal human experiences of mating, birth, and nurturance, but they also recognize that definitions of these experiences are not the same in every culture. Many people distinguish between *mating* and *marriage*. In some cultures, children whose parents are not married to each other are not seen as legitimate descendants of those parents. Understandings of descent can be even more complicated in cases of adoption, surrogacy, and conception through sperm and/or egg donation. Even nurturance is not necessarily a sign of enduring relatedness—consider, for example, foster parents in Canada: custody of foster children is officially temporary.

Forms of relatedness are thus selective. One society may emphasize women as the bearers of children and base its kinship system on this fact.

bilateral descent
A pattern of descent in which a descent group is formed based on connections of relatedness made through *both* a mother *and* a father.

unilineal descent
A pattern of descent in which a descent group is formed based on connections of relatedness made through *either* a father (patrilineal descent) *or* a mother (matrilineal descent).

Ego
The person from whose perspective the kinship associations are being mapped and/or discussed.

Another society may trace connections through men, emphasizing the paternal role in conception. A third society may encourage its members to adopt not only children but also adult siblings, blurring the link between biological reproduction and family creation. All three understandings can be justified with reference to the pan-human experiences of relatedness.

Consider the English-language kinship term *aunt*. This term most often refers to a woman occupying a unique position in one of four different ways:

1. father's sister,
2. mother's sister,
3. father's sibling's wife, or
4. mother's sibling's wife.

The women in these positions have something in common: they are sisters or sisters-in-law of your parents. But we may also refer to our mother's best friend as an *aunt*, thereby choosing to recognize her as a family member. In Chile, this concept is applied more broadly: children regularly use *tía* (Spanish for "aunt") to refer to female friends of their parents. Indeed, well into early adulthood, Chileans continue to use the term to refer to women who take on the role of "mother" but with whom they are not as intimate as they are with their own mothers.

Because understandings of relatedness differ cross-culturally, anthropologists tend to understand *kinship* as resulting from a selective interpretation of common human experiences. The principles of kinship are generally used to assign individuals to certain groups of relatedness. They also typically cover several significant issues, including

1. how to carry out the "recruiting" of legitimate group members (marriage, birthing, or adoption),
2. where group members should live (residence rules),
3. how to establish inter-generational links (descent), and
4. how to pass on social positions (succession) or material goods (inheritance).

In this way, people are located within social groups in relation to one another both in space and over time.

Patterns of Descent in Kinship

A central aspect of kinship is descent. Defined by ancestry, descent involves the transmission of group membership through parent–child links. Globally, there are two major patterns of descent: **bilateral descent** and the more common **unilineal descent**.

Bilateral Kindreds

Most Canadians are familiar with the bilateral kindred, a kinship group that forms around a particular individual. It includes all the people linked to that individual through kin of both sexes—people conventionally called *relatives* in English (Figure 6.7). These people form a group only because of their connection to the central person, known in the terminology of kinship as **Ego** (Latin for "I" or "the self"). Each person within Ego's bilateral kindred has his or her own separate kindred. For example, Ego's father's sister's daughter has a kindred that includes people related to her through her father and his siblings—people to whom Ego is not related. The major strength of bilateral kindred is that it can form broad networks; its major weakness is that it does not endure beyond the lifetime of the Ego at its centre.

A classic bilateral kindred is found among the Ju/'hoansi (see Figure 6.8; see also Ethno-Profile 6.2). Canadian anthropologist Richard B. Lee points out that every individual in Ju/'hoansi society can be linked to every other individual by a kinship term, either through male or female relatives.

> In essence, a Ju/'hoansi camp consists of relatives, friends, and in-laws who have found that they can live and work well together. Under this flexible principle a Ju/'hoansi, during his or her lifetime, may live at many water holes with many different groups but always in the presence of kin. (1992b: 62)

A wide range of kin-people makes flexibility possible. However, such social flexibility can become problematic in at least four kinds circumstances:

1. where clear-cut membership in a particular social group must be determined,

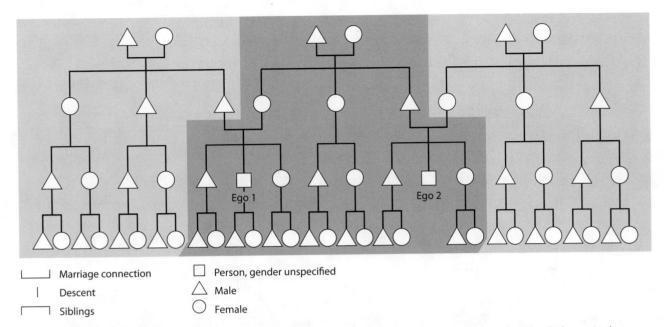

Marriage connection		▢ Person, gender unspecified
I Descent		△ Male
Siblings		◯ Female

FIGURE 6.7 A bilateral kindred includes all recognized relatives on Ego's father's and mother's sides. The dark area in the centre indicates where the kindreds of Ego 1 and Ego 2 overlap.

2. where social action requires the formation of groups that are larger than individual families,

3. where conflicting claims to land and labour must be resolved, and

4. where people want to maintain a particular social order over time.

Unilineal Descent Groups

Unilineal descent groups, found all over the world, are based on the principle that certain kinds of parent–child relationships are more important than others. In a patrilineal society, women and men belong to a patrilineage formed by father–child links (Figure 6.9); in a matrilineal society, men and women belong to a matrilineage formed by mother–child connections (Figure 6.10). Membership in the group is, on the face of it, unambiguous. Individuals belong to only one lineage. Yet, as French ethnologist Martine Segalen observes, a pattern of unilineal descent is "no more than a kind of external framework" that can support a wide range of cultural variations (1986: 51–2).

Lineages

Lineages vary in size, ranging from twenty or thirty members to several hundred or more. They can endure as long as people remember the descent lines. Generally, the memory covers five generations (grandparents, parents, Ego, children, and grandchildren). Lineages are *corporate* in their organization—that is, a lineage has a single legal character. As the Ashanti (see EthnoProfile 6.1) put it, a lineage is "one person" (Fortes 1953). To outsiders, all members of a lineage are equal *in law* to all others. Lineages are also corporate in that they control property, especially land and water, as a unit.

lineage
A descent group composed of blood relatives who believe they can trace their descent from known ancestors.

FIGURE 6.8 This Ju/'hoansi grandmother and her grandchild are members of a bilateral kinship group.

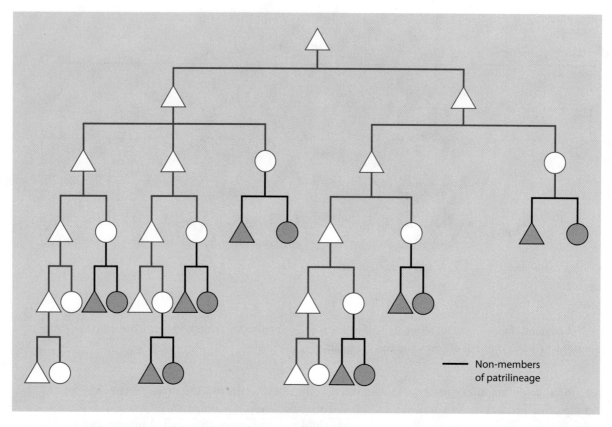

FIGURE 6.9 Patrilineal descent: all those who trace descent through males to a common male ancestor are indicated in white.

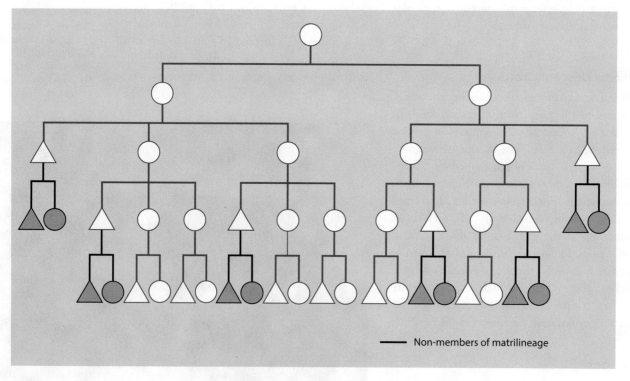

FIGURE 6.10 Matrilineal descent: all those who trace descent through females to a common female ancestor are indicated in white.

When members of a group believe that they are related to one another but can no longer specify ancient descent links, they arrange themselves in a **clan**. Members of a clan usually believe that they share a common ancestor in the distant past. This ancestor may be a powerful animal or shape shifter—for example Raven, who is recognized among many Native North American cultures and believed to have lived at the beginning of time. Often, clans transmit beliefs about their common ancestry across generations through stories or legends that offer mythical justifications for the arrangements of the society. Many clans apply the incest taboo within their group; among the Nuer of East Africa, for example, clan members recognize that they cannot marry each other, and they consider sexual relations within the group to be incestuous. In addition, as with lineage, clan membership often brings with it certain political and legal statuses.

Patrilineages

By far the most common form of lineage organization is the patrilineage. Central is the father–son relationship. Women normally leave their childhood homes when they marry, although they may have active roles in their own patrilineages for many years.

An assumption of hierarchy exists in patrilineal societies: men believe they are superior to women, and many women seem to agree. However, there is an irony at the heart of these societies, as we suggested earlier in relation to the Iteso—the future of the patrilineage depends on people (women) who do not belong to it! A second irony is that women must leave their own lineages to produce the next generation of somebody else's lineage. Women in patrilineal societies are often torn between conflicting interests and loyalties. Should they support their own children, or should they support their fathers and brothers?

A classic patrilineal system was found among the Nuer of East Africa. In the 1930s, Edward Evans-Pritchard noted twenty clans that were each segmented into separate lineages (see Figure 6.11 for an illustration of this sort of segmentation). The most basic segment constituted the *minimal lineage*, which consisted of

clan
A descent group formed by members who believe they have a common ancestor, even if they cannot specify the genealogical links.

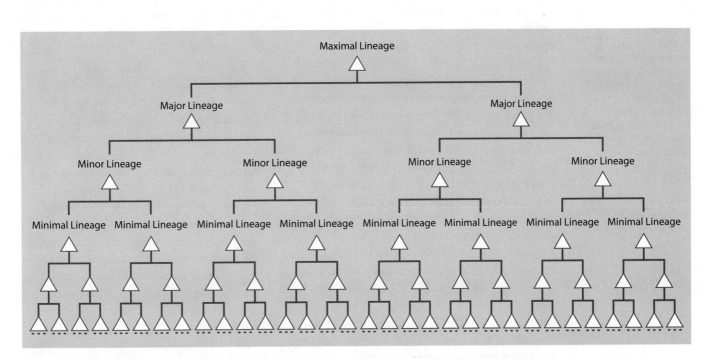

FIGURE 6.11 From a founder recognized by all descendants, lineages develop through *segmentation* across generations. The complexity of this segmentation is determined by the number and gender of the members of each generation.

three to five generations. Members of one minimal lineage could consider themselves related to another minimal lineage through ancient family connections—for example, if the founder of the first minimal lineage had been the brother of the founder of the second minimal lineage. Two minimal lineages related in such a way formed a *minor lineage*, which was composed of all those descended from the common father of the two founders. Minor lineages connected to other minor lineages by yet another presumed common male ancestor, forming *major lineages*. These major lineages were also believed to share a common male ancestor and thus formed a *maximal lineage*. The members of two maximal lineages believed their founders had been the sons of the clan's founding ancestor; thus, all members of the clan are believed to be patrilineally related.

Disputes among the Nuer emerged and dissipated along lineage lines. If a quarrel erupted between two men whose minimal lineages were in different minor lineages, each would be joined by men who belonged to his minor lineage. The dispute would be resolved when the quarrelling minor lineages recognized that they were all part of the same major lineage. Similarly, the minor lineages of one major lineage would ally if a dispute with an opposed major lineage broke out. This common social process of dispute resolution, expressed in kinship terms, is called **segmentary opposition**.

segmentary opposition
An approach to dispute resolution and social organization in which groups beyond the most basic emerge only in opposition to other groups on the same hierarchical level.

Nuer lineages are also politically significant. Members of a lineage often share rights in a given territory and in property such as cattle. Thus, men generally derive their wealth and their status from their lineage. When a man marries, members of his lineage support the union by providing the bridewealth cattle. When a man is killed, members of his lineage avenge his death and hold funeral ceremonies. Yet relationships among the members of a patrilineage are not always harmonious, and conflicts are not always easily resolved. Tension may develop, for example, when individual interests conflict with the interests of the group (see Evans-Pritchard 1951). In addition, relationships can be stressed by societal conflict. For example, the civil war that led to the separation of South Sudan in 2011, at a time of drought and famine, caused many deaths and much fragmentation of Nuer kinship.

Matrilineages

Matrilineages are more than just mirror images of patrilineages. Anthropologists find it difficult to generalize about matrilineal societies, and ethnographic evidence suggests a case-by-case approach is more helpful. However, there are a few common features. First, the central relationship is the sister–brother pair; a matrilineage may be thought of as a group of brothers and sisters connected through links made by women. Brothers marry out and often live with the family of their wives, but they maintain essential interest in the affairs of their birth lineage. Second, a matrilineage is not the same thing as a *matriarchy* (a society in which women rule); brothers often retain controlling interest in the lineage, and inheritances are generally passed to a man from his mother's brother.

A representative example of a matrilineal society comes from the Navajo (Map 6.8). For the Navajo, the traditional basic unit of social organization is composed of a head mother, her husband, some of their children, and these children's spouses and children (Witherspoon 1975: 82). The visible leader of the unit is normally a man, usually the husband of the head mother. He directs livestock and agricultural operations, deals with the outside world, and generally seems to be in charge. In actuality, it is the head mother around whom the unit is organized, as she

> is identified with the land, the herd, and the agricultural fields. All residence rights can be traced back to her, and her opinions and wishes are always given the greatest consideration and usually prevail. In a sense, however, she delegates much of her role and prestige to the leader of the unit. If we think of the unit as a corporation, and the leader as its president, the head mother will be the chairman of the board.... When there is a divorce between the leader and the head, it is always the leader who leaves and the head mother who returns, even if the land originally belonged to the mother of the leader. (82–3)

In most matrilineal societies, there are some domains of experience in which men and women are equal, some in which men are in control, and some in which women are in control.

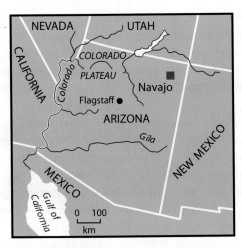

MAP 6.8 Navajo

Men living in a matrilineal society may have conflicted feelings surrounding the rules of inheritance. A man may feel great affection for his father, but he will not be his father's heir. He will inherit from his mother's brother, who lives elsewhere. And although a father may wish to have his son inherit from him, he must give to his sister's son (Richards 1954). Bronislaw Malinowski found evidence of such mixed feelings among Trobriand Islanders (see EthnoProfile 7.1). Subsequently, American anthropologist Annette Weiner argued that to understand matrilineal kinship in the Trobriand Islands, one must see the sister–brother pair as an integral unit, with each member making important contributions to the continuation of the lineage: a boy's mother gives him life, while his mother's brother gives him material inheritance (1980: 286–7).

Kinship Terminologies and Classification

People everywhere use special terms to refer to people they recognize as relatives. Table 6.4 shows the terms in general use in English. Other cultures use different terms—sometimes there are more terms, sometimes fewer. As you might expect, kinship terms do not always retain the same meanings and associations as they are translated across cultures and languages. Anthropologists David Greenwood and William Stini offer an example: "Just as the word *father* in English means a great deal more than lineal male ancestor of the first ascending generation, *aita* in Basque has many local connotations irreducible to *father*, as we understand the term" (1977: 333).

Yet despite cross-cultural differences in conceptualizing kinship connections, anthropologists have been able to identify a variety of kinship roles

TABLE 6.4 English Kinship Terms

	Position and Kinship Chart Abbreviation
Nuclear Family	mother
	father
	daughter
	son
	sister
	brother
Extended Family	aunt
	uncle
	niece
	nephew
	cousin
	grandmother
	grandfather
	granddaughter
	grandson
	great-grandmother
	great-grandfather
Affines (marriage)	wife
	husband
	sister-in-law
	brother-in-law
	mother-in-law
	father-in-law

and patterns that appear in multiple societies. Table 6.5 lists, in order from most to least common, the main criteria that anthropologists have found people use to classify kinship relationships. By examining how individuals apply these criteria within their societies, anthropologists can begin to understand the logic people use to classify and attach importance to their relatives.

Kinship and Alliance

Societies based on kinship often attempt to resolve the difficulties of intergroup relations by connecting kinship and marriage. Unilineal societies frequently promote or *prescribe* certain kinds of marriage to ensure (1) reproduction of their own memberships and (2) long-term alliances with other groups. Two major types of prescriptive marriage patterns facilitate both these needs: one in which a man must marry his father's sister's daughter, and one in which a man must marry his mother's brother's daughter. In either case, the marriage forms an alliance between two cross-cousins (see Figure 6.12).

In patrilineal systems, the father's sister's daughter pattern sets up a *direct exchange marriage* where a line that has received a wife from another line in one generation gives a wife back in the next generation. In this system, a man's *father's sister's daughter* is the prototypical spouse, but any woman of the appropriate line can be chosen if both lines agree. In contrast, the mother's brother's daughter system (which is more common) sets up a pattern of *asymmetrical exchange marriage*. Unlike direct exchange, this marriage pattern does not balance out over the generations, as men always find wives in the line their mother came from. This pattern provides a permanent alliance between two lines. While a man's mother's brother's daughter is the prototypical wife in this system, all is not lost if Ego's mother's brother does not have a daughter. In such a case, Ego could turn to another woman of his generation who is a member of his mother's patrilineage. On the rare occasion that cross-cousin marriage is found in matrilineal systems, men marry out of their lineages, thus creating direct or asymmetrical exchange alliances.

Intergroup relations can also be strengthened by members of the younger generation working to maintain the established alliances they inherit from their kin. Canadian anthropologist Naomi McPherson (2007) notes such inherited alliances in her discussion of trade networks and

TABLE 6.5 Criteria of Relatedness

Criterion	Distinction	Example
Generation	Place in descent group	*Cousin* conventionally refers to someone who is of the same generation as Ego but who is not considered a sibling.
Sex/Gender	Male or female	*Uncle* and *aunt* are distinguished on the basis of both generation and sex/gender.
Affinity	Connection through marriage	*Mother* is distinguished from *mother-in-law*.
Collaterality	Direct (linking) or indirect (linked) relative	*Mother* and *father* denote direct connections; *aunt* and *uncle* denote relations "off to one side," linked through the mother or the father.
Sex/Gender of Linking Relative	Linking relative is male or female	Not applied in English; some cultures distinguish parallel cousins (Ego's father's brother's children or Ego's mother's sister's children) from cross cousins (Ego's mother's brother's children or Ego's father's sister's children). (See Figure 6.12.)
Bifurcation	Relation on mother's or father's side	Not applied in English; some cultures distinguish the mother's brother from the father's brother.
Relative Age	Relatives of the same category who are older or younger than Ego	Not applied in English; Ju/'hoansi separate "older brother" (*!ko*) from "younger brother" (*tsin*).

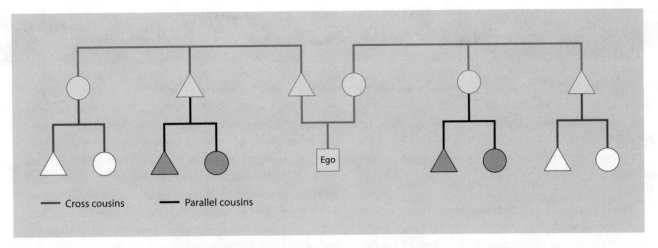

FIGURE 6.12 Cross-cousins and parallel cousins: Ego's cross-cousins are the children of Ego's father's sister and of Ego's mother's brother. Ego's parallel cousins are the children of Ego's father's brother and of Ego' mother's sister.

trade friendships among the Bariai in Northwest New Britain, Papua New Guinea (see the "In Their Own Words" box, below). In her analysis, McPherson notes the links between economics, trade networks, friendships (trade partners), and kinship affiliation (particularly that between parents and their first-born child). For example, the ceremonial dress for the first-born becomes a display of trade friendship, as it is constructed out of both locally available raw materials (e.g., red ochre and obsidian) and traded "craft" materials (e.g., armbands woven by trade partners). In effect, the items used in the ceremonial dress of the first-born advertise the extent of the trade-friendship and the family's access to the network. In the Bariai trade system, first-borns inherit their parents' trade roles; they are exemplars of parental achievement and facilitate the trade partnerships and networks for their younger siblings.

Kinship and Practice

Kinship systems may appear to be fairly rigid sets of rules that use the accident of birth to thrust people into social positions laden with rights and obligations they cannot escape. Yet in practice, people encounter a flexible series of opportunities to choose how to deal with others. Indeed, everyday lived experiences provide opportunities for individuals to *create* meaningful relationships in many different ways and for many different reasons. The following sections offer some examples.

Adoption

The accident of birth thrusts people into **ascribed statuses**. In contrast, individual or group efforts can lead to **achieved statuses**. Both statuses have rights and obligations. Adoption blurs the distinction between ascribed and achieved because it allows people to transform relationships based on nurturance into relations of kinship.

Nurturance is the central theme in Barbara Bodenhorn's (2000) discussion of adoption among the Iñupiat of northern Alaska. (Similar adoption patterns are also found among the Yupik of southwestern Alaska, the Inuit of northern Canada, and the Kalaalit of Greenland.) Most adult Iñupiat have been adopted or have lived in a household with adopted children. The reasons that the Iñupiat gave for adoption included that they "wanted to" adopt, that they had too many boys and wanted a girl (or vice versa), or that all of their "brothers and sisters [had] adopted." Often, adoption occurred because the child wanted to be adopted. In many cases, the shift was to everyone's satisfaction, but even when it was not, the question of where the child should end up was never based on the argument that he or she belonged with his or her biological parents. The degree to which a relationship is maintained between the birth parents and the adopted child is up to the child, and it ranges from no contact to regular shared activities. Recognition of the biological relationship becomes a matter of choice—there is no social stigma involved if a child ignores his or her biological parents. However, people do disapprove if the child does not act like

ascribed statuses
Social positions people are assigned at birth.

achieved statuses
Social positions people may attain later in life, often as the result of their own (or other people's) effort.

IN THEIR OWN WORDS | Myth Primogeniture and Long-Distance Trade-Friends in Northwest New Britain, Papua New Guinea

Trade-friendships form important "official" bonds, as seen in the trade-friendships of the Bariai of Northwest New Britain, Papua New Guinea. Naomi McPherson examines how trade-friendships, kinship, and economics are intimately intertwined. Note how such integrated analysis offers deep insight into the workings of a society, illustrating our dedication to holism in anthropology.

Bariai trade-friendships are, in fact, relations between individual women and men (and their spouses) rather than kin groups or communities. Although couched in an idiom of kinship, trade-friendships entail different, albeit parallel, sets of rights, obligations, and motivations from those operating among consanguineal [blood] and affinal [marriage] exchange partners....

Rules for conduct between trade-friends in the Vitiaz Strait include offering one another hospitality and protection, and both parties are under obligation to proffer, to accept, and to reciprocate pre-stations of all sorts. One ought not to lure away the trade-friends of others and, as a trade-friend host, one should act as intermediary for any exchanges between community members and one's trade-friend visitor (Harding 1967: 166–7). Harding characterizes the trade-friend relationship as "an expression of the social ethic of kinship" (166), an ethic that entails "generosity and mutual aid" (182). Rather than being the substrate out of which trade-friendships develop, "kin-like bonds develop partly as a consequence of [these] socially conducive relations" (176). The difference is that a trade-friendship depends on the two parties meeting their obligations; that is, they have a special performance of duty (Harding 1967). Kinship relations, on the other hand, are composed of a variety of acquired obligations and interests, and default in trade specifically does not sever the acquired ties. One can take advantage of kinspeople and get away with it. "Trading with relatives, therefore, may be burdensome for either side.... It is good to have kinsmen in far-away places, but it is better to have good trade-friends" (153)....

The analytical conflation of kinship and trade-friendship (prevalent in alliance theories of kinship) has made it difficult to fully appreciate trade-friendships as something other than kinship relations. For example, the idiom of kinship characterizes the Bariai concept of the trade-friend as an affine—indeed, some trade-friends are affinal kin based on contemporary intermarriages—and the trade-friend relationship is also subject to the rights and moral obligations that inform human relations in kinship-based societies. However, the majority of Bariai adults are hard pressed to trace definitive kinship connections with their trade-friends. Rather, a first-born formally inherits his or her mother's and father's trade-friendships within the context of the *mata pau* first-born ceremony. None of the first-born's subsequent siblings is the focus of a *mata pau*, but, as head of the sibling set, the first-born is expected to oversee and facilitate younger siblings' access to inherited trade-friendships. This provides a means for younger siblings to participate in the established trade-friendships while presenting them an opportunity to develop their own trade-friendships through these connections. Not unlike a system of descent reckoning, trade-friendships remain intact over generations while the origin of the relationship, which is of little immediate concern relative to the continuity, substance, and meaning of the relationship itself, is lost in the mists of antiquity. That trade-friendships resemble kinship relations should come as no surprise in societies where human relationships generally are founded on the moral obligations inherent in kinship relations. For the Bariai, trade-friendships can be distinguished from kinship in three important ways. First, the Bariai use the unique, non-kin term *sobo* to encompass the trade-friend relationship. Second, participation in trade-friendships is a household, rather than a descent group or lineage, activity (cf. Harding 1967: 182). Within the framework of day-to-day household activities, it is the spousal partners who, working as a team, produce or procure items of trade and who undertake the transactions involved in trade-friend activities, and it is their first-born who inherits the fruits and friendships of their joint labours. Finally, as noted above, the trade-friendship can be curtailed whereas the kinship relationship cannot. Bariai can and do bring pressure to bear on trade-friends and may even sever a relationship if it is

a son or daughter to his or her adoptive parents. In their view, it is the action of parenting that creates parents:

> What is real is acted on and mutually recognized.... [B]ecause [relatedness] is disconnected from anything permanent, it must be constantly reconstructed: shared

tools, food, labour, political alliance, ceremonial participation, and simply company. ... It is *this* labour—the work of being related—rather than the labour of giving birth or the "fact" of shared substance that marks out the kinship sphere from the potentially infinite universe of relatives who may or may not belong. (143)

exploitative, an outcome that is next to impossible in the entangled world of affinal and consanguineal relations of kinship. . . .

Exchange relationships with kin and trade-friendships depend upon an ability to manipulate competently the complicated system of debits and credits of the prestige economy and an ability to balance one's own self-interests and the interests of others according to the principles of morality which structure human relations. The locus of trade (and renown) is the wife/husband team. Transactions between spouses and their kin/affines and between spouses and their trade-friends occur constantly and rather inconspicuously within the context of the household. Similarly, first-born ceremonies are not group efforts but are carried out individually by parents and their *baulo* for their first-born child, when and as they have the wherewithal to do so. These public events effectively deflect individual endeavours onto the person of the first-born who exemplifies parental abilities in forging and maintaining bonds beyond the household. Without a first-born and performance of first-born ceremonies, no one can hope to achieve a reputation for renown.

The Bariai distinguish between first-born ceremonies that require "small work" (K: *ololo kaukau*) and those that require "big work" (*ololo kapei*). The difference between the two types is one of relative scale. "Small work," or minor ceremonies, usually does not require the exchange of pigs, pork, or shell money, and there is no large assembly of witnesses/kin from other villages. Minor ceremonies are contingent upon circumstances and available resources, and none of the key participants (mother and child) is dressed in ceremonial finery. Minor ceremonies celebrate "firsts" in two senses: they mark the first occasion that others receive a particular food or consumable in the name of the child, and some minor ceremonies confirm phases in the child's physical development (first tooth, first haircut, first fish, first clothing). For these ceremonies, young, inexperienced, first-time parents depend on the resources provided for them by their parents and grandparents who, for example, planned for their descendants by planting stands of sago, coconut, and areca (betel nut) palms for them. Accomplishing certain of the

minor ceremonials also serves to release the parents from various taboos on food, mobility, personal hygiene, and appearance that were imposed upon them when their child was born. Ideally, the minor ceremonies are accomplished by the time the child is four to six years of age. (I have calculated that, in an ideal world, it can take a married couple 15 to 20 years to complete the 17 first-born ceremonies; some parents never do complete them all.)

While the expenditure of energy and wealth required for the performance of minor ceremonials is anything but small, it is only a fraction of that required for major ceremonials. For their proper performance, these ceremonies require vast quantities of one or more of the following: raw/cooked foods (especially taro, sago flour, and coconuts); pigs and/or pork; shell money; and other forms of material wealth such as clay pots, carved bowls, mats, and more. In contrast to the minor ceremonials where the wealth distributed in the child's name was acquired in large part from the child's grandparents and ancestors, the wealth in the major ceremonies is produced and acquired by the child's parents. Parents use their "strength" to produce more and larger gardens, to acquire and husband numerous pigs, and to access other wealth items by actively developing and engaging in an ever-widening network of social obligations, especially trade networks. Some of the major ceremonies are also concerned with "firsts," such as the child's first trip to the reef or first wearing of clothes, first excursion to another village. Others focus on a particular item of decorative finery (such as sago fringe, arm bands, red and yellow paint), items that parents and first-born are forbidden to display as personal adornment until the appropriate ceremony is complete. Many of these objects of value are only obtainable through trade; thus, when the first-born is elaborately decorated and paraded through the village to display the item of wealth, the child publicly demonstrates parental ability to forge and maintain relations of trade and exchange.

Source: McPherson, Naomi. 2007. "Myth Primogeniture and Long-Distance Trade-Friends in Northwest New Britain, Papua New Guinea," *Oceania* 77, 2: 129–57.

This is kinship based on *active nurturance*; biology does not create parents, but actions do.

Negotiation of Kin Ties among the Ju/'hoansi

In his analysis of kinship among the Ju/'hoansi, anthropologist Richard B. Lee (1992b) notes that "the principles of kinship constitute not

an invariant code of laws written in stone, but instead a whole series of codes consistent enough to provide structure but open enough to be flexible" (62). For the Ju/'hoansi, kin terms have behavioural correlates, which Lee calls *joking* and *avoidance* (Table 6.6). Joking relationships can be relaxed and affectionate, while avoidance relationships require respect and reserve.

TABLE 6.6 Generation and Behaviour with the Ju/'hoansi

Generation	Behaviour
Grandparents'	Joking
Parents'	Avoidance
Ego's	Joking*
Children's	Avoidance
Grandchildren's	Joking

*Opposite-gender siblings of Ego's own generation are in the avoidance category.

Many avoidance relationships may be warm and friendly if the relatives show one another proper respect in public; however, people in an avoidance relationship may not marry one another.

Another, more complex part of the system is structured by the Ju/'hoansi name system, which contains 36 names for men and 32 names for women. A first-born son gets his father's father's name; a first-born daughter gets her father's mother's name. Second-born children are supposed to be named after the mother's father or mother. Later children are named after the father's brothers and sisters and the mother's brothers and sisters. All people with the same name will claim to be related. A man older than Ego who shares his or her name is called *!kun!a* ("old name"), which is the same term used for *grandfather*. A man younger than Ego who shares his or her name is called *!kuna* ("young name"), the same term used for *grandson*. By extension, Ego would call anyone with her or his father's name *father* and anyone with her or his mother's name *mother*. Additionally, names restrict potential marriage partners: "a woman may not marry a man with her father's or brother's name, and a man may not marry a woman with his mother's or sister's name" (Lee 1992b: 74)! Further, an individual may not marry anyone with the name of one of her or his avoidance kin. It does not matter how people are "really" related to others with the same name; the name relationship takes precedence, making close relatives out of distant ones.

To help resolve any confusion that might arise, the Ju/'hoansi have a third component to their kinship system: *wi*. The principle of *wi* depends on the fact that in any relationship that can be described by more than one kin term, the older party chooses the term to be used. For example, a man may get married only to discover that his wife's aunt's husband has the same name he has.

What terms will he and his wife's aunt use for each other? According to the principle of *wi*, the aunt decides because she is older. If she calls him *nephew* (rather than *husband*), he knows to call her *aunt*. The principle of *wi* means that a person's involvement with the kinship system is continually changing over the course of his or her lifetime. In youth and young adulthood, people must accept the kin terms their elders choose. After midlife, however, they begin to impose *wi* on their juniors. Thus for the Ju/'hoansi, kinship connections are open to manipulation and negotiation.

Compadrazgo in Latin America

An important set of kinship practices in Roman Catholic Latin America is *compadrazgo*, or ritual co-parenthood (Figure 6.13). In Roman Catholic tradition, the baptism of a child requires the presence of a godmother and a godfather as sponsors. In Latin America, godparents are expected to take an active interest in their godchildren and to help them wherever possible. However, the more important relationship is between the godparents and the parents. They become *compadres* ("co-parents"), and they are expected to behave toward each other in new ways. A couple often chooses godparents whose social standing is higher than their own. Participating together in the baptism changes these unequal strangers into ritual kin whose relationship, although still unequal, is now personalized, friendlier, and more open. The co-parents call each other *compadre*, and they help one another: the parents will support the godparents when that support is needed (e.g., politically), and the godparents will do favours for the parents.

Anthropologist Catherine Allen notes that the bonds of *compadrazgo*, in combination with marriage alliances and kinship, form constellations of mutual obligation and dependence that shift with time as new *compadrazgo* relationships are formed, young relatives come of age, and old bonds fall into disuse through death or quarrelling. Like kin ties, bonds of *compadrazgo* can become as much a burden as an asset, and like kin ties they can be ignored or honoured in the breach. (1988: 90)

Again we see the flexibility of kinship practices.

Euro-American Kinship and Reproductive Technologies

Euro-Americans tend to recognize kin related by blood and kin related by marriage; they also tend to believe that procreation—the process that brings kin into existence—is part of nature. Ties of kinship are supposed to stand for what is unalterable in a person's social world, in contrast to what is open to change. Yet reproductive technologies such as in vitro fertilization and surrogate motherhood reveal that even the world of "natural facts" is subject to social intervention.

Contemporary ambiguities surrounding kinship in the United States and Canada have put pressure on the courts to decide what constitutes biological parenthood and how it is related to legal parenthood. Consider, for example, the case of "Baby M" in America (see Dolgin 1995). It began as a traditional surrogacy arrangement in which the surrogate, Mary Beth Whitehead, was impregnated with the sperm of the husband in the couple who intended to become the legal parents of the child she bore. Whitehead was supposed to terminate all parental rights when the child was born, but she refused to do so. The court faced a dilemma. Existing law backed Whitehead's maternal rights, but the parties had signed a legal contract. Focussing on Whitehead's attempt to break the surrogacy contract, the court terminated her legal rights as biological mother, although they awarded her visitation rights.

More complicated than traditional surrogacy, *gestational surrogacy*—a process in which the surrogate mother is implanted with an embryo formed from the intended mother's egg and the intended father's sperm—deconstructs the role of biological mother into two roles that can be performed by two different women. In another fairly early legal case exploring issues of surrogacy, the

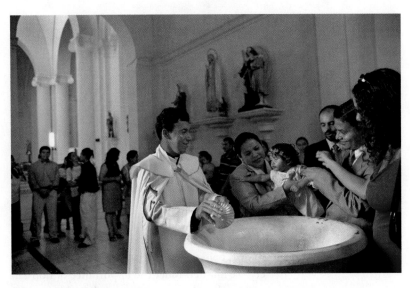

FIGURE 6.13 In Latin America, when a child is baptized according to Roman Catholic traditions, the child's godparents become *compadres*, or ritual co-parents, with the child's birth parents. Do you or anyone you know have godparents? How does the concept of *compadrazgo* differ from the concept of godparenthood?

Calverts, a childless married couple, provided egg and sperm that were used in a laboratory to create an embryo, which was then implanted in Anna Johnson's uterus. But when Johnson gave birth to the baby, she refused to give it up. As anthropologist and legal scholar Janet Dolgin points out, this case "provided a context in which to measure the generality of the assumption that the gestational role both produces and constitutes maternity" (1995: 58). While several previous court cases had emphasized the role of gestation in forming an indissoluble bond between mother and child, in this case the court referred to Anna Johnson "as a 'gestational carrier,' a 'genetic hereditary stranger' to the child, who acted like a 'foster parent'" (59). The court declared the Calverts and the child a family unit on genetic grounds and ruled that the Calverts were the baby's "natural" and legal parents.

Dolgin notes that in these cases, the courts awarded legal custody to those parties whose living arrangements most closely approximated the traditional heteronormative two-parent family. In recent years, however, popular and legal views have been shifting away from the assumption that a child should be raised by a heterosexual couple. This shift is closely tied to what sociologist Dana Berkowitz (2013) terms the "emerging trend of reproductive outsourcing" among gay men and gay couples who want to become parents through surrogacy. Such parents "are at the cutting edge of pushing society to reassess its assumptions and constructions about sex, reproduction, and parenthood" (Berkowitz 2013: 71) and thus kinship. So it seems some of our traditional ideas about kinship may not be so clear-cut after all.

Beyond Kinship

While kinship may be central to the structure and functioning of some societies, it is not equally important to all groups or all people. Indeed, all people form significant links with individuals beyond their kin group. To fully understand how human beings relate to one another in any society, we must consider the importance of non-kin relationships in composing social worlds.

At the outset, we need to recognize that the line between "kin" and "non-kin" is not always clear; often, it is a matter of interpretation. In general, non-kin social relationships are less rigidly defined than are kin relationships, and they generally involve fewer inherent obligations. Yet those involved in non-kin social relations often to refer to each other in kin terms, and they think of their roles in the relationship as being similar to those they have with their kin. Such non-kin relationships can occur on both individual and institutional levels. On the individual level, for example, ritual co-parents refer to themselves as co-parents (*compadres*) and take on the formal role obligations of family members. On the institutional level, members of organizations such as Catholic monastic orders refer to one another as *brother, sister, father*, and *mother* and model their interactions on those of a family. Such religious orders are parts of international institutions, and the connections established among members reach far beyond the contexts of everyday, face-to-face relatedness.

Cultural anthropologist David M. Schneider (1968) has argued that the emotion of North American kinship is the feeling of "enduring diffuse solidarity." This definition might just as well apply to friendship or to any other form of close companionship. Perhaps enduring diffuse solidarity is something that human beings regularly seek to establish in their relations with other people—kin or not.

Friendship

A common definition of *friend* is "one joined to another in intimacy and mutual benevolence independent of sexual or family love" (Brain 1976: 15). Yet the Western belief that friendship and kinship are separate phenomena often breaks down in practice. For example, some husbands and wives in Western societies consider each other "best friends," and we may be friends with some relatives while treating others as distant acquaintances. Definitions of *friendship* also differ cross-culturally—recall again *compadrazgo*, which many Westerners might interpret as a form of institutionalized friendship rather than kinship. In general, then, friendship might best be understood more generally, as a relatively "unofficial" bond that is personal, affective (i.e., involving feelings), and—to a varying extent from society to society—a matter of choice (Bell and Coleman 1999; Figure 6.14).

With globalization and widespread social change, ideas about friendship may be changing. In some contexts, the importance of friendship seems to be increasing: "In many shifting social contexts, ties of kinship tend to be transformed and often weakened [while] new forms of friendship are emerging" (Bell and Coleman 1999: 5). Brazilian anthropologist Claudia Barcellos Rezende (1999) has observed an example of such a relatively new form of friendship: in Rio de Janeiro, some middle-class women and their maids refer to each other as "friends" in "friendships" of affection, care, and consideration. Both sets of women value these relationships, which establish mutual trust and an "affinity that brings these people together as parts of the same social world" regardless of class distinctions (1999: 93). More recently, the rise of digital communication technologies has challenged us to consider what *friend* means in an increasingly connected world. As anthropologist Levent Soysal (2010) comments, these technologies allow us to experience intimate relationships "in virtual worlds where privacy proper . . . [is] no longer operational" (373). As friendship has become more public in online environments, in many ways it has also become less personal.

Some cultures extend their interpretation of the bonds of friendship to apply to entire groups. We can find this perspective in the network that the National Association of Friendship Centres (NAFC) has established across Canada. The NAFC focusses on providing support to First Nations peoples in urban settings, helping them overcome problems such as isolation and alienation. Thus it offers individuals the sort of emotional and practical support commonly provided by friends. Here we find a contemporary example of the importance of friendship alliances for survival.

Sodalities

Sodalities offer members a more formal organization of non-kin bonds. Such organizations can have various functions,

> among them police, military, medical, initiation, religious, economic, and recreation. Some sodalities conduct their business in secret, others in public [Figure 6.15]. Membership may be ascribed or it may be obtained via inheritance, purchase, attainment, performance, or contract. Men's sodalities are more numerous and highly organized than women's and, generally, are also more secretive and seclusive in their activities. (Hunter and Whitten 1976: 362)

Sodalities create enduring diffuse solidarity among members of a larger society. A common example of this sort of group in Western societies is the labour union—an affiliation of workers who seek certain economic and workplace conditions from employers. Sometimes union negotiations highlight issues of human rights, such as pay parity, safe working conditions, protection from harassment in the workplace, or enforcement of child labour laws.

Age Sets in Eastern Africa

Some groups establish sodalities based on generational distinctions. In eastern Africa, a number of societies assign men from different kinship groups to sodalities composed of **age sets**. These age sets "are part of the formal social order blessed by tradition, and membership is usually ascribed and is always obligatory" (Baxter and Almagor 1978: 4). These societies do not establish age-set systems for women, possibly because women are involved in domestic matters from an early age and marry shortly after puberty (11).

In a classic study, South African anthropologist Monica Wilson (1951) examined the role of age sets among the Nyakyusa (see Map 6.9). At the time of Wilson's fieldwork, the Nyakyusa were patrilineal and patrilocal, and their society was divided into many independent chiefdoms. Each Nyakyusa age set began as a group of boys about 10 to 15 years of age. When the members of this junior set were about 33 to 35 years old, an

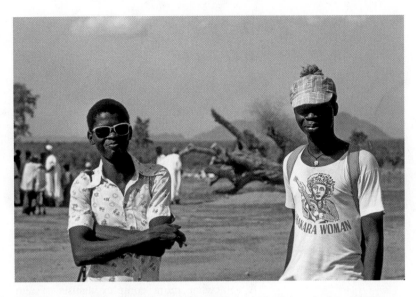

FIGURE 6.14 Friendships are based on the "unofficial" bonds that people create with one another, which vary from society to society. These two young men in Cameroon are the best of friends. What qualities do you consider necessary in a relationship in order to call someone a friend?

FIGURE 6.15 Men of the devil sodality prepare for Carnival parade in Oruro, Bolivia. Can you think of other examples of sodalities in your own society? How do members show their affiliation?

elaborate series of rituals was held to mark their "coming out." At that time, the reigning senior generation "handed the country over to them." At any point in time, there were three strata in the Nyakyusa age-set system:

1. retired elders,
2. active adult men who carried political and military responsibilities for the entire society, and
3. immature juniors.

sodalities
Non-kin social groups that may be organized on the basis of age, sex, economic role, and/or personal interest.

age sets
Non-kin social groups composed of young men born within a specified time span.

MAP 6.9 Nyakyusa

MAP 6.10 Boran

A somewhat more complex age-set system exists among the Boran of Kenya and Ethiopia (see Map 6.10; also see Baxter 1978). In this system, which the Boran call *gada*, there are five generation sets, which succeed one another over a 40-year period. Every eight years, a new generation set is formed and the oldest set retires. In many ways, *gada* is part of the Boran's traditional system of governance. Each age set has a specific role to play in social and political life, and each man has a place within his assigned age set.

Secret Societies in Western Africa

secret societies
Non-kin social groups that initiate young men or women into social adulthood and reveal "secret" knowledge to initiated members.

Several neighbouring peoples in western Africa use **secret societies** as a way of drawing members of different kinship groups into crosscutting associations. The most famous secret societies in Africa are the Poro and the Sande, which are found among the Mende, Sherbro, Kpelle, and other neighbouring peoples of Sierra Leone, Ivory Coast, Liberia, and Guinea.

Poro is a secret society for men, and Sande is a secret society for women. These sodalities are secret in the sense that members of each have certain knowledge that can be revealed only to initiates. Each is responsible for the initiation of members into social adulthood. These societies also supervise and regulate the sexual, social, and political conduct of all members of the wider society. Both are hierarchically organized. The higher a person's status within the sodality, the greater the secret knowledge revealed. To carry out their regulatory responsibilities, high-status sodality members often impersonate important supernatural figures by donning masks and performing in public. Each community has its own Poro and

Sande congregations, and a person initiated in one community is eligible to participate in the congregations of other communities. Various stages of initiation require fees. In any community where Poro and Sande are strong, authority in society is divided between a sodality of mature men and one of mature women. Together, these men and women work to keep society on the correct path in a relationship that is highly egalitarian.

Anthropologist Beryl Bellman (1984) was initiated into a Poro chapter among the Kpelle of Liberia. He describes the men's initiation as a ritual process that takes place about once each generation. In the ritual, one of the Poro's forest spirits, or "devils," metaphorically captures and eats the novices—only for the novices to be metaphorically reborn from the womb of the devil's "wife" at a later time. Cuts on the necks, chests, and backs of initiates represent the "devil's teeth marks." After this ritualistic scarring, initiates spend a year living apart from women in a special village constructed for them in the forest. During this period, they carry out various activities under the strict supervision of senior Poro members. Female Sande initiates undergo a similar experience. Bellman notes that, both during and after the process of initiation, members use kinship terminology to describe certain relationships within their secret society.

The Sherbro (see Map 6.11) have a third secret society, called *Thoma*, which initiates both men and women. Members of one society cannot be initiated into another, and families with several children usually try to initiate at least one child into each. As with Poro and Sande initiations, Thoma initiations involve elaborate rituals that create kin-like bonds between co-initiates and transform the uninitiated into initiated, fully social adult human beings. Anthropologist Carol MacCormack (1980) describes the Thoma as "a microcosm of the whole": "Its local congregations or chapters are headed by a man and a woman, co-equal leaders who are 'husband and wife' in a ritual context" (97). The Sherbro are concerned with the reproduction of their society—not just the production of children but also the continuation of the division of labour between men and women. The Sherbro say that the ritual function of the Thoma sodality is "to cleanse the land and the village from evil and restore its fertility and well-being" (98).

So what is the secret? Beryl Bellman (1984) argued that initiation rituals are primarily concerned with teaching discretion—knowing when, how, and even whether to speak about various topics. This is a valued attribute of the social adult.

Theories of Relatedness: Kin-based and Non–kin-based Societies

In the Western world, kinship has long been relegated to the realm of personal and family relations. For this reason, early Western anthropologists were struck by the ways in which the elaborate kinship systems they found in non-Western societies could regulate social life and organize behavioural patterns. Yet nineteenth-century scholars of classical antiquity recognized that kinship groups had played comparable roles in ancient European societies as well. Somehow, over time, those kin-ordered forms of social life had been displaced by the large-scale, impersonal, bureaucratically ordered forms of social life typical of a modern nation-state.

Sir Henry Maine, an English jurist who studied the roots of Roman law, described the shift as one from *status* to *contract*. Ancient societies organized people's relationships by the particular position, or status, that each person held within the group. Each status carried with it certain rights and obligations, or *roles*. Statuses and their roles complemented one another: holders of each status were responsible for particular tasks and could rely on other members of the system to perform different tasks. Ideally, these roles fit together like pieces of a puzzle, ensuring that all tasks needed for group survival were carried out. For Maine, the crucial feature of kinship-based societies was that people

MAP 6.11 Sherbro

were not free to choose their own statuses, nor could they modify the rights and responsibilities associated with those statuses. Status and role were *ascribed*. Status-based societies contrasted with contract-based societies in four major ways:

1. ideally, the parties to contractual relationships enter into them freely;
2. the contracting parties are equally free to specify the rights and obligations between them for the duration of the contract;
3. the range of possible statuses and roles is limitless, bound only by the imagination and interests of the contracting parties; and
4. once the terms of the contract are met, the parties may choose to terminate their relationship with one another.

In another interpretation, Émile Durkheim described the process as a shift from *mechanical solidarity* to *organic solidarity*. In his view, "primitive" societies (ancient and contemporary) were held together on the basis of mechanical solidarity that assigned the same social tasks to everybody who occupied the same kinship status. Tasks were based on age and sex, with each kinship group containing the full range of roles necessary for survival. Keeping kin groups together as parts of a larger whole was problematic, as nothing bound these groups together except "mechanical" similarities in language, mode of livelihood, and so on. Mechanical solidarity, therefore, was brittle, seriously affecting the group's ability to survive.

Conversely, "modern" societies were held together by organic solidarity, which depended on a highly developed *division of labour* rather than established kinship roles. In the "modern" system, each non-kin group specialized in a particular task needed for the survival of the larger whole. With organic solidarity the division of labour became more elaborate, some people specializing in food production and others in trade, government, and so on. Full-time specialization meant that each group had to depend on other groups to provide it with things it could not provide for itself, and if any one specialized group were to disappear, the society as a whole would suffer.

Essentially, Maine and Durkheim both asked: What is the social glue that ensures social cooperation? Anthropologists as well as sociologists have suggested many answers to this question over the years. Sociologist Zygmunt Bauman

A CRITICAL LOOK | Cultural Approaches to Childhood

Starting in 1869 and continuing well into the twentieth century, more than 100,000 children were shipped from the United Kingdom to Canada (Library and Archives Canada 2010; Figure 6.16). In some cases, the children were orphaned or abandoned, with no relatives willing to care for them. In other cases, impoverished parents were persuaded to send their children to be raised in what were promised to be wonderful new homes full of opportunity. Some of the children were as young as three or four, and most never saw or heard from their families again. Once in Canada, these children—who came to be known as "Home Children"—were sent to live and work on farms. In effect, many were treated as little more than slave labour—overworked and under cared for. Many were also subjected to horrific abuse, both physical and sexual.

This situation was not unique to Canada. Home Children were also sent to Australia, New Zealand, and South Africa during the same period, with the practice continuing into the 1970s in Australia. Similar child migrations were effected within the United States through programs run by the Children's Aid Society. Between 1853 and 1890, thousands of poor New York City children were transported to the Midwest and the West. Although some of these children were able to maintain links to their families, many suffered feelings of isolation, and their working conditions were far from ideal.

At the time, the people responsible for displacing these children believed that they were doing good work. They belonged to social organizations intent on bettering the situation of the poor, instilling strong work ethics, and promoting their version of Christian values. The nineteenth-century view of working-class children as "economically useful" and

capable of working full-time by the age of 12 was also a factor (see Davin 2001).

From a contemporary Western perspective, these sorts of efforts seem misguided. Undoubtedly, our cultural view of childhood has softened over the past century and a half. Today, most of us agree that childhood is a time for learning and having fun. Most of us also feel strongly that children belong with families who love and take care of them. Children are seen as innocent and vulnerable, and therefore in need of protection from the harms of the adult world. We tend to look at even older teenagers as being in need of a certain amount of protection. Our laws reflect these views, with the age of majority (i.e., the age at which an individual has the legal standing of an adult) being 18 or 19, depending on the province or territory.

Yet ideas about childhood and laws governing how children should be treated are not the same in all regions of the world. In some cultures, the age of majority is much lower. Young people (principally girls) are encouraged to marry and start a family—therefore taking on traditional responsibilities of an adult—well before they turn 18. Often more troubling, however, are practices of forced child labour. The International Labour Organization (ILO 2013) estimates that 168 million children between the ages of 5 and 17 are employed as child labourers, and that 85 million of these children work under hazardous conditions that jeopardize their "physical, mental, or moral well-being." Hazardous conditions are commonly encountered by children working in mines, in the sex trade, and in "sweatshops" that manufacture various consumer goods (e.g., clothing, fabric, and electronics).

argues that all human groups of a significant size "are first and foremost processes of collectivization of friends and enemies . . . [in which] individuals sharing a common group or category of enemies treat each other as friends" (1990: 152). Political scientist Benedict Anderson (1983) suggests that the bonds of nationalism that hold citizens of nation-states together are "imagined," as they have not existed for all time but are rather social constructions arising from historical circumstances. In this chapter, we have discussed a number of cohesive forces, notably Schneider's (1968) interpretation that it is our need for "enduring diffuse solidarity"—between kin and non-kin—that holds society together. Whatever the glue, it is clear that all people have developed patterned social relationships that aim to bind them for the long term.

In most cases, children are forced to work by poverty. But it is not only poverty that makes child labour a reality for so many children. Indeed, a major and increasingly powerful driving force is globalization—more specifically, the widespread economic processes that bind the world's economies together in a single global market. In many ways, Western demands for low-priced goods—inexpensive T-shirts, shoes, flowers, toys, and so on—have driven manufacturers to use child labour to keep costs down. So it seems that just as the Home Children of past centuries were victims of rapid urbanization, so too are many of today's child labourers victims of globalization.

—Roberta Robin Dods

FIGURE 6.16 British immigrant "Home Children" at a landing stage in Saint John, New Brunswick, in the late nineteenth century.

KEY TERMS

achieved statuses 151	conjugal family 138	friendship 131	polygamy 134
affinal 137	dowry 139	joint family 139	relatedness 131
age sets 157	ego 144	kinship 131	secret societies 158
ascribed statuses 151	endogamy 134	lineages 145	segmentary opposition 148
bilateral descent 144	exogamy 134	marriage 131	sodalities 157
blended family 139	extended family 139	monogamy 134	unilineal descent 144
bridewealth 132	family 131	non-conjugal family 138	
clan 147	family of choice 141	nuclear family 138	

CHAPTER SUMMARY

1. Human life is group life organized through relationships of marriage, family, kinship, and friendship.

2. Marriage is a social process that transforms the status of the participants, positions children, and creates relationships between the kin of the partners. Marriage patterns differ across the globe. A number of modern societies recognize same-sex marriages, while others do not. Some cultures promote monogamy, while others promote polygamy.

3. Different family structures produce different internal patterns and tensions. Families may change from one type to another over time and with the birth, growth, and marriage of children.

4. Kinship principles are based on the universal experiences of mating, birth, and nurturance.

5. Patrilineages and matrilineages are corporate groups that collectively control important property. By prescribing certain kinds of marriage, lineages establish long-term alliances with one another.

6. Kinship systems are governed by many rules, but they also offer flexibility. In some cultures, kin ties are open to negotiation; they can also be formed through relationships other than those of blood or marriage.

7. Every society provides ways of establishing links with non-kin. Close relationships—such as those between friends or co-members of a sodality—cultivate a sentiment of enduring diffuse solidarity.

CRITICAL THINKING QUESTIONS

1. What is a "prototypical" marriage? Is the prototype the same in all cultures?

2. Distinguish between *pater* and *genitor*. Are they always the same person? Similarly, are gestational, biological, and social mothers always the same person? Do adopted children struggle with such categories?

3. How are joint, extended, and blended families different from nuclear families?

4. What criteria do people use to indicate relatedness? How do you distinguish between relationships of family, kinship, and friendship in your own life?

SUGGESTED READINGS

Chute, Janet E. 1999. "Frank G. Speck's Contributions to the Understanding of Mi'kmaq Land Use, Leadership, and Land Management," *Ethnohistory* 46, 3: 481–540. An interesting article on an early Canadian ethnographer's work with an Algonquian group.

Clarke, Morgan. 2007. "Closeness in the Age of Mechanical Reproduction: Debating Kinship and Biomedicine in Lebanon and the Middle East," *Anthropological Quarterly*, 80, 2: 379–402.

A relatively recent article exploring the impact of assisted reproductive technologies from an anthropological perspective.

Ginsburg, Faye D., and Rayna Rapp, eds. 1995. *Conceiving the New World Order: The Global Politics of Reproduction* (Berkeley: University of California Press). An important collection of articles by anthropologists who address the ways human reproduction is structured across social and cultural boundaries.

Jamieson, Kathleen. 1986. "Sex Discrimination and the Indian Act," in *Arduous Journey: Canadian Indians and Decolonization*, ed. J. Rick Ponting (Toronto: McClelland & Stewart), 112–36. A discussion of the discrimination toward First Nations women found in the Indian Act and government policies associated with this Act.

Letkemann, Paul G. 2009. "Resisting Marginalization: Social Networks and 'Communication Communities' of Urban Blackfoot Teenage Girls," *Anthropologica* 51, 1: 239–50. This article examines how urban Aboriginal teens in Lethbridge, Alberta, use social networks to establish a sense of community. It reveals how social networks "serve to mitigate various forms of marginalization by creating and maintaining a sense of place in a community."

Shostak, Marjorie. 1981. *Nisa: The Life and Words of a !Kung Woman* (New York: Vintage). A wonderful book that tells the story of a Ju/'hoansi (!Kung) woman's life in her own words. Shostak provides background for each chapter, and there is much here on marriage and everyday life.

Smith, Mary F. 1981 [1954]. *Baba of Karo* (New Haven: Yale University Press). A remarkable document: the autobiography of a Hausa woman born in 1877. This text provides much information about Hausa patterns of friendship, adoption, kinship, marriage, and other intimate relationships.

Stone, Linda, ed. 2001. *New Directions in Anthropological Kinship* (Lanham, MD: Rowman & Littlefield). An excellent collection of relatively recent articles on kinship.

RELATED WEBSITES

Bill C-38: The Civil Marriage Act www.parl.gc.ca/common/bills_ls.asp?Parl=38&Ses=1&ls=c38

National Association of Friendship Centres http://nafc.ca/about

Surrogacy Options for Gay Couples: In Search of a Womb of One's Own http://itsconceivablenow.com/surrogacy

Timeline of Canadian Milestones in Marriage www.samesexmarriage.ca/evolution/timeline.htm

Vanier Institute of the Family www.vanierinstitute.ca

Online Video

The Mercer family discusses the pressures that force the young people to leave Fogo Island, Newfoundland and Labrador, and their families. www.nfb.ca/film/mercer_family

7

Making a Living

LEARNING OBJECTIVES

By the end of Chapter 7, you will be able to

- recognize how humans have devised a
  variety of subsistence strategies,
- understand the relationship between production, distribution, and consumption,
- consider economic theories as they relate
  to anthropological concerns,
- identify various forms of exchange,
- compare and contrast different explanations for consumption patterns, and
- consider change in relation to how people
  make a living, in local and global settings.

This woman participates in the economic life of her community by checking
the quality of freshly dyed fabric hanging to dry in a sari garment factory
in India. Our cultures suggest a wide range of options for making a living,
many of which are becoming increasingly tied to the global economy
through the forces of globalization.

In recent years, anthropologists have taken an increasingly holistic view on issues of livelihood, recognizing the interrelationships among the physical, biological, environmental, economic, and cultural aspects of human existence. Indeed, cross-disciplinary research encourages us to recognize that human culture is not *apart from* the natural world—rather, it is *a part of* this world and is contextualized by and interdependent with ecological processes. It is our cultural responses and our capacity for reflexivity that allow for adaptive responses.

This adaptability is evidenced by observations anthropologists have made on human beings' diverse ways of making a living at various times and in various places. At times, anthropological investigation in this area reveals surprising results. A classic example comes from the work of Canadian anthropologist Richard B. Lee (1992b). When he arrived in the Kalahari Desert to work with the Ju/'hoansi (see EthnoProfile 6.2) in 1963, Lee was asked by a man named N!eishi to drive him and his neighbours out to collect mongongo nuts—a staple of their diet and a great favourite (Figure 7.1). Lee agreed, and the men and women spent two hours gathering an impressive amount of food. Lee later weighed the food collected and calculated that "each woman had gathered enough to feed a person for ten days and each man enough for five days." Overall, Lee observed that the Ju/'hoansi were well nourished, and that they ate balanced diets. What is more, they were choosy about what they ate, unwilling to settle for food they disliked. Such behaviour is entirely familiar to us. Thus, Lee found strong evidence to counter the Western stereotype of human beings who forage for a living as leading lives that are, in Thomas Hobbes's famous words, "nasty, brutish, and short."

Much has changed in southern Africa since the 1960s, and the Ju/'hoansi no longer forage as they once did. Until relatively recently, however, the cultural knowledge of the Ju/'hoansi enabled them to live rather well in what many see as a marginal environment. Today, their adaptability and resourcefulness continue in new ways. Robert Hitchcock (2003) comments on the current activism of the Ju/'hoansi of northwestern Botswana with respect to land claims issues and herding. Their innovative response includes community-based natural mapping to gain greater control of land, water, and wildlife resources. So even as things are changing, these peoples' traditional cultural knowledge continues to frame their relationship to the natural environment around them.

Culture and Livelihood

Although our physical survival depends on our making adequate use of the material resources around us, the resources themselves do not determine how they must be used. Rather, our cultures suggest a range of options for making a living, and for furnishing the tools to pursue those options. Thus, each culture has its own **economy**. Anthropologist Richard Wilk has defined **economic anthropology** as "the part of the discipline that debates issues of *human nature* that relate directly to the decisions of daily life and making a living" (1996: xv).

Self-interest, Institutions, and Morals

Anthropologists Richard Wilk and Lisa Cliggett (2007) argue that it is possible to identify three theoretical camps in economic anthropology, each of which depends on a different set of assumptions about human nature. Further, they note that the "real heat and argument in economic anthropology comes from underlying disagreement over these starting assumptions" (2007: 40). They discuss these assumptions by highlighting three models of human nature that correspond to the three theoretical camps.

economy
The culturally specific processes used by members of a society to provide themselves with material resources.

economic anthropology
"The part of the discipline [of anthropology] that debates issues of *human nature* that relate directly to the decisions of daily life and making a living."

FIGURE 7.1 Richard B. Lee gathers mongongo nuts with the Ju/'hoansi.

The first model that Wilk and Cliggett identify is the *self-interested model*. This model of human nature originated during the Enlightenment and is based on the assumption that individuals are first and foremost interested in their own well-being, that selfishness is natural. Economists since Adam Smith (1723–1790) have argued that people's resources (e.g., money) are not and never will be great enough for them to obtain all the goods they want. This view of economy also assumes that economic analysis should focus on *individuals* who must maximize their *utility* (or satisfaction) under conditions of **scarcity**. An economizing individual sets priorities and allocates resources rationally according to those priorities. Economic anthropologists who accept the self-interest model should therefore investigate the different priorities set by different societies and study how these priorities affect the maximizing decisions of individuals.

Other economic anthropologists, however, are committed to the *social model* of human nature. These anthropologists pay attention to "the way people form groups and exercise power" (2007: 42). This view of human nature assumes that people ordinarily identify with the groups to which they belong and, in many cases, cannot even conceive of having a self with interests that diverge from the interests of the group. This view of human nature suggests that economics ought to focus on **institutions** rather than individuals. From an institutional point of view, a society's economy consists of the culturally specific processes its members use to provide themselves with material resources. Therefore, economic processes cannot be considered apart from the cultural institutions in which they are embedded (Halperin 1994).

Wilk and Cliggett's third model of human nature is the *moral model*. Economic anthropologists committed to a moral model of human nature assume that people's motivations "are shaped by culturally specific belief systems and values . . . guided by a culturally patterned view of the universe and the human place within it" (2007: 43). People are socialized and enculturated into these values and practices over a lifetime, such that they will experience distress and conflict if tempted to make decisions—including economic decisions—that are contrary to their internalized morality. From the point of view

of the moral model, "modern society . . . has lost the morality and ethics that guided behaviour in traditional cultures, replacing them with amoral selfishness" (2007: 44). Wilk and Cliggett are unwilling to take any one model as a fact and are more interested in paying close ethnographic attention to the particularities of real human beings in real sociocultural settings. "The problem is explaining why people are guided sometimes by one set of motivations and at other times by others. . . . By suspending our preconceptions about human nature, we can give more direct attention to this fundamental question, which forms the basis of each culture's practical ethics and its distinction between moral and immoral" (2007: 46).

Subsistence Strategies

Subsistence is linked to basic material survival needs: food, clothing, and shelter. The different ways to go about meeting these needs are called **subsistence strategies**. Anthropologists have devised a typology of subsistence strategies that has gained wide acceptance (Figure 7.2). The basic division is between **food collectors** and **food producers**. Yet, although this typology suggests a clear distinction, the two systems are not always separated in practice. For example, archaeological evidence shows that some of the first food producers in the world continued food collection for many generations, raising a few crops on the side and occasionally abandoning food production to return to full-time foraging.

The strategies followed by *food collectors* depend on the availability of resources in their environments. Small-scale food collectors, such as traditional Ju/'hoansi, live in environments with resources that are sufficient but patchy and frequently only seasonally available. Thus small-scale food collectors are likely to change residence often. In contrast, complex food collectors live in environments where many foods are available at all times. Thus complex food collectors may even, like the Native peoples of the northwest coast of North America, build permanent settlements.

Food producers may farm or herd, or both. Herders are often nomadic, moving their herds from place to place in search of fresh pasture. Today, nomadic herders are often in conflict with settled farmers who own the lands—and often

scarcity
A condition under which it is assumed that resources (e.g., money) will never be plentiful enough for people to obtain all the goods or services they desire.

institutions
Stable and enduring cultural practices that organize social life.

subsistence strategies
The patterns of production, distribution, and consumption that members of a society use to meet their basic material survival needs.

food collectors
People who gather wild plant materials, fish, and/or hunt for food.

food producers
People who depend on domesticated plants and/or animals for food.

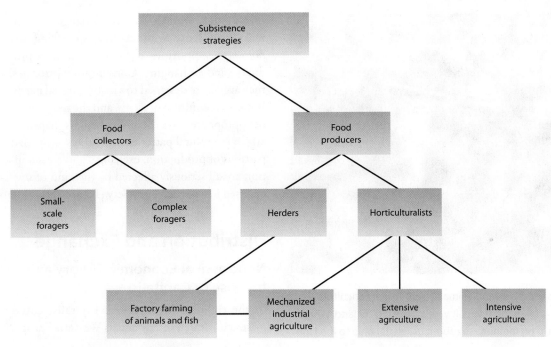

FIGURE 7.2 Subsistence strategies.

the water—that they traditionally used to sustain their herds. Among those who farm, there are three major distinctions:

1. **extensive agriculture**,
2. **intensive agriculture**, and
3. **mechanized industrial agriculture**.

In *extensive agriculture*, farmers clear plots of uncultivated land, burn the brush, and plant their crops in the ash-enriched soil. This is commonly called "*slash and burn*." Eventually, these techniques exhaust the soil, and the plot must lie fallow as a new plot is cleared and the process repeated. The length of this cycle may range from two years to twenty or thirty years, depending on the region. In *intensive agriculture*, farmers use more complex tools and technologies (e.g., crop rotation, irrigation, and fertilizers) to work on the same plot of land for a longer period of time (see Figure 7.3). In *mechanized industrial agriculture*, farming is organized along industrial lines. Most often, this type of crop production is found alongside the factory farming of animals.

Today, most of us are very familiar with the processes involved in mechanized industrial agriculture. Huge agribusinesses ("factories in the field") and animal feedlots have transformed food production into a large-scale, technology-dependent industry. Within the context of our globalized economy, food is commonly transformed into a "commodity" that is produced and distributed by transnational corporate institutions (Phillips 2006). Unfortunately, our relatively recent "scientization" of food production has led to the loss of traditional systems of production as well as the loss of traditional knowledge worked out over millennia (Brodt 2001). Indeed, many traditional ways of making a living are disappearing under the forces of modernization and globalization.

Phases of Economic Activity

Economic activity is usefully subdivided into three distinct phases:

1. **production**,
2. **distribution**, and
3. **consumption**.

Anthropologists differ in the importance they attach to each phase. Most would agree that *exchange* is central to capitalist free enterprise. However, some anthropologists argue that we cannot properly understand exchange without first studying the nature of *production* as it shapes the context in which exchange can occur, determining the kind and quantity of goods to exchange. Other anthropologists have suggested

extensive agriculture
A form of cultivation that depends on slash-and-burn techniques, rainwater, human muscle power, and a few simple tools such as digging sticks, hoes, and/or machetes.

intensive agriculture
A form of cultivation that employs plows, draft animals, irrigation, and fertilizer to bring a large amount of land under cultivation at one time.

mechanized industrial agriculture
Large-scale farming that is highly dependent on industrial methods of technology and production.

production
The transformation of nature's raw materials into a form suitable for human use.

distribution
The allocation of goods and services.

consumption
Using up material goods necessary for human survival.

FIGURE 7.3 Some farmers use plows and animals for intensive agriculture to reduce the amount of time it takes them to cultivate a large plot of land. What can a culture's dominant farming methods say about its relationship to the land?

that neither production nor exchange patterns make any sense without first specifying the *consumption* priorities of the people who are producing and exchanging. Consumption priorities, they argue, are designed to satisfy material needs. But the recognition of needs, and the recognition of appropriate ways to satisfy them, is shaped by arbitrary cultural patterns. Still others argue that patterns of production, exchange, and consumption are all seriously affected by the kind of *storage* used in a particular society (Figure 7.4).

Distribution and Exchange

Neoclassical Economic Theory and the Rise of Capitalism

In the eighteenth century, as capitalist enterprises continued to rise across Western Europe,

FIGURE 7.4 Above: A seventeenth-century drawing of storage warehouses built at the height of the Inca (Tawantinsuyu) Empire. Left: The plan of Huánuco Pampa, an Inca administration centre, which shows the location of these storage warehouses. Some anthropologists argue that food storage practices buffer a population from ecological fluctuations, making considerable cultural manipulation of the economic relations of consumption possible.

thinkers such as Adam Smith and his disciples struggled to devise theories to explain the profound changes in European economic and social life. Their work became the foundation for **neoclassical economic theory**, a theory that some economic anthropologists continue to support today.

Capitalism differed in many ways from the preceding feudal economic system, particularly in distribution. Feudal economic relations allotted goods and services to individuals on the basis of their position in society, or their *status*. Because lords had high status, they had a right to more goods and services. Peasants, who had low status, were allowed far less. This was a time-honoured system not open to modification. New capitalist economic relations, in contrast, were negotiated between buyers and sellers in the "market."

In Smith's ideal market, everyone has something to sell (if only his or her willingness to work), and everyone is also a potential buyer of the goods or services brought to the market. There is economic exchange with none of the old traditional restrictions governing who should get how much of what. Prices fluctuate depending on levels of supply and demand, and distribution is carried out in line with the preferences of individuals (needs and wants = desired goods). High demand for certain items raises the price for those items, as many buyers bargain to obtain few goods. This high demand, in turn, entices more people to produce those goods to take advantage of their higher returns. As competition among suppliers increases, however, prices go down, as each supplier attempts to obtain a greater share of the market. Ideally, prices stabilize as suppliers begin offering "desired" goods at a cost sufficiently high to allow a profit but sufficiently low for buyers to afford.

Capitalist market exchange of goods and services (including labour) for other goods, services, or cash was an important development in Western economic history. It is not surprising, therefore, that eighteenth-century Western economic theory was preoccupied with explaining how the capitalist market worked. This preoccupation grew as it became clear that markets had a new central importance in the functioning of society. Western neoclassical economics is based on the assumption that market forces are the central forces determining

levels of both production and consumption in society. Thus, neoclassical economic analysis focusses on markets, scarcity hypotheses, and "laws" of supply and demand. In such a system, everything has a price.

Modes of Exchange

Some anthropologists have argued, however, that to take self-interested, materialistic decision-making in the capitalist market as the prototype of human decision-making is both overly simplistic and ethnocentric. Further, such analyses frequently encourage the use of unilineal evolutionary models of organization and interaction in the discussion of cultures defined as "other." Thus, Lewis Henry Morgan's ethnical stages of savagery, barbarism, and civilization (discussed in Chapter 3) become embedded, overtly or covertly, in the categories used in such discussions.

At this point in the discussion, we should take a moment to remember that capitalist markets and neoclassical economic theory are relatively recent cultural inventions. We should also remember that they were developed in specific societies with certain basic values, institutions, and assumptions about the human condition—to peoples with a certain shared world view. Non-Western, non-capitalist societies also have devised modes of exchange that distribute material goods in ways that are in accordance with their basic values, institutions, and assumptions about the human condition—their world views.

Characteristic of the Western-centric analysis of non-Western cultures is the work of French anthropologist Marcel Mauss (2000 [1950]). Mauss contrasted non-capitalist *gift exchanges* with impersonal *commodity exchanges* typical of the capitalist market (Figure 7.5). Gift exchange is deeply embedded in social relations of kinship, partnerships, and acquaintanceships, always requiring a return "gift." In contrast, commodity exchange links the participants by cash—the cost of and payment for an item or labour. While Mauss associated gift exchanges with non-Western cultures, he associated commodity exchange with Western cultures. (Recall here Morgan's division between "savage" or "barbaric" non-Western societies and "civilized" European societies.)

neoclassical economic theory

A formal attempt to explain the workings of capitalist enterprise, with particular attention to distribution.

FIGURE 7.5 In his book *The Gift* (1950), Marcel Mauss examines the Kula exchange ceremony of the Trobriand Islanders. Here, men dance at a modern Kula exchange celebration in the Trobriand Islands, Papua New Guinea. What advantages might this sort of exchange system have in comparison to the typical Western exchange system involving the exchange of money for goods?

modes of exchange
Patterns according to which distribution takes place: reciprocity, redistribution, and market exchange.

reciprocity
A mode of exchange in which individuals exchange goods and/or services (1) under the assumption that the exchanges will eventually balance out, (2) with the expectation of immediate balance, or (3) in the hope that at least one party will get something for nothing.

redistribution
A mode of exchange in which a centralized social organization receives contributions from all members of the group and redistributes them in a way that provides for every member.

Consequently, Mauss did not fully address the fact that cultures may engage in *both* forms of exchange.

The work of American anthropologist Marshall Sahlins (1972) has a similarly ancient–modern directional tone. Sahlins drew on the writings of economic historian Karl Polanyi (1886–1964) to propose three **modes of exchange**: reciprocity, redistribution, and market exchange. Polanyi argued that these modes could be identified historically in many cultures. He also recognized that different modes of exchange often coexist within a single society—a recognition that makes his ideas very useful in an anthropological context.

Reciprocity

The most ancient mode of exchange, **reciprocity** is characteristic of egalitarian societies. Sahlins identified three kinds of reciprocity:

1. generalized,
2. balanced, and
3. negative.

Generalized reciprocity is found when those who exchange do so without expecting an immediate return and without specifying the value of the return. Everyone assumes that the exchanges will eventually balance out. *Balanced reciprocity* is found when those who exchange expect a return of equal value within a specified time limit. For example, Richard B. Lee noted that the Ju/'hoansi distinguish between barter, which requires an immediate return of an equivalent value, and *hxaro*, which is a kind of generalized reciprocity that encourages social obligations to be extended into the future (1992b: 103). *Negative reciprocity* is an exchange of goods and services in which at least one party attempts to get something for nothing without suffering any penalties. These attempts can range from haggling over prices to outright seizure.

Redistribution

The second mode of exchange, **redistribution**, requires some form of centralized social organization. Those who occupy the central position receive economic or material contributions from all members of the group. It is then their responsibility to redistribute the goods they receive in a way that provides for every member of the group. A well-known Canadian institution of redistribution is the Canada Revenue Agency.

The potlatch (Ýaqʷ qʷa; Figure 7.6), or gift-giving ceremony, of First Nations peoples of Canada's west coast has frequently been used erroneously to illustrate redistribution. While there are elements of exchange involved, reducing the event to a venue for redistribution of wealth ignores the complexity of the social interactions the potlatch represents: members of a community coming together to bear witness to specific culturally significant events such as births, marriages, deaths, and remembrances. Further, as anthropologist Kenneth Tollefson observes, politics plays a very large part in the potlatch:

> certain clan goals could only be fulfilled through potlatching. These include (1) installation of clan leaders, (2) evaluation and verification of clan titles to resources, (3) bestowal of clan titles, (4) resolution of inter-clan disputes, (5) establishing or reaffirming clan alliances, (6) investment and diversification of clan wealth, (7) social removal of shame, and (8) maintenance of regional stability. (1995: 71)

Thus we see the interconnections among power, politics, cultural priorities, social interaction, and economic exchange; these ties should remind us of the necessity of looking at cultural processes through the anthropological lens of holism. (Note Daisy Sewid-Smith's discussion of the potlatch in the "In Their Own Words" box, below.)

Market Exchange

Invented in capitalist society, **market exchange** is the most recent mode of exchange, according to Polanyi. Polanyi was well aware that trade, money, and market institutions had developed independently of one another. He also knew that they could be found in societies outside the West. The uniqueness of capitalism was how all three institutions were linked to one another in the societies of early modern Europe.

FIGURE 7.6 The potlatch of the Kwakiutl (Kwakwaka'wakw) was a highly complex social event that held deep cultural importance for all involved in the gathering. The ceremony was banned by the Canadian government from 1884 to 1951, although it continued in the villages even in the face of arrests and punishment through the Canadian courts.

Production

Some economic anthropologists see production as the driving force behind economic activity. Production creates supplies of goods to which demand must respond, and it determines levels of possible consumption. Anthropologists who stress the centrality of production borrow their perspective on economic activity, as well as many key concepts, from the works of German philosopher Karl Marx (1818–1883). They argue that this perspective is far more insightful than the one taken by neoclassical theorists of market exchange.

Labour

Labour is perhaps the most central Marxian concept these anthropologists have adopted. Through labour, human beings actively struggle together to transform natural substances into forms they can use. This is most clear in the case of food production but includes the production of clothing, shelter, and tools (Figure 7.7). Marx emphasized the importance of human physical labour in the material world, but he also recognized the importance of mental or cognitive labour. Human intelligence allows us to reflect on

market exchange
A mode of exchange in which the exchange of goods (trade) is calculated in terms of a multi-purpose medium of exchange and standard of value (money) and carried on by means of a supply–demand–price mechanism (the market).

labour
The activity linking human social groups to the material world around them.

IN THEIR OWN WORDS | The Continuing Reshaping of Our Ritual World by Academic Adjuncts

Daisy Sewid-Smith, a daughter of the late Chief James Sewid, is a member of the Mamaliliq la tribe of Village Island, British Columbia. Here she discusses the "grossly misunderstood" economic system known as Pðssa, which is commonly confused with the gift-giving ceremony known as Ýaqwqwa, or potlatch. She also identifies problems with traditionally academic approaches to studying and writing about Native peoples—problems that have too often led to misunderstandings about culturally significant processes such as the potlatch.

My great uncle joined with the other nobility to lament the loss of the great economic institutions of the past when he stated . . . "It's no use giving a potlatch any more. The old people don't do it; so nobody pays you back, and the young people don't even understand what it's all about." He was referring to the grossly misunderstood economic system we called Pðssa. This was the investing institution of the Kʷakʷakðwakaʷ and Liǧʷidaxʷ League of Nations. This institution charged interest, called in debts, gave credit, and kept records of all transactions for future generations. Both my father and my great uncle held hereditary positions in this complex system. It was to this institution that my great uncle was referring when he spoke of the young not understanding and the investment not being repaid.

Most of our people today have only seen what was known as Ýaqʷ qʷa, meaning *gift-giving*. That is the reason the term *potlatch*, a Chinook word meaning *to give*, was assigned to this system by the Chinook speakers of our old trade world. The Ýaqʷ qʷa, or potlatch, was a system that paid witnesses to validate such events as marriage, memorials, and the succession of ancestral names. The Ýaqʷ qʷa, or potlatch system, did not have the same principles, purpose, laws, or membership as the Pðssa.

Unfortunately, my great uncle understood too well the changing landscape of his ritual world. He and the nobility he came from had struggled so hard to keep the culture alive despite the institutionalized oppression of our beliefs by the state and by religious zealots; the loss of their sacred land and resources by the encroachment and laws of the newcomers; the loss of life due to disease, social breakdown, and the very personal identity struggles of the younger generation; and the diminished use of our precious language that holds the keys to our past, our values, and our religion. Today, our struggle is not just of legal or religious prosecution. Today our struggle is sadly the reshaping of our ritual world by academic interpretations.

The academic world must, in its need to publish accounts of my Nation, begin to subscribe to rules that are consistent with our ritual structure. They must begin to identify the trained specialists who are working within our culture and use the same rules we have of validation and authority to ensure an accurate view of our ritual world. It is not enough to read and cite from previous misinterpretations to make a theory right. When a house is built on a foundation of sand, its structure is weak and unstable. So is it for our ritual world within academic rendering. We have sorrily witnessed the reshaping of the foundations of our old institutions, the validation of those within our Nation unschooled in our complexes, and the loss of our precious rights and privileges so embedded in our history.

The last words belong to one of our chiefs addressing the first academic to come among us, Franz Boas, when he said in 1894, "It is a strict law that bids us dance. It is a strict law that bids us distribute our property among our friends and neighbours. It is a good law. Let the white man observe his law, we shall observe ours."

Source: Sewid-Smith, Daisy. 1997. "The Continuing Reshaping of Our Ritual World by Academic Adjuncts," *Anthropology and Education Quarterly* 28, 4: 594–602.

---

mode of production
"A specific, historically occurring set of social relations through which labour is deployed to wrest energy from nature by means of tools, skills, organization, and knowledge."

means of production
The tools, skills, organization, and knowledge used to extract energy from nature.

and organize productive activities. Mentally and physically, human social groups struggle together to ensure their material survival. In struggling, they reproduce patterns of social organization, production, and thought.

Modes, Means, and Relations of Production

Marx attempted to classify the ways different human groups carry out production. Each way is called a **mode of production**. Anthropologist Eric Wolf defined a mode of production as "a specific, historically occurring set of social relations through which labour is deployed to wrest energy from nature by means of tools, skills, organization, and knowledge" (1982: 75). Tools, skills, organization, and knowledge constitute what Marx called the **means of production**. The social relations linking human beings who use a given means of production within a particular mode of production are called the

relations of production. That is, different productive tasks (clearing the bush, planting, harvesting, and so on) are assigned to different social groups, all of which must work together for production to be successful.

The concept of mode of production is holistic, highlighting recurring patterns of human activity in which certain forms of social organization, production practices, and cultural knowledge co-determine one another. While he notes that Marx speaks of at least eight different modes of production in his own writings, Wolf focusses on three modes of production that he believes have been particularly important in human history:

1. a *kin-ordered mode* in which social labour is performed on the basis of kinship relations (e.g., husbands/fathers/brothers/sons clear the fields, the whole family plants, mothers/wives/sisters/daughters weed, small children keep animals out of the field);
2. a *tributary mode* in which labourers control the means of production but must provide payment (money, a percentage of the crop, or labour) to some figure of authority (e.g., a lord or ruler, as in the feudal peasant system of Europe); and
3. the *capitalist mode.*

The capitalist mode has three main features:

1. the means of production is property owned by the capitalists,
2. workers are denied access to such ownership and must sell their labour to the capitalists in order to survive, and
3. this labour produces for capitalists surpluses of wealth that capitalists may retain or plow back into production to increase output and generate further surpluses.

An overlap exists between this classification of modes of production and the traditional anthropological classification of subsistence strategies (see Figure 7.2). The kin-ordered mode of production is found among foragers and those farmers and herders whose political organization does not involve domination by one group. The tributary mode is found among farmers and herders living in a social system that is divided into classes of rulers and subjects. Subjects produce both for

FIGURE 7.7 Women weave rope out of coir, a fibre extracted from coconut husks, in Kerala, India. Human beings continuously labour to turn natural substances into useful products. Which activities do you undertake that link you to your material world?

themselves and for their rulers, who take a certain proportion of their subjects' product as tribute. The capitalist mode, the most recent to develop, is found in industrial societies around the world, but particularly those of North America and Western Europe.

Thus, in some ways the "mode of production" concept simply recognizes the same variation in the arts of subsistence that Lewis Henry Morgan recognized in the nineteenth century (see Chapter 3). Yet the concept of mode of production also highlights certain attributes of subsistence strategies that Morgan's approach tended to downplay. For example, modes of production are as much to do with forms of social and political organization as with material productive activities. That is, the kin-ordered mode of production is distinctive as much for its use of the kinship system to allocate labour to production as for the kind of production undertaken. In a kin-ordered mode of production, the *relations of kinship* serve as the *relations of production* that enable a particular *mode of production* to be carried out.

relations of production
The social relations linking the people who use a given means of production within a particular mode of production.

The Role of Conflict in Material Life

Traditionally, anthropologists have emphasized the important links between a society's social organization (kinship groups, chiefdom, or state) and the way that society meets its subsistence needs, either to demonstrate the stages of cultural evolution or to display the functional interrelationships between parts of a particular society. In both cases, however, the emphasis of the analysis was on the harmonious fashion in which societies either changed or stayed the same. This focus implied that social stability should not be tampered with. Social change was possible, but it would take place in an orderly fashion, in the fullness of time, according to laws of development beyond the control of individual members of society.

Many anthropologists have not been persuaded that social change is orderly or that social organization is by nature harmonious. They find the Marxian approach useful because it treats conflict as a natural part of the human condition. The concept of mode of production makes a major contribution to economic anthropology precisely because of the very different interpretation it gives to conflict, imbalance, and disharmony in social life.

Marx pointed out, for example, that the capitalist mode of production incorporates the workers and the owners in different and contradictory ways. These groups, which he called *classes*, have different interests, and what is good for one class may not be good for all classes. The workers' economic desires (higher wages to purchase more goods) are inevitably opposed to the owners' economic desires (lower wages to increase their profits or to reinvest in tools and raw materials).

This does not mean that warfare is constant between the different classes engaged in a particular mode of production; however, it does mean that the potential for conflict is built into the mode of production. The more complex and unequal the involvement of different classes in a mode of production, the more intense the struggle between them is likely to be. Such struggle may not always lead to outright rebellion, but minor forms of resistance—from sluggish efforts at work to intentional disruption of the status quo—are not uncommon. Marx was one of the first social analysts to document the high level of human suffering generated by certain modes of production, particularly the capitalist mode.

ideology

Those products of consciousness—such as morality, religion, and metaphysics—that purport to explain to people who they are and to justify the kinds of lives they lead.

Wolf's three modes of production (kin-ordered, tributary, and capitalist) describe not only a society's subsistence strategy but also that society's social organization. As a result, they accent the lines along which tension and conflict may develop between different segments of the society: between, say, parents and children or husbands and wives in the kin-ordered mode; between lords and peasants in the tributary mode; and between capitalists and workers in the capitalist mode.

Applying Production Theory to Social and Cultural Life

Economic anthropologists who focus on production as the main force in economic life tend to apply the metaphor of production to other areas of social life as well. They see production as involving far more than short-term satisfaction of material survival needs. If a given *mode* of production is to persist over time, the *means* and *relations* of production must also persist.

For example, farmers produce grain and leave behind harvested fields. They exchange some grain with cattle herders for milk and meat, and they permit the herders' cattle to graze in the harvested fields in exchange for manure they need to fertilize their fields. Consequently, farmers and herders alike end up with a mix of foodstuffs to sustain human life. In addition, each group has what it needs in the coming season to renew its means of production. Both groups will want to ensure that similar exchanges are carried out by successive generations who will consist of farmers and cattle herders producing the same goods and willing to exchange them. Therefore, not only must the means of production continue but so must the relations of production. The result, then, is the reproduction of society from generation to generation (Figure 7.8).

People also produce and reproduce *interpretations* of the production process and their roles in that process. Marx used the term **ideology** to refer to the cultural products of conscious reflection. As used in Marxian analysis, *ideology* refers to those beliefs that explain and justify the relations of production. Therefore, ideology was not independent of the production process, since the act of taking part in a production process alters the way participants *think*. As a result, Marxian economic anthropologists are also interested in the kinds of ideas, beliefs, and values that are produced and reproduced in societies with different modes of production. Members of the class in power usually hold to an ideology that justifies their domination. Those who are dominated may assent publicly to the ideology of the rulers, but in private they are likely to be highly critical and to offer alternative interpretations.

Unlike exchange theorists, production theorists tend to be interested in *why* the different parties to an exchange have different quantities of resources with which to bargain. They believe that access to resources is determined *before* exchange by the relations of production, which decide who is entitled to how much of what. They reject the assumption that access to valued resources is open to anyone with gumption and the spirit of enterprise. Different modes of production stack the deck in favour of some classes and against others. This is most clear in the capitalist mode, where owners have disproportionate access to wealth, power, and prestige and where workers' access to these goods is sharply restricted. Thus, the classes who fare poorly do so not because of any inherent inferiority, laziness, or carelessness; they fail to get ahead because the rules of the game (i.e., of the mode of production) were set up in a way that keeps them from winning.

Production theory also provides a perspective on cultural persistence and cultural change. It relates peoples' preferences for different goods to the interests and opportunities of the different classes to which they belong. People buy and sell as they do not out of idiosyncratic whimsy but because the choices open to them are shaped by the relations of production. From this perspective, poor people purchase cheap goods not because they have poor taste but because their position within the mode of production provides them with very limited income, and they must make do with the goods they can afford.

Finally, production theory views human beings as active social agents in the construction and reconstruction of human society through time. Traditions persist, but only because people labour to reproduce them from one day to the next. Linking production (and reproduction), social relations, and ideologies highlights the contingent nature of social life, even as it suggests how traditions are carried on.

FIGURE 7.8 Producers must find ways to pass their relations of production from one generation to the next. Here, a child fishes alongside adult fishermen in the Philippines. By participating, he is being taught to take on a role in the production process. What are some of the other ways in which the relations and means of production are reproduced from generation to generation?

Consumption

Consumption usually refers to using up material goods necessary for human survival. These goods include—at a minimum—food, drink, clothing, and shelter; they can and often do include much more. The study of consumption by economists and others was, until relatively recently, much neglected. To some extent, this is because many observers assumed that there were no interesting questions to ask about consumption. That is, it seemed clear that people either consume goods for obvious reasons, such as survival, or as a result of personal preferences. Today, consumption is often a central focus in studies of economic practices.

Explanations for Consumption Patterns

Anthropologists who make cross-cultural comparisons have always noticed striking differences in consumption patterns in different societies. Historically, they have taken three basic approaches to account for these patterns:

1. the internal explanation,
2. the external explanation, and
3. the cultural explanation.

The Internal Explanation

The internal explanation for human consumption patterns comes from the work of pioneering anthropologist Bronislaw Malinowski. His theories explain certain social practices by relating them to basic human needs (biological or psychological). If these needs go unmet, the society might not survive. Malinowski proposed a list of basic human needs, which includes nourishment, reproduction, bodily comforts, safety, movement, growth, and health. Every culture responds in its own way to these needs with some form of the corresponding institutions: food-collecting techniques, kinship, shelter, protection, activities, training, and hygiene (Malinowski 1944: 91).

Malinowski's approach was useful because it emphasized human beings' dependence on the physical world. Further, Malinowski showed that many customs that appear bizarre to Western observers are in fact "rational" because they help people satisfy their basic human needs. Nonetheless, Malinowski's approach fell short of explaining why all societies do not share the same consumption patterns.

The External Explanation

Later anthropologists looked at consumption patterns from the perspective of **cultural ecology**—that is, in terms of the ways in which we adapt in response to our physical environment. From this perspective, human consumption patterns are a response to what people can obtain in a given environment. In order to survive, people must learn to make use of the available resources. This perspective draws on the field of ecology, making note of how different **ecozones** and **ecotones** (Figure 7.9) influence the range of **econiches** available to human beings. It also draws on the findings of socioecologists, who investigate why a particular animal population—say, a troop of baboons—organizes itself the way it does in a particular environment.

The term *cultural ecology* comes to us from American anthropologist Julian Steward (1972), who was influenced by the earlier work of Franz Boas and Alfred Kroeber. Steward did fieldwork among the Shoshone in the highly inhospitable Great Basin region of the United States. In conducting his research, he developed an approach that involved

1. outlining the subsistence technologies and methods of environmental exploitation used locally,
2. seeking patterned strategies tied to such exploitations, and
3. investigating how these strategies (with associated technologies) affect other areas of the culture.

Steward's approach continues to be of use in many disciplines. Consider the work of economic anthropologist Rhoda Halperin (1994) on the relationship between ecological anthropology (an extension of the cultural ecology perspective) and economic anthropology. Borrowing concepts from Karl Polanyi, Halperin argued that every economic system can be analyzed in terms of two kinds of movements:

1. *locational movements*, or "changes of place," and
2. *appropriational movements*, or "changes of hands."

In her view, ecological relationships are properly understood as *changes of place*, as when people must move into the grasslands, gather mongongo nuts, and transport them back to camp. Economic relationships, in contrast, are more properly understood as *changes of hands*, as when mongongo nuts are distributed to all members of the camp, whether or not they helped to gather them. Thus, ecological (locational) movements involve transfers of energy (i.e., physical movement); economic (appropriational) movements, in contrast, involve transfers of rights (1994: 59).

Another way of seeing the difference between ecological and economic arrangements is to pay attention to the connection between food storage and food sharing. A socioecologist might argue that those who gather mongongo nuts are obliged to share them and consume them immediately because they have no way to store them. Ecological anthropologist Tim Ingold (1983) agrees that the obligation to share makes storage unnecessary, but he also points out that sharing with others today ordinarily obligates them to share with you tomorrow (reciprocity). Put another way, sharing food can be seen not

---

cultural ecology
The study of the ways in which human beings relate to one another and to their natural environment.

ecozones
The particular mixture of plant and animal species occupying any particular region of the earth.

ecotones
A transition area between two different ecozones that displays characteristics of both ecozones.

econiche
The sum total of relations between a species and the plants and animals on which it relies for survival; these relations define those places where a species is "at home."

only as a way of avoiding spoilage but also as a way of storing IOUs for the future!

Once societies develop ways to preserve and store food and other material goods, however, new possibilities open up (Figure 7.10). Archaeological evidence indicates that the more food there is to store, the more people invest in storage facilities, and the more quickly they become sedentary. Large-scale food-storage techniques involve a series of "changes of place" that buffer a population from ecological fluctuations for long periods of time. But techniques of food storage alone predict nothing about the "changes of hands" that food will undergo once it has been stored. Food storage techniques have been associated with all subsistence strategies, including that of complex food collectors. These findings suggest that economic relations of consumption, involving the transfer of rights in stored food, have long been open to considerable cultural manipulation (Halperin 1994: 178).

From these examples, we can see that both ecological and economic relationships affect human consumption patterns. However, economic transfers of rights to material resources cannot be separated from wider political forces that impinge on those rights. Thus, according to anthropologist Elliot Fratkin, "a shift in theoretical understanding from *cultural* ecology to *political* ecology" is necessary (1997: 236). For example, the current adaptations of eastern African herders and their animals to the semi-arid environment in which they live is strongly affected by political pressures coming from the nation-states of eastern Africa. As a result, Fratkin says, contemporary anthropological studies of herders explain human–livestock interactions "less in terms of 'carrying capacity' or 'desertification' and more in terms of loss of common property rights (land and water commons), increased economic differentiation and social stratification, and incorporation and domination of tribal pastoral groups by larger state systems" (236).

The Cultural Explanation

From the perspective of cultural anthropology, the explanations for human consumption patterns that we have discussed so far have definite limitations. Consider how each would respond to the following question: Why do people

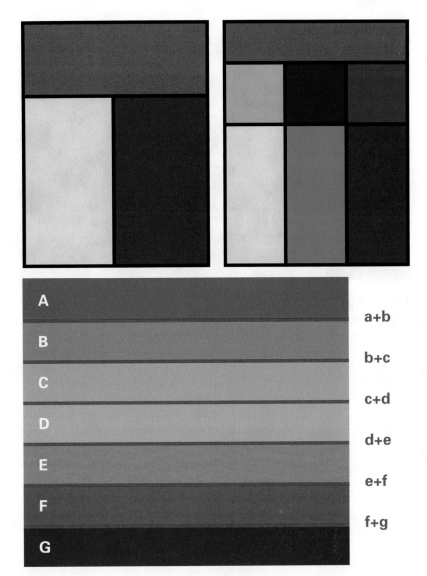

FIGURE 7.9 The composition of ecozones and ecotones is highly variable. The top left diagram represents three ecozones (red, blue, and yellow). The top right diagram adds ecotones (orange, purple, green, and brown) into the mix. Of the ecotones, the brown square has the most potential, as it has resources from all three ecozones. The lower diagram illustrates more specifically the many "tones" of transition between ecozones—for example, the forest (green) through to the coast line (orange) into the depths of the a river, a lake, or an ocean (blue).

X raise peanuts and sorghum? The internal, Malinowskian explanation would be "to meet their basic human need for food." The external, socioecological explanation would be "because peanuts and sorghum are the only food crops available in their ecozone." Both these answers are suggestive, but they remain incomplete. We might ask whether the local food sources that people X choose to exploit are the *only* local food

FIGURE 7.10 Traditional facilities for storing food in Sulawesi, Indonesia. How could the introduction of food storage change a culture's lifestyle? How about longer-term food storage?

sources available to them. Ethnographic data show that no society exploits every locally available food source to meet its consumption needs. Quite the contrary, consumption needs are selective; in other words, they *are culturally shaped*.

Here is the major shortcoming of both internal and external explanations for human consumption patterns—they ignore the possibility of *human agency*. Malinowski, and many cultural ecologists, assumed that patterns of consumption were dictated by environmental necessity that did not allow for alternatives. From such a perspective, individuals in most non-Western societies have little to no control over what they consume; they simply have no choice. Yet to rob people of choice is to dehumanize them. In contrast, by acknowledging that all people have at least some control over what they consume, and by recognizing that cultural forces influence these choices, we highlight human agency as central to the human experience.

The Cultural Construction of Needs

"Needs" is a vague concept. Hunger can be satisfied by beans and rice or steak and lobster. Thirst can be quenched by water or beer or soda pop. In effect, culture defines needs and provides for their satisfaction according to its own logic. And cultural logic is irreducible to biology, psychology, or ecological pressure.

By adopting this cultural approach to consumption, the distinctions between *needs* and *wants*, or between *necessities* and *luxuries*, disappear. As anthropologist Mary Douglas and economist Baron Isherwood propose,

> Let us put an end to the widespread and misleading distinction between goods that sustain life and health and others that service the mind and heart—spiritual goods.... The counter-argument proposed here is that all goods carry meaning. . . . The meaning is in the relations between all the goods, just as music is in the relations marked out by the sounds and not in any one note. (1979: 72–3)

For instance, a good's meaning may have to do with its edibility, but edibility is often culturally determined. Furthermore, the meaning of any individual item of food cannot be explained in isolation. That meaning becomes clear only when the item is compared with other items that are also marked by the culture as edible or inedible.

Dietary Laws

Consider the prohibition against eating pork. For Jews and Muslims, pork is inedible, culturally speaking. According to Mary Douglas (1966), this restriction has nothing to do with ecological problems associated with pigs or with defects in the digestive systems of Jews or Muslims. Douglas analyzed the Jewish dietary prohibitions detailed in the biblical Book of Leviticus. She argued that certain animals were prohibited as food because something about them violated the prototypes for edibility recognized in ancient Hebrew culture (Table 7.1). Prototypically "clean" (and therefore edible) land animals were supposed to have four legs and cloven (i.e., split) hooves and to chew the cud; pigs were an "abomination" because they were cloven-hoofed four-legged beasts that did not chew the cud. "Clean" beasts of the air were supposed to have feathers and to fly with wings; therefore, hopping insects were "unclean" because they had six legs, neither walked nor flew, and lacked feathers. "Clean" water animals were supposed to have fins and scales; shrimp were forbidden because they lacked fins and scales.

By itself, Douglas argued, a prohibition against eating pork is meaningless and appears irrational.

TABLE 7.1 Jewish Dietary Prohibitions

Realm	Class Prototype	Clean Examples	Unclean Examples	Reason Prohibited
Earth	Four-legged animals that hop, jump, or walk	Cattle, camels, sheep, goats (all cloven-hoofed and cud-chewing animals)	Hare, hyrax	Cud-chewing but not cloven-hoofed
			Pig	Cloven-hoofed but not cud-chewing
			Weasel, mouse, crocodile, shrew, chameleon, mole	Two legs, two hands, but go about on all fours
Air	Two-legged fowl that fly with wings	Chickens	Grasshoppers	Six legs, cannot walk or fly, lacks feathers
Water	Scaly fish that swim with fins	Carp, whitefish	Shrimp, clams	Possess neither fins nor scales

Source: Adapted from Douglas 1966: 41–57.

However, when this prohibition is taken together with other dietary prohibitions in Leviticus, and when these are compared with the foods that were permitted, a pattern emerges. Douglas and Isherwood write, "Goods assembled together in ownership make physical, visible statements about the hierarchy of values to which their chooser subscribes" (1979: 5). Thus, Jews who consume only "clean" foods are doing more than satisfying their hunger; they are also making a social declaration of solidarity with their religious community. Their need for food is being met, but selectively, and the selection they make carries a social message.

Dietary laws deal with food and drink and so might still be explained in biological or ecological terms. Such explanations are more difficult to construct, however, when we consider the role of banana leaves in the Trobriand Islands.

Banana Leaves in the Trobriand Islands

Anthropologist Annette Weiner travelled to the Trobriand Islands more than half a century after Malinowski carried out his classic research there (see EthnoProfile 7.1). To her surprise, she discovered a highly respected local tradition involving the accumulation and exchange of banana leaves, known locally as women's wealth (Figure 7.11;

Weiner 1980). Malinowski had never described this tradition, even though there is evidence from photographs and writing that it was in force at the time of his fieldwork. There are probably two reasons Malinowski overlooked these transactions:

1. they are carried out by women, and he did not view women as important actors in the economy; and
2. he labelled only activities that satisfied biological survival needs as "economic," and banana leaves are inedible.

However, explaining transactions involving women's wealth turns out to be crucial for understanding Trobriand kinship obligations.

Banana leaves might be said to have a "practical" use in that women make highly valued skirts out of them. But the bundles of leaves themselves are considered to be valuable. Why bother to exchange great amounts of money or other goods to obtain bundles of banana leaves? To an outsider, this would seem to be irrational consumption. And yet, as Weiner demonstrates, bundles of banana leaves are significant in that they are a "representation of the most fundamental relationships in the social system"—namely, kinship (Weiner 1980: 289).

ETHNOPROFILE 7.1 | Trobriand Islanders

Region Oceania

Nation Papua New Guinea

Language Kilivila, part of the Kilivila-Louisiades language family

Population 40,000 (2009 estimate)

Environment Tropical rainforest on main islands of Kiriwina, Kaileuna, Vakuta, and Kitava

Livelihood Subsistence horticulturalists (yams as main crop)

Political organization Traditionally, chiefs and others of rank in matriclans; today, part of a modern nation-state

For more information Malinowski, Bronislaw. 1984 [1922]. *Argonauts of the Western Pacific* (Long Grove, IL: Waveland Press); Weiner, Annette. 1988. *The Trobrianders of Papua New Guinea* (New York: Holt, Rinehart, and Winston).

FIGURE 7.11 In the Trobriand Islands, banana leaves, like the ones this woman is shaping, are recognized as women's wealth, a marker of economic, political, and social status.

Trobrianders are matrilineal, and men traditionally prepare yam gardens for their sisters. After the harvest, yams from these gardens are distributed by a woman's brother to her husband. Weiner's research suggests that what Malinowski took to be the *redistribution* of yams, from a wife's kin to her husband, could be better understood as a *reciprocal exchange* of yams for women's wealth. The parties central to this exchange are a woman, her brother, and her husband. The woman is the person through whom yams are passed from her own kin to her husband; she is also the person through whom women's wealth is passed from her husband to her own kin.

Transactions involving women's wealth occur when someone in the woman's kinship group

dies. Surviving relatives must "buy back," metaphorically speaking, all the yams or other goods that the deceased person gave to others during his or her lifetime. Each payment marks a social link between the deceased and the recipient, and the size of the payment marks the importance of their relationship. All the payments must be made in women's wealth.

The dead person's status, as well as the status of her or his family, depends on the size and number of the payments made, and the people who must be paid can number into the hundreds. Women make women's wealth themselves and exchange trade goods to obtain it from other women, but when someone in their matrilineage dies, they collect it from their husbands. Indeed, a woman's value is measured by the amount of women's wealth her husband provides. Furthermore,

> if a man does not work hard enough for his wife in accumulating wealth for her, then her brother will not increase his labour in the yam garden. . . . The production in yams and women's wealth is always being evaluated and calculated in terms of effort and energy expended on both sides of production. The value of a husband is read by a woman's kin as the value of his productive support in securing women's wealth for his wife. (Weiner 1980: 282)

Weiner argues that women's wealth upholds the kinship arrangements of Trobriand society. It balances out exchange relationships between lineages linked by marriage; it reinforces the pivotal role of women; and it publicly proclaims, during every funeral, the social relationships that make up the fabric of Trobriand society. Weiner suggests that this long-term stable system could collapse if cash ever became widely substitutable for yams. If this were to happen, then men might buy food and other items in the market; they would no longer be dependent on yams from their wives' kin, and they could therefore refuse to supply their wives' kin with women's wealth. This had not yet happened at the time of Weiner's research, but she saw it as a possible future development.

The Original Affluent Society

As the previous example suggests, Western definitions of wealth are not universal. Richard B. Lee came to a similar conclusion in his research with the Ju/'hoansi in the 1960s (see EthnoProfile 6.2). Many Westerners believe that foraging peoples lead miserable lives, spending all their waking hours searching for enough food to survive. Yet Lee and other ethnographers have shown that the Ju/'hoansi were able, until relatively recently, to maintain a lifestyle that was very rich according to their own culturally informed definition of **affluence** (see Lee 1992a; 1992b; Solway and Lee 1990).

The Ju/'hoansi provided themselves with a varied and well-balanced diet based on a *selection* from the food sources available in their environment. Although they classified more than 100 species of plants as edible, only 14 were primary or major sources of food (Lee 1992b: 45ff.). Some 70 per cent of this diet consisted of vegetable foods; 30 per cent was meat. Mongongo nuts alone made up more than one-quarter of the diet. Women provided about 55 per cent of the diet and men provided 45 per cent, including the meat. The Ju/'hoansi spent an average of 2.4 working days—or about 20 hours—per person per week in food-collecting activities (Figure 7.12). Ju/'hoansi bands periodically suffered from shortages of their preferred foods and were forced to resort to less desired items; most of the time, however, their diet was balanced and adequate and consisted of foods of preference (56ff.).

Marshall Sahlins (1972) coined the expression "the original affluent society" to refer to the Ju/'hoansi and other foragers like them. Affluence, he argued, is having more than enough

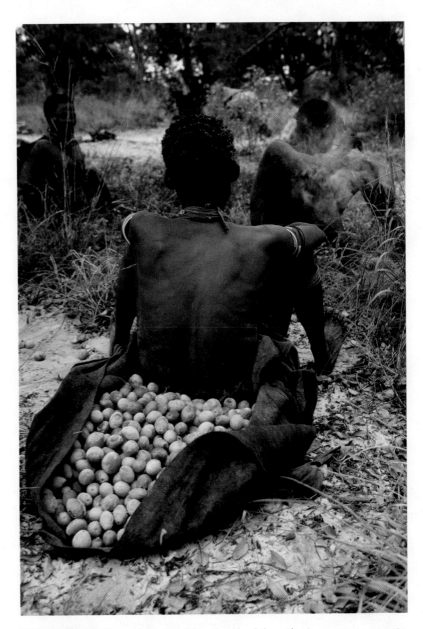

FIGURE 7.12 Ju/'hoansi women take a break while gathering mongongo nuts.

of whatever is required to satisfy consumption needs. There are two ways to create affluence:

1. to *produce much* (the path taken by Western capitalist society) and
2. to *desire little* (the option, Sahlins argues, that foragers have taken).

The wants of foraging peoples are few compared to those of most Westerners, but they are abundantly met by nature. Moreover, foragers do not suppress their natural greed; rather, their society simply does not institutionalize greed or reward the greedy. As a result, foragers cannot

affluence

The condition of having more than enough of whatever is required to satisfy consumption needs.

be considered poor, even though their material standard of living is low by Western standards. Poverty is not an absolute condition, nor is it a relationship between means and ends; it is a relationship between people and a cultural definition of *needs* and *wants*.

The Cultural Construction of Utility

Just as culture shapes needs, so too does it offer standardized ways of satisfying them. No social exchange can occur unless all parties are able to assess the value of the items to be exchanged. Because of the openness of culture and the ambiguity inherent in many social situations, values and exchange rates may well be negotiated. Such exchanges ultimately rest on cultural principles for assessing value and fairness.

By understanding consumption as the use of goods and services to communicate cultural values, we can arrive at a new understanding of wealth and poverty. We have noted Sahlins's comment that foragers with simple needs and ample means of satisfying those needs are affluent—not poor. Douglas and Isherwood also refuse to use the sheer amount of material possessions as a universal measure of wealth or poverty. They write:

> Many of the countries that anthropologists study are poor on such material criteria—no wall-to-wall carpets, no air conditioning—but they do not regard themselves as poor. The Nuer of the Sudan in the 1930s would not trade with the Arabs because the only things they had to sell were their herds of cattle, and the only things they could possibly want from trade were more cattle. (1979: 17–18)

For the Nuer, to have few or no cattle constituted poverty because cattle mattered as much for their use as markers of social relations as for their use as food. "To be rich means to be well integrated in a rich community. . . . To be poor is to be isolated" (160).

Institutionalized Sharing

Capitalist societies have passed laws and created social institutions that reward individuals for accumulating wealth. The economic practices of some non-capitalist societies, in contrast, prevent individual accumulation of wealth; the goal is to spread any wealth that exists throughout the community. This pattern is called *institutionalized sharing*.

People accustomed to capitalist practices are often either incredulous or cynical when it is suggested that institutionalized sharing can be the backbone of economic life. They assume that such widespread "generosity" can be expected only of saintly altruists, not of ordinary human beings. Nevertheless, people in societies with institutionalized sharing are not saints who never experience greed any more than people in capitalist societies are devils who never experience compassion. Both societies support the stability of established social arrangements.

Institutionalized sharing can be found among the Plains Cree of North America (see Map 7.2), studied by Swedish anthropologist Niels Braroe (1975: 143ff.). At the time of Braroe's fieldwork, the Cree still practised their tradition-based institutionalized sharing of consumption items such as food and clothing. They further practised generosity in ceremonies known as *giveaway dances*. In these ceremonies, participants danced around a room and gave away material goods, such as clothing, to other guests. Dancers aimed to give away more than they received.

The Cree ideal is that generosity should be spontaneous and contempt for material goods genuine. Nevertheless, Braroe observed that band members sometimes possessed consumption goods or money that they clearly wanted

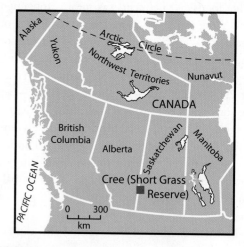

MAP 7.2 Plains Cree (across Alberta and Saskatchewan)

to keep for themselves. Individuals could enjoy such goods in private, but only if they kept the existence of those goods secret. Men sometimes hid beer to avoid having to share it with others. A woman once asked Braroe's wife to keep a sizable amount of cash for her so others would not know she had it and demand some. The rule seemed to be that "any visible resource may legitimately be requested by another" (146), and Braroe reported that direct refusals of such requests were rare.

For the Cree, institutionalized sharing is supposed to ensure that consumption goods are not hoarded but spread out and enjoyed by all in the band. This consumption pattern clashes with that of the capitalist, who views accumulation and consumption by individuals in a positive light. Some individual Cree earned money off the reserve and tried to save it in order to get ahead—by capitalist standards. Those people were considered stingy by other Cree and were resented; they could not hope to gain a position of leadership in the band.

Consumption Studies in the Age of Globalization

The foregoing examples focus attention on distinctive consumption practices in different societies and remind us forcefully not to take the Western market as the measure of all things. They also encourage respect for alternative practices that, in different times and places, have worked as well or better than capitalist markets to define needs and provide goods to satisfy those needs. Anthropologist B. Lynne Milgram (2008) gives us some insight into such markets in her analysis of Filipina entrepreneurs in Baguio City and their development of a trade in second-hand clothing between Hong Kong and the Philippines.

Examples such as these also draw attention to the way in which the arrival of capitalism, usually in the context of colonialism, has regularly undermined such alternatives, attempting to replace them with new needs and goods defined by the market. In many situations, local peoples tried to resist the influx of market commodities,

perhaps because they were aware of these commodities' capacity to destroy (Miller 1995: 144–5). In our current era of globalization, however, the consumption of market commodities occurs everywhere in the world. Moreover, the evidence is mounting that not only are Western commodities sometimes embraced by those whom we might have expected to reject them (e.g., video technology by Indigenous peoples of the Amazon), but this embrace frequently involves making use of these commodities for local purposes to defend or to enrich local culture rather than to replace it (e.g., the increasing popularity of sushi in North America).

Daniel Miller, a pioneer in this kind of consumption study, has therefore urged anthropologists to recognize that these new circumstances require that we move beyond a narrow focus on the destructive potential of mass-produced commodities to a broader recognition of the role commodities play in a globalizing world. "Desire for goods is not assumed to be natural nor goods per se as either positive or negative. Poverty is regarded as a relative lack of resources rather than the preservation of authenticity" (143). But this shift does not mean that concern about the negative consequences of capitalist practices disappears. In a global world in which everyone everywhere increasingly relies on commodities provided by a capitalist market, Miller believes that critical attention needs to refocus on "inequalities of access and the deleterious impact of contemporary economic institutions on much of the world's population" (143).

A Dialectic between the Meaningful and the Material

As we have seen in this chapter, material goods carry culturally defined meanings, and what is viewed as meaningful (as stipulated by culture) can have material consequences. It is out of this dialectic between the meaningful and the material that the modes of livelihood followed by human beings everywhere emerge.

A CRITICAL LOOK | Gendered Work

Humans have the ability to shape-shift their worlds—both cultural and natural. We could even go so far as to state that the concept of a natural world, as it is applied to the economic habitat of humans, is fully a cultural construct. As such, it has a definition that is in each case culturally specific. This is the reason the landscapes and built environments of any given culture are so different from those of other cultures. These differences are not fully founded in the actual environment or in particulars such as the geology or hydrology, the latitude or altitude, or even the biotic communities that are specific to a certain tract of land, but in how these parameters of what we call the "natural world" are turned to the marking and making of human space. In other words, land becomes landscape and is symbolic and metaphorical for a culture. Our worlds come to reflect our visions of self and culture, and as such they reflect our economic decisions—how we make a living. This living is seen in our relationships to work and in how we assign that work on the basis of gender, age, and class—how we create a division of labour.

The *shape-shifting* in the economically globalized world is not only changing "natural" landscapes but also the cultural constructs that inform how we observe and comment on the economics of life in this world. Significant here is a consideration of the place of women in the market of today. From a historical perspective, much of women's work has been "background" work done in the private sphere, while men have done the "real work" in the foreground of the public sphere. For example, women have been gatherers, not hunters; homemakers, not warriors. Furthermore, in the historical view of the colonialist—which we can access through the varied, not infrequently biased records of colonial encounters—women are almost completely absent, or by inference poignantly present as shadow people. The shadow woman is often presented as the sexualized fantasy of the colonizer, a fact that remains quite overt today in the varied pornography, sex trade, and sex tourism economies that are increasingly part of a globalized industry.

We navigate among various and conflicting subject-positions, each offering a limited perspective on the nature of women's lives in any contact zone (see Gerson 1997: 5). This is so in the analysis of women's work today as we in North America, the relatively privileged, struggle with what Canadian literary scholar Carole Gerson characterizes as "irreducible alterity." We come to recognize that men of other cultures also are seen in a paradigm of otherness, but women of these cultures fare even worse, for they are encumbered not only by the ethnocentric views generally applied to their societies but also by the misogynist aspects of the Western and local world views. Women become the "other" of the "other" in this instance, twice removed from consideration. Indeed, in many cultures, women's interactions in the public sphere are contrasted to and defined by androcentric concepts of provisioning, production, trade, commerce, and government. Under this view, the completeness of women's roles within their societies—roles that sustained life—went unseen.

American anthropologist and gender-studies scholar Carla Freeman attempts to move us toward an understanding of women in the working world of today. She notes that we need to see the contrast as well as the linkages of "global/local; masculine/feminine; production/consumption; and formal/informal sectors of the economy" (2001: 1009). She challenges us to achieve a sense of balanced reciprocity in the world of making a living. It is through her analysis of female informatics workers in the Caribbean that she cautions us to consider that the interactions between the global forces and the necessities of local life are nuanced such that we can neither consider "the local as contained within, and thus defined fundamentally by, the global" (1012) nor the local "as a space in which the heavy hand of the global makes its marks" (1031). Reality is simply too complex. As such, we cannot just "globalize" women, creating another trope for the disappeared gendered "other." Rather, our analysis needs to take in the global forces and how they affect women in the local settings in which women do the work they need to do—making a living for themselves and their families within and without the home. We need to see women as actors in their/our own modernity.

—Roberta Robin Dods

KEY TERMS

affluence   181

consumption   167

cultural ecology   176

distribution   167

econiche   176

economic anthropology   165

economy   165

ecotones   176

ecozones   176

extensive agriculture   167

food collectors   166

food producers   166

ideology   174

institutions   166

intensive agriculture   167

labour   171

market exchange   171

means of production   172

mechanized industrial
   agriculture   167

mode of production   172

modes of exchange   170

neoclassical economic theory

production   168

reciprocity   170

redistribution   170

relations of production   172

scarcity   166

subsistence strategies   166

CHAPTER SUMMARY

1. Our cultures suggest a range of options for making a living. Human beings have devised a variety of subsistence strategies to satisfy their material survival needs.

2. Human economic activity is usefully divided into three phases: production, distribution, and consumption.

3. Formal neoclassical economic theory attempts to explain how capitalism works. Building on the emphasis that this theory gives to market exchange, economic anthropologists showed that non-capitalist societies regularly relied on non-market modes of exchange, such as reciprocity and redistribution, which still play restricted roles in societies dominated by the capitalist market.

4. Marxian economic anthropologists view production as more important than exchange in determining the patterns of economic life. They argue that societies can be classified in terms of their modes of production. Each mode of production contains within it the potential for conflict between

classes of people who receive differential benefits and losses from the production process.

5. Consumption patterns are influenced by internal factors (e.g., basic human needs) as well as external factors (e.g., the availability of particular resources). In addition, our culture influences these patterns as it defines our needs and provides for their satisfaction according to its own logic—a logic that cannot be reduced to biology, psychology, or ecological pressures.

6. In our era of globalization, the consumption of Western market commodities is often embraced by non-Western peoples. Moreover, this embrace frequently involves making use of market commodities for local purposes to defend or enrich local culture rather than to replace it. In a global world in which everyone everywhere increasingly relies on market commodities, we need to pay critical attention to inequalities of access and the negative impact of contemporary economic institutions on most of the world's population.

CRITICAL THINKING QUESTIONS

1. Anthropologists distinguish between *food collectors* and *food producers*. How does this division hearken back to the ethnical stages proposed by Lewis Henry Morgan in the nineteenth century (see Chapter 3)?

2. Is reciprocity in all its forms an efficient way of distributing material goods for consumption? Why or why not?

3. Compare and contrast Wolf's *kin-ordered*, *tributary*, and *capitalist* modes of production. How would you explain the

overlap between this classification of modes of production and the traditional anthropological classification of subsistence strategies (Figure 7.2)?

4. What are some examples of human beings' abilities to adapt to a wide variety of environments? What types of environments might provide the best prospects for humans to make a living? What types of environment might threaten human survival?

SUGGESTED READINGS

Douglas, Mary, and Baron Isherwood. 1996. *The World of Goods: Towards an Anthropology of Consumption*, rev. edn (New York: Routledge). A discussion of consumption, economic theories about consumption, and what anthropologists can contribute to the study of consumption.

Lee, Richard B. 2013. *The Dobe Ju/'hoansi*, 4th edn (Belmont, CA: Wadsworth). This highly readable ethnography contains important discussions about foraging as a way of making a living.

McIntosh, Roderick J. 1996. "History of Archaeology, Intellectual" in *The Oxford Companion to Archaeology*, ed. Brian M. Fagan (Oxford: Oxford University Press), 280–5. A brief but comprehensive look at how we consider the act of "knowing" in the Western tradition and how we have wrestled with the problem of what we can never come to know.

Sahlins, Marshall. 1972. *Stone Age Economics* (Chicago: Aldine). A series of classic essays on economic life; the collection includes "The Original Affluent Society."

Steward, Julian H. 1972. *Theory of Culture Change: The Methodology of Multilinear Evolution* (Urbana: University of Illinois Press). A collection of papers in which Steward presents culture change as a complex, ongoing process.

Wilk, Richard and Lisa C. Cliggett. 2007. *Economies and Cultures: Foundations of Economic Anthropology*, 2nd edn (Boulder, CO: Westview). A relatively current, accessible guide to the conflicting views of human nature that underlie disputes in economic anthropology.

RELATED WEBSITES

Cultural Ecology www.environment.gen.tr/ecology-writings/484-cultural-ecology.html

Gifting and Feasting in the Northwest Coast Potlatch www.peabody.harvard.edu/potlatch/page2.html

Marxist Anthropology http://anthropology.ua.edu/cultures/cultures.php?culture=Marxist%20Anthropology

The Mongongo Nut www.naturalhub.com/natural_food_guide_nuts_uncommon_Ricinodendron_rautanenii.htm

8

Play, Art, Myth, and Ritual

CHAPTER OUTLINE

Play

Art

Myth

Ritual

Combining Play, Art,
Myth, and Ritual

LEARNING OBJECTIVES

By the end of Chapter 8, you will be able to

- perceive play as an open system that relates to cognition,
- consider sport and satire as forms of play that can have strong significance for adults,

- understand the significance of art,
- recognize myths as conceptual tools that explain certain aspects of social organization,

- perceive ritual as a form of metacommunication that brings text and performance together, and
- see the connections among play, art, myth, and ritual.

Band members dance in a performance celebrating African culture at the annual Carnival in Port of Spain, Trinidad. Cultural festivals bring members of a community together by combining elements of play, art, myth, and ritual in a meaningful way.

During her fieldwork in Botswana in the late 1970s, Roberta Robin Dods had a chance encounter with a group of children—three boys and eight girls about nine years of age—who were gathered at the side of the road. One boy was drawing shapes in the dusty red earth with a long stick. He had inscribed nine small circles inside a large circle. The boy stood in the middle of the large circle and pointed his stick at each girl saying "You will be the mommy." He concluded, "I will be the daddy." Each of the girls went to one of the smaller circles, and two of the boys retired to the remaining circle. And so the game of "playing house" was inscribed in the dust and described by the children playing what all children play—family.

These children were members of a culture where polygyny is practised and where adult sons may live in separate quarters in a family compound. Children at play tell us so much about how play is culturally defined and defining. Childhood is a time when adult roles can be tried on with little or no consequences. Think of the role-playing games you may have engaged in as a child—"let's pretend" school, house, doctor, and so on. These sorts of games often involve working through specific aspects of potential adult roles. Play can be fun, but for the observer it is more than fun—it is a window into many aspects of cultural identity. Children's play can reflect the changing realities of the society in which the children live—the emerging new realities in a culture. **Play** is one of four elements (along with **art**, **myth**, and **ritual**) in which the interplay of openness and creativity with rules and constraints enables people to produce powerful and moving phenomena.

As we study these sensitive aspects of culture, we must be careful not to force our own cultural interpretations on other peoples' cultural practices. Indeed, anthropologist Robin Riddington (1998) cautions us that theorizing occurs as a genre of Western academic expression and is not necessarily founded on the constructs of the peoples who provided the data (345). So we must keep in mind what he describes as "shared ethnographic authority":

The reasons for sharing authority are more than political and aesthetic. An ethnography that places the ethnographer's monologue above the voices of people being represented risks sacrificing effective engagement with its subject. . . . Its claim to objectivity may actually disguise the subjectivity of its singular isolated author. . . . A. Irving Hallowell [Anishinaabe (Ojibwe)], for instance, wrote that "a higher order of objectivity" may be obtained by "adopting a perspective which includes an analysis of the outlook of the people themselves as a complementary procedure." (1998: 344–5)

It is the "voices" of those living in and through their engagement with play, art, myth, and ritual that resonate with meaning.

Play

For the anthropologist, play has the characteristic of *openness* that we first discussed in relation to language in Chapter 4. In this case, this openness involves the ability to not only think and talk about but also *act out* or *portray* (1) the same things in different ways and (2) different things in the same way. Thus, play is a generalized form of *behavioural openness*.

Many species play, but we believe that humans play the most throughout their lives. Anthropologist Robert Fagen sees animal play as the product of natural selection that gives young animals (including young human beings) needed exercise, preparing them for the rigours of adulthood, which might include fighting, hunting, or fleeing when pursued. Importantly, during early childhood, peak brain developments associated with motor skills and peak periods of play occur at the same time. This observation suggests that the development of cognitive and motor skills may be affected by play behaviour. Playful exploration of the environment aids learning and allows for the development of behavioural versatility (see Fagen 1981: 350–5). It also seems to have a connection with the repair of certain types of brain damage caused either by injury or by trauma. All of these functions of play may help individuals survive.

Fagen proposes an additional, social function of play: the communication of the message

play

A framing (or orienting) context that is (1) consciously adopted by the players; (2) pleasurable; and (3) alludes to the non-play world by transforming the objects, roles, actions, and relations of ends and means characteristic of the non-play world.

art

A representation that relates to an object, an experience, or some other component of the world and that evokes a felt response.

myth

A representative story that embodies a culture's assumptions about the way society, or the world in general, must operate.

ritual

A repetitive social practice set off from everyday routine and composed of a sequence of symbolic activities that adhere to a culturally defined ritual schema and are closely connected to a specific set of ideas significant to the culture.

"all's well" (1992: 48–9). "It seems likely that a frequent consequence and possible biological function of play is to convey information about short-term and long-term health, general well-being, and biological fitness to parents, litter-mates, or other social companions" (51).

Thinking about Play

Joking to Ease Tensions

Joking, which can be verbal or physical (practical jokes, pranks, horseplay), is a good example of how play operates within its cultural context. American anthropologist Andrew Miracle discusses joking behaviour among Aymara people in Bolivia (see EthnoProfile 8.1). He notes that the Aymara do not laugh in the presence of strangers because it is considered disrespectful. They laugh and joke only within a circle of acquaintances and friends; this kind of joking reinforces existing social bonds (1991: 151).

Much of the joking Miracle observed took place on the crowded buses or trucks that transport rural people around the country. Ordinarily, Aymara personal space extends about one arm's length. Where there is any choice, people do not get any closer to one another. They also show respect and honour other people's privacy by not staring. Miracle notes that in everyday situations, "when stared at, the Aymara may yell at the one staring and become quite rude" (146). On buses or trucks, however, the context changes, and people who are strangers to one another are forced into artificial intimacy. They must sit or stand very close to one another for long periods of time, frequently looking right at one another. Their response is often to joke and laugh, behaviour normally reserved for intimates. Put another way, they choose to do "different things" (i.e., passing time with close friends and passing time with strangers in unusually close quarters) in the same way—by joking. This altered definition of context gives joking among strangers a new meaning; it temporarily changes strangers into friends, thus making a socially unpleasant situation more tolerable.

Metacommunication and Play

Moving from everyday reality to play reality requires a radical transformation of perspective. To an outside observer, the switch may go undetected. However, when there is potential for the switch to have serious consequences for other people and their activities, play and non-play must be signalled clearly so that one is not mistaken for the other. According to anthropologist Gregory Bateson (1972), this shift requires a level of communication called **metacommunication**, which provides information about the relationship between those who are communicating. In play there are two kinds of metacommunication: **framing** and **reflexivity**.

Framing is a cognitive boundary that marks certain behaviours as "play" or as "ordinary life." Dogs, for example, have a *play face*, a signal understood by other dogs indicating a willingness to play. If dogs agree to play, they bare their fangs and one animal attacks the other. But the bite is not a true bite; it is merely a nip. Both dogs have agreed to enter the *play frame*, an imaginative world in which bites don't mean bites. Human beings have many ways of marking the

metacommunication
Communicating about the process of communication.

framing
An understood boundary that marks certain behaviours as "play" or as "ordinary life."

reflexivity
Critically thinking about the way one thinks; reflecting on one's own experience.

ETHNOPROFILE 8.1 | Aymara

Region South America
Nations Bolivia, Peru, Chile
Language Aymara
Population 2,500,000 (2011 estimate)
Environment The Andes and Altiplano lake basin regions, with many living near Lake Titicaca

Livelihood Peasant farmers
Political organization Pre-conquest, state societies conquered first by Incas and later by Spanish; today, part of modern nation-states
For more information Miracle, Andrew. 1991. "Aymara Joking Behaviour," *Play and Culture* 4, 2: 144–52.

play frame: a smile, a particular tone of voice, a referee's whistle, or the words "let's play" or "let's pretend." The marker says that "everything from now until we end this activity is set apart from everyday life."

Reflexivity is the process of thinking about the social and cultural dimensions of the world in which we find ourselves. Because play tells us that ordinary life can be understood in more than one way, play can be a commentary on the nature of ordinary life (Handelman 1977: 186). It communicates about what *can be* rather than about what *should be* or what *is* (186). For example, jokes keep us from taking ourselves too seriously by showing us that there are alternative, even ridiculous, explanations for our experience.

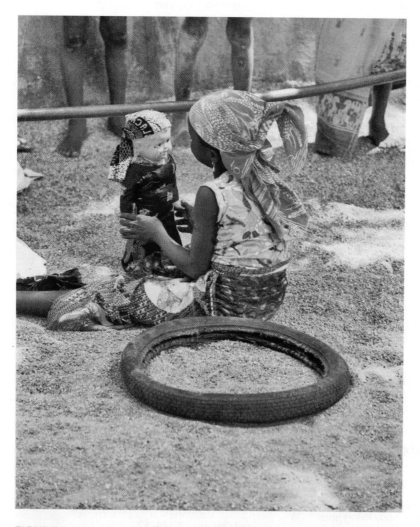

FIGURE 8.1 Play enables this girl in Guider, Cameroon, to incorporate her European doll into the world she knows. What effects could play have on the person playing?

Some Effects of Children's Play

Some scholars view children's play as a simple imitation of adult activities. Others see play as rehearsal for the "real world" (Figure 8.1). According to this view, play can validate the adult role the child is trying on, demonstrating the "rightness" of being a mommy or a daddy or the "rightness" of preparing meals to eat. It can also give children the opportunity to try on a number of roles and ways of being that may come close to their reality later in life. In North America, various forms of children's "edutainment"—cultural materials with the dual purpose of entertaining and educating—expose children to circumstances that may be beyond their first-hand experiences. For example, the children's book *The White Swan Express* (2002) gives young children a fictionalized window into international adoption practices and the situations of several non-traditional families as it tells the story of four Chinese baby girls who await adoption by four different families from across North American—a lesbian couple, a single woman, and two heterosexual married couples.

Some scholars have suggested that children's play (especially make-believe play) encourages creative interpretations of reality. In addition, it allows children to overcome the limitations of their age, experience, and maturity, thus allowing them to have a richer experience of adult life (Schwartzman 1978: 116). Further, play may allow children to comment on and criticize the world of adults by sanctioning insults of authority figures and inversions of social status (232–45).

Adult forms of play such as satire (e.g., satirical plays and novels, political cartoons) also act as commentary on the "real world." While children's play is generally viewed as harmless, this sort of adult play can threaten social norms by pointing out the folly of *what is* and suggesting better options for *what might be*. Most often, societies tend to undermine or contain this threat simply by defining play as "unserious," "untrue," "pretend," "make-believe," or "unreal" (Handelman 1977: 189). Repressive political regimes, however, frequently attempt to censor humour critical of their rulers, with the result that such humour becomes recognized as a form of political resistance.

Play and Alternative Views of Reality

We can easily see how humour shows an alternative view of reality, but what about non-joking play? For example, what about adults who climb mountains? "Is climbing a vertical face of rock at the risk of one's life play, or is it done in earnest?" (Csikszentmihalyi 1981: 16). On the one hand, it fits our definition of play—it is consciously adopted by the player, it is somehow pleasurable, and it transforms the relations of ends and means characteristic of the non-play world. On the other hand, it is a serious activity, as a rock climber risks bodily injury and is at all times "as immersed in reality as anyone can be" (17). The choice to climb a mountain, then, requires the climber to adopt an alternative view of reality—one that sees the possibility of bodily harm as an acceptable risk within the parameters of the play activity. Thus, non-joking forms of play show us that people do not always submit to the generally accepted rules of reality that govern everyday life. Indeed, it allows us to recognize that *no referential perspective is absolute*. As a result, play creates the awareness of alternatives and demonstrates the openness in human experience.

In the contemporary world, one increasingly popular type of play requires participants to adopt what are often highly creative alternative views of reality—electronic gaming. Electronic games offer players the chance to engage with elaborate simulated worlds in which many of our everyday rules of reality do not apply. Cultural scholar Derek Van Rheenen (2012) has examined the shift toward digital play in the North American landscape. He notes that "perhaps no single change in the game preferences of American children has been as dramatic as the introduction and widespread popularity of electronic games within the latter half of the twentieth century" (420). Indeed, national surveys have found that 83 per cent of teens in Canada and 87 per cent of teens in the United States have at least one gaming system in their home (CBC 2013; Rideout et al. 2010). Overall, the evidence suggests that playing electronic games may have some positive effects on overall learning, literacy, inventive problem solving, achievement motivation, and visuospatial skills (Van Rheenen 2012: 422). Although more research is required, it is likely that at least some of these benefits are connected to the creative task of fully accepting and working within an alternative view of reality.

Sport

According to a well-accepted definition, **sport** is

> a physically exertive activity that is aggressively competitive within constraints imposed by definitions and rules. A component of culture, it is ritually patterned, game-like, and of varying amounts of play, work, and leisure. In addition, sport can be viewed as having both athletic and non-athletic variations, *athletic* referring to those activities requiring the greater amount of physical exertion. (Blanchard and Cheska 1985: 60)

Sport is play embedded in the prevailing social order. Sports reflect the basic values of the cultural setting in which they are performed.

Beyond play, sport can be work for the players and an investment for the owners of professional teams. It also offers a form of personal and social identification for fans, who are invited into a make-believe world in which they may playfully identify with their heroes, rage at the opponents, imagine coaching the team, suffer the team's losses, and rejoice in the team's victories. It is framed as play, but conflict in games and sports is different from conflict in ordinary life. Competitors agree "to strive for an incompatible goal—only one opponent can win—within the constraints of understood rules" (Lever 1995: 3). As with all forms of play, the relationships of ends and means in sport are altered. Sport is struggle for the sake of struggle.

Because they can reflect a culture's values, some sports change form when they transfer from one cultural setting to another. Cricket in the Trobriand Islands (see EthnoProfile 7.1) offers us an excellent example of this transformation. An English missionary introduced the sport of cricket to the Trobrianders in the early twentieth century. By the 1970s, in the more rural parts of the islands, it had become a different game. Played between two villages, it became a substitute for warfare and a way of establishing political alliances. If the hosts had 40 men ready to play and the visitors had 36, then there were 36 to a side instead of the conventional 11. The game was always won by the home team—but not by too many runs because that would shame the visitors. War magic was employed to aid batsmen and

sport
An aggressively competitive, often physically exertive activity governed by game-like rules that are ritually patterned and agreed upon by all participants.

bowlers. Teams had dances and chants for taking the field, leaving it, and celebrating outs. These dances and chants were used to comment on current events, and they became fertile ground for additional competition beyond that of the sporting event itself. The bat was redesigned for greater accuracy, and the entire activity was associated with the ceremonial exchange of food and other goods. Cricket, the sport of the British Empire, was radically transformed.

From the perspective of some Trobrianders, in fact, their version of cricket was a way of taking the English colonizers' favourite game—a game that was supposed to teach Trobrianders how to become "civilized"—and using it to express their rejection of the colonial world. As one Trobriand leader says in the film *Trobriand Cricket* (1974), "we rubbished the white man's game; now it's our game." Here is the "openness" of play: sport can transcend its function as an enjoyable way to pass the time and become a venue for social commentary and even collective rebellion against oppression.

Sport in the Nation-State

As international sporting events reveal, sport can be a source of national pride. Moreover, it can bring citizens of a nation-state together. Indeed, the most important and universal feature of sport in the nation-state today is that it

helps complex modern societies cohere (Lever 1995: 3). Consider how the sport of hockey gives Canadians from diverse backgrounds a common interest through which they can connect with one another. Interestingly, ethnologist Michael A. Robidoux suggests that hockey may appeal to Canadians because it embodies qualities that run counter to our self-perception as unreasonably polite international peacekeepers (2002: 209; see Figure 8.2). Yet historically,

> hockey enabled Canadians to display qualities that have been valued in patriarchal relations: stoicism, courage, perseverance, and proficiency. The singularity of the game and the manner in which it was played were critical for a young and disparate nation to have as its own as it faced encroaching social, political, and cultural interests from Europe and the United States. At a more pedestrian level, hockey was accessible to men of various ethnic and class backgrounds, and thus . . . it became a game of the people. (222)

Of course, in this historical context, *people* refers only to men. Indeed, even today women are often left out of the mass culture of sport. This gendered separation often begins in childhood, when boys are more likely than girls to be encouraged to participate in team sports. In adulthood, the effects continue, as men and women cannot relate to one another through shared childhood experiences with sport. Thus there is a fundamental ambiguity in the relation of sports and integration: as sports bring people together in one domain, they separate them in another. Sports can maintain and sharpen distinctions that are already significant in many other areas of a culture.

Sport as Metaphor

In his examination of the national importance of soccer in various European and South American countries, French anthropologist Christian Bromberger (1995) observes that sport is significant because "it lays bare the major symbolic horizon of our societies: the course of a match, of a competition, resembles the uncertain fate of people in the contemporary world. Further, the combination of rules that mould the genre give this uncertainty an *acceptable* feel" (197). In this

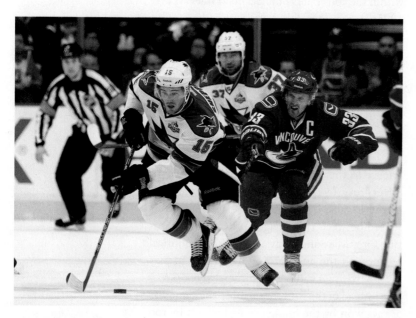

FIGURE 8.2 Hockey gives Canadians the chance to value qualities such as violence and aggression that run counter to our national identity in realms outside sport. How else might hockey impact Canadian identity?

interpretation, which could apply equally well to hockey, the game becomes a metaphor for our daily struggles. The complexity and sudden changes of a single game offer what Bromberger calls "a shortcut to the joys and dramas that make up a life" (197). A game features not only achievement on the basis of merit but also uncertainties introduced by strategy, luck, law, (in)justice (in the form of the referee), trickery, and unfairness. It offers the fan the opportunity to compare players, to reflect, to plan, to strategize, and to be surprised. And, as in life, the most innovative strategies don't always work, and the best team doesn't always win.

Art

Art is rooted in playful creativity, a birthright of all human beings. And yet, like sport, those activities defined as "art" differ from free play because they are circumscribed by rules. Artistic rules direct particular attention to, and provide standards for evaluating, the *form* of the activities or objects that artists produce.

A Definition of Art

Anthropologist Alexander Alland defines art as "play with form producing some aesthetically successful transformation-representation" (1977: 39). "Form" refers to the rules of the art game: the culturally appropriate restrictions on the way this kind of play may be organized in time and space, the culturally acceptable style and media. A painting is a form: it is two-dimensional; it is done with paint; it is intentionally made; it represents or symbolizes something in the world outside the canvas, paper, or wood on which it is created; it can be displayed. There are different kinds of paintings as well. For example, there is the painting form called *portrait*—a portrait depicts a person in some culturally appropriate way.

By "aesthetic," Alland means appreciative of, or responsive to, form (xii). "Aesthetically successful" means that the creator of the piece of art (and possibly its audience as well) experiences a positive or negative response. Indifference is the sign of something that is aesthetically unsuccessful. It is probably the case that the aesthetic response is a universal feature in all cultures and, as with play, may be part of the human condition.

Aesthetic response is holistic, involving all our faculties, including emotion, especially as these are shaped by our social and cultural experience. Linguistic theorist Valentin Voloshinov (1987 [1926]) argues that aesthetic response to form in a work of art is based largely on a culturally shaped evaluation of the appropriateness of *form* to *content*. Evaluations of appropriateness and of technical perfection involve a broad range of intellectual, emotional, and moral judgments on the part of the viewer.

Aesthetic value judgments guide the artist's choice of form, material, and presentation as she or he creates a piece of art; they also guide the observers' evaluations. This implies that art involves more than just the end product of an artist's labour. As Voloshinov notes, art is a creative "event of living communication" involving the work, the artist, and the artist's audience (107). Artists create their works with an audience in mind, and audiences respond to these works as if the works were addressed to them. Sometimes the response is enthusiastic; sometimes it is highly critical. In either case, the aesthetic event does not leave its participants indifferent.

Art also involves the *process* through which some product is made. In a practical way, archaeologists can tell us about this process by studying material culture. In the making of things there is an order archaeologists term the *chaîne opératoire* (French for "operational chain"); when followed, this order produces a specific repeatable result, such as a Clovis point (Figure 8.3). Of course, there is a certain amount of variability and creativity involved even within the constraints of artistic convention; creators of art follow a series of steps, but they do so with artistic licence.

FIGURE 8.3 A Clovis point is an artifact associated with the Clovis culture, which existed approximately 13 thousand years ago in what is now the southwestern United States.

transformation-representation
The process in which experience is transformed as it is represented symbolically in a different medium.

Transformation-Representation

To understand Alland's concept of **transformation-representation**, we must recall that symbols represent something other than themselves. They are arbitrary in that they have no necessary connection with what they represent. This means that they can be separated from the object or idea they represent and appreciated for their own sake. They may also be used to represent more than one object or idea. When a Javanese leather puppet maker makes a puppet of the mythic hero Bhima, for example, he is representing the traditional form of the hero in his work, but he is also *transforming* a three-dimensional human form into a two-dimensional flat puppet made of buffalo hide in which the colours, style, inclination of the head, and adornment stand for the internal state of the hero at a specific moment (Figure 8.4). At the same time, he is carrying out this work more or less skilfully and is embodying the meanings that Bhima has for the Javanese.

Because transformation and representation depend on each other, Alland (1977: 35) refers to them as *transformation-representations*; they are *metaphors*. A drawing, for example, is a metaphoric transformation of experience into visible marks on a two-dimensional surface. Similarly, a poem metaphorically transforms experience into concentrated and tightened language. This transformation-representation process is one place where the technical skill of the artist is involved.

But Is It Art?

In the Western view of art, there is a distinction between art and non-art. Some paintings, songs, stories, carvings, dances, and the like are considered art; some are not. People who accept this perspective might argue, for example, that the *Mona Lisa* is art but paintings of Elvis Presley on black velvet are not. Why? Part of the answer may have to do with how aesthetically successfully the painting is—the degree to which it elicits a positive or negative response from viewers. But part of the answer also involves the high degree of specialization in Western societies, which has led to the emergence of an "art establishment" that includes art critics, art historians, art teachers, journalists, schools, and museums—as well as professional artists. These people define what art is and what it is not. They distinguish between art and craft. That a painter may in fact have created an image of Elvis that is meaningful to at least some viewers does not change the art establishment's opinion. To them, Elvis on velvet is not art because it does not address problems in art theory, because it does not refer to the beautiful or the true, because it does not portray the artist's struggle to produce a new expressive style, or because the artist seems ignorant or disdainful of the stylistic experimentation that makes up Western art history.

Nevertheless, many people—anthropologists included—have resisted the notion that art is only what a group of Western experts define as art. On the one hand, convinced that all humans have a capacity for art and aesthetic response, many anthropologists have attempted to redefine the concept of art broadly enough to include, on an equal basis, aesthetic products and activities that Western art experts would describe, at best, as "primitive," "ethnic," or "folk" art. On the other hand, they recognize that not all cultures have a

FIGURE 8.4 Bhima, one of the great mythic heroes of Javanese wajang, is represented in this leather puppet. In what ways are the puppet maker's choices and skill as an artist evident in this creation?

distinct category that corresponds to the Western notion of "art." Indeed, in many cultures, the products that Westerners might call "art" play a role in various cultural activities.

In recent decades, anthropologists have become increasingly interested in the way certain kinds of material objects made by tribal peoples flow into a global art market where they are transformed into "primitive" or "ethnic" art. Cultural anthropologist Shelly Errington (1998) points out that even in the West many of the objects in fine arts museums today, no matter where they came from, were not intended by their makers to be "art." They were intended to be masks for ritual use; paintings for religious contemplation; containers for holding the relics of saints, ancestor figures, furniture, jewellery boxes, architectural details, and so on. They are in fine arts museums today because at some point they were designated as "art" by an outside "other" with the authority to put them in a museum.

For these reasons, Errington distinguishes "art by intention" from "art by appropriation." Art by intention includes objects that were made to be art, such as Impressionist paintings. Art by appropriation, however, consists of all the other objects that "became art" because at a certain moment certain people—usually those in powerful positions in colonial settings, or members of the art establishment from the countries they represented—decided that they belonged to the category of art. Because museums, art dealers, and art collectors are found everywhere in the world, it is now the case that potentially any material object crafted by human hands can be appropriated by these institutions as "art." For an example of such conflicting ideas about the nature of a specific piece of "art," we can consider the Haisla Nation's G'psgolox totem pole (Figure 8.5). It was cut down in 1929 by a government official and sold to Sweden's Museum of Ethnography, where it was preserved as a piece of art. For members of the Haisla Nation, however, the pole was a reminder of a significant event in their culture's history. They understood the pole to be situated in a specific time and place, with a "life" that had a beginning and an end—essentially, it was meant to decay over time and thus move into the realm of the ancestors.

To be transformed into art, Errington argues, an object must have *exhibition value*—someone must be willing to display it. Objects that somehow fit into the Western definition of art tend to be selected for the art market. Looking at the

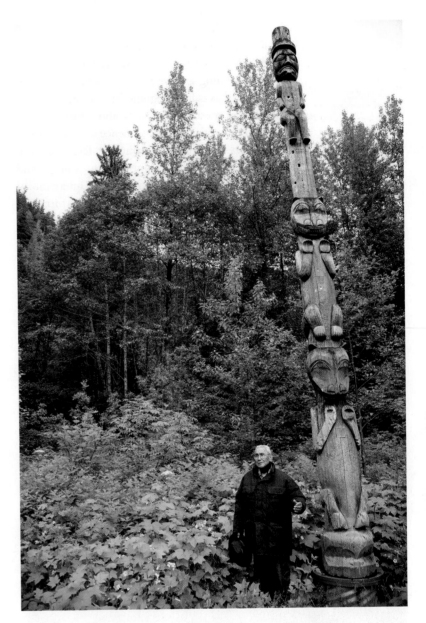

FIGURE 8.5 Cecil Paul, a Haisla elder, stands next to the G'psgolox totem pole, which now stands in the Kitlope Valley near Kitimaat, British Columbia. The totem pole was returned from Sweden's Museum of Ethnography in 2006. Why might some people object to displaying "art by appropriation" in museums?

collection of objects that have been defined as "art" over the years, Errington sees some common features: the objects are "portable (paintings preferred to murals), durable (bronze preferred to basketry), useless for practical purposes in the secular West (ancestral effigies and Byzantine icons preferred to hoes and grain grinders), representational (human and animal figures preferred to, say, heavily decorated ritual bowls)" (1998: 116–17). Errington further notes that the objects people make and "imbue with meaning" are "worthy of deep study," but they are not art until someone who carries around a particular definition of art says they are (103).

Redefining an object as art often strips it of much of its cultural significance. In their original contexts, most meaningful symbolic forms involve more than one sense: an audience watches masked dancers while hearing drumming, feeling a warm breeze, and smelling palm oil. But as masks and other objects are moved into the international art market, "they slough off their . . . performance contexts, . . . retaining only the durable part that can be set aside in a frame or on a pedestal" (84).

Traditionally, the cultural role of art was similar to that of play—it presented its creators and participants with alternative realities, a separation of means from ends, and the possibility of commenting on and transforming the everyday world. In today's global art market, however, the role is often more commercial. Errington observes that the people who make "primitive art" are no longer "tribal" but have become

> modern-day peasants. . . . They live in rain forests and deserts and other such formerly out-of-the-way places on the peripheries . . . within national and increasingly global systems of buying and selling, of using natural and human resources, and of marketing images and notions about products. Some lucky few of them make high ethnic art, and sell it for good prices, and obtain

a good portion of the proceeds. Others make objects classed as tourist or folk art, usually for much less money, and often through a middleperson. (268)

Errington points out the bitter irony that international demand for "exotic" objects is growing at the very moment when the makers of these objects are severely threatened by international economic policies and resource extraction projects that impoverish them and undermine the ways of life that give the objects they make their "exotic" allure. And, what counts as fashionable decoration this year may be unfashionable next year, leaving the producers with very little to fall back on.

"She's Fake": The Problem of the Authentic

Michelle Bigenho is an anthropologist and violinist whose multi-sited ethnography examines music performance in Bolivia, in part through her experiences performing with *Música de Maestros*. This ensemble attempts to recreate performances of contemporary cultural music that they have studied in the countryside (Bigenho 2002: 4). During Bigenho's time with the ensemble, the group was made up of both classically trained and traditionally trained Bolivian musicians as well as three foreigners: a Japanese musician who played the Andean flute, a Cuban musician who played violin, and Bigenho, an American, who also played violin. Along with a dance ensemble, the musicians were invited to represent Bolivia in a folklore festival in France (Figure 8.6). As the bands were lining up, a member of the Belgian delegation walked over to Bigenho and announced in French, "She's fake." The Belgian woman then "pointed to one of the Bolivian dancers dressed in her dancing costume with her long fake braids worked into her short brown hair. As she pointed, she said 'She's real'" (88).

In this way, Bigenho raises the question of "authenticity." What is real when it comes to music, painting, sculpture, dance, or other "folk" art forms? How do the images that people in dominant nations have of Indigenous peoples affect the production and circulation of art? And, finally, who gets to decide what is authentic? To address these issues, Bigenho distinguishes three different forms of authenticity:

FIGURE 8.6 *Música de Maestros* in costume performing in a folklore festival in France.

1. *experiential authenticity*, which exists in the sensory experience connected with a piece of art;
2. *cultural–historical authenticity*, which stems from the way in which a piece of art is represented in relation to the historical or mythical history of the art form; and
3. *unique authenticity*, which is tied to the individual artist's new, innovative, and personal production of a work of art.

Bigenho expands on these forms by relating them to her experience with music. In music performances, *experiential authenticity* is "connected to a shared experience with others, a fleeting moment of the groove, a listener's great night at a concert" (18). *Cultural–historical authenticity* makes a claim to a connection with the origin of the music. For example, the performances of *Música de Maestros* were authentic in the sense that the musicians sought to perform culturally and historically authentic renditions of Bolivian music. Bigenho also points out that in terms of Indigenous art, the power of cultural–historical authenticity derives from the Indigenous artist's position in relation to the nation-state. *Unique authenticity* is the creative activity of composing musicians. This form of authenticity raises the issue of who owns cultural products and whether it is possible to talk about collective creation and ownership of the music of a community, a people, or an ethnic group.

Issues surrounding ownership are particularly significant in relation to questions of who owns experiences and representations. Bigenho came face to face with such questions when she put together a recorded compilation of music from one of the villages in which she worked. She discussed with the villagers how to register the copyright on the compilation. While the villagers recognized that the music they played was composed by individuals, they felt strongly that ownership of the performed music was collective. When Bigenho went to La Paz to register the copyright, however, she found that it was impossible to register the compilation under collective authorship or ownership. In fact *she*, as the compiler, could register the work, but the people who created the work could not, unless they were willing to be recognized as individuals. What she discovered was that according to Bolivian law, the music in the compilation was legally folklore:

the set of literary and artistic works created in national territory by unknown authors or by authors who do not identify themselves and are presumed to be nationals of the country, or of its ethnic communities, and that are transmitted from generation to generation, constituting one of the fundamental elements of traditional cultural patrimony [i.e., inherited property] of the nation. (221)

As a result, the music was part of the "national patrimony" and belonged to the nation-state. But in the context of Bolivian cultural and ethnic politics, Bigenho observes, the villagers gained visibility and connections as a collective Indigenous entity, which they believed would provide them with possible economic advantages. Whether they were correct remains to be seen, but this example of the connections of art and authority is being repeated all over the world.

Sculpture and the Baule Gbagba Dance

The Baule of the Ivory Coast are renowned for their sculpture (see EthnoProfile 3.1: Figure 8.7). Susan Vogel (1997), who has been studying Baule

FIGURE 8.7 A Baule wood sculpture from the nineteenth century.

sculpture for several decades, identifies four forms of Baule sculpture:

1. art that is watched (performances featuring carved masks),
2. art that is seen without looking (sacred sculpture),
3. art that is glimpsed (private sculptures of personal figures for hunting and sculptures for spirit spouses), and
4. art that is visible to all (everyday objects that the Baule see as beautiful trifles).

The Western concept of "art" does not exist in Baule villages. Rather, "to approach art from a Baule perspective entails speaking of experiences that are not primarily visual and of art objects that are animate presences, indistinguishable from persons, spirits, and certain prosaic things" (Vogel 1997: 108). The Baule attribute great powers to their artwork—powers that Westerners would consider incredible. The meaning of most art objects, as well as the emotional responses that these objects evoke, derives from their ability to act. For the Baule, what Western museum-goers call *sculpture* contains enormous powers of life and death, and Baule people do not consider their sculpture apart from these powers (85).

Here we will consider one situation in which art objects are used in performance: the Gbagba dance, as described by Vogel. This event, in which sculpture and dance intersect, has deep social and cultural significance for the Baule.

The Gbagba dance is a daylong entertainment performance. It may also be performed for the funeral of an important woman. The style of mask used in the performance is called *Mblo*, and in the past, a village may have had a dozen or more such masks—some representations of animals, some portraits of people. Gbagba also includes singing, and two of the songs repeated throughout the day refer to death.

The Gbagba begins with funny morality skits based on scenes from everyday life. These skits are performed by unmasked young dancers and may include older masked performers representing domestic animals (usually sheep and goats). Next come dance-based skits in which more skilled dancers don masks representing large wild animals; these dance skits always end with the successful "killing" of the portrayed animal.

When the first masks appear, so too does the costumed figure of the trickster Ambomon. Wearing a cloth hood rather than a mask, Ambomon dances in a rapid and acrobatic way that includes somersaults and tumbling. Ambomon is a comical figure who may or may not be a god. He displays no respect for possessions, rank, or decent behaviour. He stands in direct contrast to the orderly vision of the world, as expressed by the masks; he is the spirit of disorder. Yet at the same time, Ambomon is the only figure in the dance that *must* appear—he can appear without any of the masked figures, but the masked figures cannot appear without him. When Gbagba is danced for a funeral, only Ambomon enters the courtyard to pay his respects to the deceased and to greet the mourners. Vogel proposes that the obligatory presence of Ambomon suggests to the Baule that the only certainty in life is the threat of disorder and death (167).

Ambomon's energetic style of dance is quite different from the more subtle dance style of the other performers. In a typical female solo dance, for example, the dancer moves forward very slowly in a curved line, with body and neck held upright, hands in front, palms up. Sometimes the dancer carries something in her hand. The dancer's facial features are impassive, her eyes are downcast, and the main movement is in her neck, shoulders, and back. A male dancer may be a bit more vigorous, but

> Baule dancing in general can be characterized as symmetrically balanced and essentially vertical (the dancer's knees may be flexed but the head and torso are held upright). As in so many other Baule creations, the dancer's body is closed in outline. These qualities are also characteristic of Baule sculpture and must be recognized as expressing an aesthetic preference with moral connotations that is deeply embedded in Baule culture and is expressed in myriad ways. (156)

At the end of the day, portrait masks appear, one by one. These portrait masks are usually of specific women, and the subject of each portrait always dances alongside the male who dances the mask. Only the best dancers wear these masks. During these final performances, the finest skills in the community are on display—the best dancers, the most beautiful masks, the best drummers and singers—and the distinguished women who are represented now take their places (Figure 8.8).

The Baule use the term *double* to refer to the portrait mask and its subject. The portrait mask is considered the person's true double; the mask never performs unless the person is there to dance. The "relationships between individuals and their portrait masks are close, complex, and lifelong and become elements of their identities" (166). When the subject of a portrait mask dies or cannot dance any more, a relative becomes the new double or the mask is never danced again.

In conclusion, Vogel observes that the Gbagba dance event has deep social and cultural significance for the Baule:

> The performance teaches basic lessons about the Baule world—about hierarchies and mysteries. Each skit has a simple moral lesson, evident even to children: that humans, for example, with skill and supernatural aid, can dominate even the largest and most awesome wild animals, while the portrait masks present a model of human accomplishment and beauty. At the same time, the dance provides deeper insights about blurred boundaries—about the interpenetration of bush and village and the complexity of gender. The subject of a portrait, most often a woman, sees herself impersonated by a man dancing "like a woman" and wearing a mask that is her double or namesake. A frequent theme of Baule art is opposite-sex doubling, meaning that two figures appear not as a pair of complementary beings but as manifestations of a single being having qualities of both sexes. The concept is too troubling to articulate openly in words, but in Gbagba it is available to wordless contemplation. (167–8)

The Mass Media: A Television Serial in Egypt

Contemporary anthropologists recognize the importance of the mass media (e.g., television, films, websites) as a venue for cultural productions.

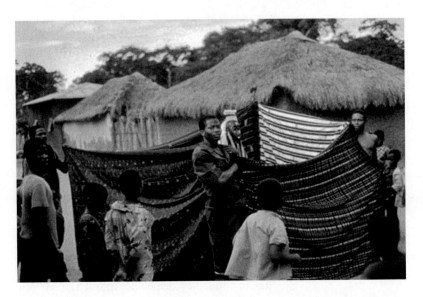

FIGURE 8.8 Portrait mask of Moya Yanso about to enter the Gbagba dance in the Baule village of Kami in 1972. The mask—an important object—is hidden by the cloths until the last moment, when the mask, its dancer, and its subject will appear dramatically.

In cases where a certain amount of creativity is involved—for example, in scripted and/or heavily edited movies and television shows—these productions can be thought of as art. Anthropological study of such productions, their creators, and their viewers can often reveal their cultural significance.

In many countries, soap operas or television serials are among the most popular mass entertainments, watched by millions. In some parts of the world, these programs are seen by their creators not simply as entertainment but also as tools, useful for teaching certain people in their societies what they need to learn to be modern citizens. But what the intended audience gets from the program is not always the message the creators thought they were transmitting.

Anthropologist Lila Abu-Lughod (1995) studied an Egyptian television serial called *Hilmiyya Nights* that was broadcast during Ramadan (the Islamic holy month of fasting) over five successive years. The serial followed the fortunes and relationships of a group of characters from the traditional Cairo neighbourhood of Hilmiyya, taking them from the late 1940s, when Egypt was under the rule of King Farouk and the British, up to the early 1990s, even incorporating Egyptian reaction to the first Gulf War. The central action revolved around the rivalry, financial dealings, and love interests of two wealthy men, and the narrative tied the lives of its characters to Egyptian national political events. Above all, the show promoted the theme of national unity. With few exceptions, all the characters were shown to be basically good and patriotic.

Abu-Lughod studied two separate groups of Egyptians during the 1990s: poor working-class women in Cairo and villagers in Upper Egypt. When she asked poor women in Cairo what they liked about the show, they volunteered not the serious political or social messages but two female characters: the glamorous, aristocratic femme fatale and the arrogant belly dancer turned cabaret owner. Although these two characters were hardly respectable, they were nevertheless favourites because they defied the moral system that kept good women quiet. Indeed, Abu-Lughod found that both the urban women and the villagers accepted the moral stances presented in the program only when they resonated with their own worlds. Overall, the women ignored the aspects of the serial that were not part of their experiences.

Most interestingly, Abu-Lughod argues that television, especially for the villagers, created its own world, one that was a small part of the viewers' daily lives. "What they experienced through television added to, but did not displace, whatever else already existed. They treated the television world not as a fantasy escape but as a sphere unto itself with its familiar time slots and specific attitudes" (Abu-Lughod 1995: 203–4). Moreover, the modern views presented on *Hilmiyya Nights* were not the only voices that brought "modernity" to the villagers. Indeed, the villagers were deeply affected in a wide variety of ways by the outside world, whether through local government policies or through multinational corporations' advertisements. As Abu-Lughod observes, "television is, in this village, one part of a complex jumble of life, and the dramatic experiences and visions it offers are surprisingly easily incorporated as discrete—not overwhelming—elements in the jumble" (205).

Television in Egypt, she notes, has had measurable social effects: for example, families prefer to stay home to watch television rather than visit among households in the evenings. Television may also have increased the number of "experiences" shared across generations and genders as young and old, men and women, now spend time together watching television.

Ultimately, the intended impact of *Hilmiyya Nights* was undermined, but not because nobody was watching television: both urban poor and villagers had their sets on almost constantly. Rather, the positive messages that the creators of *Hilmiyya Nights* and similar serials intended were lost because they were only part of the complex flow of programming in Egypt, which included many other kinds of information: news, entertainment, advertising, and so on. More important, viewers evaluated all these messages in terms of their own life experiences; hence, the messages were often neutralized or contradicted by the viewers' powerful everyday realities.

Myth

We have proposed that play lies at the heart of human creativity. However, because play has the potential to undermine the social order, societies tend to apply cultural rules meant to channel play in less destructive directions. Rules designed to limit artistic expression—for example, rules that prohibit artists from questioning certain social, religious, or sexual principles—are one result of this channelling process. All societies depend on the willingness of their members not to question certain assumptions about the way the world works. Because the regularity and predictability of social life might collapse altogether if people were free to imagine, and act upon, alternatives to the local version of reality, most societies find ways to persuade their members that the local version of reality is the only reality—period. The most widely accepted and respected way of doing this is through the use of myth.

Myths are stories whose truths seem self-evident because the narrative does such a good job of integrating personal experiences with a wider set of assumptions about the way society, or the world in general, must operate. Traditionally, these stories involve a teller and an audience; thus, myths are products of high verbal art. Frequently the official myth tellers are the ruling groups in society: the elders, the political leaders, the religious specialists. They may also be considered master storytellers. The content

IN THEIR OWN WORDS | The Grizzly Gave Them the Song

Canadian researcher Wendy Wickwire, in discussing the fieldwork of pioneer anthropologists James Teit and Franz Boas, provides some insights into bear ritual among the Aboriginal peoples of British Columbia. So many aspects of culture highlighted in this chapter can be seen in this article—myth, ritual, art (song), and the transmission of cultural knowledge from person to person.

Teit's field notes, by way of contrast (to those of Boas), present a much fuller picture of bear culture. Through the medium of songs and stories about direct encounters with bears, this source highlights the nurturing/protective role of the bear. Teit recorded 12 songs associated with bears along with contextual notes drawn from the commentary of seven singers (four men and three women). All seven focus on the close physical and spiritual bond between bears and humans. This source also highlights the prominent role of the female grizzly.

Six of the 12 songs, for example, are lullabies or cradle songs said to have been given to the Nlaka'pamux by female grizzlies. Such songs, according to Teit, were closely associated with women (CMC, cylinder collection VI.M.58). Kax.pítsa's song, catalogued by Teit as VI.M.125 "cradle song," is typical. A member of the Spences Bridge Band, Kax.pítsa told Teit that she had obtained this directly from the bear when she was a young woman.

> She had a vision in which she saw a female grizzly bear with four children under a tree. The children (or cubs) were all males and all of them were in birch bark carriers. The children were crying much and the mother was singing trying to stop them from crying. When the grizzly woman saw Kax.pítsa she called on her to come over and sing to the children. Kax.pítsa told her she did not know how to sing to them properly and the grizzly told her she would teach her. Kax.pítsa took up one after the other and sang to them as the grizzly directed and one after another they quit crying. When all were pacified (or asleep) the grizzly told Kax.pítsa,

> "You will now have this song for a cradle song and by singing it to children when they cry, you will have the power of quickly pacifying them." Kax.pítsa claims to have this power but only for male children. (VI.M.125)

The song is similar to another in the collection sung by NsElkapéskEt, a young Spences Bridge man. Teit catalogued it as a "lullaby song called the 'Black Bear's Lullaby'" (CMC, cylinder collection VI.M.195) and noted that it

> is said to be old and is said to have originated or been introduced by some person who had heard the black bear singing it. The person saw a black bear come over a hill carrying her baby. The latter was crying and as the mother came along travelling down the hill she sang this song to her baby thus quieting it. Since then the women of the Up.Ntlak (Thompson) have used the song when travelling to quiet their babies when they cried.

Chief TetlEnítsa of Spences Bridge also sang a "cradle song" with close links to the female bear. He told Teit that he had received the song in a dream in which a "dark woman and her baby" had appeared to him and led him to her den. Teit believed that this woman "was likely simply a different manifestation of the black bear woman who became manitou [a guardian spirit] of TetlEnítsa when he was a young man. She appears in different forms in his dreams. . . . [She] often carries baby" (CMC, cylinder collection VI.M.49–50). Although TetlEnítsa claimed this as his own song, he explained that the women of his band liked it and so adopted it as their cradle song. These examples . . . underscore the importance of the *female* bear in the Nlaka'pamux world. Her songs and instructions were a key component of women's culture, especially motherhood.

Source: Wickwire, Wendy. 2001. "The Grizzly Gave Them the Song: James Teit and Franz Boas Interpret Twin Ritual in Aboriginal British Columbia, 1897–1920," *American Indian Quarterly* 25, 3: 431–52.

of myths usually concerns past events (usually at or near the beginning of time) or future events (usually at or near the end of time). Sometimes, myths account for the origins of a specific cultural practice (see the "In Their Own Words" box). Myths are socially important because they tell people where they have come from, where they are going, and, thus, how they should live right now (Figure 8.9).

In some societies, myths play a relatively informal role in laying out the guidelines of social conduct. This is the case in most complex Western societies such as Canada, where many different groups, each with its own mythic tradition, often live side by side. Because the Canadian government supports cultural diversity, or multiculturalism, it regularly prohibits one group from silencing an opposing group. Yet Canada is

FIGURE 8.9 A vase painting illustrating part of the Popul Vuh, the Mayan creation story. What can a creation story communicate to people about how they should live their lives?

orthodoxy

"Correct doctrine"; the prohibition of deviation from certain generally accepted rules or beliefs.

not without its myths. For many Canadians, the notion of multiculturalism itself is the dominant myth, and our assumption is that it makes us more tolerant. Yet, as is the case with most myths, the ideal it represents is not always reflected in reality (Dods 2010).

Myths and related beliefs that are taken to be self-evident truths are sometimes arranged into an official code, or set of rules. When these rules are extreme and deviation from the code is treated harshly, we sometimes speak of **orthodoxy**. Societies differ in the degree to which they require members to adhere to orthodox interpretations of key myths. But even societies that place little emphasis on orthodoxy are likely to exert some control over the interpretation of key myths because myths have implications for action. They may justify past action, explain present action, or generate future action. To be persuasive, myths must offer plausible explanations for our experience of human nature, human society, and human history. The power of myths comes from their ability to make life meaningful for those who accept them.

The success of Western science has led many members of Western societies to dismiss non-scientific myths as flawed attempts at science or history. Only relatively recently have some scientists come to recognize the similarities between scientific and non-scientific storytelling about events such as the origin of life on earth. Scientific stories about origin—*origin myths*—are matched

against material evidence found in the *natural* world; the success of this match determines whether the myths are accepted or rejected. By contrast, non-scientific origin myths get their vitality from how well they match with the *social* world.

Myth as a Charter for Social Action

Early in the twentieth century, Bronislaw Malinowski introduced a new approach to myth. He believed that to understand myths, we must understand the social context in which they are embedded. Malinowski argued that myths serve as "charters" or "justifications" for present-day social arrangements. Myths contain some "self-evident" truth that explains why society is as it is and why it cannot be changed. If the social arrangements justified by the myth are challenged, the myth can be used as a weapon against the challengers.

Malinowski's (1948 [1926]) famous example is of the origin myths of the Trobriand Islanders (see EthnoProfile 7.1). Members of every significant kinship group know and retell the history of the place from which their group's ancestress and her brother emerged from the depths of the earth. These origin myths are set in the time before history began. Each ancestress–brother pair brought with them a distinct set of special objects, knowledge, skills, crafts, spells, and the like. On reaching the surface, the pair took possession of the land. That is why, today, the people on a given piece of land have rights to it. It is also why they possess a particular set of skills, crafts, and spells. Because the original sacred beings were a woman and her brother, the origin myth can also be used to endorse present-day social arrangements. Membership in a Trobriand clan depends on a person's ability to trace his or her kinship to that clan's original ancestress through matrilineage. A brother and a sister represent the prototypical members of a clan because they have both descended from the ancestress through female links. Should anyone question the wisdom of organizing society in this way, the myth can be cited as proof that this is indeed the correct way to live.

In Trobriand society, clans are ranked relative to one another in terms of prestige. In the Trobriand myth that explains rank, one clan's ancestor, the dog, emerged from the earth before another clan's ancestor, the pig, thus justifying ranking the dog clan above the pig clan in terms of prestige. To believe in this myth, Malinowski asserted, is to accept a transcendent justification for the ranking of clans. He made it clear, however, that if social arrangements change, the myth changes too—in order to justify the new arrangements. At some point, the pig clan became more prominent than the dog clan. This social change resulted in a modification in the mythic narrative. The dog was said to have eaten food that was taboo. In doing so, the dog gave up its claim to higher rank. Thus, to understand a myth and its transformations, one must understand the social organization of the society that makes use of it.

Myth as a Conceptual Tool

Beginning in the mid-1950s, a series of books and articles by French anthropologist Claude Lévi-Strauss transformed the study of myth (see, e.g., Lévi-Strauss 1955; 1967 [1962]). Lévi-Strauss argued that myths have meaningful structures that are worth studying in their own right, quite apart from the uses to which the myths may be put. According to Lévi-Strauss, these structures can help us understand and overcome complex issues that are otherwise difficult to comprehend.

Using a linguistic metaphor, Lévi-Strauss argued that myths are composed of smaller units—phrases, sentences, words, and so on—that are arranged in ways that give both narrative as well as structural coherence. These arrangements represent and comment upon aspects of social life that are thought to oppose each other. Examples include the male and the female, the natural world and the cultural world, life and death, the spirit and the body, and so on.

The complex syntax (or structure) of myth attempts to reconcile those opposed aspects to one another in an attempt to overcome their contradictions and achieve holism. Of course, these contradictions can never be overcome completely; for example, the opposition of life to death is incapable of any earthly resolution. But myth can transform an insoluble problem into a more accessible, concrete form. Mythic narrative can then provide the concrete problem with a solution. For example, in a myth, a hero may bridge the opposition between life and death by travelling from the land of the living to the land of the dead and back. Perhaps a myth describes the journey of a bird that travels from the earth, the home of the living, to the sky, the home of the dead. Many cultures have such myths. One of the earliest recorded is the Egyptian myth of Osiris, in which Osiris dies, is brought back to life, and becomes the ruler of the underworld.

From this point of view, myths do not just talk about the world as it is; they also describe the world as it might be. To paraphrase Lévi-Strauss, myths are good to think with; mythic thinking can propose other ways to live our lives. He insists, however, that the alternatives myths proposed are ordinarily rejected as impossible. Thus, even though myths allow for play with self-evident truths, this play remains under strict control.

Is Lévi-Strauss correct? There has been a great deal of debate on this approach since Lévi-Strauss first introduced it. But even those who are most critical of his analyses of particular myths agree that mythic structures are meaningful because they display the ability of human beings to play with possibilities as they attempt to deal with basic contradictions at the heart of human experience.

For Malinowski, Lévi-Strauss, and their followers, those who believe in myths are not conscious of how their myths are structured or of the functions their myths perform for them. More recent anthropological thinking takes a more reflexive approach. This research recognizes that ordinary members of a society *are* often aware of how their myths structure meaning, allowing them to manipulate the way myths are told or interpreted in order to effect change, to prove a point, or to buttress a particular referential perspective on human nature, society, or history. Therefore myths are the art form by which people create meaning through language (see Riddington 1998). In a myth, parts can stand for wholes, and "each story is connected to every other and to a highly contextualized discourse that assumes familiarity with biography and shared experience" (1998: 346).

Ritual

Play allows unlimited consideration of alternative referential perspectives on reality. Art permits consideration of alternative perspectives but imposes certain limitations restricting the form and the content. Myth aims to narrow the possible referential perspectives and often promotes a single, orthodox perspective presumed to be valid for everyone. It thus attempts to shape the way members of a culture think about themselves and their surroundings. But because societies aim to shape action as well as thought, art, myth, and ritual are often closely associated with one another.

A Definition of Ritual

Recall the definition of ritual given at the beginning of this chapter:

> A repetitive social practice set off from everyday routine and composed of a sequence of symbolic activities that adhere to a culturally defined ritual schema and are closely connected to a specific set of ideas significant to the culture.

This definition of ritual has four elements.

1. Ritual is *a repetitive social practice*. This means that rituals are repeated again and again, and they involve more than one person. Rituals tend to be composed of a sequence of social, symbolic activities such as dance, song, speech, gestures, the manipulation of certain objects, and so forth.

2. It is *set off from the social routines of everyday life*. Rituals occupy a special place in social life, a place separate from day-to-day activities and interactions.

3. Rituals *adhere to a characteristic, culturally defined ritual schema*. This means that members of a culture can tell that a certain sequence of activities is a ritual even if they have never seen that particular ritual before.

4. Ritual action is *closely connected to a specific set of ideas that are somehow significant to the culture*. These ideas are often encoded in myth. They might concern the nature of evil, the relationship of human beings to the spirit world, how people ought to interact with one another, and so forth.

The purpose for which a ritual is performed guides how these ideas are selected and symbolically enacted. What gives a ritual its power is that the people who perform it assert that the authorization for the ritual comes from outside themselves—from their state, society, God, ancestors, or "tradition." These people have not made up the ritual themselves; rather, it connects them to a source of power that they do not control but that controls them.

The Western idea of ritual includes the notion that it is "religious." However, in anthropological terms, ritual includes a much broader range of activities. According to the definition given above, a scientific experiment, a graduation ceremony, procedures in a court of law, and a child's birthday party are rituals just as much as weddings, bar mitzvahs, and Catholic Mass are.

Consider the example of a young child's birthday party in North America. Several children are formally invited to help celebrate the birthday. Each arrives bringing a wrapped gift, which is handed to the birthday child and then set aside. The children often put on birthday hats. They then play group games of some kind, some of which are now played *only* at birthday parties. The games culminate with the appearance of a birthday cake, illuminated by candles (one for each year of the child's life) and accompanied by the singing of "Happy Birthday." The birthday child makes a wish and blows out the candles (Figure 8.10). Following the cake and ice cream, the birthday child opens the presents. As the birthday child opens each gift, he or she examines it and thanks the guest (often with an adult's prompting). Shortly after the presents are opened, the guests' parents or guardians appear and the guests receive party favours and leave. The ritual order of these events matters. The central events of the party—the giving of gifts; the events associated with the cake, the candles, the singing of "Happy Birthday," the wish; and the opening of the gifts—must occur in this order. Additionally, if you come from a tradition in which birthday parties are celebrated, it is likely that you cannot remember *learning* how to celebrate a birthday party—it is something you have always known. It's what everyone does. It's just how it is. Its authority comes from "tradition."

In the birthday party ritual, children (both hosts and guests) learn to associate receiving gifts with important moments in life. They discover the importance of exchanging material objects (reciprocity) in defining significant social relations. They learn to defer gratification (the presents cannot be opened immediately). They live out patterns of sociability and friendship while recognizing the centrality of the individual (the child celebrating the birthday). Finally, the children participate in patterns of sharing, of celebrating the self, and of recognizing relationships with friends and kin that are important in other areas of North American life.

Ritual as Action

A ritual has a particular sequential ordering of acts, utterances, and events: that is, ritual has a *text*. Because ritual is action, however, we must pay attention to the way the ritual text is performed. The *performance* of a ritual cannot be separated from its text; text and performance shape each other. Through ritual performance, the ideas of a culture become tangible, take on a form, and shape participants' views on their society. At the same time, ritual performance can serve as a commentary on the text to the extent of transforming it. For example, Jewish synagogue ritual following the reading of the Torah (the Hebrew holy book) includes lifting the Torah scroll, showing it to the congregation, and then closing it and covering it. In some synagogues, a man and a woman, often a couple, are called to lift and cover the Torah: the man lifts it and, after he seats himself, the woman

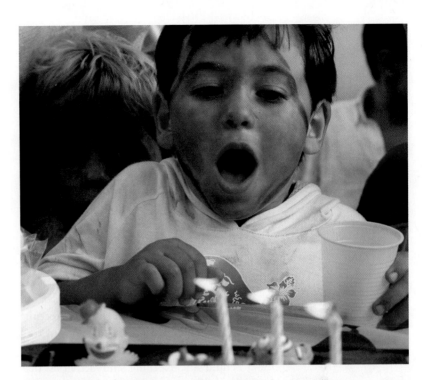

FIGURE 8.10 Part of the ritual aspect of the North American birthday party is the blowing out of candles on the cake. The birthday child blows out the candles and makes a wish. Did you celebrate such parties as a child? What aspects of the dominant North American culture do such rituals reinforce?

rolls the scroll closed, places the tie around it, and covers it with the cloth that protects it. Robert Lavenda once observed a performance of this ritual in which the woman lifted the Torah and the man wrapped it; officially, the ritual text was carried out, but the performance became a commentary on the text—on the role of women in Judaism, on the Torah as an appropriate subject of attention for women as well as for men, on the roles of men and women overall, and so on. The performance was noteworthy—indeed, many of the regular members of the congregation seemed quite surprised—precisely because it violated people's expectations and in doing so directed people's attention toward significant social issues.

Ritual performers are not robots but active individuals whose choices are guided by, but not rigidly dictated by, previous ritual texts. After all, human behaviour is fundamentally open. Rituals highlight the fact that human understanding of the world is not just mental and not just physical; instead, it is a holistic coming together of mind and body, thought and feeling. By performing our ideas, and by feeling the implications of our myths, their truths become self-evident.

Rites of Passage

Let us examine how ritual action can reaffirm certain fundamental truths by looking at one kind of ritual performance: the **rite of passage**. At the beginning of the twentieth century, French anthropologist Arnold Van Gennep noted that certain kinds of rituals around the world had similar structures. These were rituals associated with the movement (or passage) of people from one position in the social structure to another. They included births, initiations, confirmations, weddings, and funerals (Figure 8.11).

Van Gennep (1960) found that all these rituals began with a period of *separation* from the old position. During this period, the ritual passenger left behind the symbols and practices of his or her previous position. For example, military recruits leave their families behind and are moved to a new place. They are forced to cut their hair and leave behind the clothing and activities that marked who they were in civilian life.

The second stage in a rite of passage involves a period of *transition*, in which the ritual passenger is neither in the old life nor in the new one. This period is marked by rolelessness, ambiguity, and perceived danger. Van Gennep referred to this part of a rite of passage as the **liminal period**, from the Latin *limen* ("threshold"). During

this period, the individual is on the threshold, betwixt and between, neither here nor there, neither in nor out. Often, the person involved is subjected to ordeal by those who have already passed through this stage. In the military service, this is the period of basic training, in which recruits (not yet soldiers but no longer civilians) are forced to dress and act alike. They are subjected to a grinding-down process, after which they are rebuilt into something new. Another example of this sort of period of transition is the wake that precedes a funeral in many cultures; the wake is a time of transition from the here and now to the timelessness of eternity.

During the final stage—*re-aggregation*—the ritual passenger is reintroduced into society in his or her new position. In the military this involves the graduation from basic training and a visit home, but this time in uniform, on leave, and as a member of the armed forces. A more familiar rite of passage in North America is high-school graduation, which is understood as a movement from one social position (a high-school student) to another (e.g., a college or university student, a member of the workforce, or an independent adult).

British cultural anthropologist Victor Turner greatly increased our understanding of rites of passage when he concentrated on the liminal stage, which he saw as an ambiguous state. Turner notes that the symbolism accompanying this stage often expresses ambiguity and uncertainty. Liminality, he tells us, "is frequently likened to death, to being in the womb, to invisibility, to darkness, to bisexuality, to the wilderness, and to an eclipse of the sun or moon" (1969: 95). We are familiar with this concept from the tales recorded by the Brothers Grimm. Many of what we call *fairy tales* were originally folktales and have rites of passage and liminality as part of the story. Consider the original version of *Snow White*, in which a young girl is first forced to live in the woods (outside her society) and then killed before being brought back to life and back to society, at which time she is deemed ready for marriage (i.e., ready to take on the role of wife and mother). Similar themes appear in *Sleeping Beauty*, *Rapunzel*, and many other folk tales.

Turner observed that people in the liminal state tend to develop intense comradeships in which their non-liminal distinctions disappear or

FIGURE 8.11 This funeral procession in Kyoto, Japan, bears resemblance to North American funeral processions. Certain kinds of rituals around the world have similar structures.

become irrelevant. Turner calls this form of social relationship **communitas**. Turner contends that all societies need some kind of temporary communitas as much as they need more permanent structure. Communitas gives "recognition to an essential and generic human bond, without which there could be no society" (Turner 1969: 97). However, periods of communitas are brief, generally existing only within a ritual context. Communitas is dangerous, not just because it threatens structure but because it threatens survival itself. Lost in a world of communitas, an individual is cut off from the things that structure ensures (e.g., food, social support). At some point, communitas must give way to structure. In turn, this structure generates a need for the release of communitas.

The feeling of oneness associated with communitas is also possible in play and art. Indeed, in our own societies, we can find this sort of group interaction at sports games, rock concerts, or large-scale public event such as Toronto's Caribbean Carnival (Caribana), Carnaval de Québec, or the Calgary Stampede. In each case, people are temporarily brought together as equals to share in a cultural experience that exists outside the boundaries of everyday life.

Play and Ritual as Complementary

How does play differ from ritual? Play and ritual (like metaphorical and literal language) are complementary forms of metacommunication (Handelman 1977). Just as the movement from non-play to play is based on the premise of metaphor ("let's make-believe"), the movement to ritual is based on the premise of literalness ("let's believe"). The result of these contrasting premises is that play is associated with inauthenticity, while ritual is associated with truth.

Because of the connection of ritual with self-evident truth, the metacommunication of the ritual frame ("this is ritual") is associated with an additional metacommunication: "all messages within this frame are true." It is ritual that asserts *what should be* to play's *what can be*. The ritual frame is more rigid than is the play frame. Consequently, ritual is the most stable liminal domain, whereas play is the most flexible. Players can move with relative ease into and out of play, but such is not the case with ritual.

Finally, play usually has little effect on the social order of ordinary life. Thus play is allowed a wide range of commentary on the social order. Ritual is different: its role is explicitly to maintain the status quo. Societies differ in the extent to which they promote ritual behaviour. When nearly every act of everyday life is ritualized and other forms of behaviour are strongly proscribed, we sometimes speak of **orthopraxy**. Traditionally, observant Jews and Muslims, for example, lead a highly ritualized daily life, attempting from the moment they awaken until the moment they fall asleep to carry out even the humblest of activities in a manner that is ritually correct. In their view, ritual correctness is the result of God's law, and it is their duty and joy to conform their every action to God's will.

Ritual may seem overwhelming and all-powerful, but it can sometimes be manipulated to achieve non-traditional ends. This manipulation can take many forms. It might involve giving up some elements of the ritual while keeping others, as when a bride and groom have a wedding outdoors instead of in a church but still have a member of the clergy officiate at the ceremony. Or, it might involve emphasizing the importance of one ritual while downplaying another, as when Protestant Baptists downplayed the communion ritual and emphasized the baptism ritual as a way of articulating their challenge to Roman Catholicism. It might even involve exchanging one set of rituals for another, as when lone rural migrants abandoned their traditional rituals and converted to Islam shortly after their arrival in northern Cameroon.

Ethnographer Margaret Drewal (1992) argues that, at least among the Yoruba (see Map 8.2), play and ritual overlap. Yoruba rituals combine spectacle, festival, play, sacrifice, and so on. They also integrate diverse media—music, dance, poetry, theatre, and sculpture. They are spontaneous events in which the mundane order is inverted, reversed, and sometimes even subverted. For example, in everyday Yoruba life, gender roles are rigidly structured. Yoruba rituals, however, allow some cross-dressing by both men and women, providing institutionalized opportunities for men and women to cross gender boundaries and to express the traits that the Yoruba consider to be characteristic of the opposite sex. Sometimes

communitas
An unstructured or minimally structured community of equal individuals frequently found in rites of passage.

orthopraxy
"Correct practice"; the prohibition of deviation from certain generally accepted forms of behaviour.

MAP 8.2 Yoruba

MAP 8.3 Sinhalese

these performances are parody, but sometimes they are serious and respectful (190).

Combining Play, Art, Myth, and Ritual

To reiterate, play, art, myth, and ritual are often experienced together. Consider Australian anthropologist Bruce Kapferer's (1983) study of demon exorcism among the Sinhalese Buddhist working class and peasantry in Sri Lanka (see Map 8.3). The night-long ceremony, designed to cure disease, combines ritual, comedy, music, and dance. It is "a marvellous spectacle" meant "to change the experiential condition of [the] patients and to bring patients back into a normal conception of the world" (1983: 177, 236).

At the beginning of the ceremony, the patient and the audience are in different realities. The audience is in the paramount reality of everyday life; the patient is in the alternative reality of the illness. During the first part—called the Evening Watch—the audience becomes increasingly engaged in this alternative reality through music, song, and dance. The performance culminates in the appearance of the illness demons (played by actors), which are portrayed as figures of horror.

At this point, the second part—the Midnight Watch—begins. This part of the ceremony is a comic drama that lasts until nearly 3 a.m. The comic content transforms the demons into figures of ridicule and begins to fragment the demonic reality. The gods appear and reassert their dominance, and the sick person begins to see that the demons are really subordinate to the gods, not superior to them.

The last part of the exorcism is the Morning Watch, which continues until 6 a.m. During this part, the patient and the audience become re-engaged in the reality of ordinary life. The final comic drama of the performance "confirms the demonic absurdity and destroys the demonic," thus reaffirming the reality of everyday life (220). Having played on the mind, body, and emotions of the patient and the audience, the performance ends. The experience is transformative for all involved.

To understand the performance as a whole, the interactions of all aspects of the performance must be grasped. Kapferer calls this the ceremony's *aesthetics*. He argues that the ceremony succeeds because it is composed of many different parts that fit together in a way that is satisfying to the Sinhalese. In the aesthetic realm—a realm in this case created by the related forces of play, art, myth, and ritual—ideas, symbolic objects, and actions come together in a deeply meaningful way.

Play, art, myth, and ritual are different facets of the holistic human capacity to view the world from a variety of perspectives. The human capacity to play is channelled in different directions in different cultures, but it is always present. When the products of this containment process come together in key cultural productions, such as the Sinhalese curing ceremony, they display both the opportunities and the dangers that result from open human creativity.

A CRITICAL LOOK | Transitions

We all undergo transitions, great and small, throughout our lives. We experience "the coming-into-being, completion, and attenuation of personhood," and through this experience "life and death are attributed, contested, and enacted" (Kaufman and Morgan 2005: 317). In this context, we can consider "two basic anthropological models of cultural representations of death":

> The first is the journey model, in which death is considered to be a long- term transformation. In many societies, death is imagined as a continuation of the journey begun in life. Death as a journey is usually contrasted with the Western model of death as "punctual" and, insofar as it is rooted in biological understandings of death, a terminal end. (Dernbach 2005:120–1)

Both models present ways of comprehending the altered circumstances within the social fabric where the dead once lived.

Swiss anthropologist Marc-Antoine Berthod (2005) speaks of the tension that is evoked as a moment of suspended silence when the "being" of the dead or near-dead is in a state of redefinition. Our silence at such times affirms what Berthod sees as our embarrassment at asserting the radical otherness of the deceased or the nearly deceased (535). Our preoccupation with this radical otherness is emphasized by the enduring popularity of zombies in movies (e.g., *Night of the Living Dead*, *Dawn of the Dead*, and *Zombieland*), television shows (e.g., *The Walking Dead*), music videos (e.g., Michael Jackson's "Thriller" video), novels (e.g., *World War Z*, also a popular film), and other forms of entertainment. Even with the scientific discussion of zombification (see, e.g., Davis 1985, 1988), we are still left with this realm of otherness.

We seldom confront the cultural issues of the "life of the dead" (Berthod 2005: 521) during funerary rituals and mourning. In North America, these rites may be insignificant (straight and swift disposal of the corpse) or elaborate and detailed (a state funeral), but they are rarely drawn out in the fashion found in some other societies. Indeed, in some cultures, the end-of-life transition may move and change through time and be deeply integrated into the world of the living. Consider the case of the Trobriand Islanders. "Trobriand mortuary rituals, which extend over a period of five to ten years, represent an effort to deconstruct the total social person by separating elements of the body, artifacts, and spiritual essence, so that each element is reinvested in the world of the living. . . . [D]eath . . . is a process of continuity and change, a journey and an ending, mourning and memory work, an uncontrollable happening, and a complex social achievement" (Dernbach 2005: 121). In some cases, rituals even invite the deceased to actively participate, albeit in spiritual form. Among the Chuukese people of Micronesia, for example, funerary rituals involve the spirits of the recently deceased appearing to and even possessing their living relatives (Dernbach 2005). The Chuukese believe that the spirits of the dead linger in the world of the living for a period of time before moving on to the world of the dead. The purpose of this liminal phase is believed to be twofold: it provides comfort and guidance to the living, and it gives the spirit a chance to grow accustomed to its new circumstances.

Mortuary rituals of some form are universal, if only in the fulfillment of government regulations. However, in our culture, these things can become prolonged in instances where biomedical technology can project the cellular life of a body long past the point at which the individual as a social being can be defined as dead. Here we have the "modern" concept of the irreversible death of the brain. In the biotechnical world, we face the challenge of developing rites and rituals that support the living through the process of stages of death as it is variously defined in medicine and law.

For the dying, death is about departing from everything; for the remaining, it is about contemplating the space left empty by "the departed" and the ultimate destination of "the departed." Ultimately, death is a *social event*—an occurrence that has shared meaning that we mark through various rituals. These rituals reaffirm life by declaring that there was and perhaps remains a "beingness" of the dead. Thus rituals, whether religious or medical, benefit the living in various ways, mainly by providing comfort in a time of loss and support in the contemplation of our finiteness. Ultimately, ritual confirms our place in the fabric of life—the life of our family, our community, and our world.

—Roberta Robin Dods

KEY TERMS

art 188

communitas 207

framing 189

liminal period 206

metacommunication 189

myths 188

orthodoxy 202

orthopraxy 207

play 188

reflexivity 189

rite of passage 206

ritual 188

sport 191

transformation-representation 193

CHAPTER SUMMARY

1. Play is a generalized form of behavioural openness that functions as practice for the real world, increases creativity, and serves as a way of *organizing* activities. It allows us to set up a separate reality that permits reflexive consideration. Sport is a form of play that can take on a deeper significance, especially for adults.

2. Art is a kind of play that is subject to certain culturally appropriate restrictions on form and content. It aims to evoke an aesthetic response from the artist and the observer.

3. Myths are stories whose truths seem self-evident because they do such a good job of integrating personal experiences with a wider set of assumptions about the way the world works. As stories, myths are the products of high verbal art. A full understanding of a myth requires an understanding of the social context in which the myth is embedded.

4. Ritual is a repetitive social practice composed of sequences of symbolic activities such as speech, singing, dancing, gestures, and the manipulation of certain objects. In studying ritual, we pay attention not just to the symbols but also to how the ritual is performed. Cultural ideas are made concrete through ritual action. Rites of passage are rituals in which members of a culture move from one position in the social structure to another.

5. Ritual and play are complementary. Play is based on the premise "let's make-believe," while ritual is based on the premise "let's believe." As a result, the ritual frame is far more rigid than the play frame. Although ritual may seem overwhelming and all-powerful, individuals and groups can sometimes manipulate ritual forms to achieve non-traditional ends.

CRITICAL THINKING QUESTIONS

1. What adult roles do you remember learning through childhood play? Did the games you played reflect dominant cultural stereotypes within the culture (for example, that a "standard" family has both a mommy and a daddy)? In what ways did the games creatively diverge from the reality of adult life?

2. How are art and play alike in presenting alternative realities?

3. How do you think that the multiculturalism myth impacts the ways Canadians act and interpret their place in the world? What other myths do you see at work in your society?

4. How would you describe your experience as a university or college student as a rite of passage? Have you ventured through periods of separation, transition, and re-aggregation?

SUGGESTED READINGS

Alland, Alexander. 1977. *The Artistic Animal: An Inquiry into the Biological Roots of Art* (New York: Doubleday Anchor). An introductory look at the biocultural bases for art. This work is very well written, clear, and fascinating.

Blanchard, Kendall. 1995. *The Anthropology of Sport*, rev. edn (Westport, CT: Bergin and Garvey). An excellent introduction to the topic.

Errington, Shelly. 1998. *The Death of Authentic Primitive Art and Other Tales of Progress* (Berkeley: University of California Press). A sharp and witty book about the production, distribution, interpretation, and sale of "primitive art."

King, Thomas. 1993. *Green Grass, Running Water* (Toronto: HarperCollins). This novel explores contemporary Native American culture and North American literature, juxtaposing the real and the magical to show how the magical gives essential meaning to the real. It is an engaging example of both metacommunication and transformation-representation.

Riddington, Robin. 1998. "Coyote's Canon: Sharing Stories with Thomas King," *American Indian Quarterly* 22, 3: 343–62. The counterpoint of Coyote is King as he presents a Native American perspective on the American literary and cultural canon.

Turner, Victor. 1969. *The Ritual Process* (Chicago: Aldine). An important work in the anthropological study of ritual, this text is an eloquent analysis of rites of passage.

Vogel, Susan. 1997. *Baule: African Art/Western Eyes* (New Haven: Yale University Press). A book of extraordinary photographs and beautifully clear text, this work explores both Baule and Western views of Baule expressive culture.

Wickwire, Wendy. 2001. "The Grizzly Gave Them the Song: James Teit and Franz Boas Interpret Twin Ritual in Aboriginal British Columbia, 1897–1920," *American Indian Quarterly* 25, 3: 431–52. Compares and contrasts the ethnographic information collected and interpreted by two researchers in British Columbia.

RELATED WEBSITES

The Antiquity of Man www.antiquityofman.com/Solomon_myth_ritual.html

Canadian Art www.canadianart.ca

Illinois State Museum www.museum.state.il.us/muslink/nat_amer/post/htmls/il_am.html

The Museum of Anthropology at the University of British Columbia www.moa.ubc.ca

The Grimm Brothers' Children's and Household Tales (in English) www.pitt.edu/~dash/grimmtales.html

Turtle Island Native Network: Culture www.turtleisland.org/culture/culture-haisla.htm

Winnipeg Art Gallery on Inuit Art http://wag.ca/art/inuit

9

States of Being in Wellness and Illness

by Roberta Robin Dods

CHAPTER OUTLINE

Beyond the Science–Tradition Divide

Integrated Approaches and Holism in Medical Anthropology

Cultural Interpretations and Labels of Illness and Disease

Environments and Well-Being

Health Care Delivery Systems

Epidemiology

Being Applied

LEARNING OBJECTIVES

By the end of Chapter 9, you will be able to

- understand that medical anthropology draws on many disciplines to study well-being, health, illness, and disease,
- appreciate the importance of traditional knowledge and Western scientific knowledge in the management of wellness and illness,

- consider how human wellness and illness are affected by three interacting environments: the biotic (biological), the abiotic (physical), and the cultural, and

- consider the various social, cultural, personal, economic, and political factors that affect how illness is understood and how health care is provided.

A medicine man in Senegal sprays his patient with a medicinal liquid to help cure her fertility issue. Like many traditional healers, this man offers traditional cures for illnesses and diseases by mediating forces in the physical as well as the spiritual world.

In *Childhood in the Middle Ages* (1990), Shulamith Shahar writes about the lives (and deaths) of children in Europe from the twelfth through the fifteenth century. She also notes the case of one sixteenth-century English woman who had given birth to 17 children, none of whom survived to adulthood. This woman was a member of the upper class and had access to the best her society could offer in terms of education, housing, food, and health care, yet her resources were not enough to save her children from diseases and medical conditions that we would find easily treatable today. Further, considering the low life expectancy (35 years) and the high rates of maternal death related to childbirth she faced, we might marvel that this woman survived birthing so many children in the first place.

Now you may say this woman's situation is simply a product of the time in which she lived. In some sense, you would be right. After all, in Western nations, life expectancies have increased dramatically since the Middle Ages, and maternal mortality ratios are now low. Yet we must also remember that we view the situation from a privileged position. In Canada, we have access to public and private institutions that offer cutting-edge medical technologies (vaccines, medications, machines, etc.). Most of us live in communities that provide adequate sanitation programs to regulate the quality of drinking water and the disposal of sewage and garbage. Not only is our life expectancy at birth over 80 years, our quality of life is quite high well into old age. We desire relatively small families, and various birth control and fertility technologies allow us to choose when and under what conditions we will have children. Most of us take immunization for granted, and we seldom think of diseases such as diphtheria, polio, or measles—all of which contributed to high infant and childhood mortality rates in past centuries (Figure 9.1). And smallpox is unimaginable for most of us, since it was eradicated worldwide by 1979. Overall, our landscape of health and well-being has improved in ways never imagined by previous generations.

Yet conditions are much different for people in less affluent (i.e., less wealthy) regions of the world. In many areas, for example, a high proportion of children and adults still die of diseases

transmitted through unclean water. As Table 9.1 indicates, maternal mortality ratios vary greatly across the globe. All too often, when it comes to issues of health and wellness, the divide between rich and poor is starkly evident. This division was apparent when cholera broke out in Haiti in 2010; the poorest segments of the population had the least access to uncontaminated water and life-saving resources. We see this division within wealthy nations as well, as less affluent people in all societies face greater health challenges than do their more affluent neighbours. Thus, while we may look at the world of the English woman who lost 17 children so long ago as frozen in history, there are millions of people today who would recognize that world and who would understand what it is like to face the threat of deadly contagious diseases on a daily basis.

Ultimately, an individual's expectations of wellness depend on her or his cultural context. Think about how important context is in your day-to-day experiences with health matters. For example, consider the different ways in which you would describe your sense of un-wellness to your doctor, your grandmother, your instructor, or your boss, particularly if you want a day off. What words would you choose to make each understand your symptoms and the validity of your perception of un-wellness? How would your

FIGURE 9.1 This 1898 *memento mori* photograph of an infant from Hull, Quebec, suggests the preoccupation with high infant mortality rates—more than 20 per 100 live births in some regions—at the turn of the twentieth century. At the time, infectious diseases were a common cause of death. What factors have kept infant mortality rates relatively low in most Western nations in recent decades?

TABLE 9.1 Maternal Mortality Ratios (MMRs) by Specific Regions of the World

	MMR (per 100,000 live births)					
	1990	**1995**	**2000**	**2005**	**2010**	**2013**
Africa	960	920	820	670	550	500
Americas	110	92	81	71	70	68
South-east Asia	520	430	340	260	210	190
Europe	42	36	29	22	20	17
Eastern Mediterranean	340	330	300	240	190	170
Western Pacific	110	93	78	63	49	45
Global	380	360	330	270	230	210

Source: World Health Organization Global Health Observatory Data Repository, http://apps.who.int/gho/data/view.main.1370?lang=en.

traditional knowledge
Knowledge that is culturally held and passed on from generation to generation.

medical anthropology
An area of anthropological inquiry that focusses on issues of well-being, health, illness, and disease as they are situated in their wider cultural contexts.

well-being
A culturally defined state (or role) of general physical and mental comfort and good health; a lack of illness.

health
A person's general social, psychological, and physical condition.

illness
A culturally defined state (or role) of general physical and/or mental discomfort and poor health.

disease
A biomedical condition characterized by a harmful biological irregularity in an organism.

sex, gender, age, or class influence your selection of terms? Undoubtedly your statements will be informed by the familiar models of un-wellness within your culture and subculture; they will also be suited to the relationship you have with the person to whom you are talking. You live in a world of cultural concerns, and you participate in that world from a uniquely situated position.

Beyond the Science–Tradition Divide

In this complex world, there is always a dynamic tension between **traditional knowledge** and Western scientific modes of inquiry. This tension plays out in all of our lives, and it is increasingly intensified by concepts of "modernization." Thus, it is naturally a central concern in **medical anthropology**. Note that in this context the term *medical* does not refer specifically to the field of medicine as it is defined in the West. Rather, *medical* here points to a wider array of concerns that relate more broadly to human ideas of **well-being**, **health**, **illness**, and **disease**.

In the 1970s and 1980s, many medical anthropologists saw a strong opposition between medical systems based on traditional knowledge and those based on "modern" Western science. Some anthropologists even saw the characterization of these two primary categories as the "broad aims of the research" (Colson and Selby 1974: 246). In one category, there is the Western biomedical approach in which a team of medical professionals, working within an institutionalized system, combat an illness with little reference to the social or cultural

conditions of the patient or "client." Medical anthropologist Allan Young (1976) called this an *internalizing* system, as it focusses on what is happening *inside* the individual's body (e.g., a virus attacking the person's cells). In the other category, there are traditional ethnomedical approaches in which a wise, often spiritually powerful specialist fights an illness based on the knowledge and beliefs of his or her specific cultural group, generally with an awareness of the context of social relationships (Fabrega 1971: 167). Young called such systems *externalizing*, as they often focus on what is happening *outside* the individual's body (e.g., spiritual forces as the cause of an illness).

Contemporary medical anthropologists try to move beyond such "either/or" approaches for a number of reasons. First, they understand that the two systems are not mutually exclusive; indeed, many cultures in the modern world incorporate both traditional and Western concepts into their medical systems. Second, they see that they can arrive at a more holistic appreciation of all knowledges by examining the traditional in terms of the scientific and the scientific in terms of the traditional. Third, they perceive that biomedical knowledge is actually a form of traditional knowledge—after all, such knowledge is rooted in Western history, it developed as Western society developed, and it is passed along within Western cultures. Fourth, they note that the lines between "folk" medicine and "scientific" medicine are not always clear. For example, Dr Irwin Ziment, of the UCLA Collaborative Centers for Integrative Medicine, observes that chicken soup contains drug-like agents similar to those in modern cold medicines. For example, an amino acid released from chicken during cooking chemically resembles the drug acetylcysteine, prescribed for bronchitis and other respiratory problems. (quoted in Day 2010)

Finally, they understand that "modern" is a relative concept. Each culture defines its own "modernity" based on its own cultural values and its own ideas about the past and the present. Thus it is ethnocentric to see the Western version of modernity, along with its biomedical approaches, as more modern than the modernities of cultures that support ethnomedical approaches. Whether we call it "science" or "tradition," knowledge is constantly advancing, as cultures are always changing. Traditional peoples are open to new concepts, and they have often incorporated elements from Western science into their treatment regimes. At the same time, there are ideological reasons for limiting such borrowings: "in some cases, reaffirmation of traditional medicine is enacted as a defence of ethnic identity" (Menegoni 1996: 382; also see the "In Their Own Words" box on Indigenous medicine and identity in Nicaragua).

IN THEIR OWN WORDS | Indigenous Medicine and Identity in Nicaragua

Hugo De Burgos, assistant professor of anthropology at the University of British Columbia Okanagan, discusses survival of ethnic identity and the use of traditional medical practices to reinforce concepts of identity and mediate place in a wider community.

Rescuing our Indigenous medicine is to recover our Indigenous identity and culture. Using our traditional medicine is expressing our Indigenous identity.

—Antonio Guzmán, Nicaraguan Indigenous leader

Medical systems are more than social schemes for healing. They are also systems of ecological adaptation; explanatory models for physical and social suffering; and mechanisms for social control. The practical and symbolic functions of a medical system are not restricted to medical concerns. Their multiple implications pervade non-medical spheres of social life, shaping in this way their initially medical purpose. Medical beliefs and practices constitute cultural configurations that inform, shape, and mediate human experience in ways that go beyond purely medical functions.

The people of Veracruz del Zapotal, or Veracruceños, are a Spanish-speaking Indigenous community of Nahua descent from Nicaragua. Currently figuring approximately 3,800, they inhabit the Veracruz del Zapotal valley and the mountain region between the rivers of El Camarón, Guachipilín, and Rio Grande in the department of Rivas, in southern Nicaragua. In their struggle to remain culturally distinct, Veracruceños have been able to direct their medical behaviour, articulate their medical ideas, and organize their medical resources for political purposes. Since the early 1990s, they have used their Indigenous medicine as a strategy to claim and assert their precariously kept ethnic identity. In the past, these people made use of medical knowledge according to tradition, but not in a political manner. With the introduction of the "revival of Indigenous medicine," a new disposition toward their Indigenous medicine emerged.

Claiming ethnic identity through the use of medicine is informed by an elaborate discourse on how traditional medicine *is* Indigenous identity and on how Indigenous identity is conversely embedded in traditional medicine. Through the use Indigenous medicine as both *material medica* and a symbolic system, Veracruceños promote community practices that enhance an Indigenous world view. Indigenous medicine is for Veracruceños, as anthropologist and medical psychologist W.H.R. Rivers noted so long ago, a symbolic system, and all symbolic systems are valuable sites for meaning-making, at the level of the individual as well as the community. Indigenous medicine is seen by Veracruceños as a cultural trait, a part of the repertoire of practices and knowledge that makes Veracruceños culturally distinct. This sharply contrasts with the construction of scientific biomedicine, which is, categorically, non-specific to any particular people or culture.

Source: De Burgos, Hugo. 2009. "Indigenous Medicine and Identity in Nicaragua," guest editorial.

Ultimately, although Western biomedical approaches can be very effective when it comes to saving lives, they have their limitations. As anthropologist Elisa Sobo puts it, they are "asocial and highly technologized, bureaucratized, and industrialized" (2004: 5). Consequently, they stand in opposition to the anthropologist's goal of understanding individuals and their lives as situated in specific *contexts*. Medical anthropologists recognize this opposition and actively seek to remain open to non-Western, culturally defined ways of knowing and being. They understand the need to contextualize all situations. Thus, they consider various aspects of cultural systems, from the local through to the global. Perhaps most importantly, they understand that the relationship between traditional and biomedical approaches is often very complex; in practice, the two have a lot to offer one another, but they successfully work together only when cultural contexts are taken into account.

This final observation is perhaps most significant when contrasted with the Western-centric approaches of many foreign aid workers, particularly those operating in the mid-to-late twentieth century, who believed they could effectively introduce Western medical technologies around the globe without considering potential social, economic, and cultural impacts on local populations. Not surprisingly, their efforts failed in many cases, resulting in ineffective, patchy distributions of medical supplies and treatments. To avoid similar cultural bias when investigating health issues, we must keep in mind three questions at the heart of medical anthropology: How do cultures define what constitutes wellness? How do people characterize different illnesses? What degree of intervention is considered appropriate?

Integrated Approaches and Holism in Medical Anthropology

Medical anthropology is highly interdisciplinary. With roots in overlapping social, cultural, and medical studies of the late nineteenth and early twentieth centuries, the field has evolved into a productive melding of the biological sciences, the social sciences, and the humanities. Today, medical anthropologists draw on such diverse disciplines as biology, ecology, biochemistry, sociology, psychology, political science, economics, linguistics, ethics, and religious studies. While not all of these disciplines are centrally concerned with health issues, they all have components that can inform our understanding of wellness and illness. For example, a researcher interested in linguistics might record a list of plant names that could instruct us on the medicinal uses of plants and their place in religious practices. Additionally, a medical researcher who studies the transmission of a disease from person to person might offer us valuable information on the inner workings of families or larger kinship, social, or economic groups. In other cases, medical anthropologists might make useful observations on how an individual's age, sex, gender, class, geographic location, and economic status affect his or her access to treatment.

Because the approach medical anthropologists take is so broad, we often find it in settings that are not overtly anthropological. A good example comes from journalist Ingrid Peritz's (2010) exposé on lack of equal access to abortion clinics in Canada. As Peritz notes, "While decades of court battles and debates have led Canadians to view abortion access as a given, the on-the-ground reality looks like a country carved into have and have-not communities." Peritz takes a holistic approach to the topic, considering factors such as the social stigma attached to abortion, insufficient government funding, unsupportive public policy, and low numbers and geographically patchy distributions of abortion clinics. Indeed, journalistic investigations of medical issues often take into account a wide variety of personal, social, cultural, and political factors (see, e.g., Laverdière and Ashton 2014; Leung 2014; Sherman 2014).

Integrated approaches are equally informative when we consider wider health issues on a global scale. As medical anthropologist William Dressler notes, biological disease is "socially distributed between and within societies, especially societies being transformed by their increased dependency within international capitalist market systems" (2001: 456). For example, the rate at which a disease spreads within a region can be tied to transnational decisions based on political, economic, and ideological considerations. Further, as medical anthropologist Linda Whiteford points out, decisions made in one powerful nation can have an intense impact on health and well-being around the globe: "Without doubt, global health policies reflect national priorities; the role of the UN and other international agencies, such as the World Health Organization (WHO), is shaped by funders' [i.e., wealthy nations'] priorities" (2009: 106). As these examples suggest, an integrative anthropological perspective can contribute much-needed cultural context to the discussion of international health concerns.

Openness to Traditional Knowledge

Medical anthropologists' openness to a variety of integrated perspectives makes their approach particularly suited to examining both traditional knowledge and Western scientific (medical) knowledge (Dods 2004). For example, in the non-Western context, early medical anthropologists observed medical-religious practitioners, such as **shamans**, in traditional healing roles (Figure 9.2). In previous contexts, researchers had considered shamanistic practices as responses to general physical complaints (Mair 1969), as expressions of social values (Wilson 1951), or more often, as forms of religious rituals. Yet some saw such systems as analogous to science, and medical anthropologists came to see such practices as legitimate forms of healing. Their research has advanced our understanding of the importance of folk practitioners as Indigenous healers.

By accepting traditional knowledge as a source of wisdom, we open ourselves up to new discovery. Such was the case for ethnobotanist Paul Alan Cox when he was working in Samoa with a team of researchers. In his discussions with local healers, Cox learned of prostratin, an antiviral chemical compound found in the bark of the mamala tree. The compound's antiviral properties had long been known to traditional Samoan healers who use the bark of the mamala tree to treat hepatitis. Western researchers have since found that prostratin shows potential to be effective in the treatment of HIV. In a letter published in the journal *Science* in 2008, Cox and his colleagues recognize their debt to the Samoan healers:

> Because knowledge of prostratin's antiviral activity originated from ethnobotanical studies with Samoan healers, the AIDS Research Alliance (ARA) and the Government of Samoa agreed that 20 per cent of ARA's profit from prostratin will be returned to the Samoan people. Similarly, Samoa and the University of California, Berkeley, agreed to share equally in commercialization of the prostratin gene sequences. In the spirit of these previous agreements, we encourage future developers of prostratin analogs for antiviral therapy to negotiate fair and equitable benefits with the Samoan people. (Cox et al. 2008)

Here we are reminded that respecting traditional knowledge also means behaving ethically toward those who share that knowledge.

As we remain open to the views of other cultures, we must always be aware that our own perceptions are rooted in the conventions of Western medicine. As pioneering medical anthropologist George M. Foster points out,

> anthropologists filter the data of all exotic systems through the lens of belief and practice of the people they know best. Whether it be causality, diagnosis, the nature and role of the curer, or the perceptions of illness within the wider supernatural and the social universe, general statements seem strongly influenced by the writers' personal experiences. (1976: 733)

shaman
A part-time religious practitioner who is believed to have the power through altered states of consciousness to travel to or contact supernatural forces directly on behalf of individuals or groups.

FIGURE 9.2 A medicine man in Oku, Cameroon, walks down the road carrying the supplies he needs to treat various ailments. What can anthropologists learn by taking an integrated approach to understanding the sorts of healing rituals this man might use?

In effect, Foster's words remind us of the importance of remaining reflexive when we consider medical approaches within the cultures we are studying.

Cultural Interpretations and Labels of Illness and Disease

As we have suggested, interpretations of illness and even disease differ across cultures. To begin, George M. Foster (1976) notes that we can identify two principal interpretations of **etiology** (Table 9.2) when we compare traditional medical systems cross-culturally:

1. the personalistic, in which people believe that illness is caused by supernatural forces (e.g., magical powers, an evil spirit, or a deity), and
2. the naturalistic, in which people believe that the causes of illness are rooted in the physical world (e.g., dampness, cold, or an imbalance in bodily substances).

In the personalistic interpretation, all misfortune is explained by referring to illness, religion, and magic as indivisible, and a cure must be brought about by an individual with access to the supernatural. The sick are victims, and death is frequently defined as "unnatural." In the naturalistic interpretation, disease comes from *natural forces* or *conditions in nature*, and a cure can thus be found in nature. Foster observes that the naturalistic form was found in many prominent cultures

of the past—for example, in ancient Chinese civilizations. (Note the similarities between this distinction and Allan Young's distinction between *internalizing systems* and *externalizing systems*, discussed above.)

Similar systems of interpretation exist in contemporary societies as well. In the West, medical conditions are interpreted through the paradigms of Western medicine (Table 9.3). The Western interpretations tend to focus on *biological causes* of medical conditions, with a single classification covering a wide array of symptoms. Increasingly, first as a consequence of colonization and subsequently as a result of globalization, these interpretations are being accepted as definitions of illness and disease in non-Western cultures as well. Yet traditional definitions still hold sway in many areas of the world (e.g., in Sri Lanka; see Table 9.4), particularly in places where patients are cared for by traditional healers. In more traditional systems of classification, the focus tends to be on the *effect* a disease has on the person who is suffering.

Of course, cultural interpretations of disease and illness change over time. In the West, we can find evidence of such change in the evolution of the words we use to describe certain medical conditions. For example, in English, what was once called *apoplexy* (with connotations of being overwhelmed by a powerful state) is today called *stroke* (suggesting a physical assault from a tangible source). As historian Barbara Duden (1991) suggests, understandings of disease and illness are tied to the social reality at a particular period in time.

etiology
The study of the causes of a disease and/or an illness.

TABLE 9.2 Foster's Two Principal Interpretations of the Causes of Illness

	Personalistic	**Naturalistic**
Causation	Active (supernatural) agents	Natural forces; equilibrium loss
Illness and Misfortune	An illness is a special case of misfortune that can be named from a "typology" of misfortunes	Illnesses are unrelated to misfortune, although it is unfortunate that a person is ill
Religion, Magic	Ultimately tied to illness	Largely unrelated to illness
Causality	Multiple levels (e.g., a supernatural being *and* the magic this being uses)	Single level (e.g., a biological imbalance)
Prevention	Positive action (e.g., perform rituals to keep supernatural beings content)	Avoidance (i.e., avoid encountering forces that cause illnesses)
Responsibility	Beyond patient's control	Resides with patient

Source: Based on Foster 1976: 781.

TABLE 9.3 Western Medicine's Systems of Disease Classification

Broad Term	Description
Allergy	Abnormality of immune mechanisms that normally act to protect the body against foreign proteins
Developmental or Congenital Disease	Malfunction of an organ or system resulting from an abnormal environment within the uterus during fetal development
Functional Defect	Disease for which there is no obvious anatomical explanation (e.g., a disease brought on by stress)
Genetic Disease	Malfunction of an organ or system resulting from a mutation of a gene, inheritance of a harmful gene, or an alteration in the number or arrangement of chromosomes
Infection	Disease produced by viruses, prions, bacteria, or other invasive biological entities; arbitrarily distinguished from infestation with parasitic insects
Metabolic Disease	Disease due to faulty biochemical processes involved with converting food to energy on a cellular level
Neoplasm	"New growth," including benign tumours and malignancies (cancers)
Psychiatric Disease	Mental illness, including psychosis (a severe mental and emotional disorder, probably caused by a biochemical imbalance), neurosis (a moderate emotional disorder involving obsessive-compulsive behaviours, probably caused by learned behaviours in combination with biochemical factors), and addiction (a dependence on substances or behaviours that alter moods)
Thrombosis	Blood clot that forms in a blood vessel and blocks the flow of blood to an organ
Trauma	Injury produced by mechanical stress (e.g., fracture), a physical agent (e.g., frostbite), or a chemical agent (e.g., burn from a strong acid)

Source: Adapted from McElroy and Townsend 1996: 46.

TABLE 9.4 An Example of a Traditional Ethnomedical System of Disease Classification (from Sri Lanka)

Specific Demon (*Sanniya*)	Literal Translation	Associated Conditions
Amukku	Vomiting bouts	Vomiting and stomach diseases
Abutha	Non-spirit related	Non–spirit-related insanity
Butha	Spirit related	Spirit-related insanity
Bihiri	Deaf	Deafness
Deva	Divine	Epidemic diseases
Gedi	Lumps	Boils and skin diseases
Gini Jala	Great fire or flame	Malaria and high fevers
Golu	Dumb	Dumbness
Gulma	Worms	Parasitic worms and stomach diseases
Jala	Water or diarrhea	Cholera and chills
Kana	Blind	Blindness
Kora	Lame	Lameness and paralysis
Maru	Death	Delirium and death
Naga	Snake	Bad dreams about snakes
Pissu	Insanity	Temporary insanity
Pith	Bilious	Bilious diseases
Slesma	Phlegm	Phlegm and epilepsy
Vatha	Wind humour or rheumatic	Flatulence and rheumatism

Source: Bailey and de Silva 2006: 1,327.

Under European colonialism, many Indigenous peoples developed new categories to describe disease as new disease-causing agents (e.g., bacteria, viruses) invaded their world. For example, the Anishinaabe (Ojibwe) of Canada continue to divide diseases into two types:

- "white man's sickness" and
- "Anishinaabe sickness."

In the first category, they place the diseases of the colonial and neocolonial reality. This category first included smallpox, measles, chickenpox, and tuberculosis (TB); now it also includes high blood pressure, diabetes, cancer, and AIDS. The Anishinaabe believe that these diseases are best treated by Western medical personnel and techniques. In the second category are illnesses the Anishinaabe consider to be situated in "discrete and identifiable, or potentially knowable, actions of human beings, alive or dead" or in "breaches of certain rules that govern social relationships." For these conditions, sufferers can find help only through "guidance of other-than-human persons" (Garro 2004: 910–11).

The boundaries between different cultural interpretations of disease and illness can become blurred in practical situations. For example, anthropologist Jeffrey Ehrenreich (1996) describes the sickness and eventual treatment of an Awá woman named Rosa in Ecuador. Both Rosa and her husband, Ishmael, believed she was dying from a disease caused by the malice of a *brujo* ("witch"). Ishmael had insulted a specific man in their community, and he now believed that this man was a *brujo* who had brought revenge illness on Rosa for Ishmael's social mistake. Initially, Rosa underwent traditional treatment in the form of shamanic curing ceremonies. When traditional approaches failed, Ishmael carried Rosa on his back for five days to reach the post at which Ehrenreich and his fellow anthropologist Judith Kempf were working. From a Western perspective, Rosa's symptoms suggested a parasitic worm infestation and resulting starvation. Western medical approaches were unsuccessful at first, possibly because Rosa vomited up both the food and the medication she consumed. But this changed when the anthropologists adopted shamanistic methodology in addition to the Western treatment regimes. A combination of incantations (in this case Hebrew prayers), chicken soup,

and anti-parasitic medication resulted in Rosa becoming well again (1996: 137–9). Thus, while each culturally defined interpretation of Rosa's condition led to a different treatment, it was a combination of the two—made possible by the anthropologists' openness to traditional knowledge—that cured Rosa.

Historically, conflicting cultural interpretations of an illness and its appropriate treatment have not always been reconciled so harmoniously. Consider the historical debate surrounding the condition (or **folk illness**) that Western medicine and some anthropologists once referred to as Wendigo-psychosis (Figure 9.3). In Algonquian culture, the Wendigo (*witiko*) is a malevolent cannibalistic spirit that can influence human action. The Algonquians also believe that, under certain conditions, a human can transform into such a being. With the Algonquians, when such a transformation occurs, the group recognizes that the afflicted individual is in need of treatment. The purpose of treatment is not only to alleviate

folk illness

A culture-bound illness; a set of symptoms that are grouped together under a single label only within a particular culture.

FIGURE 9.3 Swift Runner, a Cree man from Alberta, killed and ate his family during a cold winter in 1878. He said that he was suffering from the influence of the Wendigo at the time of the murders. He later confessed, was remorseful, and was executed at Fort Saskatchewan.

the suffering of the individual but also, and more importantly, to protect the group as a whole. Traditionally, a shaman must treat the condition by defeating the Wendigo, and the only way to defeat the Wendigo is to kill the afflicted individual (in our culture, we might think of this treatment as a form of euthanasia).

In the nineteenth and early twentieth centuries, non-Native authorities began hearing stories of the Wendigo condition and its treatment. According to the interpretation of those authorities, the afflicted were suffering from a form of psychosis (McGee 1972). According to this interpretation, the proper treatment could be found in a mental institution, and the traditional treatment was a form of murder. Thus in 1907, Jack Fiddler, an Anishinini (Severn) chief and powerful shaman known for defeating the Wendigo, was prosecuted for murder in a Canadian court. He was found guilty but later pardoned when the cultural context was considered.

More recently, scholars have recognized that it may not be possible to fully understand the Wendigo condition from a Western perspective (see Carlson 2009). At the very least, an understanding of the condition requires Westerners to overcome their own cultural biases of interpretation. Canadian anthropologists Nadia Ferrara and Guy Lanoue (2004), for example, believe that the Wendigo condition "has been misnamed and misunderstood as an illness" by non-Natives (2004: 76). They suggest that rather than being a dangerous illness characterized by the *actual* consumption of human flesh, the Wendigo condition is in fact a culturally specific *concept* that helps members of the culture overcome certain fears and resolve internal psychological conflicts. Anthropologist Lou Marano also sees the Wendigo condition as more of a conceptual tool than an actual illness. In his view,

> the crucial question is not what causes a person to become a cannibalistic maniac, but under what circumstances a Northern Algonkian is *likely to be accused* of having become a cannibalistic maniac and thus run the risk of being executed as such. It is argued that those so executed were victims of triage homicide or witch hunts, events common in societies under stress. (Marano 1982: 385)

Essentially, Marano believes that the interpretation of the Wendigo condition as a psychosis is simply an "artifact of research" conducted from a biased Western perspective.

As these examples suggest, anthropologists can look to a culture's interpretation of illness to find deeper insight into how members of that culture collectively interpret their world and their place in that world. As Canadian medical anthropologist Sam Migliore (2001) notes in his examination of illness narratives surrounding a condition called "nerves" among Sicilian Canadians, "such narratives are an important means by which people, often in collaboration with one another, give meaning to various life experiences" (100). Migliore further notes that, when looking for meaning in cultural interpretations of illness, we need to

- address ambiguity, vagueness, and variability as central concerns in the anthropological quest for understanding;
- focus on how people use "folk" concepts (and discourse in general) in their everyday thoughts and actions;
- recognize that our definitions and explanations do not capture the essence of a particular "folk" concept but, rather, give us an insight into some of the more common or popular uses of that concept within a given group; and
- examine the decision-making processes that lead people to use or generate certain meanings rather than others (2001: 119).

An important part of this process of investigation is looking at the labels—along with the meaning attached to those labels—that people use to describe their experiences (e.g., see Table 9.4).

Medical Labels as Signifiers

Western medical labels, like all labels, are mutually agreed-upon signifiers. They denote clusters of symptoms that Western medical professionals understand to be related to one another. As such, they facilitate medical research. For example, without labels, epidemiologists would not be able to track the spread of a specific disease. In all cultures, medical labels help people identify and interpret illness. Naming is the first step to understanding and thus "illuminating relationships among illness, social forms, and social thought" (Lindenbaum 2001: 363).

Nonetheless, medical labels can be constricting on the personal level. From the perspective of the person who is unwell, the labels often reflect a position of dependence or marginalization. An afflicted individual might be defined as "the sick family member," "the supplicant," "the patient," or even "the client." Each label suggests a perceived role. More specific medical labels often carry a stigma associated with suffering, contagion, or death. As such, they can lead to stereotyping, separation, status loss, and discrimination of persons and populations who are thus labelled (Link and Phelan 2001). Consider the longstanding cross-cultural response to the term *leprosy* (Figure 9.4). For thousands of years, the name of this disease has triggered feelings of fear, not only because of the nature of the disease itself but also because of the historical "treatment," which consisted of segregating individuals afflicted with the disease into "leper colonies" for the benefit of the wider population. Thus, to be labelled as "a leper" was to be cast as a marginalized figure, someone to be feared as an outsider. Even after the discovery of effective treatments of leprosy in the early twentieth century, the disease still carries a social stigma. Today, leprosy is often referred to by its alternative name—Hansen's disease (named so after the doctor who first identified the bacterium responsible for the disease)—to evoke fewer negative associations.

In a study at McMaster University in Hamilton, Ontario, researchers have shown that the label used to name a disease influences the perceived seriousness of a specific set of symptoms. They investigated synonymous terms such as *erectile dysfunction disorder* and *impotence* and found that participants who were presented with a "newer" medicalized term perceived the condition to be more severe. They conclude: "A simple switch in terminology can result in a real bias in perception" (Young et al. 2008). Such findings also suggest that simple, non-medicalized terms might be best for communicating medical information to the general public.

The act of labelling can itself have significant social outcomes for individuals and communities. Anthropologist Sarah E. Castle (1994) illustrates this in her discussion of two folk illnesses that result in the death of children in a rural village in Mali. Local peoples refer to these illnesses as *foondu* ("the bird") and *heendu* ("the wind"), and they understand both to be caused by supernatural forces and to be "untreatable, particularly with modern medicine." As Castle observes,

> Foondu and heendu are rarely seen in living children but are frequently discussed in relation to child death. In a survey of mothers of children who had died before the age of five years . . . about half the deaths were attributed to these two illnesses. These folk illnesses act as explanatory mechanisms in this high mortality area. (314)

Labelling an illness as either *foondu* or *heendu* clears the child's caretakers from any fault (e.g., lack of care or effort to bring about a cure), as the label could not have been applied while the child was still alive. Here we see the psychotherapeutic value of the folk illness—it can offer a deflection of failure (e.g., failure to keep the child alive) from the self to other sources. Additionally, when the child is ill, family members are not resigned to the death of the child as inevitable; they have hope for a positive outcome. Such hope would be destroyed if the fatal disease were labelled before death. Finally, because the post-mortem diagnoses are conferred by senior women in a patrilineage, they also reinforce hierarchical power relationships among women while encouraging "social support from affines for the woman whose child has died" (314).

FIGURE 9.4 Leprosy has always carried a stigma, even after effective treatments were developed. How should anthropologists approach medical labels that carry stigma?

Environments and Well-Being

Researchers in many disciplines are becoming increasingly aware of the impact of physical, social, and cultural environments on human well-being. Using the integrative approach that is characteristic of their discipline, medical anthropologists examine not only the influence of environments on human health but also the many human factors—political, economic, social, and cultural—that shape those environments. Consider the landscapes that arise with the disposal of unwanted electronic goods. Such "dead" gear does not simply disappear. Rather, it is transported to less affluent nations where it sits in vast wastelands—digital dumps of frightening contamination. These dumps are mined by the poor for recyclable resources. Case in point: the Agbogbloshie dump in Accra, Ghana (Figure 9.5). Here the electronic waste of the West is burned for the retrieval of materials such as copper, brass, aluminum, and zinc; in the process, the surrounding soil and water are contaminated with lead, cadmium, antimony, PCBs, beryllium, mercury, and chlorinated dioxins. Many of the scavengers of this lethal waste are boys who labour to send money home to their impoverished families in northern Ghana. Thus are created the contentious borderlands of wellness and illness.

Integrated Worlds of the Biotic, the Abiotic, and the Cultural

The environments in which we live are made up of **biotic**, **abiotic**, and cultural components (Figure 9.6). Within these environments, all components are interlinked in complex, often invisible ways. If you tinker with one part, you risk disrupting the entire system.

Ecologically, we are tied to our surroundings. From a *medical-ecological* perspective, then, good health often results from living in an environment that is capable of supporting human life in all of its social, psychological, and physical needs. Conversely, bad health—disease and illness—is often the consequence of a disruption in the life-sustaining balance of our environment. A wide variety of environmental factors can have consequences for human health, with

FIGURE 9.5 Agbogbloshie dump in Accra, the capital city of Ghana, is a vast wasteland of unwanted electronic equipment. What kinds of impacts might your own usage of electronics have on environments both close to home and farther away?

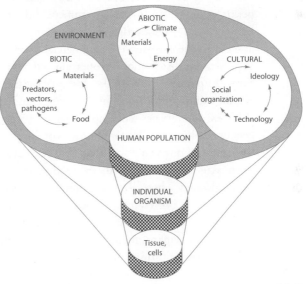

FIGURE 9.6 Human wellness and illness are affected by three interacting environments: the biotic (biological), the abiotic (physical), and the cultural.

Source: McElroy and Townsend 1996: 25.

biotic
Living; biological.

abiotic
Non-living; physical.

components of the most immediate surroundings having the greatest impact on a population. In terms of physical location, a population's immediate environment is its **realized niche**.

In many cases, realized niches face pressure from large-scale political, economic, and social processes. Certainly these processes featured in the poisoning of the Wabigoon River and the surrounding area in northwestern Ontario. Over

realized niche
The portion of the habitable world that a group of people is forced to utilize and to which it becomes highly adapted.

the course of the 1960s and early 1970s, Reed International's pulp and paper plant in Dryden, Ontario, released a dangerous amount of mercury into the Wabigoon River. The mercury was a by-product of chemical processing in the plant, and the river seemed to be the most convenient and economical place to dispose of the excess waste. In doing so, the plant's operators were not in violation of any legal restrictions. Before long, the links between the contaminated natural environment and human health were apparent. The Grassy Narrows First Nation peoples (see EthnoProfile 9.1)—who relied on the Wabigoon River for their water, food (fish), and livelihood (fisheries)—began showing signs of extensive mercury poisoning, including serious neurological symptoms. The community went from wellness to severe illness in less than a decade. Yet both the Canadian government and the operators of the plant ignored the evidence for a considerable period of time. When the government did step in, in addition to restricting chemical dumping it also closed the community's commercial fisheries to prevent the distribution of contaminated fish to the wider population. With the closing of the fishery, the community's problems were compounded as it went from 95 per cent employment to 95 per cent unemployment. The ramifications of this poisoning continue today, more than fifty years after the mercury began to move up the food chain.

For peoples whose diets contain a considerable amount of "country foods"—traditional foods such as wild game and fish taken from the natural environment—**bioaccumulation** and **biomagnification** are growing concerns (Figure 9.7). When uncontaminated, a traditional, protein-rich "country food" diet is considerably healthier than a high-carbohydrate European-style diet. Yet today, such traditional diets are not only high in protein and other nutrients but also high in toxic substances. Considering the pervasiveness of environmental toxins, and considering that most contaminated food looks no different from uncontaminated food, it has become nearly impossible for Indigenous peoples to maintain traditional diets without suffering severe consequences to their health. Here medical anthropologists recognize that emerging health problems can be identified and responded to only through the reconciliation of traditional knowledge and Western scientific knowledge, although this reconciliation has not been straightforward or in any way simple.

In nearly every case of severe contamination, the toxins come from sources beyond the affected community. Nowhere is this more distinctly the case than in the Arctic. As Aboriginal Affairs and Northern Development Canada (AANDC) notes,

Many sites in the North have been contaminated due to private sector mining, oil and gas, and government military activities that occurred before their environmental impact was fully understood. In addition, studies in the early 1990s found that a number of pollutants originating from sources outside the Arctic or in some cases outside Canada were reaching unexpectedly high levels in the Arctic ecosystem. (AANDC 2012)

bioaccumulation

An accumulation of a toxic substance in a biological organism over time.

biomagnification

An increase in the concentration of a toxic substance from the bottom to the top of a food chain.

EthnoProfile 9.1 | Grassy Narrows First Nation (Asubpeeschoseewagong Netum Anishinabek)

Region North America

Nation Canada; the Anishinaabe Nation

Language traditionally Anishinaabe (Ojibwe); today, also English

Population 1,000 (700 living on the reserve) (2014; approximate numbers)

Environment Boreal forest, threatened by deforestation

Livelihood Pre-contact, hunting, gathering, and trapping; today, various jobs, inside and outside the community

Political organization Elected tribal council operating within a modern nation state

For more information "Grassy Narrows First Nation: Protecting Traditional Lands," www.turtleisland.org/news/news-grassy.htm; "Grassy Narrows: The Right to a Healthy Environment," www.amnesty.ca/our-work/issues/indigenous-peoples/grassy-narrows.

The AANDC has created two programs to assist the peoples of Canada's Arctic: the Northern Contaminated Sites Program (NCSP), which "focusses on the cleanup and remediation of a number of contaminated sites in the North," and the Northern Contaminants Program (NCP), which "addresses human exposure to contaminants in wildlife species that are important to the traditional diets of Northern Aboriginal peoples" (AANDC 2012). Of course, the success of these programs depends on the merger of tradition and science in open cross-cultural discourse.

Large-scale programs such as the NCSP and the NCP are often created in response to the findings of studies conducted by academic researchers. One such anthropological study is Sylvie Poirier and Lorraine Brooke's 2000 examination of perceptions of ecological contaminants among the Salluit, one of 16 Inuit communities in Nunavik (northern Quebec). In many ways, the traditional Inuit view of the environment is consistent with the anthropological interpretation of the environment as composed of integrated biotic, abiotic, and cultural elements:

> In Inuit ontology, the environment is seen as complex systems of interacting agencies (and variables) and they [the Inuit] appreciate well that interface with one part of the system has implications for the other part... As hunters they view and experience their relationship with the environment and the animal world in a particularly intimate, communicative, and reciprocal manner. Human beings, animals, and the environment are all perceived as sharing partners; their modes of becoming are intrinsically linked. . . . [E]very animal [is thought of as] a sentient being or other-than-human person . . . not simply as a representative of another wildlife species that needs to be monitored or managed. (Poirier and Brooke 2000: 81, 86)

With increasing media access in the North, the Inuit have developed an understanding of pollutants. Yet, trusting their traditional knowledge and their world view, many remain convinced of their own ability to perceive and avoid dangerously sick animals and therefore guard their own health. They have not developed a confidence

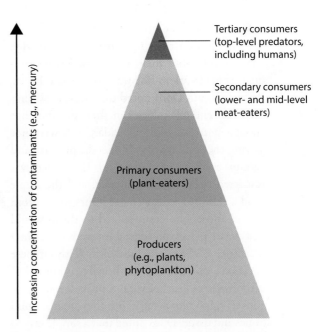

FIGURE 9.7 | Through the process of biomagnification, a toxic substance such as mercury becomes more concentrated as it moves up the food chain. The result is that organisms at the top of the food chain—including human beings—have relatively high levels of the substance in their bodies. As concentrations increase, the substance becomes more and more likely to have a negative impact on the health of the organisms.

in the southern biologists and their warnings of contaminants in the meat (86). Thus Poirier and Brooke highlight the need for cross-cultural discourse. They note a distinction between **defensive research**, which is based on the interests and methodologies of southerners, and **positive research**, which gives the Inuit the chance to have input in the research process. As Poirier and Brooke conclude, taking a "positive" approach "does not mean deterioration of the research quality . . . [but it] would give northern perceptions of southern people a much wider scope and fuller understanding, at least for those who have enough of a broad mind to grasp it" (89).

Nutritional Health

A healthy diet must be based on food that is not only free from harmful contaminants but also full of nutrients. The human body requires a regular, balanced supply of carbohydrates, proteins, fats, minerals, and vitamins in order to function properly and maintain a strong immune system. Thus, nutritional health is the basis of good health.

defensive research
Research that is designed and conducted by individuals outside the affected community without consulting members of the community about their interests or concerns.

positive research
Research that is designed with fair consideration of the interests and concerns of members of the affected community and conducted with consideration of cultural contexts within the community.

Worldwide, the availability of sufficient amounts of nutritious food has been a growing concern for more than a century. While conducting fieldwork in Botswana in the late 1970s, Roberta Robin Dods noted that most local children had enough calories in their diet but not enough nutrition—in particular, they were not getting enough vitamins, minerals, protein, and certain essential amino acids. Their diet was restricted to what was available, and the staple food was mielie-meal, a coarse flour ground from maize. Those who could afford to do so would add small pieces of vegetables and sometimes meat to the main mielie-meal dish. Without these additions, the diet was too heavily composed of carbohydrates. Carbohydrates provide energy by converting to blood sugar, but they do not build bones and tissue. Dods noted that a simple way to enhance this diet would be to add legumes such as beans, which are a good source of protein and essential amino acids. Today, medical and nutritional anthropologists continue to investigate conditions that lead to inadequate nutrition; in many cases, their work is useful to doctors and health care practitioners who work to inform local populations about the importance of good nutrition (Figure 9.8).

Anthropologists who study nutritional health tend to have very broad research interests, and their findings often contribute to national and international policies on health and nutrition,

food safety and inspection, and world hunger (Mintz and Du Bois 2002: 111). In one notable study, Canadian anthropologist Penny Van Esterik (2002) investigated food-safety regulations and the contamination of foods for infants—both breast milk and commercially available baby formulas. Other researchers have addressed issues related to child growth and development in association with nutrition, activity, and health (Dufour 1997). The expanding interest in the role of nutrition in a population's health has led to the development of a new subdiscipline in medical anthropology: nutritional anthropology.

The integrated, culturally aware approach characteristic of medical anthropology can also inform non-anthropologists attempting to improve nutritional health around the globe. A recent example comes from the research of Chris Charles, a graduate student at the University of Guelph (see Brown 2011). While conducting fieldwork in a small village in Cambodia, Charles became fixated on solving a problem: how to help locals to incorporate iron into their diets. A significant proportion of the local population, especially women and children, were suffering from iron deficiency anemia—a debilitating and potentially life-threatening condition—but they could not afford to eat meat (a source of iron) or buy iron pills on a regular basis. Charles's first solution was to suggest that the local women place a piece of iron in their cooking pots, which would transfer the much-needed nutrient to the food during the cooking process. The problem was that the women did not want to place an unappealing lump of metal in with their food. After investigating the local culture, Charles arrived at the innovative solution of providing pieces of iron shaped like a fish that the locals considered to be a symbol of good luck. The resulting product—branded as the Lucky Iron Fish (Figure 9.9)—is an example of the breakthroughs that are possible when cultural contexts are taken into account.

Health Care Delivery Systems

Health care systems take a variety of forms, based in the specifics of social and physical realities (Figure 9.10). "Clinical realities"—those realities that are tied to a health care system—vary considerably, based on factors such as

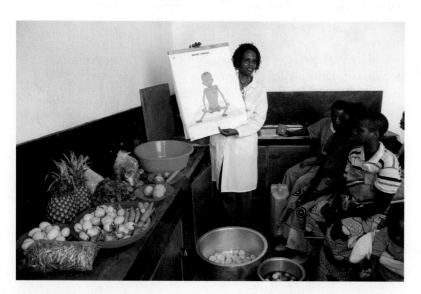

FIGURE 9.8 A health care worker in Rwinkwavu, Rwanda, teaches children and adults about nutrition. Aside from lack of knowledge about nutrition, what are some factors that might prevent people from eating a well-balanced diet?

- the patient's demographic factors (e.g., ethnicity, race, age, sex, gender, class);
- the patient's perceived situation in time (e.g., attitudes on age and life-cycle stages);
- cultural constructs (e.g., how open a woman is allowed to be in presenting her symptoms to a male doctor);
- geopolitical circumstances of place (e.g., rural or urban);
- concepts of reality (e.g., whether a disease or a symptom is perceived to be real or imagined);
- social and physical resources available to the afflicted individual or group (e.g., access to medical treatment);
- depth of interaction with other individuals or groups (e.g., relationships with kin, family, friends, and acquaintances);
- curative norms, which are often defined by class, sex, and/or age (e.g., Western treatments of heart disease are different for men than they are for women); and
- level of institutional complexity (e.g., in complex bureaucratic medical practices, patients may face alienation or problems of access).

Out of these and many other social and cultural threads, the fabric of care is woven. For some it is a warm blanket; for others it is gossamer thin indeed.

While health care systems take many different *forms* across the globe, medical anthropologist Arthur Kleinman (1980) notes that we can identify five core clinical *functions* of a health care system from a cross-cultural perspective:

1. the cultural construction of illness and/or disease as a psychosocial occurrence;
2. the evaluation of treatment approaches based on *general* criteria, independent of the individual incidents of illness;
3. the management of *specific* illness incidents through communicative operations (labelling and explaining);
4. the performance of healing activities (supportive care, healing rituals, psychotherapy, medication, and surgery; also end-of-life palliative care, where healing is not physical but can sustain the human sense of self or "spirit" and offer closure); and
5. the management of outcomes, from cure, recurrence, chronic illness, and impairment to treatment failure and death (71–2).

FIGURE 9.9 The Lucky Iron Fish is part of a relatively simple health initiative to supplement iron-deficient diets in Cambodia. What have the creators of this initiative done to tailor it to the culture whose people they are trying to help?

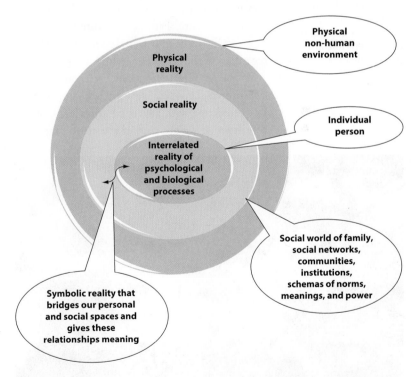

FIGURE 9.10 "Clinical reality" is constructed based on aspects of physical and social realities—cultural norms, schemas, beliefs, and behaviours, as well as various communication interactions surrounding disease and illness. Central are the practitioner–patient relationships, the therapeutic regimes, and the way outcomes are defined and evaluated.

Source: Adapted from Kleinman 1980: 28.

Kleinman notes that his list is a "summation" and that there can be great variation in the emphasis placed on each of the five functions from culture to culture and from group to group, since "the cultural construction of illness . . . is frequently a personally and socially adaptive response" (72). Yet he stresses the "profound cross-cultural similarity in clinical interest and praxis [practice]" (83).

Variety in Curing Practices

When we are faced with a mild disease, illness, or injury, we often take care of the treatment ourselves. For example, for a cold we might take over-the-counter medication; for a cut, we might use commercial bandages and antiseptics. We might also resort to home remedies or folk cures recommended by a member of our family or our community. On your grandmother's assurance that "it has always been done that way," you may swallow some vile cough syrup she has concocted or some soothing chicken soup she has prepared with care. Frequently, we find that these home remedies are effective—if only through the **placebo effect**—and we do not need to venture far beyond our home for a cure. Families are often our frontline, our fortitude, our foundation in health care regardless of the cultures in which we live.

When we feel that treatment requires more than home remedies, we will seek outside help from someone with advanced knowledge of our condition. If we are part of a culture that relies on traditional knowledge, we might appeal to a medicine woman or man or a shaman (female or male) for assistance (Figure 9.11). To a Western observer, traditional curative measures may seem no more effective than a home remedy; yet traditional cures can be highly effective for reasons not often considered in Western medicine. Canadian anthropologist Marilyn Walker (2003), for example, notes that shamanistic music used in Siberia induces altered states of consciousness, allowing the shaman to access the patient's unconscious. Other cultures use similar ceremonial activities to mediate inner and outer worlds and thus rebalance the patient in these worlds.

In other cases, even trained medical practitioners may not be able to help. For example, if you are bitten by a black mamba in a remote area, you may not be able to find medical assistance before it is too late. The venom of the black mamba is full of neurotoxins that quickly shut down the victim's nervous system. If left without treatment, an adult who is bitten will generally die within an hour; even with treatment, small children never survive a black mamba bite. What can anyone do for the patient if there is no hope of finding antivenin or reaching a hospital in time? They can comfort the victim as he or she dies and hope that coma or death will come before the worst of the symptoms appear. This is a horrific and, in some sense, extreme example, but similarly hopeless situations may arise after a traffic accident or when a patient is in the final stages of an incurable disease.

Sometimes—all too often in some places—the treatment a patient seeks may depend on his or her financial resources rather than the severity of the condition. Medical treatment can be very expensive, and the harsh reality is that class and geopolitical disparities affect an individual's access to and quality of treatment. As McGill University researchers Vinh-Kim Nguyen and Karine Peschard note,

> high levels of socioeconomic inequality correlate with worsened health outcomes across an entire society. . . . [A]ffliction must be understood as an embodiment of social hierarchy, a form of violence that for modern bodies [individual and group] is increasingly sublimated into differential disease rates and can be measured in terms of morbidity and mortality between social groups. (2003: 447)

placebo effect
An effect produced in response to an individual's belief that a treatment will have a desired effect, despite evidence that the treatment has no medicinal properties.

FIGURE 9.11 A number of members of the Altai people, who live in Siberia, still practise shamanistic rituals. In what ways might such rituals be effective in treating certain types of illnesses?

The reality of such disparities is clear when we examine the various statistics on HIV/AIDS generated by national and pan-national organizations. Consider that in excess of 95 per cent of all new infections of HIV/AIDS occur in countries commonly classified as "developing" and that at least 50 per cent of these infections are in women (WHO 2014a, 2014b). Consider also that the number of childhood cases being reported is increasing, not only among children born to infected mothers but also among children forced to work in the sex trade. Indeed, we can wonder what "development" can mean to communities where so many people are dead or dying of this disease. Socioeconomic disparity is also a significant factor in HIV transmission within more affluent Western nation-states. In Canada, rates of transmission are highest in Aboriginal communities, where many people live in what could be considered "developing" conditions. Data collected by the Public Health Agency of Canada suggests that 34.3 per cent of HIV/AIDS infections occur in Aboriginal people, while Aboriginal people make up only 4.3 per cent of the Canadian population (PHAC 2013; Statistics Canada 2011; Figure 9.12).

Patient–Practitioner Interactions

All systems of treatment have a two-step process: (1) diagnosis and (2) treatment. Both are based on effective communication between patients and their health care providers. To effectively interact with one another, all parties must be able to understand and use the languages of their culture's health and treatment institutions. For the patient, there is a need to develop an intersubjective space where meanings can be negotiated, much as anthropologists do in fieldwork. Not infrequently, negotiations are incomplete, and there remains an unresolved disconnect between what are, essentially, two or more cultures—the one of the patient and at least one of the medical practitioners.

Naming is very important in this process, as it communicates the symptoms, frames the diagnosis, and dictates the range of available treatments. Yet naming can be problematic in some instances, such as when a population considers a disease to be newly introduced from the outside world. Consider how cancer is understood among Indigenous peoples in Australia:

> Many Indigenous languages do not have a word for cancer, making it difficult to conceptualize. This emphasizes the belief

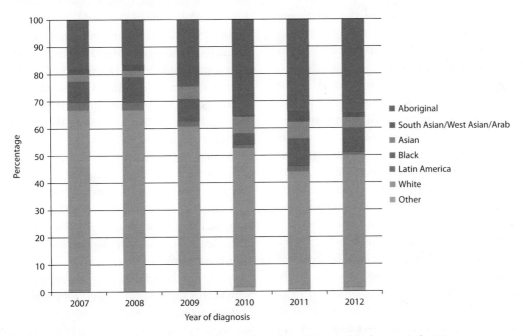

FIGURE 9.12 Proportion of HIV/AIDS cases among Canadians 15 and older by race/ethnicity.

Source: PHAC 2013.

that it is a "white man's disease" that only came about after colonization. Whether this is true or whether it was never labelled as cancer until colonization is unknown; however, many signs point to the fact that the change in Indigenous lifestyle from traditional to Westernized has increased the risk of cancer. (Shahid et al. 2010)

All systems begin by naming. We structure and make sense of our world using schema and prototypes. The naming process is universal, but the contents are culture specific. Named is the "condition" and named is the "cure."

While all health care systems recognize the importance of patient–practitioner communication, there are considerable differences between traditional systems and Western institutionalized systems in terms of how they perceive the patient's place in the system. In traditional systems, practitioners form personal relationships with their patients, investing considerable time in getting to know the patient and communicating a sense of concern. Traditional practitioners also situate the treatments in an environment that is deeply familiar to the patient—in effect their home turf. In Western medical systems, where time is money and the volume of patients affects the bottom line in a doctor's medical-business practice, the patient is viewed as a client. Doctors keep their distance from their patient/clients, and they administer treatment only in official medical environments. Of course, Western systems have their benefits: the act of "industrialization" affords a wide range of interventions supported by medical institutions, technologies, and highly trained personnel. Nevertheless, institutionalized treatment is removed from the familiar and can be very discomforting and alienating for the patient/client. Feelings of alienation can be particularly intense when the patient/client is crossing cultural and/or class boundaries and moving from traditional systems to industrialized medical systems.

Patient–practitioner relationships also differ between urban and rural locations. In the urban setting, unlike in the rural, the curer may not be a member of the community in which she or he works. Medical anthropologist Irwin Press (1978) has found that most urban curers do not become spokespersons for the communities in which they work and that they seldom know the majority of their patients on a personal level. Thus it rests with the patient to provide the symptoms and suggest the cause of the illness, while it is up to the practitioner to provide a diagnosis based on his or her understanding of the symptoms. The rural curer, in contrast, often takes the lead in searching for the cause, drawing on her or his knowledge of the patient's place within the community. Press also notes that folk practices associated with rural environments are actually flexible and capable of changing to meet the needs of urban clients. More traditional curers also can adjust their approaches to incorporate modern Western technologies and treatments when necessary.

By recording patients' narratives on illness and treatment, medical anthropologists offer us important insight into the culture clash the patient experiences when entering a system of care. Of central concern are the ways in which patients are treated—as humans or as numbers—and practitioners' willingness to incorporate elements of the patient's culture into the system of treatment. In such narratives, with embedded critique of treatment, patients are empowered to maintain or regain human identity and a sense of control over their lives.

SEARCH as an Integrative Model

Maintaining or regaining human identity and a sense of control is the objective of the Society for Education, Action, and Research in Community Health (SEARCH), a non-governmental organization (NGO) established in 1986 by spouses Dr Abhay Bang and Dr Rani Bang in the Gadchiroli district of Maharashtra, India. Two of the NGO's stated goals are promoting the reproductive health of women and improving the health of mothers, infants, and children.

In rural India, infant and maternal mortality rates are very high. According to one statistic, one woman dies every five minutes giving birth to a child in rural India (UNICEF 2004). Yet most of these deaths are preventable. SEARCH has addressed this problem by establishing public health programs in 39 villages in Maharashtra, each of which combines grassroots fieldwork with sophisticated medical monitoring, research, and advocacy. The result is a community-based health system that combines the best features of folk medicine with appropriate modern medical interventions. At the village level, the system is administered by a literate woman, herself a mother, who is trained to identify problems early and provide basic care. Physicians visit the villages every two weeks to supervise the care in place but do not give additional treatments. In the years since its inception, SEARCH has been an overwhelming success. Between 1988 and 2003, the infant mortality rate dropped from 121 to 30 deaths per 1,000 live births, and policy makers from Bangladesh, Nepal, and many African countries are currently investigating how the SEARCH approach can be implemented in their communities (Shetty 2011).

An understanding of the principles of SEARCH can help us interpret the effectiveness of different approaches to health care seen elsewhere. For example, consider medical anthropologists Carolyn Sargent and Grace Bascope's (1996) study on birthing practices in Mexico, USA (Texas), and Jamaica. In their study, the researchers focussed on "ways of knowing" about birthing and technology in high- and low-technology settings. They also considered the relationship between authoritative (biomedical) knowledge and social status. The collaborative birthing system of the Mayan women in Mexico incorporated midwives and other adult women who used their knowledge in a low-tech response. In general, patients felt at ease with their place in the system. By contrast, the women in Texas felt alienated from their public hospital system, although they appreciated the technology that provided needed caesarean deliveries. In Jamaica, the lack of communication between the English-speaking staff and the Spanish-speaking patients distanced patients from caregivers in a system dominated by authoritative knowledge but lacking adequate access to and use of biomedical technology. In each situation, the SEARCH model can help us reassess the relationship between authoritative (biomedical) knowledge and patient comfort and security. By extension, we can apply such reassessment techniques beyond birthing practices to all medicalized situations.

Political Intervention: Population Control and Management

The structure and focus of health care delivery systems frequently reflect local or national political interests, particularly when health care systems receive government funding. Most often, political and medical arenas intersect over issues surrounding population control and management. When the government's interests are aligned with those of its citizens, the health care system can function smoothly and contribute to social cohesion. But a clash between national and personal health interests can result in an array of social problems.

One example of a government's attempt to regulate health-related issues for political reasons is China's controversial one-child policy. Implemented in 1979, the policy aims at bringing control of individuals' reproduction and family size under the central government in order to lower the rate of population growth. At the local level, the program is administered by community functionaries, and health care systems must operate in line with governmental regulations. While most citizens abide by the national policy, some families attempt to circumvent the law by hiding pregnancies and births from government administrators. The 2000 national census found that 8,052,484 people were unregistered (Zhou 2005). Without official registration, these people are left without legal rights to health care or education. Additional social issues have emerged, including the preference for male children, increased female infanticide, abandoned infant girls, forced abortions for women pregnant with their second child, and forced sterilizations. The imbalance in the sex ratio has steadily increased over the past three decades, with current estimates ranging from 111 to 131 males for every 100 females. Further, it is estimated that by 2020 China will have a "bachelor army" consisting of 30 million to 40 million single men (Ross 2010; Figure 9.13). Although the Chinese government has recently adjusted the policy to allow more families to have a second child, many families still face strong restrictions, and the effects of the policy will undoubtedly be felt for decades to come.

A number of countries, including China, are facing a very different problem: how to manage the health issues of an aging population. This problem has come to the fore in recent years for a number of reasons. One major factor is the worldwide increase in life expectancy: the UN has estimated an increase in the mean global life expectancy from 47 years in 1950–55 to 69 years in 2005–10, and it projects a rise to 82

FIGURE 9.13 China's one-child policy has caused a crisis in the country, with men far outnumbering women. What social problems might this situation cause for individuals at various life stages?

managed care
A system of care, tied to the market-based delivery of medicine, particularly in the US, in which a patient's choice of treatment and of practitioner is directed by an intermediary organization that aims to provide the most cost-effective services available while generating profits for its members.

years by 2095–2100 (UN 2013). Additionally, the shift from rural (with traditional family structures) to urban (with smaller family units) living situations means that aging individuals have fewer family members to rely on for support. In the West, the demographic shift brought about by the aging of the "baby boomers" is also underway.

Elderly people face increasing rates of physical as well as cognitive conditions (e.g., Alzheimer's disease). Part of the struggle is to find financial resources to support this growing sector of patients, particularly in nation-states where universal and near universal medical interventions have been the norm. Yet the challenge is not only financial; social systems must also arrange for care that will allow the elderly to maintain their identities when they enter systems of care. Ethnographer and social scientist Joanna Latimer (1999) notes that as people age, their social status often declines, especially if they have medical conditions. Further, they are often seen as less suitable for receiving active medical care compared to their younger counterparts. Yet Latimer also finds that older patients can take steps to preserve their status and identity by actively taking part in the process of defining their place within the medical system: "If individuals participate in the authoring of the categories to which they are assigned, then selfhood is preserved" (1999: 205).

Paul Farmer has investigated the intersections between politics and health care in his work with the NGO Partners in Health, in his role as UN special envoy to Haiti, in his advocacy in the Americas and Africa, and in a number of his extensive writings (see, e.g., Farmer 2005; 2006; Farmer et al. 2013; Rylko-Bauer et al. 2009). As a physician and a medical anthropologist, Farmer explores the depth and breadth of health care issues through specific and general analysis. Additionally, with medical anthropologist Barbara Rylko-Bauer (2002), he has discussed **managed care** and the inequities that are generated when market forces focus on the management of inequality rather than the provision of the tools for delivery of care. Farmer and his colleagues direct our attention to the urban–rural divide and to the global have–have not chasm. They do not just report on conditions but seek reasons for what they see. Arguably, the most important issue is found in the succinct epilogue of *Global Health in Times of Violence*:

> If ethics are the embodiment of beliefs that individuals, groups, and cultures use to guide their behaviours and actions then we must question the violence of these ethics. We must question and challenge the contemporary moral economies that . . . tolerate the failure to provide needed and available medical assistance, and that exacerbate social and economic inequalities. . . . Connecting global violence to health requires that our analysis shift from a structural and geopolitical scale to a place that is intimate and experiential. . . . Finding the intimacy on the global requires new ways to assess, analyze, and present information . . . [that connects] the global to the personal. (Rylko-Bauer et al. 2009: 224–5)

Farmer and his colleagues argue against complacency; they challenge us to act on what they have found. They also remind us of the individuals who are affected by all the sociopolitical conditions that lead to patchy health care delivery, from the structure of political economies to the rural–urban divide to social class placement. For anthropologists, the actualities of individual lives remain as the foundation of study from which we can come to connect the personal to the global.

Epidemiology

Because disease spreads along social networks, and because social structures can facilitate this spread, collaboration between anthropologists and medical epidemiologists can be productive. Today, a number of anthropologists are looking at the cross-cultural distribution of diseases and the variables determining these distributions (race, class, religion, time, etc.). These anthropologists understand that knowledge about cultural responses can offer insight into cultural biases and how these biases play out in surveillance systems and treatment regimes for epidemics. Medical anthropologists James Trostle and Johannes Sommerfeld (1996) have suggested the term *cultural epidemiology* for this type of interdisciplinary research.

To prevent or at least slow the spread of a disease, medical personnel must identify the major paths of transmission. They must also try to anticipate how, where, and when people are most likely to become infected. Finally, they must try to inform the general population of the risks involved in certain activities. All of these goals can be accomplished most effectively if the medical personnel understand the habits and cultural situation of the affected people. For example, consider the response to the 2003 SARS (Severe Acute Respiratory Syndrome) epidemic. On a global scale, the WHO targeted travellers by advising against travel to sites where there were known infections, primarily Hong Kong, China, Taiwan, Singapore, and Toronto (see WHO 2003a). Within affected countries, local regulatory bodies targeted populations most at risk. In Hong Kong, where the rate of infection was greatest, this involved shutting down schools and placing more than a thousand people under quarantine across the country (Cheng 2004: 71). In Canada, where transmission was traced to contact with recent travellers and mainly restricted to the city of Toronto, the response included selective quarantining of individuals, increased screening for symptoms at airports, and the cancellation of many non-essential conferences and conventions in Toronto (Figure 9.14). In most countries, popular radio, print, and television media spread information about the disease and how to avoid infection. While the disease ultimately killed fewer people than did influenzas in the same period, the rapid emergence of the disease and the relative youth of its victims suggested a serious threat and a potentially devastating global pandemic.

While the widespread threat from SARS turned out to be fairly short-lived, other epidemics have proven to be more persistent. The most recent epidemic-level infections to have arisen on a global scale are Ebola and HIV/AID SID, both currently the subject of much research. Malaria also remains of particular concern, as it leads to more than 200 million clinical cases and more than 600,000 deaths every year (WHO 2014c). There has also been a concerning resurgence of tuberculosis (TB).

A first step toward fighting a disease is understanding its ecology—how it affects and is affected by its environment. Such understanding led researchers to identify that malaria is spread by mosquitoes that live in tropical and subtropical regions. Also important is knowledge of the social and cultural practices of the people who have to live in regions affected by the disease. Together, medical and cultural knowledge have

epidemiology
The study of the occurrence, spread, management, and prevention of infectious diseases.

FIGURE 9.14 A Toronto resident dons a medical mask to protect himself from the SARS virus in 2003.

led to successful control of mosquitoes through water clean-ups and the use of preventative measures such as insecticides and sleeping nets (Figure 9.15). In most cases, the ultimate goal is to develop a vaccine that can protect people from infection.

Environmental changes, whether natural or human made, can have a dramatic effect on the prevalence of certain diseases. The WHO alerts us to the need to pay attention to how diseases may spread as a result of climate change:

Changes in infectious disease transmission patterns are a likely major consequence of climate change. We need to learn more about the underlying complex causal relationships, and apply this information to the prediction of future impacts, using more complete, better validated, integrated, models. (WHO 2003b)

Researchers have already begun to apply this sort of integrated approach to the study of malaria and other diseases commonly found in tropical and subtropical regions. Based on observations of how climate change has progressed over recent decades, scientists can predict how these diseases will spread into areas in which they were uncommon in the past. While climate change is a large-scale force, smaller human-driven changes to local environments—such as building dams and cutting down forests—can also lead to increased prevalence of a wide variety of diseases (Table 9.5).

Past successes provide hope for future breakthroughs—after all, we have managed to eradicate smallpox, the disease that was largely responsible for the depopulation of the Americas shortly after European contact. At the same time, the celebration of this success is tempered by the fear that smallpox could be used as a biological weapon. Although the disease was eradicated in the general population, samples are still held in at least two controlled medical research facilities (see Chapter 14 for more on this), and few people born after 1980 have been vaccinated against the disease.

Being Applied

In some sense, this area of study we now call medical anthropology is more "applied" than many of the other areas of anthropological research. This is appropriate, as health issues affect us all on a personal level and are also tied to biological, environmental, economic, and political influences beyond our control. Taking an integrated approach to health issues allows us to avoid becoming too closely aligned with any one set of interests—for example, the interests of powerful biomedicine industries. Our approach must also be global in nature, as the forces of globalization connect us all and have the power to influence our well-being.

Being applied requires us to be present in the real world and aware of all of the factors that shape that world. When we approach a medical issue, we must place scientific knowledge in its sociohistorical context. We must also take

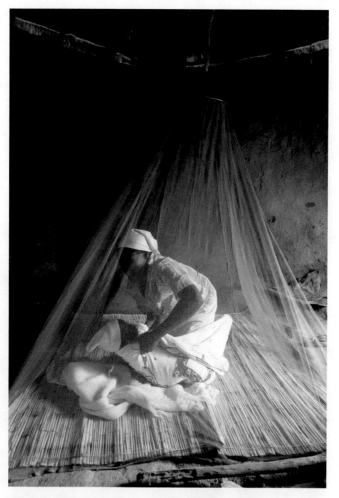

FIGURE 9.15 A woman puts her baby to bed under an insecticide-protected mosquito net in Gutu, Zimbabwe. Mosquito nets are one of the ways to prevent the spread of diseases such as malaria. How does this preventative measure fit within the cultural context in which it is being used? How might such a technology be adapted for use in other regions?

TABLE 9.5 Examples of How Environmental Changes Increase the Occurrence of Infectious Diseases in Humans

Environmental Change	Disease	Major Route of Transmission	Effect of Environmental Change
Construction of dams, canals, irrigation systems	Malaria	Bite from an infected mosquito	Increase the habitat and breeding ground of mosquitoes
	Schistosomiasis ("snail fever")	Contact with water containing parasites	Increase the habitat and breeding ground of snails that host the parasites
	Helminthiasis (parasitic worms)	Ingestion via contaminated water or food	Increased contact with larvae due to moist soil
Agricultural intensification	Malaria	Bite from an infected mosquito	Widespread use of insecticides leads to insecticide-resistant mosquitoes
	Venezuelan hemorrhagic fever	Inhalation of secretions from infected rodents	Increase the habitat and breeding ground for rodents; contact with rodents more likely
	Hantavirus diseases	Inhalation of secretions from infected rodents	Increase the habitat and breeding ground for rodents; contact with rodents more likely
Urbanization, urban crowding	Cholera	Ingestion via contaminated water or food	Increased risk of water contamination and contact with contaminated water with more people living in close proximity to one another
	Dengue fever	Bite from an infected mosquito	Increased risk associated with more people living in close proximity to one another
	Cutaneous leishmaniasis	Bite from an infected sand fly	Increased risk associated with more people living in close proximity to one another
Deforestation, new habitation	Malaria	Bite from an infected mosquito	Increase the habitat and breeding ground of mosquitoes; increased contact with infected mosquitoes
	Visceral leishmaniasis	Bite from an infected sand fly	Increased contact with infected sand flies
Reforestation	Lyme disease	Bite from an infected tick	Increased habitat and breeding ground for ticks

Source: Adapted from WHO 2003b.

an unbiased approach, giving consideration to Western scientific principles as well as traditional knowledge. This approach can help clarify health issues that are situated in a sociopolitical colonial heritage. Consider the way we as a society offer support for Aboriginal peoples living within Canada's political boundaries. We have done little to counter the inequality that results from the urban–rural divide. We have only begun to reconcile traditional Aboriginal knowledge of medicine with Western biomedical practices. We have continued to invade and pollute the Canadian "wilderness," contaminating the environments in which many Aboriginal peoples live. Additionally, we have failed to provide adequate assistance to Aboriginal individuals who are forced to live in substandard urban areas. And these conditions are not unique to Canada—they are repeated to varying degrees in post-colonial contexts around the world.

Through their health-related research, medical anthropologists can and do contribute to policy and programming at both local and international levels. Their aim is not just to understand but to work to change cultural patterns related to health care that can be seen as inappropriate, oppressive, or exploitive (Singer 1995: 81). For example, medical anthropologists have contributed to the global awareness of culturally situated forms of violence against women such as female genital mutilation, sex-selective abortion and infanticide, and dowry abuse and murder. Here one of the core ethical issues in applied anthropology arises: How do we reconcile our commitment to the principle of cultural relativism with our moral obligation to preserve the well-being of the peoples with whom we work? As medical anthropologist Merrill Singer observes,

> The anthropological tradition of cultural relativism (whatever its limitations) and the discipline's enduring concern with insider understanding . . . [results in] an appreciation of and commitment to the

principle of self-determination. Support of self-determination is further supported by the anthropological obligation to counter Western, colonial ethnocentrism and to create opportunities for the voices of so-called people without history (i.e., oppressed third-world populations) to be heard on the contemporary world stage. (Singer 1995: 98–9)

Certainly self-determination and consent are taken as core rights in the UN's Universal Declaration of Human Rights (see UN 2014).

Can we help bring about change when asked? Of course! We can effect transformations by focussing on consciousness-raising and empowering objectives directed toward "unmasking the structural roots of suffering and ill health" (Singer 1995: 99). By taking a critical approach in which we appreciate the intersubjective space of social relationships and social action, we can also foster collaborative, respectful relationships with the peoples who are the centre of our studies. Respectful interaction rests in recognizing that we all live in our own modernity and define our modernity through a process of *cultural bricolage*—the creation of something new and useful from the bits and pieces of our past and present cultural realities. Ultimately, we find that a mixture of tradition and innovation may lead us to new ways to solve the age-old problems of disease and illness.

A CRITICAL LOOK | Alternative Consciousnesses: What Constitutes Mental Illness?

In his popular and controversial work *The Origin of Consciousness in the Breakdown of the Bicameral Mind* (1976), American psychologist Julian Jaynes presents the central metaphor of the *bicameral*, or *two-chambered*, mind to explain a theory of the evolutionary development of consciousness. In his view, our ancestors had a two-part mind in which cognitive functions were divided between a speaker (often thought of as the voice of god) and a listener (the one who obeys the instructions of the speaker). Human beings were, essentially, of two minds. In this state, we lacked a sense of self-direction and purpose, a sense of the "self" as a unified being, an awareness of time, the ability to remember and think about our personal histories, and

the ability to think about and discuss non-existent objects and past and future events (Hockett's design feature of *displacement*; see Chapter 4). From a modern Western perspective, our ancestors lacked many of what we would consider to be the essential attributes of a healthy or "normal" mind. To our ancestors, however, there would have been nothing abnormal about the way their minds worked.

Questions about how we define what is and is not normal are important when we begin to think of "abnormal" or "alternative" forms of consciousness commonly labelled as "mental illnesses." In most cases, mental illnesses are harder to characterize and to diagnose than are physical illnesses. Even in our age of advanced medical knowledge, we do not fully understand how the mind works. As such, it is impossible to arrive at any absolute consensus about what constitutes mental illness.

In the institutionalized world of Western medicine, medical professionals follow the guidelines for diagnosing and treating mental illnesses outlined in two internationally respected documents:

- Chapter 5 of the *International Classification of Diseases* (*ICD; WHO* 2010), and

- the *Diagnostic and Statistical Manual of Mental Disorders* (*DSM; APA* 2013).

Yet as anthropologist Ken Jacobson reminds us, "the characterization of behaviours or abilities is a cultural process: basic concepts used to classify people, such as *normal*, *disordered*, *abnormal*, and *average*, are culturally constructed and culturally variable" (2002: 283–4). This means that patterns of thought and behaviour that seem perfectly normal in one cultural setting may seem abnormal in another. For example, Western medical practitioners would likely interpret an individual's belief that she or he has been possessed by a spirit as a sign of mental illness. Yet mediumship involving spirit possession is highly regarded among certain peoples—for example, followers of the Afro-Brazilian religion Candomblé. Thus, what is seen as an affliction in one cultural context may be viewed as a gift in another cultural context.

This observation leads us to several important questions. Do the mentally "afflicted" (or "gifted") act out the roles their culture defines for them? Might a mental state or condition that one society desires to suppress with medication be encouraged in another? Further, does cultural context influence the ways in which individuals express alternative consciousnesses? Certainly, there are no clear or easy answers to these questions. Yet they are significant and worthy of our consideration. Medical anthropologists are uniquely situated—through their commitment to openness and the use of inclusive approaches—to explore these sorts of questions. After all, such questions echo our fundamental concern: *How can we explain the human condition?*

—Roberta Robin Dods

KEY TERMS

abiotic   223
bioaccumulation   224
biomagnification   224
biotic   223
defensive research   225

disease   214
epidemiology   233
etiology   218
folk illness   220
health   214

illness   214
managed care   232
medical anthropology   214
placebo effect   228
positive research   225

realized niche   223
shaman   217
traditional knowledge   214
well-being   214

CHAPTER SUMMARY

1. Medical anthropology is highly interdisciplinary, drawing on and influencing such diverse fields as biology, ecology, biochemistry, sociology, psychology, political science, economics, linguistics, ethics, and religious studies. Thus medical anthropologists value integrated approaches and holism in their work, and they are always open to a variety of perspectives.

2. Medical anthropologists recognize the tension between traditional knowledge and Western scientific knowledge, but they also recognize that the two approaches intersect in many ways. In the past, the systems were depicted as being in opposition to each other, but contemporary medical anthropologists try to move beyond "either/or" interpretations.

3. Medical anthropologists are aware that physical (biotic and abiotic), social, and cultural environments can have a dramatic impact on human well-being. Within every environment, all components are linked in complex, often indivisible ways. Thus, researchers examine the influence of environments—especially *realized niches*—on human health. Two areas of particular interest are environmental contamination and access to a balanced diet.

4. Health care systems take many different forms around the world. Yet medical anthropologists recognize four outcomes of medical treatment that occur cross culturally, regardless of the approach to effecting a cure: (1) the treatment may cause the patient recover; (2) the patient may recover regardless of the interventions taken by caregivers because the disease/illness/injury was, in effect, self-correcting or self/healing; (3) the placebo effect may work to bring about a cure, simply because the patient believes that it will be effective, and (4) treatments may be ineffective, in some cases leading to the death of the patient.

CRITICAL THINKING QUESTIONS

1. How is the medical system in Canada an externalizing system? What evidence can you find of internalizing approaches to wellness in Canada? How can these two approaches complement one another?

2. What are the links between environmental contamination and health? How important are effort to clean up contaminated environments and prevent contamination in the future?

3. How do socioeconomic and geopolitical disparities affect treatment options? Why are Western nations often slow to act in response to the health crises in less affluent regions of the world? What can be done about disparities *within* relatively affluent Western nations?

4. Anthropologist Bruce Lincoln has observed that the human body in sickness transcends its individual psychological and physical vulnerability, becoming the "site where social pressures and tensions are experienced most acutely" and various community "contradictions and lacerations that divide a community" are played out (2001: 791). How have social pressures and tensions factored into your own experiences with disease and illness? How might Lincoln's observations relate to an epidemic within a community?

SUGGESTED READINGS

Berkes, Fikret, Peter George, Richard Preston, and John Turner. 1992. "The Cree View of Land and Resources: Indigenous Ecological Knowledge," report prepared for TASO (Technology Assessment in Subarctic Ontario), Second Series, no. 8 (Hamilton: McMaster University). An interesting paper that discusses the traditional values of the James Bay Cree with respect to their land base and the resources they use (animals, fish, and birds).

Dods, Roberta Robin. 2004. "Knowing Ways/Ways of Knowing: Reconciling Science and Tradition," *World Archaeology* 36, 4: 547–57. This paper discusses the structure of traditional ecological knowledge and Western scientific knowledge, concluding that both forms of knowledge offer access to important information and that the greatest insight can come when they are combined.

Farmer, Paul. 2005. *Pathologies of Power: Health, Human Rights, and the New War on the Poor* (Berkeley: University of California Press). A highly respected text in which Paul Farmer investigates the many intersections between politics and health care.

Mackie, Gerry. 2003. "Female Genital Cutting: A Harmless Practice?," *Medical Anthropology Quarterly*, New Series, 17, 2: 135–58. This article discusses issues of self-determination and consent in the context of cultural relativism.

Mintz, Sidney W., and Christine M. Du Bois. 2002. "The Anthropology of Food and Eating," *Annual Review of Anthropology* 31: 99–119. This article links diverse areas of research, including food security and social change. The authors note that much remains to be done in examining nutritional practices in many areas of the world.

Rylko-Bauer, Barbara, and Paul Farmer. 2002. "Managed Care or Managed Inequality? A Call for Critiques of Market-Based Medication," *Medical Anthropology Quarterly* 16, 4: 476–502. This paper challenges us to consider the actual cost of care managed by corporation who base decisions on potential profits.

Stephenson, Peter H. 2001. "Expanding Notions of Culture and Ethics in Health and Medicine to Include Marginalized Groups: A Critical Perspective," *Anthropologica* 43, 1: 3–17. A nuanced and historically contextualized paper that examines the ethical challenges involved in practising medicine—both Western and traditional—in a globalizing world.

Van Esterik, Penny. 2002. "Contemporary Trends in Infant Feeding Research," *Annual Review of Anthropology* 31: 257–78. An informative investigation into health and nutrition concerns related to infant care and feeding.

RELATED WEBSITES

Centre for Global Mental Health www.centreforglobalmentalhealth.org

Health Canada: First Nations and Inuit Health www.hc-sc.gc.ca/fni-ah-spnia/index-eng.php

The Lucky Iron Fish Project http://luckyironfish.com

Partners in Health www.pih.org

Society for Medical Anthropology www.medanthro.net

UNFPA's State of World Population www.unfpa.org/swp

UN's World Population Prospects http://esa.un.org/wpp

WHO's HIV/AIDS Data and Statistics www.who.int/hiv/data/en

10

World View

CHAPTER OUTLINE

The Role of Metaphor, Metonymy, and Symbol

Key Metaphors

Religion

World Views in Operation: Two Case Studies

Maintaining and Changing a World View

World Views as Instruments of Power

Religion and Secularism

LEARNING OBJECTIVES

By the end of Chapter 10, you will be able to

- consider the role of metaphor, metonymy, and symbol in constructing world views,
- recognize key metaphors for constructing world views,

- appreciate the role of religion and religious expression,
- understand world views as instruments of power, and

- compare and contrast the roles of religion and secularism.

Buddhist nuns in Cambodia pray during ceremonies celebrating the anniversary of Buddha's birthday. For many people around the world, religion plays a significant role in shaping the way they see themselves and the world around them.

world view

An encompassing picture of reality created by members of a society.

metaphor

A form of thought and language that asserts a meaningful link between two expressions from different semantic domains.

metaphorical subject

The first part of a metaphor, which indicates the domain of experience that needs to be clarified.

metaphorical predicate

The second part of a metaphor, which suggests the familiar domain of experience that may clarify the metaphorical subject.

metaphorical entailments

All the attributes of a metaphorical predicate that relate it to the metaphorical subject.

metonymy

The culturally defined relationship of the parts of a semantic domain to the domain as a whole and of the whole to its parts.

What guides us as we attempt to give life meaning? How do we devise cultural forms through which we can make sense of our being and belonging? How do we frame our physical and metaphysical contexts? In this chapter we attempt to answer these very complex questions by exploring **world view**.

The Role of Metaphor, Metonymy, and Symbol

Metaphor

One way to grasp a particular world view and the cultural patterns that it contains is to "follow the metaphor." In Canada, for example, we might examine the cultural metaphor of our country as a cultural mosaic to understand how Canadians interpret their place in the world. We might also contrast this metaphor with the American metaphor of the United States as a melting pot to uncover how our cultural perceptions differ from those of our neighbours to the south. Following metaphors successfully, however, requires understanding how metaphors work.

Recall from Chapter 4 that **metaphor** asserts the existence of a meaningful link between two expressions from different semantic domains. For example, metaphorical statements such as "Arnold is a turkey" create an ambiguity that can be resolved only in context. If we know Arnold is characteristically inept, ignorant, and annoying, and that turkeys are thought to be stupid and clumsy, our metaphor becomes intelligible and apt. But why resort to metaphor to represent our opinion of Arnold? Why not simply say "Arnold is inept, ignorant, and annoying"? When we choose to use metaphoric language instead of literal language, it is usually because literal language is not equal to the task of expressing the depth of meaning we intend. Our experience of Arnold may be complex and difficult to pin down in literal language. That is, there is something about the image of a turkey that encompasses more of what we think about Arnold than can ever be represented by a list of adjectives. We therefore select a figurative image whose features are familiar and use this image as a tool to help us express what kind of person Arnold is. The metaphor does not demonstrate unequivocally that Arnold *is* a turkey. Rather, it simply asserts that there is a link between Arnold and a turkey.

World views aim to encompass the widest possible understanding of how the world works. In constructing world views, people tend to examine what they already know for clues that might help them make sense of what puzzles them. Metaphor is a powerful tool for constructing world views because it clarifies areas of human experience that are vague or poorly understood. Consider the Christian metaphor "the Lord is my shepherd." This metaphor links a subject we have trouble describing (the Lord) to a familiar image (a shepherd).

Metaphors tend to be structured in a typical way. The first part of a metaphor, the **metaphorical subject**, represents the domain of experience that needs to be clarified (e.g., the Lord). The second part of a metaphor, the **metaphorical predicate**, suggests the domain of experience that is familiar (e.g., shepherding) and may help us understand what the metaphorical subject is all about (Figure 10.1). To understand the metaphor, we have to list every conceivable attribute of the metaphorical predicate and then decide which ones describe the metaphorical subject. These attributes are called **metaphorical entailments** (Lakoff and Johnson 1980). They suggest what follows from, or is entailed by, linking the metaphorical subject to the metaphorical predicate (e.g., by calling the Lord a shepherd). If we were to change the metaphorical predicate—for example, by asserting that "the Lord is my friend"—an entirely different set of metaphorical entailments would follow.

Metonymy

Metonymy is the relationship that links all of the parts of a semantic domain to one another. In the metaphor "The Lord is my shepherd," the links between the metaphorical predicate *shepherd* and its metaphorical entailments are links of metonymy (see Figure 10.1). The word *shepherd* can stand for any and all attributes (e.g., protecting sheep from wild animals) connected to the semantic domain defined by shepherding. At the same time, any of these attributes may entail the word *shepherd*. Because semantic domains are culturally defined, the meaningful elements that are linked by metonymy within any semantic

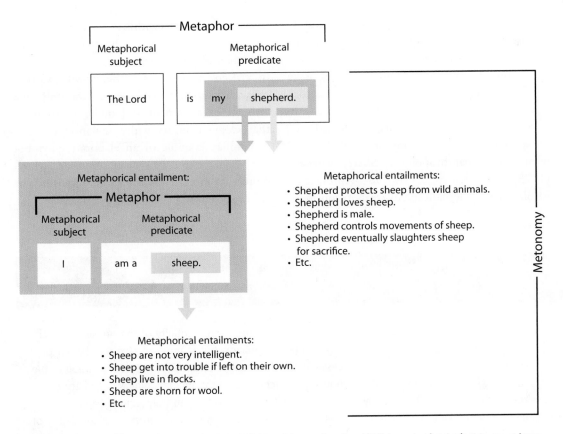

FIGURE 10.1 An analysis of the metaphor "The Lord is my shepherd." This metaphorical statement is an invitation to ponder what it means to be *a shepherd* and what it means to be *my shepherd*, and then to apply this knowledge to our understanding of the Lord.

domain are also culturally defined. Shepherding occurs in many societies, and yet the range of meanings associated with it may vary: compare a society in which shepherds are women, sheep graze freely, and mutton is primarily for family consumption with a different society in which shepherds are men, sheep graze in enclosed fields, and most animals are sold on the market for cash. Of course, members of the first society may think that theirs is the only sensible way to herd sheep and vice versa. Put another way, in any society, semantic domains defined by links of metonymy are viewed as "natural" or "true" associations.

The links of metonymy we discover within a particular semantic domain may help us make sense of experiences that seem chaotic and meaningless. Consider what happens in the case of what some people call *religious conversion*. An individual who is troubled and confused may see his personal situation suddenly come into focus when he starts thinking of himself as a lost sheep. Further, he may reason that a lost sheep must have been lost by someone—the shepherd to whom it belonged. This reflection, in turn, may lead him to ask who his shepherd might be. If he learns that some people believe that the Lord is their shepherd, he may be attracted to them and want to learn more. Thus, his exploration of the links of metonymy within a particular semantic domain in the context of his own life may lead him to conclude that the metaphor "The Lord is my shepherd" resonates with the power of divine revelation. Such reflections play an important role in religious conversion, but they are equally important in other realms—for example, in the realm of science, when a new theory is adopted because it makes sense of otherwise puzzling data.

Symbol

As people increase their understanding of themselves and the wider world by creating apt metaphors, they devise *symbols* to remind themselves of their significant insights and the connections between those insights. As noted in Chapter 1, a symbol is something—be it a word, an image, or an action—that stands for something else. Symbols signal the presence and importance of given domains of experience. They are special cases of metonymy. Some symbols—what cultural anthropologist Sherry Ortner (1973) calls *summarizing symbols*—represent a whole semantic domain and invite us to consider the various elements within it. Examples include the cross representing the Christian faith or the Canadian flag representing our country and its citizens as a whole. Others—what Ortner calls *elaborating symbols*—represent only one element of a domain and invite us to place that element in its wider semantic context. A familiar example of an elaborating symbol is the image of the cultural mosaic, which represents the relationships among different cultural groups in Canada.

IN THEIR OWN WORDS | House Re-thatching in an Andean Annual Cycle

Canadian social anthropologist Peter Gose illustrates that Andean roofing can be very complex and, at the same time, provide meaningful insights into many areas of life.

By Andean standards, house re-thatching is only a moderately ritualized labour process. Its imagery varies considerably from locality to locality, and . . . [it] is best understood through its position in the annual cycle of agrarian labour and ritual . . . . [T]he relatively modest ritual imagery of house re-thatching means little if anything in itself and cannot stand on its own as symbolism. Rather, it is motivated and given most of its significance by the practices that surround and support it in the annual cycle. House re-thatching in the Andes takes place as the dry season is giving way to the growing season. This seasonal shift involves a corresponding change in social relations from an emphasis on private appropriation by individual households during the harvest to an extensive and institutionalized inter-household co-operation that will prevail throughout the growing season. . . . [T]hese seasonally opposed moralities overlap in the house re-thatching and each lay claim to its content. . . . [C]ontradiction animates the imagery of this act and makes it signify in a way that we would miss if we considered it in abstraction from its grounding in the annual cycle. . . . [I] t is only when the imagery of the performance is subsumed by the annual cycle that it acquires the directedness necessary to "reflect and refract" another part of reality, that is, to become properly symbolic. . . . The . . . images do not function as self-contained "semantic values" that just happen to crop up around the house re-thatching but as metaphorical vehicles that intervene in and organize the very nature of the act. Put differently, this imagery does not exist for itself, in isolation from the instrumentality of the house re-thatching as a labour process, but in order to give that labour process a cultural form. And in turn, the seasonal position of the house re-thatching gives this imagery direction and entry into a real context within which it can truly signify. An example of this sort of interaction can be found in the transportation of hay down the mountain on the first day, which at first appears entirely unremarkable but, on further consideration, is seen to be embroiled in the entire "domestication" complex, including the origins of agriculture in descent. If this theme of "domestication" were not so thoroughly developed by other aspects of the rite, there would be no justification for this interpretation of the downward movement of hay. But once such a theme is established, it becomes equally hard to deny that the apparently technical act of transporting hay contributes to it. In sum, this rite teaches not only a negative lesson, that it is impossible to separate meaning from practice, but also a positive one, that the two taken together as praxis form a whole that is greater than its parts. Yet the praxis of commoners within the annual cycle is characterized not by a vapid holism but rather by a contradictory interpenetration of opposed moralities of private appropriation and collective production. This contradiction is most evident in the seasonal position of the rite, but it also works through its spatial and sequential organization and can even be identified in each of its individual symbols. Because the source of these contradictions lies beyond the act itself, house re-thatching must be understood as a moment in a larger seasonal process, not as a self-contained "text."

Source: Gose, Peter. 1991. "House Re-thatching in an Andean Annual Cycle: Practice, Meaning, and Contradiction," *American Ethnologist* 18, 1: 38, 57.

Key Metaphors

World views are attempts to answer the following question: What must the world be like for my experiences to be what they are? Over the ages, thoughtful people in all cultural traditions have drawn on different metaphors to suggest various answers to this question. Those suggestions that have become entrenched in any particular tradition are based on especially apt metaphors—**key metaphors** that make sense of experience in a variety of circumstances. Over time, as circumstances change and the established metaphors become less apt, new key metaphors replace the old, forming the basis for new world views.

Anthropologist Robin Horton suggests that people who construct a world view are searching for a way to bring "order, regularity, and predictability" to all aspects of their daily lives. As they search for key metaphors, therefore, they look at those areas of everyday experience that are most associated with order, regularity, and predictability (Horton 1982: 237). Thus, cross-culturally, key metaphors typically relate to three such realms of experience: the societal, the organic, and the technological.

Societal Metaphors

In societies where human social relations provide great order, regularity, and predictability, the central model for the world is the social order. People within these societies tend to use **societal metaphors** as they try to explain various aspects of their reality. For example, geneticist Richard Lewontin (1984) and his colleagues point out that biologists studying cells have used a societal metaphor almost from the very beginning. These biologists liken cells to a factory assembling the biochemical products needed to support the body's economy. This metaphor recurs in the twentieth-century work of Francis Crick, one of the discoverers of the structure of DNA (deoxyribonucleic acid). Lewontin and colleagues suggest: "Read any introductory textbook to the new molecular biology and you will find these metaphors as a central part of the cellular description. Even the drawings of the protein synthesis sequence are often deliberately laid out in 'assembly-line' style" (1984: 59; Figure 10.2).

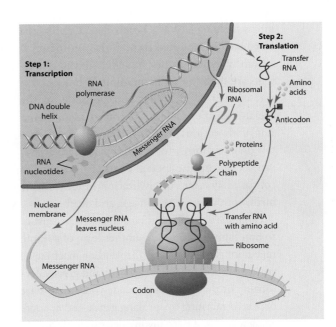

FIGURE 10.2 An example of a protein synthesis diagram laid out in "assembly-line" style.

Similarly, contemporary sociobiologists have borrowed certain concepts from modern economic thought and used them to describe the behaviour of genes or of living organisms. Sociobiologists describe the nurturing behaviour of parents toward their offspring as "parental investment." They talk about the cost–benefit analyses that people make before deciding whether or not to sacrifice themselves for others and even describe genes as "selfish." To some sociobiologists, the natural world is just the capitalist market on a larger scale. Indeed, anthropologist Marshall Sahlins (1976a) and others have argued that, from its inception in the late eighteenth century, modern biology has taken its key metaphors from the social world familiar to eighteenth-century biologists—the world of early capitalism.

Organic Metaphors

An **organic metaphor** applies the image of a living body to something else. A common organic metaphor is based on an interpretation of the body of a living organism as divisible into different systems (digestive, reproductive, respiratory, and so on), each carrying out a specialized task. When all these systems are functioning in harmony with one another, the organism is said to be healthy. If we compare society to a living organism, for example, we look for the subsystems

key metaphors
A symbolic representation that is widely understood within a culture and central to that culture's world view.

societal metaphor
A key metaphor whose predicate lies in the social order.

organic metaphor
A key metaphor whose predicate lies in the image of a living body.

into which society can be divided, identify the tasks each is supposed to perform, and describe a healthy society as one in which all the subsystems are functioning harmoniously. Indeed, this sort of organic metaphor is responsible for the social-scientific metaphor of society as an organism, with various interlinked components that rely on one another for survival. Alternatively, we can use an organic metaphor to analyze the life course of a society or civilization in terms of its birth, youth, maturity, old age, and death.

Personification (attributing human characteristics to non-human entities) is another form of organic metaphor. The belief that the vending machine in your lunch room has a malevolent and greedy personality or that you can persuade your car to start on a cold morning by speaking gentle and encouraging words to it both involve personification.

Technological Metaphors

technological metaphor
A key metaphor whose predicate lies in objects made by human beings.

A **technological metaphor** uses objects made by human beings as metaphorical predicates. Technological metaphors that use machines as metaphorical predicates have long been prominent in the world views of Western societies. For example, in the seventeenth century, French philosopher René Descartes popularized the notion that the human body was a machine, albeit one inhabited by an immortal soul. Subsequently, another French philosopher, Julien Offray de La Mettrie, carried this metaphor to its radical conclusion in *L'homme-machine* ("man-machine"), where he argued that the concept of the human soul was superfluous because machines do not have souls. As Western science and technology have grown in importance, machine metaphors have also become more widespread.

In the twentieth century, a major revolution in cognitive psychology was brought about by a shift in key technological metaphors. Psychologists rejected the steam engine metaphor of nineteenth-century industrial technology in favour of the computer metaphor of twentieth-century cybernetic technology. Computer jargon has become popular among scientists investigating the functions of the brain, the nervous system, and even the whole human body. Today, it seems impossible to avoid such language given the many suggestive insights into human mental functioning that the computer metaphor makes possible.

Using a computer as a model for the mind can produce varying interpretations. Everything depends on the kind of computer you choose as the metaphorical predicate and the aspects of computer operations you emphasize. For example, biological determinists might prefer to think of the mind as a "dedicated" computer whose functions are fully specified and wired into the hardware, allowing little flexibility. But if we think of the mind as a sophisticated general-purpose computer, we cannot predict the specific tasks it performs simply by knowing the design of its hardware (i.e., its physical structure). Rather, by loading different software programs, we direct the computer's hardware to perform particular tasks.

Were we to extend this kind of computer metaphor to explain the development of culture, we could argue that the co-evolution of brain and culture is the process by which a program hungry for system memory makes demands on hardware design. At a certain point, the computer's memory becomes full, and a flash drive is required to store the extra material. The human cultural equivalent of this flash drive would be oral tradition and forms of symbolic inscription such as writing.

Religion

religion
"Ideas and practices that postulate reality beyond that which is immediately available to the senses."

For many readers of this text, the most familiar form of world view is probably **religion**. The anthropological concept of religion, like many analytical terms, began as a description of a certain domain of Western culture. As a result, it has been very difficult for anthropologists to settle on a definition of religion that is applicable in all human societies.

Scholars have often argued that religion differs from other kinds of world views because it assumes the existence of a supernatural domain: an invisible world populated by one or more beings who are more powerful than human beings and are able to influence events in the "natural" human world. The problem is that the distinction between "natural" and "supernatural" was originally made by non-religious Western observers, where "real" was equated to the "natural" world that was separate from their defined "imaginary" or "supernatural" world. However, as we discussed in Chapter 2, each culture has its own concept of what is "real." Thus many anthropologists who study different religious traditions believe that it is less distorting to begin with their informants' statements about what exists and what does not. In this way, they are in a better position to understand the range of forces, visible and invisible, that religious believers perceive as active in their world.

Anthropological inquiry into religious world views needs to begin with broad objectives that can move to increasing specificity as the details of a particular religious tradition are revealed by its adherents. With this approach in mind, anthropologist John Bowen defines religion as "ideas and practices that postulate reality beyond that which is immediately available to the senses" (2002: 5). These ideas and practices are not individual; they are *social*: they are shared among a group of people and shape how members of the group interact with one another and with the universe in a variety of ways (Figure 10.3).

Bowen's definition of religion is significant because it emphasizes that religions involve *beliefs* as well as *actions*. Both of these components of religion can take a variety of forms. Religious beliefs may include belief in spirits and/or gods, belief in impersonal forces that affect the world, belief in the correct practice of ritual, and/or belief that ancestors continue to be active in the world of the living. Religious actions can include a wide variety of behaviours. Anthropologist Anthony F.C. Wallace (1966) has proposed a set of "minimal categories of religious behaviour" that describe many of the practices usually associated with religions. Several of the most salient are as follows:

1. *Prayer*. Where there are personified cosmic forces, there is a customary way of addressing them, usually by speaking or chanting out loud. Often people pray in public, at a sacred location and with special materials: incense, smoke, objects (such as rosary beads or a prayer wheel), and so on.

2. *Physiological exercise*. Many religious systems have methods for physically manipulating psychological states to induce an ecstatic spiritual state. Wallace suggests four major kinds of manipulation: drugs; sensory deprivation; mortification of the flesh by pain, sleeplessness, and fatigue; and deprivation of food, water, or air. In many

FIGURE 10.3 Religious beliefs and practices are social. Here, Muslim men pray together at Shah Mosque (Imam Mosque) in Isfahan, Iran. Have you engaged in religious practice in a large group? In what ways are social religious practices different from other types of social activity?

societies, the experience of ecstasy, euphoria, dissociation, or hallucination seems to be a goal of religious effort (Figure 10.4).

3. *Exhortation*. In all religious systems, certain people are believed to have closer relationships with the invisible powers than others, and they are expected to use those relationships in the spiritual interests of others. These people give orders, heal, threaten, comfort, and interpret.

4. *Mana*. Mana refers to an impersonal superhuman power that is sometimes believed to be transferable; for example, by laying her or his hands on a sick person, a healer may be able to transfer healing power to that person's body to remove or destroy an illness. In Guider, Cameroon, some people believe that the ink used to copy passages from the Quran has power. Washing the ink off the board on which the words are written, and drinking the ink, transfers the power of the words into the body of the drinker. The principle here is that sacred things are to be touched so that power may be transferred.

5. *Taboo*. People or objects that may not be touched are taboo. Some people believe that if such people or objects are touched, the cosmic power they contain will "drain away" or injure the toucher. Many religious systems have taboo objects. Traditionally,

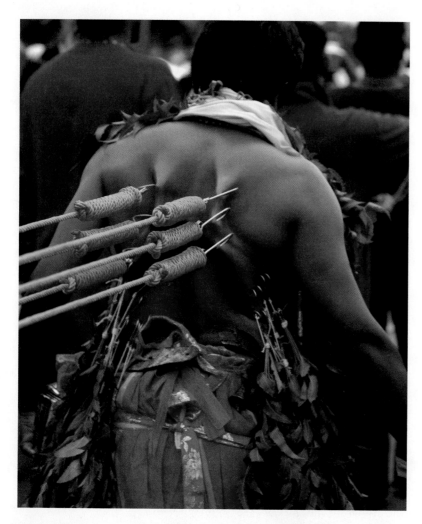

FIGURE 10.4 A Hindu devotee makes the pilgrimage to Batu Caves, near Kuala Lumpur.

FIGURE 10.5 This Balinese woman offers a sacrifice of food and flowers in prayer.

Catholics were not to touch the host (the consecrated bread) during communion; Jews may not touch the handwritten text of the biblical scrolls. In ancient Polynesia, commoners could not touch the chief's body; even an accidental touch resulted in the death of the commoner. Food may also be taboo; many societies have elaborate rules concerning the foods that may or may not be eaten at different times or by different kinds of people.

6. *Feasts*. Eating and drinking in a religious context is very common. The Holy Communion of Catholics and Protestants is a meal set apart by its religious context. The Passover Seder for Jews is another religious feast. For the Huichol of Mexico, the consumption of peyote is set apart by its religious context. Even everyday meals may be seen to have a religious quality if they begin or end with prayer.

7. *Sacrifice*. Giving something of value to the invisible forces or their agents is a feature of many religious systems. This may be an offering of money, goods, or services. It may also be the sacrificial killing of animals or, very rarely, human beings. Sacrifices may be made in thanks to the cosmic forces in hopes of influencing them to act in a certain way or simply to gain general religious merit (Figure 10.5).

Religion and Communication

Those who are committed to religious world views are convinced of the existence of beings or forces that are ordinarily invisible but actively involved in their lives. Indeed, some of the most highly valued religious practices, such as religious ecstasy or trance, produce outer symptoms that may be perceived by others, but their most powerful effects can be experienced only by the individual who undergoes them personally. If you had such a personal experience and wanted to tell others about it, how would you proceed?

You might well begin by searching for metaphors based on experiences already well known to your audience. One Hindu worshipper in Kuala Lumpur, Malaysia, who successfully went into trance during the festival of Thaipusam described his experience as "floating in the air, followed by the wind" (*Floating in the Air* 1973; Figure 10.6). And the Hebrew poet who wrote the biblical Psalm 23, which begins with the metaphor "the Lord is my shepherd," tried to express his experience of the power and love of his God by comparing this God to a shepherd and himself to a sheep. Indeed, the language human beings use to talk about omnipresent and omniscient supernatural beings is often full of metaphors. Even those religious followers who claim to have had personal experience of a supernatural reality will probably still find themselves forced to resort to poetic, metaphorical language if they want to explain that experience to other people—and perhaps even to themselves.

When societal metaphors are used, members of the tradition are likely to conceive of the forces at work in the universe as personified beings with many of the attributes of human agents at work in their own society. As societies differ from one another, so too does the way their members characterize the universe. Thus members of societies organized in strong groups based on kinship usually conceive of a universe peopled with the spirits of powerful ancestral figures who take an interest in the lives of their living descendants. However, members of societies run by vast and complex bureaucracies (e.g., the Roman Empire) are apt to picture the universe as being run by an army of hierarchically ordered gods and spirits, all of which may be supervised by a chief god.

Organic metaphors may also figure in the construction of religious understanding. Anthropologist James Fernandez (1977) reports that organic metaphors are common in the Bwiti religion of the Fang (see Map 10.1). The human heart, for example, is an apt metaphor for Bwiti devotees because "(1) it is the heart which is the most alive of the bloody organs, (2) it is traditionally conceived by the Fang to be the organ of thought, and (3) in its bloodiness it is associated with the female principle. . . . Many meanings are at work in this metaphor, for that bloody organ, the heart, has a congeries of useful associations" (1977: 112).

Societies that rely on technological metaphors tend to construct a world view in which the universe is a highly complex machine put together by a skilled builder or builders. When we say that

FIGURE 10.6 A devotee prays at the Hindu festival of Thaipusam in Kuala Lumpur. Why might a religious follower use metaphors rather than literal descriptions to describe feelings brought about by religious practices?

MAP 10.1 Fang

we are only *cogs in a machine,* or talk about social status and roles as interchangeable *parts,* we are using machine metaphors. In a mechanical world view, all processes are complex, orderly, predictable, and knowable; thus, it is possible for humans to effectively intervene in the world and alter the course of a process without the aid of a spiritual being or force. Therefore, while this world view is popular in Western societies today, many people question whether it can be called *religious.*

Religious Organization

In the societal metaphor, the forces in the universe are personalized, and people seeking to influence those forces must handle them as they would handle powerful human beings. Thus communication is the central feature. When we address each other we expect a response. The same is true when we address personalized cosmic forces. Yet communicating with supernatural forces can be a tremendously complex undertaking. It is not surprising, therefore, that some societies have developed complex social practices to ensure that it is done properly. In these societies, religion is institutionalized, and social positions are created for specialists who supervise or embody correct religious practice.

Anthropologists have identified two broad categories of religious specialists: *shamans* and *priests*. A shaman is a religious practitioner and healer who is believed to have the power to contact invisible powers directly on behalf of individuals or groups. Shamans are often thought to be able to travel to the cosmic realm to communicate with the beings or forces that dwell there. They can plead with those beings or forces to act in favour of their people and may return with messages for them. In many societies, the training that a shaman receives is long and demanding and may involve the use of powerful psychoactive substances, producing altered states of consciousness to access cosmic beings. This position can embody dangerous ambiguities: someone who can contact such beings for positive benefits may also be able to contact them to produce negative outcomes like disease or death. Cultural anthropologist Barbara Tedlock (2005) observes that shamanism was possibly the domain of women in its earliest forms. Certainly it is the world's oldest form of religious and medical practice, and it remains a force for healing today.

Priests, in contrast, are skilled in the practice of religious rituals, which are carried out for the benefit of the group (Figure 10.7). Priests do not necessarily have direct contact with cosmic forces. Often their major role is to mediate such contact by ensuring that the required ritual activity has been performed according to the established tradition. Priests are found in hierarchical societies. Status differences separating rulers and subjects in such societies are reflected in the unequal relationship between priest and other members of the religion.

Religion in Contemporary Society

Someplace in time we saw a world at once awesome and fearful. We came to contemplate the transcendental (i.e., things relating to a spiritual realm). How this happened is a mystery, but new research in evolutionary biology and cognitive behaviour gives us indications of the emergence of religious thought and the representation of the supernatural (Boyer and Bergstrom 2008). Were we *Homo sapiens*, or earlier forms of the genus *Homo*? Is it possible that some form of wonder is a trait of all living beings, as Buddhists would contend? From our traditional past, where document is the artifact, we can identify categories of sacred and/or profane that tell us of our understanding of the transformational nature of the world in which we live. This message comes to us even in the "now," and it "does not just foster conformity and stability but . . . space for invention and innovation" (Dods 2007b).

Anthropologists Garrett Cook and Thomas Offit (2008) give us an example of how religions can evolve by borrowing from surrounding cultures while still preserving their most essential aspects. During their fieldwork in Guatemala, Cook and Offit visited the small Maya town of Santiago Momostenango. To begin, they note an ongoing tension in this town between Catholics—followers of Catholicism, which was brought to the region by European colonizers beginning in the sixteenth century—and Costumbristas—followers of the local religion Costumbre. Over the years, Costumbre has evolved to incorporate elements of both traditional Maya practices and Christian traditions. For example, Costumbristas worship traditional earth lords and ancestors as well as saints and a figure known as Jesu Cristo (an interpretation of the Christian figure Jesus Christ). In recent years, Costumbre has continued to respond to external cultural influences, for example by replacing traditional dance-dramas with more modernized costumed performances, and by incorporating Westernized foods in place of more traditional fare.

Cook and Offit observe that Costumbre has changed in response to pressure from a number of forces, including the emergence of new classes and new ways of making a living, increased exposure to popular media containing messages from around the world, the introduction of new religious choices, and "a growing generation gap" (46). Despite having changed, however, Costumbre continues to retain a number of its core aspects. Indeed, it seems that it is through the process of borrowing and synthesizing elements from other cultures—what Cook and Offit refer to as **transculturation**—that traditional elements can be preserved. By changing to reflect new cultural and social realities, Costumbre is able to remain vibrant and relevant to new generations.

Even as Indigenous and quasi-Indigenous religions such as Costumbre have devised innovative ways to keep their traditions alive, a less flexible religious practice has been gaining ground in post-colonial settings: Pentecostal Christianity. Indeed, in recent decades, Pentecostal Christianity has become increasingly popular in Latin America and Africa, often replacing forms of Christianity introduced in colonial times (e.g., Catholicism). In many forms, Pentecostal Christianity strongly rejects Indigenous practices and beliefs; often, it demonizes local gods as evil forces that must be rejected (see, e.g., Cook and Offit 2008). Yet in some regions, the Pentecostal movement has brought with it positive social developments. As anthropologist Naomi Haynes (2012) observes, for example, the Pentecostal movement in Zambia has given local followers access to resources they can use to battle economic uncertainty. In particular, membership in a Pentecostal congregation offers individuals the opportunity to form interpersonal connections that can lead to social and economic gains. Singaporean sociologist Daniel P.S. Goh (2010) notes similar outcomes in Singapore, where the Pentecostal movement has exposed young Singaporeans to a world view that helps them make sense of their post-colonial surroundings.

While religious participation is growing in some regions of the world, religious attendance is declining in many Western nations, including Canada. In part, this decline stems from an increase in the number of people who choose not to align themselves with an official religion (see Eagle 2011). Of course, religious attendance varies by region, and along urban–rural lines. In Canada, for example, surveys have found that the Atlantic provinces (New Brunswick, Prince

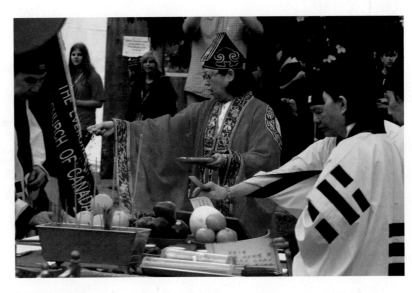

FIGURE 10.7 Priests are experts in carrying out religious rituals. This Taoist priest wears her traditional costume as she carries out a ceremony in Vancouver, British Columbia. How does a priest differ from a shaman?

Edward Island, Nova Scotia, and Newfoundland and Labrador) tend to have the highest attendance rates, while rates in British Columbia are traditionally low (Clark and Schellenberg 2006; Figure 10.8). Further, small rural communities tend to have higher attendance rates than do larger cities (Clark 2000). Factors such as age, gender, and immigration status also have an impact, with older individuals, women, and recent immigrants being more likely to attend religious services (Clark 2000; Clark and Schellenberg 2006).

American anthropologists Robert V. Kemper and Julie Adkins (2006) have taken a close look at how these and other factors impact attendance on the congregational level. In their study, they examine four specific Protestant congregations in North Texas:

1. one that has been experiencing a decline in membership for decades,
2. one that has been experiencing a decline in membership for a few years,
3. one that had experienced a decline but is now growing in membership; and
4. one that is growing in membership.

In their analysis, Kemper and Adkins hypothesize that the long-term decline they witnessed in the first congregation they investigated may be due to the fact that the congregation

transculturation
Cultural change resulting from contact between different cultures.

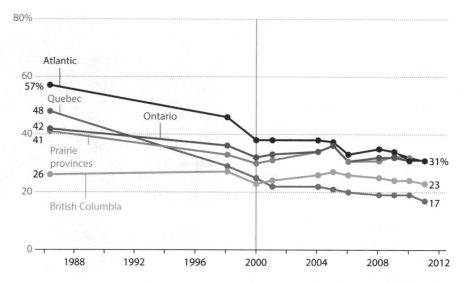

FIGURE 10.8 Decline in religious attendance in Canada, by region. Note that the numbers represent the percentage of Canadians 15 and older who attend religious services at least once a month.

Source: Pew Research. 2013. "Trends in Religious Attendance, by Region," *Religion & Public Life Project*, available at www.pewforum.org/2013/06/27/canadas-changing-religious-landscape/#_ftnref14.

is located in an older, out-of-the-way residential area that is unlikely to attract visitors. In contrast, the more recent decline they witnessed in the second congregation may be due to Protestants leaving the area and more and more Hispanic Catholics moving in. In case of the congregation experiencing a rebound in membership, Kemper and Adkins hypothesize that the recent growth may have resulted from (1) congregational members' efforts to reach out to the students, staff, and faculty of a college located across the street from the church and (2) the ability of the congregation's enthusiastic new pastor to connect with members of the community. Finally, the researchers attribute the growth experienced by the final congregation to a dramatic increase in population, including an increase in the number of Protestants moving to the area. As these case studies suggest, the ways in which various factors combine to contribute to the decline or growth within a specific congregation are varied and complex (333).

World Views in Operation: Two Case Studies

Anthropologists often say that people of different cultures live in different worlds. This itself is a metaphorical statement. It asserts that our understanding of reality depends on the particular point of view embodied in our culture. Of course, every culture contains subcultures that may draw pictures of reality that conflict with each other. The experience of juggling multiple points of view in our own society helps us to cope with unfamiliar perspectives in other societies.

As we navigate our own and other societies, we encounter world views that are fully formed. We face a rich tapestry of symbols and rituals and everyday practices linked to one another in what often appears to be a seamless web. Where do we begin to sort things out? The following examples from the field offer some valuable insights into this essential question.

Mind, Body, and Emotion in Huichol Religious Practice

American anthropologist Barbara Myerhoff (1974) discusses the world view of the Huichol in relation to their sacred peyote hunt (Figure 10.9). The Huichol are maize farmers who live in the Sierra Madre Occidental area of northwestern Mexico (see Map 10.2). Annually, they travel to a desert about 600 kilometres from their homes to hunt peyote, a small spineless cactus that contains psychoactive compounds. Because peyote is sacred to the Huichol, this journey is also sacred, representing a pilgrimage to Wirikuta, the original Huichol homeland where the First People, both deities and ancestors, once lived. The journey is hard and dangerous, both physically and spiritually. The pilgrims seek to restore and experience the original state of unity that existed at the beginning of the world.

This state of unity is symbolized by deer, maize, and peyote. The deer symbolizes the masculine, hunting past and thus connects the Huichol with their ancestors. In Huichol thought, the deer gave them peyote and appears every year in the hunt in Wirikuta. Blood from a sacrificed deer makes the maize grow and makes it nourishing. The deer is more powerful than human beings but not as remote as the gods. It symbolizes independence, adventure, and freedom.

Although the Huichol have only recently begun to grow maize, it is central to their present-day life. A life based on maize is tedious and precarious: the Huichol have to stay home to watch the crops, and even if they are careful, the maize may not grow. Maize symbolizes the labour of the present: food, domesticity, sharing between the sexes, routine, and persistent diligence. It also provides the Huichol with the language of beauty. "Maize," the Huichol say, "is our life."

Peyote, when gathered in the land of its origins, is sacred. It is used to induce personal visions, which are not shared with others. It is also used ritually, in which case so little is eaten that no visions are produced. It seems that the purpose of ritual consumption is to reach communion with the deities. The Huichol think of peyote as plant and animal at once; at the climactic moments of the peyote hunt, it is hunted like the deer. "Peyote is neither mundane, like maize, nor exotic and exciting, like deer. It is that solitary, ahistorical, asocial, asexual, non-rational domain without which [human beings] are not complete, without which life is a lesser affair" (Myerhoff 1974: 227). In Huichol religious thought, deer, maize, and peyote fit together: maize cannot grow without deer blood, the deer cannot be sacrificed until after the peyote hunt, the ceremony that brings the rain cannot be held without peyote, and the peyote cannot be hunted until the maize has been cleaned and sanctified.

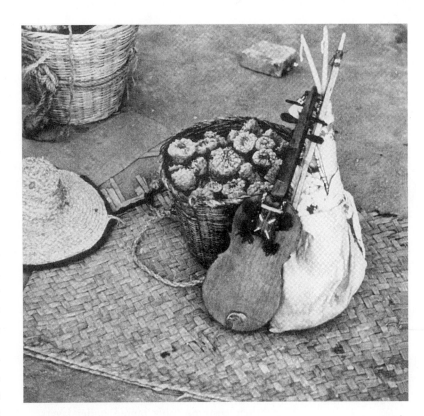

FIGURE 10.9 A Huichol shaman's violin and arrows, together with a basket of freshly gathered peyote.

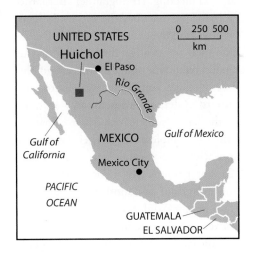

MAP 10.2 Huichol

The Peyote Hunt

In 1966, Barbara Myerhoff and her colleague Peter Furst accompanied Huichol pilgrims on the peyote hunt. Each pilgrim was given the name of a Huichol god for the duration of the pilgrimage. The pilgrims, under the guidance of a shaman, all followed strict rules about sexual continence and other behaviours, separating themselves from their everyday routine.

Once the pilgrims entered Wirikuta, many ways of speaking and acting were reversed. "Stand up" meant "sit down"; "go away" meant "come here." The van in which they travelled became a "burro" that would stop "if he ran out of tequila." The shaman who led the pilgrimage told Myerhoff that "on the peyote hunt, we change the names of things because when we cross over there, into Wirikuta, things are so sacred that all is reversed" (1974: 148).

> In the sacred land, the pilgrims became hunters, searching for peyote. Once the first peyote cactus was found, it was trapped by two arrows. The pilgrims then encircled it and presented their offerings. The shaman cut it out of the ground, sliced sections, and put one section in each pilgrim's mouth. The little group was sharply etched against the desert in the late afternoon sun—motionless, soundless, the once-bright colours of their costumes now muted under layers of dust—chewing, chewing the bitter plant. So [sixteenth-century missionary and pioneering ethnographer Bernardo de] Sahagún described the ancient Indians who wept in the desert over the plant they esteemed so greatly. The success of the undertaking was unquestionable and the faces changed from quiet wonder to rapture to exaltation, all without words, all at the same moment. . . . Their camaraderie, the completeness of their communion with one another was self-evident. The companions were radiant. Their love for life and for one another was palpable. Though they did not speak and barely moved, no one seeing them there could call the experience anything less than collective ecstasy. (155–7)

Following this moment of communitas, the pilgrims collected as much peyote as they would need for their community and hastened to depart. The reversals and other requirements remained in effect until they reached home.

The unification of deer, maize, and peyote gives the peyote hunt its power. As Myerhoff puts it, "In the climactic moments of the

rituals in Wirikuta, these symbols provide the Huichols with a formulation of the large questions dealt with by religion, the questions of ultimate meaning and purpose." She suggests that the way the Huichol's religious system answers these questions is distinctive. Some religions explain present-day moral incoherence by asserting that an original paradise was lost following an ancient sin. Other systems assert that there is an afterlife in which all the suffering of the world will be set right. The Huichol refuse to let go of their past:

> Their most precious religious heritage— their beginnings—is idealized and recovered. Even if only for a little while, by means of the peyote hunt, Paradise may be regained. Through the deer–maize– peyote complex, the deer and a life dedicated to hunting the deer is still a fact of present-day life rather than a fading, shabby memory, chewed over by old men at the end of the day. (1974: 262)

The deer–maize–peyote complex and the peyote hunt represent the union of mind, body, and emotion. Through a holistic ritual experience that is profoundly meaningful, deeply moving, and thoroughly physical, the Huichol re-experience the correctness of their way of life.

Witchcraft, Oracles, and Magic among the Azande

Anthropologist E.E. Evans-Pritchard, in his classic work *Witchcraft, Oracles, and Magic among the Azande* (1976 [1937]), describes how the Azande of central Africa (see EthnoProfile 10.1) use **witchcraft** beliefs to explain unfortunate things that happen to them, and how they employ **oracles** and **magic** to exert a measure of control over the actions of other people. Evans-Pritchard was impressed by the intelligence, sophistication, and skepticism of his Azande informants. For this reason, he was all the more struck by their ability to hold a set of beliefs that many Europeans would regard as superstitious.

witchcraft
The practice of magic, whether intentional or not.

oracles
Invisible forces to which people address questions and whose responses they believe to be truthful.

magic
A set of beliefs and practices designed to control the visible or invisible world for specific purposes.

ETHNOPROFILE 10.1 | Azande

Region Central Africa

Nations Northeast Democratic Republic of the Congo, South Sudan, southeast Central African Republic

Language Zande (Pazande), an Adamawa-Ubangi language of the Niger-Congo group

Population 1 million–4 million (2000s estimates)

Environment Sparsely wooded savannah

Livelihood Agriculture with maize, rice, and groundnuts (peanuts); cassava and sweet potatoes as main crops; hunting, fishing, and chicken raising

Political organization Traditionally, highly organized tribal kingdoms; today, part of modern nation-states

For more information Evans-Pritchard, E.E. 1976 [1937]. *Witchcraft, Oracles, and Magic among the Azande*, abr. edn (Oxford: Oxford University Press).

Azande Witchcraft Beliefs

The Azande believe that *mangu* (translated by Evans-Pritchard as "witchcraft") is a substance in the body of witches, generally located under the sternum in the chest. Being part of the body, the witchcraft substance grows as the body grows; therefore, the older the witch, the more potent his or her witchcraft. The Azande believe that children inherit witchcraft from their parents. Men and women may both be witches. Men practise witchcraft against other men, women against other women. Witchcraft works when its "soul" removes the soul of a certain organ in the victim's body, usually at night, causing a slow, wasting disease. Suffering such a disease is therefore an indication that an individual has been bewitched.

Witchcraft is a basic concept for the Azande, one that shapes their experience of adversity. All deaths are due to witchcraft and must be avenged by magic, often with the help of a witchdoctor (Figure 10.10). Other misfortunes are also commonly attributed to witchcraft, unless the victim has broken a taboo, has failed to observe a moral rule, or is believed to be responsible for his or her own problems. An incompetent potter whose pots break while firing may claim that witchcraft caused them to break, but everyone will laugh because they know that the potter lacks skill. Witchcraft is believed to be so common that the Azande are neither surprised nor awestruck when they encounter it. Their usual response is anger.

To the Azande, witchcraft is a completely natural explanation for events. Consider the circumstances that might lead to someone being crushed by a collapsing granary. Azande territory is hot, and people seeking shade often sit under traditional-style granaries, which are raised on logs. Termites are common in Azande territory, and sometimes they destroy the supporting logs, causing a granary to collapse. Occasionally, when a granary collapses, people sitting under it are killed. Why does this happen? The Azande are well aware that the termites chew up the wood until the supports give way, but to them that explanation is not enough. Why, after all, should that particular granary have collapsed at that particular moment? To skeptical observers, the only connection is coincidence in time and space. Western science does not provide any explanation for why these two chains of causation intersect. But the Azande do: witchcraft causes the termites to finish chewing up the wood at just that moment; thus, that witchcraft must be avenged.

Dealing with Witches

How to expose the witch? For this task, the Azande employ specific trials as oracles. Pre-eminent among these is the poison oracle. The poison is a strychnine-like substance imported by the Azande. The oracle "speaks" through the effect the poison has on chickens. When witchcraft is suspected, a relative of the afflicted person will take some chickens into the bush along with a specialist in administering the poison oracle. This person will feed poison to one chicken, name a suspect, and ask the oracle to kill the chicken

FIGURE 10.10 An Azande "witchdoctor."

if this person is the witch. If the chicken dies, a second chicken will be fed poison, and the oracle will be asked to spare the chicken if the suspect just named is indeed the witch. Thus, the Azande double-check the oracle carefully; a witchcraft accusation is not made lightly.

People do not consult the oracle with a long list of names. They need only consider those who might wish them or their families ill: people who have quarrelled with them, who are unpleasant or anti-social, and whose behaviour is somehow out of line. Indeed, witches are always neighbours because neighbours are the only people who know you well enough to wish you and your family ill.

Once the oracle has identified the witch, the person performing the ritual removes the wing of the chicken and has it taken by messenger to the compound of the accused person. The messenger presents the accused witch with the chicken wing and says that he has been sent concerning the illness of so-and-so's relative. "Almost invariably the witch replies courteously that he is unconscious of injuring anyone, that if it is true that he has injured the man in question he is very sorry, and that if it is he alone who is troubling him then he will surely recover because from the bottom of his heart he wishes him health and happiness" (Evans-Pritchard 1976 [1937]: 42). The accused then calls for a gourd of water, takes some water in his mouth, and sprays it out over the wing. He says aloud, so the messenger can hear and repeat what he says, that if

he is a witch he is not aware of it and that he is not intentionally causing the sick person to be ill. He addresses the witchcraft in him, asking it to become cool, and concludes by saying that he makes this appeal from his heart, not just from his lips.

People accused of witchcraft are usually astounded; no Azande thinks of himself or herself as a witch. However, the Azande strongly believe in witchcraft and in the oracles, and if the oracle says someone is a witch, then that person must be one. The accused witch is grateful to the family of the sick person for letting this be known. Otherwise, if the accused had been allowed to murder the victim, all the while unaware of it, the witch would surely be killed by vengeance magic. The witchcraft accusation carries a further message: the behaviour of the accused is sufficiently outside the bounds of acceptable Azande behaviour to have marked him or her as a potential witch. The accused witch, then, is being told to change his or her behaviour.

Patterns of Witchcraft Accusation

Compared with the stereotypes of Euro-American witchcraft—old women dressed in black, riding on broomsticks, casting spells, causing milk to sour or people to sicken—Azande witchcraft seems quite tame. People whose impression of witchcraft comes from Western European images may believe that witchcraft and witch-hunting tear at the very fabric of society. Yet anthropological accounts such as Evans-Pritchard's suggest that practices such as witchcraft accusation can sometimes keep societies together.

Anthropologist Mary Douglas looked at the range of witchcraft accusations worldwide and discovered that they fall into two basic types: (1) the witch is an evil outsider; (2) the witch is an internal enemy, either the member of a rival faction or a dangerous deviant (1970: xxvi–xxvii). These different patterns of accusation perform different functions in a society. If the witch is an outsider, witchcraft accusations can strengthen in-group ties. If the witch is an internal enemy, accusations of witchcraft can weaken in-group ties; factions may have to regroup, communities may split, and the entire social hierarchy may be reordered. If the witch is a dangerous deviant, the accusation of witchcraft can be seen as an attempt to control the deviant in defence of the wider values of the community. Douglas concludes that how people understand witchcraft is based on the social relations of their society.

Maintaining and Changing a World View

What makes a world view stable? Why is a world view rejected? These questions are related to general questions about persistence and change in human social life. Anthropologists recognize that culture change is a complex phenomenon, and they admit that they do not have all the answers.

Changes in world view must, first of all, be related to the practical everyday experiences of people in a particular society. Stable, repetitive experiences reinforce the acceptability of any traditional world view that has successfully accounted for such experiences in the past. When experiences become unpredictable, however, thinking people in any society may become painfully aware that past experiences can no longer be trusted as guides for the future, and traditional world views may be undermined.

Coping with Change

Drastic changes in experience lead people to create new interpretations that will help them cope with the changes. Sometimes the change is an outcome of local or regional struggles. The Protestant Reformation of the sixteenth century, for example, adapted the Christian tradition to changing social circumstances in northern Europe by breaking ties to the Pope, turning Church lands over to secular authorities, allowing clergy to marry, and so forth. Protestants continued to identify themselves as Christians even though many of their religious practices had changed.

In Guider, Cameroon (see Map 10.4), lone rural migrants have frequently abandoned old

religious practices and taken on urban customs and a new identity through conversion to Islam. However, the conflict between new and old need not necessarily lead to conversion. Sometimes the result is a creative synthesis of old religious practices and new ones, a process called **syncretism**. Under the pressure of Christian missionizing, Indigenous people of Central America identified some of their own pre-Christian, personalized superhuman beings with particular Catholic saints (Figure 10.11). Similarly, Africans brought to Brazil identified Catholic saints with African gods to produce the syncretistic religion Candomblé. The example of Costumbre in Guatemala, discussed above, is yet another example of a syncretic religion.

Anthropologists have debated the nature of syncretistic practices. They note that while some such practices may be viewed as a way of resisting new ideas imposed from above, others may be introduced from above by powerful outsiders deliberately making room for local beliefs within their own world view. The Romans, for example, made room for local deities within their imperial pantheon, and today's Catholicism explicitly urges non-European Catholics to worship using local cultural forms (Stewart and Shaw 1994).

When groups defend or refashion their own way of life in the face of outside encroachments,

syncretism
The synthesis of old religious practices (or an old way of life) with new religious practices (or a new way of life) introduced from outside, often by force.

MAP 10.4 Guider

FIGURE 10.11 The figure of Santa Muerte—here being venerated in Pedro Escobedo, Mexico—is a personification of death blended with Roman Catholic iconography. In what ways can syncretic figures such as this one help worshippers make sense of their worlds?

revitalization

A conscious, deliberate, and organized attempt by some members of a society to create a more satisfying culture in a time of crisis.

nativism

An attempt to return to traditional customs.

anthropologists sometimes describe their activities as **revitalization**—a deliberate, organized attempt by some members of a society to create a more satisfying culture (Wallace 1972: 75). Revitalization arises in times of crisis, most often among groups who are facing oppression and radical transformation, usually at the hands of outsiders (such as colonizing powers). Revitalization movements engage in a "politics of religious synthesis" that produces a range of outcomes (Stewart and Shaw 1994). Sometimes syncretism is embraced; other times it is rejected in favour of **nativism**, a return to the old ways. Some nativistic movements expect the appearance of a messiah or a prophet who will bring back a lost golden age of peace, prosperity, and harmony, a process often called *revivalism*, *millenarianism*, or *messianism*.

A classic New World example of a millenarian movement was the Ghost Dance movement among Indigenous peoples on the Great Plains of the United States in the 1890s. When the buffalo were exterminated, Indigenous Plains dwellers lost their independence and were herded onto reservations by Euro-Americans, who were better armed and greater in number than the Indigenous people. Out of this crisis emerged Wovoka, a prophet who taught that the existing world would soon be destroyed and that a new crust would form on the earth. All settlers and Indigenous people who followed the settlers' ways would become buried. Those Indigenous people who

abandoned the settlers' ways, led pure lives, and danced the Ghost Dance would be saved. As the new crust formed, the buffalo would return, as would all the ancestors of the believers. Together, all would lead lives of virtue and joy.

Because the world was going to change by itself, violence against the oppressors was not a necessary part of the Ghost Dance. Nevertheless, the movement frightened settlers and the US Army, who suspected an armed uprising. Those fears and suspicions led to the massacre at Wounded Knee, South Dakota, in which American soldiers killed almost all the members of a Lakota (Sioux) band, including women and children.

A revitalization movement that has enjoyed greater longevity is the syncretistic Bwiti religion of the Fang in Central Africa (Figure 10.12; Map 10.1). Since the late nineteenth century, the Fang have faced three important challenges to their world view. First, the reality of "the far away" represented by French colonialism came to challenge the reality of "the near" and familiar. Second, the protective traditional powers of "the below" were challenged by Christian missionaries' messages of divinity in "the above." Third, the pluralism of colonial life challenged the community's sense of cohesion by establishing a double standard in which the colonized were treated differently from the colonizers (Fernandez 1982: 571). Bwiti allows its members to cope with the first challenge by using the psychoactive drug *eboga* (ibogaine) to go out to the far and convert it into the near. In the second case, the Christian god of "the above" and the traditional gods of "the below'" are both incorporated into the Bwiti pantheon. For the third, Bwiti ritual promotes among members the communal feeling of "one-heartedness."

Bwiti has created a world view that allows many Fang to cope with the strains of exploitation. Within Bwiti, some old metaphors (the forest, the body social, the kinship system) have been reanimated, some new ones (red and white uniforms, a path of birth and death, the world as a globe or a ball) have been created, and all have been fitted together in a satisfying way. This world has, however, closed itself off from the wider society of Gabon. Bwiti represents a kind of escape from the pressures of the outside world (Fernandez 1982: 566).

Nativistic movements may, however, represent resistance to, rather than escape from, the outside

FIGURE 10.12 Fang women perform the Belebele dance during a Bwiti ceremony. How do revitalization movement such as this one differ from nativistic movements?

world. They may attempt to actively remove or avoid any cultural practices associated with outsiders. One such "anti-syncretistic" group is the Kwaio, living on the island of Malaita in the Solomon Islands (Figure 10.13; see also Map 10.5). Almost all their neighbours have converted to Christianity, and the nation of which they are a part is militantly Christian. Members of other groups wear Western-style clothing, work on plantations or in tourist hotels, attend schools, and live in cities. The Kwaio have refused all this: "Young men carry bows and arrows; girls and women, nude except for customary ornaments, dig taro in forest gardens; valuables made of strung shell beads are exchanged at mortuary feasts; and priests sacrifice pigs to the ancestral spirits on whom prosperity and life itself depend" (Keesing 1982: 1).

America anthropologist Roger Keesing (1992), known for his work with the Kwaio people, admits that he does not know exactly why the Kwaio responded to colonial influence in this way. He suspects that pre-colonial social and political differences between the Kwaio and their coastal neighbours influenced later developments. The colonial encounter was certainly relevant. In 1927, some Kwaio attacked a British patrol, killing the district officer and 13 Solomon Islands troops. The subsequent massacre of many Kwaio by a police force of other Malaitans, and their marginalization and persecution by the colonial government, contributed to Kwaio resistance.

The Kwaio maintain their old ways deliberately, in the face of alternatives; their traditional way of life is therefore lived in a modern context. "In the course of anti-colonial struggle, *kastomu* (custom) and commitment to ancestral ways have become symbols of identity and autonomy" (Keesing 1982: 240). In the eyes of the Kwaio, the many Solomon Islanders who became Christianized and acculturated lost their cultural ties and thereby their ties to the land and to their past, becoming outsiders in their own homeland. Thus, maintaining tradition is a form of political protest. From this perspective, many contemporary anti-syncretistic movements in the world, from various religious fundamentalisms to movements for national identity and cultural autonomy, can be understood as having aims very similar to those of the Kwaio, sparked by many of the same forces.

FIGURE 10.13 Although the Kwaio have recently adopted some outsider practices, such as wearing manufactured clothing, they continue to adhere to many of their traditional ways.

MAP 10.5 Kwaio

World Views as Instruments of Power

We have discussed the process that people use to build their world views, and we have noted how world views vary enormously from culture to culture. But within any particular cultural tradition, there are probably always different world views.

How does a particular picture of reality become the "official" world view for a given culture? And once that position is achieved, how is it maintained? To be in the running for the official picture of reality, a world view must be able, however minimally, to make sense of some people's personal and social experiences. Sometimes, however, it may seem to

IN THEIR OWN WORDS | Custom and Confrontation

In the following passage, the late Roger Keesing recorded the words of one of his Kwaio informants, Dangeabe'u, who defends Kwaio custom.

The government has brought the ways of business, the ways of money. The people at the coast believe that's what's important and tell us we should join in. Now the government is controlling the whole world. The side of the Bible is withering away. When that's finished, the government will rule, unchallenged. It will hold all the land. All the money will go to the government to feed its power. Once everything—our lands, too—are in their hands, that will be it.

I've seen the people from other islands who have all become Christians. They knew nothing about their land. The white people have gotten their hands on their lands. The whites led them to forget all the knowledge of their land, separated them from it. And when the people knew nothing about their land, the whites bought it from them and made their enterprises. . . .

That's close upon us too. If we all follow the side of the Bible, the government will become powerful here, too, and will take control of our land. We won't be attached to our land, as we are now, holding our connections to our past. If the government had control of our land, then if we wanted to do anything on it, we'd have to pay them. If we wanted to start a business—a store, say—we'd have to pay the government. We reject all that. We want to keep hold of our land, in the ways passed down to us.

Source: Keesing, Roger. 1992. *Custom and Confrontation: The Kwaio Struggle for Cultural Autonomy* (Chicago: University of Chicago Press), 184.

---

some members of society that barely credible views of reality have triumphed over alternatives that seem far more plausible. Thus, something more than persuasive ability alone must be involved, and that something is power. As cognitive linguists George Lakoff and Mark Johnson put it, "People in power get to impose their metaphors" (1980: 157). Powerless people may be unable to dislodge the official world view of their society. They can, however, refuse to accept the imposition of someone else's world view and develop an unofficial world view based on metaphors that reflect their own condition of powerlessness (Scott 1990). Such unofficial world views may even suggest appropriate action for transforming that condition.

How can metaphors, or the symbols that represent them, be used as instruments of power and control? First, a symbol can be used to refer to a self-evident truth when people in power seek to eliminate or impose certain forms of conduct. Thus, a deceased parent, whose memory must be respected, may be invoked to block some actions or to stimulate others. Holy books such as the Quran may also be used in this way. For example, a legal record from Guider indicates that a son once brought suit against his father for refusing to repay him a certain amount of money. The father claimed that he had paid. Both father and son got into an increasingly heated argument in which neither would give ground. Finally, the judge in the case asked the father to take a copy of the Quran in his hand and swear that he was telling the truth. This he did. The son, however, refused to swear on the Quran and finally admitted that he had been lying. In this case, the status of the Quran as the unquestioned word of God, which implied the power of God to punish liars, controlled the son's behaviour.

Second, a symbol may be under the direct control of a person wishing to affect the behaviour of others. Consider the role of official interpreters of religious or political ideology, such as priests or kings. Their pronouncements define the bounds of permissible behaviour. As Keesing points out:

> Senior men, in Melanesia as elsewhere in the tribal world, have depended heavily on control of *sacred knowledge* to maintain their control of earthly politics. By keeping in their hands relations with ancestors and other spirits, by commanding magical knowledge, senior men could maintain a control mediated by the supernatural. Such religious ideologies served too, by defining rules in terms of ancient spirits and by defining the nature of men and women in supernatural terms, to reinforce and maintain the roles of the sexes—and again to hide their nature. (1982: 219)

Keesing's observations remind us that knowledge, like power, is not evenly distributed throughout a society. Some people possess knowledge and control symbols to which others are denied access. Furthermore, this distribution of knowledge is not random: different kinds of people know different things. In some societies, what men know about their religious system is different from what women know, and what older men know may be different from what younger men know. Such discrepancies can have important consequences. Keesing suggested that men's control over women and older men's control over younger men are based on differential access to knowledge (14). It is not just that these different kinds of people know different things; rather, the different things they know (and don't know) enable them (or force them) to remain in the positions they hold in the society.

Religion and Secularism

The European Enlightenment gave birth to a world view that has come to be called **secularism**, and the spread of this world view has had repercussions across the globe. The development of secular ideas and practices profoundly transformed the religious and political institutions that had dominated European society in the Middle Ages. Earlier generations of anthropologists took secularism for granted as the expected outcome of cultural evolution. More recently, however, anthropologists have been led to reconsider the nature of both the Enlightenment and secularism, prompted most sharply by resistance to the secular institutions of Western nation-states. Strong resistance has come from some immigrant groups living within those states as well as some groups in non-Western nation-states who insist that citizenship and religious identity belong together.

Perhaps the most difficult struggles to adapt to life in secular Western nation-states have been those of some Muslim groups. The distinction between what the liberal democratic state expects and what some Muslims want has recently been explored by anthropologist Talal Asad. His efforts to develop an "anthropology of secularism" highlight the ways in which notions of the secular were shaped in the course of European history, particularly by the Protestant Reformation of Christianity, the subsequent wars of religion in the sixteenth and early seventeenth centuries, and

the Enlightenment and the French Revolution of the eighteenth century. Secularism is usually defined as the separation of religion and state, and it is commonly understood as the Enlightenment solution to the bloody and irresolvable wars of religion that followed the Reformation. But Asad's account shows that European secularism presupposed a specific post-Reformation concept of "religion" and a very specific post-Enlightenment concept of "the state," as well as a notion of secular citizenship that owes much to the notion of individual agency developed in Protestant theology. "The secular," he argues, "is a concept that brings together certain behaviours, knowledges, and sensibilities in modern life" (Asad 2003: 25).

The particularities of modern secularism may be clarified if we return to the distinction made in Chapter 8 between orthodoxy and orthopraxy. Religious disputes in the Reformation and the wars of religion concerned questions of *orthodoxy*—that is, correct religious beliefs. In European secularism, thus, *religion* is defined primarily in terms of the beliefs to which its adherents are committed. Similarly, the secular *state* is always understood to be the modern nation-state within a capitalist economy. It is from these understandings of *religion* and *state* that the Enlightenment concept of *citizenship* developed. Secular citizenship, Asad explains, is supposed to "transcend the different identities built on class, gender, and religion, replacing conflicting perspectives by unifying experience. In a sense, this transcendent mediation *is* secularism" (2003: 5). Secular citizens are first and foremost individuals unencumbered by ties to other social groups who possess *within themselves* the motivation to formulate goals, who have the resources to initiate action to pursue those goals, and who are responsible for the consequences of their actions. This concept of agency, absolutely crucial to the successful functioning of democratic government and the capitalist market, was itself the product of Protestant theology. In the religious context, independent, self-motivating individuals were responsible before God; in their role as citizens of a liberal secular state, they are individually responsible before the law.

Thus, secularism as a political doctrine clearly emerged as a response to specific religious, political, and economic developments in early modern

secularism
The separation of religion and state.

Europe. Secularism depends, for example, on the notion that a "worldly" domain of social life exists that is distinct from a realm in which religion holds sway. In Christian Europe, this domain was recognized when proponents of what would become "science" successfully argued that the "supernatural," spiritual realm of God was separate and distinct from the "natural," material world of lifeless, inert matter (Keller 1997). This distinction between supernatural and natural worlds "signals the construction of a secular space that begins to emerge in early modernity" (Asad 2003: 27). That secular space would be the ground to which the modern nation-state would lay claim.

Religion and state remained entangled after the wars of religion, however, since "religious freedom" was left in the hands of the states themselves. In most cases, citizens were to profess the faith of their rulers, and if their rulers changed allegiance, the allegiance of citizens was to follow. But in every state, this arrangement created religious minorities of "dissenters" whose rights as citizens were regularly curtailed. Protest against these inequalities led to the French Revolution, which brought a more democratic form of secularism to Europe. Now religious affiliation was a matter of individual conscience and could not be imposed by the state. One consequence of this change was the "eventual emergence of 'minority rights.' But this consequence contained a paradox. Religious minorities in a secular state were at once equal to other citizens [and] . . . unequal to the majority, requiring special protection" (Asad 2003: 174).

Secularism is "not a simple matter of absence of 'religion' in the public life of the modern nation-state. For even in modern secular countries the place of religion varies" (Asad 2003: 5–6). But Asad's analysis suggests that adaptation to life in a liberal secular state is likely to be difficult and painful for those whose religious commitments are rooted primarily in forms of religious *orthopraxy*—correct practice. Many traditions, he notes,

> attribute to the living human body the potential to be shaped (the power to shape itself) for good or ill. . . . The living body's materiality is regarded as an essential means for cultivating what such traditions define as virtuous conduct and for discouraging what they consider as vice. The role of fear and hope, of felicity and pain, is central to such practices. . . . [The] more one exercises a virtue, the easier it becomes; . . . the more one gives into vice, the harder it is to act virtuously. (89–90)

Islamic religious traditions are rooted in such orthopraxy, and cultivation of correct practice depends upon one being embedded within a community of like-minded practitioners. When successful, such orthopraxy is understood to produce "the virtue of faithfulness, [which is] an unquestioning habit of obedience." Faithfulness is "a disposition that has to be cultivated like any other and that links one to others who are faithful, through mutual trust and responsibility" (90). Religious orthopraxy of this kind can be sustained only by faithful practitioners whose entire way of life is informed by, and acts to reinforce, these unquestioning habits of obedience. If this is the case, then such forms of orthopraxy would appear to be incompatible with secularism.

> For many Muslim minorities (though by no means all) being Muslim is more than simply belonging to an individual faith whose private integrity needs to be publicly respected by the force of law, and being able to participate in the public domain as equal citizens. It is more, certainly, than a cultural identity recognized by the liberal democratic state. It is being able to live as autonomous individuals in a collective life that extends beyond national borders. (180)

World views represent comprehensive ideas about the structure of the world and the place of one's own group, or one's own self, within that world. The ethnographic record offers a broad array of different world views, each testifying to the imaginative, meaning-making cultural capacity of humans. These models of the world, moreover, do not exist apart from everyday social practices; on the contrary, they are heavily implicated in our interactions with others. And when those interactions lead to crisis, humans respond by seeking ways to make the crisis appear meaningful and therefore manageable. We are meaning-making, meaning-using, meaning-dependent organisms, and nowhere is this clearer than when a meaningful way of life is under assault.

A CRITICAL LOOK | Religion: From the Dark Seeking Our Brighter Selves

From the distant past emerge early memories of our transcendental selves. These memories come to us through artifacts, monuments, and, eventually, fragmentary scripts in ancient languages—some of which we have deciphered, some of which we have not. While the visions and voices of people in strictly oral traditions became silent over time, writing made things more permanent. Written religious texts became testaments that preserved ideas across time, and translations of these testaments allowed their messages to transcend cultural and linguistic barriers. Thus certain religions came to frame world views and afterworld views that resonated for many. They became "world religions," transcending space and time.

Judaism, Christianity, and Islam are all examples of world religions that have flourished for many centuries. All three focus on a single supreme deity and inform on obligations to this deity and to our fellow humans. Do these three religions exist in their original forms? Yes and no. Their core messages have remained the same, passed down to followers through their written holy texts, but in many cases their interpretations have changed in response to emerging social and cultural needs. These interpretations have been recorded and passed along in "subsidiary" or "secondary" texts, which are numerous and continue to expand as these religions evolve.

Each of these three religions has developed wide and various "sects," and each has spawned alternative ways of representing its core messages in daily life. Internal divisions have not always been peaceful, at times leading to religious conflict and even war. When conflict arises, concepts of God are often co-opted as one or both sides come to believe that God is on "their side" and, therefore, that their actions are "right." Indeed, religious texts have at times been used to give legitimacy to various rulers or to state structures and actions, including acts of violence against certain groups. This has been and remains a challenge.

Unfortunately, the connection between religious beliefs and violence against other human beings is not new. Archaeological evidence suggests that fighting wars and killing to eliminate groups and individuals to appease various spirits or deities seems to run deep in our human past. For example, we can look to the First Sacred War of the ancient Greeks, which lasted from 595 BCE to 585 BCE. War may even be part of our primate heritage if we consider chimpanzee "wars" (see Jane Goodall's [2010] discussion of the "Four-Year War" among chimpanzees of Gombe). Although it is stretching it to attribute such wars to concepts of the transcendental held by humans, the concepts of "us" and "them," and of territory, are evident in such examples.

While religion can lead us to our better selves, it can also be used for horrible things. Too often, it drives fanatics who are focussed on specific scripts or egotistically entrenched in their own visions of meaning to become leaders of destructive movements devised for self-aggrandizement or political objectives. In the relatively recent past, we could cite the 1978 mass suicide of 909 members of Jim Jones's cult in Jonesville, Guyana. Or we could cite Marshall Applewhite's UFO–millenarian cult Heaven's Gate, which led to 38 members committing suicide in March 1997, after Applewhite told them that by doing so they could hitch a ride on a "spacecraft" that was trailing the Hale–Bopp comet. And Canada has not been immune to this form of religious cultism. The Order of the Solar Temple, operating mainly in Quebec, France, Switzerland, Australia, and Martinique, is another significant example; it resulted in the deaths of an estimated 77 people. Initially, the Order's objectives placed emphasis on the spiritual over the secular in preparation for the second coming of Christ, but the movement turned deadly as its leaders (Joseph Di Mambro and Luc Jouret) came to focus on money and political power.

Deadly groups with toxic religious interpretations or idiosyncratic pseudo-religious messages seem to dominate in areas of conflict. Such dominance is not new—consider the Crusades (1095–1269), which were driven by the Catholic pope's direction to "take back" the Holy Land from the Muslims. This was a time of great unrest in Europe, a time of deep poverty for most people and economic upheaval in a corrupt feudal system. In some senses, the Crusades were much like the violent shows at the Colosseum in Rome—spectacle instead of substance, cruel circuses that provided diversion for the masses while elites maintained their positions of power and domination.

Today we live in a world of great change where certain pseudo-religious messages resonate in horrible and destructive ways. These messages are often promoted by destructive groups that maintain their own twisted interpretations of religious beliefs. Indeed, the difference today is the size of the leaders' operational forces, their acquisition of armaments, and the scope of their ambitions at the expense of other human beings. And truly we live in a

continued

new world of communication, a world with an immediacy that would boggle the mind of the Jim Jones types of the past. That these new leaders and their messages of death resonate with so many young men from diverse backgrounds is a matter for serious consideration and deep critical analysis.

Cynical designs to destroy in the name of religion are manipulations of our better selves as we seek meaning in our lives. Here we must ask: Who profits, and to what end? Such machinations take away the potential to celebrate our beingness and to bring positive change to our world. But we can turn to the light and be there for a moment of brightness, and we can invite others to witness, in their way, with us. Together, we can celebrate life and diversity, and we can try to effect positive change in a world that is full of both beauty and challenges.

—Roberta Robin Dods

KEY TERMS

CHAPTER SUMMARY

1. Shared cultural assumptions about how the world works are called *world views*.

2. Metaphors are valuable tools for constructing world views. They can give us insight into aspects of our world that are at times difficult to understand. Metonymy is the relationship that links the parts of a semantic domain to one another, making metaphor possible. Symbols remind us of the cultural links and insights established through metaphor and metonymy.

3. Differences in world views derive from differences in experience that people try to explain by means of metaphor. People use at least three kinds of key metaphors as foundations for particular world views: societal metaphors, organic metaphors, and technological metaphors.

4. Followers of a particular religion tend to share a world view. Over time, religious beliefs and practices change in response to external cultural forces. By evolving, religions remain vibrant and relevant to new generations.

5. Power and knowledge are not evenly distributed throughout a society. More powerful individuals and groups often impose their preferred key metaphors on the rest of society. Those without power can resist this imposition by creating their own contrasting metaphors and constructing alternative world views.

CRITICAL THINKING QUESTIONS

1. How do *summarizing symbols* and *elaborating symbols* differ? What do the symbols of the Canadian flag and the cultural mosaic mean to you? Can you think of any other examples of these sorts of symbols within the Canadian context?

2. Key metaphors that have served as the foundation of world views in different societies include societal, organic, and technological metaphors. What is an example of each type of key metaphor?

3. Consider the Canadian metaphor of the cultural mosaic. If we "follow the metaphor," what will we find as the Canadian world view?

4. Drastic changes in experience lead people to create new interpretations that will help them cope with the changes. How can metaphors, or the symbols that represent them, be used as instruments of power and control in such times?

SUGGESTED READINGS

Bowen, John. 2014. *Religions in Practice: An Approach to the Anthropology of Religion*, 6th edn (Boston: Pearson). A contemporary introduction to the anthropology of religion focussing on religious practice and interpretation, with a very wide range of case studies.

Boyer, Pascal, and Brian Bergstrom. 2008. "Evolutionary Perspectives on Religion," *Annual Review of Anthropology* 37: 111–30. A relatively recent article exploring perspectives on the evolutionary emergence of religious thought and the representation of the supernatural.

Evans-Pritchard, E.E. 1976 [1937]. *Witchcraft, Oracles, and Magic among the Azande*, abr. edn (Oxford: Oxford University Press). An immensely influential and very readable anthropological classic.

Frazer, James George. 2006 [1922]. *The Golden Bough* (NuVision Publications), available online in various formats. An example of the "armchair" anthropology of the nineteenth century, this book nonetheless developed the theoretical background used for the anthropological analysis of religion.

Lambek, Michael. 2008. *A Reader in the Anthropology of Religion*, 2nd edn (Malden, MA: Blackwell). An excellent collection of classic and contemporary readings in the anthropology of religion.

Malinowski, Bronislaw. 1948 [1926]. *Magic, Science, and Religion, and other Essays* (New York: Doubleday Anchor), excerpt available at www.adolphus.nl/xcrpts/xcmalinow.html. The essays in this book cover many aspects of Malinowski's fieldwork in the Trobriand Islands and subsequently in Africa. Malinowski's lifelong interest in the ideational life of the people he worked with is evident in this book.

Robidoux, Michael A. 2002. "Imagining a Canadian Identity through Sport: A Historical Interpretation of Lacrosse and Hockey," *Journal of American Folklore* 15, 456: 209–25. Do we have a key metaphor as a country based on the game of hockey? Here, we can examine this in a historical perspective.

RELATED WEBSITES

Canada's Office of Religious Freedom www.international. gc.ca/religious_freedom-liberte_de_religion/

Human Rights Watch: France: Face-Veil Ruling Undermines Rights www.hrw.org/news/2014/07/03/france-face-veil-ruling-undermines-rights

Pew Research: Canada's Changing Religious Landscape www.pewforum.org/2013/06/27/canadas-changing-religious-landscape

We Do Not Have Shamans: The Case against "Shamans" in North American Indigenous Cultures www.angelfire.com /electronic/awakening101/not_shamans.html

Wounded Knee Museum www.woundedkneemuseum.org

III

Organization of Life: Local to Global

HUMAN BEINGS HAVE USED THEIR CULTURAL CREATIVITY, TOGETHER WITH POLITICAL AND ECONOMIC RESOURCES, TO CREATE IMAGINED COMMUNITIES THAT NOW ENCOMPASS THE ENTIRE WORLD. These communities have complex hierarchical forms of social organization. In the following chapters, we look at some of the most significant ways in which social inequality has been institutionalized, and we turn to the rise of global forms of inequality, particularly as they are associated with European colonial empires and their aftermath. Finally, we examine the work of those anthropologists who have tried to do more than record and analyze contemporary social change—anthropologists who have taken on the task of applying anthropological information to the solution of contemporary human social problems.

11

Social Organization and Power

CHAPTER OUTLINE

LEARNING OBJECTIVES

By the end of Chapter 11, you will be able to

- consider that social organization refers to the patterning of human interdependence,
- understand power as a transformative capacity that is exercised

- by both coercive and persuasive means,
- appreciate the power of the imagination for investing the world with meaning, and

- recognize how people bargain for control over interpretations of reality.

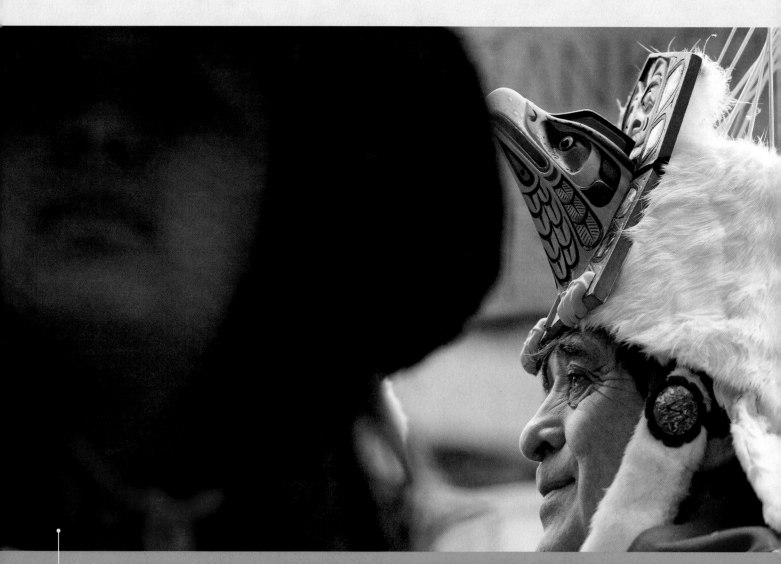

Chief Harvey Humchitt of the Heiltsuk Nation participates in a protest against the building of oil pipelines in British Columbia. Aboriginal peoples living in modern nation-states often struggle to exercise agency over their lives and to make their voices heard from politically marginalized positions.

In 1992, following twelve years of civil war and two years of intensive negotiation, representatives of the government of El Salvador and of the Salvadoran guerrilla movement known as the Farabundo Martí National Liberation Front (FMLN) signed a peace accord. The civil war had cost over 75,000 lives and had turned a million Salvadorans into refugees. It was one of the bloodiest insurrections in twentieth-century Latin America. How could so many years of fierce fighting end at the negotiator's table?

The roots of the conflict go back to the nineteenth century, when a tiny elite of Salvadoran landowners managed to monopolize 60 per cent of the land in order to raise coffee for export. The result was one of the most highly polarized class structures in all of Latin America. Close to 98 per cent of the citizens were forced to survive on plots too small to support them, to live as tenant farmers or labourers on land they did not own, or to become landless migrants. When the coffee market crashed during the depression of the 1930s, the majority on the bottom rebelled against their exploitation, and the Salvadoran army crushed them in a brutal massacre known as *la matanza* ("the massacre").

During the Cold War between the United States and the Soviet Union that began in the late 1940s, even comparatively mild efforts to reform the system were repressed. After 1958, the US government interpreted challenges to the Salvadoran government as signs that El Salvador might be vulnerable to a Cuban-style communist revolution and viewed Salvadoran repression of reformers and rebels as a fight against the spread of communism, an explanation the Salvadoran government willingly endorsed. By the late 1970s, convinced that peaceful social change would never occur, political moderates in El Salvador swelled the ranks of five guerrilla groups that united to form the FMLN. The government response in the 1980s was as brutal as it had been in the 1930s and included a new *matanza* in the peasant village of El Mozote in which over two hundred men, women, and children were massacred for their supposed collaboration with the guerrillas (Danner 1994).

By 1990, Salvadoran society was still polarized, but the prospect of endless war caused Salvadorans on both sides to rethink their positions. Members of the Nationalist Republican Alliance (ARENA) party had won national elections in 1989 and seemed less hostile to democracy, and their elite supporters had become convinced that continued fighting would only hurt their business interests. The United States was also tiring of the war and could no longer ignore highly publicized human rights violations committed by the Salvadoran government. Furthermore, the notion that supporting the Salvadoran government was stemming the spread of communism lost its force following the collapse of communism in Eastern Europe. At the same time, Salvadoran guerrillas concluded that military victory offered no permanent guarantees. Led by guerrilla leaders, the FMLN eventually agreed to meet their enemies at the peace table.

What drives people to take up arms against powerful, well-armed government forces? What convinces battle-hardened fighters who believe that their cause is just to lay down their arms and negotiate when they have no certainty of success? Historian Peter Winn observes that the 1992 UN-brokered accord in El Salvador "was a political compromise that allowed both sides to claim victory while leaving the future in doubt" (1992: 535). Not all Salvadorans supported the negotiated settlement, and sporadic violence directed against some guerrillas-turned-politicians after 1992 threatened the fragile peace it brought about. In May of 1994, however, the first national elections held since the signing of the peace accord were peaceful. The ARENA presidential candidate won two-thirds of the vote against the left coalition, whose candidate won one-third of the vote. By late 1996, the FMLN was reflecting on the experiences of its first legislative session and planning on making alliances with other parties for future elections.

To be sure, the absence of violence at one moment of political crisis does not mean that violence will not be used later. The UN accord did not end economic and political inequality in El Salvador. And the damage caused by various natural disasters over the past decades have only added to these continuing woes. But the peace settlement of 1992 has not been broken to date (Figure 11.1), and the mere fact that violence is not automatic suggests that the exercise of power,

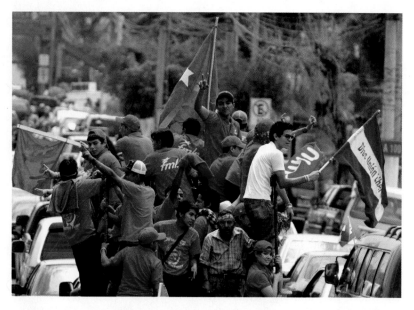

FIGURE 11.1 Young Salvadorans wave FMLN party flags in a non-violent show of support as they ride through downtown San Salvador in 2009. What do you notice about how the FMLN represented in this photo? What do you think this may say about how the status of the FMLN has changed?

social organization

The patterning of human interdependence in a given society through the actions and decisions of its members.

even in a highly stratified society, is more complicated than it may appear.

There are always choices to be made about how a society is to be organized or how that organization may be changed. Who has the power to make and enforce these choices? Where does that power come from? What forms can power take? To answer these questions, this chapter focusses on social organization and the power that human beings have to produce, reproduce, or change that organization.

Varieties of Social Organization

We have already described, in Chapter 3, the variety of forms of human society and some attempts by anthropologists to analyze that variation. American anthropologist and social theorist Lewis Henry Morgan (1871, 1877) urged anthropologists to pay close attention to what he called the *arts of subsistence*. But he ran into difficulties when he observed significant differences in ways of life that were *not* connected with significant differences in ways of making a living. In terms of Morgan's scheme of "ethnical stages," for example, both "barbarians" and "civilized peoples" relied on farming and herding, and in many cases their technologies were quite similar.

What did distinguish them were differences in who did what, how it was done, and for whom. That is, they differed from one another in terms of **social organization**.

The Search for the Laws of Social Organization

Even before the birth of the social sciences, Western thinkers searched for the inflexible laws of society that would explain differences in social organization in a non-arbitrary way. Biological determinists look for biological processes operating deeply within human beings, forcing them to act in some ways and forbidding them to act in other ways. Other thinkers explain similarities and differences in social organization as adaptations to particular ecological conditions. In the nineteenth century, unilineal evolutionists such as Lewis Henry Morgan and Karl Marx believed that the laws of society are rooted in the dynamics of history and work themselves out over time for each human group. Although Marxist analysis still has its adherents, the use of the unilineal evolutionary approach is now seen as somewhat counterproductive to understanding the diversity of historical realities manifest in all cultures.

The Arbitrariness of Social Organization

Perhaps the most important and controversial contribution of anthropology to the debate about laws of social organization is the argument that social relations in any society are ultimately arbitrary. This does not mean that societies are free to do or be whatever they like; rather, it means that there is no way to reduce the complexities of human societies to a single underlying cause.

For example, the adaptive flexibility of the human brain and body would be impossible if our behaviour were under rigid genetic control. Environmental determinism is implausible because no society has ever been left on its own long enough for so-called "environmental pressures" to exert their forces without outside human interference. European colonial conquest vividly demonstrated how the most delicately balanced societal adaptation to a given environment can be totally disrupted, if not destroyed, when outsiders arrive with plans of their own and the power to enforce those plans. Yet even

MAP 11.1 Somalis (Northern)

if societies could be isolated from one another and left to work out their own destinies in their own environments, it is unlikely that identical societies would develop in identical step-by-step sequences as Morgan argued. British anthropologist I.M. Lewis pointed out, for example, that the northern Somalis and the various Cushitic-speaking peoples of Kenya and Ethiopia live next to each other in semi-arid scrubland (see Map 11.1) and even herd the same kinds of animals (1967: 166ff.). Despite these similarities, the Somalis and the neighbouring Cushitic-speaking peoples are quite different in social structure: they engage in much less fighting and feuding than do the Somalis; their families split up to take care of the animals, whereas Somali families do not; and lineage organization is less significant among them than it is among the Somalis.

The Power to Act

Human beings actively work to reshape the environments in which they live to suit themselves. Because the resources available in any environment can be used to sustain more than one way of life, however, human beings must choose which aspects of the material world to depend on. Human choice is equally important in the domain of social organization.

Some archaeologists suggest that population growth, for example, is a constant aspect of the human condition that determines forms of social organization. American anthropologist Marshall Sahlins (1976b: 13) reminds us, however, that population pressure determines nothing more than the number of people that can be supported when the environment is used in a particular way. Members of a society can respond to that pressure in various ways: they can try to get along on less, they can intensify food production by inventing new technologies, they can reduce their numbers by inventing new social practices (e.g., infanticide, birth control), or they can migrate. Indeed, the manner in which a group might choose to implement any of these options is equally undetermined by population pressure. Which members of the group will have to do with less? Which members will control technological innovation? Who will be expected to migrate? And will the ultimate decision be imposed by force or voluntarily adopted? Population pressure alone cannot determine the answer to any of these questions.

The ability to choose implies the ability to transform a given situation. Thus, the ability to choose implies **power**, which we can understand broadly as "transformative capacity" (Giddens 1979: 88). When the choice affects an entire social group, we speak of **social power**. In any social situation, we all have some degree of social power, although some people have more influence than do others. When one group is officially recognized as having more social power than any other group has, we speak of **political power**. Social activists Lisa VeneKlasen and Valerie Miller (2002) note three levels of political power: the visible, the hidden, and the invisible. On the visible level are the "definable aspects of political power—the formal rules, structures, authorities, institutions, and procedures of decision-making" (47). Individuals who are not part of the dominant governing group can observe the operations of visible power, and they can assert their social power in support of or in resistance to visible political decisions. Hidden power is exerted when a group with a great deal of social power discreetly influences the decisions that are made on the visible level, often with negative consequences for groups and individuals with less social power (47–8). Invisible power is "the most insidious of the three": it is embedded in cultural norms and makes certain issues, interests, and problems invisible by shaping "people's beliefs, sense of self, and acceptance of their own superiority or inferiority" (48). This form of power is what keeps certain minorities from protesting when they are treated as less than equal to others.

power
Transformative capacity; the ability to transform a given situation.

social power
The ability to transform a situation that affects an entire social group.

political power
Social power held by a group that is in a position to affect the lives of many people.

When thinking about how political power impacts social organization, we can also consider Eric Wolf's (1999) concept of *structural power*. Structural power is power that organizes social settings themselves and controls the allocation of social labour. Uncovering the patterns of structural power requires paying attention to (1) the large-scale and increasingly global division of labour among regions and social groups, (2) the unequal relations between these regions and groups, and (3) the way these relations are maintained or modified over time. The way in which clothing for sale in wealthy nations (e.g., Canada, the United States) is manufactured in countries with cheap labour forces (e.g., Indonesia, El Salvador, China) is an example of structural power. People are hired to work long hours for low wages in unpleasant conditions to make clothing that they cannot afford to buy; their labour disproportionately benefits the companies for which they work and the foreign consumers who will buy the clothing they produce.

The study of social and political power in human society is the domain of **political anthropology**. In an overview of the subfield, anthropologist Joan Vincent has argued that political anthropology is vital because it involves a complex interplay between ethnographic fieldwork, political theory, and critical reflection on political theory (2002: 1). Vincent divides the history of political anthropology into three phases. The first phase, from 1851 to about 1939, she considers the "formative" era in which basic

political anthropology

The study of social and political power in human society.

orientations and some of the earliest anthropological commentaries on political matters were produced. The second phase, from 1942 to about 1971, is the "classic" era in the field; this phase developed under conditions of the post–World War II British Empire through the period of decolonization in the 1950s and 1960s. This phase is most closely associated with the flourishing of British social anthropology rooted in structural-functionalist theory, and it produced well-known works by such eminent figures as E.E. Evans-Pritchard, Max Gluckman, Edmund Leach, and Fredrik Barth (Figure 11.2). Topics of investigation during this period include classifying pre-industrial political systems and attempting to reconstruct their evolution, displaying the characteristic features of different kinds of preindustrial political systems and demonstrating how these functioned to produce political order, and studying local processes of political strategizing by individuals in non-Western societies (see, e.g., Lewellen 1983).

Decolonization drew attention to emerging national-level politics in new states and the effects of "modernization" on the "traditional" political structures that had formerly been the focus of anthropological investigation. But the turbulent politics of the 1960s and early 1970s called into question not only received social forms but also received forms of anthropological scholarship. Beginning in the 1960s, political anthropologists developed new ways of thinking about political issues and new theoretical orientations to guide them, inaugurating in the 1970s and 1980s a third phase in which political anthropology posed broader questions about power and inequality (Vincent 2002: 3). Under conditions of globalization, anthropologists interested in studying power have joined forces with scholars in other disciplines who share their concerns, and they have adopted ideas from influential political thinkers such as Antonio Gramsci and Michel Foucault to help them explain how power shapes the lives of those they describe in their ethnographies.

The cross-cultural study of social power reveals a paradox of the human condition. On one hand, open cultural creativity allows humans to imagine worlds of pure possibility; on the other hand, we all live in material circumstances that make many of those possibilities profoundly unrealistic. We can imagine many

FIGURE 11.2 Norwegian anthropologist Fredrik Barth conducted some of his earliest fieldwork in the Swat District of Pakistan in the 1950s. Here, a shepherd brings his herd to a local market in modern-day Swat District.

different ways to organize ourselves into groups, but the situations in which we live have been firmly shaped by history, and the opportunity to restructure social organization is ordinarily quite limited. Therefore, we will look closely at the ways in which the material circumstances of everyday life generate fields of power that channel and inhibit agency and cultural creativity—and how human beings can sometimes creatively exercise power and agency in order to evade or subvert those restrictions.

The Role of the State

In the beginning, political anthropologists were strongly influenced by other Western thinkers who had investigated the same topics. Many of these earlier thinkers had assumed that the state was the prototype of "civilized" social power. The absence of a state, therefore, had to represent anarchy and disorder. Although the state often perpetrated injustice or exploitation as a side effect of its monopoly of force, this could be viewed as a necessary price for social order.

Early anthropologists such as Lewis Henry Morgan, however, showed that kinship institutions organized social life in societies without states. A later generation of political anthropologists showed how different kinship institutions distribute power among their members and how non-kin institutions, such as secret societies, sometimes carry out important political roles. They were able to show repeatedly that societies without states can reach and carry out decisions affecting the entire social group by means of orderly traditional processes. More recently, archaeologist Gary M. Feinman and his colleagues (2000) have proposed a network–corporate/hierarchical–egalitarian matrix (see Figure 11.3) that applies to power organization and application in all societies regardless of their complexity. This approach

expands on traditional evolutionary models through the recognition that an unequal distribution and ostentatious display of wealth does not always correlate tightly with the concentration of power or proscribed inheritance rules. It also recognizes a wide range of power-wielding strategies, which in themselves have

marked organizational and integrative implications. (Feinman et al. 2000: 453)

(Note Gary Feinman et al.'s discussion of political hierarchies and organization within societies in the "In Their Own Words" box, below.)

Coercion: With and without Traditional State Institutions

The traditional Western prototype of power in human social relations is based on physical coercion. A typical "natural" manifestation might be a fist fight. This prototype represents an exceedingly pessimistic view of human nature. It suggests that co-operative social living is not natural for humans, as innate instincts drive us toward **free agency**. By extension, political activity is competition between individual free agents over political control. When free agents make decisions, no larger groups, no historical obligations, and no collective beliefs can or ought to stand in their way. In this view, cultural evolution took a giant leap forward when our ancestors first realized that sticks and stones could be used as weapons, not only against non-human predators but especially against human enemies, and human history is a chronicle of the production of better and better weapons. Thus the civilizations we are so proud of have been born and sustained in violence.

Even in many stateless societies of the past, coercion played a role in maintaining control. While there was no central political power, other institutions often functioned to punish those who deviated from cultural norms. Members of such societies did not fear the king or the police but rather the ancestors, supernatural forces, or the lineage elders. Power still often involved physical coercion, with co-operation resulting largely from the fear of punishment.

In the global systems of today, pressure from power-seeking states—states bent on acquiring control over new territories and resources—impinges on the lives of those who traditionally lived in what were essentially stateless societies. (Note John Wagner's discussion in the "In Their Own Words" box, below.) Additionally, when political and institutional coercion comes into play in an atmosphere of ethnic, racial, religious, and economic power struggles, the Darfurs of the

free agency
The freedom of self-contained individuals to pursue their own interests above everything else and to challenge one another for dominance.

IN THEIR OWN WORDS | Political Hierarchies and Organizational Strategies in the Puebloan Southwest

American archaeologist Gary M. Feinman and his colleagues have investigated alternative ways to explain organization within societies. Although this example comes from researchers investigating ancient Puebloan societies, it is informed by ethnography of several contemporary peoples of the southwestern United States. Thus, in attempting to find explanations for the past, they have given us insight for today.

The network strategy of political action is associated with heavily personalized or centralized forms of leadership [see Table 11.1]. Wealth is concentrated in the hands of a few, who use their network of personal connections to enhance and expand their individualized power and authority. The network strategy broadly corresponds to descriptions of accumulators (Hayden 1990), aggrandizers (Clark and Blake 1994), strivers (Maschner 1995), and entrepreneurial elites (Hayden 1995), which are well entrenched in Western leader-centric ideas about power and individualism. In contrast, the corporate strategy bears certain similarities to [Gregory] Johnson's sequential hierarchies and [Dean] Saitta's communal mode and adheres closely to descriptions of [Colin] Renfrew's (1974) group-oriented chiefdoms and [Edward] Lehman's (1969) concept of systemic power. In corporate organizations, economic resources are more dispersed, leadership is less personalized, and ostentatious displays and individual aggrandizement are less apt to be found. Instead, communal ritual, public construction, large co-operative labour tasks, shared power, social segments that are woven together through broad integrative ritual and ideological means, and suppressed economic differentiation are emphasized [see Table 11.1]. . . . Corporate–network strategies of political action represent a continuous comparative dimension. We stress that these strategies are not an explicit substitute for the familiar dimensions of hierarchical complexity. Instead, corporate–network strategies are an orthogonal comparative dimension to that of hierarchies [see Figure 11.3]. In other words, corporate–network tendencies may be found in political organizations with little hierarchical development or in those characterized by complex bureaucracies with multiple levels of decision-making. . . . As a consequence, we propose that there are at least two important comparative dimensions (corporate–network and hierarchical complexity) relevant to explaining long-term change and variation.

TABLE 11.1 Tendencies of Corporate–Network Modes

Network	Corporate
Concentrated wealth	More even wealth distribution
Individual power	Shared power arrangements
Ostentatious consumption	More balanced accumulation
Prestige goods	Control of knowledge, cognitive codes
Patron/client factions	Corporate labour systems
Attached specialization	Emphasis on food production
Wealth finance	Staple finance
Princely burials	Monumental ritual spaces
Lineal kinship systems	Segmental organization
Power inherited through personal glorification	Power embedded in group association/affiliation
Ostentatious elite adornment	Symbols of office
Personal glorification	Broad concerns with fertility, rain

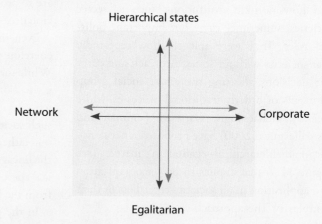

FIGURE 11.3 Two comparative dimensions for the examination of social organization.

Source: Feinman, Gary M., et al. 2000. "Political Hierarchies and Organization Strategies in the Puebolan Southwest," *American Antiquity* 65, 3: 453–4.

world emerge (Figure 11.4). Nothing can focus our understanding of these power struggles more than the personal accounts of those who have lived through such violence (see, e.g., Bashir 2008).

Domination and Hegemony

Our reasons for accepting social power structures are often ambiguous. Do we submit to institutionalized power because we have been coerced and fear punishment? Or do we submit because we believe that the power structures in our society are legitimate given our understandings about the way the world works? What leads people to accept coercion by others as legitimate (Figure 11.7)?

Karl Marx argued that rulers consolidate their power by successfully persuading their subjects to accept a ruling-class ideology that portrays their domination as legitimate. Thus, in his view,

FIGURE 11.4 The people of regions such as Darfur suffer when power struggles erupt in violence. People displaced by armed conflicts are often forced to live in refugee camps, where they have few resources and little power to improve their situation.

IN THEIR OWN WORDS | Water as Commodity in the Okanagan Valley of British Columbia

John Wagner, of the University of British Columbia Okanagan, works in Papua New Guinea and the Okanagan region in Canada. His research interest could be broadly described as environmental. More specifically, he focusses on water and the consequences of its commodification.

Conflict is a normal and inevitable part of life in all societies, but wars involving the loss of thousands or even millions of human lives are not. Why do human beings go to war? Many recent and ongoing civil wars such as those in Rwanda, Sudan, or the former Yugoslavia are described in the media as either *ethnic* or *religious* in nature. In fact, the causes of war are always more complex than these simplistic explanations indicate, and *competition over resources* is almost always a significant, if not a determining, factor. An increasing number of resource conflicts today are also global in scale, an outcome of the increasingly integrated nature of the world economy. Many analysts . . . have proposed that water may well replace oil as the chief source of armed conflict in the twenty-first century.

The economic, military, and technological control of water has, in fact, been essential to the emergence of state-level human societies since they first occurred several thousands of years ago in Mesopotamia, Egypt, China, India, and the Americas. These *hydraulic societies*, as they are often called, typically acquired

their economic strength through construction of large irrigation systems that facilitated greater agricultural productivity, food surpluses, and thus the capacity to maintain professional armies and bureaucracies.

As human demands on freshwater resources grow, and clean water in particular becomes an increasingly scarce resource, armed conflicts and other less immediately destructive forms of conflict are likely to become more frequent. Intensive commoditization of water under these conditions can worsen the divide between rich and poor, leaving the poor of many countries without sufficient access to clean water for even their most basic needs. Over the past few decades, bottled water has become a billion-dollar-per-year industry, water utility services are being privatized in both affluent and less developed nations, and bulk water transfers are occurring on a massive scale.

The Okanagan Valley of British Columbia illustrates another way in which water is being commoditized within today's global marketplace. Home originally to the *Syilx*, an Indigenous hunting/gathering society, this arid and mountainous region was settled by Europeans in the late nineteenth and early twentieth centuries. Irrigation systems were constructed by land development companies to carry water from upland reservoirs to subdivided lots on the valley bottom. Once irrigated, those

continued

FIGURE 11.5 An historic apple box image from the Okanagan Valley. How can the images used to depict a place influence how that place is understood?

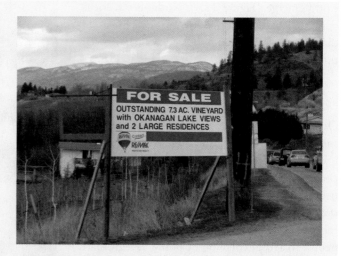

FIGURE 11.6 The conversion of family-farm agricultural land in the Okanagan Valley to waterfront properties for affluent hobby-farmers fetches a high price in the real estate market.

lands were ideally suited to the intensive cultivation of tree fruits. A family-farm orchard industry thus emerged and became a dominant feature of Okanagan culture and landscape [Figure 11.5]. That economy is being displaced today, however, by an economy based on the region's growing popularity as a resort destination and retirement centre. Water as a commodity lies at the heart of this new form of development but in a very different sense than previously. Despite low levels of rainfall in the region, a series of large lakes stretch along the valley bottom, remnants of a glacier that covered the area 10,000 years ago. The lakes are valued for recreational purposes: for boating, scuba diving, and swimming; and waterfront and lake-view properties fetch a high premium in today's booming real estate market [Figure 11.6]. The orchard

oases that surround the lakes at lower elevations enhance the aesthetic and economic value of lake-view properties, but, ironically, the orchard industry is in decline precisely because of this new form of commoditization. As a commodity, water has much higher value in the recreational tourism and housing industries than it does in the agricultural industry. As a consequence, land prices have escalated beyond the level at which they are affordable for agricultural purposes. In the Okanagan Valley, as elsewhere in Canada, conflict over water is not likely to result in armed conflict, but it is likely to result in long-term social and economic change and a sharper divide between water haves and have-nots.

Source: Wagner, John. 2009. "Water as Commodity in the Okanagan Valley of British Columbia," guest editorial.

---

dominated groups suffer from *false consciousness*. However, the concept of false consciousness is problematic because it views people as passive and incapable of withstanding ideological indoctrination.

More promising was the approach taken by Italian political theorist Antonio Gramsci (1971). Writing in the 1930s, Gramsci pointed out that coercive rule—what he called **domination**—is expensive and unstable. Rulers do better if they can persuade the dominated to accept their rule as legitimate. To do so, they may provide some genuine material benefits to their subjects and also use schools and other cultural institutions to disseminate an ideology

justifying their rule. If they achieve all this—while also ensuring that none of these concessions seriously undermine their privileged position—they have established what Gramsci called **hegemony**.

Hegemony is never absolute; it is always vulnerable to challenges. Struggles may develop between rulers trying to justify their domination and subordinate groups who exercise agency by challenging "official" ideologies and practices that devalue or exclude them. Hegemony may be threatened if subordinate groups maintain or develop alternative, or *counter-hegemonic*, cultural practices. Successful hegemony, by contrast, involves linking the understandings of dominant

domination
Coercive rule.

hegemony
A system of leadership in which rulers persuade subordinates to accept the ideology of the dominant group by offering mutual accommodations that nevertheless preserve the rulers' privileged position.

FIGURE 11.7 Prior to colonial conquest by outsiders, Muslim emirs from northern Cameroon had coercive power.

women. Sociologist R.W. Connell has suggested that early societies' gendered divisions of labour in which men occupied the dominant positions constitutes the genesis of hegemonic class systems that later emerged. Connell observes that the structure of relationships between women and men

> operates at every level of human experience, from economic arrangements, culture, and the state to interpersonal relationships and individual emotions. . . . Moving toward a gender-equal society involves profound institutional change as well as change in everyday life and personal conduct. To move far in this direction requires widespread social support, including significant support from men and boys. (2005: 1801)

However, as historian Robert Nye points out, hegemonic masculinity remains the dominant model of identity in heteronormative societies:

> allowing for variations in class, the kind of masculinity that is performed by most men in groups is usually of the hegemonic kind, no matter what the men's education, occupation, or ideological outlook. Even if men stake out and perform masculinities at odds with the hegemonic masculinity of their own society, they must know the code in order to oppose it, and so they know, in a pinch, how to enact it. (2005: 1952)

Despite women's many successful challenges to male-dominated hegemonic power structures over the past century or so, gendered power differentials continue to have a strong influence on the lives of many.

As another example, consider the Azande of central Africa (see EthnoProfile 10.1), who believe that people use witchcraft only against those they envy. This seems highly plausible to people who experience daily friction with their neighbours. At the same time, however, this belief makes it impossible to accuse Azande chiefs of using witchcraft against commoners—because, as the Azande themselves ask, why would chiefs envy their subjects? In this way, hegemonic ideology deflects challenges that might be made against those in power.

and subordinate groups into what appears to be mutual accommodation.

Anthropologists who study the exercise of power in different types of societies have found Gramsci's contrast between domination (rule by coercive force) and hegemony (rule by persuasion) to be very useful. This contrast allows anthropologists to move beyond some of the tortuous and implausible accounts of power that depend on fear of punishment or false consciousness. In place of these determinants, researchers can examine the verbal skills and personal charisma of leaders who have limited coercive force at their disposal but who can nonetheless persuade others to follow them by skilfully aligning shared meanings, values, and goals with a particular interpretation of events or proposed courses of action.

The concept of hegemony is also attractive because it draws attention to the central role of cultural beliefs and symbols in struggles to consolidate social organization and political control. One particularly pervasive cultural belief that has influenced how hegemonic relationships take shape is the belief that men should be dominant over

In other settings, however, hegemonic ideology may justify certain individuals' engagement in social action that would be condemned if engaged in by others. Consider the connection between witchcraft and kingship among the Beng of Ivory Coast (see Map 11.2). The Beng are organized into two regions, each ruled by a king and a queen who come from a specific matrilineal clan. The king is said to be the owner of the Earth, which is the primary focus for worship among the Beng. Violations of taboos concerning the Earth are believed to endanger the entire region and therefore must be dealt with by the king of the region, who is said to have the power to foresee those natural calamities that are punishment for sins committed. In general, "the king is responsible for not only the legal but also the moral and spiritual well-being of the people living in this region" (Gottlieb 1989: 249).

The legitimate power of the king is in direct contrast to the power of witches, who are considered to be utterly immoral. Using illegitimate power, working in secret, they kill and "consume" their close matrilineal kin. Nevertheless, when a man becomes king, he has one year to "bewitch: (i.e., kill) three close relatives in his matriline. If he fails to do so, he will die. Rather than destroying his power, this exercise of illegitimate power legitimates his rule. By killing three close matrilineal relatives, the king shows his commitment to the greater public "good." He is demonstrating his control over, and independence from, the narrow interests of his own kinship group. Operating on a plane beyond that of common morality, the king, who has sacrificed part of himself, will rule the kingdom fairly. From the point of view of the

Beng, including members of the king's own matrilineal clan, the king's actions not only are legitimate but also make it possible for him to rule.

Gramsci was particularly interested in how hegemony is (or is not) successfully established in state societies. In a post-colonial and globalizing world, where all people are presumed to be citizens of one nation-state or another, understanding the effects of decisions and actions of state authorities becomes crucial for making sense of many events on a local level. Anthropologists have often focussed on the processes by which ruling groups in former colonies attempt to build national identities. For example, the British colony of Ceylon became independent in 1948, later changing its name to Sri Lanka. The majority of residents of Ceylon belonged to two populations: the Tamils, concentrated in the northern part of the island (see EthnoProfile 11.1), and the Sinhalese, who lived elsewhere and in much greater numbers. After independence, however, new Sinhalese rulers worked to forge a national identity rooted in their version of local history, which excluded the Tamils. In 1956, Sinhala was made the only official language; in the 1960s and 1970s, the Tamils' access to education was restricted and they were barred from the civil service and the army (Daniel 1997: 316). The Tamils became a persecuted minority. In 1979, when some Tamils began to agitate for a separate state of their own, the Sri Lankan government responded with severe and violent repression, sending many of the Tamils into exile and stimulating the rise of the nationalist Liberation Tigers of Tamil Eelam (LTTE), which grew "into one of the most dreaded militant organizations in the world" (323) (see Figure 11.8). The period of the Sri Lankan Civil War (1983–2009) was marked by escalating violence, with both sides committing "gross human rights abuses, including war crimes"; today, instances of "torture and enforced disappearances" continue to be reported, but still no one is held responsible (Amnesty International 2013).

Over the years, the Sri Lankan government used violent means of coercion to force Tamil residents out of Sri Lanka. But it has also used violence against Sinhalese citizens who objected to state policies. Between 1987 and 1990, Indian troops were brought into Sri Lanka to supervise a peace agreement between Tamils and Sinhalese. These troops found themselves fighting the LTTE in the north and facing violent resistance in Sinhalese areas:

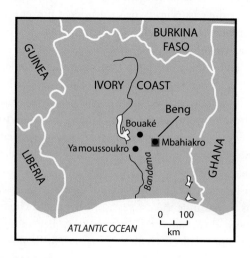

MAP 11.2 Beng

ETHNOPROFILE 11.1 | Tamils

Region South Asia

Nation Northeastern Sri Lanka, also south-eastern India

Language Tamil, one of the many Dravidian languages

Population 3.1 million in Sri Lanka (several hundred thousand have fled the country), nearly 70 million in India (2012 estimates)

Environment Low plains; tropical monsoon climate

Livelihood Planation agriculture; clothing manufacture

Political organization Part of a modern nation-state

For more information Trawick, Margaret. 2002. "Reasons for Violence: A Preliminary Ethnographic Account of theLTTE," in *Conflict and Community in Contemporary Sri Lanka*, eds Siri Gamage and I.B. Watson (Thousand Oaks, CA: Sage); Indrapala, K. 2007. *The Evolution of Ethnic Identity: The Tamils of Sri Lanka* (Colombo: Vijitha Yapa).

---

the rest of the country was convulsed by a wave of terror as young members of a group called the JVP (Janata Vimukti Peramuna, or People's Liberation Front) attacked the government not only for betraying the nation by allowing the Indian presence but also for its own unjust political and economic policies. . . . The government responded with a wave of terror, directed at young males in particular, which reached its climax with the capture and murder of the JVP leadership in late 1989. As far as we can tell, the government won the day by concentrated terror—killing so many young people, whether JVP activists or not, that the opposition ran out of resources and leadership. (Spencer 2000: 124–5)

After 1990, violence directed by the state against Sinhalese citizens lessened, and in 1994, a new government promised to settle the ethnic conflict by peaceful means. But even before then, Sri Lankan government efforts at nation-building had not rested entirely on violence. Leaders also tried to exercise persuasive power to convince Sinhalese citizens that the state had their welfare in mind and was prepared to take steps to improve their lives. For example, anthropologist Michael Woost (1993) has described how the government of Sri Lanka used a wide range of cultural media (television, radio, newspapers, the school system, public rituals, and even a lottery) to link the national identity to development.

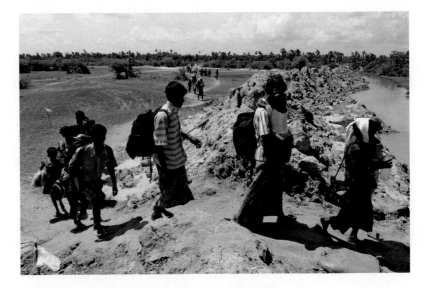

FIGURE 11.8 Sri Lankan Tamil civilians enter a government-controlled area in 2009 after fleeing territory controlled by Liberation Tigers of Tamil Eelam (LTTE) rebels in northeast Sri Lanka.

National development strategies were presented as attempts to restore Sinhalese village society to its former glory under the pre-colonial rule of Sinhalese kings. The ideal village, in this view, is engaged in rice-paddy cultivation carried out according to harmonious principles of Sinhala Buddhist doctrine. The villagers Woost knew could hardly escape this nationalist development discourse, but they did not resist it as an unwelcome imposition from the outside. On the contrary, they incorporated development goals into their own values and accepted that state-sponsored development would improve their lives.

This acceptance might suggest that the state's attempt to establish hegemony had succeeded, but collaboration with the state was undermined as three different village factions selectively manipulated development discourse in their struggle to gain access to government resources. For example, nationalistic rhetoric connected development with "improvement of the land." One village faction claimed it had "improved the land" first by building houses or planting tree crops. A second faction claimed it had "improved the land" first by introducing paddy cultivation in the village. A third faction claimed it had "improved the land" first since its members had intermarried with early settlers who had planted a large mango tree, a sign of permanent residence. Each faction made what the other factions interpreted as unjust claims, and each blamed the lack of village unity on the un-Buddhist greed of its opponents. These disagreements eventually led the state to withdraw its offer of resources, ultimately preventing the implementation of a village development scheme that all factions wanted!

Woost argued that the outcome of this political wrangling demonstrated the contradictory and fragile nature of the hegemonic process: paradoxically, the villagers' active appropriation of nationalist ideology undermined efforts to establish the very social order it was supposed to create. Gramsci himself was well aware that establishing successful hegemony in a nation-state was a difficult process whose outcome was not assured; indeed, it was the very inability of Italians to achieve this goal that stimulated many of his reflections on domination and hegemony.

Biopower and Governmentality

Is there a set of skills that would bring into existence—and sustain—a peaceful, prosperous nation-state in places like Sri Lanka? This question was addressed by French philosopher Michel Foucault, who looked at the way European thinkers from the end of the Middle Ages onward had posed (and attempted to answer) similar questions. Together with colleagues, he identified the emergence of a new form of power in the nineteenth century. He called this form of power **biopower** or *biopolitics*. Biopower is preoccupied with managing bodies—both the bodies of individual citizens and the "body" of the population as a whole.

According to Foucault, a state based on biopolitics is very different from states in the Middle Ages based on the rule of law or administrative states of the fifteenth and sixteenth centuries based on regulation and discipline. Of prime concern in those states was making sure that the ruler maintained *control* of the state. It was generally thought that a ruler should preserve his or her control by any means necessary, even if those means harmed the ruler's subjects. But by the seventeenth century, this approach to state rule was proving increasingly inadequate. Political thinkers began to speak instead about *governing* a state, likening such government to the practices that preserved and perpetuated other social institutions, such as family households and religious orders (Foucault 1991: 90). The example of household management, at that time called *economy*, was a preferred model of government, and debate concerned how to incorporate "the correct manner of managing individuals, goods, and wealth within the family . . . into the management of the state" (92). Thus the concept of *political economy* was born. But running the state in terms of political economy—managing citizens and their relations with goods and resources, with the territory, and with customs, and coping with misfortunes such as famines, epidemics, and death—could not be undertaken effectively until rulers possessed adequate knowledge about such things. In the eighteenth century, such knowledge was produced by state bureaucracies that began to count and measure people and things subject to state control, giving birth to the discipline of *statistics*. Statistics suggested that populations had unique attributes, and rulers concluded that management of the population through the use of statistics was the proper task of government.

The art of governing appropriate to biopolitics—what Foucault calls **governmentality**—requires rulers to anticipate calamities and intervene to prevent such calamities from harming the state or its population. In this arrangement, statistics were powerful tools that could identify a series of possible and probable events, calculate their potential cost, and prescribe a form of intervention that would render such events tolerable, such that they would not undermine the security of the state. For example, such interventions include forms of insurance that protect economic activities in the event of a catastrophe that would otherwise curtail or destroy them (Gordon 1991: 18–20).

biopower
Power held by a modern government over the bodies of its individual citizens and over the "body" of all its citizens.

governmentality
The art of governing appropriate to promoting the welfare of populations within a state.

To an extent, governmentality is a form of power at work in the contemporary world, and institutions that rely on it count and measure their members in a variety of ways (Figure 11.9). Although, as Canadian philosopher Ian Hacking insists, not all bureaucratic applications of such statistical knowledge are evil (1991: 183), the fact remains that providing the government (or any bureaucratic institution) with detailed vital statistics can be very threatening, especially in cases where people are concerned that the state does not have their best interests at heart. After all, states want to tax citizens, vaccinate and educate their children, restrict their activities to those that benefit the state, control their movements beyond (and sometimes within) state borders, and otherwise manage what citizens do. In a globalizing world full of nation-states, anthropologists are increasingly likely to encounter in their fieldwork both the pressures of governmentality and attempts to evade or manipulate governmentality.

The Ambiguity of Power

The contrasts between domination and hegemony and Foucault's explorations of the machinery of governmentality demonstrate that the exercise of power cannot be equated with physical violence alone. Moreover, the occasional violent outburst of one member of a foraging society against another is not the same thing as the organized violence of one army against another in a conflict between modern nation-states. No one can deny that human beings can be violent with one another. But is this the whole story?

"It is useful to accept the proposition that while men have in some sense always been equal (i.e., in that each always has some independent power), they have in another sense never been equal (in that some always have more power than others)" (Adams 1979: 409). Some political anthropologists who think of power as coercion have traditionally emphasized the universality of human inequality. Some have concentrated on power in societies without states, whereas others have taken a more Gramscian approach and reconsidered the nature of independent power available to individuals living in societies with states. The first focus involves looking at power as an independent entity. The second looks at the power of the human imagination to define the nature of social interactions and to persuade other actors to accept these definitions of the situation.

FIGURE 11.9 Censuses are one way in which a state collects information in order to govern effectively. What is the census form pictured above measuring about the people who are answering it? How does this census define kinship and marriage?

Power as an Independent Entity

In some of the traditionally stateless societies of Native peoples in North and South America, power is understood to be an entity existing in the universe independent of human beings. As such, it cannot be produced and accumulated through the interactions of human beings. Strictly speaking, power does not belong to human beings at all. At most, people can hope to *gain access* to power, usually through ritual means. From this point of view, "control over resources is evidence of power rather than the source of power" (Colson 1977: 382).

resistance
The power to refuse being forced against one's will to conform to someone else's wishes.

consensus
An agreement to which all parties collectively give their assent.

persuasion
Power based on verbal argument.

Societies that see power as an independent force usually embed this understanding within a larger world view in which the universe consists of a balance of different forces. Individuals may seek to manipulate those natural forces to their own ends, but only if they can do so without upsetting the universal balance. As a consequence, coercive means of tapping power sources are ruled out in such societies. Violence threatens to undo the universal balance. Thus, in many Native North and South American societies, gentler measures were required. A person approached power through prayer and supplication. The vision quest (as among the Lakota) is a good example of such

FIGURE 11.10 The Aché people of Paraguay were a central example in Pierre Clastres's studies of stateless societies. Formerly nomadic, the Aché now reside in permanent settlements but continue to make hunting trips, as shown here.

an approach: through fasting and self-induced suffering, individuals hoped to move the source of power to pity so that the source might then freely bestow on them the power they sought in the form of a vision or a song or a set of ritual formulas. Power freely bestowed would not disrupt the balance of the universe. (Power mobilized through suffering is a theme that arises in other cultural contexts as well. Consider the use of hunger strikes as political tools, most memorably employed by Mahatma Gandhi in his decades-long struggle for political reform in India.)

In a world view that sees power as an independent force, violence and access to power are mutually contradictory. Cultures that conceive of cosmic power in this way also tend to view individual human beings as independent entities who cannot be coerced but must be supplicated. Individuals in such societies are not free agents in the Western sense (i.e., free of social ties and responsibilities); rather, they are free in the sense that they can refuse to be forced against their will to conform to someone else's wishes. They exercise the power of **resistance**. The power of individuals to resist emphasizes the importance of **consensus** as the appropriate means to decide issues affecting the group. In seeking consensus, proponents of a particular course of action must use **persuasion** rather than coercion to get other members of the group to support their cause. They resort to verbal argument, not physical intimidation. As a result, the most respected members of stateless societies, those generally regarded as leaders, are persuasive speakers. Indeed, as French anthropologist Pierre Clastres (1977) points out, such respected individuals are often referred to by other members of their society as "those who speak for us." The shamans (or *mara'akate*) of the Huichol people of northern Mexico serve this function. By virtue of their verbal ability, they see themselves (and are seen by their fellows) as especially well-suited to negotiate with outsiders on behalf of all the Huichol.

Clastres suggests that stateless forms of social organization are strongly resistant to the emergence of hierarchy (1977: 35; Figure 11.10). Indeed, he argues that members of stateless societies struggle to prevent such authority from emerging. They sense that the rise of state power spells the end of individual autonomy and disrupts beyond repair the harmonious balance between human beings and the forces of the wider world. Canadian anthropologist Richard

Lee agrees, arguing that band societies, and some farmers and herders, have found ways to limit "the accumulation of wealth and power":

> Such societies operate within the confines of a metaphorical ceiling and floor: a ceiling above which one may not accumulate wealth and a floor below which one may not sink. These limits . . . are maintained by powerful social mechanisms known as levelling devices. . . . Such societies therefore have social and political resources of their own and are not just sitting ducks waiting to adopt the first hierarchical model that comes along. (1992a: 39–40)

Here you may recall our discussion of institutionalized sharing, a common levelling device, in Chapter 7.

The Power of the Imagination

Gramsci's discussion of the interplay between coercion and persuasion and Foucault's discussions of governmentality and biopolitics offer more nuanced understandings of the different levels on which social power can operate. Many anthropologists feel that a discussion of social power is incomplete if it does not also pay attention to the way individuals make sense of and use the constraints and opportunities for action open to them, however limited they may be.

All people have the power to interpret their experiences, regardless of the complexity of a social system and whether or not the power of coercion is monopolized by a central authority. People retain this power even under totalitarian dictatorship. It is notoriously difficult to erase the sense of self from human consciousness, even in the face of degradation and imminent death, as can be seen in the art and writings of inmates of the concentration camps of Nazi Germany. Anthropologist Hoyt Alverson argues that "a belief in one's power to invest the world with meaning (the 'will to believe') and a belief in the adequacy of one's knowledge for understanding and acting on personal experience are essential features of all human self-identity" (1978: 7). This is the power to resist outside influences, to reject alternative choices that others want to impose. This does not mean that individuals work out the meanings of their experiences in isolation.

All human activities, including the growth and development of self-identity, take place in a social, cultural, and historical context. Still, each individual retains the power to interpret that context from his or her unique vantage point, in terms of his or her unique experiences. Cynics might argue that the power of the imagination must, in the real world, be restricted to private opinions; the mind can resist, but the body must conform. From this perspective, for example, the actions of a miner who labours underground daily for a meagre wage are clear-cut and unmistakable: he works for money to buy food for his family. However, ethnographic data suggest that this may not be the whole story.

The modern prototype of the downtrodden and exploited human being is the industrial labourer, the sufferer of the dislocations of the Industrial Revolution. Social scientists in the early twentieth century attempted to describe these changes. Émile Durkheim coined the term **anomie** to refer to the pervasive feelings of rootlessness and normlessness that people were experiencing. Karl Marx used the term **alienation** to describe the deep separation workers seemed to experience between their innermost sense of identity and the labour they were forced to do in order to earn enough money to live.

Do industrial workers in what used to be called "the Third World" similarly suffer from anomie and alienation? The issue has been hotly debated. Some argue that their condition could well be far worse than that of Western workers, at least in part because of the lingering effects of colonialism in these regions. This argument is rooted in what has been called "the scars of bondage" thesis. This thesis predicts that the more complete the political domination and exploitation of a people, the more deeply they will be scarred, brutalized, and dehumanized by the experience. For people suffering the twin exploitations of colonialism and industrialism, the outcome could only be the most bitter, unrelieved tragedy. However, as American anthropologist Hoyt Alverson (1977) showed, the "scars of bondage" thesis was not confirmed by his ethnographic research among Tswana migrants who worked in South African mines in the 1960s. When these miners later described their experiences in South Africa, instead of seeing themselves as victims, they drew on their own cultural traditions, identifying themselves with resilient culture heroes.

Similarly, American anthropologist June Nash (1979), working among Bolivian tin miners (see

anomie
A pervasive sense of rootlessness and normlessness.

alienation
The deep separation that individuals experience between their innermost sense of identity and the labour they are forced to perform in order to survive.

Map 11.4), has made interesting observations about the power of the human imagination to transform experiences by investing them with meaning. At the time of her fieldwork, the labour force in Bolivian mines was drawn from local Indigenous populations who had been effectively separated from their involvement in traditional Indigenous communities. Nonetheless, the Bolivian tin miners she knew were able to combine elements of the dominant industrial culture with elements drawn from Indigenous traditions. These Bolivian miners had created new, cohesive cultural patterns; far from being dissonant and alienating, the miners' culture provides an intact

MAP 11.4 Bolivian Tin Miners

FIGURE 11.11 The offerings of cigarettes and coca leaves placed in front of a statue of "El Diablo," a guardian of a government-run Bolivian tin mine complex, is an example of how Bolivian miners have created new, cohesive cultural patterns. The roots of this custom date from much earlier times. How is this process of cultural adaptation political?

sense of self and belonging and an ability to celebrate life as meaningful (Figure 11.11).

How can we explain, in the lives of these Bolivian miners, the combination of what appears to be both genuine suffering and genuine celebration? Exploitation certainly leaves its mark on its victims: poor health, high infant mortality rates, shattered hopes. Yet many of these Bolivian miners were not irrevocably brutalized by these experiences. Their powers to invest their experiences with meaning remained intact, despite crushing conditions of exploitation. Nash notes, "My experience living in mining communities taught me, more than anything else, how a people totally involved in the most exploitative, dehumanizing form of industrialization managed to resist alienation" (1979: 319–20). She argues that the events people experience are less important than how they interpret those events. Nash concludes that the ethnocentrism of Western observers has kept them from recognizing the creative, revolutionary potential embodied in hybrid cultures like that of the Bolivian tin miners.

Bargaining for Reality

The power that people have to invest their experiences with meanings of their own choosing suggests that a ruler's power of coercion is limited, which was Gramsci's key insight. Thought alone may be unable to alter the material circumstances of coercion, yet it has the power to transform the meaning of those material circumstances.

Any hegemonic establishment runs the risk that the dominated may create new, plausible accounts of their experiences of domination. American anthropologist and political scientist James Scott (1990) refers to these unofficial accounts as "hidden transcripts." Occasionally, those who are dominated may be able to organize themselves socially in order to transform their hidden transcripts into a counter-hegemonic discourse aimed at discrediting the political establishment. Those who are dominated may be able to persuade some or all of those around them that their counter-hegemonic interpretation of social experience is better or truer than the hegemonic discourse of the current rulers. Such challenges to incumbent political power are frequently too strong to be ignored and too widespread to be simply obliterated by force. When coercion no longer works, what remains is a struggle between alternative accounts of experience.

Anthropologist Lawrence Rosen (1984) worked in the Moroccan city of Sefrou (see Map 11.5). As he listened to the local people discussing and defining their relationships with one another, he realized that none of the traditional concepts they used could be said to have a fixed meaning. Any definition offered by one person would be verbally challenged by another. Rosen concluded that political and social life in Sefrou could not be understood unless one accepted that, for the locals, negotiation was the norm. Rosen calls this sociopolitical negotiation "bargaining for reality."

The reality bargained for is not an impersonal, unchangeable set of truths about the world. Moroccans aim to persuade one another to accept alternative ways of understanding a particular situation. Persuasive accounts must be *coherent*: they must explain events and processes central to the experiences of those to whom they are addressed, they must be expressed in language that other members of society can understand, and they must hang together in a way that is not blatantly contradictory.

The power relationship between men and women in Sefrou illustrates this process. In his fieldwork, Rosen found that men viewed women as less intelligent, less self-controlled, and less altruistic, and they expected women to obey them. Although women often assented to the male account of this relationship, they did not accept it in all circumstances. Women had developed an alternative account that explained elements in their lives that the male account either overlooked or interpreted differently.

Women in Sefrou depended on men—first their fathers, later their husbands, and perhaps eventually their sons—for material support. But marriages were fragile, and women often had to rely on males of their patriline when their husbands divorced them (a wife could not legally divorce her husband). Consequently, security for women depended on women strengthening their positions within their families. In particular, women attempted to influence marriage negotiations because marriage automatically rearranges social relationships within the family. Women were eager to protect themselves and their daughters from oppressive demands by a husband and his kin. They viewed their actions as sensible and compassionate, not as misplaced interference. Nor did they accept the view that men are intellectually and morally superior to women. Indeed, they often viewed men as self-centred and childish.

In effect, Moroccan men and women lived side by side in different worlds. They shared experiences but interpreted those experiences differently. In everyday life, women had little direct contact with men, so these different interpretations of experience did not constantly come into conflict. But marriage negotiations inevitably brought these different perspectives into contention. The outcome was reality bargaining, as several different actors attempted to make their definitions of the situation prevail.

Rosen described one marriage negotiation that he encountered in Sefrou (1984: 40–7). A girl refused to marry the suitor her family chose, and her continued resistance had disrupted the harmony of her father's household. Rosen visited the household in the company of a respected male informant who was an old friend of the family. During their visit, the family friend and the girl's mother discussed the betrothal and the girl's refusal to consent to it. Both parties interpreted the girl's refusal differently. The family friend described the girl's behaviour as a typical case of female selfishness and immorality. What other reason could there be for her refusal to obey her father, as dutiful daughters should? He spoke harshly of her and repeatedly asserted that when her father returned they would force her to come to her senses and make the marriage. Her mother never openly contradicted these

MAP 11.5 Sefrou

assertions. All the while, however, she quietly and insistently continued to make counter-assertions of her own. She reported her daughter's reason for rejecting the match: her intended husband came from a distant city. If she married him, she would have to leave her family behind and go live among strangers. It was not that she objected to an arranged marriage; rather, she did not want to marry this particular man because to do so would take her so far away from home. From a woman's perspective, the daughter's anxieties were entirely rational given the powerlessness and isolation that she would endure as a result of the marriage.

As it turned out, after a year and a half of successful resistance, the young girl was eventually persuaded to marry the suitor. She changed her mind when she became convinced that consenting to the marriage was an economically sound move, not a submission to patriarchal authority. So women may agree with the male position in general terms and yet successfully dispute its relevance in a particular situation. Men may get women to comply with their wishes, and yet the women's reasons for doing so may have nothing to do with the reasons men offer to justify their demands.

James Scott carried out two years of ethnographic research among peasant rice farmers in a Malaysian village he called Sedaka (a pseudonym) (see Map 11.6). He found that poor Malaysian peasants were at the bottom of a social hierarchy, dominated locally by rich farmers and nationally by a powerful state apparatus. These peasants were not kept in line by some form of state-sponsored terrorism; rather, the context of

MAP 11.6 Sedaka

their lives was shaped by what Scott calls *routine repression*: "occasional arrests, warnings, diligent police work, legal restrictions, and an Internal Security Act that allows for indefinite preventive detention and proscribes much political activity" (1985: 274).

Scott wanted to find out how this highly restrictive environment affected political relations between members of dominant and subordinate classes in the village. He quickly realized that the poor peasants of Sedaka were not about to rise up against their oppressors. But this was not because they accepted their poverty and low status as natural and proper. One reason was that organized overt defence of their interests would have been difficult given the conflicting loyalties generated by local economic, political, and kinship ties. Another reason was that the peasants knew that overt political action in the context of routine repression would be foolhardy. And they had to feed their families. Their solution was to engage in what Scott calls *everyday forms of peasant resistance*: this included "foot dragging, dissimulation, desertion, false compliance, pilfering, feigned ignorance, slander, arson, sabotage, and so forth" (1985: xvi). These actions may have done little to alter the peasants' situation in the short run; however, Scott argues, in the long run they may have been more effective than overt rebellion in undercutting state repression.

What we find in everyday forms of peasant resistance are indirect attempts to challenge local hegemony. Scott says: "The struggle between rich and poor in Sedaka is not merely a struggle over work, property rights, grain, and cash. It is also a struggle over the appropriation of symbols, a struggle over how the past and present shall be understood and labelled, a struggle to identify causes and assess blame" (1985: xvii). When peasants criticize rich landowners or rich landowners find fault with peasants, the parties involved are not just venting emotion. According to Scott, each side is simultaneously constructing a world view. Rich and poor alike are offering "a critique of things as they are as well as a vision of things as they should be. . . . [They are writing] a kind of social text on the subject of human decency" (23).

Scott described the dynamics of this struggle during the introduction of mechanized rice harvesting in Sedaka. Traditionally, rice harvesting was manual labour (Figure 11.12). In the late 1970s, however, the introduction of combine harvesters eliminated the rich farmers' need for hired labour, a loss that dealt poor families a severe economic blow. When the rich and poor talked about the harvesters, each side offered a different account of their effect on economic life in the village.

While both sides agreed that using the machines hurt the poor and helped the rich, consensus evaporated when each side was asked whether the benefits of the machines outweighed their costs. The poor offered practical reasons against the use of combine harvesters: they claimed that the heavy machines were inefficient and that their operation destroyed rice paddies. They also offered moral reasons: they accused the rich of being "stingy," of ignoring the traditional obligation of rich people to help the poor by providing them with work and charity. The rich denied both the practical and the moral objections of the poor. They insisted that using harvesters increased their yield. They accused the poor people of bad faith. They claimed that the poor suffered because they were bad farmers or lazy, and they attributed their own success to hard work and prudent farm management.

Rich rice farmers would never have been able to begin using combine harvesters without the outside assistance of both the national government and the business groups who rented the machines to them at harvest time. Poor peasants were aware of this, yet they directed their critique at the local farmers and not at the government or outside business organizations. After all, the rich farmers "are a part of the community and therefore *ought* not to be indifferent to the consequences of their acts for their neighbours" (Scott 1985: 161). The stinginess of the rich did not just bring economic loss. It also attacked the social identity of the poor, who vigorously resisted being turned into non-persons. The poor insisted on being accorded the "minimal cultural decencies in this small community" (xviii). The only weapon they controlled in this struggle was their ability, by word and deed, to undercut the prestige and reputation of the rich.

This strategy worked in Sedaka because rich local farmers were not ready to abandon the traditional morality that had regulated relations between rich and poor. They had not yet become so Westernized that they no longer cared what other villagers thought of them. A shrewd campaign of character assassination

FIGURE 11.12 Until recently, rice harvesting in rural Malaysia was manual labour that regularly allowed poor peasants to earn cash and receive grain from their employers as a traditional form of charitable gift. The peasants worked against routine repression not by revolting, but by resisting in the everyday. Do you witness everyday forms of resistance in your own life? What do they look like?

may have caused at least some of the rich to hesitate before ignoring their traditional obligations. The improvement might have been minor, strictly in economic terms, but it would have been major in terms of the ability of the poor to defend their claims to citizenship in the local community. In addition, the wider political arena could always change in the future. Scott was convinced that many of the poor peasants he knew might well engage in open, active rebellion if routine repression disappeared.

When disputes are settled in this manner, experience is transformed. As Scott observed:

> The key symbols animating class relations in Sedaka—generosity, stinginess, arrogance, humility, help, assistance, wealth, and poverty—do not constitute a set of given rules or principles that actors simply follow. They are instead the normative raw material that is created, maintained, changed, and above all manipulated by daily human activity. (1985: 309)

In a similar way, Rosen referred to central Moroccan values such as intelligence, self-control, and generosity as **essentially negotiable concepts**: "There is an element of uncertainty inherent in these terms such that

essentially negotiable concepts
Culturally recognized concepts that evoke a wide range of meanings and whose relevance in any particular context must be negotiated.

their application to any situation by one person can be contested by another" (1984: 43). Bargaining for reality involves just this sort of manoeuvre: "What is negotiable, then, is less one's view of reality as such than its scope, its impact, and its differential importance" (47). In articulating their particular world views, social groups aim "not just to convince but to control; better stated, they aim to control by convincing" (Scott 1985: 23).

IN THEIR OWN WORDS | Canaries in the Mines of Citizenship

Joyce Green, a political scientist from the University of Regina, discusses the issues of citizenship and membership for First Nations women in Canada.

So what is an excluded Indian woman to do? The standard responses to citizen dissatisfaction with an aspect of the political regime include legal challenge, political activism, partisan activity, and building new social consensus. Indian women concerned about citizenship and membership issues have tried all of these but have not yet found the political leverage to have their concerns ranked high by predominantly white or Aboriginal male politicians, mainstream political parties, and colonial courts.

Law, democratic mainstream politics, and Indigenous politics seem unable or unwilling to contend with the issues raised by this problematic minority. Denied band membership, meaningful exercise of Aboriginal and treaty rights, and, perhaps most importantly, denied the right to practise identity by living and raising children in their own communities, the affected women and their children are exiled to the dominant society where, thanks to racism, they are seen forever as "Indian."

Nor will the state apply its emerging view of rights in a way that works to the advantage of these women. Rather, the federal government retreats behind its self-serving rhetoric of respect for "self" government, washing its hands of any responsibility to guarantee these women's rights. Meanwhile, Indian Act band governments claim to be governments of First Nations, practising a constitutionally recognized Aboriginal and treaty right which includes control of membership or citizenship.

The Sawridge pleadings suggest some of these invoke colonial sexist practices as constitutionally protected "tradition." In sum, neither the state nor band governments defended these women with rights discourse, though both use it when it suits them. Neither has affirmed their value as human resources to society. Neither guarantees equality of citizenship by taking the steps needed to permit these women to live in a way that honours their identity and values their participation.

Democracy fails these women. Premised on majority rule, and on the theoretical cultural-neutral and gender-neutral citizen and politician, it is unable to ensure their representation in a political system implicitly premised on their sex and ethnic inferiority. Privileging mythical notions of undifferentiated equality, the ideology grounding Canadian democracy is inherently hostile to affirming rights-bearing specificity, especially where Aboriginal rights may result in constitutional and public policy measures that benefit Aboriginal people in ways not available to non-Aboriginal Canadians; that is, where differing kinds of citizenship result. This hostility has been evident in non-Aboriginal opposition to treaty fishing rights and to land and governance rights sustained by the Supreme Court of Canada.

To date, Canadian law has failed these women, even with rights discourse foregrounded. The Lavell case of 1974, eight years prior to the entrenchment of the Canadian Charter of Rights and Freedoms, is infamous for dignifying sex discrimination as non-discrimination in law. The Sawridge case 21 years later sought to define Indian women's sexual equality rights out of existence. Lawmakers fail to see that any law affirming these women's rights must affirm them in their specificity as Indigenous women, part of colonized societies, to whom the state is historically an oppressor and only potentially an ally. While the Charter protections from discrimination on the basis of gender have motivated the federal government to eliminate the most egregious forms of legislative discrimination against Indian women, the measures are inadequate and stem from incomplete analyses that ignore the centrality to these women of their Aboriginal identities and rights, and their right to be fully acknowledged as part of their communities.

Yet citizenship may have the capacity to transcend the contradictions and pitfalls of decolonization in conditions defined by liberal and neo-liberal ideology and by the realpolitik of contemporary Canada. Even though Aboriginal rights constitute a different kind of right belonging only to members of Aboriginal nations, in addition to other citizenship rights enjoyed by all citizens of Canada, in the final analysis, people are not so incommensurable as to not share fundamental and inalienable human rights. All governments are impositions of authority upon those they govern, no matter how democratic or culturally authentic their processes. Authority must be held accountable for protecting the conditions fundamental to our humanity. In addition to human rights, which may be expressed and practised in different culturally specific fashions, Aboriginal rights must also be protected for all Aboriginal women and men.

Source: Green, Joyce. 2001. "Canaries in the Mines of Citizenship: Indian Women in Canada," *Canadian Journal of Political Science* 34, 4: 736–8.

The issues arising from the post-colonial environment also extend into basic definitions and negotiations of rights of citizenship and who controls these definitions and negotiations. This is of concern to anthropologists as well as scholars working in other disciplines, such as political science. (Note Joyce Green's discussion in the "In Their Own Words" box, above.) The rights of those designated by a society as *the least amongst us* are essentially the only rights existing under law for all. What can be granted by authorities to the "least" can become the reality for the "most" in any regime of subjugation. This point moves beyond contested world views to contested human rights.

History as a Prototype of and for Political Action

When individual actors within a particular cultural and situational context attempt to impose their definition of the situation on those with whom they interact, they draw on elements of a shared tradition of values and beliefs. This shared tradition, however, does not consist of values and beliefs divorced from experience and history. To some degree, people in all cultures continue to reshape—to bargain over—not merely which part of an agreed-on tradition is relevant in a particular situation but also which version of the tradition ought to be agreed on. The combinations they come up with are sometimes surprising.

Consider the development of rural justice groups called *rondas campesinas* ("peasants who make the rounds") in the northern Peruvian highlands (see Map 11.7). Rondas consist of armed groups of peasants who walk the paths around their hamlets at night keeping an eye out for animal rustlers (Figure 11.13). The rondas began in one small hamlet in the northern Peruvian department of Cajamarca in 1976. During the 1980s, they spread hundreds of miles within Cajamarca and surrounding departments. At the same time, their functions were radically expanded: they became an alternative justice system with open peasant assemblies to resolve problems ranging from wife-beating to land disputes. By the early 1990s, rondas operated in 3,400 hamlets in the northern Peruvian Andes.

American anthropologist Orin Starn (1992) notes that at least five forces spurred campesinas to establish their alternative justice system.

1. The theft of animals shot up dramatically with the onset of the Peruvian economic crisis of the mid-1970s. The rise in theft was extremely serious for the poor farmers of the northern Andes, most of whom had small flocks and earned less than two thousand dollars per year.
2. Peasants got no relief from the official justice system. As the economy worsened,

MAP 11.7 Northern Peruvian Highlands

FIGURE 11.13 Rondas campesinas have become an alternative justice system in highland Peru. Here, a group of ronderos pose with a stolen donkey recovered from rustlers in 1986.

many government authorities tried to enlarge their shrinking salaries through bribery, kickbacks, and extortion, and poorer peasants were increasingly unable to pay.

3. The government had a weak presence in the mountains, providing an opportunity for peasants to develop a new form of community organization.

4. Country people in northern Peru value toughness and bravery in the face of violence and were able to channel their aggressiveness into the service of order and discipline in the rondas.

5. Local organizers had outside supporters. In the province where the rondas began, these were activists from the Maoist Red Homeland (Communist) party. In a neighbouring province, peasant teachers of Christianity became early ronda leaders and were defended by priests and nuns as well as the local bishop.

During the 1980s, rondas were transformed from vigilante groups to dispute-resolution groups. Compared to the expensive, time-consuming, humiliating, and ineffective official justice system, the rondas were inexpensive, efficient, effective, and local. By the late 1980s, rustling was virtually eliminated and rondas in some communities were adjudicating over one hundred cases a month. The rondas also involve the elaboration of political identity and culture. Songs and poems celebrate the rondas, and festivals commemorate their anniversaries.

To create the rondas, peasants drew on national and local cultural patterns. Peasants had served on patrols to stop thieves on haciendas (expansive estates) before the haciendas were broken up in the late 1960s. Men in the hamlets who had served in the Peruvian military incorporated military strategies and forms into the rondas. The peasants also employed local patterns, keeping the ronda patrols under the collective authority of the community. Likewise, when the rondas took on adjudication roles, they adopted some forms from the state bureaucracy, using a table like a judge's bench, rubber stamps, a recording secretary

with notarized minutes, and so on. But the openness of the ronda system is very different from the state bureaucracy, for the final decision rests on the ronda president's evaluation of the response of the people attending. Assemblies of rondas are often held outside, where the event occurred, such as a farmyard. All attending have detailed knowledge of some kind that may be brought into play, and everyone jumps in to attempt to settle the dispute.

But the rondas, for all their effective innovation, are sometimes still enmeshed in old practices.

- They are connected with political parties in Peru, and squabbles involving the parties have weakened the ronda movement.

- They see themselves as the genuine upholders of the law and the Peruvian constitution. Thus, even though they have challenged the government's monopoly on the administration of justice, they are not working to overthrow the state.

- In some rondas, the leaders stay on for many years, hoard power, and begin to show favouritism. (More often, communities encourage constant rotation of leaders to avoid this problem.)

- The rondas perpetuate patriarchy. Although the rondas have given women a place in order to censure wife-beating, and a number of offenders have received a stern warning or whipping, only men patrol; female participation in assemblies is limited and mostly passive, and women are never ronda officers.

- The rondas sometimes use violent measures to bring about justice. While their ultimate aim is to create peace and order in a violent environment, the ronderos employ some of the techniques of the Peruvian police—for example, whipping with barbed wire and hanging accused rustlers by their arms—to achieve their goal.

Starn concludes that, on the whole, the rondas have given Peruvian peasants the vision of an alternative modernity and have renewed among them a powerful sense of independent identity.

Negotiating the Meaning of History

The meanings of the central symbols of any cultural tradition are essentially negotiable. That is, each symbol evokes a wide range of meanings among those who accept it. But what that symbol means in any particular situation, as well as the appropriateness of applying that symbol to the situation, is never obvious. Such matters are cultural dilemmas that people struggle to resolve. Consider the Moroccan and Peruvian examples discussed in this chapter, and consider the power to invest experience with one's own meanings. This is a very real power. And yet many anthropologists are divided about the effectiveness of resistance as a solution to the problems of those at the very bottom of society. While some individuals and groups have been able to successfully assert themselves and their view of the world in the face of tremendous oppression, others have been destroyed by such oppression. Political anthropologist John Gledhill observes that it would be "dangerous to be over-optimistic"; after all, "counter-hegemonic movements exist, but much of the world's population is not participating in them" (1994: 198). He is particularly skeptical about the power of everyday forms of peasant resistance: the ability of such practices to undermine the local elite, he warns, may "merely provide the scenario for the replacement of one elite by another, more effective, dominant group" (92). At the beginning of the twenty-first century, with no utopian solutions in sight, the most that anthropologists may be able to do is agree with historian A.R. Tawney, who wrote about the agrarian disturbances in sixteenth-century England: "Such movements are a proof of blood and sinew and of a high and gallant spirit. . . . Happy the nation whose people has not forgotten how to rebel" (quoted in Wallerstein 1974: 357).

A CRITICAL LOOK | Interpretations of War

In our modern, technologically connected world, we are continually bombarded with descriptions and images of intense power struggles that are taking place around the globe. Newspapers, TV news broadcasts, and online news sites of all sorts bring us graphic reports and photographs depicting armed uprisings, terrorist attacks, military invasions, and other large-scale acts of violence. These depictions both draw our attention to and mediate the reality of those conflicts. Through the lens of Western media, wars lose much of the intense meaning they hold for those participating in the conflict. Most often, they filter through to us as remote, depersonalized experiences in which lost human lives are nothing more than "collateral damage."

German linguist Uwe Poerksen (1995) would define *collateral damage* as a "plastic" phrase—a phrase made up of words that are malleable (like plastic) and that, through their malleability, can shape aspects of our reality by disguising their true nature. More common examples of plastic words include "development," "project," "strategy," and "problem." Plastic words are often used by hegemonies of various forms—governments, economic organizations, military forces, and so on. They are the real-world realization of the "newspeak" described by George Orwell in his dystopian, oddly prophetic novel *1984*: "war is peace," "freedom is slavery," "ignorance is strength." Such words and phrases warp our perceptions, hiding the true consequences of war.

Images can have an equally distorting effect. Filmmaker and political activist Susan Sontag (2003) challenges us to think deeply about how we use and interpret photographs of "hellish events" such as war. She notes that the stories and descriptions that accompany photographs give these visual representations most of their meaning. In turn, we assume that pictures give credibility to the stories they accompany. Yet through this relationship, the truth is open to manipulation. Imagine, for example, a photograph of a building that has been destroyed in an explosion. On its own, the photograph carries little meaning; it simply reveals that a building, somewhere, has been destroyed by someone for some reason. Now imagine that the photograph is accompanied by a caption telling you that the building was an elementary school, and that the school was bombed by enemy forces in an attempt to scare locals into submission. This caption makes sense of the image, and it implicitly encourages you to side with the locals. Now imagine that

continued

the photograph is accompanied by a caption declaring that the building was an abandoned warehouse, and that members of the local community destroyed it in order to frame their enemies for an attack. This caption also makes sense of the image, but it offers a very different explanation. Which caption describes what really happened? Without access to additional information, it is impossible to be sure.

Whenever we are faced with a representation of reality, we must remember that someone *created* that representation. People write stories and take pictures, and people always leave their mark on their creations, even if only subtly. Whether or not they intend to have an impact, creators always have the power to influence the minds of those who encounter their creations. In addition, we must be aware that in reading or viewing a representation, we are making our own interpretations. Thus, the information contained within a representation of any human experience—including, but not limited to, war—passes through three cultural filters: that of the culture of the people being represented, that of the culture of the photographer, and that of the culture of the reader or observer. Each filter adds a perspective that is based on certain beliefs, interests, and experiences.

Now take a moment to reflect. What stories and images of war flood your view of today? More importantly, what concepts can you rely on to inform how you interpret those representations? Anthropologist R. Brian Ferguson (2008) suggests 10 points that can help us interpret modern wars in a meaningful way:

1. "Our species is not biologically destined for war."
2. "War is not an inescapable part of social existence."
3. "Understanding war involves a nested hierarchy of constraints."
4. "War expresses both pan-human practicalities and culturally specific values."
5. "War shapes society to its own ends."
6. "War exists in multiple contexts."
7. "Opponents are constructed in conflict."
8. "War is a continuation of domestic politics by other means."
9. "Leaders favour war because war favours leaders."
10. "Peace is more than the absence of war."

These points give us an alternative way of understanding the large-scale violent conflicts often simplified by the news media as unavoidable and unresolvable. Peace is created—it does not just happen. It is hard to achieve and hard to keep. And it begins with each of us working toward building an open and inclusive society in which all members respect and value one another.

—Roberta Robin Dods

KEY TERMS

alienation 281
anomie 281
biopower 278
consensus 280
domination 274

essentially negotiable
   concepts 285
free agency 271
governmentality 278
hegemony 274

persuasion 280
political anthropology 270
political power 269
power 269
resistance 280

social organization 268
social power 269

CHAPTER SUMMARY

1. Social organization refers to the patterning of human interdependence in a given society through the actions and decisions of its members. Anthropologists understand that the complexities of human social organizations can never be reduced to a single cause. The power that human beings have to reproduce or to change their social organization is an important focus of anthropological study.

2. The ability to act implies power. Power operates according to principles that are culturally constructed. Anthropologists

interested in how power is exercised in states have been influenced by the works of Antonio Gramsci and Michel Foucault. Gramsci distinguished coercive domination from hegemony, arguing that coercion alone is rarely sufficient for social control. Foucault's concept of governmentality emphasizes the importance of practices that create and sustain peaceful and prosperous social life. These sorts of practices can be tailored to specific populations through the use of statistics.

3. Anthropological research in societies without states has shown how social obligations can restrict individuals from pursuing their own self-interests. In those societies, power is usually seen to be an independent entity to which one may gain access by supplication, not coercion. Likewise, individuals cannot be coerced but must be persuaded to co-operate. They are not free agents in the modern Western sense, but they are empowered to resist conforming to another's wishes.

4. All human beings possess the "power to invest the world with meaning." Rulers always face the risk that those they dominate may create new, persuasive accounts of their experience of being dominated, organize themselves to defend and disseminate their account, acquire a following, and unseat their rulers. When people bargain for reality, they draw on elements of a shared culture and shared history in order to persuade others of the validity of their position. Much political debate concerns which lessons from the past are relevant to the present. When disputes are settled in this manner, experience is transformed.

CRITICAL THINKING QUESTIONS

1. Why would the anthropological contention that social relations in any society are ultimately arbitrary be a controversial idea?

2. What are the similarities and differences between domination and hegemony?

3. What was the initial bureaucratic role of statistics, and why were (are) they considered important?

4. If power is part of the natural order of things yet independent of direct human control, what are the consequences that follow? Consider personal access to power, social constructs and relationships related to power, and the individual's ability to change the balance in a power relationship.

SUGGESTED READINGS

Arens, W., and Ivan Karp, eds. 1989. *Creativity of Power: Cosmology and Action in African Societies* (Washington, DC: Smithsonian Institution Press). Contains 13 essays exploring the relationship among power, action, and human agency in African social systems and cosmologies.

Barrett, Stanley R., Sean Stokholm, and Jeanette Burke. 2001. "The Idea of Power and the Power of Ideas: A Review Essay," *American Anthropologist*, New Series, 103, 2: 468–80. A critique of Eric Wolf's *Envisioning Power: Ideologies of Dominance and Crisis* (1999). The authors argue that the concept of structural power is redundant and expendable as it is presented by Wolf.

Bashir, Halima. 2008. *Tears of the Desert: A Memoir of Survival in Darfur* (New York: One World). One woman's description of her survival of torture and gang-rape, inflicted for speaking out about an attack on primary school children.

Fogelson, Raymond, and Richard N. Adams, eds. 1977. *The Anthropology of Power* (New York: Academic Press). A classic collection of 28 ethnographic essays on power all over the world.

Vincent, Joan, ed. 2002. *The Anthropology of Politics: A Reader in Ethnography, Theory, and Critique* (Malden, MA: Blackwell Publishers). A challenging but worthwhile collection of key texts in political anthropology ranging from the eighteenth-century Enlightenment to twenty-first-century critique.

RELATED WEBSITES

Ronda Campesinas www.mundoandino.com/Peru/Ronda-Campesina

Council on Hemispheric Affairs (COHA) www.coha.org/a-new-face-to-salvadoran-politics

Pueblo Indian History and Resources www.puebloindian.com

Sawridge Band v. Canada http://reports.fja.gc.ca/eng/2004/2004 fca16.html

12

Inequality in the Contemporary World

CHAPTER OUTLINE

Class

Caste

Race

Ethnicity

Nation and Nationalism

LEARNING OBJECTIVES

By the end of Chapter 12, you will be able to

- identify aspects of social stratification resulting in class and caste structures,
- consider and challenge the concept of race,

- appreciate the forms ethnicity may take, and
- discuss how issues of inequality relate to nationalism.

Roma women beg for money on a busy street Sweden. People like the Roma who face widespread discrimination tend to be forced to the margins of society, where they have little access to wealth, power, or prestige.

While anthropologists have documented some distinctive forms of social organization that are relatively egalitarian, in today's increasingly globalized world we most often find **stratified societies**. In stratified societies, higher-ranking groups have a disproportionate access to wealth, power, and prestige. At times, stratification is minimal—for example, in societies that anthropologists call *chiefdoms* (see Chapter 3), the chief may be the only person with a permanently superior status, while social and economic relations among other members of the group may remain relatively egalitarian. More elaborate social stratification is found in societies classified as *states*, which not only are much larger than chiefdoms but also employ a variety of mechanisms to bind different subgroups together into a hierarchy that regulates each group's access to wealth, power, and prestige.

All people in the world today, including the stateless and refugees, must deal with the authority of one or another nation-state, and all nation-states are socially stratified. But the inequality that exists in any given nation-state may be constructed out of multiple categories arranged in different hierarchies of stratification. Here we could consider the problems of sexism, discrimination based on sexual orientation, and the biases involved in ageism; however, we shall confine our discussion in this chapter to five categories of inequality:

1. **class**,
2. **caste**,
3. **race**,
4. **ethnicity**, and
5. **nationality**.

It is important to understand that *every one* of these categories is a cultural invention designed to create boundaries around one imagined community or another. *None* of these categories maps onto permanent biological subdivisions within the human species, although members of societies that employ these categories often will invoke "nature" to support their legitimacy.

Some patterns of inequality appear to reach back through deep historic time, while others seem to have gained currency far more recently and are closely associated with the spread of colonialism and capitalism. In many cases, capitalist and colonialist forces introduced new forms of stratification to formerly independent, egalitarian societies; in others, these forces reshaped forms of stratification that predated European contact. Anthropologists and other social scientists have argued with one another about how the categories of inequality should be defined, and they have asked whether these categories can be usefully applied cross-culturally. We will look at some of their arguments.

Class

In general, classes are hierarchically arranged social groups defined on economic grounds. That is, members of higher-ranked social classes have disproportionate access to resources and sources of wealth, whereas members of lower-ranked classes have much more limited access to wealth and most resources (Figure 12.1).

FIGURE 12.1 Social classes often live within easy sight of one another. Here, luxury apartments and squatter settlements rub shoulders in Caracas, Venezuela. Where in your own life do you see social classes coming together?

stratified societies
Societies in which there is a permanent hierarchy that accords some members privileged access to wealth, power, and prestige.

class
A ranked group within a hierarchically stratified society whose membership is defined primarily in terms of wealth, occupation, and/or access to power.

caste
A ranked group within a socially stratified society that is closed, prohibiting individuals from moving from one caste into another.

race
A broad human population category that allegedly corresponds to distinct, heritable sets of biological attributes and often conflates geographic ancestry and physical type.

ethnicity
A social classification based on a common cultural heritage and selected cultural features such as language, religion, or dress.

nationality
A sense of identification with and loyalty to a nation-state; membership, defined by citizenship, in a geopolitical sovereign state.

client
The party of lower status in a clientage.

The concept of class has a double heritage in modern anthropology, one stemming from Europe, the other from North America. European social scientists lived in states with a long history of social-class divisions reaching back to ancient times. In their experience, entrenched social classes were relatively closed groups. The Industrial Revolution and the French Revolution promised to end the oppressive privileges of the ruling class and to equalize everyone's access to wealth. However, class divisions did not wither away in Europe during the nineteenth century; they just changed their contours. Followers of Karl Marx judged that, at best, an old ruling class had been displaced by a new one: feudal aristocrats had been replaced by bourgeois capitalists. The lowest level in European societies—rural peasants—were partially displaced as well with the appearance of the urban working class. But the barriers separating those at the top of the class hierarchy from those at the bottom seemed just as rigid as ever.

Significantly, Marx defines classes in terms of their members' different relations to the means of production. This means that as long as a particular set of unequal productive relations flourishes in a society, the classes defined by these unequal roles in the division of labour will also persist. The French Revolution had triggered the displacement of aristocrats and peasants, who had played the key roles in European feudalism, only to replace them with new key classes—industrial entrepreneurs and the industrial working class—that were linked together within the capitalist mode of production. In time, Marx predicted, these industrial workers would become the new "leading class," rising up to oust capitalists when the socialist revolution came.

As Marx was well aware, all those who are linked to the means of production in the same way (e.g., as workers) do not often recognize what they have in common and may therefore fail to develop the kind of solidarity—the "class consciousness"—that could, in Marx's view, lead to revolution. Indeed, the possibility of peasant- or working-class solidarity in many of the stratified societies studied by anthropologists is actively undercut by institutions of **clientage**. Clientage describes relationships between individuals—**patrons** and

clientage
Institution linking individuals from upper and lower levels in a stratified society.

patron
The party of higher status in a clientage.

clients—rather than groups. Stratified societies united by links of clientage can be very stable. Low-status clients believe their security depends on finding a high-status individual who can protect them. For example, clientage is characteristic of *compadrazgo* relationships (discussed in Chapter 6), especially when the ritual parents are of higher social status than the biological parents. In fact, the Latin American societies in which *compadrazgo* flourishes are class societies, and parents who are peasants or workers often seek landowners or factory owners as *compadres*.

Marx's view of class is clearly different from the traditional view of class in North America. For generations, North Americans have assumed that individuals may pursue wealth, power, and prestige unhampered by the unyielding class barriers characteristic of "Old World" societies. This assumption is the basis for what is commonly referred to as the "American Dream," but this "dream" of equal opportunity for upward class mobility has more than a little currency here in Canada as well. As a result, many social scientists trained in North America have tended to define social classes primarily in terms of income level and to argue that such social classes are open, porous, and permeable rather than rigid and exclusionary. Yet the promise of equal opportunity for upward class mobility has not been fully realized.

In the early twentieth century, social scientists began to investigate race as a class mobility–limiting factor in North America. In the United States, black and white social scientists concluded that an unyielding "colour bar" prevented upward class mobility. First applied to citizens with African ancestry, the analysis could also be extended to Indigenous peoples and other non-white racial groups. One participant in these early studies, an anthropologist named W. Lloyd Warner (1936), argued that the colour bar looked more like the rigid barrier reported to exist between castes in India than the supposedly permeable boundary separating social classes. In Warner's interpretation, membership in a caste is ascribed at birth, and individuals are not allowed to move from one caste into another. While membership in a social class is also ascribed at birth, individual social mobility between classes is possible. Warner's distinction between *caste* and *class* became standard for decades in North American cultural anthropology.

Is this a plausible contrast? The aspect of caste that impressed Warner was the reported rigidity of the barrier between castes, which seemed much like the barrier separating blacks and whites in the United States. But in 1948, a black Trinidadian American sociologist named Oliver Cromwell Cox rejected an equation between caste and race. Cox pointed out that many authorities on caste in India claimed that Hindu castes were harmoniously integrated within a *caste system* shaped by Hindu religious beliefs about purity and pollution. Most importantly, it appeared that members of low-ranked "impure" castes did not challenge the caste system even though it oppressed them. If this were true, Cox concluded, caste relations were *unlike* race relations in the United States, and by extension Canada, because whites had imposed the colour bar and only by force had they been able to repress black resistance to this injustice. Social scientist Ursula Sharma (1999) points out, however, that both Warner and Cox were relying on an understanding of Hindu castes that, today, is considered highly misleading. Indeed, more recently, both *race* and *caste* have been considered as metaphorical constructs that have been employed to various ends in sociopolitical struggles (Reddy 2005).

Caste

The word *caste* comes from the Portuguese word *casta*, meaning "chaste." Portuguese explorers applied the term to the stratification systems they encountered in South Asia in the sixteenth century. They understood that these societies were divided into a hierarchy of ranked subgroups, each of which was "chaste" in the sense that sexual and marital links across group boundaries were forbidden. Most Western scholars have taken the stratification system of India as the prototype of caste stratification, and some insist that caste cannot properly be said to exist outside India. Others, however, do find value in applying the term to forms of social stratification, developed elsewhere, that bear a certain resemblance to the Indian pattern.

Caste in India

The term *caste*, as most Western observers use it, collapses two different South Asian concepts:

1. **varna**, which refers to the widespread notion that Indian society is ideally divided into four functional subdivisions: priests, nobility (rulers and warriors), commoners (farmers and merchants), and labourers or servants; and
2. **jāti**, which refers to localized, named, endogamous groups.

Although jāti names are frequently the names of occupations (e.g., farmer, saltmaker), there is no conventional way to group the many local jātis within one of the four varnas, which is why jāti members can disagree with others about where their own jāti ought to belong. In any case, varna divisions are more theoretical in nature, whereas jāti divisions are more significant in most of the local village settings where anthropologists have traditionally conducted fieldwork.

Villagers in the southern Indian town of Gopalpur (see Map 12.1) defined a jāti for American anthropologist Alan Beals while he was working among them in the 1950s. They described it as "a category of men thought to be related, to occupy a particular position within a hierarchy of jātis, to marry among themselves, and to follow particular practices and occupations" (Beals 1962: 25). They also compared the relationship between jātis of different rank to the relationship between brothers. Ideally, they said, members of low-ranking jātis respect and obey members of high-ranking jātis, just as younger brothers respect and obey older brothers.

varna

Traditional social ranks that divide Indian society into four functional subdivisions: priests, nobility (rulers and warriors), commoners (farmers and merchants), and labourers or servants.

jāti

A localized, named, endogamous group.

MAP 12.1 Gopalpur

The villagers were aware of at least fifty different jātis, although not all were represented in their village. Because jātis have different occupational specialties that they alone can perform, these villagers were sometimes dependent on the services of outsiders. For example, there was no member of the Washerman jāti in Gopalpur. As a result, a member of that jāti from another village had to be employed when people in Gopalpur wanted their clothes cleaned ritually or required clean cloth for ceremonies. Indeed, it is often in the context of ritual that jāti interdependence is most clear:

> To arrange a marriage, to set up the doorway of a new house, to stage a drama, or to hold an entertainment, the householder must call on a wide range of jātis. The entertainment of even a modest number of guests requires the presence of the Singer. The Potter must provide new pots in which to cook the food; the Boin from the Farmer jāti must carry the pot; the Shepherd must sacrifice the goat; the Crier, a Saltmaker, must invite the guests. To survive, one requires the co-operation of only a few jātis; to enjoy life and do things in the proper manner requires the co-operation of many (Beals 1962: 41).

FIGURE 12.2 Gautam Ganu Jadhao, a city worker, removes a cart full of sewage waste from a Mumbai neighbourhood in July 2005. People like him, whose occupations are characterized as polluting, are ranked at the bottom of Hindu caste society.

Traditionally, members of certain Jātis are restricted from eating certain foods. Food taboos have a ritual significance that affects interactions between members of different jātis. In Hindu belief, certain foods and occupations are classed as pure and others as polluting. In theory, all jātis are ranked on a scale from purest to most polluted. Ranked highest of all are the vegetarian Brahmins (priests), who are pure enough to approach the gods. Carpenters and Blacksmiths, who also eat a vegetarian diet, are also assigned a high rank. Below the vegetarians are those who eat "clean," or "pure," meat. In Gopalpur, this group of jātis included Saltmakers, Farmers, and Shepherds, who eat sheep, goats, chicken, and fish but not pork or beef. The lowest-ranking jātis are "unclean" meat-eaters, who include Stoneworkers and Basketweavers (who eat pork) as well as Leatherworkers (who eat pork and beef). Occupations that involve slaughtering animals or touching polluted things are themselves polluting (Figure 12.2). Jātis that traditionally carry out such activities as butchering and washing dirty clothing are ranked below jātis whose traditional work does not involve polluting activities.

Hindu dietary rules also deal with the circumstances in which members of one jāti may accept food prepared by members of another. Members of a lower-ranking jāti may accept any food prepared by members of a higher-ranking jāti. Members of a higher-ranking jāti, however, may accept only certain foods prepared by a lower-ranking jāti. In addition, members of different jātis should not eat together. In practice, these rules are not as confining as they appear. In Gopalpur, "eating together" means "eating from the same dish or sitting on the same line.... Members of quite different jātis may eat together if they eat out of separate bowls and if they are facing each other or turned slightly away from each other" (Beals 1962: 41). Members of jātis that are close in rank often share food and eat together on a daily basis. Strict observance of the rules is saved for ceremonial occasions.

In Gopalpur, certain non-Hindus were also loosely incorporated into the jāti system. Muslims, for example, were given a place based on the characteristics locals attributed to them as a group. Muslims had long held political power in the region, so political powerfulness was considered to be an important attribute of Muslim identity. In addition, Muslims do not eat pork or the meat of animals that have not been ritually slaughtered. Taken together, these characteristics allowed Muslims to be ranked above the Stoneworkers and Basketweavers, who eat pork. However, they were considered to be eaters of unclean meat because they eat beef.

There is no direct correlation between the status of a jāti on the scale of purity and pollution and the class status of members of that jāti. For example, the high status of Brahmins meant that "there are a relatively large number of ways in which a poor Brahmin may become wealthy" (Beals 1962: 37). Similarly, members of low-status jātis may find their attempts to amass wealth curtailed by the opposition of their status superiors. In Gopalpur, a group of Farmers and Shepherds attacked a group of Stoneworkers who had purchased good rice land in the village. Those Stoneworkers were eventually forced to buy inferior land elsewhere. In general, however, regardless of jāti, a person who wishes to advance economically "must be prepared to defend his gains against jealous neighbours. Anyone who buys land is limiting his neighbour's opportunities to buy land. Most people safeguard themselves by tying themselves through indebtedness to a powerful landlord who will give them support when difficulties are encountered" (39).

Beals's study of Gopalpur documented three dimensions of caste relations that remain particularly relevant to our understanding of caste in India. First, Beals noted that jāti membership mattered most on ritual occasions. In the years since Beals's study, many village rituals that were once associated with caste have become less widely practised. In large part, this development has resulted from the fact that large numbers of Indians have moved to large cities where they are surrounded by strangers whose caste membership they do not know (Sharma 1999: 37). City dwellers still use the idiom of purity and pollution in debates on castes and status, but these debates usually have nothing to do with rituals.

Second, Beals described members of middle-ranking jātis who treated one another as equals outside of ritual contexts. Political scientist Subrata Mitra points out that "by the 1960s, electoral mobilization had led to a new phenomenon called *horizontal mobilization*, whereby people situated at comparable levels within the local caste hierarchy came together in caste associations," many of which formed new political parties to support their own interests (1994: 61). Moreover, increased involvement of Indians in capitalist market practices has led to "a proliferation of modern associations that use traditional ties of jāti and varna to promote collective economic well-being" (65). The interests that draw jātis into coalitions "often turn out to be class interests. . . . This does not mean that caste and class are the same, since commentators note caste as blurring class divisions as often as they express them. Rather it tells us that class and caste are not . . . antithetical" (Sharma 1999: 68).

Third, Beals showed that members of middle-ranking jātis were willing to use violence to block the upward economic mobility of members of a low-ranking jāti. Similar behaviour has been reported in the work of other anthropologists working in India around the same time. Gerald Berreman, for example, who did fieldwork in a peasant village in northern India during the late 1950s, observed that members of higher-ranking castes "rely heavily on threats of economic and physical sanctions to keep their subordinates in line" (1962: 15–16).

In recent years, a number of low-caste groups in urban India have undertaken collective efforts to lift themselves off the bottom of society, either by imitating the practices of higher castes (a process called *Sanskritization*) or by converting to a non-Hindu religion (such as Buddhism or Christianity) in which caste plays no role. Typically, however, these moves have had no effect in changing the negative stereotypes of so-called "untouchables" held by the so-called "clean" castes. However, the constitution of India prohibits the practice of untouchability, and the national government has acted to improve the lot of the low castes by regularly passing legislation designed to improve their economic and educational opportunities. In some cases, these measures seem to have succeeded, but caste-related violence continues to be a serious problem in both rural and urban settings.

Caste in Other Societies

Over the years, anthropologists have applied the concept of caste to systems of social stratifications outside of India as well. For example, Jacques

Maquet (1970) used it to describe the closed, endogamous ranked strata of the Tutsi, Hutu, and Twa peoples in the central African kingdom of Rwanda prior to 1959. Pierre van den Berghe (1970) documented caste-like relationships in southern Africa, beginning with white settlement in the area and culminating in the twentieth-century "colour caste" system that was enforced in apartheid South Africa. George De Vos and Hiroshi Wagatsuma (1966) used the term *caste* to describe the Burakumin of Japan—low-ranking endogamous groups, traditionally associated with polluting occupations, who have been subject to dehumanizing stereotypes and residential segregation from other Japanese people. Similarly low-ranking "caste" groups include the Cagots in Spain and France and the Al-Akhdam in Yemen. Ursula Sharma (1999) has also suggested that the concept of caste might be fruitfully used to characterize the relations between the Roma people of Europe and their non-Roma neighbours, who for centuries have subjected the Roma to stigmatization, social segregation, and economic exclusion (1999: 85–6; Figure 12.3).

A key element recognized by all anthropologists who use the concept of caste is the endogamy that is forced, at least in theory, on the members of each ranked group. As van den Berghe puts it, membership in such groups is "determined by birth and for life" (1970: 351). Sharma highlights the significance of the link between descent and caste, observing that "in societies where descent is regarded as a crucial and persistent principle (however reckoned, and whatever ideological value it is given), almost any social cleavage can become stabilized in a caste-like form" (1999: 85).

But the principle of descent has also played a central role in the identification and persistence of race, ethnicity, and nationality. These three categories are all closely bound with historical developments over the past five hundred years that have built the modern world. Indeed, these categories are particularly significant in nation-states, and many contemporary nation-states are of very recent, post-colonial origin. Clearly, to make sense of contemporary post-colonial forms of social stratification, we will also need some understanding of the categories of race, ethnicity, and nationality.

racialism

Belief in the existence of biologically distinct races.

Race

The concept of race developed in the context of European exploration and conquest beginning in the fifteenth century. Europeans conquered Indigenous peoples in the Americas and established colonial political economies that soon depended on the labour of Africans imported as slaves. By the end of the nineteenth century, light-skinned Europeans had established colonial rule over large territories inhabited by darker-skinned peoples, marking the beginnings of a global racial order (see Smedley 1998; Painter 2010). Both as a way of explaining the existence of the human diversity they had encountered, and as a way of justifying their domination over Indigenous peoples and enslavement of Africans, European intellectuals argued that the human species was subdivided into "natural kinds" of human beings called *races* that could be sharply distinguished from one another on the basis of outward physical (or *phenotypic*) appearance. All individuals assigned to the same race were assumed to share many features other than just clearly visible physical characteristics.

Belief in the existence of biologically distinct races (sometimes called **racialism**) was then joined to an ancient Western notion called the "Great Chain of Being," which proposed that all "natural kinds" could be ranked in a hierarchy. In the latter half of the nineteenth century,

FIGURE 12.3 Social and economic segregation of the Roma people continues to this day. The problem is particularly problematic in western Europe, where longstanding prejudices against the Roma influence political decisions in many countries, and Roma people must often participate in alternative economies to support themselves.

IN THEIR OWN WORDS | The Slave Narrative in Life History and Myth

American anthropologist Susan J. Rasmussen draws on her experiences with the Tuareg people of Niger as she speaks to us on the slave "story" and identity.

Anthropologists and narrators may become mutually implicated with one another in a variety of ways. As a researcher among the Tuareg, I stood in a relationship of friendship, but also of marginality, to the community. In effect, I became a sign facilitating the storytellers in making their points. The act of constructing a life narrative can expand historical and ethnographic consciousness by compelling the author to move from accounts of discrete experiences to an account of why and how his or her life took the shape it did, at a given time, and why this was revealed from a particular viewpoint. The Personal Narratives Group (1989: 4–5) observes that the dynamics of gender emerge more clearly in personal narratives of women than in those of men. Likewise, it would seem to follow that the dynamics of social differentiation, inequality and domination, negotiation and resistance, would also emerge more clearly in slave narratives than in non-slave narratives. Or do they? Former slave and noble both used the experience of marginality and interdependence as a device by which to express their sense of how they have been treated in the post-colonial era. The tales of Tama the noble woman, as a discourse on servitude, in effect complement the narrative of the former slave man although they are not mirror images of each other. Gender and age were shown to be significant in both of them, in historical memory as well as social practice. Women and former slaves were also revealed as united in certain contexts, rather than always competing or opposed.

Discourse about past servitude offers an expressive vocabulary that provides not only reflection about social stratification and gender but also meaning for suffering from any basis of declared social difference. Additionally, these slave narratives—both in life history and myth—empower, each in their own manner. They enable an inversion of deprivation and effect a recasting of roles and relationships in a way that does not merely recreate social difference or redirect oppression but that reconciles the interests of all the parties to the narratives. There emerges from them an expanded consciousness, on the part of local residents of diverse origins and outside anthropologists in the audiences. The personal slave narrative/life history and the mythology about slavery constitute a counterpoint through which Atakor and other Tuareg remember, but also recast, their social and political history.

Source: Rasmussen, Susan J. 1999. "The Slave Narrative in Life History and Myth, and Problems of Ethnographic Representation of the Tuareg Cultural Predicament," *Ethnohistory* 46, 1: 67–108.

European thinkers, including many anthropologists, devised schemes for ranking the "races of mankind" from lowest to highest. Not surprisingly, the "white" Europeans at the apex of imperial power were placed at the top of this global hierarchy. Darker-skinned peoples, like the Indigenous inhabitants of the Americas or of Asia, were ranked somewhere in the middle. But Africans, whom Europeans had bought and sold as slaves, ranked lowest of all. In this way, the identification of races was transformed into **racism** (Figure 12.4).

However, it is important to emphasize that races are *imagined communities* that *do not correspond to major biological differences* within the human species. Although our species as a whole exhibits great variation in phenotypic attributes such as skin colour, hair texture, and stature, these variations do not naturally clump into separate populations with stable boundaries that can be sharply distinguished from one another. Put another way, the traditional concept of race in Western society is biologically and genetically meaningless.

Even though the concept of race is biologically meaningless, however, racial thinking persists in the twenty-first century, and the concept of race continues to be used as a culturally constructed social category. The end result is a highly distorted, but seemingly coherent, set of criteria that members of a society can use to assign people to one culturally defined racial category or another. Once this happens, members of a society can treat racial categories *as if* they reflect biological reality, using them to build institutions that include or exclude particular "races." In this way, race can become "real" in its consequences, even if it has no reality in biology.

Since the days of colonialism, white domination of Euro-American and Euro-Canadian racial hierarchies has been a constant. However, some anthropologists who study the cultural construction of whiteness point out that, even in North America, "whiteness" is not monolithic

racism
The systematic oppression of members of one or more socially defined "races" by members of another socially defined "race" that is justified within the ruling society by the rulers' faulty belief in their own biological superiority.

FIGURE 12.4 Racism has been common in countries that were colonized by Europeans. In South Africa, for example, apartheid policies forced the majority population of non-whites into positions of subordination under the ruling white minority. Think back to Chapter 11. What types of power do policies such as these give to those implementing them?

and that the cultural attributes supposedly shared by "white people" have varied in different times and places. Some members of white ruling groups in the southern United States, for example, have traditionally distanced themselves from lower-class whites, whom they call "white trash." And in South Africa, the meaning of "whiteness" has been complicated by differences of class and culture separating British South Africans from Afrikaners (Hartigan 1997). Moreover, the sharp "caste-like" racial divide between blacks and whites in North America has become complicated by increasing numbers of citizens who identify with so-called "brown" (Latin American/Hispanic or South Asian) and yellow (Asian) racial categories. Anthropologists and others recognize that racial categorization and repression take different forms in different places. As we shall see, anthropologists working in Latin America describe racial practices that do not match those characteristic of the United States and Canada.

Race in Colonial Oaxaca

Anthropologist John Chance studied the development of ideas about race and class in the city of Oaxaca, Mexico (see EthnoProfile 12.1). Oaxaca (known as *Antequera* during the period of Spanish colonial domination) is a highland city founded in an area that was densely populated, prior to the Spanish conquest, by Indigenous people. Chance (1978) examined how social stratification changed from the period of Spanish conquest, in 1521, to the early years of the Mexican war of independence, in 1812. He used an anthropological perspective to interpret census records, wills, and other archival materials preserved in Mexico and Spain. As a result, he was able to show that changes occurred both in the categories used to describe social groups and in the meanings attached to those categories, with associated changes in the dynamics of social stratification itself.

When the Spanish arrived in Mexico in 1521, they found a number of Indigenous societies organized into stratified states. The Aztecs, for example, were divided into an upper ruling stratum of nobles and a lower, commoner stratum. The Spanish conquerors also came from a society stratified into a system of *estates*, which were legally recognized social categories entitled to a voice in government. European estates prototypically included the nobility, the clergy, and the common people. By 1529, African slaves had been brought to New Spain. The colonizers in colonial Oaxaca reworked the European notion of estates to accommodate these new arrivals by assigning people membership into one or another estate on the basis of their observable physical traits, including skin colour.

In general, the "white" Spanish formed the nobility and the clergy; Indigenous groups were merged together to form the common people, and "black" African slaves formed a final layer at the bottom of the colonial hierarchy. There were exceptions to this system, however. Indigenous nobles were given special status in post-conquest society and were used by the colonial administration to control the common people. Moreover, the conquistadors, who brought no Spanish women with them, soon established sexual relationships with local Indigenous women. In the early years, if these unions involved marriage, the offspring were usually considered Spanish, but if they were casual or clandestine, the offspring were more likely to be considered Indigenous. Over the years, sexual relations between Europeans, Indigenous peoples, and Africans created a population of mixed descent. According to the system of estates, people of mixed ancestry were not supposed to exist. By

EthnoProfile 12.1 | Colonial Oaxaca (1521–1812)

Region North America

Nation Mexico

Language Mixtec, an Oto-Manguean language

Population 18,000 (1792)

Environment High mountain river basin; temperate

Livelihood Administrative centre; clothing and textile industries

Political organization Colony of Spain

For more information Chance, John. 1978. *Race and Class in Colonial Oaxaca* (Stanford: Stanford University Press).

the mid-sixteenth century, however, their numbers and their economic importance made them impossible to ignore. As a result, the rulers of New Spain developed the *sistema de castas* to classify all people of mixed racial heritage (Figure 12.5). The first castas recognized were *mestizos* (people of mixed Spanish and Indigenous descent) and *mulattos* (people who showed evidence of African ancestry).

As soon as there were enough mestizos and mulattos to attract attention, the colonial government tried to limit their social mobility by legal means. Yet their status was ambiguous. Mestizos were ranked above mulattos because they had no African ancestry, but they were ranked below the Spanish because of their "illegitimacy." In cases where Indigenous and Spanish people were legally married, their children were called *españoles* (Spaniards). They were distinguished from *españoles europeos* (Spaniards born in Spain). In later years, the term *creole* (*criollo*) was also used to refer to people of mixed Indigenous and Spanish ancestry. Some mestizos managed to obtain elite privileges, such as the right to carry arms. Most mulattos were classed with Africans and could be enslaved. Yet free mulattos could also apply for the right to carry arms, which shows that even their status was ambiguous.

During the seventeenth century, the castas were acknowledged as legitimate strata in the system of colonial stratification. A number of new castas were recognized: *castizo* (a person of mixed Spanish and mestizo descent), *mulatto libre* ("free mulatto"), *mulatto esclavo* ("mulatto slave"), *negro libre* ("free black"), and *negro esclavo* ("black slave"). Perhaps most striking

FIGURE 12.5 By the late eighteenth century, the number of castas recognized in Mexico had proliferated. This painting displays 16 different outcomes of various cross-casta matings. Note that the child of a castizo (who has three Spanish grandparents) and an española (who has four Spanish grandparents) would be an español. The painting attempts to represent not only the phenotypes of different castas but also the relative social statuses their members might occupy, as suggested by the clothing they wear (note especially the presence or absence of shoes).

is the *castizo* category. This seems to have been designed by the colonial elite to stem the tide of ever "whiter" mestizos who might be mistaken for genuine Spaniards. Chance points out that racial mixing was primarily an urban phenomenon and that individuals of Spanish–Indigenous descent perceived themselves, and were perceived by the elite, as belonging to Hispanic rather than Indigenous society (1978: 126). It is perhaps not surprising that lighter-skinned castas became increasingly indistinguishable from middle-class and lower-class creoles. In fact, census records in Oaxaca list creoles as the largest segment of the city's population throughout the entire colonial period.

Other Stratification Systems

As if the *sistema de castas* were not enough, colonial society in Oaxaca recognized three additional systems of classification that cut across the castas. One distinguished groups required to pay tribute to the Spanish crown (Indigenous groups, Africans, and mulattos) from everyone else. The second distinguished *gente de razon* ("rational people," who practised the Hispanic culture of the city) from *indios* (the rural, culturally distinct Indigenous population). And a third distinguished *gente decente* ("respectable people") from *la plebe* (the "common people"). Chance suggests that the last distinction, which made the most sense in the urban setting, represented the beginning of socioeconomic classes (1978: 127).

Mobility in the Casta System

Throughout the colonial period, the boundaries of the stratification system in Oaxaca were most rigid for those of "unmixed" Indigenous, African, and European descent. Those of mixed background had the most ambiguous status and therefore the greatest opportunity to improve it. For example, when a couple married, the priest decided the casta membership of the bride and groom. The strategy for upward mobility called for choosing a marriage partner who was light-skinned enough for the priest to decide that both spouses belonged in a high-ranking casta. Over time, such manoeuvring swelled the ranks of the creoles.

The growth of the population coincided with the transformation of the colonial economy from one based on tribute and mining to one based on commercial capitalism. The prosperity this transformation brought to Oaxaca was greatest in the eighteenth century, when the city became the centre of an important textile and dye-manufacturing industry. People from lower castas were able to accumulate wealth, which together with light skin and adoption of the urban culture made it possible for them to achieve the status of creole.

Chance argued that during the late colonial period, racial status had become an achieved, rather than an ascribed, status. By that time, the increasing rate of legitimacy in all castas meant that descent lost its importance as a criterion of group membership. Creole status could be claimed by anyone who was able to show that his or her ancestors had not paid tribute. At the same time, people's idea of what high-status people looked like had changed. As people with Indigenous and African ancestry moved up the social scale, their phenotypes widened the range of phenotypes considered prototypical for creoles.

Chance concludes that the *sistema de castas* is best understood as "a cognitive and legal system of ranked socio-racial statuses" (1978: viii). Anthropologists have called this sort of status **social race**. The stratification system in Oaxaca was a hybrid, beginning with closed, caste-like racial categories whose "purity" could not be maintained and ending up with open, class-like categories with racial labels.

Colourism in Nicaragua

Some observers might expect that once race becomes an achieved status, racism has disappeared. But the situation is not so simple. Let us compare the case of Oaxaca, Mexico, with that of Managua, Nicaragua. American anthropologist Roger Lancaster argues that, in Nicaragua, racism exists, but it is "not as absolute and encompassing a racism as that which one encounters in the United States" (1992: 215). One dimension of Nicaraguan racism contrasts the Spanish-speaking mestizo majority of the highlands with the Indigenous Miskitos and African Caribbeans along the Atlantic coast. Highland mestizos tend to regard these coastal groups as backward, inferior, and dangerous—notions overlain with political suspicions deriving from the fact that

social race
An achieved status with a racial label in a system of stratification that is composed of open, class-like categories to which racial labels are assigned.

some Miskito factions had fought with the contras against the Sandinistas.

But Lancaster came to see racism toward the coastal peoples as an extension of the pattern of race relations internal to highland mestizo culture that he calls **colourism**. In colourism, no fixed race boundaries exist. Instead, individuals negotiate their colour identity anew in every social situation they enter. Thus, in this system, the colour a person might claim or be accorded changes from situation to situation.

Lancaster identified three different systems of colour classification at work among the mestizos of Nicaragua, all of which presupposed white superiority and black inferiority:

1. a *phenotypic* system composed of three categories—*blanco* (white), *moreno* (brown, the category into which most mestizos fell), and *negro* (black);
2. a *polite* system composed of three categories that roughly correspond to the categories in the phenotypic system—*chele* ("blue," as in "blue eyes," used for Europeans), *blanco* (used for *morenos*), and *moreno* (used for *negroes*); and
3. a *pejorative/affectionate* system composed of only two terms: *chele* (lighter skin and hair) and *negro* (darker skin and hair).

Each system was considered appropriate to different contexts. The phenotypic system was appropriate for discussing colour distinctions generally. The polite system was appropriate for use in the presence of the person about whom one was speaking. As Lancaster noted, it was "a grave and violent offence to refer to a black-skinned person as *negro*" (1992: 217). Finally, the *pejorative/affectionate* system was appropriate in two situations: when a less powerful person wanted to express her or his displeasure toward a more powerful person, and, somewhat paradoxically, when family members wanted to express affection for one another. In both cases, this system was appropriate because it was relatively "informal" and violated the rules of "polite" discourse (218).

Lancaster discovered that "whiteness is a desired quality, and polite discourse inflates its descriptions of people" (1992: 219). People compete in different settings to claim whiteness. In some settings, individuals may be addressed as *blanco* if everyone else has darker skin; in other settings, they may be addressed as *moreno* if someone else has lighter skin. Because it allows people some freedom to negotiate their colour status, Nicaraguan colourism may seem less repressive than the more rigid forms of racism found in other countries. Yet, in Lancaster's opinion, it still represented "a significant social problem" (215).

Lancaster is not optimistic about the possibility of successfully overturning this system in Nicaragua any time soon. Similarly, anthropologist Faye Harrison argues that racial solidarity and rebellion are hard to achieve or sustain in societies where social race is present, and she is not optimistic that similar systems would have the same effect in other countries. For example, considering race relations in the United States, she fears that a "more multi-shaded discourse" would be more likely to contribute to "an enduring stigmatization of blackness" than to "democratization and the dismantling of race" (1998: 618–19).

Ethnicity

For anthropologists, **ethnic groups** are social groups whose members distinguish themselves (and/or are distinguished by others) in terms of *ethnicity*—that is, in terms of distinctive cultural features such as language, religion, or dress (Figure 12.6). Ethnicity, like race, is a culturally constructed concept. Many anthropologists today would agree with anthropologists John Comaroff and Jean Comaroff that ethnicity is created by historical processes that incorporate distinct social groups into a single political structure under conditions of inequality (1992: 55–7). Comaroff and Comaroff point out that ethnic consciousness existed in pre-colonial and pre-capitalist societies; however, they and most contemporary anthropologists have been more interested in forms of ethnic consciousness that were generated under capitalist colonial domination.

Ethnicity develops as members of different groups try to make sense of the struggle between *self-ascription* (i.e., insiders' efforts to define their own identity) and *other-ascription* (i.e., outsiders' efforts to define the identities of other groups). In Comaroff and Comaroff's view, furthermore, the ruling group turns both itself and

colourism

A system of social identities negotiated, based on the situation, along a continuum of skin colours between white and black.

ethnic groups

Social groups that are distinguished from one another on the basis of ethnicity.

the subordinated groups into *classes* because all subordinated social groupings lose independent control "over the means of production and/or reproduction" (1992: 56).

FIGURE 12.6 A train station sign in French and Euskara (Basque) languages advises that the station will be open at 9 a.m. every morning, with trains departing every 35 minutes during peak times. The Euskara language, which has at various periods in history been suppressed by governments, is a key element of ethnic identity in the Basque region, which crosses the border between France and Spain. Why is language important to a people's sense of ethnicity?

One outcome of this struggle is the appearance of new ethnic groups and identities that are not continuous with any single earlier cultural group (Comaroff and Comaroff 1992: 56). In northern Cameroon, for example, Emily Schultz (1984) found that successive German, French, and British colonial officials relied on local Muslim chiefs to identify significant local social divisions for them, and they adopted the Muslim practice of lumping together all the myriad non-Muslim peoples of the hills and plains and calling them *Haabe* or *Kirdi*—that is, "Pagans." To the extent, therefore, that Guidar, Daba, Fali, Ndjegn, Guiziga, and other non-Muslim peoples were treated the same by colonial authorities and came to share a common set of interests, they developed a new, more inclusive level of ethnic identity. This new, post-colonial identity, like many others, cannot be linked to any single pre-colonial cultural reality but has been constructed out of cultural materials borrowed from a variety of non-Muslim Indigenous groups who were incorporated as "Pagans" within the colonial political order.

Comaroff and Comaroff argue that a particular structure of *nesting identities* was quite common throughout European colonies in Africa. The lowest and least inclusive consisted of local

IN THEIR OWN WORDS   The Emergence of a New Political Paradigm

Canadian anthropologist John Matthiasson first went to Baffin Island, in the Canadian Arctic, to do fieldwork among the Inuit in 1963. He returned a decade later to carry out additional fieldwork and has kept up with events in the Canadian Arctic since then. Here, he writes about a people's name.

The names by which we refer to ourselves or others can also be used to manipulate our identity and to align with or isolate ourselves from others, as well as to rationalize our treatment of others. When I lived with the Aullativikmiut in the 1960s they referred to themselves as Eskimos, as did all of the Tununermiut. By the 1970s many of them had ceased to use the term, which was now considered pejorative. (Its etymological origins have always been murky, although many sources claim that it means "eaters of raw meat.") It was, of course, replaced in both singular and plural by Inuk and Inuit, for "a person" and "the people." The change in terminology of self-reference had, I am convinced, enormous political significance.

Not everyone accepted the change readily, and in some instances it was never adopted. One elderly man who had lived virtually all of his life in the camps told me in 1973, "I was born an Eskimo and I will die an Eskimo." However, his was to become a minority position. Others—even of his generation—soon saw the political significance of rejecting the term, and certainly that man's children and grandchildren did. This change, which was so important in the construction of new individual and group identities, was the work of the Inuit Tapirisat of Canada (ITC), or Inuit Brotherhood, a new organization that sought to create a pan-Inuit consciousness. The ITC was external to the Tununermiut, but when it offered them a new political agenda, they responded and, in the process, took further steps toward a renewed sense of self-determination.

Source: Matthiasson, John S. 1992. "The Emergence of a New Political Paradigm," in *Living on the Land: Northern Baffin Inuit Respond to Change* (Peterborough, ON: Broadview Press), 161–2.

groups, often called *tribes*, who struggled to dominate one another within separate colonial states. The middle levels consisted of a variety of entities that crossed local boundaries, sometimes called *supertribes* or *nations*. For example, the British administered the settler colony of Southern Rhodesia (later to become Zimbabwe) according to the policy of "indirect rule," which used Indigenous "tribal" authorities to maintain order on the local level. The effect of indirect rule was thus both to reinforce "tribal" identities where they existed and to create them where they had been absent in pre-colonial times. Two such tribal identities, those of the Shona and the Ndebele, became pre-eminent, and each gave rise to its own "(supratribal) nationalist movement."

Both movements joined together in a "patriotic front" to win a war of independence fought against white settlers. This confrontation took place at the highest level of the ethnic hierarchy where "Europeans" and "Africans" opposed one another, and each group developed its own encompassing ethnic identity with race as a defining feature. Africans regularly dealing with Europeans began to conceive of such a thing as "African culture" (as opposed to European culture) and "pan-African solidarity" (to counter the hegemony of the European colonizers). Conversely, in the British settler colonies of southern and eastern Africa, European immigrants defined themselves in opposition to Africans by developing their own "settler–colonial order" based on a caricature of aristocratic Victorian English society (Comaroff and Comaroff 1992: 58).

Because ethnic groups are incorporated into the colony on unequal terms, it is not surprising to discover that many individuals in colonies attempted to achieve upward mobility by manipulating ethnicity. For example, Emily Schultz

(1984) investigated ethnic mobility in Guider, Cameroon, in 1976 (Figure 12.7). Guider began as a small settlement of non-Muslim Guidar people. In 1830, it was brought into the Muslim Fulbe empire of Yola and remained a Fulbe stronghold under subsequent colonial rule. The Fulbe remained numerically dominant in town until after World War II; by 1958, individuals from over a dozen non-Fulbe groups had migrated to town, primarily from the neighbouring countryside. By 1976, 83 per cent of household heads in town were recent migrants, and 74 per cent did not claim Fulbe origins.

In Comaroff and Comaroff's terms, all these groups, including the Fulbe, had lost political and economic independence with the coming of colonial rule and, under conditions of inequality, were incorporated as ethnic groups into first the German and later the French colony of Cameroon. The colonizers uniformly admired the political, cultural, and religious accomplishments of the Muslim Fulbe. In their own version of indirect rule, they allowed Fulbe chiefs to administer territories they had controlled prior to colonization and, in some cases, handed over additional territories, whose residents had successfully resisted Fulbe domination in pre-colonial times.

In 1976, the local ethnic hierarchy in Guider placed Fulbe at the top and recent non-Muslim, non-Fulfulde-speaking migrants from rural areas at the bottom. But in the middle were numerous individuals and families of Fulfulde-speaking Muslims who could claim, and in some cases be accorded, recognition as Fulbe by others in the town. These people's narrower identity as Ndjegn or Fali, for example, nested within the broader identity of Fulbe (see Figure 12.7). Depending on the situation, they would emphasize one

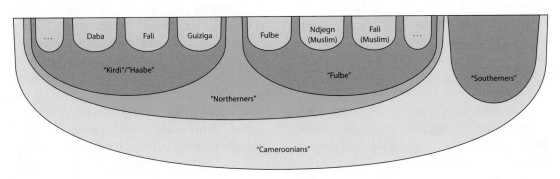

FIGURE 12.7 Nesting identities in northern Cameroon, in 1976.

Source: Adapted from Schultz 1984.

ethnic identity over the other. When with family, they emphasized their narrower ethnic identity; in urban public settings, they emphasized their Fulbe identity.

Indeed, by 1976, Fulbe identity had become an achieved status; it was the ethnicity claimed by the upwardly mobile in Guider. People born outside the dominant Fulbe ethnic group could achieve Fulbe status in their lifetimes (Schultz 1984). To do this, they had to be successful in three tasks: (1) they had to learn the Fulbe language (Fulfulde), (2) they had to practise to the Fulbe religion (Islam), and (3) they had to adopt the Fulbe "way of life," which was identified with urban customs and the traditional high culture of western Sudan. Many Fulbe claimed that descent from one Fulbe lineage or another was needed in order to claim Fulbe identity. Nevertheless, they seemed willing to accept "Fulbeized Pagans" as Fulbe (e.g., by giving their daughters to them as brides) because those people were committed defenders of the urban Fulbe way of life. Those who were "Fulbeizing," however, came from societies in which descent had never been an important criterion of group membership. For those people, ethnic identity depended on territorial affiliation of the group to which they were currently committed. In becoming Fulbe, they had simply chosen to commit themselves to Fulfulde, Islam, and life in "Fulbe territory"—the town.

This example illustrates some of the key attributes often associated with ethnicity: ethnicity is fluid, malleable, and something that can be voluntarily embraced or successfully ignored in different situations. Ambitious individuals and groups in an ethnically stratified society can manipulate ethnicity as a resource in order to pursue their interests. When nesting identities are present, people may regularly alternate between different identities in different contexts. Ethnic "Fulbeization" in northern Cameroon might be described as the formation of a "super-tribe." Like the formation of caste alliances in India, it involves the expansion of group boundaries, allowing for the creation of stronger solidarity linkages among more people of different backgrounds. When such expanded alliances actually achieve increased success in political, economic, and social struggles, they may affect the very structures that gave rise to them (as

the Shona–Ndebele alliance did in Zimbabwe) (Comaroff and Comaroff 1992: 61).

For dominant groups, however, defence of ethnic identity can be a way of defending privilege. Members of the dominant ethnic group may stress their cultural superiority and question the eligibility (and even the humanity) of subordinate groups who challenge them. It is at this point that Faye Harrison would argue that ethnicity becomes *racialized*. In her view, race differs from ethnicity precisely because it is used to "mark and stigmatize certain peoples as essentially and irreconcilably different, while treating the privileges of others as normative. This quality of difference, whether constructed through a bio-determinist or culturalist idiom, is what constitutes the social category and material phenomenon of 'race'" (Harrison 1998: 613). Racialization in Western societies would thus bear a family resemblance to castification in South Asian societies.

Harrison argues that by the middle of the nineteenth century, white northern Europeans, connecting their growing colonial power with their whiteness, began to racialize ethnic, religious, and class stereotypes associated with other Europeans (e.g., Irish, Jews, Italians, Poles, Slavs), viewing them as less human or, at any rate, differently human from themselves and attributing this difference to biologically inherited factors (1995: 52). Conversely, some racialized ethnic groups, such as the Irish, were able to reverse this process once they moved to Canada or the United States, shedding their stigma and *ethnicizing* into just another Canadian or American ethnic group. Some social scientists might argue, or at any rate hope, that all racialized groups should be able to ethnicize sooner or later. But such a perspective risks ignoring the plight of racialized groups whose status never seems to change. Historians argue, for example, that the Irish were able to ethnicize in the United States precisely because they accepted the racialization of black Americans (Allen 1994–97). With the presupposition of white privilege, non-white races in the United States "historically have defined layers of the social bottom" (Harrison 1995: 49). For these reasons, Harrison argues that attempts to interpret race relations in the United States as ethnic relations "euphemize if not deny race" by failing to address the social, political, and economic factors responsible for keeping groups like African

Americans excluded and stigmatized at the bottom of society (1995: 48).

As we have seen, anthropologists have argued about which technical terms ought to be used to describe which forms of identity under which circumstances. We would agree with Ursula Sharma that social scientists should use a particular term only if it highlights a dimension of social relationships that would otherwise go unnoticed (1999: 93). Thus, ethnicity probably needs to be supplemented by the discredited but yet used notion of race in order to distinguish the dehumanizing confinement of certain social groups to the bottom layers of society, and caste's emphasis on endogamy and hierarchical ranking highlights features of social organization that elude the usual scope of race, class, or ethnicity. Anthropologist Pnina Werbner (1997) further builds on these distinctions when she argues that in order to make progress in analyzing ethnic violence as a social force, practices of "everyday" ethnic identification need to be distinguished from racism. Therefore, ethnicity's "form and substance must be related to other social phenomena and to historical changes that contextualize ethnic identification" (Lindgren 2005).

Research on multicultural social relations distinguishes two different social processes at work in multicultural societies: **objectification** and **reification** (Werbner 1997). *Objectification* refers to the intentional construction of a collective public identity; it is the process that produces "everyday" or "normal" ethnicity. Ethnic identities are distinguished by the fact that they are "evoked situationally[,] . . . highlighted pragmatically, and objectified relationally and contingently" (Werbner 1997: 241). They are also distinguished by the fact that they focus on two key issues: "a demand for ethnic rights, including religious rights, and a demand for protection against racism" (241). Social relations between objectified ethnic groups are based on a "rightful performance" of multiple shifting, highly valued forms of collective identification based on religion, dress, food, language, and politics. Interaction between groups that differentiate themselves along such lines ordinarily do not lead to violent confrontations (229). *Reification*, in contrast, is a form of negative racial or ethnic absolutism that encourages the violent elimination of targeted groups and is central to the

practice of racism. Reification "distorts and silences"; it is "essentialist in the pernicious sense" (229). Violence differentiates racism from everyday ethnicity, and if ethnic confrontation becomes violent, then it turns into a form of racism (234–5). Making this distinction is crucial in multi-ethnic situations because when people fail to distinguish non-violent forms of everyday ethnicity from racism, they are, in effect, criminalizing valid ethnic sentiments and letting racists off the hook (233).

Nation and Nationalism

As we saw earlier, state societies are not new social forms. **Nation-states**, however, are a far more recent invention. For Europeans, prior to the French Revolution, states were ruled by kings and emperors whose access to the throne was officially believed to have been ordained by God. After the French Revolution in 1789, which thoroughly discredited the divine right of kings, rulers needed to find a new basis on which to found legitimate state authority. The solution that was eventually adopted rooted political authority in **nations**: groups of people believed to share the same history, culture, language, and even physical substance. Nations were associated with territories, as were states, and a nation-state came to be viewed as an ideal political unit in which national identity and political territory coincided.

The building of the first nation-states is closely associated with the rise and spread of capitalism and its related cultural institutions during the nineteenth century. Following the demise of European colonial empires and the end of the Cold War, the final decades of the twentieth century witnessed a scramble in which former colonies or newly independent states struggled to turn themselves into nation-states capable of competing successfully in a "transnational culture of nationalism" (Malkki 1992).

On the one hand, the ideology of the nation-state implies that every nation is entitled to its own state. (Here we could consider the aspirations of the Kurds to establish their own nation-state in West Asia.) On the other hand, it also suggests that a state containing heterogeneous populations *might be made into a nation* if all peoples within its borders could somehow be made to adopt a common nationality: a sense

nation-state
An ideal political unit in which national identity and political territory coincide.

nation
A group of people believed to share the same history, culture, language, and even physical substance.

objectification
The intentional construction of a collective public identity; the process that produces what we commonly think of as ethnicity.

reification
A form of negative racial or ethnic absolutism that encourages the violent elimination of targeted groups and is central to the practice of racism.

nationalism

The attempt made by government officials to instill a sense of nationality into the citizens of a state.

transformist hegemony

A nationalist program to define nationality in a way that preserves the cultural domination of the ruling group while including enough cultural features from subordinated groups to ensure their loyalty.

of identification with and loyalty to the nation-state. The attempt made by government officials and state institutions to instill this sense of nationality into the citizens of a state has been called *nation-building*, or **nationalism**.

States are the very political structures that generate ethnic identities among the various cultural groupings unequally incorporated within them. Thus, anthropologists studying state formation often find themselves studying ethnicity as well as nationalism. However, groups with different forms of identity that continue to persist within the boundaries of the nation-state are often viewed as obstacles to nationalism. If such groups successfully resist assimilation into the nationality that the state is supposed to represent, their very existence calls into question the legitimacy of the state. Indeed, if their numbers are sufficient, they might well claim that they are a separate nation, entitled to a state of their own. Canadians have seen this sort of separatist impulse arise over the years among French-speaking people in Quebec. This impulse led to two provincial referendums on the topic, one in 1980 and one in 1995; in both cases, the proposal for separation was rejected by the voters of Quebec. Today, the separatist movement continues to find favour among some, particularly older, French-speaking Quebecers, but overall support for the movement has dwindled over time (Patriquin 2014; Figure 12.8).

To decrease the likelihood that an ethnically distinct group will separate to form its own nation-state, nationalist ideologies typically include some cultural features of subordinate cultural groups. In Canada, the strongest example of this sort of inclusion is the promotion of French as well as English as an official language. Such inclusion is possible because nationalist traditions are often carefully thought out. A national identity is usually based on cultural attributes of the dominant group, but it also integrates specially

chosen cultural elements of other, subordinated groups. Those who control the nation-state try to define nationality in ways that "identify and ensure loyalty among citizens," with the goal of creating "criteria of inclusion and exclusion to control and delimit the group" (Williams 1989: 407). The hope seems to be that if at least some aspects of their ways of life are acknowledged as essential to national identity, subordinated groups will identify with and be loyal to the nation. Following Italian political theorist Antonio Gramsci (see Chapter 11), Williams calls this process a **transformist hegemony** in which nationalist ideologues are attempting to "create purity out of impurity" (429, 435).

FIGURE 12.8 Although Quebecers did not ultimately separate from Canada following the 1995 referendum on the question of separation, the preservation of a distinct national identity remains important to many people in the province. One reminder of this identity is Saint-Jean-Baptiste Day, officially known in Quebec as "la fête nationale" ("the national holiday"), celebrated annually on June 24.

National leaders will measure the trustworthiness and loyalty of citizens by how closely they copy (or refuse to copy) the cultural practices that define national identity (Williams 1989: 407). Unfortunately, the practices of subordinated groups that do not get incorporated into nationalist ideology are regularly marginalized and devalued, and continued adherence to such practices may be viewed as subversive. Some groups, moreover, may be totally ignored. Anthropologist Ana María Alonso (1994) points out, for example, that Mexican nationalism is "mestizo nationalism" rooted in the official doctrine that the Mexican people are a hybrid of European whites and the Indigenous people they conquered. As we saw in colonial Oaxaca, African slaves were also a part of early colonial Mexican society. Nationalist ideology, however, erases their presence entirely (Alonso 1994: 396).

Australian Nationalism

Australia began its existence as a penal then settler colony of Great Britain. Early settlers laid claim to the land and other resources under the doctrine of *terra nullius*: the idea that before the arrival of the Europeans, the land had been owned by nobody. Of course, this position ignored the fact that the land was being used by the Aboriginal peoples who lived there. In European capitalist terms, "ownership" meant permanent settlement and "improvement" of the land by clearing it and planting crops or grazing animals. Since the Aboriginal peoples were foraging peoples who did not depend on domesticated plants or animals, European settlers felt justified in displacing them and "improving" the land as they saw fit. In general, Aboriginal peoples were viewed as a "dying race," and white settler domination was taken as a foregone conclusion. This was not so different from what happened in North America.

It was against this backdrop that the Australian national identity developed. Not surprisingly, this identity was based primarily on the racial and cultural features of the British colonialists. Until relatively recently, non-Aboriginal Australians did not recognize the need to incorporate aspects of Aboriginal culture into this identity.

But times change and, for the past few decades, Australians have been rethinking the nature of Australian national identity. Indeed, according to Australian anthropologist Robert Tonkinson (1998), two kinds of nation-building are going on at the same time. First, an intense national debate has developed over the possibility of creating a new nation-state whose constitution would affirm the existence and rights of the country's Indigenous peoples. For that to happen, however, "the nation as a whole must re-imagine itself via a myth-making process, in which the search for distinctively Australian national symbols may well include elements drawn from Indigenous cultures" (Tonkinson 1998: 287–8). This will not be easy because such a myth-making process (or transformist hegemony) immediately runs up against a second, alternative myth-making process generated by Australia's Indigenous minorities who have, for decades, struggled to construct a sense of identity that is inclusive of all Aboriginal Australians. Since the 1970s, a central theme in this struggle has been the demand for land rights, which was given an enormous boost in 1992 by the court decision in the case of *Eddie Mabo and Others v. The State of Queensland*. The *Mabo* decision rejected the doctrine of *terra nullius*, proclaiming that the Native title of Australia's Indigenous people was part of Australian common law.

The symbolic significance of the *Mabo* decision has been enormous. The Australian federal government has made reconciliation with Indigenous minorities a major policy goal, well aware that "unless Australia achieves a formal and lasting reconciliation with its Indigenous people, its self-image as a fair and just land will continue to be mocked by the history of its oppression of them" (Tonkinson 1998: 291). Many white Australians and the national government are seeking ways of incorporating Aboriginality into Australian national identity. A measure of success is indicated by increasing interest on the national level in the artistic, literary, and athletic accomplishments of Aboriginal people (Figure 12.9).

While all this might augur favourably for a reconstructed Australian national identity that includes Aboriginal people, many problems remain. Some come from white Australians who reject a multicultural national identity or who see their economic interests threatened by the *Mabo* decision. But even Aboriginal people, whom the decision is supposed to help, criticize the *Mabo* decision because of its limitations and unresolved complexities. For example, the only lands eligible

FIGURE 12.9 Australian Aboriginal people marching in protest over the Australian Bicentennial celebrations, which, they argued, did not pay appropriate attention to them. Does this sort of argument constitute nationalism? How does nation-building look in your own society?

for Indigenous claims turn out to be those that have demonstrable historical connection to contemporary Aboriginal groups who continue to practise "traditional" Aboriginal customs. This not only exempts most of Australia from Indigenous land claims, it also bars most of Australia's Aboriginal people from making land claims because they live in large towns and cities and have, for generations, been separated from the lands of their ancestors.

Since the *Mabo* decision, however, expressions of Aboriginality seem to be moving toward "a more culture-centred—and to non-Aboriginal Australians more easily accommodated—emphasis on Aboriginal commonalities, continuity, and survival" (Tonkinson 1998: 289). The *Mabo* decision has recognized the legitimacy not only of Aboriginal land rights but also of Aboriginal customs. This has stimulated the explosion of Aboriginal cultural expression that white Australians have come to appreciate, as well as numerous programs that have brought urban Aboriginals into remote areas to work, to learn about rural Aboriginal traditions, and to contribute to the growth of biculturalism among rural Aboriginal people. Even in a multicultural Australia, however, many Aboriginal people would insist that they must not be lumped together with other "ethnic minorities," given their special status as descendants of the original inhabitants and victims of centuries of exploitation. Tonkinson concludes that "despite the limitations of *Mabo* . . .

its symbolic force is such that it may provide the basis for reconciliation between Indigenous and other Australians" (300). Australian legal scholar Janice Gray likewise recognizes the mixed effect of the *Mabo* decision:

> The fact that the *Native Title Act* ([Cth] 1993), which was a response to the [*Mabo*] decision, has generated no successful Native title claims leads one to conclude that the decision has not had very radical consequences. That, however, does not mean . . . that the decision is undeserving of praise. What the decision has done is put Aboriginal issues on the national agenda and paved a path for reconciliation. (1997: 67)

And it is reconciliation that is the most promising outcome of the Aboriginal civil rights movement in Australia and the *Mabo* case of 1992. At the same time, in the early twenty-first century, the struggle for Aboriginal rights is far from over in Australia, and it has experienced reversals as well as advances.

Naturalizing Discourses

We have emphasized that all the social categories under discussion—class, caste, race, ethnicity, and nationality—are culturally created and cannot be justified with reference to biology or nature. Yet many people around the world argue just the opposite, employing what some anthropologists call *naturalizing discourses*—the deliberate representation of particular identities (e.g., caste, class, race, ethnicity, and nationality) as if they were a result of biology or nature rather than history or culture, making them appear eternal and unchanging.

Naturalizing discourses rely on the imaginary reduction or conflation of identities to achieve persuasive power (Williams 1989). For example, every one of the forms of identity we have discussed in this chapter has been described or justified by someone, at some time, in terms of *shared bodily substance*. Thus, living within the same borders is conflated with having the same ancestors and inheriting the same culture, which is conflated with sharing the same blood or the same genes. Culture is reduced to blood, and "the magic of forgetfulness and selectivity, both deliberate and inadvertent, allows the once recognizably arbitrary classifications of one generation to become the given inherent properties of reality several generations later" (Williams 1989: 431).

Nation-states frequently use trees as national symbols, rooting the nation in the soil of its territory (Figure 12.10). Sometimes they use kinship imagery, referring to the nation-state as a "motherland" or "fatherland"; sometimes the territory of a nation-state itself can be a unifying image, especially when portrayed on a map (Alonso 1994). The case of Australia shows, however, that doctrines like *terra nullius* enable newcomers to deny Indigenous inhabitants' "natural" links to the land in order to make way for their own "natural" links to the land through "improvement."

The Paradox of Essentialized Identities

The struggle of Aboriginal people to defend themselves and claim their rights after centuries of exploitation and neglect was extraordinarily important in making the *Mabo* decision possible. In response to dominant groups that attempted to conflate their humanity with a narrow, unflattering stereotype, these people chose to accept their racial designation but to view it as a positive *essence*, an

FIGURE 12.10 The tree-like symbol at the centre of the Mexican coat of arms (the cactus on which the eagle stands) is a pre-Conquest Aztec symbol. It symbolizes the connection between the nation-state of Mexico and the land on which this nation-state exists. Does Canada have any national symbols that connect the nation-state to the land on which it exists?

"inner something or distinctive 'spirituality' possessed by everyone who is Aboriginal" (Tonkinson 1998: 294–5). Similar kinds of essentialist rhetoric have helped many stigmatized groups build a positive self-image and unite politically.

Many anthropologists and other observers would argue that the essentialist rhetoric of Aboriginal activists does not, in fact, reflect what those activists believe about Aboriginality at all. They would describe what the activists are promoting as ***strategic essentialism***, a term coined by social theorist Gayatri Chakravorty Spivak (1987). Most activists are perfectly aware that essentialized racial or ethnic identities have no scientific validity. Nevertheless, they press their claims, hoping that by stressing their difference they may be able to extract concessions that the national government cannot refuse without violating its own laws and sense of justice. The concessions may be substantial, as in the case of the *Mabo* decision. At the same time, strategic essentialism is troubling to many observers and participants in these struggles, for those who promote it as a political strategy risk "reproducing the same logic that once oppressed them" (Hale 1997: 547). Thus, rather than bringing about a more just society, it may simply "serve to perpetuate an ethnically ordered world" (Comaroff and Comaroff 1992: 62).

Over the years, the concept of *strategic essentialism* has gained ground in the analysis of political action in various human-rights areas. In recent years, it has also been extended into other areas of application. In the realm of environmental sustainability, for example, analysis shows that environmental groups with different agendas have come together as a single political force to add weight to the environmental movement as a whole (Dourish 2008). In our increasingly globalized world, forming this sort of alliance may prove to be an effective strategy for relatively small or marginalized "action" groups to get their message heard.

Nation-Building in a Post-colonial World: The Example of Fiji

While the citizens of nation-states need to construct a shared public identity, they also need to establish concrete legal mechanisms for taking group action to influence the state. As anthropologists John Kelly and Martha Kaplan (2001) argue, nation-states are more

strategic essentialism The use of essentialist rhetoric as a conscious political strategy to create a temporary solidarity to facilitate a specific social action.

than imagined communities; they are also *represented* communities. For this reason, nation-building involves more than constructing an image of national unity; it also requires institutions of political representation that channel the efforts of citizens into effective state support. But what happens when citizens of a nation-state do not agree about what nation they are building or what kinds of legal and political structures are necessary to bring it about? One answer to this question can be seen in the South Pacific island nation of Fiji, which became independent from Britain in 1970 and experienced four political coups in twenty years (between 1987 and 2006).

At independence, the image of the Fijian nation was that of a "three-legged stool"; each "leg" was a separate category of voters:

1. "general electors" (a minority of the population that includes Europeans),
2. "Fijians" (ethnic Fijians, descended from the original inhabitants of the island), and
3. "Indians" (or Indo-Fijians, descendants of indentured labourers brought to Fiji by the British from Mumbai [Bombay] and Kolkata [Calcutta] in the nineteenth century).

Kelly and Kaplan show that these three categories have deep roots in the colonial period, where they were said to correspond to separate "races." In the British Empire, race was an accepted way to categorize subordinated peoples, even though in many cases—as in the case of the Indo-Fijians—the people so labelled had shared no common identity prior to their arrival in their new home.

These distinctions were recognized in colonial law, and the legal status of ethnic Fijians was different from the legal status of Indo-Fijians. The status of ethnic Fijians was determined by the Deed of Cession, a document signed by some Fijian chiefs with the British in 1874, which linked ethnic Fijians to the colonial government through their hierarchy of chiefs. The status of Indo-Fijians, however, was determined by the contracts of indenture that each individual labourer had signed in order to come to Fiji. Thus, ethnic Fijians

were accorded a hierarchical, collective legal identity, whereas Indo-Fijians had the status of legal individuals, with no legally recognized ties to any collectivity.

Inspired by the freedom movement in India in the early twentieth century, Indo-Fijians began to resist racial oppression and struggle for equal rights in Fiji, but their efforts were repeatedly blocked by the British. When it became possible for them to vote after 1929, for example, Indo-Fijians lobbied for equal citizenship and the abolition of separate racial voting rolls, and they lost: the voting rolls were divided by race in order to limit representation for Indo-Fijians in government. At the time of World War II, Indo-Fijians agreed to serve in the armed forces, but only if they were treated as equal with white soldiers. These efforts were resisted: they spent the war serving in a labour battalion for very low wages, while ethnic Fijians joined a Fijian Defence Force. It was primarily Indo-Fijians who pushed for independence in the late 1960s, and once again they engaged in difficult negotiations for equal citizenship and a common voting roll; they eventually had to consent to separate race-based voting rolls in order to obtain independence.

> Thus, when Fiji's independence became real in 1970, the constitution insisted that races still existed in Fiji and had to vote separately. Since then parties have generally and increasingly followed racial lines, and the army has remained an enclave of Indigenous Fijians. When political parties, backed mostly by Indo-Fijian voters, won Fiji's 1987 election, this army took over the country within a month. The constitution that was then installed in 1990 returned to even more naked discrimination against Indo-Fijians in regard to voting rights. (Kelly and Kaplan 2001: 77)

The constitution was revised yet again, in a manner that favoured ethnic Fijian interests and seemed guaranteed to prevent parties backed by Indo-Fijian voters from winning control of the government in the 1999 election. To everyone's surprise, parties backed by ethnic Fijians lost this election as well. Another coup came on 19 May

2000. Finally, after new elections in 2001, ethnic Fijians won control of the government. The military coup of 2006 was a direct result of the continuing consequences of the coup of 2000. It focussed primarily on the Reconciliation, Tolerance, and Unity Bill that proposed amnesty legislation for those involved in the 2000 coup. The coup of 2006 resulted in the military effectively taking control of the country (Figure 12.11). In October 2008, the Fijian High Court ruled that the resulting government was the legal government.

What lessons does this history suggest about nation-building in post-colonial states? The issues are many and complex. But one key factor is that the image of a united Fijian nation projected at independence was severely undermined by legal mechanisms of political representation carried over from the colonial period, particularly the race-based voting rolls. What became apparent in the years after independence was the fact that Indo-Fijians and ethnic Fijians had imagined very different national communities. Indo-Fijians had supported the image of a Fijian nation in which all citizens, Indo-Fijian or ethnic Fijian or other, would have equal status, voting on a single roll, working together to build a constitutional democracy. However, "few among the ethnic Fijians have yet come to see themselves as partners with immigrants" (2001: 41). Ever since independence, and particularly after each coup, ethnic Fijians worked to construct an image of the Fijian nation based solely on their own traditions—traditions in which Indo-Fijians had no meaningful place. Thus, Kelly and Kaplan conclude, in Fiji (and in many other parts of the world) "'the nation' is a contested idea, not an experienced reality" (142).

Nationalism and Its Dangers

The most horrifying consequence of nation-building movements in the twentieth century has been the discovery of just how far the ruling groups of some nation-states are willing to go in order to enforce their version of national identity.

After World War II, the world was shocked to learn about Nazi programs to "liquidate" Jews, Roma, and other groups that failed to conform to Nazi ideals of Aryan purity. Many people

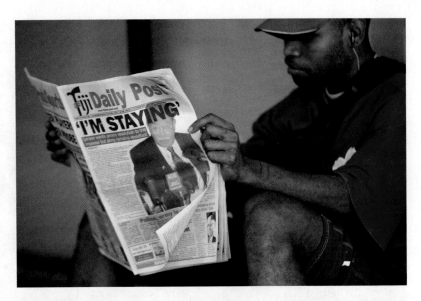

FIGURE 12.11 A Fijian citizen reads a newspaper in November 2006 as tensions rise between Prime Minister Laisenia Qarase and the Fijian military. The military took control of the government on 6 December 2006.

hoped that the Nazi Holocaust was exceptional, but subsequent developments suggest that it may have been the most dramatic example of an exterminationist temptation that accompanies all drives to nationalism. Sociologist Zygmunt Bauman argued in his book *Modernity and the Holocaust* (1989) that modern nation-states with rationalized bureaucracies and industrial technology were the first societies in history to make efficient mass extermination of deviants technically possible. In a transnational culture of nationalism, not to belong to a nation-state made up of loyal, ambitious, like-minded citizens is a severe, possibly fatal, handicap. Using violence against all citizens who undermine claims of national homogeneity and common purpose may thus be a peculiarly modern way for insecure rulers of embattled nation-states to try to bring about solidarity and stability. In the late twentieth century, warring nationalities in the former Yugoslavia used selective assassinations and forced migration to rid their fledgling nation-states of unwanted *others*, a policy known as *ethnic cleansing* (Figure 12.12). And reports of ethnic cleansing have continued into the first decades of the twenty-first centuries; many of these reports come from Congo, Libya, South Sudan, and other chronically war-torn regions of Africa and the Middle East. Additionally, in 2014 the people of the world were challenged

FIGURE 12.12 Relatives of 8,000 Muslim men and boys slaughtered in the 1995 Srebrenica massacre walk between rows of coffins next to freshly dug graves, looking for those belonging to their relatives, in a field in the town on 31 March 2003. Reflect back on the discussions of social trauma in Chapter 5. How can the concept of social trauma be applied here? Is this a case of structural violence?

for a response to the ethnic murders (as well as the murders not directly related to ethnicity) of men, women, and children in Syria and Iraq by the Islamic State of Iraq and al-Sham (ISIS). Thus, rather than relics of a barbarian past, ethnic cleansing, *ethnocide* (the destruction of a culture), and *genocide* (the extermination of an entire people) may constitute a series of related practices that are all signs of things to come. All are measures of the high stakes for which rulers of these nation-states see themselves competing.

Inevitably, such policies create populations of immigrants and refugees whose social status is unclear in a world of nation-states. As these people are forced to relocate, they may be seen as a threat in the countries in which they settle; as a result, they could be faced with new rounds of social struggle that may lead to violence.

A CRITICAL LOOK | How Do We Decide Who Gets to Shape Our Nation's Identity?

Most people do not play a direct role in constructing the identity of their nation. Rather, it is a nation's leaders who choose, on behalf of the entire group, which cultural attributes to build on as they decide what shape the nation's identity will take. The resulting identity is significant not only because it fosters a sense of community among group members, but also—and perhaps more importantly—because it defines who does and does not belong to the group. Group membership offers security and status, a place near the top (or at least somewhere in the middle) of the social hierarchy. Those who are denied group membership are relegated to the bottom of the hierarchy, with little to no social support. Thus, those who define national identity control what shape inequality will take within a nation. When these leaders are our representatives within a *nation-state*, the stakes become even higher, as they have the full force of governmental institutions, binding laws, and police and military forces behind them. The question of choosing the best leaders for the job, then, becomes paramount.

As Canadians, we must ask ourselves an important question: How do we choose our political leaders—those select few whose job it is to represent us and who, at the same time, have great power to influence our daily lives? Undoubtedly, this is a complex question. Different people have different priorities, and not everyone agrees on what makes a good leader. Yet we can begin to investigate some of the forces at work in this crucial decision-making process and, as a result, come to better understand ourselves and our society.

To begin, let's take a step back to consider what is important to us in a nation-state. For guidance, we can turn to the ideas of Clifford Geertz, one of the foremost anthropologists of the twentieth century. Geertz understood the state not as a singularity but as the consolidation of three "themes":

1. status, or *estate* ("standing, rank, condition");
2. pomp, or *stateliness* ("splendor, display, dignity, presence"); and
3. governance, or *statecraft* ("regime, dominion, mastery") (1980: 121).

As Geertz observes, modern political discourse tends to focus on the third of these themes: governance, or *statecraft*. This is true not only in considerations of the state itself but also in considerations of state leaders. However, a major problem arises with this focus on statecraft: it "obscure[s] our understanding of the multiplex nature of high authority" (121). Indeed, too often it seems that we are so "impressed with command [that] we see little else" (121).

Yet the status and pomp of our political leaders *do* often influence how we perceive these leaders' ability to govern (i.e., their statecraft). This is especially true in our world of visual media, which bombards us with photographs, video recordings, and even live video streams that show us in high definition the stateliness—or lack thereof—of our political leaders. An early example of the power of video broadcasts to colour our perceptions of political leaders comes from the first televised US presidential debate, which took place in 1960 between Richard Nixon and John F. Kennedy. The debate was broadcast simultaneously on television and radio. Americans who heard the debate on the radio found Nixon more compelling, while those who watched it on TV felt that Kennedy was the stronger leader. These stark differences in perception were attributed to appearance: Nixon, who had recently been ill and refused to wear makeup for the camera, looked sickly, pale, and tired; Kennedy, on the other hand, appeared healthy, tanned, and well-rested. In short, on TV, Kennedy outshone Nixon in terms of pomp and apparent status. Canada saw a similar drama play out in the first televised leaders' debate, which took place in 1968 among Tommy Douglas, Pierre Trudeau, Robert Stanfield, and Réal Caouette. In terms of public perception, the results echoed those of the earlier Kennedy–Nixon debate, with Trudeau coming out on top and Stanfield suffering a fate similar to Nixon's.

Today, pomp, pageantry, and posing for the camera are the order of the day among politicians in North America and elsewhere. These public figures are well aware just how much image counts, and most take great pains to always look the part of a leader when appearing in public. Top politicians even hire publicists and "image-makers" to help them create and control their public persona. Most citizens take it for granted that politicians will appear polished and play the part of the politician. At the same time, few are consciously aware of the degree to which appearance and performance influence their perception—and ultimately their selection—of their leaders.

Is our cultural focus on the public image of our politicians necessarily a bad thing? No, but only as long as it is tempered with awareness that there is more to leadership than appearance. A key responsibility of the state is to care for its citizens, and we must assess our leaders with this responsibility in mind. Given Geertz's assertion that the real business of politics is "social domination" (1980: 122), we would do well to choose carefully when selecting those by whom we will be dominated.

—Roberta Robin Dods

KEY TERMS

caste 293

class 293

client 294

clientage 294

colourism 303

ethnic groups 303

ethnicity 293

jāti 295

nation 307

nationalism 308

nationality 293

nation-state 307

objectification 307

patron 294

race 293

racialism 298

racism 299

reification 307

social race 302

strategic essentialism 311

stratified societies 293

transformist hegemony 308

varna 295

CHAPTER SUMMARY

1. All people in the world today must deal with the authority of one nation-state or another, each of which contains multiple hierarchies of stratification. Every one of these hierarchies is a cultural invention designed to create boundaries around imagined communities. Some patterns of stratification reach back thousands of years, but others are closely associated with the rise of European capitalism and colonialism.

2. The concept of class in anthropology has a double heritage: Europeans tended to view class boundaries as closed and rigid, whereas North Americans tended to view them as open and permeable. Class solidarity may be undercut by clientage relations that bind individuals to one another across class boundaries.

3. India has been taken as the prototype of caste stratification, although anthropologists have applied the concept to social hierarchies encountered elsewhere in the world. Contemporary anthropologists reject views of caste in India that portray it as internally harmonious and uncontested by those at the bottom of the caste hierarchy.

4. The contemporary concept of race developed in the context of European colonialism beginning in the fifteenth century, as lighter-skinned Europeans came to rule over darker-skinned peoples in different parts of the world. In many regions today, a hierarchy persists in which whiteness symbolizes high status and blackness symbolizes low status.

5. Although ethnic consciousness existed in pre-colonial and pre-capitalist societies, contemporary anthropologists have been most interested in forms of ethnicity that were generated under capitalist colonial domination, when different groups were subordinated within a single political structure under conditions of inequality. This process frequently creates "nesting identities" that individuals often manipulate in order to achieve upward mobility. When dominant ethnic groups feel threatened, they may attempt to stigmatize subordinate groups by "racializing" them.

6. Nation-states were invented in nineteenth-century Europe, but they have spread throughout the world. Nationalist thinking aims to create a political unit in which national identity and political territory coincide, and this has led to various practices designed to force subordinate social groups to adopt a national identity defined primarily in terms of the culture of the dominant group. If the creation of such an imagined hybrid identity is not accompanied by legal and political changes that support it, however, the end result may be political turmoil.

CRITICAL THINKING QUESTIONS

1. How has the "American Dream" been realized in the Canadian context? Does our interpretation of class mobility differ from that of our neighbours to the south?

2. Which aspects of social stratification do you consider to be associated with capitalism?

3. Discuss open and closed stratification systems. Beyond their permeable or non-permeable boundaries, what would you consider to be their main differences?

4. In what ways does the national identity of Canada incorporate elements from French Canadian culture? Does it incorporate elements from any other subordinate social groups?

SUGGESTED READINGS

Domhoff, G. William. 2013. *Who Rules America? Challenges to Corporate and Class Dominance*, 7th edn. New York: McGraw-Hill. This book has become a classic in sociology, and it is also relevant to the anthropologist interested in theory on elites, as it discusses how power and politics operate in the United States.

Magat, Ilan N. 1999. "Israeli and Japanese Immigrants to Canada: Home, Belonging, and the Territorialization of Identity," *Ethos* 27, 2: 119–44. This article investigates identity formation, management, and change, and the interrelationship of the personal, the cultural, and the national for immigrants to Canada from Israel and Japan.

Nash, Manning. 1989. *The Cauldron of Ethnicity in the Modern World* (Chicago: University of Chicago Press). Nash looks at ethnicity in the post-colonial world and sees more of a seething cauldron than a melting pot. He examines the relations between Ladinos and Maya in Guatemala, Chinese and Malays in Malaysia, and Jews and non-Jews in the United States.

Painter, Nell Irvin. 2010. *The History of White People* (New York: W.W. Norton and Company). A great book that looks at the development of the concept of "whiteness" and what it has led to in recent times.

Razack, Sherene. 2000. "From the 'Clean Snows of Petawawa': The Violence of Canadian Peacekeepers in Somalia," *Cultural Anthropology* 15, 1: 127–63. This article discusses the violence of Canadian peacekeepers in the context of gender roles and racist responses.

Schryer, Frans J. 2001. "Multiple Hierarchies and the Duplex Nature of Groups," *Journal of the Royal Anthropological Institute* 7, 4: 705–21. This article examines the links between multiple hierarchies and broad-based groups to create a theoretical framework for integrating group phenomena, social identities, and political mobilization.

Sharma, Ursula. 1999. *Caste* (Philadelphia: Open University Press). A brief survey of anthropological scholarship dealing with caste in South Asia.

Smedley, Audrey, and Brian Smedley. 2011. *Race in North America: Origin and Evolution of a World View*, 4th edn (Boulder, CO: Westview Press). This book offers a comprehensive historical overview of the development of the concept of race in North America, beginning in the late eighteenth century. The authors show how the concept of race is a cultural construct that has been used in different ways, for different purposes.

RELATED WEBSITES

French Canadian Nationalism www.thecanadianencyclopedia.com/en/article/french-canadian-nationalism

Immigration and Refugee Board of Canada www.irb-cisr.gc.ca

Politics of Racism www.japanesecanadianhistory.ca

Racism against Aboriginals www.theprovince.com/news/racism/aboriginals/index.html

Reconciliation (Australia) http://australia.gov.au/about-australia/australian-story/reconciliation

13

A Global World

LEARNING OBJECTIVES

By the end of Chapter 13, you will be able to

- understand various theories that explain how different cultures and nations have related to one another,

- consider globalization and the pressures on the nation-state,
- recognize the challenges of human rights in a "globalized world," and

- compare and contrast cultural imperialism, cultural hybridization, and cosmopolitanism.

Bedouin men take a break from their travels to check their cellphones in the Sahara Desert in Tunisia.
Around the world, modern technologies are reshaping traditional ways of life.

In March 1989, anthropologist Terence Turner published a report describing how Indigenous Amazonians had organized themselves to resist outside encroachment on their traditional lands. These peoples had long been affected by the destruction of the Amazonian rainforest, and anthropologists and other observers had often feared that they were destined for extinction. No one imagined that they would become leaders in defence of the environment, working successfully with national and international allies.

Yet this is exactly what happened. Some 28 Indigenous nations came together to prevent the construction of a hydroelectric dam complex in the state of Pará in northern Brazil. Instrumental to this movement were the Kayapó (see EthnoProfile 13.1). The Kayapó leader Payakan combined traditional Indigenous political skills with a keen understanding of the international media. He and other Kayapó chiefs toured Europe and appeared publicly with well-known celebrities, including the musician Sting, who supported their cause. As Turner observes, "The boldness and global vision of this project are breathtaking; nothing like such a concerted action by even a few, let alone 28 unrelated Indian societies, has ever taken place in the Amazon. The Indians are trying to tell us something important; we should listen" (1989: 21–2).

Unfortunately, in 2010, the government of Brazil signed a contract renewing plans for a hydroelectric dam complex in Pará. Despite continued protests from the Kayapó, other Indigenous peoples, and activist groups around the globe, the dam complex—now known as the Belo Monte Dam—is currently under construction. Upon completion, it is expected be the world's third-largest hydroelectric dam complex. It is estimated that the Belo Monte Dam will displace 20 to 40 thousand Indigenous people and devastate approximately 1,500 square kilometres of Amazonian rainforest (see Amazon Watch 2014).

This example is but one of many that illustrate how Indigenous peoples continue to struggle in neocolonial environments. In the discussions that follow, we explore just how closely the Western world and the societies where anthropologists have traditionally worked are interrelated. We also explore how those interrelationships have changed over the years. We look at ourselves as much as we look at the peoples on which anthropological research traditionally focussed. Through this reflexive exercise, we try to establish a context for contemplating the common fate of humankind.

Views of the Political Economy

Looking back, we can distinguish two important phases of anthropological theorizing in the last seventy years or so. The first phase corresponds to the period of the Cold War—from the end of World War II to the break-up of the Soviet Union in 1991—which was also the period in which European colonial empires were dismantled. The struggle was between the Western capitalist-style nations (collectively known as the First World)

ETHNOPROFILE 13.1 | Kayapó

Region South America

Nation Brazil

Language Kayapó, part of the Gê language family.

Population 7,000 (2012 estimate)

Environment Rainforest and savannah; wet and dry seasons

Livelihood Extensive agriculture, hunting and gathering

Political organization Headmen with no formal power; age grades

For more information Rabben, Linda. 1999. *Unnatural Selection: The Yanomami, the Kayapó and the Onslaught of Civilization* (London: Pluto Press); "About the Kayapó," available at www.kayapo.org.

modernization theory
A theory that argues that the social change occurring in non-Western societies under colonial rule was a necessary and inevitable prelude to higher levels of social development that had been reached by the more "modern" nations.

dependency theory
A theory that argues that the success of "independent" capitalist nations has required the failure of "dependent" colonies or nations whose economies have been distorted to serve the needs of dominant capitalist outsiders.

globalization
Reshaping of local conditions by powerful global forces on an ever-intensifying scale.

and the "communist world" (the Second World). Control of the "non-aligned world" (the Third World) was the objective. This struggle affected anthropologists who were engaged in major debates about the efficacy of first **modernization theory** and then **dependency theory** (see below).

The second phase began in the late 1980s, with the dismantling of economic and political barriers that had separated the First, Second, and Third worlds from one another. These events unleashed new patterns of movement and exchange that have come to be called **globalization**. Issues connected to globalization now dominate anthropological discussions of local, regional, and international issues.

Even today, the three-world analysis structure developed during the Cold War still has some currency. The First World continues to consist of powerful, wealthy nations, and the Third World consists of less powerful, less wealthy nations. While the Second World is no longer strictly represented by states that fit the "communist" mould, perhaps here we could now place those states and societies in conflict with First World aspirations of "development" and "democratization"—for example, Islamic societies whose ideologies oppose those of the West. To this structure, we can add a fourth category—the Fourth World—to describe the world of Indigenous peoples living in neocolonial areas of the world. Examples of Fourth World societies include those of the First Nations and Inuit peoples of Canada. Major concerns for peoples of the Fourth World include issues of Indigenous identity and the pressures of globalization.

Before we can begin to understand the complex forces of globalization, however, we must look more closely at earlier perspectives on global relationships.

Decolonization: Modernization versus Dependency

In the early days of decolonization, many Western leaders and scholars interpreted the meaning of colonialism and its consequences through modernization theory. As colonial empires were reframed as newly independent states, Western thinkers postulated that these states would become prosperous, self-sustaining countries so long as they imitated the policies and practices

believed to have been responsible for the successes of "modern" Western nation-states. Colonization was viewed as a positive process. Former colonies were viewed as "young" nation-states in need of paternal guidance from more "mature" modern states. Modernization theory became a road map that promised self-sustaining prosperity.

Yet many observers, particularly those living in former colonies, rejected modernization theory. Some criticized it for promoting a form of unilineal evolutionism in which tradition and modernity were seen as polar opposites. Others criticized it for failing to recognize that the prosperity of Western nations had *depended on* the exploitation of cheap raw materials, cheap labour, and the captive markets that colonies provided. This observation led to the development of dependency theory.

Dependency theory, developed in the 1960s by Latin American economists and social scientists, explained why most of the former colonies remained poor and weak long after they obtained independence from colonial domination. Challenged was the assumption that nations are naturally autonomous and independently responsible for their own success or failure at modernizing. Indeed, it became clear that the West would never have prospered if colonial powers had not exploited other peoples' resources to fuel their own development. As anthropologist James Peoples puts it, "capitalistic economic relations that have produced development for a few countries are also responsible for the underdevelopment of the many. People in the less developed countries [have been] robbed of their economic surplus by the economic agents of the rich nations" (1978: 535). Without the ability to similarly exploit foreign resources, the former colonies could never hope to achieve the levels of economic prosperity experienced by the former colonizers.

Although more widely accepted than modernization theory, dependency theory was not without its critics. Primarily, the theory was criticized for assuming a simple exploitative relationship between rich nations and poor nations. As such, it failed to recognize and investigate the economic strategies of peoples in areas categorized as dependent. Moreover, it treated formerly colonized peoples as passive rather than active agents, thus dismissing their efforts in shaping their own modernity (see Peoples 1978: 536).

Despite its shortcomings, however, dependency theory resonated in the post-colonial world. It drew attention to the way that dependent nations endure the reshaping of their economic structures to meet demands generated outside their borders. For example, land that could be used to raise food crops for local consumption is used to grow export goods such as flowers, bananas, sugar, coffee, and even illegal drugs (Figure 13.1). In such cases, local needs are often neglected in order to satisfy the wants of rich nations. Thus the international capitalist economic order was accused of distorting the economies of dependent nations. Analysis suggested that "underdevelopment" would persist until dependent countries took control of their own destinies and restructured their economies and their societies to meet local needs. Thus anti-capitalist revolutionary movements arose in various Third World countries, such as Cuba.

World-System Theory

An extension of dependency theory is Immanuel Wallerstein's (1974) **world-system theory**, which describes how societies across the globe are linked together through a large-scale economic system. Thoroughly rejecting modernization theory, Wallerstein set forth a global framework for understanding development and underdevelopment. He traced exploitative relations between First World and Third World countries to the late fifteenth and early sixteenth centuries, when emerging European capitalism began incorporating other regions and peoples into a world economy based on the capitalist mode of production. The Hudson's Bay Company, established in 1670, is a Canadian example of an organization that profited from this arrangement.

Originally, the European world economy was not the only world economy in existence. Perhaps its most important competitor was China. Nevertheless, the European mode was able to surpass other forms because of capitalism. "The secret of capitalism was in the establishment of the division of labour within the framework of a world economy that was *not* an empire" (Wallerstein 1974: 127). Banking, finance, and highly skilled industrial production became central, and nations with these specialties became the **core** of the European world economy. The core (i.e., powerful Western nations) exploited the

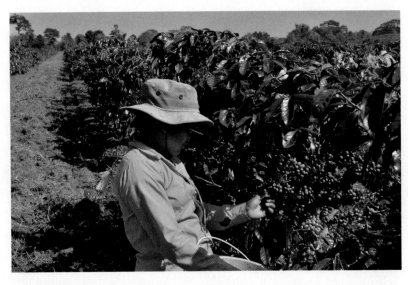

FIGURE 13.1 A farmer picks coffee berries on a plantation in Laos. Because of its low nutritional value and high resource requirements, coffee is considered a luxury good. Why do farmers in "dependent" nations grow luxury crops? How might using land to grow luxury crops for export rather than nutritional crops for domestic consumption impact local populations?

periphery to support its own high standard of living. The periphery, in contrast, practised various forms of coerced labour to produce goods to support core industries, and the standard of living for coerced workers was generally low. There also existed a **semi-periphery**, which consisted of states like Mexico and Brazil that initially played peripheral roles but eventually accumulated sufficient industrial capacity and other resources to possibly achieve core status in the future.

The main critique of Wallerstein's model is that it offers only two possibilities for change:

1. units within the system may change roles (e.g., a semi-peripheral state may move to the core, or vice versa), or
2. the system as a whole may be transformed into something else as the result of a system-wide socialist revolution.

In its abstraction, the model misses the actual vibrancy of local activity.

Globalization: Developments and Debates

By the end of the twentieth century, no part of the world was unaffected by capitalist economic practices. For some individuals and groups, the emerging era of globalization seemed to

world-system theory
A theory that argues that capitalism incorporates various regions and peoples into a world system whose parts are linked economically but not politically.

core
In world-system theory, the nations specializing in banking, finance, and highly skilled industrial production.

periphery
In world-system theory, those exploited former colonies that supply the core with inexpensive food, goods, and raw materials.

semi-periphery
In world-system theory, states that have played peripheral roles in the past but that now have sufficient industrial capacity and other resources to possibly achieve core status in the future.

present an opportunity to challenge the previously unquestioned truths about development and underdevelopment. Such challenges often came in the form of new social movements (Figure 13.2). Examples include vigilante movements (such as the *rondas campesinas* of Peru; see Chapter 11), squatter movements in cities, movements defending the rights of women and of minorities, and movements protecting fragile environments. Through these movements, people were attempting to construct cultural institutions that met their needs in ways that often bypassed national governments or development agencies. Observing these widespread social changes, anthropologists began pointing out that many of the new social movements—especially those arising in formerly colonized nations—involved struggles over meanings as well as material conditions (see, e.g., Escobar 1992).

The apparent triumph of capitalism over communism at the end of the Cold War reanimated the defenders of modernization theory, now repackaged as **neoliberalism**, as Marxian analysis was dismissed. States were encouraged by international institutions like the World Bank and the International Monetary Fund to accept that prosperity depended on their finding a niche in the growing global capitalist market. The widely held belief was that market discipline would allow state officials to support economic enterprises that would earn income in the market; as a result, individuals' personal income would increase,

neoliberalism
A political perspective that promotes individual freedom, open markets, and free trade while opposing strong state involvement in personal and economic affairs.

thus eliminating the need for state-supported safety nets for the poor. Western leaders enthusiastically embraced the beckoning opportunity to bring the entire world within the encompassing capitalist economy.

At the same time, many anthropologists and others attacked the notion of "development" promoted by Western governments and international aid agencies. They argued that the source of the problems in "underdeveloped" countries was misidentified as a simple lack of wealth or resources (see, e.g., Ferguson 2002). Rather, the problems of these countries were rooted in complex political, economic, social, and cultural forces. In the more than twenty years since the end of the Cold War, the truth of these arguments has become clear. Forces unleashed on a global scale have reconstructed the global political economy in unprecedented ways, with outcomes that no one could have predicted. Today, an event that occurs in one nation can easily have an impact—whether obvious or subtle—on people living on the other side of the world. (See the "In Their Own Words" box titled "Global Fractures.") Anthropologists have found that the best way to begin understanding the intricacies of global interconnections is through a holistic approach.

Cultural Processes in a Global World

Most theories that were developed before the final decades of the twentieth century presupposed a world of relatively clear-cut geographic and cultural boundaries. In our globalized world, however, these boundaries are not nearly as well defined as they once were. Consider how various advances in communications technologies have made it relatively easy to stretch social relationships of all kinds over huge distances that previously would have been unbridgeable. Indeed, globalization is essentially an "intensification of . . . interconnectedness" on a global scale, and it involves "a world full of movement and mixture, contacts and linkages, and persistent cultural interaction and exchange" (Inda and Rosaldo 2002: 2). Yet this "interconnectedness" requires that "globalizing processes . . . come to terms with the realities of particular societies" (Inda and Rosaldo 2002: 4).

Under globalization, cultural practices have the opportunity to stretch far beyond the societies in

FIGURE 13.2 In the last decades of the twentieth century, a number of new social movements developed around the world, including the Green Belt Movement, a tree-planting project in Kenya, run mostly by women. In what ways do movements like this one challenge capitalist economic practices?

IN THEIR OWN WORDS | Global Fractures

Carolyn Nordstrom is a professor of anthropology at the University of Notre Dame. Her specialties include political and economic anthropology, anthropology of war and peace, globalization, and culture theory. In the reading that follows, Nordstrom introduces the concept of "fracture zones" as she challenges us to see the depth of the danger we face when the local becomes global in the world of war.

People don't want to look at the big picture, because they are opening Pandora's box. What happens when they open the box and see all kinds of trails. Who's linked in? What are the linkages? There are always bigger boys out there.

So it remains an unspoken topic.

It's like there are two levels of knowledge. The first is the face people want out there: "Sure, there's security, sure, we trust the reputable corporations . . ."

And then there's what is really going on.

—Sheila Gonzales, LA Port Authority, personal interview, 2004

This article introduces the idea of "fracture zones"—lines of instability that radiate out from specific and discernible crises. Fractures constitute vulnerabilities in trade networks, financial systems, economic enterprises, and socio-political services so great that the very viability of these institutions (as they define the modern state) is undermined. I followed these pathways ethnographically for over three years between 2001 and 2006—from the frontlines of political violence in Southern Africa into global supply chains and the complex relationships of extra/legal and extra/state networks passing through Europe, the US, and parts of Southern Asia. During this fieldwork, I spoke with, and at times travelled with, those working all sides of the law and state.

The example I focus on here is war, but this is not the only crisis that generated such zones. Fracture zones are often hidden in the shadows of analysis of global power relations, and thus their impact on the economic and political realities of the world often goes unrecognized. There is a logical reason for this. Fracture lines run internationally and follow power abuses, pathological profiteering, institutional inequalities, and human rights violations—actions that fill the pockets and secure the dominance of some while damaging the lives of others. . . . [W]hat are taken to be commonplace international acts of power surrounding political violence are neither logical nor innocent. They set in motion lethal instabilities that can topple political and economic systems in peacetime locales around the globe that are far removed from the site of crisis. Fractures radiating out from a war zone along countries at peace do not appear dangerous. Until a small shock. All that is needed is a slight pressure—an economic downturn, a political conflagration, a natural disaster, an armed attack—and

the lines of instability splinter, no longer able to support the society's basic service institutions. Peacetime nations that are instrumental in creating these fractures can crumble along these lines if fractures are sufficiently widespread and institutionalized.

The irony is that people often take these actions as pathways to achieving and maintaining power when the truth is far different. . . .

But what, exactly, constitutes a crisis? What are the boundaries we draw around it? Perhaps more accurately, what boundaries are we taught to see and not see, and what politics defines these? This is situated in [Ernesto] Laclau's (2000) fundamental question: "What is inherent in the hegemonic relationship?"

Philosopher Alain Badiou (2003, 2004) suggests that delving into the question of ontology is in fact delving into what he has termed "multiple multiplicities." He breaks with modernist-based ideas, which posit that all complex phenomena—all multiplicity—can be broken into constituent parts that can ultimately be traced to singularities. In other words, he does not accept the modernist equation that underneath complexity (many/much) is a singularity (isolatable "ones"). Underneath all multiplicity is multiplicity. Complexity *is*. Reducing any question to a single causal equation, a linear sequence of isolate factors, or a combination of individual generative foci is misleading—the result of knowledge traditions that break the flow of reality into unrealistic divisions.

For example, violence is first and foremost an ontological reality. . . . Certainly, the bomb is a locatable event and a personal experience. But it is not singular. It is (quite literally) simultaneously embedded in the person hit, the larger networks of interplay among people and events, the war itself, and the global values and structures that sustain these realities. All of these arenas mutually define one another—a fact critical to understanding the ontology of fractures. . . .

Taken as multiplicity, the ways in which these fractures are inculcated into the defining dynamics of the world's econo-political systems, plus the ways in which they cause dangerous vulnerabilities to the very foundations of governing and market systems, can be seen and perhaps changed. But these realities are not transparent: those who benefit from exploiting them work hard to render these processes invisible. Fractures are etched as undetectably as possible into the institutions grounding political and economic relations worldwide. The tendency in research analysis to focus on a single issue (economics, political studies, criminal investigations) helps hide the very realities that it purports to explain.

Source: Nordstrom, Carolyn. 2008. "Global Fractures," *Social Analysis: The International Journal of Social and Cultural Practice* 52, 2: 71–86.

which they first developed. Along the way, they may change form and take on new meaning, but this doesn't necessarily mean that they will lose their original significance. As anthropologist Theodore Bestor tells us, "globalization doesn't necessarily homogenize cultural differences nor erase the salience of cultural labels. Quite the contrary, it grows the franchise" (2005:18). The example Bestor uses to illustrate his point is the relatively recent popularity of sushi—specifically, bluefin tuna—in many Western nations:

> The tuna trade is a prime example of the globalization of a regional industry, with intense international competition and thorny environmental regulations; centuries-old practices combined with high technology; realignments of labour and capital in response to international regulation; shifting markets; and the diffusion of culinary culture as tastes for sushi, and bluefin tuna, spread worldwide. (Bestor 2005: 14)

In Japan, sushi remains, despite its global spread, a continuation of traditional, local food customs. For us in the West, it is a mark of the global economy.

However, not all reactions to globalization's impact on local cultural practices are positive. Anthropologist Susan J. Terrio (1996) observes how traditional French chocolatiers have faced intense international competition that threatens their livelihood as well as their cultural identity. She notes that in France there exists a strong desire to preserve the "authenticity" of the French culture:

> A universalist notion of civilization still survives in France and is strongly linked to the view that French culture itself best embodies it (Rigby 1991). Many French people see their achievements in literature, philosophy, and the arts, both high and popular, as evidence of this. Moreover, the French state and its representatives take seriously the protection of their language and culture forms from intrusive foreign influences. Current debates on the ubiquitous spread of English and the effect of European norms on traditional foods . . . illustrate this. (Terrio 1996: 68)

To the French in general, "the area of culture remains highly charged and contested" (68). This is particularly true today, as the European Union continues to strengthen the political, cultural, and other ties among European nations.

Perhaps not surprisingly, globalization does not affect all individuals and all cultures equally. Consequently, different groups and actors interpret and experience global processes in different—often very personal and unique—ways. One factor that impacts how a particular group experiences globalization is location. Even today, there exist "large expanses of the planet" that are, due to their geographical remoteness, "only tangentially tied to the webs of interconnection that encompass the globe" (Inda and Rosaldo 2002: 4). Another factor is the sort of "temporal conflict" that arises when interactions such as business meetings occur between individuals in different time zones (Birth 2007). While the meeting might fall in the middle of the day for some of the individuals involved, it might force others to lose sleep or miss out on important social events. Yet other factors involve different cultural interpretations—of everything from commodities, wealth, and consumption to "the nature of sociality and the politics of democratic empowerment" (Mukhopadhyay 2005: 59).

Anthropologists Faye Ginsburg and Rayna Rapp (1995) identify one particularly troublesome consequence of unequal experiences of globalization: *stratified reproduction*. Whereas some categories of people (Westerners, the wealthy) are empowered to nurture and reproduce, others (non-Westerners, the poor) are not. Consider, for example, how members of the elite in some nations "import" childcare workers. These workers then send their earnings home to support their own children, who are raised by parent surrogates, frequently grandmothers. Anthropologist Faye Harrison presents an analysis of feminist political ecology, noting that "the most problematic effects of globalization are engendering gross disparities in wealth, health, and life expectancy that disproportionately compromise the well-being of women and the families and communities that depend on their knowledge and labour" (2004: 1)

Undoubtedly, the forces of globalization are transforming the world in which we live. We have seen this transformation at work in the growth of transnational corporations that relocate their manufacturing operations from core to periphery, and in the transformation of locally significant cultural products (e.g., tribal masks, ceremonial costumes) into commodities to be marketed throughout the world. We have seen it in tourism, which has grown into the world's largest industry (Figure 13.3), and in migration patterns that have brought people from very different cultures closer together.

In many areas of the world, migration now happens on such a massive scale that observers speak of the "de-territorialization" of peoples and cultures that, in the past, were presumed to be firmly attached to specific geographical locations. When de-territorialized peoples re-territorialize in a new location, social conflicts may arise. Re-territorialization also generates new forms of cultural identity, as relocated populations struggle for recognition in their new surroundings while also trying to preserve connections to their culture of origin. Globalization has drawn the attention of many anthropologists to areas where people from different cultures have found themselves forced to interact with one another. Such contexts exhibit a "diffusion of culture traits gone wild, far beyond that imagined by the Boasians" (Kearney 1995: 557). Since this sort of cultural mixing is now happening worldwide, it undermines views of culture that depend upon settled peoples with distinct cultural attributes.

Where does Wallerstein's portrayal of the global processes as part of a world *system* fit now? Anthropologist Arjun Appadurai (1990) points out that ever-intensifying global flows of people, technology, wealth, images, and ideologies are highly contradictory, generating global processes that are fundamentally disorganized and unpredictable. Meanwhile, anthropologist Jonathan Friedman (1994) argues that the disorder may be real, but it is also a predictable consequence of the breakdown of Western global hegemony. In his view, these developments exemplify a pattern of commercial expansion and contraction that began at least five thousand years ago with the rise of the first commercial civilizations, each of which was characterized by its own form of "modernity." Thus, the capitalist world system of the West "tends, as in previous mercantile civilizations, to become decentralized and more competitive. Weakened and crisis-ridden, the centre is likely to decline and lose its hegemonic power

FIGURE 13.3 Tourism has grown into the world's largest industry, and tourists have begun to encroach on people and cultures all over the world. This Bonda woman presents her handmade necklaces for sale to Western tourists in a market in Odisha, India.

to new rising centres of imperialist accumulation" (1994: 2–3). As a result, "modernity in this sense is just another tradition, labile and fragile, that has emerged, however partially, and disappeared numerous times on the stage of human history"— for example, in ancient Greece, Rome, China, and India, and in the Arab Middle Ages (229–30). Awareness of this oscillating pattern reveals that "the variety of social structures documented in the anthropological literature can be understood as transformations of one or two basic types of organization in changing conditions of marginality in larger systems," based on whether they occur as a new commercial civilization begins to spread or as that civilization begins to decline (40).

Recognition of this pattern makes Friedman even more pessimistic than Wallerstein about possibilities for the future. He sees current changes in the capitalist world system as simply the latest example of "a more cyclically sinister history of civilizational systems" that have risen and fallen repeatedly throughout history (1994: 99). Friedman remains unmoved by those who suggest that anything new or hopeful might emerge from the current state of the world: "The capacity to even conceive of consciously changing the world for the better lies, perhaps, in changing the system as a whole, a system whose more general properties have eluded the storms of innumerable revolutions and cataclysm" (41). Not all anthropologists accept Friedman's arguments, as his conclusions cannot account for the "local structures" and "autonomous cultural schemes" that appear at any point in the cycle. It is this historically specific local detail—what Inda and Rosaldo (2002: 27) call "the conjectural and situated character of globalization"—that anthropologists aim to document and analyze.

Consider this: we have always lived in a world where elements of culture—ideas and material things—have made their way from culture area to culture area and across time, down through the ages. What may be challenging in the modern world, however, are (1) the speed at which this cultural transmission takes place and (2) the complexity of the range of cultural elements and other factors involved in this process.

composed of disparate ethnic groups with diverging self-interests. National governments are virtually powerless to control what their citizens read or watch in the media. Nation-states allow migrants, businesspeople, students, and tourists to cross their borders because they need their labour or expertise or tuition or vacation dollars, but in doing so states must contend with the political values or religious commitments or families that these outsiders bring with them (Figure 13.4). Is the weakening of boundaries between states a good thing?

Massive global displacements of people have characterized the modern world. In the nineteenth century, developing capitalist markets pushed and pulled waves of emigrants out of their homelands and installed them in different parts of the globe. When immigration volumes were fairly low and jobs were plentiful, newcomers could often assimilate into their new homes with relative ease. But globalization has changed all that. Today, desperate economic and political situations in migrants' home territories, plus ease of transportation, have increased the volume and speed of migration; at the same time, market crises in the countries where migrants have settled have sharply reduced the economic opportunities available to them. Thus, migrants often find themselves caught between the hope for better opportunities and the threat of failure. Additionally, their visibility in enclaves of settlement, often in the

Globalization and the Nation-State

Are Global Flows Undermining Nation-States?

In the recent past, one of the fundamental suppositions about global social organization was that the world was a mosaic of independent nation-states. The flow of people, technology, wealth, images, and ideologies unleashed by globalization, however, has seemed to suggest that the conventional ideas about nation-states require revision. Further, many nation-states are actually

FIGURE 13.4 A foreign-born student sits among her Japanese classmates. Japan is an example of a nation-state where foreigners struggle to understand cultural values, customs, and beliefs that often differ from their own.

poorer areas of cities, and the hostility sometimes directed against them by locals promotes the sense that hopes of assimilation are unrealistic. In such an atmosphere, many migrants have strong reasons for maintaining ties to their homeland.

Migration, Transborder Identities, and Long-Distance Nationalism

The term *diaspora* is commonly used to refer to migrant populations with a shared identity who live in a variety of different locales around the world. However, anthropologists Nina Glick Schiller and Georges Fouron (2002) point out that not all such populations see themselves in the same way. In their work, they describe different types of *transborder identities*, and they prefer to use the term *diaspora* to identify a form of transborder identity that does not focus on nation-building. Should members of a diaspora begin to organize in support of nationalist struggles in their homeland, or to agitate for a state of their own, they become **long-distance nationalists** (2002: 360–1).

The term *long-distance nationalism* was coined by political scientist Benedict Anderson to describe the efforts of émigrés to offer moral, economic, and political support to the nationalist struggles of their countries of origin. Anderson emphasizes the dangerous irresponsibility of the "citizenshipless participation" of long-distance nationalists: "while technically a citizen of the state in which he comfortably lives, but to which he may feel little attachment, he finds it tempting to play identity politics by participating (via propaganda, money, weapons, any way but voting) in the conflicts of his imagined *Heimat* [homeland]" (2002 [1992]: 269–70). Schiller and Fouron argue, however, that the conditions of globalization have led to new forms of long-distance nationalism that do not correspond to Anderson's original description. They point to the emergence of the **transborder state**: a form of state "claiming that its emigrants and their descendants remain an integral and intimate part of their ancestral homeland, even if they are legal citizens of another state" (2002: 357). This form of long-distance nationalism creates what Schiller and Fouron call a **transborder citizenry**: a group of people—some living in the homeland, some living abroad—who maintain strong ties to a shared homeland.

Transborder states and transborder citizenries are more than symbolic concepts: they have become formalized in law. Canada and many other nations allow their citizens to hold dual citizenship. Some countries go so far as to set up special government ministries to address the needs of citizens living abroad. This situation is very different from Anderson's notion of "citizenshipless participation." Schiller and Fouron stress that transborder states and citizenries "cannot be seen as top-down fostering of elite beliefs"; rather, they spring "from the life experiences of migrants of different classes" and are "rooted in the day-to-day efforts of people in the homeland to live lives of dignity and self-respect that compel them to include those who have migrated" (2002: 359).

But some transborder citizens face difficulties. In some cases, their efforts at nation-building may be blocked by political forces in the homeland who do not welcome their contributions. In other cases, the state in which they have settled may not welcome their continued involvement in the affairs of their homeland. Often, the severity of these difficulties depends on the tone of the relationship between the country of settlement and the country of origin.

The globalizing forces that produce long-distance nationalism and transborder states and citizens have undermined previous understandings of what nation-states should look like. In addition, they have revealed unacknowledged problems and weaknesses within certain nation-states. For example, the existence and strength of transborder states and citizenries show that some nation-states—especially those sending migrants—are actually what Schiller and Fouron call *apparent states*: they have all the outward attributes of nation-states—government bureaucracies, armies, a seat at the United Nations, and so on—but in fact they are unable to meet the needs of their people (2002: 363).

The strength of long-distance nationalism and transborder citizenries also exposes inconsistencies and paradoxes in the meaning of *citizenship*. Schiller and Fouron contrast **legal citizenship** with **substantive citizenship**. They point out that, for transborder citizens, these two types of citizenship do not necessarily coincide. *Legal citizenship* is granted by state laws and can be difficult for migrants to obtain. But even those transborder citizens who obtain legal citizenship often experience a gap between what legal citizenship promises and the way they are treated by the state. For example, a state may its treat citizens

diaspora
Migrant populations with a shared identity who live in a variety of different locales around the world; a form of transborder identity that does not focus on nation-building.

long-distance nationalists
Members of a diaspora who begin to organize in support of nationalist struggles in their homeland or to agitate for a state of their own.

transborder state
A state in which it is claimed that those people who left the country and their descendants remain part of their ancestral state, even if they are citizens of another state.

transborder citizenry
A group made up of citizens of a country who continue to live in the homeland plus the people who have emigrated from the country and their descendants, regardless of their current citizenship.

legal citizenship
The rights and obligations of citizenship granted by the laws of a state.

substantive citizenship
The actions people take, regardless of their legal citizenship status, to assert their membership in a state and to bring about political changes that will improve their lives.

who have lived their entire lives within its borders more favourably than it treats its recently naturalized citizens. *Substantive citizenship*, in contrast, is defined by the actions people take to assert their membership in a state and to bring about political changes to improve their lives. Some transborder citizenries call for the establishment of fully fledged **transnational nation-states**. That is, "they challenge the notion that relationships between citizens and their state are confined within that territory," and they work for the recognition of a new political form that reflects the realities of their experiences of national identity (Schiller and Fouron 2002: 359).

The contrast between formal and substantive citizenship illustrates that traditional, seemingly straightforward notions of citizenship have begun to break down in the context of globalization. While such developments may provide new opportunities for some, they create difficulties for others. For example, individuals with complicated or ambiguous citizenship status may have a hard time accessing state-supported social programs (see Clarke 2004; Gledhill 2001). Too often, globalization can have a marginalizing effect on the powerless. As our world continues to globalize, we must ensure that those in need are not left behind.

Flexible Citizenship among Diasporic Chinese Families

In her research on diasporic communities of elite Chinese families, anthropologist Aihwa Ong (2002 [1999]) has examined the concept of **flexible citizenship**. As she describes it, flexible citizenship is defined by "the strategies and effects of mobile managers, technocrats, and professionals seeking both to circumvent *and* [to] benefit from different nation-state regimes by selecting different sites for investment, work, and family relocation" (174). This form of citizenship has clear benefits for individuals working in business or commerce.

Although the successes of Chinese business people are often attributed by outsiders to "Chinese culture," Ong's research challenges this simplistic explanation. Many Chinese business people have responded creatively to opportunities and challenges they have encountered since the end of the nineteenth century, when Chinese merchants first became involved in the capitalist economic centres of European colonial empires in East and Southeast

Asia. They succeeded because they were able to cultivate values and practices that allowed them to evade or exploit the rules governing three different kinds of institutions: (1) Chinese kinship and family, (2) the nation-state, and (3) the marketplace.

The break from mainland Chinese ideas of kinship and Confucian filial piety came when Chinese merchants first moved into the capitalist commercial circuits of European empires. Money could be made in these settings, but success required Chinese merchant families to cut themselves off from ties to mainland China and to reinforce bonds among family members and business partners in terms of *guanxi*: "relationships of social connections built primarily upon shared identities such as native place, kinship, or attending the same school" (Smart 1999: 120).

Diasporic Chinese merchant and industrial families developed a set of values and practices that centred on the well-being of the family.

> An individual's sense of moral worth is based on endurance and diligence in income-making activities, compliance with parental wishes, and the making of sacrifices and deferral of gratification, especially on the part of women and children. . . . Children, especially sons, are expected to collect symbolic capital in the form of educational certificates and well-paying jobs that help raise the family class position and prestige. (Ong 2002 [1999]: 178)

Having managed to evade the discipline of mainland Chinese kinship and family practices, the family discipline of overseas Chinese individuals enabled them to become wealthy and provided the resources to subvert the control of the nation-state. The orientation of these wealthy families toward national identity and citizenship, Ong explains, is "market-driven." In Hong Kong, for example, in the years leading up to its return to mainland China in 1997, many wealthy Chinese thought of citizenship "not as the right to demand full democratic representation but as the right to promote familial interests apart from the well-being of society" (178). None of the overseas Chinese people she knew expressed any commitment to nationalism, either local or long-distance.

Rather, overseas Chinese families actively worked to evade the regulations of nation-states. For example, Chinese from Hong Kong who

---

transnational nation-states
Nation-states in which the relationships between citizens and their states extend to wherever citizens reside.

flexible citizenship
Strategies employed by individuals who regularly move across state boundaries in order to circumvent and benefit from different nation-state regimes.

wanted to migrate to Britain in the 1960s were able to evade racial barriers that blocked other "coloured" immigrants because of their experience with capitalism and their reputation for peaceful acquiescence to British rule. When the British decided to award citizenship to some Hong Kong residents in the 1990s, they used a point system that favoured applicants with education, fluency in English, and training in professions of value to the economy, such as accountancy and law. Wealthy applicants were also highly favoured, in Britain and elsewhere (Figure 13.5). In many countries, citizenship, or at least a passport, could be purchased by those who had the money.

Although they had managed to evade or subvert both the traditional principles governing Chinese kinship and family and the regulations of nation-states, these overseas Chinese families remained vulnerable to the discipline of the market. This was a very different market from the one that existed before the development of the transportation, communication, and manufacturing technologies that enabled people to move money and factories around the world with ease. Making money in the context of globalization required the flexibility to take advantage of economic opportunities wherever and whenever they appeared; accordingly, overseas Chinese families took steps to position family members in different settings. Ong describes one family in which the eldest son remained in Hong Kong to run part of the family hotel chain located in the Pacific region while his brother lived in San Francisco and managed the hotels located in North America and Europe. Sometimes even younger children are separated from their parents for business-related reasons—for example, they might be sent away to attend a good school while their parents manage businesses in other countries on different continents. Yet these flexible business arrangements are not without costs. "Familial regimes of dispersal and localization . . . discipline family members to make do with very little emotional support; disrupted parental responsibility, strained marital relations, and abandoned children are . . . common circumstances." At the same time, individual family members truly do seem to live comfortably as citizens of the world. A Chinese banker in San Francisco told Ong: "I can live anywhere in the world, but it must be near an airport" (2002: 190).

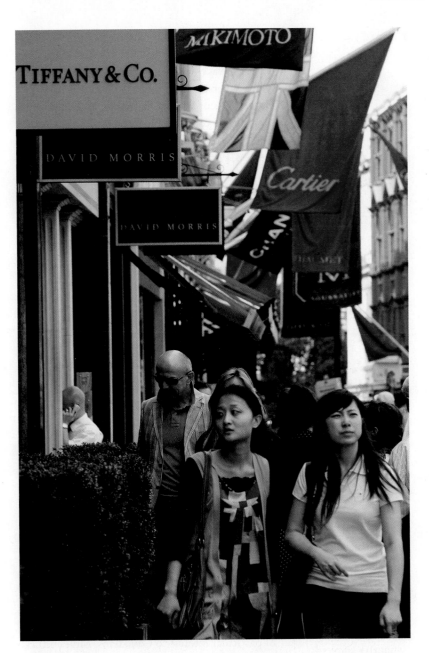

FIGURE 13.5 Chinese shoppers flock to the luxury stores in London's West End. Historically, wealthy Chinese families have been able to use their money, along with their business experience, to succeed in Western society.

The values and practices to which overseas Chinese families adhere, and which seem responsible for their tremendous achievements in a globalized capitalist economy, suggest to Ong that, for these elite Chinese, the concept of nationalism has lost its meaning. Instead, she says, they seem to subscribe to a **post-national ethos** in which they submit to the regulations of the capitalist market while trying to evade the regulations of nation-states, ultimately because their only true loyalty is to the family business (2002: 190). Ong notes, however, that flexible citizenship informed

post-national ethos
An attitude toward the world in which people submit to the regulations of the capitalist market while trying to evade the regulations of nation-states.

by a post-national ethos is not an option for non-elite migrants: "whereas for bankers, boundaries are always flexible, for migrant workers, boat people, persecuted intellectuals and artists, and other kinds of less well-heeled refugees, this . . . is a harder act to follow" (190).

Ong also points out that, on the way to their success, contemporary Chinese merchants "have also revived pre-modern forms of child, gender, and class oppression" (2002: 190). Yet neither the positives nor the negatives should, she insists, be attributed to any "Chinese" essence; instead, she thinks these strategies are better understood as "the expressions of a habitus [i.e., a general constitution created by lifestyle, values, interests, etc.] that is finely tuned to the turbulence of late capitalism" (191).

Human Rights, Globalization, and the Language of Social Justice

The original UN Declaration on Human Rights in 1948 and numerous subsequent declarations, accompanied by the intensification of processes of globalization, have created conditions for growing discussions of **human rights**. The challenge has been the emerging, different understandings about what it means to be human, or what kinds of rights people may be entitled to under radically changed conditions of everyday life. Questions of human rights become most salient in settings defined by **multiculturalism**, a situation found almost everywhere in today's globalized world but of particular interest to Canadians. Multicultural settings combine different cultural understandings of what it means to be human.

For the past few decades, rights discourses have also extended to gender politics. For example, in 1992, the Committee on the Elimination of Discrimination against Women (CEDAW) declared that violence against women was a form of gender discrimination that violated the human rights of women. This declaration was adopted by the UN General Assembly in 1993. Anthropologist Sally Engle Merry sees that this declaration "demonstrates the creation of new rights—rights which depend on the state's failure to protect women rather than its active violation of rights"; further, "the emergence of violence against women as a distinct human

human rights
A set of rights that should be accorded to all human beings everywhere in the world.

multiculturalism
A situation in which people of various cultural backgrounds live in close proximity to one another.

rights violation depends on redefining the family so that it is no longer shielded from legal scrutiny" (2001: 36–7). Although CEDAW has proven contentious over the years, other human rights documents have been signed without controversy by many national governments.

Signing on to a human rights declaration ostensibly binds governments to take official action to implement changes in local practices that might be seen to violate the rights asserted in the declarations. Human rights discourses are common currency in all societies, at all levels. After all, it is "no use imagining a 'primitive' tribe which has not yet heard of human rights," since "what it means to be 'Indigenous' is itself transformed through interaction with human rights discourses and institutions" (Cowan et al. 2001: 5).

Because of the wide adoption of human rights discourses throughout the world, some people have come to speak of an emerging "culture of human rights" that has now become "the pre-eminent global language of social justice" (Merry 2001: 38). These developments mean that anthropologists need to take note of the important influence this human rights discourse is having in the various settings where they do their research. What counts as "human rights" has changed over time, in part due to the efforts of an increasing number of non-governmental organizations (NGOs) that have become involved in various countries of the world. Many of these organizations are deeply committed to projects designed to improve people's lives and protect their rights. As Merry says, these developments "have created a new legal order" that has given birth to new possibilities throughout the world for the elaboration and discussion of what human rights are all about (2001: 35; see also the "In Their Own Words" box on the female inheritance movement in Hong Kong). In addition, because the "culture of human rights" is increasingly regarded as the "culture of globalization," it would seem to be a topic well-suited to anthropological analysis.

On the face of things, defending human rights for all people seems unproblematic. Few people who are aware of the devastation wrought by colonial exploitation, for example, would want to suggest that the victims of that exploitation did not have rights that needed to be protected at all costs. And yet, when we look closely at particular disputes about human rights, the concept no longer seems so simple. Anthropologist Jane Cowan and

IN THEIR OWN WORDS | The Female Inheritance Movement in Hong Kong

Sally Engle Merry is a professor of anthropology, law, and society at New York University. Rachel E. Stern is an assistant professor of law and political science at the University of California, Berkeley. In the discussion that follows, they discuss how universal ideas about human rights were adopted and transformed by local women in Hong Kong during the "female inheritance movement" of the early to mid-1990s. Through this movement, "rural indigenous women joined forces with Honk Kong women's groups" to fight for the reform of laws that prohibited them from inheriting land.

How do places like Hong Kong manage to employ rights language in a way that taps the power of universalism while responding to local conditions? Using an anthropological perspective, we examine the female inheritance movement . . . [and] develop a framework for thinking about . . . how and why human rights ideas moved from their global sites of creation to local social movements. Two ideas are important here: *layers* and *translators*.

We see the female inheritance movement as a coalition of distinct layers. We call the different camps "layers" rather than "groups" as a way of conceptualizing their relationship to rights language and their relative distance from transnational ideas. . . . [W]e see rights as a resource. . . . The layers of the female inheritance movement formed a rough hierarchy in terms of the degree to which they tapped into this resource. For example, one layer emphasized the rights dimension of female inheritance while another framed the issue in terms of patriarchy and feudal thinking. The indigenous women themselves, whose stories formed the narrative core of the movement, generally saw themselves as the victims of unfeeling and rapacious male relatives, although they also came to see themselves as subject to gender discrimination. The movement was an amalgamation of the ways in which these different layers perceived the issue, incorporating both particularistic understandings of grievances and the more generalized framework of human rights. . . .

[T]hese layers were able to communicate through . . . "translators" . . . [who] were able to switch between different ways of framing the problem, facilitating collaboration between people in various layers. . . . Translators, for example, helped the indigenous women recast their stories as violations of a right to protection from gender discrimination, something guaranteed by the Hong Kong government. These few intermediaries provided critical bridges between a human rights discourse connected to modernity and universalism and more particular and individualized ways of thinking about injuries. . . .

For a focus on human rights to be an effective political strategy . . . timing is critical. The Chinese crackdown at Tiananmen Square in 1989 and the anticipated handover to China in 1997 worried Hong Kong leaders and citizens concerned about protection for individual rights (Petersen 1996; Chan 1995: 27). At this historical juncture, human rights were an important source of what Kevin O'Brien terms "rightful resistance" (1996). By citing the gulf between international norms and the situation in Hong Kong, the women and their allies gained both legitimacy and public support. . . .

The female inheritance movement illustrates the localization of global ideas. Gender equality, feminism, and human rights are ideas borrowed from another cultural context, spread through the UN system of treaties and major world conferences which draw government and nongovernmental activists together from all parts of the globe. This language was clearly critical to this movement at all levels, although to varying degrees. Much has been written about the importance of technology, particularly the Internet, as a force behind the globalization of ideas, but the female inheritance movement underscores the importance of people. Much of the rights discourse was introduced by expatriates. It was subsequently picked up by Hong Kong residents who had either spent time abroad . . . or been exposed to this kind of language by others. As people flow across borders in search of jobs or education, they carry ideas with them. Cultural translators reinterpret these ideas in ways that make sense in more particular and local terms.

Success is important to the spread of travelling theories such as that of human rights. During the campaign, the indigenous women expected that the new law would allow them to inherit their fathers' property, although some also filed lawsuits (Chan 1995: 48). However, the land exemption ordinance was not retroactive, so the original claimants whose fathers had already died did not benefit. They had to file lawsuits under Chinese customary law. . . . Lack of success probably contributed to these women's disappearance from rights-based movements. Yet some of the indigenous women in the movement continued to talk about their misfortunes in terms of gender discrimination, injustice, and the land exemption ordinance. They still articulated their grievances in rights terms, even if they did not regain their property or become recognized as daughters in the lineage system. In contrast, the passage of the law gave the women's groups, some legislators, and the expatriates a dramatic victory. And it is these groups rather than the indigenous women who sustained a long-term commitment to a rights framework.

Source: Merry, Sally Engle, and Rachel E. Stern. 2005. "The Female Inheritance Movement in Hong Kong: Theorizing the Local/Global Interface," *Current Anthropology* 46, 3: 387–409.

her colleagues (2001) have noted that there are two major arguments that have developed for talking about the way human rights and culture are related:

1. that *human rights are opposed to culture* (and cannot be reconciled with each other) and
2. that a key universal human right is precisely one's *right to culture*.

Below, we will consider each in turn. We will also consider two ways in which anthropologists have been able to contribute something new to the discussion:

1. by exploring the concept of "human rights as culture" and
2. by examining some of the ways the concept of culture has been mobilized in the discussion of human rights.

Rights versus Culture

Arguments that pit human rights against culture depend on the assumption that (1) "cultures" are homogeneous, bounded, and unchanging sets of

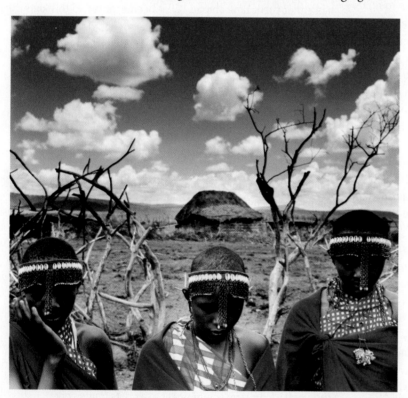

FIGURE 13.6 Among many East African people, including the Maasai, female genital cutting is an important part of the transformation of girls into women. Do you think this practice constitutes a human rights violation? Why, or why not?

ideas and practices and (2) each society has only one culture, which its members are obligated to follow. As we saw in Chapter 1, this view of culture has been severely criticized by cultural anthropologists. But it is a view of culture that is very much alive in many human rights disputes. Adherents of this view consider interference with customs of any sort—even customs that appear to outsiders to violate human rights—to constitute a human rights violation. They see such interference as disrupting a supposedly harmonious way of life and preventing those who are committed to such a way of life from observing their own culturally specific understandings about rights. Ultimately, they believe that cultures should be allowed to enjoy absolute, inviolable protection from interference by outsiders. This has been the position adopted, for example, by some national governments that have refused to sign the CEDAW declaration that violence against women violates women's human rights.

Some people defend cultural practices against international human rights discourse because they feel that such discourse echoes back to the colonial period, when colonialists blindly imposed their ethnocentric views and practices on those they dominated. However, such a dismissal of human rights discourse needs to be closely examined. In the case of the right of women to protection from violence, for example, Merry (2001) points out that although some forms of violence against women may be culturally sanctioned in some societies, there are many forms that violence against women can take even in those societies, and not all of these are accorded the same amount of cultural support. Even practices like wife-beating or female genital cutting (Figure 13.6), which in the past could be justified in some circumstances as culturally appropriate actions, are now being questioned and even outlawed in the societies where they were practised. Thus "culture values" cannot be held responsible for everything, and members of the same society can disagree about these matters and sometimes change their minds.

As talk about human rights has become incorporated into local cultural discussions in recent decades, anthropologists are not surprised to discover that the notion undergoes transformation as people try to make sense of what it means in their own local contexts (Cowan et al. 2001: 8). Being forced to choose between rights *or* culture, however, seems increasingly unviable in a global, multicultural world, especially when the rights-versus-culture debate often *exaggerates* cultural differences. Finally, it is worth asking if "culture" is sometimes used as a scapegoat to mask the unwillingness of a government to extend certain rights to its citizens. Indeed, a government's appeal to "culture" or "traditional values" is often a weak excuse for condoning the violation of its citizens' human rights.

Rights to Culture

A second popular argument about the relationship between rights and culture begins from very different premises. Far from viewing universal "human rights" as alien and opposed to "cultures," this argument states that all peoples have a universal human right to maintain their own distinct cultures. This right has been made explicit in a number of international rights documents, and it draws strength from the ideas, popularized by earlier generations of anthropologists, that cultural diversity is intrinsically valuable and that people should be free to observe their own cultural practices without outside interference. The right-to-culture argument seems to involve conceding that such things as universal human rights actually do exist. The right-to-culture position therefore shows exactly the kind of transformation that the ideas of rights and culture undergo when caught in global–local struggles provoked by globalization.

One of the key issues in the struggle to protect the right to culture—as well as any human rights deemed worthy of protection—concerns the kinds of legal mechanisms needed to ensure such protection. The great promise of international documents like the UN Declaration on Human Rights seems to be that people are now free to bring allegations of human rights abuses to an international forum to seek redress. But in fact, this is not the case.

- First, as human rights activists have discovered, human rights are legally interpreted as *individual* rights, not group rights.
- Second, the way in which people are to seek protection of their individual human rights is to demand that the *governments of the nation-states in which they are citizens* recognize and enforce the individual rights defended in international documents.

This second point has proven particularly problematic. International institutions like the UN have been unwilling to challenge the sovereignty of individual nation-states. Making the defence of all human rights, including a right to culture, dependant on the policies of particular national governments has been viewed by activists and others as a serious contradiction in human rights discourse that undermines its effectiveness. (See the letter from the Assembly of First Nations to the Canadian government in the "In Their Own Words" box, below.)

Rights as Culture

As with all cultures, the "culture of human rights" is based on certain ideas about human beings, their needs, their ability to exercise agency, and the kinds of social connections between human beings that are considered legitimate or illegitimate. The entire question of "legitimacy" in human rights discourse points to the central role played by *law*, both as a way of articulating specific human rights and as a tool for defending those rights. Under the rights-as-culture interpretation, *law* is understood to be the "world view" or "structuring discourse" that shapes the culture of human rights (Cowan et al. 2001: 11). Further, the "facts" upon which this culture depends "are socially constructed through rules of evidence, legal conventions, and the rhetoric of legal actors" (11).

Analysts who talk about a "culture of human rights" as the new culture of a globalizing world note that it focusses on the rights of *individuals*. Additionally, they note that it proposes to relieve human suffering through *technical* rather than *ethical* solutions, and it emphasizes *rights* over *duties* or *needs* (Cowan et al. 2001: 12). As such, it may have the power to de-politicize conflicts that are caused and/or shaped by cultural differences. In our contemporary world, where state structures are under stress and the dynamics of transnational and multicultural living sometimes provoke violent and bloody political confrontations, a human rights discourse capable of de-politicizing such confrontations could very well have an important role to play.

Some anthropologists see the development of such de-politicizing discourses as a vital necessity and a key challenge in a globalized world. In the meantime, to the extent that human rights discourse is conceived to be a "culture," most

IN THEIR OWN WORDS | Open Letter to All Political Parties

Living with the contradictions between international policy and governmental implementation, the Assembly of First Nations, with their significant allies, wrote an open letter to all political parties on the one-year anniversary of the UN's adoption of its Declaration on the Rights of Indigenous Peoples. Following the release of this letter in 2008, it took the Canadian government another two years to formally endorse the UN's Declaration.

Tomorrow, 13 September 2008, we celebrate the one-year anniversary of the United Nations Declaration on the Rights of Indigenous Peoples. The Declaration was adopted by the UN General Assembly on 13 September 2007 after more than two decades of negotiation and debate.

Despite having previously played a positive role in building international support for this human rights instrument, Canada was one of only four states to oppose the Declaration.

There are over 370 million Indigenous people worldwide. Indigenous peoples urgently require international affirmation and protection of their human rights. Their rights are routinely ignored and trampled by national governments, even when these rights are entrenched in domestic laws.

The Declaration affirms minimum human rights standards necessary for the "survival, dignity, and well-being of the Indigenous peoples of the world." These include the right of self-determination, protections from discrimination and genocide, and recognition of rights to lands, territories, and resources that are essential to the identity, health, and livelihood of Indigenous peoples.

The Declaration also explicitly requires that all provisions are to be balanced with the rights of others and interpreted in accordance with principles of justice, democracy, non-discrimination, good governance, and respect for the human rights of all.

On 8 April 2008, the Canadian House of Commons passed a resolution to endorse the UN Declaration, calling on Parliament and the Government of Canada to "fully implement the standards contained therein." Unfortunately, the minority Conservative government has persisted with its unfounded claims that the Declaration cannot be applied in Canada and should not be used as a standard of human rights protection in countries that voted against it.

Human rights declarations become universally applicable upon their adoption by the UN General Assembly, regardless of how individual states vote. To claim that countries should be exempt from principles and standards they vote against flies in the face of six decades of Canadian human rights advocacy at the United Nations and sets a dangerous example for other countries of the world.

Indigenous peoples and human rights organizations urge Canada to join the global community in implementing this long overdue and much needed universal human rights instrument. To continue in any other manner undermines Canada's commitment to human rights at both the domestic and international levels.

In June, a private members bill was introduced in the House of Commons, calling for concrete measures to advance the Declaration in Canada. This includes requiring the Minister of Indian Affairs and Northern Development to report regularly to Parliament on implementation. Regretfully, Parliament will not have the opportunity to vote on this bill before the 14 October election. We recommend that this worthy initiative be re-introduced and embraced by all political parties in the new Parliament.

In February 2009, Canada's human rights record will be examined as part of the UN Human Rights Council's Universal Periodic Review process. As a sign of its commitment to respecting the human rights of all, Canada should endorse the Declaration.

Our organizations take the occasion of the anniversary of the adoption to call on all political parties to affirm their support for the UN Declaration on the Rights of Indigenous Peoples. In accordance with the 8 April 2008 Motion, all parties should commit themselves to take action to ensure effective implementation of the Declaration when the new Parliament begins its work.

Source: Union of BC Indian Chiefs. 2008. "First Nations Pressure Canada to Endorse the UN Declaration on the Rights of Indigenous Peoples" (12 Sept.), available at www.ubcic.bc.ca/News_Releases/UBCICNews09120801.htm.

anthropologists would probably agree that this culture concept would be more illuminating if it reflected current anthropological understandings of culture as open, heterogeneous, and flexible (Cowan et al. 2001: 13). This understanding of culture can become an effective tool to help us understand how human rights processes work.

Culture as a Way of Thinking about Rights

To use the culture concept as a tool for analyzing human rights processes means looking for "patterns and relationships of meaning and practice" that are related to the culture of human rights

(Cowan et al. 2001: 13). Since human rights are articulated in legal documents and litigated in courts, one of the most important emergent patterns is the way these rights are shaped to accommodate the law. Groups and individuals who assert that their human rights have been violated regularly take their cases to courts of law. But this means that in order to get the courts to take them seriously, they need to understand how the law operates. They must have a realistic awareness of the kinds of claims that the law considers admissible. Further, they must know how to craft cases that will fit the laws.

Many groups among whom anthropologists work have engaged in political struggles with national governments in which they argue for protection of their rights to practise their culture freely. These kinds of political struggles regularly involve claims about protecting the culture's distinct and unchanging values and practices from state policies. As we saw in Chapter 12, these kinds of arguments for a right to culture are often cases of "*strategic essentialism*" in which the unity and unchanging homogeneity of a particular "culture" is deliberately constructed in order to build group solidarity and to engage the state in a focussed and disciplined way. Such "essentialism" often comes to dominate discussions of group rights, since the law tends to take an essentialist view of culture (Cowan et al. 2001: 11).

Because human rights law recognizes only certain kinds of rights violations, groups with grievances must tailor their claims to fit the violations that human rights law recognizes. For example, groups involved in the Hawaiian sovereignty movement have successfully achieved some of their political goals by making claims based on the requirements of their "traditional culture" (Merry 2001; Figure 13.7). Their approach is effective because they live in a society that is "willing to recognize claims on the basis of cultural authenticity and tradition but not reparations based on acts of conquest and violation" (Merry 2001: 42–3).

Outside the courtroom, many members of Indigenous groups think of their culture the way contemporary anthropologists think about culture: there are some common patterns, but culture is basically unbounded, heterogeneous, and open to change. But human rights law is ordinarily written in such a way that claims for cultural rights will be considered only if the culture in question is presented as bounded, homogenous, and unchanging. As a result, Indigenous peoples are often forced to portray themselves and their cultures in ways that are very different from their own everyday understandings of who they are. While doing so may enable them to win legal judgments in their favour, it can also reshape their ideas about what their culture is. Groups that enter into the human rights process, thus, are entering into ethically ambiguous territory that is "both enabling and constraining" (Cowan et al. 2001: 11).

Human Rights in Thailand: Child Prostitution

Reaching successful accommodations between human rights discourse and local cultural practices is not always easy. A particularly difficult set of issues must be confronted when attempting to enforce the rights of children. Anthropologist Heather Montgomery (2001) did field research in a slum settlement in Thailand (Map 13.2). The settlement, known as Baan Nua, was located near a prosperous seaside resort catering to foreign tourists. Those who lived in this settlement had broken all ties to other kin and other places from which they had migrated, which meant that the bonds linking parents and children in the settlement had become especially strong. Of overriding importance among these families was the duty of children to work to help support their families. Children did their best to fulfill this duty as soon as they were able, trying many

FIGURE 13.7 Members of Hawaiian sovereignty groups protest in the streets of Honolulu.

MAP 13.2 Thailand

different jobs, including begging. But none of these options earned very much. And so, sooner or later, children began working as prostitutes for wealthy foreign tourists who visited the resort. At the time of Montgomery's research, 65 children in the community were working as prostitutes in the local sex tourism industry.

Children could earn five times as much money working as prostitutes as they could get from begging; plus they were able to visit fancy hotels and were well fed. Many of the clients, moreover, developed long-term relationships with the families of the child prostitutes, often lending them large sums of money—in one case, enough to rebuild the family home. It was friends and neighbours of the children, not their mothers, who recruited them into prostitution. When faced with the reality of the nature of their children's employment, mothers were able to claim that they had not found out until it was too late, and they interpreted the children's acts as evidence of their strong sense of filial duty in fulfilling obligations to help support the family. "Both adult and child were aware of the child's duties, but there was a degree of unease about how far a child had to go to fulfill them" (Montgomery 2001: 90). The children claimed not to hate the men whom they worked for, especially those who kept in touch even when not in Thailand and who continued to send them money. Because of the financial generosity and long-term involvement of these men with their children, mothers said they felt the men were trustworthy. The actual sexual acts for which the children were paid took place outside the settlement and were never publicly discussed.

Commercial sex and even child prostitution are not new in Thailand, and the situation in Baan Nua is not unique. On the basis of estimates from UNICEF, between 60,000 and 200,000 Thai children are prostitutes, and HIV/AIDS is a serious and continuing issue. In recent years, many Thais, especially those working in the media and for NGOs, have denounced child sex tourism and tried to force the national government to put a stop to it (Figure 13.8). Human rights discourse—particularly discourse about the rights of the child—have played a prominent role in this campaign.

Children's rights are based on Western ideas about what constitutes an acceptable human childhood and when childhood begins and ends. For example, the 1989 Convention on the Rights of the Child defines a child as anyone less than 18 years of age, and Anti-Slavery International has claimed that child-marriage is a form of slavery and therefore violates human rights. But as Montgomery observes, "it does not take an anthropologist to recognize that a child marrying at 15 in full accordance with traditional norms and local custom in India is very different from a child marrying at 15 in the UK" (2001: 82). In common with other forms of human rights discourse, declarations on the rights of the child normally emphasize the importance of *rights* over *duties*. As Montgomery notes, this issue is particularly significant when it comes to the rights of children working as prostitutes.

The model of ideal Western childhood contained in the UN Convention on the Rights of the Child includes the idea that "every child has a right to a childhood that is free from the responsibilities of work, money, and sex" (Montgomery 2001: 83). The problem with this standard is that it fits so poorly with understandings of childhood in which, for example, children are expected (or needed) to work for money to support the family, and it seems unable to imagine situations in which the entire support of a family depends on a child's earnings from prostitution. Yet that is an accurate description for many families and children in Baan Nua.

Local Thai activists have been particularly interested in enforcing Article 34 of the UN Convention, which aims to protect children "from all forms of sexual exploitation and sexual abuse" (Montgomery 2001: 86). But the Convention also recognizes many other children's rights, including the notion that the child's best interests must always be kept uppermost and that children have a right to live with their families. The problem is that "the assurance of one right often occurs at the expense of others. How these rights are prioritized is not culturally neutral" (85). "Too often . . . Article 34 is quoted in isolation, decontextualizing sexual abuse and presenting it as the paramount difficulty that poor children face without linking it to global issues of poverty, cultural background, and discrimination" (86–7). The child's best interests are certainly compromised through prostitution, but they are also compromised when children are removed from their families and communities or when they have nothing to eat. This is particularly poignant in the case of the children of Baan Nua, many of whom claimed that they were not exploited, and all of whom were strongly motivated to engage in prostitution based on the cultural belief that children are obliged to support their parents. Montgomery concludes:

> By ensuring that their families could stay together and have a sustainable income, it would be possible to eradicate child prostitution without enforcing punitive measures against their parents. . . . Thailand's positions in globalized political and economic relations are as important as cultural specificities in perpetuating that sexual exploitation. . . . Article 34 would be redundant if the other rights enshrined in the convention . . . could be reliably enforced. (97–8)

This example suggests two important conclusions, which are also relevant to broader discussions of human rights:

1. it is possible to find ways of accommodating the universal discourse of human rights to the particularities of local conditions, and
2. no single model of the relationship between rights and culture will fit all cases.

Moreover, as the culture of human rights becomes better established, it increasingly becomes enmeshed in political and legal institutions that go beyond the local level. As activists become more experienced operating in globalized

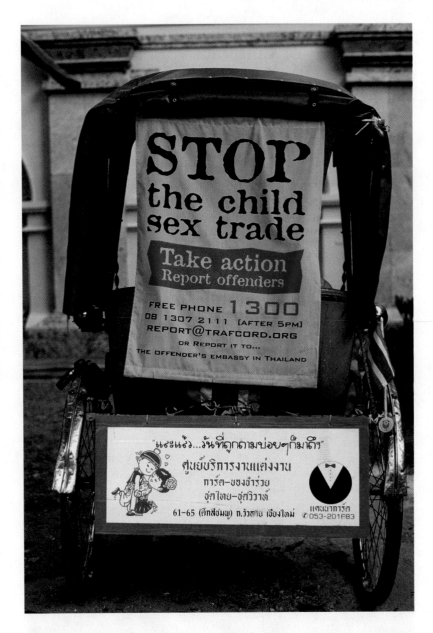

FIGURE 13.8 This sign, attached to the back of a trishaw taxi in Chiang Mai, Thailand, encourages bystanders to help fight child sex tourism by reporting offenders. To whom do you think the sign's message is directed? How might the effect be different if the message were written in the local Thai language?

circumstances, they are likely to become more sophisticated about making use of these different settings as they plan their human rights strategies (Cowan et al. 2001: 21). Struggles over human rights are hardly likely to go away; indeed, along with struggles over global citizenship, they can be seen as the prime struggles of our time (Mignolo 2002). Anthropologists are well positioned to help make sense of these complex developments as they unfold.

Cultural Imperialism, Cultural Hybridization, and Cosmopolitanism

Cultural Imperialism or Cultural Hybridization?

The global spread of people, technology, wealth, images, and ideologies has clearly had a profound impact on local social settings. But how should anthropologists characterize the processes by which these changes have come about? One explanation, formulated during the Cold War debates about modernization and dependency, was in the concept of **cultural imperialism**. Cultural imperialism is based on two notions:

1. The notion that some cultures dominate other cultures. In recent history, it is the culture(s) of "the West" that are seen to have come to dominate all other cultures of the world, due to the spread of colonialism and capitalism.
2. The notion that cultural domination by one culture leads inevitably to the destruction of subordinated cultures and their replacement by the culture of those in power.

Thus, Western cultural imperialism is seen as responsible for destroying, for example, local music, technologies, dress, and food traditions and replacing them with Western popular music, MP3 players, flashlights, cellphones, T-shirts, blue jeans, McDonald's hamburgers, and Coca-Cola. The inevitable outcome of Western cultural imperialism is seen to be "the cultural homogenization of the world," with the unwelcome consequence of "dooming the world to uniformity" (Inda and Rosaldo 2002: 13–14).

The discourse of cultural imperialism developed primarily outside anthropology, but anthropologists could not ignore it. After all, it purported to describe what was happening to the people they studied. Anthropologists, too, were aware that Western music, fashion, food, and technology had spread among those they worked with. But cultural imperialism did not seem to be a satisfactory explanation for this spread for at least three reasons:

1. Cultural imperialism denies *agency* to non-Western peoples who make use of Western cultural forms. It assumes that they are passive and without the resources to resist anything of Western origin that is marketed to them.
2. Cultural imperialism assumes that non-Western cultural forms never move "from the rest to the West." Yet non-Western music, food, and material culture have large and eager followings in Western nations.
3. Cultural imperialism ignores the fact that cultural forms and practices sometimes move from one part of the non-Western world to other parts of the non-Western world, bypassing the West entirely. For examples, Indian movies have been popular for decades in northern Nigeria, Mexican soap operas have large followings in the Philippines, and karaoke is popular all over the world (Inda and Rosaldo 2002: 22–4; Figure 13.9).

Thus anthropologists began to search for alternative ways of understanding global cultural flows.

From the days of Boas and his students, anthropologists have not only recognized the significance of cultural borrowing but also emphasized that borrowing cultural forms or practices from elsewhere always involves *borrowing-with-modification*. Indeed, people never adopt blindly; they

cultural imperialism The idea that some cultures dominate other cultures and that cultural domination by one culture leads inevitably to the destruction of subordinated cultures and their replacement by the culture of those in power.

FIGURE 13.9 Outdoor karaoke in the Mauerpark in Berlin, Germany. Karaoke machines were first patented in Japan in the 1970s. Now, karaoke is enjoyed all over the world. What does the international popularity of karaoke suggest about cultural borrowing in the contemporary globalized world?

always adapt what they borrow for local purposes. Importantly, and put another way, people rarely accept ideas or practices or objects from elsewhere without **indigenizing** them—that is, finding a way of reconciling them with local practices in order to serve local purposes.

In the 1980s, for example, a number of weavers in Otavalo, Ecuador, organized small production firms and purchased television sets to entertain their employees while they worked at their looms. In addition, some men had so much business that they encouraged their wives to take up weaving, even though women were not traditionally weavers. In order to spend more time weaving, women started to use indoor cookstoves, which relieved them from the time-consuming labour of traditional meal preparation over an open fire (Colloredo-Mansfeld 1999). From the perspective of anthropologist Rudi Colloredo-Mansfeld (1999), these adoptions of items of Western technology could not be understood as the consequences of Western cultural imperialism because they had nothing to do with trying to imitate a Western lifestyle. It made more sense to interpret these changes as Otavalan *indigenization* of televisions and cookstoves, since these items from elsewhere were adopted precisely in order to promote Indigenous Otavalan weaving. Thus, borrowing-with-modification involves *customizing* that which is borrowed to meet the purposes of the borrowers, which may be quite remote from the purposes of those among whom the form or practice originated (Inda and Rosaldo 2002: 16). This form of cultural change is very different from having something from elsewhere forced upon you against your will.

At the same time, it is necessary to recognize that the consequences of borrowing-with-modification can never be fully controlled. Thus, Otavalan weavers may start watching television because local reruns of old American television series relieve the tedium of weaving, but once television-watching becomes a habitual practice, it also exposes them to advertising and news broadcasts that may stimulate unpredictable local changes. The indigenization of cultural forms from elsewhere makes it possible *both* to do old things in new ways *and* to do new things as well (Figure 13.10). Cultural borrowing is double-edged; borrowed cultural practices are both amenable to indigenization and yet able to escape it. The challenges are particularly acute

in globalizing conditions—colonial or postcolonial—where borrowed ideas, objects, or practices remain entangled in relationships with donors even as they are made to serve new goals by recipients. It is not surprising, therefore, that people in multicultural settings who must deal with tempting cultural alternatives emanating from more powerful groups regularly struggle to control processes of cultural borrowing and to contain indigenized cultural practices within certain contexts.

indigenization
The process of bring something foreign under the control of local people, or of adapting something foreign to serve local purposes.

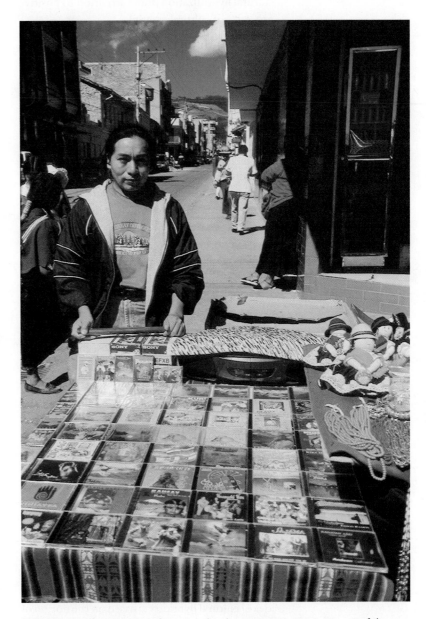

FIGURE 13.10 Musical performance has become an important part of the Otavalo economy, as musicians from Otavalo travel throughout the world performing and selling woven goods. They have indigenized CD production as well and have been quite successful in selling CDs of their music to tourists in Otavalo and to listeners abroad.

cultural hybridization
Cultural mixing that produces a new cultural form.

When discussing this sort of complex globalized cultural exchange, anthropologists often speak of **cultural hybridization** or *cultural hybridity*. Cultural hybridization is more than simple cultural borrowing: it is a form of *cultural mixing* that produces something new, something that cannot be collapsed or subsumed either within the culture of the donor or within the culture of the recipient. Further, it is a highly positive form of cultural mixing: rather than indicating a regrettable loss of original "purity," cultural hybridization draws attention to positive processes of cultural creativity.

The move from talk of dependency and cultural imperialism to talk about globalization and cultural hybridization is widely seen as a move from *modernist* discourse to *postmodernist* discourse. Modernist discourse embodies Enlightenment assumptions about rationality, science, progress, capitalism, and democracy. Postmodernist discourse calls all of these Enlightenment assumptions into question. While modernists tend to portray non-Western societies and cultures as bounded, orderly, and unchanging, postmodernists argue that all social and cultural borders have always been porous and thus open to people, ideas, and practices from elsewhere. This postmodern position is not confined to academic contexts; it has had important implications for everyday cultural choices. If hybridity is a normal part of human social experience, social groups can legitimately challenge the idea that "authentic" traditions never change. Thus, they can feel free to revise or discard cultural practices as they see fit. Possessing this sort of freedom means that they possess agency—the capacity to exercise at least some control over their lives. And exercising agency calls into question charges that a group is succumbing to cultural imperialism or losing cultural "authenticity."

However, close examination of talk about cultural hybridization reveals at least three problems. First, it is not clear that the concept actually frees anthropologists from the modernist commitment to the existence of bounded, homogeneous, unchanging "cultures." That is, the idea of cultural hybridity is based on the notion of cultural mixing. But what is it that is mixed? Two or more non-hybridized, original, "pure" cultures! But such "pure," homogeneous, bounded, unchanging cultures are not supposed to exist. Thus we are caught in a paradox. For this reason

anthropologist Jonathan Friedman, among others, is highly critical of discussions of cultural hybridity; in his view, cultures have *always* been hybrid, and it is the existence of *boundaries*, not cultural borrowing, that anthropologists need to explain. Besides, hybrid cultural mixtures often get transformed into new, unitary cultural identities. This process can be seen, Friedman argues, in the way in which the "mixed race" category in the US has been transformed into a "new, unitary group of mixtures for those who feel 'disenfranchised' by the current single-race categories" (1997: 83). Friedman also points out that hybrid identities are not liberating when they are thrust upon people rather than being adopted freely. He draws attention to cases in Latin America where the "mestizo" (mixed European–Native) identity has been used "as a middle-/upper-class tool" against Indigenous groups by hybridizing them "from above": that is, criticizing their claims to a common Indian identity in order to undermine their sense of solidarity as members of a single group. "We are all part-Indian, say members of the elite who have much to lose in the face of minority claims" (81–2).

These examples highlight a second difficulty with hybridity talk: those who celebrate cultural hybridization often ignore the fact that its effects are experienced differently by those with power and those without power. As Friedman says, "the question of class becomes crucial" (1997: 81). The complexity of this issue is seen in many popular discussions of "multiculturalism" that celebrate cultural hybridization and that, in the context of globalizing capitalism, turn hybridity into a marketable commodity. The commodification of hybridity is problematic because it glosses over differences in the experience of cultural hybridization, offering multiculturalism as an array of tempting consumables for outsiders. "Multiculturalism is aimed at nourishing and perpetuating the kind of differences which do not [threaten]," writes cultural theorist Nira Yuval-Davis (1997: 197). International folk festivals, festivals of nations, and the like—events that emphasize costume, cuisine, music, and dance—spring to mind (Figure 13.11). But the troubling fact is that cultural hybridity is experienced as both non-threatening and very threatening, depending on the terms on which it is available. Because of power differences among groups challenged by cultural hybridization, any globalized "multicultural" setting reveals active processes of cultural hybridization *together with* the defence of discrete cultural identities that seem to *resist* hybridization (Werbner 1997: 3). Cultural hybridization is unobjectionable when actors perceive it to be under their own control, but it is resisted when it is "perceived by actors themselves to be potentially threatening to their sense of moral integrity" (Werbner 1997: 12). The threat is greatest for those with the least power who feel unable to control forms of cultural hybridization that threaten to undermine the fragile survival structures on which they depend in an unwelcoming multicultural setting.

Examinations of class and power also lead us to a third problem with the concept of cultural hybridization. Fashionable hybridity talk can actually *hide* the differences between elite and non-elite experiences of multiculturalism, potentially diverting attention away from social problems that exist in multicultural or culturally hybridized environments. Anthropologist John Hutnyk, for example, deplores the way "world music" is marketed to middle-class consumers, noting that such sales strategies divert attention "from the urgency of anti-racist politics" (1997: 122). When cultural hybridization becomes fashionable, it easily turns the experiences of hybridized elites into a hegemonic standard, suggesting that class exploitation and racial oppression are easily overcome or no longer exist. In Brazil, a country with a long history of tensions along racial and class lines, the hybridization of local and Western ideals of physical attractiveness has resulted in a new "culture of beauty" that overshadows discussions of social inequality (Edmonds 2007). Rather than focussing on the social problems that promote inequality, lower- and middle-class Brazilians—particularly Brazilian women—blame their lack of opportunity on their lack of "beauty." To remedy the perceived problem, they turn to surgeons to perform cosmetic procedures that are common among the more affluent members of societies. Many believe that fixing their physical "flaws" through cosmetic surgery will lead to upward social mobility as well as "First World modernity and glamour" (370). While cosmetic surgery has led to improved self-esteem for some, it rarely brings about a great degree of economic or social change.

FIGURE 13.11 Ukrainian dancers from Alberta, Canada, perform at an international dance festival in Zagreb, Croatia. How should we understand this cultural performance? Is it Ukrainian, Canadian (Albertan), Croatian, or some hybrid of all three?

In some cases, dismissing or ignoring differences in how elites and non-elites experience cultural hybridization can spark dangerous confrontations. Anthropologist Peter van der Veer (1997) argues that such a dynamic ignited the furor in Britain that followed the publication of Salman Rushdie's novel *The Satanic Verses* (1988). Rushdie is an elite, highly educated South Asian migrant to Britain who experienced cultural hybridity as a form of emancipation from oppressive religious and cultural restrictions. His novel contained passages describing Islam and the Prophet Muhammad that, from his elite point of view, embodied "transgression" that was liberating. But migrants from South Asia in Britain are not all members of the elite. Most South Asian Muslim immigrants in Britain are part of the working class, and they saw *The Satanic Verses* not as a work of artistic liberation but as a deliberate attempt to mock their beliefs and practices. "These immigrants, who are already socially and culturally marginalized, are thus double marginalized in the name of an attack on 'purity' and Islamic 'fundamentalism'" (van der Veer 1997: 101–2). Even more important, however, may be the way popular interpretations of their objections in the press and among Western intellectuals ignored these immigrants' own, very different but very real, *non-elite* experiences of cultural hybridization. Van der Veer stresses that British Muslims who objected to the novel were

> not necessarily fundamentalists at all; their religious ideas are just as hybrid and syncretic as those of the author. They, too, are migrants, but the sources of their identity are authenticated not by profane literary texts but by what are to them sacred religious traditions. (1997: 102)

Put simply, elites experience cultural hybridization in ways that are often very different from the ways non-elites experience cultural hybridization. We all ignore this fact at our peril.

From Cultural Hybridity to Cosmopolitanism

The era of globalization in which we live is exciting and offers opportunities for some. But it is also an era of uncertainty and insecurity. Possibilities for new and liberating ways of life are undercut by sharpening economic and political differences and looming threats of violence. Is it possible, in the midst of all this confusion and conflict, to devise productive ways of coping with our changing circumstances and addressing cultural differences? No one expects such efforts to be easy. But anthropologists and other concerned scholars are currently struggling to come up with concepts and practices that might be helpful.

Our era is not the first to have faced such challenges. Cultural theorist Walter Mignolo (2002)

cosmopolitanism
Being at ease in more than one cultural setting.

argues that multiculturalism was born in the sixteenth century when European conquest in the New World first raised troubling issues among Western thinkers about the kinds of relationships that were possible and desirable between the conquerors and the Indigenous peoples whom they had conquered. During the ensuing centuries, the challenges posed by a multicultural world did not disappear.

In the late eighteenth century, in an attempt to identify the proper way for human beings to live in the world, German philosopher Immanuel Kant revived a concept that was first coined by the Stoic philosophers of ancient Rome: **cosmopolitanism** (Mignolo 2002). Kant's cosmopolitanism was firmly embedded within the values and practices of Enlightenment civilization, which meant that it was embedded in Western elite forms of cultural hybridization. That is, Kantian cosmopolitanism "by and large meant being versed in Western ways, and the vision of 'one world' culture was only a sometimes unconscious, sometimes unconscionable, euphemism for 'First World' culture" (Abbas 2002: 210). To the extent that discussions of cosmopolitanism continue to focus on Western elites only, they would seem to offer little to anthropologists and others who are interested in finding a place for non-elite and non-Western experiences of cultural hybridization.

Nevertheless, is it possible to rework our understandings of cultural hybridity to stretch the notion of cosmopolitanism beyond its traditional association with privileged Western elites? Many anthropologists have become comfortable talking about "alternative" or "minority" modernities that depart from the Western norm. In a similar fashion, any new anthropological understanding of cosmopolitanism would have to be plural, not singular, and it would have to include non-elite experiences of cultural hybridization that reflect the experiences of those who have been the victims of modernity (see Breckenridge et al. 2002). The goal would be to develop new, broader ways of understanding peoples' lived experiences from multiple perspectives at once.

Does anthropological talk about a world of "cosmopolitanisms" offer any advantage over earlier anthropological talk about a world of "cultures"? It might, if anthropologists can find a way to think about cultural hybridization (and resistance to hybridization) that overcomes the problems discussed above. Anthropologist Pnina Werbner

(1997) suggests that this might be possible if we can think about cultural hybridization as a *process* rather than as a series of momentary, shocking, "transgressive" challenges that periodically disrupt the ongoing, tense standoff among defenders of different cultural positions. Rather than assuming that all hybridity (or all resistance to hybridity) is the same—either all "good" or all "bad"—Werbner's approach would make it possible to distinguish *different processes* of cultural hybridization and cultural resistance. To illustrate, Werbner distinguishes between cultural processes that lead to *ethnicity* and cultural processes that lead to *racism* (see Chapter 12). In her view, a process-oriented theory of cultural hybridization "must differentiate . . . between a politics that proceeds from the legitimacy of difference [ethnicity] and a politics that rests on coercive unity [racism]," and it "must explain how and why cultural hybrids are still able to disturb and 'shock' . . . in a postmodern world that celebrates difference" (Werbner 1997: 21). To arrive at such a theory, we would need to examine "the way discourses interact to create bridges or precipitate polarizing processes" (21).

Werbner's approach to cultural hybridization as a process has much in common with what Walter Mignolo calls *border thinking*. That is, in a globalized world, concepts like "democracy" and "justice" can no longer be defined within a single Western logic—or, for that matter, from the perspective of the political left or the political right. *Border thinking* involves detaching these concepts from their hegemonic "Western" meanings and practices, and using them as "connectors"—tools for imagining and negotiating new, cosmopolitan forms of democracy or justice informed by the ethical and political judgments of non-elites (Mignolo 2002: 179, 181).

Finally, in re-imagining what cosmopolitanism might mean, it is important not only to go beyond Kantian limitations but also to go beyond standard anthropological orientations to other ways of life. An understanding of cosmopolitanism that is limited to being open to other cultures or to being inclusive—the traditional orientation of cultural relativism—is insufficient to cope with the challenges presented by a globalizing world. For one thing, "Otherness has lost its innocence as a result of the colonial experience" (Abbas 2002: 226). And for another, "silenced and marginalized voices are bringing themselves into the conversation of cosmopolitan projects rather than waiting to be included" (Mignolo 2002: 174).

The hope is that border thinking can produce a *critical cosmopolitanism* capable of negotiating new understandings of human rights and global citizenship in ways that can dismantle barriers of gender and race that are the historical legacies of colonialism (Mignolo 2002: 161, 180). In many cases, this will require creative new ways of understanding and interacting with others. It will also require overcoming power differentials and giving equal attention to non-elites.

Many of the cases in this chapter demonstrate the human ability to cope creatively with changed life circumstances. They remind us that human beings are not passive in the face of the new, that they actively and resiliently respond to life's challenges. Changing circumstances that may benefit some human groups can overwhelm and destroy others. Western capitalism and modern technology have exploded into a vortex of global forces that resist control. A critical cosmopolitanism involving concerted practical action to lessen violence and exploitation may be all that can prevent these forces from destroying us all.

A CRITICAL LOOK | Diaspora and Identity

If we consider culture as a performance art, we can see why it must be that culture is in a constant state of change. The performance is by nature unscripted and unbounded, shaped not only by what the performers bring to the performance—their knowledge, experiences, perspectives, beliefs, and so on—but also by the context in which it takes place. Changing the context changes the performance.

When people leave their homeland to re-establish themselves in a new place, they bring with them elements of their culture. Once they reach their destination, however, they must adapt what they have brought with them to their new context. For immigrants to Canada, this new context is often a major city made up of people from many different cultural backgrounds. In many cases, the most comfortable

continued

place for immigrants to settle is in ethnic enclaves where they can be close to people whose cultural backgrounds are similar to their own and who are likewise negotiating a hybridized cultural identity in a new homeland. As they draw on experiences from their old and new worlds, these people develop complex cultural identities based on their uniquely transnational world views.

Anthropologist Nicholas Harney has made some general observations on migrants' experiences with diaspora and identity:

First, the experience of dispersal is to more than one place. Second, there is active communication, both institutional and kin, between different locations within the diaspora and also with the homeland. Third, a collective sentiment of groupness is cultivated and distinct from the host society. Fourth, there is a collective memory about the past, real or imagined. Fifth, diasporas are also disciplined, structured, and influenced by their location within the political, bureaucratic, and cultural sphere of a host society which may adopt strategies for managing diversity. (2002: 44)

These features remain central and salient regardless of the origins or destinations of migrants.

In his field research, Harney has taken a more specific look at how processes of identity formation operate among Italian Canadians living in Toronto. As he observes, "Italian immigrants and their descendants negotiate identity in locally specific circumstances . . . within the context of state-sponsored multiculturalism in Canada and multiple diasporic discourses linking peoples in Italy and Canada" (43). Central to this identity is the family as the "pragmatic transnational link" (Levin 2002: 8). For example, in the home, family members generally speak Italian, but with English words and phrases incorporated into the discussion. Such language environments not only maintain Italian-ness, they mark regional dialectical differences of the homeland.

Family dinners also contribute to identity formation. In Italian Canadian households, dinners often feature regional dishes from the homeland. Food of *home* is more than nutrition. It is a metaphor for identity, and it marks boundaries of distinctiveness within and between culture areas. Food touches us on so many levels—smell, taste, visual appeal. It becomes "embodied forms of memory" (Holtzman 2006: 361)—memories of family meals and special occasions, memories of other times and places.

As Harney observes, modern technologies make it easier for immigrants to stay in touch with people "back home" and to learn about cultural developments in the homeland:

In an accelerated fashion, Italian immigrants and their children can interact with and expend emotional energy on ties with their "homeland" in every sphere of social life. Magazines arrive from regions of origin in Italy, and hometown websites seek out rite-of-passage life histories, photographs, and social activities of co-villagers dispersed around the world. (2002: 48)

These sorts of close connections help Italian Canadians feel connected to their homeland despite the great physical distance that separates them from it.

In many cases, migrants leave their homeland for better opportunities elsewhere. In some cases, these opportunities materialize into success and security; in others, the result is disappointment. Either way, immigrants often imagine an "idealized return" to the homeland (Levin 2002). In the past, this return often remained imagined, but the relative ease of international travel today has made it a possibility for many. Indeed, "travel allows frequent and well-timed returns, for example, on ritual occasions marking life-cycle events and to socialize children in the homeland, which express relationships more concretely than does verbal or written contact alone" (Levin 2002: 4). While these sorts of brief visits can be refreshing and identity affirming, more permanent migrations back to the homeland can be difficult.

In her recent travels to a northern Italian city, Roberta Robin Dods met an elderly woman who had returned to the region after having lived in Ottawa for 45 years. This woman was a widow without children, now living with relatives "back home" in Italy. Yet her return was not what she had hoped it would be. She was lonely, living with a family she barely knew and missing her Italian Canadian friends in Ottawa. Here was a painful reversal—a woman seeing herself as foreign in her country of origin. "Home" remained elsewhere, in the place where she had made a life with her husband even while she maintained the almost mythic idea of "back home." Her story of Canada had the nostalgia often found in immigrants' "back home" memories. Her life was book-ended by two places, each calling to her through their defining metaphors of identity.

—Roberta Robin Dods

KEY TERMS

core   321
cosmopolitanism   342
cultural hybridization   339
cultural imperialism   337
dependency theory   320
diaspora   326

flexible citizenship   328
globalization   320
human rights   330
indigenization   338
legal citizenship   327
long-distance
    nationalists   327

modernization theory   320
multiculturalism   330
neoliberalism   322
periphery   321
post-national ethos   329
semi-periphery   321

substantive citizenship   327
transborder citizenry   327
transborder state   327
transnational
    nation-states   327
world-system theory   321

CHAPTER SUMMARY

1. Anthropologists have made use of a variety of theoretical perspectives to explain the relationship between the West and the rest of the world. Three significant examples from the twentieth century are *modernization theory*, *dependency theory*, and *world system theory*. Today, most theorists see the situation through the lens of globalization. Most anthropologists agree that the effects of globalization are uneven—some groups in some parts of the world benefit, whereas others do not.

2. The contrasts between formal and substantive citizenship suggest that conventional notions of citizenship are breaking down. People who migrate across national borders often develop transborder identities, which in some cases allow them to both circumvent and benefit from different nation-state regimes by investing, working, and living in different places.

3. Discussions of human rights have intensified in recent decades. Some arguments about human rights include the right to one's culture. Some anthropologists have identified a relatively new "culture of human rights"—an international

culture that emphasizes individual rights over duties or needs and that proposes technical rather than ethical solutions to human suffering.

4. Some anthropologists discussing globalization prefer to speak about borrowing-with-modification or indigenization of practices or objects imported from elsewhere. Many anthropologists describe these processes as examples of cultural hybridization or hybridity. At the same time, some criticize talk of cultural hybridization for assuming that "pure" cultures existed prior to mixing or for failing to recognize differences between how the powerful and the powerless experience cultural change. Others would like to revive the notion of cosmopolitanism and rework it in order to be able to speak about alternative cosmopolitanisms that reflect the experiences of those who have been the victims of modernity. The ideal end result would be a critical cosmopolitanism capable of negotiating new understandings of human rights and global citizenship in ways that can dismantle barriers of gender and race that are the historical legacies of colonialism.

CRITICAL THINKING QUESTIONS

1. What would you consider to be the main factor(s) in the emergence of globalization?

2. What would you consider to be the key factor(s) in local variations on the acceptance of globalization?

3. Are national boundaries being challenged by the Internet? How, and to what possible ends?

4. What are some of the ways elites and non-elites experience cultural hybridization differently? Why do you suppose these differences occur?

SUGGESTED READINGS

Barber, Benjamin R. 1995. *Jihad versus McWorld: How Globalism and Tribalism Are Reshaping the World* (New York: Times Books). This book examines the basis for the misunderstanding between the Muslim world and the capitalist Western world.

Dyck, Noel, and James B. Waldram. 1993. *Anthropology, Public Policy, and Native Peoples in Canada* (Montreal and Kingston: McGill-Queen's University Press). A comprehensive review of governmental policy issues and the conditions experienced by First Nations peoples up to the beginning of the 1990s.

Harney, Nicholas. 2002. "Building Italian Regional Identity in Toronto: Using Space to Make Culture Material," *Anthropologica* 44, 1: 43–54. This paper is a close and highly nuanced examination of the ways in which Italian Canadians create meaningful spaces and identities in the city of Toronto.

Inda, Jonathan Xavier, and Renato Rosaldo, eds. 2007. *The Anthropology of Globalization: A Reader*, 2nd edn (Malden, MA: Blackwell). A comprehensive collection of articles by anthropologists who address the process of globalization from varied points of view and different ethnographic situations.

Lewellen, Ted C. 2002. *The Anthropology of Globalization: Cultural Anthropology Enters the Twenty-First Century* (Westport, CT: Greenwood). A relatively recent anthropological look at the ways in which the forces of globalization are shaping our world.

Murray, David A.B. 2000. "Between a Rock and a Hard Place: The Power and Powerlessness of Transnational Narratives among Gay Martinican Men," *American Anthropologist* 102, 2: 261–70. Murray explores the narratives gay men tell each other in Martinique, arguing that these stories often depict life in Quebec as utopic in comparison to life in either France or Martinique.

No'eau Warner, Sam L. 1999. "'Kuleana': The Right, Responsibility, and Authority of Indigenous Peoples to Speak and Make Decisions for Themselves in Language and Cultural Revitalization," *Anthropology and Education Quarterly* 30, 1: 68–93. This paper addresses the issue of Hawaiian language and cultural revitalization becoming highly politicized by non-Indigenous Hawaiian language educators.

Sylvain, Renée. 2005. "Disorderly Development: Globalization and the Idea of Culture in the Kalahari," *American Ethnologist* 32, 3: 354–70. This article discusses issues of identity, struggles for rights, and other challenges facing the San of southern Africa.

RELATED WEBSITES

Conservation International www.conservation.org

Fairtrade Canada http://fairtrade.ca

Foreign Affairs, Trade, and Development Canada: Development www.international.gc.ca/development-developpement/index.aspx

International Bureau for Children's Rights www.ibcr.org

International Women's Rights Project (IWRP), CEDAW http://iwrp.org/projects/cedaw

Women Activities and Social Services Association http://wassa-af.org/en

14

Applying Anthropology in Everyday Life

CHAPTER OUTLINE

Anthropology in the World at Large

Two Examples of Practical Applications

Anthropology and Policy

Anthropology and the Challenges of Global Citizenship

Awareness and Uncertainty

Freedom and Constraint

LEARNING OBJECTIVES

By the end of Chapter 14, you will be able to

- understand the value of applied anthropology,
- appreciate anthropology's value in addressing the challenges of global citizenship,

- consider the world of uncertainty and the awareness needed to confront this world (reflexivity), and

- challenge views on freedom and constraint.

Tourists and locals enjoy the midway attractions at the Calgary Stampede in Alberta. When viewed through the anthropological perspective, even familiar situations that we encounter here in Canada can be a source of new insight into the many ways in which beliefs and behaviours are shaped by culture.

Anthropology in the World at Large

Why study anthropology? Perhaps the best initial answer comes from French anthropologist Maurice Godelier:

> anthropology . . . is one of the social science disciplines that is best able to help us understand the complexity of our now globalized world and the nature of the conflicts and the crisis we are experiencing. In such a world, it would be irresponsible and indecent for anthropologists to stop trying to understand others—and themselves at the same time—and making their results known. (2010: 217)

Here Godelier highlights the power of anthropology to help us understand our world. It can help us make sense of a wide variety of issues that impact human beings' lived experiences. Certainly, it can teach us about others, but it can also teach us about ourselves (Figure 14.1).

Many anthropologists now work in the area called *applied anthropology*. As we saw in Chapter 1, applied anthropology involves the practical application of information provided by the four main anthropological specialties (cultural anthropology, linguistic anthropology, archaeology, and

FIGURE 14.1 Studying anthropology can help us understand our own culture. Here, anthropology graduate students help Professor Bill Rathje examine the dirt at a landfill in San Francisco in an effort to understand local human behaviour through waste habits.

biological anthropology). Medical anthropology, discussed in detail in Chapter 9, is one important area of work that falls under the umbrella of applied anthropology. Medical anthropologists often engage in practical research with significant applied results—for example, research that explores issues of aging and can lead to the development of programs that assist the elderly in culturally appropriate ways. Additionally, medical anthropologists draw attention to practical issues of medical ethics. As Canadian medical anthropologist Margaret Lock notes in her discussion of medicalization and resistance,

> Ethnography makes it possible to examine the way in which scientific knowledge is selectively deployed in different global contexts by drawing on morals and value systems that are historically, politically, and culturally informed. . . . I find culture (used reflexively and in conjunction with a political/economy framework) a necessary concept for most research projects, especially when culture is explicitly made to do work by the particular people or institutions that one is studying. (2001: 488)

Of particular interest are the health and well-being of women and children in a world where access to prenatal care, adequate nutrition, clean water, immunization programs, and treatment is patchy, while diseases like malaria and HIV are rampant (Figure 14.2). Indeed, many applied anthropologists work on HIV-related projects. One example is medical anthropologist Holly Wardlow's work on HIV infections in rural Papua New Guinea. Through her work, Wardlow demonstrates how a researcher's site-specific observations often point to broader cultural concerns. She notes that "married women are at risk for HIV primarily because of their husbands' extramarital sexual liaisons, and wives have little control over this risk, which is not lessened by their own fidelity. . . . [T]he dynamics of marital HIV transmission [are embedded in] economic, social, and cultural factors that propel and structure men's extramarital sexuality" (2007: 1006). Thus the intimacies of their lives and the structures of their social worlds creates a dangerous space for women in many parts of the world.

Anthropologists have gone into public policy and planning as interpreters, mediators, civil servants, and urban planners. A few are psychotherapists, employing the insights of anthropologist Gregory Bateson and others on family systems and family therapy, while some are cross-cultural social workers. Some have taken on activist roles, working with Indigenous peoples' organizations or human rights organizations such as Survival International and Cultural Survival. Others have become involved in international development, working with various agencies on projects such as devising appropriate technologies, resolving fuel shortages, locating potable water, arranging financial assistance, conducting feasibility studies for dams and other enterprises, implementing bilingual education programs, and improving and managing livestock and crops. In looking at how anthropologists have contributed to meaningful change, anthropologist Melissa Checker lists six core themes in this sort of "action" anthropological work:

1. war and peace;
2. climate change;
3. natural, industrial, and development-induced disaster recovery;
4. human rights;
5. health disparities; and
6. racial understanding, politics, and equity. (2009).

To this list we could add a seventh—alienation and resettlement, which are often the outcomes of issues that arise in these six core areas (especially the first, second, third, and sixth).

When participating in "action" or "advocacy-oriented" work, anthropologists must remain acutely aware of two things. First, they must be aware of the "potential ramifications of [their] engagement" (Johnston 2010: 235). Indeed, they must constantly examine the ethical implications of their work, and they must consider how their actions might have unintended consequences (see Mullins 2010). Second, they must be aware that their work is by nature *collaborative*. This collaboration involves not only anthropologists and other advocates, but also the people they are trying to help (see Lassiter 2005).

FIGURE 14.2 Medical anthropologist Andrea Wiley (left) in the Himalayas of Ladakh, India, where she studied maternal and child health. Think back to the example of SEARCH used in Chapter 9. How can anthropologists use their skills to contribute to grassroots efforts and community-based health initiatives?

Two Examples of Practical Applications

The case studies that follow reveal in greater detail the value of applied anthropology.

Doing Business in Japan

Doing business in a cultural setting that is very different from your own requires you to be aware of and sensitive to local customs and cultural norms. When working in such a setting, we can learn a great deal from the work of Edward T. Hall, the father of intercultural communication. Hall's work in diverse cultures and understanding of cultural perceptions of space and time constraints allowed us to start to see through the eyes of others. What popped into view were the dynamics of intersubjective space in intercultural (and intracultural) contexts, as well as ways to understand to be sensitive to these dynamics. (For more on this topic, see Hall 1959; 1966; 1976; 1983; Hall and Hall 1987.)

Anthropologist Richard Reeves-Ellington (1993) has built on this earlier work in the field of intercultural dynamics. In the early 1990s, he designed and implemented a cross-cultural training program for a North American company doing business in Japan (see Map 14.1).

MAP 14.1 Japan

He found that many of the traditional methods of anthropology—cultural understanding, ethnographic data, and participant-observation—helped managers conduct business in Japan. Reeves-Ellington began the training program by having employees gather general *cultural information artifacts*. To complete this task, he asked them to focus on questions such as the following:

- "How are things classified?" and
- "What are the artifacts of an agreed classification system?"

He also had them gather *social knowledge* by asking questions such as the following:

- "What are proper principles for behaviour?" and
- "What are the values that drive the categories and artifacts?"

Finally, he had them investigate *cultural logic*. This task revolved around answering the following question:

- "What is the world view?"

Social knowledge or values are based on an underlying, taken-for-granted cultural logic. Coming to understand Japanese cultural logic is of great importance to foreigners wishing to live and work in Japan.

The managers at the company decided to learn how to carry out introductions,

meetings, leave-taking, dinner, and drinking in Japan. Each practice was analyzed according to the framework of artifacts, social knowledge, and cultural logic, and each was taught by a combination of methods that included collecting observations while visiting Japanese museums, theatres, shrines, baseball games, and business meetings. The managers analyzed these observations and discussed stories that show how badly things can go when cultural knowledge is not sufficient.

One thing the managers needed to learn about introductions involved the presentation of the business card (*meishi*). In Japan, the proper presentation and use of the *meishi* is the central element in the practice of making introductions at business meetings (Figure 14.3). Reeves-Ellington explained that, to a Japanese business

FIGURE 14.3 A Japanese man presents his *meishi* to a colleague. The *meishi* exchange is a central part of Japanese business culture. How can the applied anthropological method used by Reeves-Ellington (1993) help us understand the significance of this exchange? In what other situations might a similar methodological framework be useful?

person, the *meishi* is an extension of the self. Damage to the card is damage to the individual. Therefore, mistreatment of a *meishi* will ruin a relationship. Reeves-Ellington notes that his students did not fully appreciate the consequences of these beliefs until he told them a story:

> A major US company was having problems with one of its distributors, and the parties seemed unable to resolve their differences. The president of the US company decided to visit Japan, meet with his counterpart in the wholesaler organization, and attempt to resolve their differences. The two had not met previously and, upon meeting, each followed proper *meishi* ritual. The American, however, did not put the Japanese counterpart's *meishi* on the table; instead he held on to it. As the conversation became heated, the American rolled up the *meishi* in his hand. Horror was recorded on the face of the Japanese businessman. The American then tore the *meishi* into bits. This was more than the Japanese could stand; he excused himself from the meeting. Shortly afterward the two companies stopped doing business with each other. (1993: 209)

Table 14.1 shows the information regarding introductions and the use of the *meishi* that Reeves-Ellington's students derived from their work based on their analytic framework of artifacts, social knowledge, and cultural logic.

On three critical measures—effective working relationships with Japanese executives, shortened project times, and improved financial returns—the anthropologically based training program that Reeves-Ellington designed was a success. Both employees and their Japanese counterparts felt more comfortable working with each other. Prior to the program, joint projects required an average of 15 months to complete; projects run by executives applying the methodologies of the program cut completion time to an average of 8 months. Financial returns based on contracts negotiated by personnel who had not participated in the program averaged a gross income of 6 per cent of sales, whereas those negotiated by personnel applying the anthropological techniques averaged a gross income equal to 18 per cent of sales.

TABLE 14.1 Introductions at Business Meetings

Artifacts	Social Knowledge	Cultural Logic
Technology • Business cards (*Meishi*).	• Once given, a card is kept—not discarded. • *Meishi* are not exchanged a second time unless there is a position change.	**Human relations** • *Meishi* provide understanding of appropriate relations between parties. • *Meishi* take uncertainty out of relationships.
Visual Behaviour • Presentation of *meishi* by presenting card, facing recipient. • Senior people present *meishi* first. • Guest presents first, giving name, company affiliation, and bowing. • Host presents *meishi* in same sequence. • Upon sitting at conference table, all *meishi* are placed in front of recipient to assure name use.	• Before the next meeting between parties, the *meishi* are reviewed for familiarization with the people attending the meeting. • The *meishi* provide status for the owner.	**Environment** • *Meishi* help establish insider/outsider environment. • *Meishi* help establish possible obligations to environment. **Human activity** • *Meishi* help to establish human activities.

Source: Reeves-Ellington 1993: 203–16. Reproduced by permission of the Society for Applied Anthropology.

As this example illustrates, cross-cultural understanding—a major focus of anthropological research—is important to work in disciplines other than anthropology. For more examples of lessons that are central to anthropology and also useful in other areas, see the "In Their Own Words" box called "What Can You Learn from an Anthropology Major?" (Also see Niemeier et al. [1998] and Reeves-Ellington [2009] for more examples specific to business and organizational leadership.)

Urban Social Planning and Restructuring in Canada

Alexander Ervin is an anthropologist in Saskatoon, Saskatchewan, who has had considerable experience participating in collaborative, community-based research that involves social service and health agencies (see EthnoProfile 14.1). In his view, anthropologists seem to be particularly well-suited for this kind of applied work because they "have been trained conceptually and methodologically to seek linkages among behaviours, institutions, and values, and to attempt to construct integrated overviews of whatever is the phenomenon under investigation" (1996: 324). As government policy-makers move to cut costs by downsizing, few policy disciplines are able to provide information about how the different social-service providers and their services fit together, and few are able to listen effectively to

---

IN THEIR OWN WORDS │ What Can You Learn from an Anthropology Major?

The Career Development Centre at SUNY Plattsburgh developed a document that highlights what students typically learn from a major in anthropology. Note that the skills listed below are valuable not only in anthropological settings but also in other situations—especially those commonly encountered in the business world.

1. **Social agility**

   In an unfamiliar social or career-related setting, you learn to quickly size up the rules of the game. You can become accepted more quickly than you could without this anthropological skill.

2. **Observation**

   You must often learn about a culture from within it, so you learn how to interview and observe as a participant.

3. **Analysis and planning**

   You learn how to find patterns in the behaviour of a cultural group. This awareness of patterns allows you to generalize about the group's behaviour and predict what they might do in a given situation.

4. **Social sensitivity**

   Although other people's ways of doing things may be different from your own, you learn the importance of events and conditions that have contributed to this difference. You also recognize that other cultures view your ways as strange. You learn the value of behaving toward others with appropriate preparation, care, and understanding.

5. **Accuracy in interpreting behaviour**

   You become familiar with the range of behaviour in different cultures. You learn how to look at cultural causes of behaviour before assigning causes yourself.

6. **Ability to appropriately challenge conclusions**

   You learn that analyses of human behaviour are open to challenge. You learn how to use new knowledge to test past conclusions.

7. **Insightful interpretation of information**

   You learn how to use data collected by others, reorganizing or interpreting the data to reach original conclusions.

8. **Simplification of information**

   Because anthropology is conducted among publics as well as about them, you learn how to simplify technical information for communication to non-technical people.

9. **Contextualization**

   Although attention to details is a trait of anthropology, you learn that any given detail might not be as important as its context and can even be misleading when the context is ignored.

10. **Problem solving**

    Because you often function within a cultural group or act on culturally sensitive issues, you learn to approach problems with care. Before acting, you identify the problem, set your goals, decide on the actions you will take, and calculate possible effects on other people.

11. **Persuasive writing**

    Anthropologists strive to represent the behaviour of one group to another group and continually need to engage in interpretation. You learn the value of bringing someone else to share—or at least understand—your view through written argument.

12. **Assumption of a social perspective**

    You learn how to perceive the acts of individuals and local groups as both shaping and being shaped by larger socio-cultural systems. The perception enables you to "act locally and think globally."

Source: Omohundro, John. 2000. "What Can You Learn from an Anthropology Major?," in *Careers in Anthropology* (New York: McGraw-Hill).

ETHNOPROFILE 14.1 | Saskatoon

Region North America

Nation Canada

Language English is the official language, but Cree is also spoken, as there is a large population of First Nations peoples, mostly from Plains Cree communities

Population 253,000 (2014 estimate)

Environment Northern plains

Livelihood Industrial, commercial, agricultural, educational centre

Political organization City in contemporary nation-state

For more information "City of Saskatoon," www.saskatoon.ca.

grassroots perceptions of issues, needs, and solutions. Anthropologists, however, are trained to do precisely these things.

To illustrate, Ervin discusses his work with the Saskatoon Social Planning Council. The council was established in 1992 with a push from activists working with organizations that specialize in the delivery of human services in Saskatoon. The council was created to investigate and work toward resolving local social issues. As with other social planning councils in Canada, it is involved in an extremely wide range of policies and issues, and it carries out policy research to assess local needs and problems, and to evaluate local programs. Ervin's main task has been to design a plan for conducting investigations of issues that fall under the council's domain. The goal of the research is to provide information that the human service organizations can use to help solve some of the problems the research identifies.

The council's first investigation project was a multi-dimensional study of the well-being of children in the city. The investigation took a wide variety of issues into account, including poverty, hunger, recreation, education, family, Aboriginal and immigrant issues, substance abuse, and general health concerns. Several organizations collaborated on the project, including the regional health board, the Catholic and public school boards, and the social services district office. A working group of representatives from each organization was formed to analyze the data, much of which was collected by anthropology students at the University of Saskatchewan. When the group released its report, the council called together the organizations that had

collaborated on the project, as well as other organizations and individuals involved with children's issues in Saskatoon, to consider the results and discuss possible solutions.

Ervin believes that anthropologists can make important contributions in urban policy contexts, especially in needs assessment, through "the process of identifying and seeking solutions to problems of particular populations, irrespective of whether programs have already been designed to address them" (1996: 330). Anthropologists seem particularly well suited for participating in these projects, given their commitment to participatory research and holism. Indeed, from Ervin's point of view, there is a major need in urban policy research for anthropologists who are *flexible* in their approach—that is, anthropologists who can move from one policy domain to another and construct integrated overviews of the phenomenon under investigation.

Anthropology and Policy

Central to applied anthropology is, as illustrated throughout this text, the use of holism, comparison, and cultural relativism. Because anthropologists contextualize their work and consider alternative perspectives, they are frequently hesitant to make policy recommendations that are as detailed as those often made by individuals working in other professional disciplines. This may be because anthropologists are particularly aware of the problems in applied work, the problems in trying to make people, or systems, change. Anthropologists are trained to analyze social and cultural systems, and when they are asked how to change these systems, they begin to ask questions. These questions are based on an awareness of the enormous complexity of human life when it is viewed from ground level.

Anthropologists have developed a keen awareness that not everyone makes the same basic assumptions about the world that planners and officials make. They know that sometimes technical experts providing help in other cultures know less about the issues they are investigating than do the people they are advising; further, they know that these "experts" are not always qualified to give culturally appropriate advice (Figure 14.4). Anthropologists realize that no change benefits everyone equally and that some people gain as others lose. They also understand that even if they get involved in planning a program, implementation of that program depends on diverse external factors over which they have no control. And they know that they get to go home while others remain to deal with the outcomes of policy-makers' decisions. Anthropologists believe they have much to contribute in helping to build a better world, yet they are also highly sensitive to the kinds of issues that arise when dealing with complex human systems. Applied anthropologists are well aware of the ambiguities of the human experience.

FIGURE 14.4 A Palestinian widow in Gaza confers with a field worker in the greenhouse she built, with the help of an international humanitarian aid organization, on ground that she cleared herself. She uses the garden to grow seasonal food to feed her six children.

Anthropology and the Challenges of Global Citizenship

One of the challenges faced by people everywhere in the world today is that of defining citizenship in a complex, diverse, and difficult world. Can anthropologists provide ways for people to understand the issues involved?

Anthropology and Democracy

In the decades since the end of the Cold War, the capitalist market has spread into nearly all parts of the globe; as a result, many observers have assumed that other Western institutions will also eventually spread into all regions. The fall or mutation of dictatorial political regimes in a number of Latin American and European countries, for example, was viewed as an opportunity to introduce Western political practices, including political parties and formal elections. Many members of the Western political and economic elite eagerly proclaimed the arrival of democracy as soon as the first elections were held, and they have often been very suspicious of political movements that challenge formal electoral institutions "in the name of democracy."

But anthropologists and other social scientists working in these same countries are often able to present a different perspective on the "transition" to democracy. Fieldwork brings them into close, regular contact with citizens who have their own ideas about what kinds of social institutions do or do not operate in a democratic fashion. Taking these observations seriously has drawn anthropologists into a growing debate about what democracy is, what it has been, and what it can be. In particular, their work has helped to show that formal Western electoral politics may produce less democratic outcomes than other, traditional institutions could produce.

For example, anthropologist Serge Tcherkézoff (1998) has followed debates about the shape democracy ought to take in the independent nation of Samoa (see EthnoProfile 4.1). Traditionally, Samoa was a land of villages, each of which was governed by a council of *matai*, or "sacred chiefs." This system survived Christian missionaries, German colonization, and decades of foreign administration (during the time that the area was a protectorate of New Zealand). A referendum sponsored by the UN in 1962 led to independence, and the people then voted to set up a parliamentary system of national government. However, their constitution specified that only *matai* could vote and run for office. In 1990, the law was changed to allow all citizens to vote, but even today *matai* remain the only ones allowed to run for office (Figure 14.5).

Does this hybrid of a Western parliamentary system and the Samoan *faamatai*, or "chief-system," represent an undemocratic attempt by chiefly "aristocrats" to maintain power within formally democratic political institutions? In Tcherkézoff's opinion, the question is deeply misleading because it rests on a fundamental misunderstanding of how the Samoan chief-system functions. He points out that if outsiders insist on thinking of *matai* as aristocrats, then there are no families in Samoa who are not aristocratic. This is because each *matai* is actually the head of an extended family. Each extended family is held together by kinship connections, joint ownership of land, and joint participation in rituals directed to their founding ancestor. *Matai*, in fact, means "the one who bears the family name," and members of each extended family choose the person who will be ritually invested with this title. It is the job of each *matai* to serve his family and his *matai* name by leading worship directed to the ancestor and engaging in other activities designed to elevate the reputation of his extended family. If a *matai* fails to live up to these expectations, his extended family can strip him of his title and give it to someone else. Every family has a *matai*, which is why Tcherkézoff says that there are no families that are not chiefly families. Further, *matais* serve at the will of the kin who choose them, which is why he tells us, "when Samoans heard about 'democracy,' they said that they 'already have it'" (1998: 423).

So why are Samoans arguing about the connection between the *matai* system and democracy? As Tcherkézoff explains, this debate involves a variety of different ideas about what *democracy* means and which kinds of institutional arrangements are most likely to ensure it. Some Samoans favour a view of democracy in which the emphasis is on individual freedom: anyone can run for office and anyone can vote. They point out, for example, that traditionally nobody becomes a *matai* until he has served his family for many years

FIGURE 14.5 The parliament building in Samoa. Today, Samoans continue to take part in a debate that involves a variety of ideas about what *democracy* means and what kinds of institutional arrangements are most likely to ensure it. What does democracy mean to you?

and his predecessor has died, which limits the field of possible parliamentary candidates to one relatively old man per extended family. How can it be democratic to restrict the opportunities of younger people to run for office? These sorts of arguments fit well with traditional Western arguments that speak of democracy in connection with individual freedom from arbitrary restrictions.

But those Samoans who want the *matai* system to continue stress that it is more democratic than typical Western-style stems of democracy because it creates representatives who can never forget that they are responsible to those who elected them—the other members of their extended family. In thinking about democracy in this way, these Samoans are refusing to reduce democratic citizenship to the right to vote. Rather, they take the view that democracy involves not just being treated as an equal by others but also the obligation of those who make political decisions for others to remain accountable and accessible to those whom they represent. Thus, the *matai* system can be viewed as highly democratic because it ensures that every extended family will be represented in some form in the electoral process and that any *matais* elected to parliament will not be able to ignore the wishes of those who put them in office.

Politics in Samoa also has a regional dimension. Tcherkézoff points out that Samoa was primarily a nation of villages in the past, but the capital city has been growing in size in recent years. Many of those who live in the growing urban area depend more on wage labour and less on agriculture and fishing, the activities central to live in villages, where *matais* traditionally exercised their authority. Thus, those who want to preserve the *matai* system also defend it as a way of maintaining equality between those who live in the city and those who still live in rural areas. They fear that if any citizen were allowed to run for office, Samoa would be fractured into two societies: an urban sector with a Western political system, which would have no way to hold their parliamentary representatives accountable, and a rural sector in which *matais* still exist but only as powerless guardians of local folklore. Should this happen, "then some Samoans say that 'democracy' will not be achieved and will even go backwards" (Tcherkézoff 1998: 427).

As Tcherkézoff makes clear, the debate about democracy in Samoa is complex and nuanced: Samoans have a sophisticated understanding of the advantages and drawbacks of different democratic political forms, some of which are indigenous to Samoa and some of which came from elsewhere. "The problem is that Samoa has the chance to build its future on ideas and experiences that come both from the *faamatai* tradition and from the Western tradition of democracy, and to maybe create a new synthesis where the advent of democracy will not just be the replacement of hierarchy (in the *faamatai*) by inequality (in the Western-style politics). There lies the real question of the future of the country" (Tcherkézoff 1998: 430).

Anthropology and Multicultural Politics in the New Europe

One of the more interesting things about the late twentieth and early twenty-first centuries is that Europe—the continent that gave birth to the Enlightenment and colonial empires, and to anthropology itself—has now become a key setting for the anthropological study of social and cultural changes. Europeans are struggling with the concept of multiculturalism in ways we in Canada can recognize. Indeed, we are the people with the Canadian Multiculturalism Act, passed in Parliament in 1988, which recognizes "the diversity of Canadians as regards race, national or ethnic origin, colour, and religion as

a fundamental characteristic of Canadian society . . . while working to achieve the equality of all Canadians in the economic, social, cultural, and political life of Canada" (Preamble). How are European nations dealing with the influx of people they consider non-European?

Let us look at an example from Italy. In 1999, British anthropologist Michael Herzfeld (2003) moved into Rione Monti, a working-class Roman neighbourhood close to the Coliseum (see Map 14.3), to do fieldwork exploring social change in the way people use the concept of the past. Long-time residents of Monti share a common local culture, which includes use of the *romanesco* dialect rather than standard Italian and a strong sense of local identity that distinguishes them from "foreigners," including diplomats and non-Roman Italians. Their identity survived fascist dictator Benito Mussolini's demolition of part of the neighbourhood in the early twentieth century. They successfully dealt with a local criminal underworld by mastering a refined code of politeness. The underworld had faded away by the 1970s, but beginning in the 1980s, residents began to face two new challenges to their community.

1. Historic Roman neighbourhoods became fashionable, and well-to-do Italians began to move into Rione Monti, pushing many workers into cheaper housing elsewhere.
2. In the 1990s, another group of newcomers arrived: immigrants from eastern Europe.

Italy is one of the more recent destinations of immigration into Europe, reversing the country's

MAP 14.3 Rione Monti

historical experience as a source, rather than a target, of immigration. After Germany, France, and Britain passed laws curtailing immigration in the 1970s, Italy became an increasingly popular destination for immigrants from Africa, Asia, Latin America, and, after the Cold War, other European nations, particularly those of eastern Europe. Until relatively recently, laws regulating immigration were few, and the country appeared welcoming. But this is changing (Figure 14.6). "Italy has not historically been a racist country, but intolerant attitudes toward immigrants have increased. To a large extent, this seems to be the result of a long-standing underestimation of the magnitude of the changes and thus poor policy implementation for a lengthy period, in spite of the best intentions officially proclaimed" (Melotti 1997: 91).

Italian anthropologist and political sociologist Umberto Melotti (1997) contrasts the distinctive ways in which immigration is understood by the governments of France, Britain, and Germany. According to him, the French project is *ethnocentric assimilationism*: since the early nineteenth century, when French society experienced a falling birth rate, immigration was encouraged and immigrants were promised all the rights and privileges of native-born citizens as long as they adopted French culture completely, dropping other ethnic or cultural attachments and assimilating the French language, culture, and character (75). The British project, in contrast, is *uneven pluralism*: that is, the pragmatic British expect immigrants to be loyal and law-abiding citizens, but they do not expect immigrants to "become British," and they tolerate private cultivation of cultural differences as long as these do not threaten the British way of life (79–80). Finally, Melotti describes the German project as *the institutionalization of precariousness*, by which he means that despite the fact that Germany has within its borders more immigrants than any other European country, and began receiving immigrants at the end of the nineteenth century, its government continues to insist that Germany is not a country of immigrants. Immigrants were generally considered "guest workers," and even today it remains somewhat difficult for immigrants to obtain German citizenship.

Some European countries face issues of multiculturalism that are rooted in longstanding

FIGURE 14.6 In recent years, intolerance toward immigrants has increased in Italy. As part of a 2002 protest in Rome against increased restrictions on immigration, this young immigrant from Africa displayed a silencing sticker that reads "never more racism." How would you use your anthropological skills to look at both sides of this situation? What questions would you ask?

tensions between two or more ethnic groups that are equally established within the same country. This is the case in Belgium, for example, where there has been historic conflict between the Dutch-speaking Flemings in the north and the French-speaking Walloons in the south. The country has found a partial solution to cultural tension by allowing both groups to enjoy considerable autonomy, and the state's role is to protect the rights of each community in the public sphere.

Coming to terms with increasing numbers of Muslims living in countries where Christianity has historically been dominant is a central theme in multicultural debates within Europe. Although almost all European states consider themselves secular in orientation, the relation between religion and state is far from uniform. France is unusual because of its strict legal separation between religion and state. In Britain, the combination of a secular outlook with state funding of the established Anglican Church has allowed citizens to support forms of religious inclusion such as state funding of "faith schools" (i.e., schools that combine religious and secular content) for non-Protestant immigrants. Today, there are over a dozen state-funded Muslim schools in England (AMS 2014). In Germany, where a secular outlook also combines with state-subsidized religious institutions, the state has devised curricula for elementary schools designed to teach all students about different religious traditions, including Islam, in ways that emphasize the possibility of harmonizing one's religious faith with one's obligations as a citizen. Although this approach may be seen as presumptuous or paternalistic, its supporters counter that its advantages outweigh its costs. Perhaps as a result of their country's history, many contemporary Germans have less faith than the British that a civic culture of religious tolerance will automatically lead to harmony without state intervention, and less faith than the French in the existence of a separate secular sphere of society from which religion can be safely excluded (Schiffauer 1997).

These are, of course, thumbnail sketches of more complex attitudes and practices. But they illustrate the fact that there is no single "European" approach to the challenges posed by immigration and multiculturalism. In a way, each European state, with its own history and institutions, is experimenting with different ways of coping, and their failures and successes will influence the kinds of multicultural relations and institutions that develop in the future. This experimentation is particularly significant in light of the fact that European nation-states have joined together in the European Union (EU), a superstate with 28 members as of 2014. Reconciling the diverse, culturally informed interests and needs of member states poses enormous challenges for the EU as a whole.

Many scholars and activists hope that solutions can be found that will involve extensions of social justice throughout the EU. But there is still a lot of work to be done, and there are no guarantees about the outcome. British Pakistani professor of public policy Tariq Modood points out, for example, that European multiculturalism requires supporting conceptions of citizenship that allow the "right to assimilate" as well as the "right to have one's 'difference' . . . recognized and supported in the public and the private spheres" (1997: 20). Further, in Modood's view, European multiculturalism must recognize that "participation in the public or national culture is necessary for the effective exercise of citizenship" while at the same time defending the "right to widen and adapt the national culture" (20). The potential and actual contradictions among some of these goals are apparent, but insofar as they are seen as necessary, the challenge becomes finding ways

to move forward. And here, with no blueprint to follow, all parties find themselves involved in creating new cultural practices. Based on her experience in France, anthropologist Marie-Bénédicte Dembour is convinced that "we need to accept the discomfort of moving in-between, as a pendulum" (2001: 71–2). Modood agrees: "There is indeed a tension here, and perhaps it can only be resolved in practice through finding and cultivating points of common ground between dominant and subordinate cultures, as well as new syntheses and hybridities. The important thing is that the burdens of change . . . are not all dependent on one party to this encounter" (1997: 20).

Anthropologists are inevitably drawn into these discussions, not only because they carry out research in the communities struggling for resolution but also because many of them are citizens of the societies whose future depends on the solutions that are implemented. As a result, theoretical debates in the field are intertwined with political debates in society, and scholars can disagree with one another just as political activists do. For example, Norwegian anthropologist Thomas Eriksen (2001) reports on the outcome of a formal debate organized by the Department of Anthropology at the University of Oslo in 1997, in which the thesis to be contested was the assertion that cultural freedom protects not only a group but also the rights of every individual within a group. Eriksen notes that those supporting the thesis and those arguing against it "not only reached opposite conclusions but also failed to engage in a proper dialogue: they tended to depict each other . . . as hopeless Romantics and cynical modernists, respectively" (144). In the end, Eriksen observes, the debate raised the same kinds of issues and provoked the same kinds of responses and standoffs that can be found in the wider society. After the debate, the audience was invited to vote for the side they thought had made the best case. The results were 78 in favour of the motion, 75 against. This almost perfect standoff, Eriksen points out, is very different from what the outcome would likely have been 10 or 15 years earlier, when there would have been "almost certainly a massive 'yes' vote" (145). As Eriksen speculates, "perhaps the tide will turn again" (145).

Thus, the struggles and dilemmas facing residents of Rione Monti are widespread across the new Europe. But the specifics of the situation in

Rione Monti, and the cultural resources available to longstanding residents, have their own particularity. For the most part, the traditionally left-wing Monti residents have resisted turning against immigrant families in the neighbourhood. Still, they are unhappy with many of the ways in which immigration has impacted their lives (Figure 14.7). For example, they do not like the location of the Ukrainian church in a building that overlooks the neighbourhood's central square because churchgoers gather there twice a week, invading "their" space (Herzfeld 2003: 4). Herzfeld reports that the residents of Monti, like other Romans, claim not to be racist (which accords with Melotti's views of Italians in general) and that they seem less hostile to immigrants of colour than to Ukrainians. Ukrainians are more numerous in Monti and more threatening because they look like local people and compete with local people for work and space in the neighbourhood (5). At the same time, the Monti code of politeness "underlies the facility with which democratically inclined residents today construct a popular street democracy, a system of neighbourhood associations" (2). At the beginning of the twenty-first century, immigrants were not able to deploy this code, a fact that signalled their outsider status and could lead to misunderstandings and bad feelings. If they could learn to use the code, however, fresh opportunities for political co-operation might be forged. This arrangement could be decisive, for the code of politeness is the foundation of local democratic processes.

More recently, Herzfeld has made the following observations on the situation in Rione Monti:

> People are being kicked out of their homes by a variety of implacable forces ranging from the underworld and the banks to religious institutions claiming a charitable identity. Loansharking is rife; so are prostitution, racism against immigrant populations, police intolerance, political extremism. The economic pressures that these facts indicate are being exacerbated by the current problems of the country as a whole and of the European Union, but in some form they have always been part of Roman life, and Romans know how to deal with them—not always successfully, but usually with aplomb and dignity. (2013)

FIGURE 14.7 In the neighbourhood of Rione Monti in central Rome, long-time residents and new immigrants are negotiating new forms of relationships.

As these observations suggest, codes can mutate, indeed disintegrate, with changing economic conditions and demography. Tolerance can be eroded in tough and/or changing times and be shown to be merely skin deep—and not an integrated component of our definition of self.

Anthropology and Human Rights

Anthropologists have long been involved in an intensifying understanding of human rights, and they have contributed to the recognition by human rights legal advocates that the collective rights of groups deserve as much attention as do the rights of individuals. Anthropologist Ellen Messer observes that anthropologists have examined, and continue to examine,

> the contexts of human rights abuses to understand how the political economic conditions that create cultural customs such as infanticide, underfeeding of women and children, and other abuses of women might be improved and make the customs of less evident utility. They also continue to work with interpreters of local traditions, so that through persuasion and contextualization, and by drawing on the authority of multiple traditions, people might be empowered to improve human rights in their own lives. (1993: 241)

FIGURE 14.8 Kuna women work with Cultural Survival radio producer Rosy Sul González on grassroots Kuna language maintenance efforts in Panama. What sorts of things can organizations and anthropologists do to ensure that Indigenous peoples are actively involved in their projects?

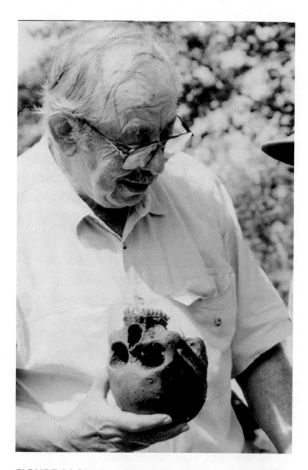

FIGURE 14.9 Some applied anthropologists, like the late Clyde Snow (shown here), use their knowledge and skills in skeletal identification to defend human rights around the world.

Perhaps one of the foremost anthropologically oriented organizations involved with human rights is Cultural Survival, founded in 1972 by anthropologists Pia Maybury-Lewis and David Maybury-Lewis. The organization is dedicated to helping Indigenous people and ethnic minorities deal as equals in their encounters with industrial society (Figure 14.8). Over the years, many Canadian anthropologists have contributed to projects with similar aims across the globe. Indeed, in this and other contexts, "Canadian anthropology has been on the leading edge of engaged anthropology for decades," essentially avoiding the energy-sapping debate on the merits of theoretical versus applied anthropology that often dominates anthropological discussions in the United States and elsewhere (Waldram 2010: 225).

Biological anthropologists have also contributed in an important way to the defence of human rights in the world. Until his death in 2014, forensic anthropologist Clyde Snow was at the forefront of such efforts (Figure 14.9). Snow was often called on by police departments, medical examiners, and other law-enforcement officials to try to identify human remains and to determine the cause of death. Snow was involved in a number of international human rights cases. Beginning in 1984, he worked with the American Association for the Advancement of Science to help the Argentinian National Commission on Disappeared Persons to determine the fate of some of the more than 10,000 people who had vanished during the "dirty war" waged by the Argentine military government against supposed subversives. Snow began his work in Argentina by training a team of medical and anthropology students in the techniques of forensic investigation, both skeletal and archaeological, and then helped them exhume and examine the remains of many *desaparecidos* ("those who have disappeared"). Their efforts helped convict a number of leaders, including high-ranking military and police officers, responsible for the deaths (Huyghe 1988). Snow has commented on the importance of this sort of work: "There are human rights violations going on all around the world. But to me murder is murder, regardless of the motive. I hope that we are sending a message to governments who murder in the name of politics that they can be held to account" (55).

Social anthropologists Paul Oldham and Miriam Frank (2008) have considered the adoption of the UN's 2007 Declaration on the Rights of Indigenous Peoples. Declarations are important, but only insofar as they become the road map for action. They challenge us to consider the role that anthropology might play in promoting human rights. In Canada, for example, we might ask what anthropologists can do to help ease the suffering of Aboriginal peoples who continue to struggle with the after-effects of the residential school system.

Awareness and Uncertainty

At this point, let us return to the question we posed at the beginning of this chapter: Why study anthropology? The second part of our answer is more personal.

Anthropology brings all of us into contact with different ways of life—past and present. It makes us aware of just how arbitrary our own

---

Changes in the contemporary world are producing what anthropologist George Marcus calls "transcultural 'traditional' peoples," whose members live in many different places and whose sense of cultural identity involves a mix of many cultural elements.

The power of global cultural homogenization in the late twentieth century challenges the conventions and rationales by which anthropology has so far produced its knowledge of other cultures. The reorganization of the world economy through technological advances in communication, production processes, and marketing has thoroughly de-territorialized culture. For example, the Tongan Islanders of Polynesia that I studied in the early 1970s now constitute a diaspora of communities in locales around the Pacific Rim. As many, if not more, Tongans now live permanently in Australia, New Zealand, and the United States as in the islands themselves. One might fairly ponder where both the cultural and geographical centre of the Tongan people resides. Their identity is produced in many locales and through the mix of many cultural elements. And their conditions are similar to those of numerous other peoples that anthropologists have traditionally studied. It is no longer just the most powerful, large-scale, and most modern societies, such as the United States and Japan, that exist in international, transcultural science.

Among such transcultural "traditional" peoples, levels of cultural self-consciousness and alternatives increase. The authenticity of performances, rituals, or apparently deep-seated norms like those of kinship cannot be merely assumed, either by locals or by visitors such as anthropologists. To some extent, media documentaries have absorbed anthropology's function of presenting vividly the life-ways of other cultures to Euro-American publics that themselves can no longer be considered as homogeneous or mainstream. And, finally, the subjects of anthropological study independently and articulately translate their own perspectives with sensitivity to the effects of different media.

Peoples who in particular have become classic anthropological subjects, such as the Samoans, the Trobriand Islanders, the Hopi of the Southwest USA, and the Todas of India, know their status well, and have, with some ambivalence, assimilated anthropological knowledge about them as part of their sense of themselves. A recent example was the visit of a Toda woman to Houston, Texas. A trained nurse among her people, as well as a cultural broker, she was on tour in the United States giving talks about the Todas, of the sort that anthropologists might have given in past decades. By chance, she was visiting the home of a colleague just as a British documentary about the Todas appeared on the television—a documentary in which the visitor was featured prominently as the filmmaker's prime source of information. The visitor's comments as she watched the program along with my colleague did not much concern the details of Toda culture but rather dealt with the ironies of the multiple representations of her people—by herself, by anthropologists, and by the British Broadcasting Corporation.

The lesson of this story is compelling. The penetrations of a world economy, communications, and the effects of multiple, fragmented identities on cultural authenticity, once thought restricted to advanced modernity, have increased markedly among most local and regional cultures worldwide. They have thus engendered an ethnography in reverse among many peoples who not only can assimilate the professional idioms of anthropology but can relativize them among other alternatives and ways of knowledge. This does not mean that the traditional task of anthropology to represent distinctive and systematic cultural forms of life has been fundamentally subverted by its own subjects. Rather, anthropology's traditional task is now much more complicated, requiring new sensibilities in undertaking fieldwork and different strategies for writing about it.

Source: Marcus, George. 1990. "Into the Warp and Woof of Multicultural Worlds," guest editorial in *Cultural Anthropology: A Perspective on the Human Condition*, 2nd edn, eds Emily Schultz and Robert Lavenda (St Paul: West), 254–5.

understanding of the world is as we learn how other people have developed satisfying but different ways of living. In addition, if we are from Western countries that were responsible for colonialism and its consequences, it makes us painfully aware of just how much our own tradition has contributed to the form of the modern world. Further, it makes us aware of just how much our well-being is situated in the wealth and resources generated elsewhere in the world.

Knowing and experiencing cultural variety gives rise, perhaps inevitably, to doubt. We come to doubt the ultimate validity of the central truths of our own cultural tradition, which have been ratified and sanctified by the generations who preceded us. We doubt because a familiarity with alternative ways of living makes the ultimate meaning of any action, of any object, a highly ambiguous matter. Ambiguity is part and parcel of the human condition. Human beings have coped with ambiguity from time immemorial by means of culture, which places objects and actions in contexts and thereby makes their meanings plain. This doubt can lead to anxiety, but it can also be liberating.

Such liberation leads to a recognition of themes of central concern for informed global citizens—freedom, health, divisions of wealth, environment, personhood, governance, transnationalism, and the like. An excellent example is how these themes combine in the context of the debate about who should control the remaining samples of the "eradicated" disease smallpox (see the "In Their Own Words" box on this topic). Western scientists and politicians argue that the samples are necessary for research purposes. Yet other people—especially people living in Africa, where the disease was most devastating during the twentieth century—argue that all samples should be destroyed to prevent them from leaking out into the public. Between these two positions, other individuals and groups have developed their own unique perspectives based on their own unique situations. By employing the anthropological perspective, anthropology

In Their Own Words | Homes for the Smallpox Virus

This editorial article considers the efficacy of keeping samples of the smallpox virus—one of the most deadly virus known to humans—decades after its eradication from human populations. Similar ethical discussions will arise in other world-health situations (e.g., in efforts to reconstruct the virus that caused the 1918 "Spanish flu" pandemic, or to study the Ebola virus in laboratories across the globe).

19 January 2011

At a May meeting of the World Health Assembly—a gathering of delegates from all WHO member states—the United States and Russia will once again face a clamour, led by African countries, to eliminate the last known live samples of the smallpox virus—thirty years after the WHO declared it eradicated. Unfortunately, humanity cannot dispense with this destroyer of life so easily.

The scourge is believed to have killed more people over the millennia than any other, its victims running into the hundreds of millions. Legions more were blinded and permanently disfigured. The last natural outbreaks occurred in Africa as late as the 1970s, within living memory, and it is understandable that African countries are pushing most vehemently to bring about its extinction.

The fact of smallpox's survival three decades after its eradication through a global program of vaccination, even in maximum-containment, "biosafety level 4" laboratories at the US Centers for Disease Control and at a research institution in Russia, constitutes a real and constant danger. But the elimination of the live virus would not remove that threat. On the contrary, it might serve in a perverse way to exacerbate it.

Live viruses might well persist in unknown laboratories, or even, it has been theorized, lie in wait in permafrost cemeteries. It is also possible that the virus could be artificially reconstructed and used in a bioterrorism attack. For that reason, the US ordered the emergency production of 168 million doses of smallpox vaccine after 11 September 2001 and continues to add to its stocks.

This is not bioterror hysteria. It is a sensible precaution. Such a threat is much greater than any risk posed by the collections maintained at two WHO-authorized high-security laboratories. These samples, frozen in liquid nitrogen, are the source of anxiety for those who want to declare total victory in the war against smallpox. But such chest-thumping would harm research into the human immune system and undermine the capacity of science to identify and research antiviral agents and next-generation vaccines. Surely this is a case of its being better to know thy enemy.

Source: "Homes for the Smallpox Virus." 2011. Editorial in *The Globe and Mail* (19 Jan.), available at www.theglobeandmail.com/news/opinions/editorials/homes-for-the-smallpox-virus/article1876412/. © The Globe and Mail Inc. All Rights Reserved.

allows us to understand the many sides of the debate and respect the validity of the many perspectives involved in seeking a positive outcome.

Freedom and Constraint

So why study anthropology? The third part of our answer is humanistic—it relates to our interest in our fellow human beings and our desire to learn about and from the diversity of humanity.

All human beings live in culturally shaped worlds, enmeshed in webs of interpretation and meaning. It has been the particular task of anthropologists to go out to bear witness to and record the vast creative diversity in *world-making* that has been the history of our species. In our lifetimes, we will witness the end of many of those ways of life. This loss can be tragic, for as these worlds disappear so too does something special about humanity: variety, creativity, and awareness of alternatives. We are also witness to change—a loss also but also a gain—as we face the challenge of moving into an unknown, unknowable future. Our survival as a species, and our viability as individuals, depends on the possibility of choice, of perceiving and being able to act on alternatives in the various situations we encounter during our lives. If we think of human life as a minefield, then the more paths we can see and imagine through that minefield, the more likely we are to make it through. As alternatives are destroyed, wantonly smashed, or thoughtlessly crushed, our own human possibilities are reduced.

Anthropologists have, for the last century or so, gone out into the world to write the record of human accomplishment, learn from it, and teach its meaning to others. Surely our greatest human accomplishment is the creation of the sometimes beautiful worlds in which we all

---

A CRITICAL LOOK | Going Somewhere?

And so we arrive at the end of this book with a sense that we are on a metaphorical road to *somewhere*. Without an awareness of where we have come from and where we are now, the map for this road lacks context. It is context that situates us in the meaning of things, indeed the meaning of *us* and the potential meanings of *future destinations*.

In archaeological findings from very ancient times—the Paleolithic, or Old Stone Age—we have some indicators of material culture altering our relationship to the natural world we were and remain a part of. One was the invention of tools—first simple and later more complex—made from stone. Then came fire. Without fire we would have remained in the long-running and deeply stable Paleolithic, chipping away and staying near to what warmth we could find.

Fire came to us first in its wild form from the sky—a place where fire shone in the day and sparkled in the night. It came from a brilliant light show in the sky, through a bolt of lightning striking the ground, essentially a gift from above. Once found, this gift had to be cherished, fed, and protected. Of course, it could be a difficult gift as well—a fire raging over the grasslands of Africa had the power to burn us out of our place in the world.

Who was our first ancestor to understand that stone struck on stone could make fire? That friction could warm? That fire could be "domesticated"? Once this discovery had been made, we became the keepers of a crucial technology, one that must have seemed magical and that was certainly transformative. Fire allowed us to alter our relationship with our world. It turned cold to warmth, night to day. It altered what and how we ate, and it provided a circle of protective light from the predators and scavengers of the night. It gave us a cozy, intimate place for family and friends to gather and a way to communicate over great distances. Its heat altered materials, allowing us to shape malleable metals and create pottery. It allowed us to fashion diverse forms of weapons. As we studied the light and the heat of fire, and its ability to transform our world, we became chemists and physicists. Much later, fire gave us the Industrial Revolution—the steam engine to drive us into a different cultural world. Of course there were other "great" inventions and innovations: domestication of plants and animals (food economies) and the wheel (transportation), to name only two, but fire was transformative in a foundational way.

Today, with the dawn of the digital age and the diffusion of information technologies around the globe, we are in the midst of another unparalleled transformation. Technology lights our minds, sparks our imagination in new ways! For the younger generations born into this

continued

world of change, these technologies are not so surprising. They are merely a part of daily life, and the immense changes they have brought about are generally taken for granted. But for many others, the change has been quite startling.

Of course, there were a number of forward-thinking individuals who anticipated the ways in which such technologies might change our lives. We can find many examples in the realm of science fiction, perhaps most notably Arthur C. Clarke, whose mid-twentieth-century works explore such contemporary concepts as artificial intelligence, nanotechnology, and gene mapping. In the realm of anthropology, Edward T. Hall was a similarly forward-thinking individual. In his 1976 book *Beyond Culture*, he discussed *extension transference*, a term he coined for the relationship between our biology and our technology. Hall understood that technological change could lead to biological change, although our human culture (both ideational and material) is capable of adapting much more quickly than is our genetic makeup.

What does our future hold? No one knows, but many continue to speculate. Theoretical physicist Michio Kaku, for example, gives us some insight into what might be possible in the world of the future. One troubling question that Kaku poses is "Can consciousness exist by itself, free from the constraints of the physical body?" (2014: 266)? This question speaks to our deep desire not to be transient. While Kaku cannot give us a definitive answer to this question, he explores a number of new and evolving technologies that may one day make it possible for us to separate our consciousness from our body—for example, cloning and mind transfer, and computer-based "backups" of the human mind. He even suggests the possibility of our consciousnesses existing as beams of light, pure energy able to roam free through the universe. While such developments may seem far off and even fanciful to some, they also represent the unlimited possibilities available through human creativity and agency.

While we wait with anticipation to see what the future holds, we should consider what we are currently giving of ourselves to technology. How deeply do we rely on our gadgets to make our way through the world? How much of what makes us *us* have we given over to their digital systems? What might we be losing as we increasingly choose to connect with one another through digital technologies rather than face-to-face interactions? Can digital connections ever replace the sensation of sharing the same physical space with another person, perhaps sitting around a nice warm fire roasting marshmallows and eating s'mores? As anthropologists, we cannot help but ask these sorts of questions as we contemplate what our technological advancements might mean for the future of humanity.

—Roberta Robin Dods

live. Anthropologists have rarely given in to the romantic notion that these other worlds are all good, all life-enhancing, all fine or beautiful. They are not. Ambiguity and ambivalence are, as we have seen, hallmarks of the human experience. There are no guarantees that human cultures will be compassionate rather than cruel or that people will agree they are one or the other. There are not even any guarantees that our species will survive. But all anthropologists have believed that these are *human* worlds that have given those who have lived in them the ability to make sense out of their experiences and to derive meaning for their lives, and that we are a species at once bound by our culture and free to change it.

This is a perilous and fearsome freedom. Nevertheless, the freedom is there, and in this dialectic of freedom and constraint lies our future. It is up to us to create it.

CHAPTER SUMMARY

1. Anthropological research can be challenging to conduct in today's world, but it is also very rewarding. Applied anthropology can contribute to contemporary solutions of various social issues. Applied anthropologists do their work using holism, comparison, relativism, and a concern for particular cases.

2. Anthropology teaches many lessons that are relevant to a wide variety of situations. Even if you do not go on to work as an anthropologist, you can refer to your knowledge of anthropology as a guide for a way of living in the world in a state of reflexivity—a state of constant engagement and growth.

3. Anthropologists involved in expanding the understanding of human rights have participated in organizations for the defence of human rights. In particular, they have contributed to the recognition by human rights legal advocates that the collective rights of groups (such as Indigenous peoples) deserve as much attention as the rights of individuals.

4. Cultural anthropology brings us into contact with different ways of life and challenges our awareness of just how arbitrary our own understanding of the world is as we learn how other people have developed satisfying but different ways of living.

CRITICAL THINKING QUESTIONS

1. How would you describe the potential of applied anthropology to address various issues of concern in today's world? Give at least three specific examples.

2. Review the list of the 12 main skills you can learn from a major in anthropology (p. 351). Which have been the greatest challenges for you?

3. Why do you suppose anthropologists are particularly aware of the problems in applied work—the problems in trying to make people, or systems, change? What is it about anthropology that engenders such sensitivity?

4. How would you describe the ambiguity and ambivalence of the human experience in the sometimes beautiful worlds in which we all live?

SUGGESTED READINGS

Oldham, Paul, and Miriam Anne Frank. 2008. "'We the People . . .': The United Nations Declaration on the Rights of Indigenous Peoples," *Anthropology Today* 24, 2: 5–9. A report on the adoption of the UN document on the rights of Indigenous peoples worldwide. Note that not all states have signed on.

Rylko-Bauer, Barbara, Merrill Singer, and John Van Willigen. 2006. "Reclaiming Applied Anthropology: Its Past, Present, and Future," *American Anthropologist*, New Series, 108, 1: 178–90. An examination of the central role that application has played throughout anthropology's evolution, as well as the role of advocacy in relation to greater engagement as well as the relationship of theory to practice.

Smith, Susan E., Dennis G. Willms, and Nancy A. Johnson, eds. 1997. *Nurtured by Knowledge: Learning to Do Participatory Action Research* (New York: Apex Press). A discussion of PAR (participatory action research), a methodology that enables people to take control of their lives through the integration of formal and informal knowledge and by using this integrated knowledge in a transformative way to challenge their assumed realities.

Wardlow, Holly. 2007. "Men's Extramarital Sexuality in Rural Papua New Guinea," *American Journal of Public Health* 97, 6: 1006–14. A consideration of the role of extramarital activity in the spread of HIV/AIDS.

RELATED WEBSITES

Canadian Multiculturalism www.cic.gc.ca/english/multiculturalism/citizenship.asp

Foreign Affairs, Trade, and Development Canada's International Youth Internship Program www.international.gc.ca/development-developpement/partners-partenaires/iyip-psij

Cultural Survival www.culturalsurvival.org

Truth and Reconciliation Commission of Canada www.trc.ca

Society for Applied Anthropology www.sfaa.net

Survival International www.survivalinternational.org

USAID www.usaid.gov

GLOSSARY

abiotic Non-living; physical.

achieved statuses Social positions people may attain later in life, often as the result of their own (or other people's) effort.

affinal Related through marriage.

affluence The condition of having more than enough of whatever is required to satisfy consumption needs.

agency An individual's ability to make choices and to effect change through her or his actions.

age sets Non-kin social groups composed of young men born within a specified time span.

alienation The deep separation that individuals experience between their innermost sense of identity and the labour they are forced to perform in order to survive.

anomie A pervasive sense of rootlessness and normlessness.

anthropological perspective An approach to the human condition that is holistic, comparative, and evolutionary.

anthropology The integrated study of human nature, human society, and human history.

applied anthropology The use of information gathered from the other anthropological specialties to solve practical problems within and between cultures.

archaeology The specialty of anthropology interested in what we can learn from material remains left behind by earlier human societies.

art A representation that relates to an object, an experience, or some other component of the world and that evokes a felt response. In the words of anthropologist Alexander Alland, art is "play with form producing some aesthetically successful transformation-representation" (1977: 39).

articulated style A field-independent way of viewing the world that breaks it up into small pieces, which can then be organized into larger chunks.

ascribed statuses Social positions people are assigned at birth.

band A form of social organization that consists of a small group of foragers (usually fewer than fifty people), in which labour is divided according to age and sex, and social relations are highly egalitarian.

bilateral descent A pattern of descent in which a descent group is formed based on connections of relatedness made through *both* a mother *and* a father.

binary opposition A pair of opposites used as an organizing principle (e.g., body–soul; yin–yang; male–female).

bioaccumulation An accumulation of a toxic substance in a biological organism over time.

biocultural organisms Organisms whose defining features are co-determined by biological and cultural factors. Anthropologists use this term to describe human beings.

biological (or physical) anthropology The specialty of anthropology that looks at humans as biological organisms and tries to discover what characteristics make us different from and/or similar to other living things.

biological evolution Change (through mutation) in genetic makeup (the DNA/RNA) of a population that is passed on through the generations. Mutations can be beneficial, nonbeneficial (lethal), or neutral; thus, they can be overtly noticeable or not noticeable.

biomagnification An increase in the concentration of a toxic substance from the bottom to the top of a food chain.

biopower Power held by a modern government over the bodies of its individual citizens and over the "body" of all its citizens.

biotic Living; biological.

blended family A family created when previously divorced or widowed people marry, bringing with them children from their previous marriages.

bridewealth The transfer of certain symbolically important goods from the family of the groom to the family of the bride, representing compensation to the wife's lineage for the loss of her labour and for child-bearing capacities.

capitalism An economic system dominated by a supply and demand market designed to create capital and profit.

caste A ranked group within a socially stratified society that is closed, prohibiting individuals from moving from one caste into another.

chiefdom A form of social organization in which the leader (a chief) and the leader's close relatives are set apart from the rest of society and allowed privileged access to wealth, power, and prestige.

clan A descent group formed by members who believe they have a common (sometimes mythical) ancestor, even if they cannot specify the genealogical links.

class A ranked group within a hierarchically stratified society whose membership is defined primarily in terms of wealth, occupation, and/or access to power.

client The party of lower status in a clientage.

clientage Institution linking individuals from upper and lower levels in a stratified society.

co-evolution The relationship between biological processes and symbolic cultural processes in which each makes up an important part of the environment to which the other must adapt.

cognition (1) The mental process by which human beings gain knowledge, and (2) the nexus of relations between the mind at work and the world in which it works.

cognitive style Recurring patterns of cognitive activity that characterize an individual's perceptual and intellectual activities.

colonialism The cultural domination of a people by larger, wealthier powers.

colourism A system of social identities negotiated, based on the situation, along a continuum of skin colours between white and black.

communicative competence A term coined by anthropological linguist Dell Hymes to refer to the mastery of adult rules for socially and culturally appropriate speech.

communitas An unstructured or minimally structured community of equal individuals frequently found in rites of passage.

comparative A characteristic of the anthropological perspective that requires anthropologists to consider similarities and differences in a wide a range of human societies before generalizing about human nature, human society, or human history.

conjugal family A family based on marriage; at minimum, a spousal pair and their children.

connotative meaning Additional meanings of a word that derive from the typical contexts in which they are used and rely on personal and cultural associations.

consensus An agreement to which all parties collectively give their assent.

consumption Using up material goods necessary for human survival.

core In world-system theory, the nations specializing in banking, finance, and highly skilled industrial production.

cosmopolitanism Being at ease in more than one cultural setting.

creole A complex language with native speakers that has developed over one or more past generations from two or more distinct languages. Alternatively, a complex language that has developed from two or more distinct languages and that is used as a main language, whether or not it has native speakers.

cultural anthropology The specialty of anthropology that studies how variation in beliefs and behaviours is shaped by culture and learned by different members of human groups.

cultural ecology The study of the ways in which human beings relate to one another and to their natural environment.

cultural evolution Evolution of the beliefs and behaviours we incorporate into human development through the experiences of teaching and learning.

cultural hybridity See **cultural hybridization**.

cultural hybridization Cultural mixing that produces a new cultural form.

cultural imperialism The idea that some cultures dominate other cultures and that cultural domination by one culture leads inevitably to the destruction of subordinated cultures and their replacement by the culture of those in power.

cultural pattern A behaviour or idea that members of a specific society repeatedly pass on to one another, across generations, and that is thus recognizable to all members of that society. See also **schema**.

cultural relativism "Understanding another culture in its own terms sympathetically enough so that the culture appears to be a coherent and meaningful design for living" (Greenwood and Stini 1977: 182).

cultural synaesthesia A culturally shared response to a sense other than the one being stimulated (e.g., hearing a sound and seeing it as a colour).

culture Sets of learned behaviours and ideas that humans acquire as members of a society. We use culture to adapt to and transform the world in which we live.

culture area A geographical region in which cultural traditions share similar culture traits.

culture shock The feeling of physical and mental dislocation/discomfort a person experiences when in a new or strange cultural setting. It can manifest most deeply on returning "home," with home seeming exceedingly strange after extended stays in the fieldwork situation.

culture traits Particular features or parts of a cultural tradition such as a dance, ritual, or style of pottery.

decolonization The withdrawal of a colonial power from a territory that had been under its control.

defensive research Research that is designed and conducted by individuals outside the affected community without consulting members of the community about their interests or concerns.

denotative meaning The formal meaning(s) of a word, as given in a dictionary.

dependency theory A theory that argues that the success of "independent" capitalist nations has required the failure of "dependent" colonies or nations whose economies have been distorted to serve the needs of dominant capitalist outsiders.

design features of language The characteristics of language that, when taken together, differentiate it from other known animal communication systems.

determinism The philosophical view that one simple force (or a few simple forces) causes (or determines) complex events.

dialectic of fieldwork The process of building a bridge of understanding between anthropologist and informant so that each can begin to understand the other.

diaspora Migrant populations with a shared identity who live in a variety of different locales around the world; a form of transborder identity that does not focus on nation-building.

discourse In speech, a meaningful utterance or series of utterances united by a common theme.

disease A biomedical condition characterized by a harmful biological irregularity in an organism.

distribution The allocation of goods and services.

domination Coercive rule.

dowry The transfer of wealth from parents to their child (usually a daughter) at the time of the child's marriage.

dualism The philosophical view that reality consists of two equal and irreducible forces.

econiche The sum total of relations between a species and the plants and animals on which it relies for survival; these relations define those places where a species is "at home."

economic anthropology "The part of the discipline [of anthropology] that debates issues of *human nature* that relate directly to the decisions of daily life and making a living" (Wilk 1996: xv).

economy From an institutional perspective, the culturally specific processes used by members of a society to provide themselves with material resources.

ecotones A transition area between two different ecozones that displays characteristics of both ecozones.

ecozones The particular mixture of plant and animal species occupying any particular region of the earth.

Ego The person from whose perspective the kinship associations are being mapped and/or discussed.

elementary cognitive processes Mental tasks common to all humans without cognitive impairment.

emotion The product of entanglements connecting bodily arousal and cognitive interpretation. It comprises states, values, and arousals.

enculturation The process by which human beings living with one another must learn to come to terms with the ways of thinking and feeling that are considered appropriate in their respective cultures.

endogamy Marriage within a defined social group.

epidemiology The study of the occurrence, spread, management, and prevention of infectious diseases.

essence An unchanging core of features that is unique to things of the same kind (whether they are chairs, cows, ideas, or people) and makes them what they are.

essentially negotiable concepts Culturally recognized concepts that evoke a wide range of meanings and whose relevance in any particular context must be negotiated.

ethnic groups Social groups that are distinguished from one another on the basis of ethnicity.

ethnicity A social classification based on a common cultural heritage and selected cultural features such as language, religion, or dress. Ethnicity emerges from historical processes that incorporate distinct social groups into a single political structure under conditions of inequality.

ethnocentrism The opinion that one's own way of life is the most natural, correct, or fully human way of life.

ethnography An anthropologist's recorded (e.g., written, filmed) description of a particular culture.

ethnology The comparative study of two or more cultures.

ethnopragmatics The study of language use in a specific culture, grounded in an ethnographic approach, with close attention to the relationships among language, communication, and social interaction.

etiology The study of the causes of a disease and/or an illness.

evolutionary A characteristic of the anthropological perspective that requires anthropologists to place their observations about human nature, human society, or human history in a flexible framework that takes into consideration change over time.

exogamy Marriage outside a defined social group.

extended family A family pattern made up of three generations living together: parents, married children, and grandchildren.

extensive agriculture A form of cultivation that depends on slash-and-burn techniques, rainwater, human muscle power, and a few simple tools such as digging sticks, hoes, and/or machetes; it exhausts the land, requiring farmers to move plots every few years

fact A widely accepted observation, a taken-for-granted item of common knowledge, that becomes intelligible only when it is interpreted and placed in a context of meaning.

family At minimum, a woman or a man and her or his dependent children.

family of choice A family created over time by new kin ties as friends and lovers demonstrate their genuine commitment to one another.

fieldwork An extended period of close involvement with the people in whose way of life anthropologists are interested, during which anthropologists ordinarily collect most of their data.

flexible citizenship Strategies employed by individuals who regularly move across state boundaries in order to circumvent and benefit from different nation-state regimes.

folk illness A culture-bound illness; a set of symptoms that are grouped together under a single label only within a particular culture.

food collectors People who gather wild plant materials, fish, and/or hunt for food.

food producers People who depend on domesticated plants and/or animals for food.

framing An understood boundary that marks certain behaviours as "play" or as "ordinary life."

free agency The freedom of self-contained individuals to pursue their own interests above everything else and to challenge one another for dominance.

friendship The relatively unofficial bonds that people construct with one another that tend to be personal, affectionate, and chosen.

functional cognitive systems Culturally linked sets of cognitive processes that guide perception, conception, reason, and emotion.

gender The culturally constructed beliefs and behaviours considered appropriate for each sex.

gender roles Sets of behaviours that are commonly perceived as masculine or feminine within a specific culture.

globalization Reshaping of local conditions by powerful global forces on an ever-intensifying scale.

global style A field-dependent way of viewing the world that first sees it as a bundle of relationships and only later sees the smaller pieces involved in these relationships.

governmentality The art of governing appropriate to promoting the welfare of populations within a state.

grammar A set of rules that describes the patterns of linguistic usage observed by members of a particular speech community.

habitus Everyday, routine social activity rooted in habitual behaviour.

health A person's general social, psychological, and physical condition. Generally, good health is what allows an individual to function within his or her society.

hegemony A system of leadership in which rulers persuade subordinates to accept the ideology of the dominant group by offering mutual accommodations that nevertheless preserve the rulers' privileged position.

heteroglossia The co-existence of multiple varieties of a specific language.

heteronormativity An ideology that promotes heterosexuality as the social ideal, supported by the cultural definition of "appropriate" behaviour based on culturally defined categories of "male" and "female," "masculine" and "feminine."

historical particularism The study of cultures in their own historical contexts, an approach developed by Franz Boas as an alternative to unilineal cultural evolutionism.

holism A perspective on the human condition that assumes that mind and body, individual and society, and individual and environment interpenetrate and even define one another.

human agency Human beings' ability to exercise at least some control over their lives.

human rights A set of rights that should be accorded to all human beings everywhere in the world.

idealism The philosophical view (dating back as far as Plato in Western thought) that pure, incorruptible ideas—or the mind that produces ideas—constitute the essence of human nature.

ideology According to Marx, those products of consciousness—such as morality, religion, and metaphysics—that purport to explain to people who they are and to justify the kinds of lives they lead.

illness A culturally defined state (or role) of general physical and/or mental discomfort and poor health; a personal experience of suffering that prompts the afflicted to seek intervention and that underlies all culturally defined interventions to alleviate suffering.

imperialism A system in which one country controls other, less powerful territories through colonization, often augmented by military force.

indigenization The process of bring something foreign under the control of local people, or of adapting something foreign to serve local purposes.

informants People in a particular culture who work with anthropologists and provide them with insights about local ways of life; also called respondents, teachers, *consultants*, or friends.

institutions Stable and enduring cultural practices that organize social life.

intensive agriculture A form of cultivation that employs plows, draft animals, irrigation, and fertilizer to bring a large amount of land under cultivation at one time.

intersubjective meaning Meaning rooted in the symbolic systems of a culture and shared by participants in that culture.

jāti A localized, named, endogamous group. A jāti provides ascribed identity.

joint family A family pattern made up of brothers and their wives (or sisters and their husbands) along with their children and sometimes their parents living together.

key metaphors A symbolic representation that is widely understood within a culture and central to that culture's world view.

kinship Social relationships that are prototypically derived from the universal human experiences of mating, birth, and nurturance.

labour The activity linking human social groups to the material world around them. Human labour is always social labour.

language The system of symbols we use to encode our experiences of the world and of one another.

language ideology A system of beliefs about how language features relate to social features and what they reveal about the people who use them.

legal citizenship The rights and obligations of citizenship granted by the laws of a state.

liminal period The ambiguous transitional state in a rite of passage in which the person or persons undergoing the ritual are outside their ordinary social positions.

lineage A descent group composed of blood relatives who believe they can trace their descent from known ancestors.

linguistic anthropology The specialty of anthropology concerned with the study of human languages.

linguistic competence A term coined by linguist Noam Chomsky to refer to the mastery of adult grammar.

linguistic relativity principle The assertion, also known as the Sapir–Whorf hypothesis, that language has the power to shape the way people see the world.

linguistics The scientific study of language.

long-distance nationalists Members of a diaspora who begin to organize in support of nationalist struggles in their homeland or to agitate for a state of their own.

magic A set of beliefs and practices designed to control the visible or invisible world for specific purposes.

managed care A system of care, tied to the market-based delivery of medicine, particularly in the US, in which a patient's choice of treatment and of practitioner is directed by an intermediary organization that aims to provide the most cost-effective services available while generating profits for its members.

market exchange A mode of exchange in which the exchange of goods (trade) is calculated in terms of a multi-purpose medium of exchange and standard of value (money) and carried on by means of a supply–demand–price mechanism (the market).

marriage An institution that prototypically (1) involves a man and a woman, (2) transforms the status of the participants, (3) carries implications about sexual access, (4) gives offspring a position in society, and (5) establishes connections between the kin of a husband and the kin of a wife.

materialism The philosophical view that the activities of our physical bodies in the material world constitute the essence of human nature.

means of production The tools, skills, organization, and knowledge used to extract energy from nature.

mechanized industrial agriculture Large-scale farming that is highly dependent on industrial methods of technology and production. This type of agriculture is often found in conjunction with factory farming of animals.

medical anthropology An area of anthropological inquiry that focusses on issues of well-being, health, illness, and disease as they are situated in their wider cultural contexts.

metacommunication Communicating about the process of communication.

metalanguage Language used to talk about language. Metalanguage often shapes discourse, either directly (e.g., by making language the topic of discussion) or indirectly (e.g., by revealing our awareness of language as a system of symbols that is open to interpretation).

metanarrative A grand-scale story or theme that members of a given culture recognize and that often drives ideas and actions within that culture. See also **world view**.

metaphor A form of thought and language that asserts a meaningful link between two expressions from different semantic domains.

metaphorical entailments All the attributes of a metaphorical predicate that relate it to the metaphorical subject.

metaphorical predicate The second part of a metaphor, which suggests the familiar domain of experience that may clarify the metaphorical subject.

metaphorical subject The first part of a metaphor, which indicates the domain of experience that needs to be clarified.

metonymy The culturally defined relationship of the parts of a semantic domain to the domain as a whole and of the whole to its parts.

mode of production "A specific, historically occurring set of social relations through which labour is deployed to wrest energy from nature by means of tools, skills, organization, and knowledge" (Wolf 1982: 75).

modernization theory A theory that argues that the social change occurring in non-Western societies under colonial rule was a necessary and inevitable prelude to higher levels of social development that had been reached by the more "modern" nations.

modes of exchange Patterns according to which distribution takes place: reciprocity, redistribution, and market exchange.

monogamy A marriage pattern in which a person may be married to only one person at a time.

morphemes The shortest meaning-bearing units in any language (e.g., /bɔɪ/ refers to a young male) The change to plural form has the morpheme for plural added (in this case /z/, which we write as *boys* [/boɪz/]). (Compare to **phonemes**.)

morphology The study of the smallest units of meaning (morphemes) in a language.

motivation The inner impulse to set (or accept) and accomplish goals.

multiculturalism A situation in which people of various cultural backgrounds live in close proximity to one another.

multi-sited ethnography Ethnographic research on cultural processes that are not contained by social, ethnic, religious, or national boundaries, in which the ethnographer follows the process from site to site, often doing fieldwork in sites and with persons that were traditionally never subject to ethnographic analysis.

myth A representative story that embodies a culture's assumptions about the way society, or the world in general, must operate.

nation A group of people believed to share the same history, culture, language, and even physical substance.

nationalism The attempt made by government officials to instill a sense of nationality into the citizens of a state.

nationality A sense of identification with and loyalty to a nation-state; membership, defined by citizenship, in a geopolitical sovereign state.

nation-building See **nationalism**.

nation-state An ideal political unit in which national identity and political territory coincide.

native speaker A person who has spoken a particular language since early childhood.

nativism An attempt to return to traditional customs.

naturalizing discourse The deliberate representation of particular identities (e.g., caste, class, race, ethnicity, and nationality) as if they were a result of biology or nature rather than history or culture, making them appear eternal and unchanging.

neoclassical economic theory A formal attempt to explain the workings of capitalist enterprise, with particular attention to distribution.

neocolonialism The persistence of profound social and economic ties linking former colonial territories to their former colonial rulers despite political sovereignty.

neoliberalism A political perspective that promotes individual freedom, open markets, and free trade while opposing strong state involvement in personal and economic affairs.

non-conjugal family A woman (or, less commonly, a man) and her (or his) children, with or without a second parent.

norms Rules (usually unwritten) for behaviour assumed to be typical within a specific social or cultural group.

nuclear family A family made up of two generations: parents and their unmarried children.

objectification The intentional construction of a collective public identity; the process that produces what we commonly think of as *ethnicity*.

objective knowledge Knowledge about reality that is absolute and true for all people, in all times and places.

oracles Invisible forces to which people address questions and whose responses they believe to be truthful.

organic metaphor A key metaphor whose predicate lies in the image of a living body.

orthodoxy "Correct doctrine"; the prohibition of deviation from certain generally accepted rules or beliefs. These rules and beliefs are often recorded in approved mythic (or religious) texts.

orthopraxy "Correct practice"; the prohibition of deviation from certain generally accepted forms of behaviour. These forms of behaviour are often part of (or are at least closely connected to) rituals.

paleoanthropology The study of the fossilized remains of human beings' earliest ancestors.

participant-observation The method anthropologists use to gather information by living and working with the people whose culture they are studying while participating in their lives as much as possible.

patron The party of higher status in a clientage.

perception The processes by which people organize and experience information that is primarily of sensory origin.

periphery In world-system theory, those exploited former colonies that supply the core with inexpensive food, goods, and raw materials.

personality The relative integration of an individual's perceptions, motives, cognitions, and behaviour within a sociocultural matrix.

persuasion Power based on verbal argument.

phonemes Basic units of distinct sound that are characteristic of a language and that come together to form words (e.g., /b/ and /ɔɪ/ in boy). On their own, phonemes carry no referential or lexical meaning. (Compare to **morphemes**.)

phonology The study of the sounds (phones and phonemes) of a language.

pidgin A simple language with no native speakers that develops in a single generation between members of communities that possess distinct native languages. Alternatively, a shared secondary language in a speech community in which speakers also use some other main language.

placebo effect An effect produced in response to an individual's belief that a treatment will have a desired effect, despite evidence that the treatment has no medicinal properties.

play A framing (or orienting) context that is (1) consciously adopted by the players; (2) pleasurable; and (3) alludes to the non-play world by transforming the objects, roles, actions, and relations of ends and means characteristic of the non-play world.

political anthropology The study of social and political power in human society.

political economy A social structure that is organized around material (economic) interests, in which these interests are protected and enhanced through the use of power (politics).

political power Social power held by a group that is in a position to affect the lives of many people.

polygamy A marriage pattern in which a person may be married to more than one person at a time. Polygamy is called *polygyny* when it involves multiple wives; when it involves multiple husbands, it is called *polyandry*.

positionality A person's uniquely situated social position, which reflects his or her gender, nationality, political views, previous experiences, and so on. See also **situated knowledge**.

positive research Research that is designed with fair consideration of the interests and concerns of members of the affected community and conducted with consideration of cultural contexts within the community.

positivism The view that there is a single reality "out there" that can be detected through the senses and that there is a single, appropriate scientific method for investigating that reality.

post-national ethos An attitude toward the world in which people submit to the regulations of the capitalist market while trying to evade the regulations of nation-states.

power Transformative capacity; the ability to transform a given situation.

pragmatics The study of language in the context of its use.

primatology The study of non-human primates, the closest living relatives of human beings.

production The transformation of nature's raw materials into a form suitable for human use.

prototypes Examples of a typical instance, element, relation, or experience within a culture.

race A broad human population category that allegedly corresponds to distinct, heritable sets of biological attributes and often conflates geographic ancestry and physical type.

racialism Belief in the existence of biologically distinct races.

racism The systematic oppression of members of one or more socially defined "races" by members of another socially defined "race" that is justified within the ruling society by the rulers' faulty belief in their own biological superiority.

realized niche The portion of the habitable world that a group of people is forced to utilize and to which it becomes highly adapted.

reasoning style Culture- and context-dependent ways in which we appraise, come to understand, and think about a cognitive task.

reciprocity A mode of exchange in which individuals exchange goods and/or services (1) under the assumption that the exchanges will eventually balance out, (2) with the expectation of immediate balance, or (3) in the hope that at least one party will get something for nothing.

redistribution A mode of exchange in which a centralized social organization receives contributions from all members of the group and redistributes them in a way that provides for every member.

reflexivity Critically thinking about the way one thinks; reflecting on one's own experience.

reification A form of negative racial or ethnic absolutism that encourages the violent elimination of targeted groups and is central to the practice of racism.

relatedness The socially recognized ties that connect people in a variety of ways.

relations of production The social relations linking the people who use a given means of production within a particular mode of production.

religion "Ideas and practices that postulate reality beyond that which is immediately available to the senses" (Bowen 2002: 5).

resistance The power to refuse being forced against one's will to conform to someone else's wishes.

revitalization A conscious, deliberate, and organized attempt by some members of a society to create a more satisfying culture in a time of crisis.

rite of passage A ritual that serves to mark the movement and transformation of an individual from one social position to another.

ritual A repetitive social practice set off from everyday routine and composed of a sequence of symbolic activities that adhere to a culturally defined ritual schema and are closely connected to a specific set of ideas significant to the culture.

Sapir–Whorf hypothesis See **linguistic relativity principle.**

scarcity A condition under which it is assumed that resources (e.g., money) will never be plentiful enough for people to obtain all the goods or services they desire.

schemas Patterned, repetitive experiences that are shared and easily understood by members of a particular culture.

secret societies Non-kin social groups that initiate young men or women into social adulthood and reveal "secret" knowledge to initiated members.

secularism The separation of religion and state.

segmentary opposition An approach to dispute resolution and social organization in which groups beyond the most basic emerge only in opposition to other groups on the same hierarchical level.

self The result of the process of socialization and enculturation for an individual.

semantics The study of meaning.

semi-periphery In world-system theory, states that have played peripheral roles in the past but that now have sufficient industrial capacity and other resources to possibly achieve core status in the future.

sex The conventional biological distinction between male and female based on *morphological sex* (observable sex characteristics), *gonadal sex* (ovaries in females; testes in males), and *chromosomal sex* (XX or XY chromosomes).

sexuality An individual's sense of his or her own sexual desires, orientation, and preferences.

shaman A part-time religious practitioner who is believed to have the power through altered states of consciousness to travel to or contact supernatural forces directly on behalf of individuals or groups.

situated knowledge Knowledge that is set within or specific to a precise context or situation. For the ethnographer, situating knowledge based on field observations means explicitly stating his or her personal details, such as gender, nationality, political views, class/ethnic/educational backgrounds, and so on. See also **positionality**.

small-scale society A community of several dozen to several hundred people usually held together by family (kinship) ties and often engaged in traditional subsistence activities.

social forms Culturally conforming collective ways of interacting with our surroundings and the people we encounter; these forms of interaction, often taken for granted, are encoded forms of behaviour that are enforced by the group.

socialization The process by which human beings learn to become members of a group, both by interacting appropriately with others and by coping with the behavioural rules established by the group.

social organization The patterning of human interdependence in a given society through the actions and decisions of its members.

social power The ability to transform a situation that affects an entire social group.

social race An achieved status with a racial label in a system of stratification that is composed of open, class-like categories to which racial labels are assigned.

social structure The enduring aspects of the social forms in a society, including its political and kinship systems.

social trauma Individual and group experience of negative physical, mental, and emotional effects resulting from powerfully disturbing occurrences caused by forces and agents external to the person or group. Social trauma is commonly the result of armed conflict or war, widespread drought and famine, and/or an epidemic.

societal metaphor A key metaphor whose predicate lies in the social order.

sodalities Non-kin social groups that may be organized on the basis of age, sex, economic role, and/or personal interest.

sport An aggressively competitive, often physically exertive activity governed by game-like rules that are ritually patterned and agreed upon by all participants.

state A stratified society that possesses a territory that is defended from outside enemies with an army and from internal disorder with police. A state, which has a separate set of governmental institutions designed to enforce laws and collect taxes and tribute, is run by an elite that possesses a monopoly on the use of force.

strategic essentialism The use of essentialist rhetoric as a conscious political strategy to create a temporary solidarity to facilitate a specific social action.

stratified societies Societies in which there is a permanent hierarchy that accords some members privileged access to wealth, power, and prestige.

structural violence Violence that results from the way that political and economic forces structure risk for various forms of suffering within a population.

structural-functional theory A position that explores how particular social forms function from day-to-day in order to reproduce the traditional structure of the society.

structured interviews A method for gathering information whereby an anthropologist (or another researcher) asks a set of predetermined questions and records participants' responses. Structured interviews can be used as an opening to move into intersubjective discussions and then into participant observation.

subject position An individual's unique position the world, which is shaped by social variables such as class, gender, and socioeconomic status.

subjective meaning Meaning that seems true to a particular person, based on his or her personal values, beliefs, opinions, and assumptions.

subjectivity An individual's awareness of his or her own agency and position as a subject.

subsistence strategies The patterns of production, distribution, and consumption that members of a society use to meet their basic material survival needs.

substantive citizenship The actions people take, regardless of their legal citizenship status, to assert their membership in a state and to bring about political changes that will improve their lives.

syllogism A series of three statements in which the final statement (the conclusion) must follow logically from the first two statements (the premises). A typical example is (1) All men are mortal. (2) Socrates is a man. (3) Therefore, Socrates is mortal.

syllogistic reasoning A form of reasoning based on the syllogism.

symbol Something that stands for something else.

syncretism The synthesis of old religious practices (or an old way of life) with new religious practices (or a new way of life) introduced from outside, often by force.

syntax The study of sentence structure.

taxonomies Hierarchical systems that sort groups of things that share at least one quality (e.g., dogs) into subgroups that share a greater number of qualities (e.g., poodles, collies, boxers). Thus, all things belonging to a subgroup share the defining characteristic(s) of the overall group but at least one characteristic that makes them exclusive to their subgroup.

technological metaphor A key metaphor whose predicate lies in objects made by human beings.

thinking The active cognitive process of going beyond the information given.

traditional knowledge Knowledge that is culturally held and passed on from generation to generation.

transborder citizenry A group made up of citizens of a country who continue to live in the homeland plus the people who have emigrated from the country and their descendants, regardless of their current citizenship.

transborder state A state in which it is claimed that those people who left the country and their descendants remain part of their ancestral state, even if they are citizens of another state.

transculturation Cultural change resulting from contact between different cultures.

transformation-representation The process in which experience is transformed as it is represented symbolically in a different medium.

transformist hegemony A nationalist program to define nationality in a way that preserves the cultural domination of the ruling group while including enough cultural features from subordinated groups to ensure their loyalty.

transnational nation-states Nation-states in which the relationships between citizens and their states extend to wherever citizens reside.

tribe A form of social organization generally larger than a band, in which members usually farm or herd for a living; social relations are relatively egalitarian, although there may be a chief who speaks for the group.

typology A classification system based on systematic organization into *types* on the basis of shared qualities.

unilineal cultural evolutionism A nineteenth-century theory that proposed a series of stages through which all societies must go (or had gone) in order to reach civilization.

unilineal descent A pattern of descent in which a descent group is formed based on connections of relatedness made through *either* a father (patrilineal descent) *or* a mother (matrilineal descent).

varna Traditional social ranks that divide Indian society into four functional subdivisions: priests, nobility (rulers and warriors), commoners (farmers and merchants), and labourers or servants.

visuality The ways that individuals from different societies learn to interpret what they see and to construct mental pictures using the visual practices that their own cultural system favours.

vocabulary The words used in a particular language or by members of a particular speech community.

well-being A culturally defined state (or role) of general physical and mental comfort and good health; a lack of illness.

white man's burden Europeans' sense that it was their duty to colonize, rule, and "civilize" all peoples they viewed as "savage."

witchcraft The practice of magic, whether intentional or not.

world view An encompassing picture of reality created by members of a society.

world-system theory A theory that argues that capitalism incorporates various regions and peoples into a world system whose parts are linked economically but not politically.

zone of proximal development (ZPD) The difference between what an individual can achieve on her or his own and what she or he can achieve under the guidance of more experienced individuals.

REFERENCES

AAA (American Anthropological Association). 2009. *Code of Ethics of the American Anthropological Association*, available at www.aaanet.org/issues/policy-advocacy/upload/AAA-Ethics-Code-2009.pdf.

AANDC (Aboriginal Affairs and Northern Development Canada). 2012. "Contaminants in the North," available at www.aadnc-aandc.gc.ca/eng/1100100035295/1100100035299.

Abbas, Ackbar. 2002. "Cosmopolitan Description: Shanghai and Hong Kong," in *Cosmopolitanism*, ed. Carol A. Breckenridge et al. (Durham, NC: Duke University Press), 209–28.

Aboriginal Language Task Force Report. 2005. "Towards a New Beginning: A Foundational Report for a Strategy to Revitalize First Nations, Inuit and Métis Languages and Cultures." Report to the Minister of Canadian Heritage, June 2005, available at www.afn.ca/uploads/files/education2/towardanewbeginning.pdf.

Abu-Lughod, Lila. 1991. "Writing against Culture," in *Recapturing Anthropology*, ed. Richard Fox (Santa Fe, NM: SAR), 137–62.

———. 1995. "The Objects of Soap Opera: Egyptian Television and the Cultural Politics of Modernity," in *Worlds Apart: Modernity through the Prism of the Local*, ed. Daniel Miller (London: Routledge), 109–210.

Adams, Richard Newbold. 1979. *Energy and Structure: A Theory of Social Power* (Austin: University of Texas Press).

Adesope O.O., Lavin T., Thompson, T., and Ungerleider C. (2010). "A Systematic Review and Meta-analysis of the Cognitive Correlates of Bilingualism," *Review of Educational Research* 80, 2: 207–45.

Agar, Michael. 1996. *The Professional Stranger: An Informal Introduction to Ethnography*, 2nd edn (San Diego: Academic Press).

Alland, Alexander. 1977. *The Artistic Animal* (New York: Doubleday Anchor).

Allen, Catherine J. 1988. *The Hold Life Has: Coca and Cultural Identity in an Andean Community* (Washington, DC: Smithsonian Institution Press).

Allen, Theodore. 1994–7. *The Invention of the White Race*, 2 vols (London: Verso).

Allen, Timothy F.H., and T.W. Hoekstra. 1991. "Role of Heterogeneity in Scaling of Ecological Systems under Analysis," *Ecological Heterogeneity (Ecological Studies)*, vol. 86, ed. J. Kolasa and S. Pickett (New York: Springer Verlag), 47–68.

Alonso, Ana María. 1994. "The Politics of Space, Time, and Substance: State Formation, Nationalism, and Ethnicity," *Annual Review of Anthropology* 23: 379–405.

Alverson, Hoyt. 1977. "Peace Corps volunteers in Rural Botswana," *Human Organization* 36, 3: 274–81.

———. 1978. *Mind in the Heart of Darkness* (New Haven: Yale University Press).

Amazon Watch. 2014. "Brazil's Belo Monte Dam: Sacrificing the Amazon and Its Peoples for Dirty Energy," available at http://amazonwatch.org/work/belo-monte-dam.

Amnesty International. 2013. "Sri Lanka Human Rights," available at www.amnestyusa.org/our-work/countries/asia-and-the-pacific/sri-lanka.

AMS (Association of Muslim Schools). 2014. "FAQ," available at http://ams-uk.org/faq.

Anderson, Benedict. 1983. *Imagined Communities*. (London: Verson).

———. 2002 [1992]. "The New World Disorder," in *The Anthropology of Politics*, ed. Joan Vincent (Malden, MA: Blackwell), 261–70.

APA (American Psychiatric Association). 2013. *Diagnostic and Statistical Manual of Mental Disorders*, 5th edn, available at www.psychiatryonline.org.

Apfel, Roberta J., and Bennett Simon. 2000. "Mitigating Discontents with Children in War: An Ongoing Psychoanalytic Inquiry," in *Cultures under Siege: Collective Violence and Trauma*, ed. Antonius C.G.M. Robben and Marcelo M. Suárez-Orozco (Cambridge: Cambridge University Press), 102–30.

Appadurai, Arjun. 1990. "Disjuncture and Difference in the Global Cultural Economy," in *Global Culture*, ed. Mike Featherstone (London: Sage), 295–310.

———. 2002. "Grassroots Globalization and the Research Imagination," in *The Anthropology of Politics*, ed. Joan Vincent (Malden, MA: Blackwell), 271–84.

Asad, Talal, ed. 1973. *Anthropology and the Colonial Encounter* (London: Ithaca Press).

———. 2002. "From the History of Colonial Anthropology to the Anthropology of Western Hegemony," in *The Anthropology of Politics*, ed. Joan Vincent (Malden, MA: Blackwell), 133–42.

———. 2003. *Formations of the Secular: Christianity, Islam, Modernity* (Palo Alto, CA: Stanford University Press).

Bacigalupo, Ana Mariella. 2004. "The Mapuche Man Who became a Woman Shaman: Selfhood, Gender Transgression, and Competing Cultural Norms," *American Ethnologist* 31, 3: 440–57.

Badiou, Alain. 2003. *Infinite Thought: Truth and the Return of Philosophy*, ed. and trans. Oliver Feltham and Justin Clemens (London: Continuum).

———. 2004. *Theoretical Writings*, ed. and trans. Ray Brassier and Alberto Toscano (London: Continuum).

Bailey, A.G. 1969 [1937]. *The Conflict of European and Eastern Algonquian Cultures, 1504–1700*, 2nd edn (Toronto: University of Toronto Press).

Bailey, Mark S., and H. Janaka de Silva. 2006. "Sri Lankan *Sanni* Masks: An Ancient Classification of Disease," *BMJ*, 333(7582), 1327–1328. **BMJ** by British Medical Association.

Bakhtin, Mikhail. 1981 [1975]. *The Dialogical Imagination* (Austin: University of Texas Press).

Barad, Karen. 1999. "Agential Realism: Feminist Interventions in Understanding Scientific Practices," in *The Science Studies Reader*, ed. Mario Biagioli (New York: Routledge), 1–11.

Barron, Lee. 2013. "The Sound of Street Corner Society: UK Grime Music as Ethnography," *European Journal of Cultural Studies* 15, 5: 531–47.

Bashir, Halima. 2008. *Tears of the Desert: A Memoir of Survival in Darfur* (New York: One World).

Bateson, Gregory. 1972. "A Theory of Play and Fantasy," in *Steps to an Ecology of Mind*, ed. Gregory Bateson (New York: Ballentine Books), 177–93.

Bauman, Zygmunt. 1989. *Modernity and the Holocaust* (Ithaca, NY: Cornell University Press).

———. 1990. "Modernity and Ambivalence," in *Global Culture*, ed. Mike Featherstone (London: Sage), 143–69.

Baxter, P.T.W. 1978. "Boran Age Sets and Generation Sets: *Gada*, a Puzzle or a Maze?," in *Age, Generation, and Time*, ed. P.T.W. Baxter and Uri Almagor (New York: St Martin's Press), 151–82.

———, and Uri Almagor, eds. 1978. *Age, Generation, and Time* (New York: St Martin's Press).

Beals, Alan. 1962. *Gopalpur, A South Indian Village* (New York: Holt, Rinehart, and Winston).

Bell, Sandra, and Simon Coleman, eds. 1999. "The Anthropology of Friendship: Enduring Themes and Future Possibilities," in *The Anthropology of Friendship* (Oxford: Berg), 1–19.

Bellman, Beryl. 1984. *The Language of Secrecy* (New Brunswick, NJ: Rutgers University Press).

Benedict, Ruth. 1934. *Patterns of Culture* (New York: Houghton Mifflin).

Berger, Carl. 1990. "Wilson, Sir Daniel," in *Dictionary of Canadian Biography*, vol. 12, available at www.biographi.ca/en/bio/wilson_daniel_12E.html.

Berkowitz, Dana. 2013. "Gay Men and Surrogacy, in *LGBT-Parent Families: Innovations in Research and Implications for Practice*, ed. Abbie E. Goldberg and Katherine R. Allen (New York: Springer), 71–85.

Bernhardt, B., J. Ball, and J. Deby. 2007. "Cross-cultural Interaction and Children's Speech Acquisition," in *The International Guide to Speech*

Acquisition, ed. S. McLeod (Clifton Park, NY: Delmar).

Berreman, Gerald D. 1962. *Behind Many Masks: Ethnography and Impression Management in a Himalayan Village* (Lexington, KY: Society for Applied Anthropology).

Berthod, Marc-Antoine. 2005. "La Vie des Morts dans le Regard des Anthropologues," *Anthropos* 100, 2: 521–36.

Bestor, Theodore. 2005. "How Sushi Went Global," in *The Cultural Politics of Food and Eating: A Reader*, ed. James L. Watson and Melissa L. Caldwell (Malden, MA: Blackwell), 13–20.

Bickerton, Derek. 1981. *Roots of Language* (Ann Arbor, MI: Karoma).

Bigenho, Michelle. 2002. *Sounding Indigenous: Authenticity in Bolivian Music Performance* (New York: Palgrave).

Birth, Kevin. 2007. "Time and the Biological Consequences of Globalization," *Current Anthropology* 48, 2: 215–36

Bishop, C.A. 1970. "The Emergence of Hunting Territories among the Northern Ojibwa," *Ethnology* XI, 1: 1–15.

———. 1973. "Ojibwa Cannibalism," paper presented at the IX International Congress of Anthropological and Ethnological Sciences (Chicago).

———. 1981. "Northeastern Indian Concepts of Conservation and the Fur Trade: A Critique of Calvin Martin's Thesis," in *Indians, Animals, and the Fur Trade*, ed. S. Krech III (Athens: University of Georgia Press), 39–58.

Blackwood, Evelyn, and Saskia E. Wieringa, eds. 1999. "Preface," in *Female Desires: Same-Sex Relations and Transgender Practices across Cultures* (New York: Columbia University Press), ix–xiii.

Blanchard, Kendall, and Alyce Cheska. 1985. *The Anthropology of Sport* (South Hadley, MA: Bergin and Garvey).

Bledsoe, Caroline. 1993. "The Politics of Polygyny in Mende Education and Child Fosterage Transactions," in *Sex and Gender Hierarchies*, ed. Barbara Diane Miller (Cambridge: Cambridge University Press), 170–92.

Bock, Philip K., ed. 1994. *Psychological Anthropology* (Westport, CT: Praeger).

Bodenhorn, Barbara. 2000. "'He Used to Be My Relative': Exploring the Bases of Relatedness among Iñupiat of Northern Alaska," in *Cultures of Relatedness: New Approaches to the Study of Kinship*, ed. Janet Carsten (Cambridge: Cambridge University Press), 128–48.

Boellstoroff, Tom. 2007. "Queer Studies in the House of Anthropology," *Annual Review of Anthropology* 36: 17–35.

Bowen, John. 2002. *Religions in Practice: An Approach to the Anthropology of Religion*, 2nd edn (Needham Heights, MA: Allyn and Bacon).

Boyer, Pascal, and Brian Bergstrom. 2008. "Evolutionary Perspectives on Religion," Annual Review of Anthropology 37: 111–30.

Bradburd, Daniel. 1998. *Being There: The Necessity of Fieldwork* (Washington, DC: Smithsonian Institution Press).

Brain, Robert. 1976. *Friends and Lovers* (New York: Basic Books).

Braroe, Niels. 1975. *Indian and White* (Stanford: Stanford University Press).

Breckenridge, Carol A., et al. 2002. "Cosmopolitanisms," in *Cosmopolitanism* (Durham, NC: Duke University Press), 1–14.

Brenneis, Donald, and Ronald K.S. Macauley, eds. 1996. *The Matrix of Language* (Boulder, CO: Westview Press).

Briggs, Charles L. 2007. "Anthropology, Interviewing, and Communicability in Contemporary Society," *Current Anthropology* 48, 4: 551–80.

Briggs, Jean. 1980. "Kapluna Daughter: Adopted by the Eskimo," in *Conformity and Conflict: Readings in Cultural Anthropology*, 4th edn, ed. J. Spradley and D. McCurdy (Glenview, IL: Scott Foresman), 44–62.

Brodt, Sonja B. 2001. "A Systems Perspective on the Conservation and Erosion of Indigenous Agricultural Knowledge in Central India," *Human Ecology* 29, 1: 99–120.

Bromberger, Christian. 1995. *Le match de football: Etnologie d'une passion partisane à Marseille, Naples et Turin* (Paris: Éditions de la maison des sciences de l'homme).

Brown, Louise. 2011. "Canadian's Lucky Iron Fish Saves Lives in Cambodia," *The Toronto Star* (12 Nov.), available at www.thestar.com/news/gta/2011/11/12/canadians_lucky_iron_fish_saves_lives_in_cambodia.html.

Bruner, Jerome S. 1957. "Going beyond the Information Given," in *Contemporary Approaches to Cognition*, ed. Jerome S. Bruner, Egon Brunswik, Leon Festinger, Fritz Heider, Karl F. Muenzinger, Charles E. Osgood, and David Rapaport (Cambridge, MA: Harvard University Press), 41–69).

Burch Jr, Ernest S. 1970. "Marriage and Divorce among the North Alaskan Eskimos," in *Divorce and After*, ed. Paul Bohannan (Garden City, NY: Doubleday), 152–81.

Canadian Multiculturalism Act. 1988. Revised Statutes of Canada, 1985, c. 24 (4th Supp.), available at http://laws.justice.gc.ca/en/C-18.7.

Carlson, Nathan D. 2009. "Reviving Witiko (Windigo): An Ethnohistory of 'Cannibal Monsters' in the Athabasca District of Northern Alberta, 1878-1910," *Ethnohistory* 56, 3: 355–94.

Carrithers, Michael. 2005. "Anthropology as a Moral Science of Possibilities," *Current Anthropology* 46, 3: 433–56.

Castle, Sarah E. 1994. "The (Re)negotiation of Illness Diagnoses and Responsibility for Child Death in Rural Mali," *Medical Anthropology Quarterly* 8, 3: 314–35.

CBC. 2013. "Most Families with Kids Have Gaming Consoles," *CBC News* (11 Apr.), available at www.cbc.ca/news/technology/most-families-with-kids-have-a-gaming-console-1.1325831.

Chan, Eliza Chong-lai. 1995. "Negotiating Daughterhood: A Case Study of the Female Inheritance Movement in the New Territories, Hong Kong," MA Thesis, Chinese University, Hong Kong.

Chance, John K. 1978. *Race and Class in Colonial Oaxaca* (Stanford: Stanford University Press).

Checker, Melissa. 2009. "Anthropology in the Public Sphere, 2008: Emerging Trends and Significant Impacts," *American Anthropologist*, New Series, 111, 2: 162–9.

Cheng, Cecilia. 2004. "To Be Paranoid Is the Standard? Panic Responses to SARS Outbreak in the Hong Kong Special Administrative Region," *Asian Perspective* 28, 1: 67–98.

Chevannes, Barry. 2002. *Learning to Be a Man: Culture, Socialization, and Gender Identity in Five Caribbean Communities* (Kingston, Jamaica: University of the West Indies Press).

Cheyfitz, E. 1991. *The Poetics of Imperialism: Translation and Colonization from the Tempest to Tarzan* (New York: Oxford University Press).

Childs, Becky, and Mallinson, Christine. 2004. "African American English in Appalachia: Dialect Accommodation and Substrate Influence," *English World-Wide* 25: 27–50.

Chomsky, Noam. 1957. *Syntactic Structures* (The Hague: Mouton).

———. 1965. *Aspects of the Theory of Syntax* (Cambridge, MA: MIT Press).

Chrisjohn, Roland, Sherri Young, and Michael Maraun. 1997. *The Circle Game: Shadows and Substance in the Indian Residential School Experience in Canada* (Penticton: Theytus Books Limited).

CIHR, NSERC, SSHRC (Canadian Institutes of Health Research, Natural Sciences and Engineering Research Council of Canada, Social Sciences and Humanities Research Council of Canada). 2010. *Tri-Council Policy Statement: Ethical Conduct for Research Involving Humans*, available at www.pre.ethics.gc.ca/pdf/eng/tcps2/TCPS_2_FINAL_Web.pdf.

Clark, Gracia. 1994. *Onions Are My Husband* (Chicago: University of Chicago Press).

Clark, Warren. 2000. "Patterns of Religious Attendance," *Canadian Social Trends*, available at www.statcan.gc.ca/pub/11-008-x/2000003/article/5389-eng.pdf.

——— and Grant Schellenberg. 2006. "Who's Religious?," *Canadian Social Trends*, available at www.statcan.gc.ca/pub/11-008-x/2006001/pdf/9181-eng.pdf.

Clarke, John. 2004. *Changing Welfare, Changing States: New Directions in Social Policy* (London: Sage).

Clastres, Pierre. 1977. *Society against the State*, trans. Robert Hurley (New York: Urizen Books).

Cohen, I.B. 1994. "An Analysis of Interactions between the Natural and Social Sciences," *Boston Studies in the Philosophy of Science* 150 (Dordrecht: Kluwer), 1–99.

Cole, Michael. 1994. *Cultural Psychology: A Once and Future Discipline* (Cambridge, MA: Harvard University Press).

———, and Sylvia Scribner. 1974. *Culture and Thought: A Psychological Introduction* (New York: Wiley).

Collier, Jane, and Sylvia Yanagisako, eds. 1987. "Toward a Unified Analysis of Gender and Kinship," in *Gender and Kinship: Essays Toward a Unified Analysis* (Stanford: Stanford University Press), 14–50.

Colloredo-Mansfeld, Rudi. 1999. *The Native Leisure Class: Consumption and Cultural*

Creativity in the Andes (Chicago: University of Chicago Press).

Colson, Anthony C., and Karen E. Selby. 1974. "Medical Anthropology," *Annual Review of Anthropology* 3: 245–63.

Colson, Elizabeth. 1977. "Power at Large: Meditation on 'The Symposium on Power,'" in *The Anthropology of Power: Ethnographic Studies from Asia, Oceania, and the New World*, ed. R. Fogelson and R.N. Adams (New York: Academic Press), 375–86.

Comaroff, John, and Jean Comaroff. 1992. *Ethnography and the Historical Imagination* (Boulder, CO: Westview Press).

Connell, R.W. 2005. "Change among the Gatekeepers: Men, Masculinities, and Gender Equality in the Global Arena," *Signs* 30, 3: 1801–25.

Connolly, Jennifer. 2009. "Forbidden intimacies: Christian–Muslim Intermarriage in East Kalimantan, Indonesia," *American Ethnologist* 36, 3: 492–506.

Cook, Garrett, and Thomas Offit. 2008. "Pluralism and Transculturation in Indigenous Maya Religion," *Ethnology* 47, 1: 45–59.

Côté, J.E. 2000. "The Mead–Freeman Controversy in Review," *Journal of Youth and Adolescence* 29, 5: 525–38.

Cowan, Jane, Marie-Bénédicte Dembour, and Richard A. Wilson, eds. 2001. "Introduction," in *Culture and Rights: Anthropological Perspectives* (Cambridge: Cambridge University Press), 1–26.

Cox, Oliver Cromwell. 1948. *Caste, Class, and Race: A Study in Social Dynamics* (Garden City, NY: Doubleday).

Cox, Paul Alan, Holly E. Johnson, Gaugau Tavana. 2008. "Giving Samoan Healers Credit for Prostratin," *Science*, New Series, 320, 5883: 1589.

Crehan, Kate. 2002. *Gramsci and Cultural Anthropology* (Berkeley: University of California Press).

Croom, Adam M. 2013. "How to Do Things with Slurs: Studies in the Way of Derogatory Words," Language and Communication 33, 3: 177–204.

Csikszentmihalyi, Mihalyi. 1981. "Some Paradoxes in the Definition of Play," in *Play and Context*, ed. Alyce Cheska (West Point: Leisure Press), 14–25.

Dalsgaard, Steffen. 2008. "Facework on Facebook: The Presentation of Self in Virtual Life and Its Role in the US Elections," *Anthropology Today* 24, 6: 8–12.

Daly, Mary. 1978. *Gyn/ecology: The Metaethics of Radical Feminism* (Boston: Beacon Press).

———. 1984. *Pure Lust: Elemental Feminist Philosophy* (Boston: Beacon Press).

———. 2001. Interview, in *Philosophy Now* 33, available at http://philosophynow.org/issues/33/Mary_Daly.

D'Andrade, Roy G. 1992. "Cognitive Anthropology," in *New Directions in Psychological Anthropology*, ed. Theodore Schwartz, Geoffrey M. White, and Catherine A. Lutz (Cambridge: Cambridge University Press), 47–58.

Daniel, E. Valentine. 1997. "Suffering Nation and Alienation," in *Social Suffering*, ed. Arthur Kleinman, Veena Das, and Margaret Lock (Berkeley: University of California Press), 309–58.

Danner, Mark. 1994. *The Massacre at El Mozote* (New York: Vintage).

Darnell, Regna. 2000. "Canadian Anthropologists, the First Nations, and Canada's Self-image at the Millennium," *Anthropologica* 42, 2: 165–174.

———. 2009. "Anthropological Approaches to Human Nature, Cultural Relativism, and Ethnocentrism," *Anthropologica* 51: 187–94.

Das, Veena, and Arthur Kleinman. 2000. "Introduction," in *Violence and Subjectivity*, ed. Veena Das et al. (Berkeley: University of California Press), 1–18.

Davies, B., and R. Harré. 1990. "Positioning: The Discursive Production of Selves," *Journal for the Theory of Social Behaviour* 20, 1: 44–63.

Davin, Anna. 2001. "Waif Stories in Late Nineteenth-Century England," *History Workshop Journal* 52: 67–98.

Davis, Wade. 1985. *The Serpent and the Rainbow* (New York: Simon and Schuster).

———. 1988. *Passage of Darkness: The Ethnobiology of the Haitian Zombie* (Chapel Hill: University of North Carolina Press).

Day, Chet. 2010. "Chicken Soup: Nature's Best Cold and Flu Remedy," available at http://chetday.com/coldfluremedy.htm.

Deacon, Terrence W. 1997. *The Symbolic Species: The Co-evolution of Language and the Brain* (New York: Norton).

de Gobineau, A. 1967 [1915]. *The Inequality of Human Races*, trans. A. Collins, with Introduction by O. Levy (New York: Howard Fertig).

Dembour, Marie-Bénédicte. 2001. "Following the Movement of a Pendulum between Universalism and Relativism," in *Culture and Rights: Anthropological Perspectives*, ed. Jane Cowan, Marie-Bénédicte Dembour, and Richard A. Wilson (Cambridge: Cambridge University Press), 26–79.

Dernbach, Katherine Boris. 2005. "Spirits of the Hereafter: Death, Funerary Possession, and the Afterlife in Chuuk, Micronesia," *Ethnology* 44, 2: 99–123.

De Vos, George, and Hiroshi Wagatsuma. 1966. *Japan's Invisible Race* (Berkeley: University of California Press).

Dods, Roberta Robin. 2002. "The Death of Smokey Bear: The Ecodisaster Myth and Forest Management Practices in Prehistoric North America," *World Archaeology* 33, 3: 475–87.

———. 2003. "Wondering the Wetland: Archaeology through the Lens of Myth and Metaphor in Northern Boreal Canada," *Journal of Wetland Archaeology* 3: 17–36 (Oxbow Books).

———. 2004. "Knowing Ways/Ways of Knowing: Reconciling Science and Tradition," *World Archaeology* 36, 4: 547–57.

———. 2007a. "Pyrotechnology and Landscapes of Plenty in the Northern Boreal," in *The Archaeology of Fire: Understanding Fire as Material Culture*, ed. D. Gheorghiu and G. Nash (Budapest: Archaeolingua).

———. 2007b. "Intersubjectivity and the Meaning of Things," *International Journal of the Humanities* 4, 9: 99.

———. 2010. "Nation/First Nations: Conflicts in Identity and the Role of Archaeology," in *Unquiet Pasts*, ed. Stephanie Koerner and Ian Russell (Ashgate: Aldershot), 49–53.

Dolgin, Janet. 1995. "Family Law and the Facts of Family," in *Naturalizing Power*, ed. Sylvia Yanagisako and Carol Delaney (New York: Routledge), 47–67.

Douglas, Mary. 1966. *Purity and Danger* (London: Routledge and Kegan Paul).

———. 1970. "Introduction," in *Witchcraft Confessions and Accusations*, ed. Mary Douglas (London: Tavistock), vi–xxxviii.

———, and Baron Isherwood. 1979. *The World of Goods: Towards an Anthropology of Consumption* (New York: Norton).

Dourish, Paul. 2008. "Points of Persuasion: Strategic Essentialism and Environmental Sustainability," Pervasive 2008 Workshops.

Dressler, William W. 2001. "Medical Anthropology: Toward a Third Moment in Social Science?," *Medical Anthropology Quarterly* 15: 455–65.

Drewal, Margaret. 1992. *Yoruba Ritual* (Bloomington: Indiana University Press).

Duden, B. 1991. *The Woman beneath the Skin: A Doctor's Patients in Eighteenth-Century Germany* (Cambridge, MA: Harvard University Press).

Dufour, Darna L. 1997. "Nutrition, Activity, and Health in Children," *Annual Review of Anthropolgy* 26: 541–65.

Duranti, Alessandro. 1994. *From Grammar to Politics: Linguistic Anthropology in a Western Samoan Village* (Berkeley: University of California Press).

Eagle, David E. 2011. "Changing Patterns of Attendance at Religious Services in Canada, 1986–2008," *Journal for the Scientific Study of Religion* 50: 187–200.

Edberg, Mark. 2004. "The Narcotrafficker in Representation and Practice: A Cultural Persona from the US–Mexican Border," *Ethos* 32, 2: 257–77.

Edmonds, Alexander. 2007. "The Poor Have the Right to Be Beautiful: Cosmetic Surgery in Neoliberal Brazil," *Journal of the Royal Anthropological Institute* 13, 2: 363–81.

Ehrenreich, Jeffrey David. 1996. "Worms, Witchcraft, and Wild Incantations: The Case of the Chicken Soup Cure," *Anthropological Quarterly* 69, 3: 137–41.

Ekman, Paul. (1965). Communication Through Nonverbal Behaviour: A Source of Information about an Interpersonal Relationship," in *Affect, Cognition, and Personality: Empirical Studies*, ed. Silvan Solomon Tomkins and Carroll Ellis Izard (Oxford, England: Springer), 390–442.

Elliot, Alison. 1981. *Child Language* (Cambridge: Cambridge University Press).

Epprecht, Marc. 2006. "'Bisexuality' and the Politics of Normal in African Ethnography," *Anthropologica* 48: 187–201.

Eriksen, Thomas Hylland. 1995. *Small Places, Large Issues: An Introduction to Social and Cultural Anthropology* (London: Pluto Press).

———. 2001. "Between Universalism and Relativism: A Critique of the UNESCO Concept of Culture," in *Culture and Rights: Anthropological Perspectives*, ed. Jane Cowan, Marie-Bénédicte Dembour, and Richard A. Wilson (Cambridge: Cambridge University Press), 127–48.

Errington, Shelly. 1998. *The Death of Authentic Primitive Art and Other Tales of Progress* (Berkeley: University of California Press).

Ervin, Alexander M. 1996. "Collaborative and Participatory Research in Urban Social Planning and Restructuring: Anthropological Experiences from a Medium-sized Canadian City," *Human Organization* 55, 3: 324–33.

Escobar, Arturo. 1992. "Culture, Economics, and Politics in Latin American Social Movements Theory and Research," in *The Making of Social Movements in Latin America*, ed. Arturo Escobar and Sonia Alvarez (Boulder, CO: Westview Press), 62–85.

Etienne, Mona. 1980. "Women and Men, Cloth and Colonization: The Transformation of Production–Distribution Relations among the Baule (Ivory Coast)," in *Women and Colonization: Anthropological Perspectives*, ed. Mona Etienne and Eleanor Leacock (New York: Praeger), 270–93.

Evans, Mike. 2004. "Ethics, Anonymity, and Authorship in Community Centred Research, or Anonymity and the Island Cache," *Pimatisiwin: A Journal of Aboriginal and Indigenous Community Health* 2, 1: 60–75.

Evans-Pritchard, E.E. 1951. *Kinship and Marriage among the Nuer* (Oxford: Oxford University Press).

———. 1963. *Social Anthropology and Other Essays* (New York: Free Press).

——— 1976 [1937]. *Witchcraft, Oracles, and Magic among the Azande*, abr. edn (Oxford: Oxford University Press).

Fabrega, Horacio. 1971. "Medical Anthropology," in *Biennial Review of Anthropology*, ed. J. Siegel (Stanford, CA: Stanford University Press), 167–229.

Fagen, Robert. 1981. *Animal Play Behavior* (New York: Oxford University Press).

———. 1992. "Play, Fun, and Communication of Well-being," *Play and Culture* 5, 1: 40–58.

Farmer, Paul. 2002 [1996]. "On Suffering and Structural Violence: A View from Below," in *The Anthropology of Politics*, ed. Joan Vincent (Malden, MA: Blackwell), 424–37.

———. 2005. *Pathologies of Power: Health, Human Rights, and the New War on the Poor* (Berkeley: University of California Press).

———. 2006. *AIDS and Accusation: Haiti and the Geography of Blame*, 2nd edn (Berkeley: University of California Press).

———, Arthur Kleinman, Jim Kim, and Matthew Basilico, eds. 2013. *Reimaging Global Health: An Introduction* (Berkeley: University of California Press).

Feinman, Gary M., Kent G. Lightfoot, and Steadman Upham. 2000. "Political Hierarchies and Organizational Strategies in the Puebloan Southwest," *American Antiquity* 65, 3: 449–70.

Ferguson, James. 2002. "The Anti-politics Machine," in *The Anthropology of Politics*, ed. Joan Vincent (Malden, MA: Blackwell), 399–408.

Ferguson, R. Brian. 2008. "Ten Points on War," *Social Analysis* 52, 2: 32–49.

Fernandez, James W. 1977. "The Performance of Ritual Metaphors," in *The Social Use of Metaphors*, ed. J.D. Sapir and J.C. Crocker (Philadelphia: University of Pennsylvania Press).

———. 1980. "Edification by Puzzlement," in *Explorations in African Systems of Thought*, ed. Ivan Karp and Charles Bird (Bloomington: Indiana University Press), 44–69.

———. 1982. *Bwiti: An Ethnography of the Religious Imagination in Africa* (Princeton: Princeton University Press).

Ferrara, Nadia, and Guy Lanoue. 2004. "The Self in Northern Canadian Hunting Societies: 'Cannibals' and Other 'Monsters' as Agents of Healing," *Anthropologica* 46, 1: 69–83.

Fischer, Michael M.J. 1999. "Emergent Forms of Life: Anthropologies of Late or Postmodernities," *Annual Review of Anthropology* 28: 455–78.

Floating in the Air, Followed by the Wind. 1973. Film distributed by Indiana University Instructional Support Services. Produced by Michigan State University.

Fortes, Meyer. 1950. "Kinship and Marriage among the Ashanti," in *African Systems of Kinship and Marriage*, ed. A.R. Radcliffe-Brown and Daryll Forde (Oxford: Oxford University Press).

———. 1953. "The Structure of Unilineal Descent Groups," *American Anthropologist* 55: 25–39.

———, and E.E. Evans-Pritchard. 1940. *African Political Systems* (Oxford: Oxford University Press for the International African Institute).

Foster, George M. 1976. "Disease Etiologies in Non-Western Systems," *American Anthropologist* 78, 4: 773–82.

Foucault, Michel. 1991. "Governmentality," in *The Foucault Effect: Studies in Governmentality*, ed. Graham Burchell, Colin Gordon, and Peter Miller (Chicago: University of Chicago Press), 87–104.

Fratkin, Elliot. 1997. "Pastoralism: Governance and Development Issues," *Annual Review of Anthropology* 26: 235–61.

Freeman, Carla. 2001. "Is Local : Global as Feminine : Masculine? Rethinking the Gender of Globalization," *Signs* 26 4: 1007–37.

Freeman, Derick. 1983. *Margaret Mead and Samoa: The Making and Unmaking of an Anthropological Myth* (Cambridge: Harvard University Press).

———. 1998. *The Fateful Hoaxing of Margaret Mead: A Historical Analysis of Her Samoan Research* (Boulder, CO: Westview Press).

Friedman, J. 1994. *Cultural Identity and Global Process* (London: Sage).

———. 1997. "Global Crises, the Struggle for Cultural Identity, and Intellectual Porkbarrelling: Cosmopolitans versus Locals, Ethnics, and Nationals in an Era of Dehegemonisation," in *Debating Cultural Hybridity: Multicultural Identities and the Politics of Anti-racism*, ed. Pnina Werbner and Tariq Modood (London: Zed Books), 70–89.

Gampel, Yoland. 2000. "Reflections on the Prevalence of the Uncanny in Social Violence," in *Cultures under Siege: Collective Violence*

and Trauma, ed. Antonius C.G.M. Robben and Marcelo M. Suárez-Orozco (Cambridge: Cambridge University Press), 48–69.

Gardner, Katy. 2008. "Keeping Connected: Security, Place, and Social Capital in a 'Londoni' Village in Sylhet," *Journal of the Royal Anthropological Institute* 14 3: 477–95.

Garro, Linda C. 2004. "Overview of Culture: Ojibwa," in *Encyclopaedia of Medical Anthropology: Health and Illness in the World's Cultures*, vol. 2, ed. Carol R. Ember and Melvin Ember (New York: Springer Science + Business Media, Inc.), 903–15.

Geertz, Clifford. 1973. *The Interpretation of Cultures* (New York: Basic Books).

———. 1980. *Negara: The Theatre State in Nineteenth Century Bali* (Princeton, NJ: Princeton University Press).

Geller, Pamela L. 2009. "Bodyscapes, Biology, and Heteronormativity," *American Anthropologist*, New Series, 111, 4: 504–16.

Gentner, Dedre, and Susan Goldin-Meadow. 2003. "Whither Whorf," in *Language in Mind: Advances in the Study of Language and Thought*, ed. Dedre Gentner and Susan Goldin-Meadow (Cambridge, MA: MIT Press).

Georges, Eugenia. 1990. *The Making of a Transnational Community: Migration, Development, and Cultural Change in the Dominican Republic* (New York: Columbia University Press).

Gerson, Carole. 1997. "Nobler Savages: Representation of Native Women in the Writings of Susanna Moodie and Catharine Parr Traill," *Journal of Canadian Studies* 32, 2: 5–21.

Gerson, Jen. 2013. "The Heartbreaking Tale of a Pregnant, Brain-Dead BC Woman and Her Husband Hoping for Their Son's Healthy Arrival," *National Post* (3 Feb.), available at http://news.nationalpost.com/2014/02/03/the-heartbreaking-tale-of-a-pregnant-brain-dead-b-c-woman-and-her-husband-hoping-for-their-sons-healthy-arrival.

Gibbon, John Murray. 1938. *Canadian Mosaic* (Toronto: McClelland and Stewart).

Giddens, Anthony. 1979. *Central Problems in Social Theory* (Berkeley: University of California Press).

Gilligan, Carol. 1982. *In a Different Voice* (Cambridge, MA: Harvard University Press).

Gilsenan, Michael. 1982. *Recognizing Islam: Religion and Society in the Modern Arab World* (New York: Pantheon).

Ginsburg, Faye D., and Rayna Rapp, eds. 1995. *Conceiving the New World Order: The Global Politics of Reproduction* (Berkeley: University of California Press).

Gledhill, John. 1994. *Power and Its Disguises* (London: Pluto Press).

———. 2001. "'Disappearing the Poor?': A Critique of the New Wisdoms of Social Democracy in an Age of Globalization," *Urban Anthropology and Studies of Cultural Systems and World Economic Development* 30, 2–3: 123–56.

Godelier, Maurice. 2010. "In Today's World, Anthropology Is More Important than Ever," *Paideuma* 56: 205–20.

Goh, Daniel P.S. 2010. "State and Social Christianity in Post-colonial Singapore," *Sojourn:*

Journal of Social Issues in Southeast Asia 25, 1: 54–89.

Goodall, Jane (2010). *Through a Window: My Thirty Years with the Chimpanzees of Gombe* (Boston: Houghton Mifflin Harcourt).

Goody, Jack, and S. Tambiah. 1973. *Bridewealth and Dowry* (Cambridge: Cambridge University Press).

Gordon, Colin. 1991. "Governmental Rationality: An Introduction," in *The Foucault Effect: Studies in Governmentality*, ed. Graham Burchell, Colin Gordon, and Peter Miller (Chicago: University of Chicago Press), 1–52.

Gottlieb, Alma. 1989. "Witches, Kings, and the Sacrifice of Identity, or the Power of Paradox and the Paradox of Power among the Beng of Ivory Coast," in *Creativity of Power: Cosmology and Action in African Societies*, ed. W. Arens and Ivan Karp (Washington, DC: Smithsonian Institution Press), 245–72.

Goulet, Jean-Guy A. 1996. "The 'Berdache'/'Two-Spirit': A Comparison of Anthropological and Native Constructions of Gendered Identities among the Northern Athapaskans," *Journal of the Royal Anthropological Institute* 2, 4: 683–701 (published by Royal Anthropological Institute of Great Britain and Ireland).

Gramsci, Antonio. 1971. *Selections from the Prison Notebooks*, trans. Q. Hoare and G.N. Smith (New York: International Publishers).

Gray, Janice. 1997. "The *Mabo* Case: A Radical Decision?," *Canadian Journal of Native Studies* 17, 1: 33–74.

Gravel, Pierre Bettez. (1976). "'And Sometimes All for Nought' or Reflections from an Anthropologist upon His Return from the Field," *Western Canadian Journal of Anthropology* 6, 4: 103–23.

Greenwood, David, and William Stini. 1977. *Nature, Culture, and Human History* (New York: Harper and Row).

Gregory, Richard. 1983. "Visual Perception and Illusions: Dialogue with Richard Gregory," in *States of Mind*, ed. Jonathan Miller (New York: Pantheon), 42–64.

Gupta, Akhil, and James Ferguson. 1997. "Discipline and Practice: 'The Field' as Site, Method, and Location in Anthropology," in *Anthropological Locations: Boundaries and Grounds of a Field Science*, ed. Akhil Gupta and James Ferguson (-Berkeley: University of California Press), 1–46.

Gutierrez Muñiz, Jose A., Josefina Lopez Hurtado, and Guillermo Arias Beatón. 1997. "La educacion ambiental en el proceso docente educativo en las montañas de Cuba," available at www.monografias.com/trabajos11/eduamb/eduamb.shtml?monosearch.

Hacking, Ian. 1991. "How Should We Do the History of Statistics?," in *The Foucault Effect: Studies in Governmentality*, ed. Graham Burchell, Colin Gordon, and Peter Miller (Chicago: University of Chicago Press), 181–96.

Hale, Charles. 1997. "Cultural Politics of Identity in Latin America," *Annual Review of Anthropology* 26: 567–90.

Hall, Edward T. 1959. *The Silent Language* (New York: Doubleday).

———. 1966. *The Hidden Dimension* (New York: Doubleday).

———. 1976. *Beyond Culture* (New York: Anchor Press).

———. 1983. *The Dance of Life: The Other Dimensions of Time* (New York: Doubleday).

———, and Mildred Reed Hall. 1987. *Hidden Differences: Doing Business with the Japanese* (New York: Anchor Press).

Halperin, Rhoda. 1994. *Cultural Economics: Past and Present* (Austin: University of Texas Press).

Handelman, Don. 1977. "Play and Ritual: Complementary Frames of Metacommunication," in *It's a Funny Thing, Humour*, ed. A.J. Chapman and H. Foot (London: Pergamon), 185–92.

Hanks, William. 1996. *Language and Communicative Practices* (Boulder, CO: Westview Press).

Haraway, Donna. 1991. *Simians, Cyborgs, and Women: The Reinvention of Nature* (New York: Routledge).

Harding, T.G. 1967. *Voyagers of the Vitiaz Strait: A Study of a New Guinea Trade System*. University of Washington Press: Seattle and London.

Harney, Nicholas. 2002. "Building Italian Regional Identity in Toronto: Using Space to Make Culture Material," *Anthropologica* 44, 1: 43–54.

Harrison, Faye. 1995. "The Persistent Power of 'Race' in the Cultural and Political Economy of Racism," *Annual Review of Anthropology* 24: 47–74.

———. 1998. "Introduction: Expanding the Discourse on 'Race'," *American Anthropologist* 100, 3: 609–31.

———. 2004. "Global Apartheid, Environmental Degradation, and Women's Activism for Sustainable Well-Being: A Conceptual and Theoretical Overview," *Urban Anthropology* 33, 1: 1–35.

Hartigan Jr, John. 1997. "Establishing the Fact of Whiteness," *American Anthropologist* 99, 3: 495–504.

Hastrup, Kirsten, and Peter Elsas. 1990. "Anthropological Advocacy: A Contradiction in Terms?," *Current Anthropology* 31, 3: 301–11.

Hatzfeldt, Sophie. 2011. "Queer Deconstruction of Heteronormative Identity," *Imponderabilia: The International Student Anthropology Journal*, available at http://imponderabilia.socanth.cam.ac.uk/articles/article.php?articleid=30.

Hayden, Brian. 1990. "Nimrods, Piscators, Pluckers, and Planters: The Emergence of Food Production," *Journal of Anthropological Archaeology* 9: 31–69.

———. 1995. "Pathways to Power: Principles for Creating Socioeconomic Inequalities," in *Foundations of Social Inequality*, ed. T.D. Price and G.M. Feinman (New York: Plenum), 15–86.

Hayden, Robert M. 2000. "Rape and Rape Avoidance in Ethno-National Conflicts: Sexual Violence in Liminalized States," *American Anthropologist*, New Series, 102, 1: 27–41.

Haynes, Naomi. 2012. "Pentecostalism and the Morality of Money: Prosperity, Inequality, and Religious Sociality on the Zambian Copperbelt,"

Journal of the Royal Anthropological Institute 18, 1: 123–39.

Hedican, Edward J. 2008. *Applied Anthropology in Canada: Understanding Aboriginal Issues*, 2nd edn (Toronto: University of Toronto Press).

Heider, Karl. 1979. *Grand Valley Dani* (New York: Holt, Rinehart, and Winston).

Henriksen, Georg. 1985. "Anthropologists as Advocates—Promoters of Pluralism or Makers of Clients?," in *Advocacy and Anthropology*, ed. Robert Paine (St John's: Institute of Social and Economic Research).

Herdt, Gilbert. 1994. "Mistaken Sex: Culture, Biology, and the Third Sex in New Guinea," in *Third Sex, Third Gender*, ed. Gilbert Herdt (New York: Zone Books), 419–45.

Herring, D. Ann. 1994. "'There Were Young People and Old People and Babies Dying Every Week': The 1918–1919 Influenza Pandemic at Norway House," *Ethnohistory* 41, 1: 73–105.

Herring, Susan C., and Sharon Stoerger. 2014. "Gender and (A)nonymity in Computer-Mediated Communication," in *The Handbook of Language, Gender, and Sexuality*, 2nd edn, ed. Susan Ehrlich, Miriam Meyerhoff, and Janet Holmes. (Oxford, UK: Wiley Blackwell), 567–86.

Herskovits, Melville. 1973. *Cultural Relativism*, ed. Frances Herskovits (New York: Vintage).

Herzfeld, Michael. 2001. *Anthropology: Theoretical Practice in Culture and Society* (Malden, MA: Blackwell Publishers).

———. 2003. "Competing Diversities: Ethnography in the Heart of Rome," *Plurimundi* 3, 5: 147–54.

———. 2013. "Interview with Michael Herzfeld," *Romeing* (16 Apr.), available at www.romeing.it/interview-with-michael-herzfeld-author-of-evicted-from-eternity-the-restructuring-of-modern-rome.

Hess, David J. 1997. *Science Studies: An Advanced Introduction* (New York: New York University Press).

Hill, Jane, and Judith Irvine. 1992. *Responsibility and Evidence in Oral Discourse* (Cambridge: Cambridge University Press).

Hinton, Alexander Laban. 2002. "The Dark Side of Modernity: Toward an Anthropology of Genocide," in *Annihilating Difference: The Anthropology of Genocide*, ed. Alexander Laban Hinton (Berkeley: University of California Press), 1–40.

Hinton, Leanne. 2000. "New Writing Systems," in *The Green Book of Language Revitalization in Practice*, ed. Leanne Hinton and Kenneth Hale (San Diego: Academic Press), 239–50.

Hitchcock, Robert K. 2003. "Land, Livestock, and Leadership among the Ju/'hoansi San of North Western Botswana," *Anthropologica* 45, 1: 89–94.

Hockett, C.F. 1966. "The Problems of Universals in Language," in *Universals of Language*, ed. J.H. Greenberg (Cambridge, MA: MIT Press), 1–29.

Holm, John. 1988. *Pidgins and Creoles: Theory and Structure*, vol. 1 (Cambridge: Cambridge University Press).

Holtzman, Jon D. 2006. "Food and Memory," *Annual Review of Anthropology* 35: 361–78.

Horton, Robin. 1982. "Tradition and Modernity Revisited," in *Rationality and Relativism*, ed. M. Hollis and Steven Lukes (Cambridge, MA: MIT Press), 201–60.

Howell, Nancy. 1988. "Health and Safety in the Fieldwork of North American Anthropologists," *Current Anthropology* 29, 5: 780–7.

Høygaard, A. 1941. *Studies on the Nutrition and Physiopathology of Eskimos*. [Skrifter utgitt av Det Norske Videnskaps-Akademi i Oslo. I. Mat.-Naturv. Klasse 1940, No. 9.] (Oslo: I Kommisjon Hos Jacob Dybwad).

Hudson, R.A. 1980. *Sociolinguistics* (Cambridge: Cambridge University Press).

Hunter, David, and Phillip Whitten, eds. 1976. *Encyclopedia of Anthropology* (New York: Harper and Row).

Hutnyk, John. 1997. "Adorno at Womad: South Asian Crossovers and the Limits of Hybridity-talk," in *Debating Cultural Hybridity: Multicultural Identities and the Politics of Anti-racism*, ed. Pnina Werbner and Tariq Modood (London: Zed Books), 106–36.

Huyghe, Patrick. 1988. "Profile of an Anthropologist: No Bone Unturned," *Discover* (Dec.), 51–6.

Hymes, Dell. 1972. "On Communicative Competence," in *Sociolinguistics: Selected Readings*, ed. J.B. Pride and J. Holmes (Baltimore: Penguin), 269–93.

Ignace, Ron, George Speck, and Renee Taylor. 1993. "Some Native Perspectives on Anthropology and Public Policy," in *Anthropology, Public Policy and Native Peoples in Canada*, ed. Noel Dyck and James B. Walram (Montreal and Kingston: McGill-Queen's University Press), 166–91.

ILO (International Labour Organization). 2013. "What Is Child Labour?," available at www.ilo.org/ipec/facts/lang--en/index.htm.

Inda, Jonathan Xavier, and Renato Rosaldo, eds. 2002. "Introduction: A World in Motion," in *The Anthropology of Globalization* (Malden, MA: Blackwell).

Ingold, Tim. 1983. "The Significance of Storage in Hunting Societies," *Man* 18: 553–71.

Jacobson, Ken. 2002. "ADHD in Cross-cultural Perspective: Some Empirical Results," *American Anthropologist* 104, 1: 283–7.

Jaynes, Julian. 1976. *The Origin of Consciousness in the Breakdown of the Bicameral Mind* (Boston, MA: Houghton Mifflin).

Johnston, Barbara Rose. 2010. "Social Responsibility and the Anthropological Citizen," *Current Anthropology* 51, S2: 235–47.

Jourdan, Christine. 1991. "Pidgins and Creoles: The Blurring of Categories," *Annual Review of Anthropology* 20: 187–209.

Judy. 2010. "Bad Words," *Society for Linguistic Anthropology* (6 Aug.), available at http://linguisticanthropology.org/blog/2010/08/06/bad-words.

Kaku, Michio. 2014. *The Future of the Mind* (New York: Doubleday).

Kapferer, Bruce. 1983. *A Celebration of Demons* (Bloomington: Indiana University Press).

Karp, Ivan. 1978. *Fields of Change among the Iteso of Kenya* (London: Routledge and Kegan Paul).

Kaufman, Sharon R., and Lynn M. Morgan. 2005. "The Anthropology of the Beginnings and Ends of Life," *Annual Review of Anthropology* 34: 317–41.

Kearney, M. 1995. "The Local and the Global: The Anthropology of Globalization and Transnationalism," *Annual Review of Anthropology* 24: 547–65.

Keesing, Roger. 1982. *Kwaio Religion* (New York: Columbia University Press).

———. 1992. *Custom and Confrontation: The Kwaio Struggle for Cultural Autonomy* (Chicago: University of Chicago Press).

Keller, Evelyn Fox. 1997. "Secrets of God, Nature, and Life," in *The Gender/Sexuality Reader*, ed. Roger Lancaster and Micaela di Leonardo (New York: Routledge), 209–18.

Kelly, John D., and Martha Kaplan. 2001. *Represented Communities: Fiji and World Decolonization* (Chicago: University of Chicago Press).

Kemper, Robert V., and Julie Adkins. 2006. "Who Are My Neighbours? Congregation and Community in North Texas," *Urban Anthropology* 35, 2–3: 295–339.

Kenny, Michael G. 1999. "A Place for Memory: The Interface between Individual and Collective History," *Comparative Studies in Society and History* 41, 3: 420–37. © 1999 Society for Comparative Studies in Society and History.

Kesterton, Michael. 2007. "Stone Age Campaign," in Social Studies column, *The Globe and Mail*, sec. L6 (18 July).

King, Jeanette. 2000. "Te Kōhanga Reo: Māori Language Revitalization," in *The Green Book of Language Revitalization in Practice*, ed. Leanne Hinton and Kenneth Hale (San Diego: Academic Press), 119–28.

Kinsey, Alfred C., Wardell B. Pomeroy, and Clyde E. Martin. 1948. *Sexual Behaviour in the Human Male* (Philadelphia: Saunders).

———, ———, ———, and Paul H. Gebhard. 1953. *Sexual Behaviour in the Human Female* (Philadelphia: Saunders).

Kinsey Institute. 2014. "Kinsey's Heterosexual–Homosexual Rating Scale," *The Kinsey Institute*, available at www.kinseyinstitute.org/research/ak-hhscale.html.

Klein, Fritz. 1978. *The Bisexual Option* (New York: Arbor House).

Kleinman, Arthur. 1980. *Patients and Healers in the Context of Culture* (Berkeley: University of California Press).

Knapp, Mark L., Judith A. Hall, and Terrence G. Horgan. 2013. *Nonverbal Communication in Human Interaction*, 8th edn (Boston: Wadsworth).

Knorr Cetina, Karin. 2000. *Epistemic Cultures* (Cambridge, MA: Harvard University Press).

Kroeber, Alfred L. 1939. "Cultural and Natural Areas of Native North America," *University of California Publications in American Archaeology and Ethnology* 38: xii.

Kulick, Don. 2000. "Gay and Lesbian Language," *Annual Review of Anthropology* 29: 243–85.

Kumar, Nita. 1992. *Friends, Brothers, and Informants: Fieldwork Memoirs of Banaras* (Berkeley: University of California Press).

Kuper, Adam. 1982. *Wives for Cattle: Bridewealth and Marriage in Southern Africa* (London: Routledge and Kegan Paul).

———. 1999. *Culture: The Anthropologists' Account* (Cambridge, MA: Harvard University Press).

Labov, William. 1972. *Language in the Inner City: Studies in the Black English Vernacular* (Philadelphia: University of Pennsylvania Press).

Laclau, Ernesto. 2000. "Identity and Hegemony: The Role of Universality in the Constitution of Political Logics," in *Contingency, Hegemony, Universality: Contemporary Dialogues on the Left*, ed. Judith Butler, Ernesto Laclau, and Slavoj Žižek (London: Verso), 44–89.

Lakoff, George, and Mark Johnson. 1980. *Metaphors We Live By* (Berkeley: University of California Press).

Lamphere, Louise. 2005. "Replacing Heteronormative Views of Kinship and Marriage," *American Ethnologist* 32, 1: 34–6.

Lancaster, Roger. 1992. *Life Is Hard: Machismo, Danger, and the Intimacy of Power in Nicaragua* (Berkeley: University of California Press).

Lanehart, Sonja L., ed. 2009. *African American Women's Language: Discourse, Education, and Identity* (Newcastle, UK: Cambridge Scholars Publishing).

Laqueur, Thomas. 1990. *Making Sex* (Cambridge, MA: Harvard University Press).

Lassiter, Luke Eric. 2005. "Collaborative Ethnography and Public Anthropology," *Current Anthropology* 46, 1: 83–106.

Latimer, Joanna. 1999. "The Dark at the Bottom of the Stairs: Performance and Participation of Hospitalized Older People," in *Medical Anthropology Quarterly* 13, 2: 186–213.

Lave, Jean. 1988. *Cognition in Practice* (Cambridge: Cambridge University Press).

Laverdière, Hélène, and Ashton, Niki. 2014. "Canada Must Do More to Prevent Unsafe Abortions," *The Globe and Mail* (28 May), available at www.theglobeandmail.com/news/politics/canada-must-do-more-to-prevent-unsafe-abortions/article18883298.

Lee, Jamie Shinhee. 2006. "Linguistic Constructions of Modernity: English Mixing in Korean Television Commercials," *Language in Society* 35, 1: 59–91.

Lee, Richard B. 1992a. "Art, Science, or Politics? The Crisis in Hunter–Gatherer Studies," *American Anthropologist* 94: 31–54.

———. 1992b. *The Dobe Ju/'hoansi*, 2nd edn (New York: Holt, Rinehart, and Winston).

———. 2013. *The Dobe Ju/'hoansi*, 4th edn (Belmont, CA: Cengage).

Lehman, Edward W. 1969. "Toward a Macrosociology of Power," *American Sociological Review* 34: 453–65.

Leikin, Mark. 2012. "The Effect of Bilingualism on Creativity: Developmental and Educational Perspectives," *International Journal of Bilingualism* 17, 4: 431–47.

Leve, Lauren. 2011. "Identity," *Current Anthropology* 52, 4: 513–35.

Lever, Janet. 1995. *Soccer Madness*, rev. edn (Prospect Heights, IL: Waverland Press).

Levin, Michael D. 2002. "Flow and Place: Transnationalism in Four Cases," *Anthropologica* 44, 1: 3–12.

Levine, Nancy. 1980. "Nyinba Polyandry and the Allocation of Paternity," *Journal of Comparative Family Studies* 11, 3: 283–8.

———. 1988. *The Dynamics of Polyandry: Kinship, Domesticity, and Population on the Tibetan Border* (Chicago: University of Chicago Press).

———, and Walter Sangree. 1980. "Women with Many Husbands," *Journal of Comparative Family Studies* 11, 3: 283.

Levinson, S.C. 1998. "Studying Spatial Conceptualization across Cultures," *Ethos: Journal of the Society for Psychological Anthropology* 26, 1: 7–24.

Lévi-Strauss, Claude. 1955. "The Structural Study of Myth," *Journal of American Folklore* 68, 270: 428–44.

———. 1967 [1962]. *L'antropologie structurale* (Paris: Plon), trans. under the title *Structural Anthropology*, ed. Claire Jacobson and Brooke Grundfest Schoepf (New York: Doubleday Anchor).

Lewellen, Ted. 1983. *Political Anthropology: An Introduction*. (South Hadley, MA: Bergin and Garvey).

Lewis, I.M. 1967. *A Pastoral Democracy: A Study of Pastoralism and Politics among the Northern Somali of the Horn of Africa* (London: Oxford University Press).

Lewontin, Richard, Steven Rose, and Leon J. Kamin. 1984. *Not in Our Genes* (New York: Pantheon).

Leung, Marlene. 2014. "Calgary Doctor Refuses to Prescribe Birth Control due to Personal Beliefs," *CTV News* (28 Jun.), available at www.ctvnews.ca/canada/calgary-doctor-refuses-to-prescribe-birth-control-due-to-personal-be-liefs-1.1890724.

Library and Archives Canada. 2010. "Home Children," available at www.collectionscanada.gc.ca/022/022-908.009-e.html.

Liebersohn, Harry. 1994. "Discovering Indigenous Nobility: Tocqueville, Chamisso, and Romantic Travel Writing," *American Historical Review* 99, 3: 746–66.

Lincoln, Bruce. 2001. "Revisiting 'Magical Fright,'" *American Ethnologist* 28, 4: 778–802.

Lindgren, Björn. 2005. "The Politics of Ethnicity as an Extended Case: Thoughts on a Chiefly Succession Crisis," *Social Analysis: The International Journal of Social and Cultural Practice* 49, 3: 234–53.

Lindenbaum, Shirley. 2001. "Kuru, Prions, and Human Affairs: Thinking about Epidemics," *Annual Review of Anthropology* 30: 363–85.

Link, Bruce G., and Jo C. Phelan. 2001. "Conceptualizing Stigma," *Annual Review of Sociology* 27: 363–85.

Linke, Uli. 1997. "Gendered Difference, Violent Imagination: Blood, Race, Nation," *American Anthropologist* 99, 3: 559–73.

Lock, Margaret. 2001. "The Tempering of Medical Anthropology: Troubling Natural Categories," *Medical Anthropology Quarterly* 15: 478–92.

Lukács, Georg. 1971. *History and Class Consciousness: Studies in Marxist Dialectics* (Cambridge, MA: MIT Press).

Lutz, Catherine. 1988. *Unnatural Emotions: Everyday Sentiments on a Micronesian Atoll and Their Challenge to Western Theory* (Chicago: University of Chicago Press).

Lyotard, Jean-François. 1987. "The Postmodern Condition," in *After Philosophy: End or Transformation?*, ed. Kenneth Baynes, James Bohman, and Thomas A. McCarthy (Cambridge, MA: MIT Press), 73–94.

MacCormack, Carol P. 1980. "Proto-social to Adult: A Sherbro Transformation," in *Nature, Culture, and Gender*, ed. Carol MacCormack and Marilyn Strathern (Cambridge: Cambridge University Press), 95–118.

McElroy, Ann, and Patricia K. Townsend. 1996. *Medical Anthropology in Ecological Perspective*, 3rd edn (Boulder, CO: Westview Press).

McGee Jr, Harold Franklin. 1972. "Windigo Psychosis," *American Anthropologist*, New Series, 74, 1–2: 244–6.

McGregor, G. 1985. *The Wacousta Syndrome* (Toronto: University of Toronto Press).

MacKay, Donald G., et al. 2004. "Relations between Emotion, Memory, and Attention: Evidence from Taboo Stroop, Lexical Decision, and Immediate Memory Tasks," *Memory and Cognition* 32, 3: 474–88.

MacPherson, C.B. 1962. *The Political Theory of Possessive Individualism* (Oxford: Oxford University Press).

McPherson, Naomi. 2007. "Myth Primogeniture and Long-Distance Trade-Friends in Northwest New Britain, Papua New Guinea," *Oceania* 77, 2: 129–57.

Mafeje, A. 1976. "The Problem of Anthropology in Historical Perspective: An Inquiry into the Growth of the Social Sciences," *Canadian Journal of African Studies* 10, 2: 307–33.

Mair, Lucy Philip. 1969. *Witchcraft* (New York: McGraw-Hill).

Malinowski, Bronislaw. 1929. *The Sexual Life of Savages in North-Western Melanesia* (New York: Eugenics Publishing Company).

———. 1944. *A Scientific Theory of Culture and Other Essays* (New York: Oxford University Press).

———. 1948 [1926]. *Magic, Science, and Religion, and Other Essays* (New York: Doubleday Anchor).

Malkki, Liisa. 1992. "National Geographic: The Rooting of Peoples and the Territorialization of National Identity among Scholars and Refugees," *Cultural Anthropology* 7, 1: 24–44.

Mallinson, Christine, and Becky Childs. "The Intersection of Regional and Ethnic Identity: African American English in Appalachia," *Journal of Appalachian Studies* 10: 129–42.

Mandler, George. 1975. *Mind and Emotion* (New York: Wiley).

Maquet, Jacques. 1970. "Rwanda Castes," in *Social Stratification in Africa*, ed. Arthur Tuden and Leonard Plotnicov (New York: Free Press).

Marano, Lou. 1982. "Windigo Psychosis: The Anatomy of an Emic-Etic Confusion," *Current Anthropology* 23, 4: 385–412.

Marcus, George. 1995. "Ethnography in/of the World System: The Emergence of Multi-sited Ethnography," *Annual Review of Anthropology* 24: 95–117.

Marks, Jonathan. 1995. *Human Biodiversity* (New York: Aldine).

Martin, Emily. 2000. "Mind-Body Problems," *American Ethnologist* 27, 3: 569–90.

Marx, Karl. 1963 [1852]. *The 18th Brumaire of Louis Bonaparte* (New York: International Publishers).

Matthiasson, John S. 1992. "The Emergence of a New Political Paradigm," *Living on the Land: Change Among the Inuit of Northern Baffin Island* (Peterborough, ON: Broadview Press).

Maschner, Herbert D.G. 1995. "Review of *A Complex Culture of the British Columbia Plateau: Traditional Stl'atl'imx Resource Use*," *American Antiquity* 60: 378–80.

Mauss, Marcel. 2000 [1950]. *The Gift: The Form and Reason for Exchange in Archaic Societies* (New York: W.W. Norton).

Mead, George Herbert. 1934. *Mind, Self, and Society* (Chicago: University of Chicago Press).

Mead, Margaret. 1995. *Blackberry Winter: My Earlier Years* (New York: Kodansha International).

Meisch, Lynn. 2002. *Andean Entrepreneurs: Otavalo Merchants and Musicians in the Global Arena* (Austin: University of Texas Press).

Melotti, Umberto. 1997. "International Migration in Europe: Social Projects and Political Cultures," in *The Politics of Multiculturalism in the New Europe: Racism, Identity and Community*, ed. Tariq Modood and Pnina Werbner (London: Zed Books), 73–92.

Menegoni, Lorenza. 1996. "Conceptions of Tuberculosis and Therapeutic Choices in Highland Chiapas, Mexico," *Medical Anthropology Quarterly* 10: 381–401.

Merry, Sally Engle. 2001. "Changing Rights, Changing Culture," in *Culture and Rights: Anthropological Perspectives*, ed. Jane Cowan, Marie-Bénédicte Dembour, and Richard A. Wilson (Cambridge: Cambridge University Press), 31–55.

Mertz, Elizabeth, and Jonathan Yovel. 2010. *Handbook of Pragmatics Highlights*, ed. Jef Verschueren and Jan-Ola Östman (Dordrecht, Netherlands: Kluwer).

Messer, Ellen. 1993. "Anthropology and Human Rights," *Annual Review of Anthropology* 22: 221–49.

Michelson, Truman. 1916. "Terms of Relationship and Social Organization," *Proceedings of the National Academy of Sciences of the United States of America* 2, 5: 297–300.

Migliore, Sam. 2001. "From Illness Narratives to Social Commentary: A Pirandellian Approach to 'Nerves,'" *Medical Anthropology Quarterly* 15, 1: 100–25.

Mignolo, Walter D. 2002. "The Many Faces of Cosmopolis: Border Thinking and Critical Cosmopolitanism," in *Cosmopolitanism*, ed. Carol A. Breckenridge et al. (Durham, NC: Duke University Press), 157–87.

Milgram, B. Lynne. 2008. "Activating Frontier Livelihoods: Women and the Transnational Second-Hand Clothing Trade between Hong Kong and the Philippines," *Urban Anthropology and Studies of Cultural Systems and World Economic Development*, 37, 1: 5–47.

Miller, Daniel, ed. 1995. *Acknowledging Consumption: A Review of New Studies* (New York: Routledge).

———, and Don Slater. 2000. *The Internet: An Ethnographic Approach* (Oxford: Berg).

Mills, Anthony J. 2013. "Dakhleh Oasis Project," *Monash University Arts*, available at http://artsonline.monash.edu.au/archaeology/excavations-in-dakhleh-oasis-egypt.

Minturn, Leigh. 1993. *Sita's Daughters* (New York: Oxford University Press).

Mintz, Sidney W., and Christine M. Du Bois. 2002. "The Anthropology of Food and Eating," *Annual Review of Anthropology* 31: 99–119.

Miracle, Andrew. 1991. "Aymara Joking Behaviour," *Play and Culture* 4, 2: 144–52.

Mishra, Charudutt, Herbert H.T. Prins, and Sipke E. Van Wieren. 2003. "Diversity, Risk Mediation, and Change in a Trans-Himalayan Agropastoral System," *Human Ecology* 31, 4: 595–609.

Mitra, Subrata. 1994. "Caste, Democracy, and the Politics of Community Formation in India," in *Contextualizing Caste: Post-Dumontian Approaches*, ed. Mary Searle-Chatterjee and Ursula Sharma (Oxford: Blackwell Publishers/The Sociological Review), 49–71.

Modood, Tariq. 1997. "Introduction: The Politics of Multiculturalism in the New Europe," in *The Politics of Multiculturalism in the New Europe: Racism, Identity, and Community*, ed. Tariq Modood and Pnina Werbner (Cambridge: Cambridge University Press), 1–25.

Moll, Luis, ed. 1990. *Vygotsky and Education* (Cambridge: Cambridge University Press).

Montgomery, Heather. 2001. "Imposing Rights? A Case Study of Child Prostitution in Thailand," in *Culture and Rights: Anthropological Perspectives*, ed. Jane Cowan, Marie-Bénédicte Dembour, and Richard A. Wilson (Cambridge: Cambridge University Press), 80–101.

Morgan, Lewis Henry. 1871. *Systems of Consanguinity and Affinity of the Human Family* (Washington: Smithsonian Institute).

———. 1877. *Ancient Society: Researches in the Lines of Human Progress from Savagery through Barbarism to Civilization* (New York: Holt).

Morgan, Marcyliena. 1995. "Theories and Politics in African American English," *Annual Review of Anthropology* 23: 325–45.

Morris, A. 1877. *The Treaties of Canada with the Indians of Manitoba and the North-West Territories, including the Negotiations on Which They Were Based, and Other Information Relating Thereto* (Toronto: Belford, Clarke, and Co.).

Mukhopadhyay, Bhaskar. 2005. "The Rumour of Globalization: Globalism, Counterworks, and the Location of Commodity," *Dialectical Anthropology* 29, 1: 35–60.

Mullins, Paul R. 2010. "Practising Anthropology: Practising Anthropology and the Politics of Engagements: 2010 Year in Review," *American Anthropologist*, New Series, 113, 2: 235–45.

Murphy, Robert, and Yolanda Murphy. 1974. *Women of the Forest* (New York: Columbia University Press).

Mushquash, Christopher J., and Dana Bova. 2007. "Cross-cultural Measurement and Assessment Issues," *Journal on Developmental Disabilities* 12: 53–66.

Myerhoff, Barbara. 1974. *Peyote Hunt* (Ithaca, NY: Cornell University Press).

Nader, Laura. 1972. "Up the Anthropologist—Perspectives Gained from Studying Up," in *Reinventing Anthropology*, ed. Dell H. Hymes. New York, Pantheon Books. 284–311

———. 1994. "Comparative Consciousness, " in *Assesing Cultural Anthropology*, ed. R. Borofski (New York: Hawaii Pacific University Press), 84–94).

Naiman, R.J., J.M. Melillo, and J.E. Hobbie. 1986. "Ecosystem Alteration of Boreal Forest Streams by Beaver (*Castor Canadensis*)," *Ecology* 67, 5: 1254–69.

Nanda, Serena. 1994. "Hijras: An Alternative Sex and Gender Role," in *Third Sex, Third Gender*, ed. Gilbert Herdt (New York: Zone Books), 373–417.

Nash, June. 1979. *We Eat the Mines, and the Mines Eat Us* (New York: Columbia University Press).

Niemeier, Susanne, Charles P. Campbell, and Rene Dirven, eds. 1998. *The Cultural Context in Business Communication* (Philadelphia: John Benjamin Publishing).

Nguyen, Vinh-Kim, and Karine Peschard. 2003. "Anthropology, Inequality, and Disease: A Review," *Annual Review of Anthropology* 32: 447–74.

Nwoye, Augustine. 2006. "Remapping the Fabric of the African Self: A Synoptic Theory," *Dialectical Anthropology* 30: 119–46.

Nye, Robert A. 2005. "Locating Masculinity: Some Recent Work on Men," *Signs* 30, 3: 1937–62.

Obeyesekere, Gananath. 1981. *Medusa's Hair* (Chicago: University of Chicago Press).

———. 1990. *The Work of Culture* (Chicago: University of Chicago Press).

O'Brien, Kevin. 1996. "Rightful Resistance," *World Politics* 49, 1: 31–55.

Oldham, Paul, and Miriam Anne Frank. 2008. "'We the People…': The United Nations Declaration on the Rights of Indigenous Peoples," *Anthropology Today* 24, 2: 5–9.

Ong, Aihwa. 2002 [1999]. "The Pacific Shuttle: Family, Citizenship, and Capital Circuits," in *The Anthropology of Globalization*, ed. Jonathan Xavier Inda and Renato Rosaldo (Malden, MA: Blackwell), 172–97.

Ortner, Sherry. 1973. "On Key Symbols," *American Anthropologist* 75, 5: 1338–46.

———, ed. 1999. *The Fate of "Culture": Geertz and Beyond* (Berkeley, CA: University of California Press).

Overholt, T.W., and J.B. Callicott. 1982. *Clothed-in-Fur and Other Tales: An Introduction to an Ojibwa World View* (Washington: University Press of America).

Oyama, Susan, Griffiths, Paul E., and Gray, Russell D., eds. 2001. *Cycles of Contingency: Developmental Systems and Evolution* (Cambridge, MA: MIT Press).

Pack, Sam. 2006. "How They See Me vs How I See Them: The Ethnographic Self and the Personal Self," *Anthropological Quarterly* 79, 1: 105–122.

Painter, Nell Irvin. 2010. *The History of White People* (New York: W.W.Norton and Company).

Parkin, David. 1984. "Mind, Body, and Emotion among the Giriama," paper presented at Humanity as Creator lecture series (St Cloud State University).

Patriquin, Martin. 2014. "The Epic Collapse of Quebec Separatism, *Maclean's* (11 Apr.), available at www.macleans.ca/politics/the-epic-collapse-of-separatism.

Peletz, Michael. 2006. "Transgenderism and Gender Pluralism in Southeast Asia since Early Modern Times," *Current Anthropology* 47, 2: 309–40.

Peoples, James. 1978. "Dependence in a Micronesian Economy," *American Ethnologist* 5, 3: 535–52.

Peritz, Ingrid. 2010. "Despite Being Legal, Abortions Still Not Accessible for All Canadians," *The Globe and Mail* (18 Jun.), available at www.theglobeandmail.com/news/national/despite-being-legal-abortions-still-not-accessible-for-all-canadians/article1610254.

Petchauer, Emery. 2011. *Hip-Hop Culture in College Students' Lives: Elements, Embodiment, and Higher Edutainment* (New York: Routledge).

Petersen, Carole. 1996. "Equality as a Human Right: The Development of Anti-discrimination Law in Hong Kong," *Columbia Journal of Transnational Law* 34: 335–87.

PHAC (Public Health Agency of Canada). 2013. "At a Glance: HIV and AIDS in Canada: Surveillance Report to December 31st, 2012," available at www.phac-aspc.gc.ca/aids-sida/publication/survreport/2012/dec/index-eng.php.

Phillips, Lynne. 2006. "Food and Globalization," *Annual Review of Anthropology* 35: 37–57.

Pickering, Andrew. 1995. *The Mangle of Practice: Time, Agency, and Science* (Chicago: University of Chicago Press).

Poerksen, Uwe. 1995. *Plastic Words: The Tyranny of a Modular Language* (University Park: Pennsylvania State University Press).

Poirier, Sylvie, and Lorraine Brooke. 2000. "Inuit Perceptions of Contaminants and Environmental Knowledge in Salluit, Nunavik," *Arctic Anthropology* 37, 2: 78–91.

Potts, Richard. 1996. *Humanity's Descent* (New York: Morrow).

Press, Irwin. 1978. "Urban Folk Medicine: A Functional Overview," *American Anthropologist* 80, 1: 71–84.

Rabinow, Paul. 1977. *Reflections on Fieldwork in Morocco* (Berkeley: University of California Press).

Reddy, Deepa S. 2005. "The Ethnicity of Caste," *Anthropological Quarterly* 78, 3: 543–84.

Reeves-Ellington, Richard H. 1993. "Using Cultural Skills for Co-operative Advantage in Japan," *Human Organization* 52, 2: 203–16.

———. 2009. "Enviroscapes: A Multi-level Contextual Approach to Organizational Leadership," in *Multi-Level Issues in Organizational Behavior and Leadership (Research in Multi-level Issues, Volume 8)*, ed. Francis J. Yammarino and Fred Dansereau (Bringley, UK: Emerald Group Publishing Limited), 337–420.

Renfrew, Colin. 1974. "Beyond a Subsistence Economy: The Evolution of Social Organization in Prehistoric Europe," in *Reconstructing Complex Societies,* ed. C.B. Moore (Cambridge: American Schools of Oriental Research), 69–85.

Rezende, Claudia Barcellos. 1999. "Building Affinity through Friendship," in *The Anthropology of Friendship,* ed. Sandra Bell and Simon Coleman (Oxford: Berg), 79–97.

Rich, E.E. 1961. *The Hudson's Bay Company, 1670–1870: Vol. I, 1670–1763* (New York: Macmillan).

Richards, Audrey. 1954. *Chisungu* (London: Methuen).

Richardson, Sarah S. 2012. "Sexing the X: How the X became the 'Female Chromosome,'" *Signs* 34, 4: 909–33.

Riddington, Robin. 1998. "Coyote's Canon: Sharing Stories with Thomas King," *American Indian Quarterly* 22, 3: 343–62.

Rideout, Victoria J., Ulla G. Foehr, and Donald F. Roberts. 2010. *Generation M²: Media in the Lives of 8- to 18-Year-Olds.* The Henry J. Kaiser Family Foundation, available at http://kaiserfamilyfoundation.files.wordpress.com/2013/04/8010.pdf.

Ringrose, Kathryn M. 1994. "Living in the Shadows: Eunuchs and Gender in Byzantium," in *Third Sex, Third Gender,* ed. Gilbert Herdt (New York: Zone Books), 85–109.

Robidoux, Michael A. 2002. ""Imagining a Canadian Identity through Sport: A Historical Interpretation of Lacrosse and Hockey," *Journal of American Folklore* 115, 456: 209–25.

Rodriguez, Jeanette, and Ted Fortier. 2009. *Cultural Memory: Resistance, Faith, and Identity* (Austin: University of Texas Press).

Rogers, Edward S., and Mary B. Black. 1976. "Subsistence Strategy in the Fish and Hare Period, Northern Ontario: The Weagomow Ojibwa, 1880–1920," *Journal of Anthropological Research* (SWJA) 32, 1: 1–43.

Ronan, Colin A., and Joseph Needham. 1978. *Shorter Science and Civilisation in China* (Cambridge: Cambridge University Press).

Rosaldo, Renato. 2008. "Of Headhunters and Soldiers: Separating Cultural and Ethical Relativism," *Markkula Center for Applied Ethics,* available at www.scu.edu/ethics/publications/iie/v11n1/relativism.html.

Roscoe, Will. 1994. "How to Become a Berdache: Toward a Unified Analysis of Gender Diversity," in *Third Sex, Third Gender,* ed. Gilbert Herdt (New York: Zone Books), 329–72.

Rosen, Lawrence. 1984. *Bargaining for Reality: The Constructions of Social Relations in a Muslim Community* (Chicago: University of Chicago Press).

Rosenblatt, Daniel. 2004. "An Anthropology Made Safe for Culture: Patterns of Practice and the Politics of Difference in Ruth Benedict," *American Anthropologist* 106, 3: 459–72.

Ross, Kaz A. 2010. "An 'Army of Bachelors'? China's Male Population as a World Threat," *Journal of Asia Pacific Studies* 1, 2: 338–63.

Roy, Srila. 2008. "The Grey Zone: The 'Ordinary' Violence of Extraordinary Times," *Journal of the Royal Anthropological Institute* 14, 2: 316–33.

Rylko-Bauer, Barbara, and Paul Farmer. 2002. "Managed Care or Managed Inequality? A Call for Critiques of Market-Based Medication," *Medical Anthropology Quarterly* 16, 4: 476–502.

———, Linda Whiteford, and Paul Farmer, eds. 2009. *Global Health in Times of Violence* (Santa Fe, NM: School for Advanced Research Press).

Sabloff, Jeremy A. 2008. *Archaeology Matters: Action Archaeology in the Modern World* (Walnut Creek, CA: Left Coast Press, Inc.).

Sahlins, Marshall. 1972. *Stone Age Economics* (Chicago: Aldine).

———. 1976a. *The Use and Abuse of Biology* (Ann Arbor: University of Michigan Press).

———. 1976b. *Culture and Practical Reason* (Chicago: University of Chicago Press).

Salzman, Philip Carl. 1994. "The Lone Stranger in the Heart of Darkness," in *Assesing Cultural Anthropology,* ed. R. Borofski (New York: Hawaii Pacific University Press), 29–40.

———. 2002. "On Reflexivity," *American Anthropologist* 104, 3: 805–13.

San Roque, Lila. 2010. "Ill-Advised, Enlightened, Obstructive and Essential: Diverging Views on Vernacular Language Education in Papua New Guinea," paper presented at the American Anthropological Association's annual conference, in the panel Vernacular Education in Melanesia and North America (New Orleans, 18 November).

Sapir, Edward. 1966 [1933]. *Culture, Language, and Personality,* ed. David Mandelbaum (Berkeley: University of California Press).

Sargent, Carolyn, and Grace Bascope. 1996. "Ways of Knowing about Birth in Three Cultures," *Medical Anthropology Quarterly* 10, 2: 213–36.

Schiffauer, Werner. 1997. "Islam as a Civil Religion: Political Culture and the Organization of Diversity in Germany," in *The Politics of Multiculturalism in the New Europe: Racism, Identity, and Community,* ed. Tariq Modood and Pnina Werbner (London: Zed Books), 147–66.

Schiller, Nina Glick, and Georges Fouron. 2002. "Long-distance Nationalism Defined," in *The Anthropology of Politics,* ed. Joan Vincent (Malden, MA: Blackwell), 356–65.

Schneider, David M. 1968. *American Kinship: A Cultural Account* (Englewood Cliffs, NJ: Prentice-Hall).

Schultz, Emily. 1984. "From Pagan to Pullo: Ethnic Identity Change in Northern Cameroon," *Africa* 54, 1: 46–64.

———. 1990. *Dialogue at the Margins: Whorf, Bakhtin, and Linguistic Relativity* (Madison: University of Wisconsin Press).

Schwartzman, Helen. 1978. *Transformations: The Anthropology of Children's Play* (New York: Plenum).

Scott, James C. 1985. *Weapons of the Weak* (New Haven: Yale University Press).

———. 1990. *Domination and the Arts of Resistance: Hidden Transcripts* (New Haven: Yale University Press).

Segalen, Martine. 1986. *Historical Anthropology of the Family* (Cambridge: Cambridge University Press).

Shahar, Shulamith. 1990. *Childhood in the Middle Ages* (New York: Routledge).

Shahid, Shaouli, Ryan Bleam, Dawn Bessarab, and Sandra C. Thompson. 2010. "'If You Don't Believe It, It Won't Help You': Use of Bush Medicine in Treating Cancer among Aboriginal People in Western Australia," *Journal of Ethnobiological Medicine,* 6: 18.

Shankman, Paul. 2009. *The Trashing of Margaret Mead: Anatomy of an Anthropological Controversy* (Madison: University of Wisconsin Press).

Sharma, Ursula. 1999. *Caste* (Buckingham: Open University Press).

Sherman, Mark. 2014. "Some Employers Can Avoid Covering Birth Control, US Supreme Court Rules," *CTV News* (30 Jun.), available at www.ctvnews.ca/health/some-employers-can-avoid-covering-birth-control-u-s-supreme-court-rules-1.1892666.

Shetty, Priya. 2011. "Rani and Abhay Bang—Pioneers of Health Care in Rural India," *The Lancet* 377, 9761, doi: 10.1016/S0140-6736(11)60034-2.

Shostak, Marjorie. 1981. *Nisa: The Life and Words of a !Kung Woman* (New York: Vintage Books).

Sidoroff-Dorso, Anton. 2014. "Synaesthesia, Culture, and Neuroimaging," presentation given to the Department of Medical Electronics (BMS College of Engineering, Karnataka, India), slides available at www.academia.edu/2556437/Synesthesia_Culture_and_Neuroimaging.

Sims, Christine P. 2005. "Tribal Languages and the Challenges of Revitalization," *Anthropology and Education Quarterly* 36, 1: 104–6.

Singer, Merrill. 1995. "Beyond the Ivory Tower: Critical Praxis in Medical Anthropology," *Medical Anthropology Quarterly* 9, 1: 80–106.

Slobin, Dan. 1987. "Thinking for Speaking," *Proceedings of the Annual Meeting of the Berkeley Linguistics Society* 13: 435–44.

Smart, Alan. 1999. "Expressions of Interest: Friendship and *Guanzi* in Chinese Societies," in *The Anthropology of Friendship,* ed. Sandra Bell and Simon Coleman (Oxford: Berg), 119–36.

Smedley, Audrey. 1998. "'Race' and the Construction of Human Identity," *American Anthropologist* 100, 3: 690–702.

Smith, Antonia. 2007. "Canadian Citizenship in the Work of John Murray Gibbon," *Race/Ethnicity: Multidisciplinary Global Contexts* 1, 1: 37–60.

Smith, Wilfred Cantwell. 1982. *Towards a World Theology* (Philadelphia: Westminster).

Sobo, Elisa J. 2004. "Theoretical and Applied Issues in Cross-cultural Health Research," in *Encyclopedia of Medical Anthropology,* ed. Carol R. Ember and Melvin Ember (New York: Kluwer Academic/Plenum Publishers), 3–11.

Solway, Jacqueline, and Richard Lee. 1990. "Foragers, Genuine or Spurious: Situating the

Kalahari San in History," *Current Anthropology* 31: 109–46.

Sommer, Iris E.C., et al. 2004. "Do Women Really Have More Bilateral Language Representation than Men? A Meta-analysis of Functional Imaging Studies," *Brain* 127, 8: 1845–52.

Sontag, Susan. 2003. *Regarding the Pain of Others* (New York: Picador).

Soysal, Levent. 2010. "Intimate Engagements of the Public Kind," *Anthropological Quarterly* 83, 2: 373–99.

Spencer, Jonathan. 2000. "On Not Becoming a 'Terrorist': Problems of Memory, Agency, and Community in the Sri Lankan Conflict," in *Violence and Subjectivity*, ed. Veena Das, Arthur Kleinman, Mamphela Ramphele, and Pamela Reynolds (Berkeley: University of California Press), 120–40.

Spivak, Gayatri Chakravorty. 1987. *In Other Worlds: Essays in Cultural Politics.* (New York: Taylor and Francis).

Starn, Orin. 1992. "'I Dreamed of Foxes and Hawks': Reflections on Peasant Protest, New Social Movements, and the *Rondas Campesinas* of Northern Peru," in *The Making of Social Movements in Latin America: Identity, Strategy, and Democracy*, ed. Arturo Escobar and Sonia E. Alvarez, Series in Political Economy and Economic Development in Latin America (Boulder, CO: Westview Press), 89–111.

Statistics Canada. 2011. *Aboriginal Peoples in Canada: First Nations People, Métis, and Inuit* (National Household Survey, 2011), available at www12.statcan.gc.ca/nhs-enm/2011/as-sa/99-011-x/99-011-x2011001-eng.pdf.

Steward, Julian H. 1972. *Theory of Culture Change: The Methodology of Multilinear Evolution.* (Urbana: University of Illinois Press).

Stewart, Charles, and Rosalind Shaw. 1994. *Syncretism/Anti-syncretism* (London: Routledge).

Suárez-Orozco, Marcelo M., and Antonius C.G.M. Robben, eds. 2000. "Interdisciplinary Perspectives on Violence and Trauma," in *Cultures under Siege: Collective Violence and Trauma* (Cambridge: Cambridge University Press), 1–41.

Sullivan, Nikki. 2003. *A Critical Introduction to Queer Theory* (Melbourne, Australia: Circa Books).

Sullivan-Blum, Constance R. 2006. "Discourses in the Christian Same-Sex Marriage Debate," *Anthropologica* 48: 203–15.

Survival International. 2014. "Stamp It Out," available at www.survivalinternational.org/stampitout.

Sussman, Nan M., and Dianne H. Tyson. 2000. "Sex and Power: Gender Differences in Computer-Mediated Interactions," *Computers in Human Behaviour* 16: 381–94.

Tannen, Deborah. 1990. *You Just Don't Understand: Women and Men in Conversation* (New York: Ballantine).

Tcherkézoff, Serge. 1998. "Is Aristocracy Good for Democracy? A Contemporary Debate in Western Samoa," in *Pacific Answers to Western Hegemony: Cultural Practices of Identity Construction*, ed. Jürg Wassmann (Oxford: Berg), 417–34.

Tedlock, Barbara. 2005. *The Woman in the Shaman's Body: Reclaiming the Feminine in Religion and Medicine* (New York: Random House).

Terrio, Susan J. 1996. "Crafting *Grand Cra* Chocolates in Contemporary France," *American Anthropologist* 98, 1: 67–79.

Thomsen, Christian Jürgensen. 1936 [1836]. *Ledetraad til Nordisk Oldkyndighed* [*A Guide to Northern Antiquities*] (Copenhagen).

Tollefson, Kenneth D. 1995. "Potlatching and Political Organization among the Northwest Coast Indians," *Ethnology* 34, 1: 53–73.

Tonkinson, Robert. 1998. "National Identity: Australia after Mabo," in *Pacific Answers to Western Hegemony: Cultural Practices of Identity Construction*, ed. Jürg Wassmann (Oxford: Berg), 287–310.

Trigger, B.G. 1975. "Review of Culture and Nationality by A.G. Bailey," *American Anthropologist* 77, 3: 636–7.

———. 1981. "Ontario People and the Epidemics of 1634–1640," in *Indians, Animals, and the Fur Trade*, ed. S. Krech III (Athens: University of Georgia Press), 21–38.

Trostle, James A., and Johannes Sommerfeld. 1996. "Medical Anthropology and Epidemiology," *Annual Review of Anthropology* 25: 253–74.

Trouillot, Michel-Rolph. 1991. "Anthropology and the Savage Slot: The Poetics and Politics of Otherness," in *Recapturing Anthropology*, ed. Richard Fox (Santa Fe, NM: **SAR** Press), 17–44.

Turgeon, Laurier, and Madeleine Pastinelli. 2002. "'Eat the World': Postcolonial Encounters in Quebec City's Ethnic Restaurants," *Journal of American Folklore* 115, 456: 247–68.

Turnbull, Colin. 1961. *The Forest People* (New York: Simon and Schuster).

Turner, Terence. 1989. "Amazonian Indians Fight to Save Their Forest," *Anthropology Newsletter* 30, 3: 21–2.

Turner, Victor. 1969. *The Ritual Process* (Chicago: Aldine).

Tylor, Edward B. 1958 [1871]. *Primitive Culture* (New York: Harper and Row).

———. 2013. *World Population Prospects: The 2012* (Highlights and Advance Tables), available at http://esa.un.org/wpp/Documentation/pdf/WPP2012_HIGHLIGHTS.pdf.

UN (United Nations). 2014. *The Universal Declaration of Human Rights*, available at www.un.org/en/documents/udhr.

Undie, Chi-Chi. 2007. "My Father's Daughter: Becoming a 'Real' Anthropologist among the Ubang of Southeast Nigeria," *Dialectical Anthropology* 31: 293–305.

UNICEF (United Nations Children's Fund). 2004. "Building Health and Hope for Soon-to-Be Mothers in Rural India," available at www.unicef.org/infobycountry/india_fight_mortality.html.

Urciuoli, Bonnie. 2008. "Skills and Selves in the New Workplace," *American Ethnologist* 35: 211–28.

Valentine, Bettylou. 1978. Hustling and Other Hard Work: Life Styles in the Ghetto (New York: Free Press).

van den Berghe, Pierre. 1970. "Race, Class, and Ethnicity in South Africa," in *Social Stratification in Africa*, ed. Arthur Tuden and Leonard Plotnicov (New York: Free Press), 345–71.

van der Veer, Peter. 1997. "'The Enigma of Arrival': Hybridity and Authenticity in the Global Space," in *Debating Cultural Hybridity: Multicultural Identities and the Politics of Anti-racism*, ed. Pnina Werbner and Tariq Modood (London: Zed Books), 90–195.

Van Esterik, Penny. 1985. "Confronting Advocacy Confronting Anthropology," in *Advocacy and Anthropology*, ed. Robert Paine (St John's: Institute of Social and Economic Research).

———. 2002. "Contemporary Trends in Infant Feeding Research," *Annual Review of Anthropology* 31: 257–78.

Van Gennep, Arnold. 1960. *The Rites of Passage* (Chicago: University of Chicago Press).

Van Rheenen, Derek. 2012. "A Century of Historical Change in the Game Preferences of American Children," *Journal of American Folklore* 125, 498: 411–43.

Van Willigen, John, and V.C. Channa. 1991. "Law, Custom, and Crimes against Women," *Human Organization* 50, 4: 369–77.

Van Wolputte, Steven. 2004. "Hang on to Your Self: Of Bodies, Embodiment, and Selves," *Annual Review of Anthropology* 33: 251–69.

VeneKlasen, Lisa, and Valerie Miller. 2002. A New Weave of Power, People, and Politics: The Action Guide for Advocacy and Citizen Participation (Oklahoma: World Neighbors).

Vincent, Joan, ed. 2002. "Introduction," in *The Anthropology of Politics* (Malden, MA: Blackwell), 1–13.

Vogel, Susan M. 1997. *Baule: African Art, Western Eyes* (New Haven: Yale University Press). © Susan M. Vogel.

Voloshinov, Valentin N. 1986 [1929]. *Marxism and the Philosophy of Language*, trans. Ladislav Matejka and I.R. Titunik (Cambridge, MA: Harvard University Press).

———. 1987 [1926]. "Discourse in Life and Discourse in Art," in *Freudianism*, trans. and ed. I.R. Titunik in collaboration with Neil H. Bruss (Bloomington: Indiana University Press), 93–116.

Vonnegut Jr, Kurt. 1976. *Slapstick, or Lonesome No More!* (New York: Dell Publishing).

Vygotsky, Lev. 1978. *Mind in Society: The Development of Higher Psychological Processes* (Cambridge, MA: Harvard University Press).

Wagner, Andrew. 2012. "Reclamation: Taking Back, Giving Away, and the Future of (Queer) Language," *Broad Recognition* (22 April), available at http://broadrecognition.com/politics/reclamation-taking-back-giving-away-and-the-future-of-queer-language.

Waldram, James B. 2010. "Engaging Engagement: Critical Reflections on a Canadian Tradition," *Anthropologica* 52, 2: 225–32.

Walker, Marilyn. 2003. "Music as Knowledge in Shamanism and Other Healing Traditions of Siberia," *Arctic Anthropology* 40, 2: 40–8.

Wallace, Anthony F.C. 1966. *Religion: An Anthropological View* (New York: Random House).

———. 1972. *The Death and Rebirth of the Seneca* (New York: Vintage).

Wallerstein, Immanuel. 1974. *The Modern World System* (New York: Academic Press).

Walsh, Michael. 2005. "Will Indigenous Languages Survive?," *Annual Review of Anthropology* 34: 293–315.

Wardlow, Holly. 2007. "Men's Extramarital Sexuality in Rural Papua New Guinea," *American Journal of Public Health* 97, 6: 1006–14.

Warner, W. Lloyd. 1936. "American Caste and Class," *American Sociological Review* 42, 2: 234–7.

Washington, Julie A. and Craig, Holly K. 1998. "Socioeconomic Status and Gender Influences on Children's Dialectal Variations," *Journal of Speech, Language, and Hearing Research* 41: 618–26.

Waubageshig, ed. 1970. *The Only Good Indian: Essays by Canadian Indians* (Toronto: New Press).

Weiner, Annette. 1976. *Women of Value, Men of Renown* (Austin: University of Texas Press).

———. 1980. "Stability in Banana Leaves: Colonization and Women in Kiriwina, Trobriand Islands," in *Women and Colonization: Anthropological Perspectives*, ed. Mona Etienne and Eleanor Leacock (New York: Praeger), 270–93.

———. 1988. *The Trobrianders of Papua New Guinea* (New York: Holt, Rinehart, and Winston).

Werbner, Pnina. 1997. "Afterword: Writing Multiculturalism and Politics in the New Europe," in *The Politics of Multiculturalism in the New Europe: Racism, Identity, and Community*, ed. Tariq Modood and Pnina Werbner (London: Zed Books), 261–7.

Weston, Kath. 1991. *Families We Choose* (New York: Columbia University Press).

———. 1998. *Longslowburn: Sexuality and Social Science* (New York: Routledge).

Whiteford, Linda. 2009. "Failure to Protect, Failure to Provide: Refugee Reproduction Rights," in *Global Health in Times of Violence*, ed. Barbara Rylko-Bauer, Linda Whiteford, and Paul Farmer (Santa Fe, NM: School for Advanced Research Press), 89–112.

WHO (World Health Organization). 2003a. "Summary Table of SARS Cases by Country, 1 November 2002–7 August 2003," available at www.who.int/csr/sars/country/2003_08_15/en/index.html.

———. 2003b. "Climate Change and Human Health," in *Climate Change and Human Health*, available at www.who.int/globalchange/climate/summary/en/index5.html.

———. 2010. *ICD*-10 (Version: 2010), available at http://apps.who.int/classifications/icd10/browse/2010/en.

———. 2014a. "WHO–UNAIDS HIV Vaccine Initiative," available at www.who.int/immunization/research/forums_and_initiatives/HIV_vaccine_initiative/en.

———. 2014b. "Women's Health," available at www.who.int/mediacentre/factsheets/fs334/en.

———. 2014c. "Malaria," available at www.who.int/mediacentre/factsheets/fs094/en.

Whorf, Benjamin. 1956. *Language, Thought, and Reality*, ed. John B. Carroll (Cambridge, MA: MIT Press).

Wilk, Richard. 1996. *Economies and Cultures* (Boulder, CO: Westview Press).

——— and Lisa Cliggett. 2007. *Economies and Cultures: Foundations of Economic Anthropology*. Boulder, CO: Westview Press.

Williams, Brackette. 1989. "A Class Act: Anthropology and the Race to Nation across Ethnic Terrain," *Annual Review of Anthropology* 18: 401–44.

Wilson, Monica. 1951. "Witch Beliefs and Social Structure," *American Journal of Sociology* LVI, 4: 307–13. (Oxford: Oxford University Press).

Winn, Peter. 1992. *Americas* (New York: Pantheon).

Witherspoon, Gary. 1975. *Navajo Kinship and Marriage* (Chicago: University of Chicago Press).

Wolcott, Harry F. 1999. *Ethnography: A Way of Seeing* (Walnut Creek, CA: AltaMira Press).

Wolf, Eric. 1969. *Peasant Wars of the Twentieth Century* (New York: Harper and Row).

———. 1982. *Europe and the People without History* (Berkeley: University of California Press).

———. 1999. *Envisioning Power: Ideologies of Dominance and Crisis* (Berkeley: University of California Press).

Woodbury, Anthony. 2012. "Endangered Languages." Linguistic Society of America, available at www.linguisticsociety.org/content/endangered-languages.

Woolard, Kathryn A. 1998. "Introduction: Language Ideology as a Field of Inquiry," in *Language Ideologies: Practice and Theory*, ed. Bambi Schieffelin, Kathryn Woolard, and Paul V. Kroskrity (New York: Oxford University Press), 3–47.

Woost, M.D. 1993. "Nationalizing the Local Past in Sri Lanka: Histories of Nation and Development in a Sinhalese Village," *American Ethnologist* 20, 3: 502–21.

Young, Allan. 1976. "Some Implications of Medical Beliefs and Practices for Social Anthropology," *American Anthropologist* 78, 1: 5–24.

Young, Diana. 2005. "The Smell of Greenness: Cultural Synaesthesia in the Western Desert (Australia)," *Etnofoor* 18, 1: 61–77.

Young, Meredith E., Geoffrey R. Norman, and Karin R. Humphreys. 2008. "The Role of Medical Language in Changing Public Perception of Illness," *PLoS One*, doi: 10.1371/journal.pone.0003875.

Yuval-Davis, Nira. 1997. "Ethnicity, Gender Relations, and Multiculturalism," in *Debating Cultural Hybridity: Multicultural Identities and the Politics of Anti-racism*, ed. Pnina Werbner and Tariq Modood (London: Zed Books), 193–208.

Zhou, Yingying. 2005. "Uncovering Children in Marginalization: Explaining Unregistered Children in China," paper prepared for the International Union for the Scientific Study of Population's General Conference (Tours, France), available at http://iussp2005.princeton.edu/download.aspx?submissionId=50479.

Zuckerhut, Patricia. 2011. "Feminist Anthropological Perspectives on Violence," *Gender and Violence in the Middle East*, ed. Moha Ennaji and Fatima Sadiqi (New York: Routledge): 13–25.

CREDITS

INDEX

abiotic world, 223–5
Aboriginal Affairs and Northern Development Canada, 224–5
Aboriginal peoples: *see* First Nations; Indigenous peoples; Inuit; specific groups
abortion, 216, 231; "selective female," 138
Abu-Lughod, Lila, 199–200
activism: anthropology and, 349
adoption, 151–3
affinity, 132, 137
affluence, 181–2
Africa: caste in, 298; colonialism in, 55–7, 64; ethnicity in, 304–6; sexuality in, 69; *see also* specific countries, groups
African American English (AAE), 89–90, 91
Agar, Michael, 33
agency: consumption and, 178; free, 271; human, 21–2, 112; neoliberal, 113
age sets, 157–8
agribusiness, 167
agriculture, extensive/intensive/mechanized/industrial, 167
AND: *see* HIV/AIDS
Akmajian, A., et al., 95
Algonquian peoples: disease and, 220–1
alienation, 281
Alland, Alexander, 193, 194, 210
Allen, Catherine, 154–5
Alonso, Ana María, 309
Alverson, Hoyt, 281
Amazon: Indigenous people in, 319
ambiguity, structural, 83, 92
ambilocal residence, 133
American Anthropological Association, 32
"American Dream," 294
American Sign Language, 87
Anderson, Benedict, 161, 327
anemia, 226
Anishinaabe people: disease and, 220, 224
anomie, 281
anthropological knowledge, 46–7
anthropological perspective, 5–12, 22
anthropology: active, 11; applied, 11–12, 234–6, 347–65; biological, 6–8, 115; British, 64–7; Canadian, 51–2; cognitive, 103–7; colonialism and, 59–60, 61; contemporary, 70; cultural, 1–25; economic, 164–86; as evolutionary, 6; forensic, 7, 11–12; global citizenship and, 354–61; history and, 20–2, 50–73; human rights and, 359–61; language and, 77–8; linguistic, 9; medical, 212–38, 348; molecular, 7–8; physical, 6–8; policy and, 352–4; political, 270–1; psychological, 96–129; skills of, 352; social, 9, 65; sociocultural, 9; study of, 348, 352, 363–4; subdisciplines of, 6–12; urban planning and, 352–3; *see also* cultural anthropology

anti-capitalist movements, 321
Anti-Slavery International, 336
apes, 14, 79
Apfel, Roberta, and Bennett Simon, 122
Appadurai, Arjun, 36, 325
Applewhite, Marshall, 261
arbitrariness, linguistic, 79–80
archeology, 8–9
Arctic: pollution in, 224–5
Arens, W., and Ivan Karp, 291
Argentina: dirty war in, 360
art, 187, 188, 193–200; definition of, 193; "by intention/appropriation," 195; as metaphor, 194; myth, play, ritual and, 208; non-art and, 194–200; ownership of, 198; primitive/ethnic/folk, 194–5, 196–7
articulated style, 104, 105
Asad, Talal, 59, 259–60
Ashanti people, 140
Assembly of First Nations, 60, 334
Association of Social Anthropologists, 63–4
Australia: Indigenous peoples in, 309–10; nationalism in, 309
authenticity: art and, 196–7; cultural–historical, 197; experiential, 197; unique, 197
authority, "shared ethnographic," 188
authorization: field work and, 32
avunculocal residence, 133
Aymara people, 189
Azande people, 252–4, 275–6

"Baby M," 155
Bacigalupo, Ana Mariella, 117
Badiou, Alain, 323
Bailey, A.G., 51–2
Bakhtin, Mikhail, 84, 85
Baldikas, Biruté, 7
band, 65
Bang, Abhay, and Rani Bang, 230
Barbados: gay men in, 119
"barbarism," 63
Barber, Benjamin, 41, 42, 346
"bargaining for reality," 282–7
Bariai people, 151–3
Barnard, Alan, 72
Barrett, Stanley R., et al., 291
Barth, Frederik, 270
Bashir, Halima, 291
Bateson, Gregory, 189, 349
battle fatigue, 122
Baule people, 58–9, 102–3, 197–9
Bauman, Zygmunt, 160–1, 313
Beals, Alan, 295, 297
beaver, 54
Belgium, 357
beliefs, religious, 245
Bellman, Beryl, 158

Benedict, Ruth, 18, 97, 109
Beng people, 276
Benhabib, Seyla, 24
berdache, 115–16
Berkes, Fikret, et al., 238
Berkowitz, Dana, 155
Berlin, Brent, and David G. Casagrande, 129
Berreman, Gerald, 297
Berthod, Marc-Antoine, 209
Bestor, Theodore, 324
Bettelheim, Bruno, 123
Bickerton, Derek, 88
Bigenho, Michelle, 196–7
binary opposition, 3
bioaccumulation, 224
biocultural organisms, 12–14, 97
biology, 6, 12; culture and, 97; sex and, 115
biomagnification, 224
biopower/biopolitics, 278–9, 281
biotic world, 223–5
bisexuality, 69, 120
Bishop, Charles A., 55
black people, 294–5, 300; *see also* specific groups
Blackwood, Evelyn, and Saskia Wieringa, 120
Blanchard, Kendall, 210; and Alyce Cheska, 190
Bledsoe, Caroline, 138
Boas, Franz, 7, 11, 16, 18, 25, 28, 172; consumption and, 176; culture area studies and, 67; typologies and, 63
Bock, Philip K., 112, 129
Bodenhorn, Barbara, 151
bodily arousal, 107–8
Bolivia: miners in, 281–2
Borofsky, Robert, et al., 24
Bourdain, Anthony, 48
Bowen, John, 245, 263
Boyer, Pascal, and Brian Bergstrom, 263
Bradburd, Daniel, 46, 49
Brahmins, 296, 297
Braroe, Niels, 182–3
Brazil: culture of beauty in, 341; fieldwork in, 37
bride-burning, 138
bridewealth, 132–3, 136–7, 141
Briggs, Charles L., 27
Briggs, Jean, 38–40
British Columbia: water in, 273–4
Bronberger, Christian, 192–3
brother–sister relationships, 140, 148–9
Bruner, Jerome, 106
Bwiti religion, 247, 256
Bylko-Bauer, Barbara, et al., 365

Caesar, Julius, 62
call systems, 79
Cameroon, 304–6